Studies in Latin American Ethnohistory & Archaeology

Joyce Marcus, General Editor

Volume I	*A Fuego y Sangre: Early Zapotec Imperialism in the Cuicatlán Cañada, Oaxaca,* by Elsa Redmond, Memoirs of the Museum of Anthropology, University of Michigan, No. 16. 1983.
Volume II	*Irrigation and the Cuicatec Ecosystem: A Study of Agriculture and Civilization in North Central Oaxaca,* by Joseph W. Hopkins, Memoirs of the Museum of Anthropology, University of Michigan, No. 17. 1984.
Volume III	*Aztec City-States,* by Mary G. Hodge, Memoirs of the Museum of Anthropology, University of Michigan, No. 18. 1984.
Volume IV	*Conflicts over Coca Fields in Sixteenth-Century Peru,* by María Rostworowski de Diez Canseco, Memoirs of the Museum of Anthropology, University of Michigan, No. 21. 1988.
Volume V	*Tribal and Chiefly Warfare in South America,* by Elsa Redmond, Memoirs of the Museum of Anthropology, University of Michigan, No. 28. 1994.
Volume VI	*Imperial Transformations in Sixteenth-Century Yucay, Peru,* transcribed and edited by R. Alan Covey and Donato Amado González, Memoirs of the Museum of Anthropology, University of Michigan, No. 44. 2008.
Volume VII	*Domestic Life in Prehispanic Capitals: A Study of Specialization, Hierarchy, and Ethnicity,* edited by Linda R. Manzanilla and Claude Chapdelaine, Memoirs of the Museum of Anthropology, University of Michigan, No. 46. 2009.
Volume VIII	*Yuthu: Community and Ritual in an Early Andean Village,* by Allison R. Davis, Memoirs of the Museum of Anthropology, University of Michigan, No. 50. 2011.
Volume IX	*Advances in Titicaca Basin Archaeology–III,* edited by Alexei Vranich, Elizabeth A. Klarich, and Charles Stanish, Memoirs of the Museum of Anthropology, University of Michigan, No. 51. 2012.
Volume X	*Regional Archaeology in the Inca Heartland: The Hanan Cuzco Surveys,* edited by R. Alan Covey, Memoirs of the Museum of Anthropology, University of Michigan, No. 55. 2014.
Volume XI	*The Northern Titicaca Basin Survey: Huancané-Putina,* by Charles Stanish, Cecilia Chávez Justo, Karl LaFavre, and Aimée Plourde, Memoirs of the Museum of Anthropology, University of Michigan, No. 56. 2014.
Volume XII	*Coastal Ecosystems and Economic Strategies at Cerro Azul, Peru: The Study of a Late Intermediate Kingdom,* edited by Joyce Marcus, Memoirs of the Museum of Anthropology, University of Michigan, No. 59. 2016.
Volume XIII	*The Burials of Cerro Azul, Peru,* by Joyce Marcus, Memoirs of the Museum of Anthropology, University of Michigan, No. 65. 2023.

Memoirs of the Museum of Anthropology
University of Michigan

Number 65

The Burials of Cerro Azul, Peru

Joyce Marcus

Ann Arbor, Michigan
2023

©2023 by the Regents of the University of Michigan
The Museum of Anthropology
All rights reserved

Printed and bound by CPI Group (UK) Ltd, Croydon, CR0 4YY
ISBN (print): 978-1-951538-75-0
ISBN (ebook): 978-1-951538-76-7

Cover design by Bruce Worden

Buy this book and browse all of our books at **sites.lsa.umich.edu/archaeology-books**
Visit the Museum website at **lsa.umich.edu/ummaa**

The University of Michigan Museum of Anthropological Archaeology (UMMAA) publishes books on archaeology and anthropology.

For permissions, questions, or manuscript queries, contact Museum publications in Ann Arbor, Michigan, by email at umma-pubs@umich.edu.

Library of Congress Control Number: 2023952181

The paper used in this publication meets the requirements of the ANSI Standard Z39.48-1984 (Permanence of Paper).

Table of Contents

List of Illustrations — vii
Overview and Acknowledgments — xv

Part I. Background

Chapter 1: Mortuary Analysis — 3
Chapter 2: Introduction to the Site of Cerro Azul — 21

Part II. Early Excavations at Cerro Azul

Chapter 3: Burials Excavated at Cerro Azul by Alfred L. Kroeber — 31

Part III. Excavations in Quebrada 5a at Cerro Azul

Chapter 4: The Structure 4 burial cist — 41
Chapter 5: The Structure 5 burial cist — 109
Chapter 6: The Structure 6 burial cist — 143
Chapter 7: Burial 1 — 175
Chapter 8: Burial 2 — 187
Chapter 9: Burial 3 — 190
Chapter 10: Burial 4 — 194
Chapter 11: Burial 5 — 256
Chapter 12: Burial 6 — 262
Chapter 13: Burial 7 — 267
Chapter 14: Burial 8 — 272
Chapter 15: Burial 9 — 283

Part IV. Excavations in Quebrada 5-south at Cerro Azul

Chapter 16: The Structure 12 burial cist — 299

Part V. Cerro Azul's Burials in Regional and Historical Perspective

Chapter 17: Mortuary Archaeology and Andean Culture — 331

References — 341
Index — 363

List of Illustrations

Front cover designed by Bruce Worden

Figure 1.1. An Andean *chullpa*, a funerary tower, 4
Figure 1.2. A royal Inca mummy and his mummified spouse are honored by their descendants, 5
Figure 1.3. November, the month when the dead were put on litters and transported through the streets, 8
Figure 1.4. Nineteen gourds in a woman's grave at the site of Pacatnamu, Peru, 10
Figure 1.5. George Dorsey's typology of graves at the archaeological site of Ancón, Peru, 12
Figure 1.6. Weaving on a backstrap loom, 15
Figure 1.7. William Safford's 1891 sketch of a grave at Ancón, 18

Figure 2.1. Map showing the limits of the *señorío* of Huarco in the lower Cañete Valley, Peru, 22
Figure 2.2. Sketch map of the *señorío* of Huarco showing prominent roads, canals, and other landmarks, 23
Figure 2.3. Contour map showing the location of Lunahuaná and Huarco, 24
Figure 2.4. Map showing the valleys that bracket the Cañete Valley, 25
Figure 2.5. The archaeological site of Cerro Azul, overlooking the Pacific Ocean, 26
Figure 2.6. Aerial photo of Cerro Azul showing Cerro Camacho and the sea cliffs, 27
Figure 2.7. Location of the 13 quebradas at Cerro Azul, 28

Figure 3.1. Map of Cerro Azul, showing the quebradas where Kroeber excavated, 32
Figure 3.2. Ceramic vessels found in Cerro Azul's Burial K1, a grave containing 18 individuals, 33
Figure 3.3. Sherds found by Kroeber in Burial K3 at Cerro Azul, 34
Figure 3.4. Carved wooden block found in Burial K3 at Cerro Azul, 35
Figure 3.5. Two of the four *balanzas* found at Cerro Azul, 36
Figure 3.6. Four *balanzas*, from various sites on the Peruvian coast, 37
Figure 3.7. Two of the ten pottery vessels found by Kroeber in Cerro Azul's Burial K4, a grave containing six adults and six children, 38

Figure 4.1. Map of Cerro Azul showing where the University of Michigan Project found looted burials, 42
Figure 4.2. Evidence of looting in Quebrada 5a at Cerro Azul, 43
Figure 4.3. Quebrada 5a at Cerro Azul, showing looters' holes and the start of the University of Michigan's salvage excavations, 44
Figure 4.4. Excavation in Quebrada 5a at Cerro Azul revealed Structures 4, 5, 6, and 7, 45
Figure 4.5. Vessels broken by looters, found next to Structure 4, 47
Figure 4.6. Cross section of the 5 x 5 m excavation in Quebrada 5a, Cerro Azul, 48
Figure 4.7. Fragment of twill mat that lined the interior of the Structure 4 burial cist, 49
Figure 4.8. A second mat fragment from the lining of the Structure 4 burial cist, 50
Figure 4.9. A bundle of bulrushes, possibly used as a pillow for one of the burials in Structure 4, 50
Figure 4.10. Miniature Camacho Black amphora, found next to Structure 4, 51
Figure 4.11. Two Camacho Black amphorae, discarded by looters next to Structure 4, 52
Figure 4.12. A Camacho Black miniature jar, found in looters' backdirt next to Structure 4, 53
Figure 4.13. A Camacho Reddish Brown miniature jar, found next to Structure 4, 54
Figure 4.14. An amphora, found next to Structure 4, with coca leaves in the bottom of the amphora, 55
Figure 4.15. One of several *mates* or gourd vessels associated with Structure 4, 56
Figure 4.16. Rim profiles of two gourd bowls found just outside Structure 4, 57
Figure 4.17. Gourd bowl found adjacent to Structure 4, 57
Figure 4.18. A second gourd bowl found adjacent to Structure 4, 58

Figure 4.19. A pyroengraved gourd bowl, found on the surface adjacent to Structure 4, *58*
Figure 4.20. A gourd bowl from Structure 4, *59*
Figure 4.21. Two miniature containers, created by drilling holes in *lúcuma* seeds, *59*
Figure 4.22. Molluscs associated with Structure 4, *60*
Figure 4.23. Net 1 from Structure 4, *62*
Figure 4.24. Net 2 from Structure 4, *63*
Figure 4.25. Net 3 from Structure 4, *64*
Figure 4.26. Net 4 from Structure 4, *65*
Figure 4.27. Net 5 from Structure 4, *66*
Figure 4.28. Net 6 from Structure 4, *67*
Figure 4.29. Net 7 from Structure 4, *68*
Figure 4.30. Net 8 from Structure 4, *69*
Figure 4.31. Net 9 from Structure 4, *70*
Figure 4.32. Net 10 from Structure 4, *71*
Figure 4.33. Net 11 from Structure 4, *72*
Figure 4.34. Net 12 from Structure 4, *73*
Figure 4.35. Net 13 from Structure 4, *74*
Figure 4.36. Net 14 from Structure 4, *75*
Figure 4.37. Net 15 of Structure 4, *76*
Figure 4.38. Net 16 of Structure 4, *77*
Figure 4.39. A *mallero*, or wooden template used to create uniform mesh openings in a net, found near Structure 4, *77*
Figure 4.40. Examples of the knots used to make fishing nets at Cerro Azul, *78*
Figure 4.41. Net 017, a fragment of trammel net discarded by looters adjacent to Structure 4, *79*
Figure 4.42. Net 022 from Structure 4, made from three different yarns of varying thicknesses, *80*
Figure 4.43. Net 034 from Structure 4, a fragment of a trammel net, *83*
Figure 4.44. Net 037, found just below Structure 4, a fragment of cotton net, *84*
Figure 4.45. Four views of Net 038m from Structure 4, a fragment of trammel net, *85*
Figure 4.46. A damaged leather pouch, found inside Structure 4, *86*
Figure 4.47. A complete slit-cradle sling, found next to Structure 4, *88*
Figure 4.48. Two sling fragments from Structure 4, *89*
Figure 4.49. Two slit-cradle sling fragments from Structure 4, *90*
Figure 4.50. Possible sling fragments, found just outside Structure 4, *91*
Figure 4.51. Two combs from Cerro Azul, *91*
Figure 4.52. Two bundles of cordage, found just outside Structure 4, *92*
Figure 4.53. Artist's rendition of a design on a textile band found next to Structure 4, *92*
Figure 4.54. A warp-faced plain weave textile, found next to Structure 4, *94*
Figure 4.55. A cloth with faded blue, brown, and off-white stripes, found next to Structure 4, *95*
Figure 4.56. A warp-stripe plain weave cotton textile, found next to Structure 4, *96*
Figure 4.57. A slit tapestry associated with Structure 4, *97*
Figure 4.58. The remains of a possible tunic, found next to Structure 4, *99*
Figure 4.59. A decorated cloth associated with Structure 4, *100*
Figure 4.60. Remains of a possible blouse or tunic, found inside Structure 4, *101*
Figure 4.61. A warp-stripe plain weave textile, found next to Structure 4, *102*
Figure 4.62. A textile from Structure 4, featuring narrow brown stripes alternating with tan stripes, *103*
Figure 4.63. A warp-stripe plain weave cotton textile, found inside Structure 4, *104*
Figure 4.64. A warp-stripe plain weave textile, found inside Structure 4, *104*
Figure 4.65. An all-cotton textile with brown and white stripes, associated with Structure 4, *105*
Figure 4.66. A *wara*, or shaped breechclout, associated with Structure 4, *106*
Figure 4.67. Frayed spindle with its whorl still attached, associated with Structure 4, *106*

Figure 4.68. Yarn balls and cane tube found inside Structure 4, *107*
Figure 4.69. Fragment of belt loom with unfinished textile still attached, associated with Structure 4, *108*
Figure 4.70. The Structure 4 burial cist, now empty, *108*

Figure 5.1. Workman shown salvaging items left inside Structure 5, *110*
Figure 5.2. Human remains discarded next to Structure 5, *111*
Figure 5.3. Two miniature jars found inside Structure 5, *112*
Figure 5.4. Two vessels associated with Structure 5, *113*
Figure 5.5. Vessel 5 of Structure 5, a Camacho Black miniature vessel, *113*
Figure 5.6. A miniature gourd bowl from Structure 5, *114*
Figure 5.7. Gourd bowl from Structure 5 that contained one guinea pig, two molluscs, one anchoveta, and an unidentified second fish, *114*
Figure 5.8. Miniature gourd vessel from Structure 5, containing a *lúcuma* seed wrapped in cloth, *115*
Figure 5.9. Structure 5 contained cobs of two maize varieties, *116*
Figure 5.10. An *Erythrina* pod found in Structure 5, *116*
Figure 5.11. A well-preserved potato found beside Structure 5, *117*
Figure 5.12. Five figurines from Cerro Azul, *118*
Figure 5.13. Items of metal associated with Structure 5, *119*
Figure 5.14. Pieces of metal found in Structure 5, *120*
Figure 5.15. Nets used today at Cerro Azul, *122*
Figure 5.16. Fragments of a cast net, found in looters' debris next to Structure 5, *123*
Figure 5.17. A complete sling with webbed cradle from Structure 5, *124*
Figure 5.18. Three examples of the decorative wool designs on slings, *124*
Figure 5.19. A brown and white warp-stripe plain weave textile associated with Structure 5, *125*
Figure 5.20. Two-sided, reversible loom backstrap found in Structure 5, *126*
Figure 5.21. Band of slit tapestry from Structure 5, showing birds and hexagons, *127*
Figure 5.22. Possible headband made of slit tapestry, featuring fish with raised eyeballs, found in Structure 5, *128*
Figure 5.23. Band of eccentric slit tapestry with edge embroidery, found in Structure 5, *128*
Figure 5.24. Textile consisting of two bands of eccentric slit tapestry found in Structure 5, *129*
Figure 5.25. Bag found inside Workbasket #1 of Structure 5, *130*
Figure 5.26. Cloth found wrapped around Workbasket #1 of Structure 5, *131*
Figure 5.27. A possible bag, found inside a gourd vessel associated with female mummy in Structure 5, *132*
Figure 5.28. Textile remains from Structure 5, *133*
Figure 5.29. Cotton cloth from Structure 5, *134*
Figure 5.30. Cloth with alternating brown and white stripes, associated with Structure 5, *135*
Figure 5.31. Plain weave textile, associated with an infant buried in Structure 5, *136*
Figure 5.32. Wool band found in Structure 5, *136*
Figure 5.33. Cotton cloth from Structure 5, *138*
Figure 5.34. Workbasket #1, found lying at the bottom of the Structure 5 burial cist, *139*
Figure 5.35. Four spindle whorls and five spindles, found inside Workbasket #1, Structure 5, *140*
Figure 5.36. Workbasket #2, found at the bottom of the Structure 5 burial cist, *141*
Figure 5.37. A *kallwa*, or weaving sword, found inside Structure 5, *142*

Figure 6.1. A north-south cross section of Terrace 9, Quebrada 5a at Cerro Azul, *144*
Figure 6.2. Leaves of *pacay* (*Inga* sp.) from the floor of the Structure 6 burial cist, *144*
Figure 6.3. A skull discarded by looters next to Structure 6, *145*
Figure 6.4. Partially mummified individual, discarded by looters next to Structure 6, *146*
Figure 6.5. Remains of a second individual, discarded by looters next to Structure 6, *147*
Figure 6.6. Cane and wood construction that was either a litter or roof of the Structure 6 cist, *148*
Figure 6.7. Remains of a mat found inside Structure 6, *149*

Figure 6.8. Bundle of willow twigs, found on the floor of Structure 6, may have served as a pillow, *150*
Figure 6.9. Camacho Black miniature jar, found inside Structure 6, *150*
Figure 6.10. Camacho Black miniature jar, the second of two vessels found inside Structure 6, *151*
Figure 6.11. Six pieces of silver or silver foil, found in the Structure 6 burial cist, *152*
Figure 6.12. Two stone mace heads from the Cañete Valley, *153*
Figure 6.13. Webbed cradle from a sling, found in Structure 6, *154*
Figure 6.14. Two spherical stones from Cerro Azul, *154*
Figure 6.15. A two-stone bolas, found in Structure 6, *155*
Figure 6.16. Close-up photo of the repair made on the bolas seen in Figure 6.15, *156*
Figure 6.17. A second bolas from Structure 6, *157*
Figure 6.18. Two additional bolas from Structure 6, *157*
Figure 6.19. Two grinding stones associated with Structure 6, *158*
Figure 6.20. Tied bundle of loom parts, found inside Structure 6, *159*
Figure 6.21. Parts of a backstrap loom, *160–161*
Figure 6.22. A brown-and-white-striped textile, found inside Structure 6, *162*
Figure 6.23. Cloth from Structure 6, found wrapped around the workbasket shown in Figure 6.30, *163*
Figure 6.24. Two views of a striped textile from Structure 6, *164*
Figure 6.25. One of the textiles used as the outermost wrapping of a mummy bundle in Structure 6, *165*
Figure 6.26. Fragment of blue cotton textile found in Structure 6, *166*
Figure 6.27. Band from Structure 6, *167*
Figure 6.28. Bands found in Structure 6, *167*
Figure 6.29. Twill basketry found in Structure 6, *168*
Figure 6.30. A workbasket from Structure 6, *169*
Figure 6.31. The same workbasket seen in Figure 6.30, with its lid open, *170*
Figure 6.32. Twenty grams of cotton from the Figure 6.30 workbasket, found in Structure 6, *171*
Figure 6.33. Three spindle whorls found in the Structure 6 workbasket, *172*
Figure 6.34. More items from the Structure 6 workbasket seen in Figure 6.30, *172*
Figure 6.35. Mummified hand holding a yarn ball, discarded by looters near Structure 6, *173*
Figure 6.36. Sweeping the floor of Structure 6, a looted burial cist, *174*

Figure 7.1. Location of Burials 1–9 within our 5 x 5 m salvage unit in Quebrada 5a, Cerro Azul, *176*
Figure 7.2. Uppermost level of Burial 1, exposing grinding stones, pottery vessels, and human crania, *177*
Figure 7.3. Vessel 1 of Burial 1, a Camacho Reddish Brown amphora with a face modeled on its neck, *179*
Figure 7.4. Wad of human hair found at the bottom of Vessel l, Burial 1, *179*
Figure 7.5. Vessel 2 of Burial 1, a Camacho Black amphora with two animal effigy lugs on its shoulder, *180*
Figure 7.6. Vessel 3 of Burial 1, a misfired Camacho Black amphora with two lugs on its shoulder, *181*
Figure 7.7. Vessel 4 of Burial 1, a Camacho Black amphora with two animal effigy lugs on its shoulder, *182*
Figure 7.8. Vessel 5 of Burial 1, a drum-shaped miniature vessel, *183*
Figure 7.9. Vessel 6 of Burial 1, a miniature gourd found inside a cloth bag, *184*
Figure 7.10. Two grinding stones found with Burial 1, *185*
Figure 7.11. The cranium of a dog whose complete remains accompanied Burial 1, *1986*
Figure 7.12. An orange garment from Burial 1, possibly a tunic or blouse, *186*

Figure 8.1. A gourd bowl found with Burial 2, *188*
Figure 8.2. A Camacho Black jar from Burial 2, featuring two possible "kill" holes, *189*

Figure 9.1. Vessel 1, Burial 3, an amphora with a harness of grass rope that passed through the handles, *191*
Figure 9.2. Vessel 2, Burial 3, an amphora with loop handles, each at a different height, *192*
Figure 9.3. Vessel 3, Burial 3, a gourd bowl, *193*
Figure 9.4. Vessel 4, Burial 3, a miniature gourd bowl, *193*

Figure 10.1. Burial 4 of Quebrada 5a, a multiperson burial, *195*
Figure 10.2. Items from Burial 4, *197*
Figure 10.3. A globular jar from Burial 4, *198*
Figure 10.4. An amphora from Burial 4, *199*
Figure 10.5. A gourd vessel from Burial 4, *199*
Figure 10.6. Gold foil from Burial 4, embossed with sun-shaped *intis*. When discovered, it was folded over the silver foil shown in Figure 10.7, *200*
Figure 10.7. Silver foil, found folded inside the gold foil shown in Figure 10.6, *201*
Figure 10.8. Associated with Individual 1a of Burial 4 was silver foil, with a red painted fingernail still adhering to it, *201*
Figure 10.9. Items associated with Individual 1a of Burial 4 included a bag, pigment pouches, and seed bracelet, *203*
Figure 10.10. Brocaded textile, found in a hole made by looters when they penetrated the side of the Burial 4 pit, *204*
Figure 10.11. Artist's rendering of Chumpi 7, found with Individual 1a of Burial 4, *206*
Figure 10.12. Artist's rendering of Chumpi 8, found with Individual 1a of Burial 4, *207*
Figure 10.13. Artist's rendering of Chumpi 9, found with Individual 1a of Burial 4, *208*
Figure 10.14. Contents of disintegrated workbasket associated with Individual 1a of Burial 4, *209*
Figure 10.15. Contents of disintegrated workbasket associated with Individual 1a of Burial 4, *210*
Figure 10.16. Eight spindle whorls, found in workbasket associated with Individual 1a of Burial 4, *211*
Figure 10.17. Items found near Individual 1a's disintegrated workbasket, *211*
Figure 10.18. Weaving implements found beneath Individuals 1a and 2 of Burial 4, *213*
Figure 10.19. Needles found beneath Individuals 1a and 2 of Burial 4, *214*
Figure 10.20. Yarn balls and skeins of yarn, found near Individuals 1a and 2 of Burial 4, *215*
Figure 10.21. Individual 3 of Burial 4, a woman, with two tattoos on her left arm, *217*
Figure 10.22. Decorative cords held in the hand of Individual 3 of Burial 4, *218*
Figure 10.23. Two miniature flasks associated with Individual 3 of Burial 4, *220*
Figure 10.24. A double-chambered bridgespout vessel, associated with Individual 3 of Burial 4, *221*
Figure 10.25. Rim fragment from a gourd vessel, found mixed in with the yarn balls at the bottom of the Burial 4 pit, *222*
Figure 10.26. A stone bead necklace, found in place around Individual 3's neck when her mummy bundle was opened, *222*
Figure 10.27. Two silver *tupus* found inside the mummy bundle of Individual 3 in Burial 4, *223*
Figure 10.28. Pieces of silver foil decorated with the *inti* motif, associated with Individual 3 of Burial 4, *224*
Figure 10.29. Needlecase #1, associated with Individual 3 of Burial 4, *225*
Figure 10.30. Needlecase #2, associated with Individual 3 of Burial 4, *226*
Figure 10.31. Needlecase #3, associated with Individual 3 of Burial 4, *226*
Figure 10.32. Figurine found inside Bag 1, associated with Individual 3 of Burial 4, *227*
Figure 10.33. Black seeds, perforated for suspension, found in Bag 1 with Individual 3 of Burial 4, *228*
Figure 10.34. Some of the 58 items found in Bag 1 of Individual 3, Burial 4, *229–230*
Figure 10.35. Mussel shells used as pigment palettes, found inside Bag 2 of Individual 3, Burial 4, *231*
Figure 10.36. Pigment pouch found in Bag 2 with Individual 3, Burial 4, *231*
Figure 10.37. Cloth found inside Bag 2 of Individual 3 that had been wrapped around pigment pouches, *232*
Figure 10.38. Bag 2, a bag associated with Individual 3, Burial 4, *233*
Figure 10.39. Bag 3a, found inside Bag 2, associated with Individual 3, Burial 4, *234*
Figure 10.40. Two of eight pigment pouches found in Bag 3b, associated with Individual 3 of Burial 4, *234*
Figure 10.41. Bag 3b, associated with Individual 3 of Burial 4, is similar to a bag with Individual 1a of Burial 4, *235*
Figure 10.42. Bag 4, found with Individual 3 of Burial 4, *236*
Figure 10.43. Contents of Bag 4 with Individual 3 of Burial 4, *237*
Figure 10.44. Bone *balanza*, found inside Bag 5a, associated with Individual 3 of Burial 4, *238*
Figure 10.45. Bag 5a, found with Individual 3 of Burial 4, *239*
Figure 10.46. Bag 5b, found inside Bag 5a with Individual 3, *240*
Figure 10.47. Bag 5c, found inside Bag 5a, contained gold and silver foil, *241*
Figure 10.48. Bag 5c, found inside Bag 5a, held pieces of metal, *241*

Figure 10.49. Bag 6, associated with Individual 3 of Burial 4, contained cords, *242*
Figure 10.50. Belt loom, found inside the mummy bundle of Individual 3, Burial 4, *243*
Figure 10.51. Belt loom shown in Figure 10.50, unwrapped, *244*
Figure 10.52. Artist's rendering of Chumpi 1, associated with Individual 3 of Burial 4, *245*
Figure 10.53. Artist's rendering of Chumpi 2, associated with Individual 3 of Burial 4, *246*
Figure 10.54. Artist's rendering of Chumpi 3, associated with Individual 3 of Burial 4, *247*
Figure 10.55. Artist's rendering of Chumpi 4, associated with Individual 3 of Burial 4, *248*
Figure 10.56. Artist's rendering of Chumpi 5, associated with Individual 3 of Burial 4, *249*
Figure 10.57. Artist's rendering of Chumpi 6, associated with Individual 3 of Burial 4, *250*
Figure 10.58. A twill workbasket associated with Individual 3 of Burial 4, *252*
Figure 10.59. The contents of the workbasket shown in Figure 10.58, *253*
Figure 10.60. Two pairs of barcoded spindles with identical whorls, found inside workbasket belonging to Individual 3 of Burial 4, *254*
Figure 10.61. A sample of yarn balls and skeins that had fallen to the bottom of the Burial 4 pit, *255*

Figure 11.1. Vessel 1 of Burial 5, a Camacho Black jar plugged with *algodón blanco*, *257*
Figure 11.2. Loom and weaving tool from Burial 5, with a flint flake attached to the loom by a string, *258*
Figure 11.3. Loom from Burial 5, unrolled to show an unfinished textile, *258*
Figure 11.4. A close-up of the unfinished textile shown in Figure 11.3, *259*
Figure 11.5. Weaving components rolled up with the loom from Burial 5, including spindles, bobbins, and an ungulate long bone that displayed cut marks probably made by taut yarn, *260*

Figure 12.1. Burials 6 and 7 at Cerro Azul, *263*
Figure 12.2. Exposing the remains of the adult in Burial 6, *264*
Figure 12.3. Gourd vessel, placed at the feet of the adult in Burial 6, contained a guinea pig, *265*
Figure 12.4. Seeds strung on a thread, associated with the child in Burial 6, *266*

Figure 13.1. Associated with the child in Burial 7 was an unusual vessel with two appliqué snakes, *268*
Figure 13.2. Decorated gourd vessel associated with the child in Burial 7, *269*
Figure 13.3. Gourd bowl associated with the adult man in Burial 7, *270*
Figure 13.4. Jar found with adult man in Burial 7 that shows it was blackened from cooking, *271*

Figure 14.1. Burial 8 contained a woman, her loom, workbasket, and gourd vessel, *273*
Figure 14.2. Vessel 1 of Burial 8, found inside the woman's funerary bundle, in the first cloth wrapping, *274*
Figure 14.3. Vessel 2 of Burial 8, a Camacho Black amphora with two possible "kill" holes, *275*
Figure 14.4. Vessel 3 from Burial 8, a broken gourd bowl containing a guinea pig, *276*
Figure 14.5. Two *tupus*, or cloak pins, found with the woman from Burial 8, *278*
Figure 14.6. Five pieces of silver foil that had fallen to the chest of the woman in Burial 8, *279*
Figure 14.7. Around the hips of the woman in Burial 8 we found cotton, *279*
Figure 14.8. Loom parts with the woman in Burial 8, *280*
Figure 14.9. Woman in Burial 8, holding a bag of yarn balls, pieces of chalk, and a pigment pouch, *281*
Figure 14.10. Contents of the disintegrated workbasket found with Burial 8, including two barcoded spindles with whorls, three spindles without whorls, and a possible piece of chalk, *282*

Figure 15.1. View of the Structure 8 cist, which contained Burial 9, *284*
Figure 15.2. Structure 8, the only burial cist at Cerro Azul whose shape resembled a keyhole, *285*
Figure 15.3. Burial cists at Cerro Azul were built from *cantos rodados* or cobblestones, *286*
Figure 15.4. Vessel 1 from Burial 9, a Camacho Black jar, *286*
Figure 15.5. Vessel 2 from Burial 9, a miniature Camacho Black amphora, *287*

Figure 15.6. Gourd bowl from Burial 9, with guinea pigs, sardines, razor clams, mussels, false abalone, bean pod, *pacay*, *lúcuma* seed, maize cob, and maize tassel, *288*

Figure 15.7. Individual 3, Burial 9, accompanied by gourd bowl containing a bundle of *totora* (*Scirpus* sp.), *289*

Figure 15.8. Chumpi 10, a double-sided loom backstrap, found in place around the hips of Individual 3, the woman in Burial 9, *291*

Figure 15.9. Textile 114a, associated with Burial 9, was a multicolored warp-stripe plain weave, *292*

Figure 15.10. Textile 171 of Burial 9 appears to be a bag, *293*

Figure 15.11. Textile 173 of Burial 9, a bag containing food, *294*

Figure 15.12. Textile 149b, associated with Burial 9, consisted of two types of cords, knotted together, *295*

Figure 15.13. Two skeins of wool, six spindles, and spindle whorls were among the contents of a disintegrated workbasket from Burial 9, *296*

Figure 16.1. View of Quebrada 5 with workmen salvaging items discarded by looters from Structure 12, *300*

Figure 16.2. Quebrada 5-south, showing locations of Structure 11 and Structure 12, *301*

Figure 16.3. Two views of the Structure 12 burial cist, *302*

Figure 16.4. Broken amphora, found in looters' backdirt next to Structure 12, *303*

Figure 16.5. Two vessels from Cerro Azul depicting the "fat skeleton," a motif featuring incised ribs as well as modeled arms and vertebral column, *304*

Figure 16.6. A broken Pingüino Buff shallow dish from Structure 12, *305*

Figure 16.7. Gourd #1, one of two gourd bowls found on the floor of Structure 12, included dried anchovetas, *lúcuma* seeds, tiny molluscs, and maize cobs, *306*

Figure 16.8. A vessel lid made from a gourd, found in Structure 12, *307*

Figure 16.9. Gourd #2, the second of two gourd bowls on the floor of Structure 12, contained beans, anchovetas, a guinea pig, and a bag, *308*

Figure 16.10. A white cotton bag found in Gourd #2 of Structure 12, *309*

Figure 16.11. A possible "medicine bundle," discovered in Structure 12, *310*

Figure 16.12. Two views of a silver disc, found in looters' backdirt adjacent to Structure 12, *311*

Figure 16.13. A *balanza* from Structure 12, Cerro Azul, *312*

Figure 16.14. A *balanza* found in Room 2, Structure D, Cerro Azul, *313*

Figure 16.15. A net fragment from Structure 12, *314*

Figure 16.16. A net fragment from Structure 12, with a potsherd attached as a weight, *315*

Figure 16.17. A *mallero* (wooden template used to create uniform mesh openings in fishing nets) discovered in Structure 12, *316*

Figure 16.18. Ungulate astragalus drilled through the condyles, found in Structure 12 of Cerro Azul, *316*

Figure 16.19. Cotton cloth from Structure 12 that contained maize fragments, *318*

Figure 16.20. Cotton cloth from Structure 12 that contained maize fragments, *319*

Figure 16.21. Colorful band from Structure 12, *320*

Figure 16.22. A round cord featuring bird motifs, found in Structure 12, *320*

Figure 16.23. Possible children's toys (wooden tops) from a burial and from *canchones* at Cerro Azul, *321*

Figure 16.24. Items kept in a storage bin in the Northeast Canchón of Structure D at Cerro Azul, *323*

Figure 16.25. Broken flute from Structure 12, Cerro Azul, *324*

Figure 16.26. Contents of a disintegrated workbasket found in Structure 12, *324*

Figure 16.27. Spindles from a disintegrated workbasket found in Structure 12, *325*

Figure 16.28. More spindles from a disintegrated workbasket found in Structure 12, *325*

Figure 16.29. Artist's rendering of spindles and whorls from a disintegrated workbasket found in Structure 12, *326*

Figure 16.30. Three of the yarn balls from one of the disintegrated workbaskets found in Structure 12, *326*

Figure 16.31. Structure 12, after we had salvaged all the artifacts, *327*

Figure 17.1. Four miniature Camacho Black vessels, said to be from the Cañete Valley, *340*

Overview and Acknowledgments

It was never our intention to excavate cemeteries at Cerro Azul. Our goal was to gather data on coastal ecosystems, economic specialization, and the lives of fishermen. Unfortunately, looters had arrived at Cerro Azul before we did, and they left human bones scattered across the slopes of Cerro Camacho. We could not bear to ignore this appalling destruction, so we decided to salvage as much information as we could. This volume reports on those burials, all of which dated to A.D. 1000–1470 (this timespan is called the Late Intermediate Period, and it precedes the Inca conquest of the coast).

At that time Cerro Azul was a fishing community. Like many other coastal sites, Cerro Azul focused on exploiting the rich marine life of the Pacific (Aland 2018; Coker 1908; Marcus 1987b, 2016b; Prieto and Sandweiss 2020; Weinberg et al. 2022). The fishermen at Cerro Azul caught many species of fish but specialized in drying and storing vast quantities of anchovies and sardines, apparently for export to farming communities within the Huarco [Warku] polity. This coastal polity was small and encircled by irrigation canals and defensive walls that extended across the lower Cañete Valley (Larrabure y Unanue 1935[1893]; Marcus 2008: Figs. 1.1, 1.2). In exchange for its dried fish, Cerro Azul acquired agricultural products from inland sites (Marcus 1987a, 1987b, 2016b, 2016d, 2016f).

Huarco and Lunahuaná

According to sixteenth-century ethnohistoric documents, the lower half of the Cañete Valley was divided into two polities—(1) Huarco, in the *yunga* or coastal plain, which included the fishing community of Cerro Azul, and (2) Lunahuaná, 28 kilometers upstream in the *chaupi yunga* or piedmont zone (Barraza Lescano et al. 2022; Chu 2015; Díaz Carranza 2015; Harth-Terré 1933; Hyslop 1984, 1985; Marcus 2008; Rostworowski de Diez Canseco 1978–1980).

One of the concerns of the Huarco *señorío* was defense; on its inland border, it was protected by a *gran muralla* or "great wall" (Larrabure y Unanue 1935[1893]; Marcus 2008: Fig. 1.2; Rostworowski de Diez Canseco 1978–1980). We have yet to identify the capital of the Huarco polity. One possibility is the site of Canchari, given its defensible hilltop location and its private supply of water for drinking and irrigating fields (Harth-Terré 1923, 1933; Rostworowski 1978–1980). Another possibility, advocated by Barraza Lescano et al. (2022) and by Hyslop (1984:89), is the huge site of Los Huacones-Vilcahuasi (Areche Espinola 2019; Campos Napán 2007). Ungará, a large fortified site overlooking the Cañete River, was perfectly situated to protect the takeoff point of Huarco's main irrigation canal (Harth-Terré 1923; Hyslop 1985; Marcus 2008:6).

The Inca strategy for annexing the lower Cañete region was to conquer the upvalley polity of Lunahuaná first, later descending to the coast to attack the Huarco polity. The Inca emperor Topa Inca Yupanqui subdued Lunahuaná around A.D. 1450 (Hyslop 1985; Marcus 2017). There the Inca constructed from scratch a "new Cusco"—the site of Inkawasi—which featured enormous storage facilities (Chu 2015; Hyslop 1985; Urton and Chu 2018). Using Inkawasi as its staging ground, the Inca initiated multiple attacks on Huarco. Cerro Azul valiantly refused to submit to the Inca, causing the imperial army to retreat on multiple occasions. The stalemate was finally broken when the Inca ruler announced that he had a desire for peace. In celebration, the people of Huarco got into their watercraft and went out to hold a ceremony at sea. While the celebrants were offshore, Inca troops descended upon Huarco and defeated it (Acosta 1954[1590]: Book 3, Chapter 15; Cieza de León 1932[1553], Chapters 73–74; Cieza de León 1959[1553]:337–344; Rostworowski 1978–1980).

Bernabé Cobo (1956[1653]: Tomo 92, Capítulo 15) provides additional information on this conquest. He notes that Huarco was administered by a *cacica* (a female ruler) who resisted Inca rule. When the *coya* (the empress, the wife of the Inca ruler) heard that the *cacica* of Huarco would not submit to the will of her husband, she laughed and devised a plan to deceive the *cacica*. Cobo says that it was the *coya* who sent a messenger telling the *cacica* of Huarco that the Inca ruler had decided to leave her in office, suggesting that she should hold a great celebration in honor of the sea to confirm the peaceful end to hostilities. Believing in the word of the Inca ruler, the *cacica* of Huarco ordered that preparations be made, and on the day of the celebration, all of her people set out to sea accompanied by music and drumbeats. When the celebrants were far from the coast, Inca troops took control of the lower Cañete Valley (Hyslop 1985; Marcus 2017; Rostworowski 1978–1980).

Community Specialization

From sixteenth-century accounts we learn that each coastal polity included fisherfolk at oceanfront sites and agriculturalists at inland sites (Castro and Ortega Morejón 1936[1558]; Rostworowski 1975, 1977a, 1977b, 1978–1980, 1981, 1999; Slovak and Paytan 2009; Zaro 2007). These communities were not merely economically specialized; each consumed a different mix of foods, displayed different cranial deformation, and appeared ethnically distinct (Chan 2011; Lozada and Buikstra 2002; Lozada and Rakita 2013:115; Marsteller et al. 2017a, 2017b; Tomczak 2003). Some fishermen on Peru's north coast even spoke their own distinct dialect, known as the "la lengua pescadora" (Rabinowitz 1980, 1983).

Unfortunately, the sixteenth-century documents do not tell us when such occupational specializations first appeared, nor do they reveal how goods circulated between specialists during earlier times. Archaeologists have been working to address these (and other) topics at large sites such as Pachacamac, La Centinela, and Inkawasi (e.g., Aguirre Morales 2008; Chu 2015; Daggett 1988; Eeckhout 2000, 2003, 2004a, 2004b, 2010, 2012, 2013; Eeckhout and López Hurtado 2018; Eeckhout and Owens 2008, 2015; Hyslop 1985; Marcone 2022; Morris 1988, 1998; Morris and Santillana 2007; Owens and Eeckhout 2015; Palma Málaga and Makowski 2019; Patterson 1985; Rostworowski 1973, 1978, 1991; Shimada 1991, 2015; Shimada et al. 2022; Takigami et al. 2014; Tello and Mejía Xesspe 1979; Tiballi 2020; Uhle 1903, 1924).

Less is known about smaller sites and the roles they played in (1) community specialization, (2) supplying goods to larger centers, and (3) the consumption of goods produced at the latter.

It was with these topics in mind that I began my excavations at Cerro Azul. Based on Kroeber's (1937) work at the site, I expected to find fish bones and fishing nets. What I did not expect was that the large tapia-walled compounds at Cerro Azul would have rooms with so many different functions: the industrial-level processing of fish, the brewing of maize beer, the raising of guinea pigs, and the weaving of both cotton and camelid wool textiles. Nor was I expecting to find the burials of elite women with their twill workbaskets, decorated needlecases, tapestry belts, backstrap looms, pouches containing pigment of different colors, metal *tupus* (cloak pins), and pieces of gold, silver, or copper in their mouths.

Previous Publications

My previous publications on Cerro Azul have discussed the architecture and pottery (Marcus 2008); fishing and the coastal ecosystems (Marcus 1987a, 2016b; Marcus et al. 1999, 2020; Marcus and Flannery 2010); the drying of fish for export (Marcus 2016d); the hunting of birds and mammals (Marcus 2016e); the barcoding of painted spindles (Marcus 2016a); the double-sided backstraps and slit tapestry belts (*chumpis*) (Marcus 2015); the brewery (Marcus 2009); and the impact of the Inca conquest on the Huarco polity (Marcus 1987a, 1987b, 2017; Marcus et al. 1985). This volume is designed to give a full account of the Late Intermediate burials that we salvaged.

Acknowledgments

The success of any archaeological project depends on having a talented team of excavators and analysts. Lending their expertise to the Cerro Azul project were Sonia Guillén, who analyzed the human skeletons; María Rostworowski de Diez Canseco, who provided ethnohistoric data; Kent Flannery, Jeffrey D. Sommer, and Christopher P. Glew, who analyzed the animal remains; Ramiro Matos Mendieta, who helped excavate the burial cists; C. Earle Smith, Jr., Lawrence Kaplan, and Linda Perry, who analyzed the plant remains; Charles M. Hastings, who mapped the site; John G. Jones, who analyzed the coprolites; James B. Stoltman, who conducted a petrographic analysis of the pottery; James Burton, who studied the pigments; Max Saltzman, who studied the yarn dyes; and Dwight Wallace, who studied the textiles. Wallace's descriptions of the textiles are given throughout this book.

The Cerro Azul project received substantial financial support, for which I am very appreciative. The 1982 field season was supported by a University of Michigan Faculty Fund Grant. The next four seasons of the project—entitled Archaeology and Ethnohistory of Cerro Azul, Cañete Valley, Peru—were supported by funds from the National Science Foundation (Grant BNS-8301542).

Excavation permits were awarded by Peru's Instituto Nacional de Cultura (Credencial 102-82-DCIRBM, Credencial 041-83-DCIRBM, Credencial 018-84-DPCM, and Resolución Suprema 357-85-ED).

The illustrations in this volume are the work of Kay Clahassey, John Klausmeyer, David West Reynolds, and Bruce Worden, four very talented artists. Seung-Og Kim printed the black and white photographs. I also want to thank our gifted editor, Elizabeth Noll, for steering this book through every phase of production.

Many colleagues encouraged me to publish the results of our excavations, and they include Robert McCormick Adams, Guillermo Algaze, Will Andrews, Rodrigo Areche Espinola, Kathryn Bard, Brian Bauer, Robin Beck, Véronique Bélisle, Duccio Bonavia, Elizabeth Boone, Geoffrey Braswell, Matthew Brown, Bob Carneiro, Lacey Carpenter, Luis Jaime Castillo Butters, Guillermo Cock, R. Alan Covey, Jordan Dalton, Allison Davis, Christopher B. Donnan, Robert Drennan, Tim Earle, Gary Feinman, Robert Feldman, Chelsea Fisher, Soren Frykholm, Michael Galaty, Sonia Guillén, John Henderson, Ken Hirth, Frank Hole, Judy Irvine, Patrick Kirch, Conrad Kottak, Jennifer Larios, Ashley Lemke, Tom Levy, Leonardo López Luján, Bruce Mannheim, Giancarlo Marcone Flores, Ramiro Matos Mendieta, Brett Meyer, Alicia Ventresca Miller, Bryan Miller, Craig Morris, Michael Moseley, Linda Nicholas, Jo Osborn, John O'Shea, Bill Parkinson, Stephen Plog, Tatiana Proskouriakoff, Rogger Ravines, Elsa Redmond, Don S. Rice, Prudence Rice, María Rostworowski de Diez Canseco, Jeremy Sabloff, Paula Sabloff, Robert Sharer, Jorge Silva, Charles Spencer, Jeffrey Splitstoser, Charles Stanish, Brian Stewart, Loa Traxler, John Verano, Evon Z. Vogt, Joseph Wardle, Gordon R. Willey, Ryan Williams, and Jason Yaeger.

I also appreciate the help of our workmen and local informants in the town of Cerro Azul—Edalio Aguidos, Marcelina Aguidos, Urbano Aguidos, Zenobio Aguidos, Pedro Álvarez, Alberto Barraza, Adolfo Casella, José Chumpitaz, Ruperto Corral, Cirilo Cruz, Víctor de la Cruz Álvarez, Pablo Cubillas, Víctor Cubillas, Ramón Espinosa, César (Chinaco) Francia, Iván Francia, Roberto García, José Huaratapaira, Ramón Landa, Carlos Manco Flores, José Antonio Manco Flores, Rufino Manco Flores, Francisco Padilla, Camilo Quispe, Edgar Zavala, and Pedro Manuel (Pato Loco) Zavala.

Part I

Background

Chapter 1

Mortuary Analysis

In areas with great preservation, such as the Peruvian coast, burials often provide much more information than the age and sex of the deceased. Cerro Azul's burials supplied data on weaving and other craft activities, personal style preferences, sexual division of labor, and interregional exchange. In some cases, even the functions of rare perishable artifacts can be suggested simply because they were included with a burial. We also found evidence for the storage of mineral pigments in waterproof pouches; gourd bowls with well-preserved corn on the cob; unfinished textiles still in place on loom bars; and matted human hair or coca leaves in the bottom of ceramic vessels.

The Role of Burials in the Built Environment

For more than a century, Andean archaeologists have been studying cemeteries and burial towers. Once such mortuary constructions were present, the landscapes they occupied were converted from unmodified spaces to a built environment with important new landmarks (Hyslop 1977; Stanish 2012; Tuan 1991). These formerly unaltered spaces could then become destinations for relatives, pilgrims, and others.

Archaeologists in many parts of the world have shown how adding cemeteries and monumental crypts to the landscape affected the use of a region. In the Andes, the construction of mortuary towers and cemeteries affected both the location of settlements and later mortuary features (Bongers 2019; Hyslop 1977; Nielsen 2008; Stanish 2012; Valdez et al. 2002). The mortuary towers called *chullpas* became gathering places; descendants came to them to honor their ancestors by offering coca, maize beer, and textiles (Figure 1.1). These visits were occasions during which descendants reinforced descent group membership and ethnic identity; they were opportunities to communicate with ancestors and honor family and *ayllu* members (Allen 1982, 1988, 2015; Guaman Poma de Ayala 1980[1615]; Lau 2021; Salomon 1995). Mortuary towers and cemeteries could also be used to redefine ethnic membership as well as reinforce social boundaries and territorial claims.

Once the landscape was dotted with mortuary constructions, the residents incorporated their ancestors' final resting places into their cognitive map. Burials came to serve as geographic landmarks, as reference points, as

Figure 1.1. An Andean *chullpa,* a funerary structure that could be seen from a distance, often served as a pilgrimage destination. The door at the base of the stone tower could be entered when necessary to add or remove mummy bundles. (This image was created by Kay Clahassey from illustrations in Gasparini and Margolies 1980:149, 151–153.)

symbols that could be manipulated to legitimize one's status or to help descendants reinforce claims to resources (Barrett 2001; Bartel 1982; Beck 1995; Bongers 2019; Chapman 1987, 1995, 2003, 2005, 2013; Chapman et al. 1981; Dillehay 1995; Doyle 1988; Fortes 1976; Goodenough 1965; Goody 1962; Hertz 1960; Hyslop 1977; Isbell 1997; Moore 1996; Newell 1976; Stanish 2012; Velasco 2022; Weinberg et al. 2015; Whitley 2002).

Burial towers housing relatives from different generations were used to bolster genealogical claims. In Figure 1.2 we see elite descendants standing in front of a burial tower (at left). One of them pours maize beer into a large two-handled vessel to honor the deceased couple (at right). In the background, we see the open door of the tomb and the bones of the ancestors. The label *yllapa* (lightning) refers to the deceased (*defunto* [sic]), according to Guaman Poma de Ayala (1980[1615], Volume I:262–263).

Initially, the people of the south-central Andes buried their dead below ground. By the third century B.C., however, some highland groups were experimenting with aboveground tumuli. By the twelfth century A.D., the highlanders were burying their ancestors in stone towers. Such aboveground tombs became a locus of offerings and ritual performances, a place where descendants could communicate with their ancestors (Stanish 2012).

The open doors and wall niches of *chullpas* suggest that they were designed for repeated use and the insertion of new interments (Bongers 2019; Hyslop 1977; Nielsen 2008). Keeping such tombs accessible was important not only for Andean populations, but also for groups such as the Zapotec and Maya of Mesoamerica and the Merina of Madagascar. By entombing multiple generations in one family crypt, Zapotec nobles reinforced lineage rights for their descendants (Marcus 2020; Middleton et al. 1998; Miller 1991, 1995). In speaking of the Merina, Bloch (1971:35) says "The tombs stand for the permanent unity of people and land; they place the ancestors in the land."

Prehistoric societies differed in their use of individual burials and actual cemeteries. Chapman (1999) has argued that when early farming communities in central Europe began to create cemeteries, it marked the use of the ancestors to symbolize claims to resources. Some ancient societies, to be sure, lacked separate burial grounds; instead, their burials were incorporated within the settlement. In some cases, the bodies of nobles might be inserted into public buildings, temples, or family shrines, where rituals could be conducted by their descendants on designated anniversaries (e.g., Becker 1992; Cobo 1990[1653]:250–251; Doyle 1988; Fitzsimmons 1998, 2002, 2006; Huntington and Metcalf 1979; Isbell and Korpisaari 2015; Kidder et al. 1946; Marcus 2020; Metcalf and Huntington 1991; Millaire 2004; Sharer and Traxler 2006; Trik 1963). In contrast, commoners could be buried below their own houses (e.g., Cobo 1990[1653]:40; Flannery and Marcus 2005; Mantha 2015; Marcus 2004; Quilter 1989). In such societies, nobles affected the built environment in ways that commoners did not.

Many of these practices have continued into the ethnographic present. For example, Kopytoff (1971:129) says, "The African emphasis is clearly not on how the dead live but on the manner in which they affect the living." Among the Suku of the Congo, for example, some individuals were worshiped as ancestors. In Mexico, many Zapotec nobles were also worshiped; these deceased nobles

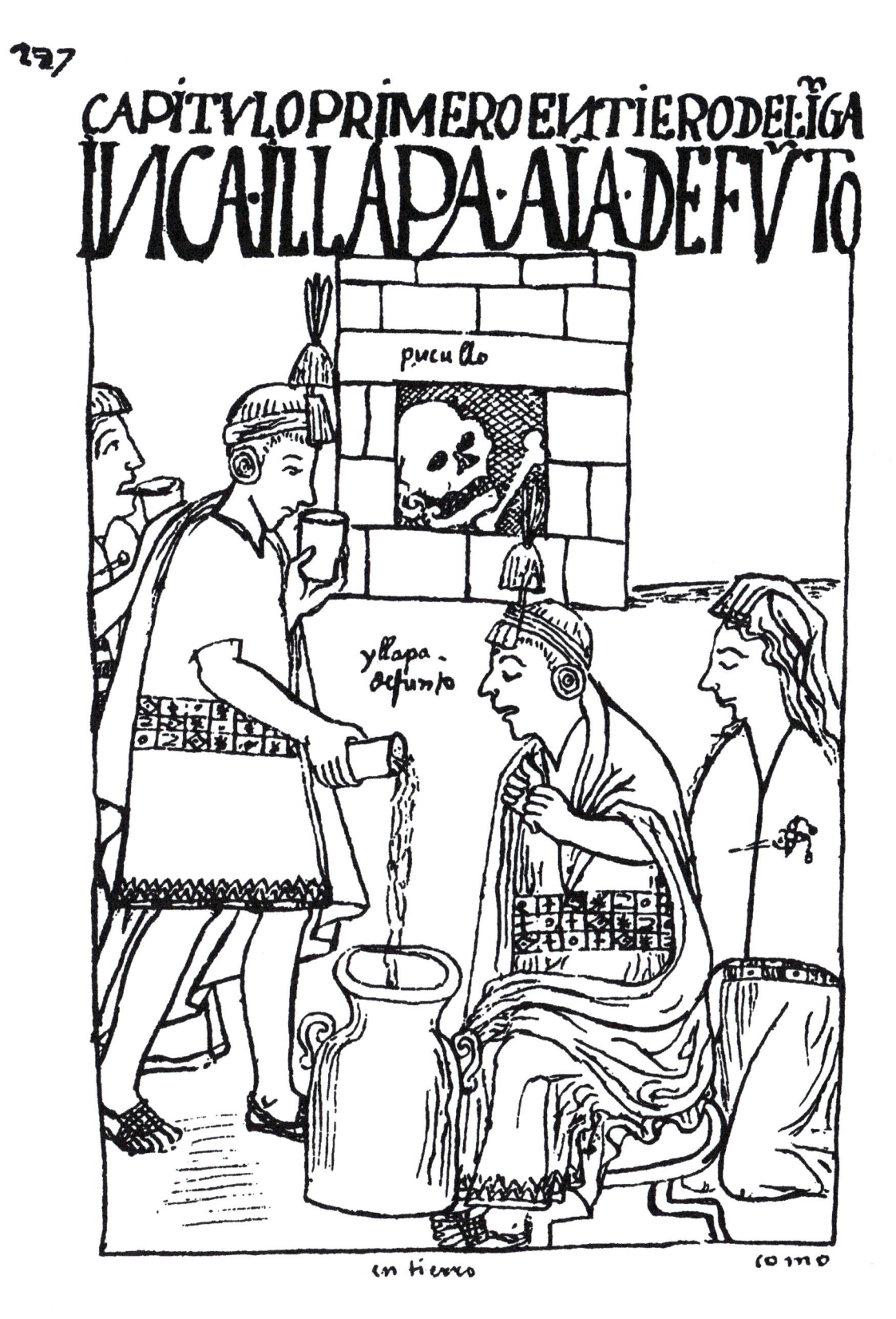

Figure 1.2. In this seventeenth-century drawing, a royal Inca mummy and his mummified spouse (lower right) are honored by their descendants. On the left, one attendee drinks *chicha* while another pours it into a vessel in front of the mummies. The labels *yllapa* (lightning) and *defunto* (deceased) are written in front of one mummy's face. In the background is the open door of a funerary structure, with the bones of ancestors visible inside (Guaman Poma de Ayala 1980 [1615], I:262–263).

acted as intermediaries between their living offspring on the one hand, and divine beings, supernatural forces, and ancestors on the other. And even among today's Zapotec, "Dead kin, especially parents, continue to exert great influence on the living, not infrequently receiving as much attention as during life" (Chiñas 1973:60).

Andean societies still revere the dead, who are "perceived to be powerful and sacred"; ancestors watch "over the welfare of their descendants, affecting their health and well-being, their crops, human and animal fertility, the weather, and their fortunes in general" (Dean 2010:29).

These Andean, Mexican, and African societies did not draw a sharp line between the living and the dead. For example, the Suku of Africa still regard their dead as elders, as generic ancestors whose distinctive individual characteristics disappear at the time of their death. Simply stated, the dead occupy the oldest age grade and are still part of the living world.

The Ongoing Use of Tombs

Mortuary studies have often highlighted cultures that reenter tombs on multiple occasions. In such societies the burial ritual is not a single moment (e.g., Chase and Chase 1996, 1998, 2003, 2011; Hecker and Hecker 1992; Lind 2003; Millaire 2002, 2004; Nelson 1998; Rakita et al. 2005; Reese-Taylor et al. 2006; Shimada and Fitzsimmons 2015; Shimada et al. 2004, 2015; Takigami et al. 2014; van Gennep 1960; Weiss-Krejci 2001, 2004), but rather a series of visits, with tomb contents altered over time.

We now know that some tombs were reentered to add burials, offerings, and new quantities of pigment (Bloch and Parry 1982; Bongers et al. 2023; Caso 1969; Chase and Chase 1996, 1998, 2003; Middleton et al. 1998; Millaire 2004; Quinn 2015; Sharer and Traxler 2006; Weiss-Krejci 2003). When such reentries occurred, older skeletons were often shoved to the back of a tomb to make room for new bodies (Bloch 1971; Caso 1969; Kenyon 1960:189–190; Middleton et al. 1998; Millaire 2004; Miller 1991; J. Rowe 1995; Takigami et al. 2014). Certain bones, such as crania and femora, might be removed at that time (Chase and Chase 2011; Coe 1959; Feinman et al. 2010; Lind 2003; Marcus 1983, 2020). In other cases, bones might be defleshed and sprinkled with red pigment (Bongers et al. 2023; Verano 2003, 2016). Sometimes older remains were wrapped in new cloth and relocated within the tomb (e.g., Ashmore 2013; Bloch 1971; Marcus 2020). Some reentries could also involve the removal of entire mummy bundles and the insertion of others (Bloch 1971; Eeckhout and Owens 2015; Marcus 2020:237; Shimada et al. 2015; Tello and Mejía Xesspe 1979).

Evidence for Reentry

Various clues indicate that a tomb has been reentered. One clue is the presence of artifacts from different time periods, with contrasting dated texts and styles (e.g., Bernal 1976; Miller 1995). In the case of Tomb 7 at Dainzú in the Valley of Oaxaca (Mexico), the tomb lintel had been turned 180 degrees and vessels from more than one period were present (Bernal 1976:297; Marcus 2020:221). In the case of Tomb 28 at Yagul in Oaxaca, the tomb door had been removed and left to one side (Marcus 2020:332–333). Tombs were reentered multiple times at Lambityeco (also in Oaxaca). For example, Lambityeco's Tomb 6 contained the skeletons of six individuals; not only was a new body periodically inserted into the tomb, but the femur of a deceased ancestor was removed at that time. Friezes on the tomb exterior proclaim dynastic continuity by providing the names of marital pairs; they also show the firstborn son of each married couple brandishing the femur of his father (Lind and Urcid 1983; Marcus 2020; Miller 1995; Rabin 1970). These scenes of femur brandishing were not merely symbolic; nine of the expected twelve femora from six individuals had been removed from the tomb. Another Oaxaca case was Tomb 5 at Cerro de la Campana, in which each reentry led to the painting of a new hieroglyphic text on a lintel inside the tomb (Miller 1995).

One of our best-known ethnographic cases of tomb reentry is that of the Merina of Madagascar, where relatives of the deceased entered their family tomb after each death to add a new corpse. These reentries facilitated close physical interaction with all previously dead relatives (Bloch 1971). During these reentries, the Merina removed some old corpses from the tomb to dance with them, sing to them, and carry them in processions, all the while recounting the past deeds of each ancestor. Relatives might then rewrap a corpse in red cloth and return it to the family tomb. The introduction of each body obviously required the rearrangement of those already in the tomb.

Similar interactions between the living and the dead are known for the Inca. Friar Bernabé Cobo's comments, largely based on Juan Polo de Ondegardo's 1559 account, were as follows:

> They celebrated the anniversary of the man's death by coming at certain times to the tomb. Opening it, they put new clothing and fresh food in place of what had been

put there before, and they offered some sacrifices. ..... The way of putting the body into the tomb was not the same everywhere. In the Valley of Jauja, the body was placed in a fresh llama skin, and it was sewn up so as to show the face with the nose, mouth, and the rest. In Chincha, the burial was performed with the bodies placed on *barbacoas*, a cane framework of a bed. But most of the kingdom followed the custom of the Incas and natives of Cuzco, who buried their dead seated on the ground, the head over the knees, and if they were lords, they were placed on their *duhos* or low benches (translated by Roland Hamilton, from Cobo 1990[1653]:250–251).

In some cases, bodies were mummified so that they could be periodically removed and displayed in public. Mummified Inca emperors, seated on litters, were carried to distant parts of the empire (see Figure 1.3). These trips enabled the dead ruler to visit his people and deliver in-person messages through his oracle or spokesperson (Guaman Poma de Ayala 1980[1615], Volume I:230–231). From sixteenth-century documents, we learn that the mummy of the ruler continued to play major political, religious, and social roles, thanks to official litter-bearers who carried him across the landscape. His mummy also attended ceremonies in Cuzco, where he sat alongside the mummies of earlier rulers (e.g., Bauer 2004; Sillar 1992).

At Late Intermediate Cerro Azul, as we will see, the venue for reentry or collective mass burials was a stone-lined burial cist on the slopes of Cerro Camacho.

The Social Construction of Value

The objects included in a burial, whether they were the deceased's possessions or the mourners' gifts, had a value of some kind. It falls to the archaeologist to deduce that value—not an easy task, given the elapsed time and the sociocultural differences involved.

In some cases, the value of the object derived from the fact that it was an heirloom owned by an earlier individual. For example, some of the items in King Tutankhamun's tomb bore labels indicating that they had been owned by his Egyptian relatives; included was a lock of his royal grandmother's hair. I mention this because at Cerro Azul, the hair of other individuals was sometimes included with a burial.

As for the "value" of burial objects, Papadopoulos and Urton (2012:21–22) have isolated four types—"place value," "body value," "object value," and "number value." Running through each of their four categories were aspects of identity, biography, memory, and nostalgia.

A recent example will show how difficult it can be to interpret value without knowing the backstory. Actress Lauren Bacall placed a whistle in Humphrey Bogart's coffin because it evoked the lines she spoke to him in the 1944 movie, *To Have and Have Not*: "You know how to whistle, don't you, Steve? You just put your lips together and blow." Bacall had the burial whistle engraved with another of her lines, "If you want anything, just whistle." That one sentence evoked the memory of their first movie together; it symbolized their love.

This example, for which we know the backstory, emphasizes that objects have a value that may only be known to the people involved, such as a widow and her deceased husband. If we were to find a whistle in a man's grave today—especially one without an inscription—we would not know the meaning it held for the person who contributed it. We might conclude that the man buried with the whistle was a basketball referee, a high school football coach, or even a policeman, any of whom could be associated with a whistle.

Christopher Donnan (2012) and Donnan and Mackey (1978) have also tackled the topic of value and the ways it manifested itself among the Moche of the north coast of Peru. In his study of more than 130 Moche burials, Donnan (2012:186) concluded: "The Moche put a high value on precious materials, extraordinary craftsmanship, the use of color, and the creation of shiny surfaces. They also valued forms derived from nature and objects that rattled and shimmered in reflected light—features that gave the objects an animated, lifelike quality."

By gilding a copper *tupu*, the Moche could convert an ordinary cloak pin into a shimmering object that appeared to be solid gold, increasing its value. By pyroengraving a common gourd, they made it more valuable. By adding colorful embroidery or dyed wool decoration to a plain weave white cotton garment, they increased that textile's value.

A problem for the archaeologist, of course, is that value can change over time. At one moment, an item might be totally restricted to the upper class, and in subsequent periods more accessible to commoners. In Mesoamerica, for example, access to jade ornaments was restricted in some periods and more widely available in others.

In Peru, metal often played the same role that jade played in Mesoamerica. When metal first appeared on the north coast of Peru, it seems to have been regarded as a prestige item for high-status people. Gold was seemingly the most inaccessible, restricted to royalty or nobles. As objects of metal became more common over time, even prosperous commoners might have access to copper and silver.

Figure 1.3. At the top of another Colonial drawing, we read Noviembre Aia Marcai Quilla, which refers to "November, the month of the dead." That was the month the dead were traditionally put on litters and transported through the streets. At the bottom we read "la fiesta de los defuntos," referring to the fact that after the dead were removed from the funerary structures, they were fed, given beverages, and dressed, while mourners sang and danced (Guaman Poma de Ayala 1980[1615] I:230–231).

Setting Land Aside as a Cemetery

The concept of "value" also comes into play when previously undedicated land is converted to a cemetery. As Tuan (1977:6) has noted, "what begins as undifferentiated space becomes place as we get to know it better and endow it with *value*...". An unused piece of land, once regarded as undifferentiated space, can become endowed with meaning after the remains of the dead are buried there.

In the case of Cerro Azul, the cemetery was the endproduct of multiple stages. The first step was to convert the rocky slopes of Cerro Camacho's quebradas into a series of midden-filled terraces. Residents of the site's large tapia (or poured mud wall) compounds originally began to use some quebradas as places to dump their garbage. As midden accumulated, they added rough stone retaining walls to prevent the discarded material from sliding downslope; this strategy allowed the deposits to deepen. Once its fill was sufficiently deep, a terrace could be employed as a site for earth ovens or burial cists (Marcus 2008).

One of the localities used for burial cists was Terrace 9 of Alfred Louis Kroeber's Quebrada 5a. We found no evidence that this terrace had been selected in advance as a cemetery; its midden deposits had simply accumulated to the point where they provided an adequate matrix to insert subterranean cists. We assume that looters found some of these cists by trial and error, testing one terrace after another. Certainly, there were no signs on the surface that Terrace 9 had been used as a cemetery.

The burials on Terrace 9 included a wide variety of artifacts, many of which had been discarded or ignored by the looters. Each burial object varied in terms of (1) its raw material; (2) the distance it had traveled; (3) the place where it was manufactured; and (4) the skill and workmanship involved (Appadurai 1986; Bailey and Mills 1998; Papadopoulos and Urton 2012). The difficulty faced by the archaeologist, of course, is inferring what value was placed on any given object by members of the Late Intermediate society.

Some of these burial items appeared to be new and unused; others were broken, worn, or repaired. Some gourd vessels, for example, had clearly been repaired multiple times; in such cases, we suspected that we were seeing one of the deceased's personal possessions. Similarly, when we found fishing nets that had been repaired, we assumed that we were seeing the deceased's property, rather than a gift contributed by a mourner. In the case of a woman's burial, we suspected that a workbasket filled with spindles, needles, and yarn balls was her personal property. On the other hand, a relatively new water jar or gourd bowl—filled with food for the afterlife—was more likely to be a contributed item.

To be sure, in many cases the looting had made it impossible to associate all of an individual's objects with his or her mummy. Fortunately, we found a few mostly intact burials—enough to conclude that a *fardo*, or mummy bundle, likely contained a mixture of personal property and contributed goods.

We were aided in our interpretation of the Cerro Azul burials by mortuary analyses from other sites. The burials from Pacatnamu, for example, reinforced the inference that gourd vessels were highly valued in the afterlife (Donnan and Cock 1986; Donnan and McClelland 1997). Burial 42 at that site, a woman in her thirties, had 19 gourd vessels (Figure 1.4). Burial 44, a woman 25–35 years old, had the same number (Donnan and McClelland 1997:119, 123). Most of these gourds had been shaped into cups, bowls, and plates, while others had the shape of bottles (Donnan 1995: Fig. 19). Some gourd vessels were empty when found, while others still held corn, beans, cotton seeds, or *yuyu* (edible seaweed).

Metals, especially gold and silver, are some of the burial objects relied on by archaeologists to determine social status in Peru. Once again, however, we are faced with the problem of determining whether such metal objects were personal property or contributed goods. In the case of the Moche, only the graves of high-status individuals contained metals in large quantities, particularly gold, silver, and gilded copper (Alva and Donnan 1993). Lower-status burials seem to have contained mostly copper or no metal at all. In addition, copper objects were generally bent or broken prior to their placement in Moche graves, while objects of gold were generally not intentionally damaged.

When only a few objects of metal were put in a Moche grave, they were usually placed in the mouth or hand of the deceased. In the case of the mouth, folded or rolled-up wedges of metal were common. We can assume that such acts were performed by the persons who prepared the body for burial. Such rolled-up wedges of metal also appeared in the mouths of Cerro Azul men, women, and children.

By Inca times, burial customs varied from one quarter (*suyu*) of the empire to another; we can read about these in descriptions of Chinchaysuyu, Antisuyu, Collasuyu, and Cuntisuyu (e.g., Guaman Poma de Ayala 1980[1615]:262–271). For the quarter called Collasuyu, Guaman Poma de Ayala says that burial rites took place five days after death. If the individual was wealthy, he was richly dressed, placed in a seated position, and given vessels of gold, silver, and clay. If the individual was poor, only food was offered. To celebrate

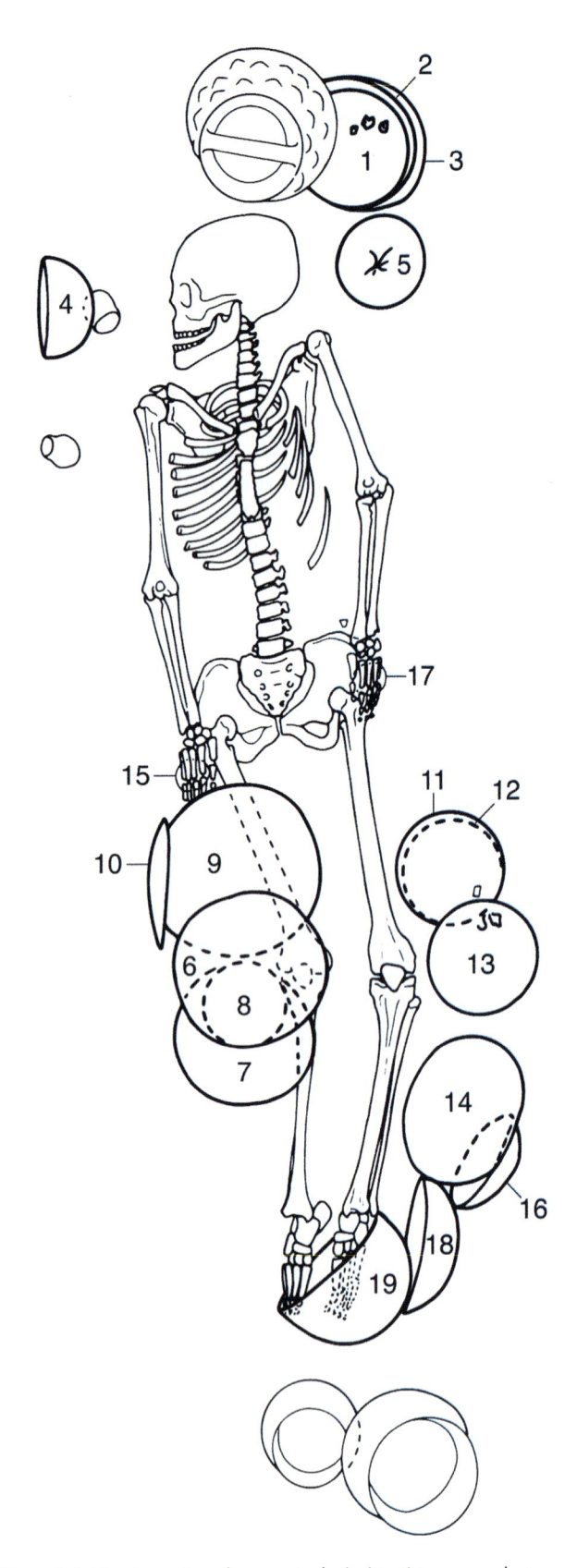

Figure 1.4. Nineteen gourds were included in this woman's grave at the site of Pacatnamu, on the north coast of Peru (redrawn from Donnan and McClelland 1997:119).

the life of the deceased, living mourners came back after ten days to offer food and liquid, especially maize beer and water. In this *suyu* of the Inca Empire, the rites were repeated after six months had elapsed, and again after one year.

The Inca set aside the month of November to honor their ancestors (*mes de llevar difuntos*, "the month to carry the dead"). They removed the dead from the open tombs called *pucullo*; they fed them, gave them beverages, and dressed them in lavish or elegant clothing and put feathers on their head; they sang and danced with them. They put them on litters and transported them from house to house and through the streets and through the plaza and later returned them to their tomb, giving the rich their silver and gold, and the poor their objects of clay. They gave llamas and cloth, which they buried with them. In November they carried them on litters during *aya marcai*, "carrying the dead" (Guaman Poma de Ayala 1980[1615], Volume I:231).

The Inca emperor's mummy was seated and displayed in elaborate textiles, wearing a cloak with a feather collar and ruff, holding a coca bag, and wearing a headband signifying Chinchaysuyu (drawn by Guaman Poma de Ayala 1980[1615], Volume I:230–231). Mourners referred to the ruler's corpse as *yllapa* ("lightning"); the other corpses were called *aya* ("the deceased"). Those servants who were to accompany him in death were forced to become drunk and had powdered coca inserted into their mouths. After an emperor's death, there was a month filled with songs, dances, and crying; at the end of the month he was buried in a stone tomb.

Guaman Poma de Ayala (1980[1615]) illustrates a Chinchaysuyu mummy being carried on a litter while his widow (*yquima*) walks along nearby. They are shown passing a *pucullo* (Guaman Poma de Ayala 1980[1615], Volume I:264–265).

Inferring Social Status from Grave Goods

Archaeology has a long history of inferring social status from the number and nature of grave goods (e.g., Binford 1971; Braun 1981; Brown 1971a, 1971b, 1995; Carmichael 1988, 1995; Deetz 1967; Degano and Colombini 2009; Donnan and McClelland 1997; Goldstein 1976, 1980, 1981, 1995, 2006; Milner 1984, 1995; O'Shea 1981, 1997; Saxe 1970, 1971; Tainter 1978; Turner et al. 2010; Yarrow 1880).

Given the enormous variation in prehistoric societies, however, there is no agreed-upon standard for all times and regions. Wherever possible, archaeologists tend to rely on the "direct historical approach" (Parker 1922; Ritchie

1932, 1938; Strong 1933, 1935; Wedel 1938), tying their inferences to the known historical or ethnohistorical record of a particular culture. Fortunately, the Andean area is one where considerable ethnohistoric data are available.

In the Peruvian highlands, inferences rely largely on nonperishable items such as pottery and precious metals. The arid Pacific coast, however, adds countless perishable items, such as multicolored textiles, carved wooden scales (*balanzas*), pyroengraved gourds, or even tattooed designs on the skin of mummies (Allison et al. 1981; Kroeber and Strong 1924:38; van Dalen Luna et al. 2018; Vásquez Sánchez et al. 2013).

Pottery is often the least impressive category in an elite burial, a cautionary tale for those working in regions with no preservation of perishable goods. At Cerro Azul, we found elite women with impressive perishable items, yet only the most drab pottery beside them. The full range of their possessions came to light only because their incised needlecases, exquisite textiles, barcoded spindles, and imported alpaca wool yarn balls were preserved. We were encouraged to infer not only their social status but also some of their favorite craft activities. In some cases, we found that a dying individual might be buried with medicinal coca tea, a final meal of crayfish soup, a pyroengraved gourd, or clutching an unfinished braided cord in her hand.

One last benefit of coastal preservation has to do with baskets and cloth bags. We recovered many items that, in the highlands, would simply have been found loose in the dirt of a burial. At Cerro Azul, every item was found inside a bag or basket, or wrapped in a cloth. One of my favorite examples was a nondescript chunk of chalk-like material which, if found loose, would have been assigned no function. Because it was found inside a woman's spinning and sewing basket, Kroeber's workers suggested that the chalk-like material might have been used to coat one's fingers (or coat the yarn itself) during one of these activities (Kroeber 1937:248). Vreeland (1986:367) says that his informants use powdered chalk when spinning "to dust their fingers to absorb sweat and oils, which lessen their ability to rotate the spindle effectively."

Sample Size and Representativeness

A universal problem for archaeologists is wondering whether their sample of burials is representative, including examples of every status category. At Cerro Azul, neither Kroeber nor I recovered the full range of burials. Kroeber generally found the burials of fisherfolk; among the burials I salvaged, I found the remains of elite women. When Kroeber's discoveries are added to mine, a richer picture of Cerro Azul emerges.

Even at sites where excavation has gone on for decades, archaeologists often remain unconvinced that they have an adequate sample of burials. In Mesoamerica, Teotihuacan is estimated to have had a peak population of 125,000; Tikal is estimated to have had 50,000 (e.g., Haviland 1969; Millon 1992; Sanders and Price 1968). At neither site does the current sample of burials seem adequate. Sometimes our samples are small and unrepresentative because less important people did not receive the same burial treatment, and, in some instances, the cemeteries lie outside the settlement. Even the small Formative site of Tomaltepec (Oaxaca, Mexico) provides a cautionary tale: its cemetery was found 100 meters outside the limits of the early village, as defined by surface sherds (Whalen 1981).

The largest possible sample of burials is needed to detect patterns and trends, and to say something significant about society as a whole (e.g., Cock and Goycochea Díaz 2004; van Dalen Luna and Majchrzak 2019). After studying hundreds of burials from seven cemeteries, O'Shea (1984, 1995) provided an overview of the Early and Middle Bronze Age tribal societies of southeast Hungary and adjacent portions of Romania. Among his conclusions were the following: "The central role of funerary activities in the assertion of common identity and in the demarcation of tribal boundaries is particularly striking. It equally is clear, however, that under such circumstances a meaningful understanding of past funerary practices can only be obtained when viewed in light of multiple sites and multiple archaeological contexts" (O'Shea 1995:126).

The potential for a similar study can be found in Julio C. Tello's sample of one thousand mummy bundles from three different cemeteries on Peru's Paracas Peninsula (Wari Kayan, Cerro Colorado, and Cabeza Larga). Unfortunately, relatively few of these mummy bundles have been opened for study. At Wari Kayan, for example, where Tello found 429 mummies, only about 50 bundles have been opened and subjected to detailed study (Peters 2000).

Other large burial samples from Peru include 500 tombs from 40 Late Intermediate cemeteries in the Chincha Valley (Weinberg et al. 2015). At the site of Pachacamac on Peru's central coast, Uhle (1903:12) found six cemeteries and divided the burials into three types based on their location: (1) those in cemeteries, (2) those in temples, and (3) those in other buildings. At Ancón, near Lima, Dorsey had excavated 127 graves by 1894; hundreds more have been recovered since the nineteenth century. Dorsey divided his

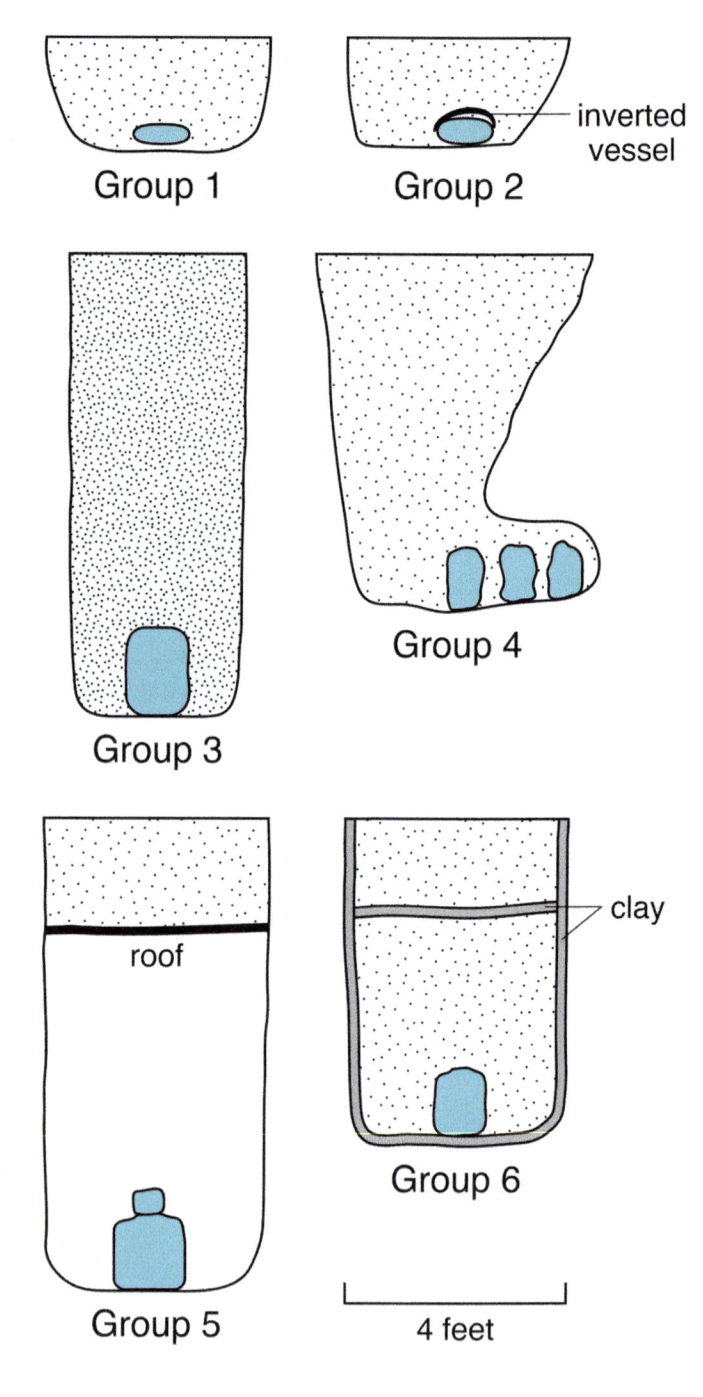

Figure 1.5. While excavating in 1891 at Ancón, George Dorsey divided the graves he found into six groups. Group 1 consisted of a pit containing one individual, wrapped in cloth; Dorsey considered this burial type to be that of a poor person. Group 2 consisted of the same kind of pit, but with the added feature of an inverted vessel above the body. Seven of the nine Group 2 burials were those of children. Dorsey classified only four graves as belonging to Group 3, defined by a stone-lined shaft that could be more than eight feet deep. Group 4 graves, more than six feet deep, contained more than one person (in one instance, 17 individuals). Group 5 (Dorsey's most numerous category) consisted of graves nine feet deep, with a single mummy and a roof of hard clay. Group 6 consisted of three graves that were lined with white clay, carefully smoothed, and with finger impressions still visible. Dorsey noted that most individuals had their toes and fingers tied together with string; a few had their hair held in place by a sling. Mummy bundles in this illustration are shown in blue. [Here we retain Dorsey's original scale, which used "feet," rather than meters.]

Ancón graves into six types (see Figure 1.5), some of which are known from other coastal sites.

Much larger samples from coastal cemeteries are providing abundant data on mortuary practices—for example, the 1286 mummy bundles from Puruchuco (Cock and Goycochea Díaz 2004) and the 1500 burials from Cerro Colorado in the Huaura Valley, in the area known locally as the "Norte Chico" (van Dalen Luna and Majchrzak 2019; van Dalen Luna et al. 2021).

Even by combining my sample with Kroeber's, Cerro Azul has provided only 70 individuals, a number much too small to allow for sweeping generalizations. In such a limited sample, it is unlikely that the full range of ages, statuses, professions, burial treatments, and offerings are represented. For example, as we shall see later in this volume, elite men seem to be underrepresented in our current sample.

The Cerro Azul sample is similar in size to the 64 burials recently excavated in the Huarmey Valley by Więckowski (2019). Equally similar is the fact that a number of elite women were recovered from the site, known today as the Castillo de Huarmey. Of the 64 individuals buried in the Castillo's centrally located chamber, only 52 could be sexed and all 52 were females. As was the case with the elite women from Cerro Azul, Huarmey's elite women were associated with spindles and spindle whorls. At Huarmey, however, the excavators found a greater number—more than 350 spindle whorls and hundreds of spindles, some of which were of gold.

Based on signs of skeletal stress, biological anthropologists concluded that these Huarmey women were longtime users of backstrap looms (Figure 1.6 a, b). They had all been buried in the seated position, their faces covered with red pigment, and their bodies wrapped in textiles. The central woman of the group was distinguished by elaborate ear ornaments, a *tupu* cloak pin, a stone *kero* or drinking vessel, gold and silver whorls and spindles, and Wari style pottery. Three percent of the females in the group were 10 years of age or younger; 17 percent were 10 to 20 years of age. The remainder were adults, but less than 10 percent of them were over the age of 50. The central woman in the group was accompanied by two skeletons whose left feet were missing, a mutilation sometimes performed on sacrificed captives.

Let us turn now to the Moche, for whom a large sample is available. By 1995 Christopher Donnan had amassed a database of 326 Moche burials from 18 archaeological sites in eight north coastal valleys. He divided his study into five categories: (1) preparation of the corpse; (2) the manner in which the corpse was encased (from shroud wrap to plank coffin); (3) the type of funerary chamber (from simple pit to large rectangular chamber); (4) the quantity and quality of grave goods (from low to extremely high); and (5) the burial location (from sterile soil to inside pyramids).

More than 55 percent of Donnan's burials came from two sites: the Pyramids at Moche and the site of Pacatnamu. The majority was buried fully extended, supine. Although some boot-shaped chambers at Pacatnamu and San José de Moro contained several individuals, most Moche graves held just one person (Donnan 1995:136; Donnan and Donnan 1997). Most of the well-preserved Moche burials had unspun cotton pads covering the eyes or face; these pads were placed there before the whole body was wrapped in cloth (Donnan 1995:123–125). In a few instances, men were found wearing a shirt and loincloth, but many of the well-preserved individuals were naked, with their clothing placed nearby. Several Moche burials had a wad of unspun cotton placed under their heads, evidently to serve as a pillow. Bodies were often tied with cords and had camelid wool yarn wrapped around the deceased's head, hands, fingers, wrists, or ankles. While one should never be overconfident, Donnan's sample is more likely to be representative than most.

Lifetime Modifications to the Body

Individuals in some societies had their bodies modified by piercing, tattooing, and/or cranial deformation. Such modifications often conveyed information about age, gender, marital status, political standing, wealth or other factors (e.g., Houston et al. 2006; Joyce 1998, 2005, 2008; Meskell and Joyce 2003; Romero Molina 1958, 1970; Tiesler 2012; Verano 2003, 2016; Weiss 1932; Yacovleff and Muelle 1932). Because of excellent preservation on the Peruvian coast, it is the ideal venue to study such body modification.

Each major rite of passage in a person's life could be accompanied by the alteration of physical features. Parents could tighten headbands, cords, or wooden boards around an infant's head to reshape the cranium; many varieties of head deformation were practiced in ancient Peru. One example can be seen at the site of Cabeza Larga on the Paracas Peninsula, so named by Tello for the presence of skulls with that type of cranial deformation (Tello 1959; Tello and Mejía Xesspe 1979). Tello first examined 50 skulls lying on the surface, and then augmented them by excavating an additional 135 burials (DeLeonardis 2012; Tello 1929, 2009; Tello and Mejía Xesspe 1979; Tomasto-Cagigao 2009; Tomasto-Cagigao et al. 2015; Verano 2016: Fig. 5.8).

In addition to cranial deformation, Paracas populations practiced trephining (removing small, usually circular, pieces of bone from the skull). Verano (2016:103) studied 59 trephined skulls from Paracas and showed that 68 percent were males and 29 percent were females. In these cases, however, it was more likely that the individuals were seeking to alleviate pain than commemorate a life milestone. Verano (2016:105) suggests that many Paracas males had suffered blunt force trauma in battle and were trephined to relieve the pain and pressure. Trephinations were most common on the frontal bone (43 percent), less often on the occipital (21 percent) and on the left side or midline of the skull (14 percent). The least common location was on the right side of the skull (8 percent). One inference is that such head trauma was most often the result of a blow from a right-handed enemy wielding a club.

It is generally believed that a Paracas "surgeon" first made a groove to delimit the boundaries of the area to be cut. Then he or she slowly scraped the outer bone table and spongy bones, starting on the outside and working inward to the center, all the while leaving a thin portion of the inner bone table to be carefully broken and removed. Tello found a possible surgical kit in one of the Paracas Cavernas tombs (Tello 1929:147–148; Tello and Mejía Xesspe 1979:204). This kit included obsidian knives stained with blood; the knives were of various sizes and still bore wooden handles.

The fact that both men and women were trephined suggests that while men were regarded as warriors, women may have also been injured while fighting in raids and in defending their communities.

Natural and Artificial Mummification

Long fascinated by mummification, archaeologists are only now realizing what an ancient and widespread process it was. We now know that coastal hunting-gathering groups of southern Peru and northern Chile (ca. 7000–2000 B.C.) engaged in both natural and artificial mummification. It is possible that natural mummification—caused by the sun and hot sand—occurred first, and led to deliberate attempts to preserve bodies (especially those of children) by defleshing them, then wrapping them in reed mats, camelid fur, or pelican skin. The hands and feet of some of the earliest mummies had string tied around each finger and toe, evidently placed there to keep the digits together. This practice of tying digits together with a string survived into the Late Intermediate Period at places like Cerro Azul.

In northern Chile and southernmost Peru, some early mummies were given headbands or even wigs. In our sample of burials at Cerro Azul, we found headbands, but no wigs.

Some of our earliest examples of artificial mummification come from the Chinchorro culture of southern Peru and northern Chile (Bittmann and Munizaga 1976, 1979; Guillén 1992; Marquet et al. 2012; Rivera 1995; Standen 1997; Standen et al. 2014). Chinchorro populations engaged in the removal of flesh from the body, the drying of bones by the application of hot ash, the reapplication of human skin, or the substitution of skin from sea lions or pelicans (Allison et al. 1984; Arriaza 1995a, 1995b, 2016; Arriaza et al. 2005; Aufderheide 2003; Aufderheide et al. 1993; Guillén 1992). In a sample of more than 280 Chinchorro mummies, 30 percent were found to be naturally mummified while 70 percent were artificially mummified. Some Chinchorro mummies (including children) had wooden sticks or reeds that either substituted for, or reinforced, arm and leg bones.

Arguably, the oldest known Chinchorro mummy is Acha Man, a naturally desiccated body found in the Quebrada Acha near Arica in southernmost Peru. One of the Chinchorro sites there, known as Acha 2, was a camp occupied by what seems to have been an egalitarian hunting-gathering band. Located six kilometers inland from the Pacific Ocean, the site consisted of eleven circular huts. Each hut had a central hearth, one of which yielded a date of 6950 B.C. Also found at Acha 2 was a body wrapped in a mat and camelid fur, dating to 7020 B.C. (Arriaza 1995b; Muñoz et al. 1993). The earliest 153 mats from funerary contexts have recently been discussed by Santos and Standen (2022).

Some Chinchorro mummies were buried with net bags. A few men were buried with a harpoon foreshaft held in their hands, or with shell and cactus fishhooks, stone knives, fishhook weights, throwing sticks, darts, or lanceolate points. Other individuals were associated with camelid or sea lion ribs attached to a handle, a tool allegedly used to pry shellfish off the sea cliff.

Chinchorro cemeteries were small but densely packed, and regardless of whether the mummification was natural or artificial, bodies shared a series of postmortem practices (such as having the face coated in mud or painted red or black). It is striking that even at this early date, we see that about 25 percent of the bodies had healed skull fractures, showing that interpersonal violence was not infrequent.

At the Chinchorro site of Morro 1, 37 percent of the 96 burials were naturally mummified, while 63 percent had been artificially mummified. The latter were assigned to three categories—black, red, and mud-coated (Arriaza et al. 2005). Black mummies had their flesh replaced with clay; their bodies were painted with black manganese pigment, and they wore short wigs made of human hair. Red

Figure 1.6. Weaving on a backstrap loom. (Top) a Colonial drawing of a 33-year-old woman weaving on her backstrap loom; her *chumpi* or backstrap bears a diamond pattern (Guaman Poma de Ayala 1980[1615], I:190–191). (Bottom) a woman at Cerro Azul sitting in front of her house, weaving a belt on her backstrap loom.

mummies had eviscerated bodies painted with red ochre and were given wigs with long human hair. Mud-coated mummies simply had their bodies encased in mud.

Obviously, such detailed data can only be recovered from environments with unusual preservation, such as the Egyptian desert and the Peruvian coast. There the human body can be remarkably well preserved, often with the skin, hair, muscles, tendons, organs, and other tissues still present. Then there is the Scottish island of South Uist, where bodies placed in peat and sphagnum moss were also well preserved; those bodies were later transferred to a storage room aboveground, where they were kept for centuries. Some of the South Uist bodies were further manipulated when bones selected from different individuals were used to create a composite body. The excavators have concluded that these South Uist mummified bodies were used in rites of ancestor veneration (Booth et al. 2015; Parker Pearson et al. 2004, 2005, 2007).

In ancient Egypt, a special salt called natron was used to create artificial mummies. The extent to which one was preserved in this way had to do with one's wealth and social status (Aufderheide 2003; Ikram and Dodson 1998).

Deceased Inca rulers often had their internal organs removed, after which they were artificially mummified. For example, Huayna Capac, the last king to rule over a unified Inca Empire, died in Quito and was mummified there. His intestines were removed and his body dried in the sun; after this, he was elegantly dressed and seated on a litter adorned with feathers and gold. His mummy was then carried around the empire by litter-bearers (see Guaman Poma de Ayala 1980 [1615]:210).

The mummies of several Inca emperors were kept aboveground for periodic display. Their preserved bodies continued to participate in social events and political ceremonies in the plazas at Cuzco, the capital of the Inca Empire. We are told that when the Spaniards entered Cuzco, they were amazed to see the mummies of these kings being displayed at an array of political events.

The descendants of each Inca ruler maintained elaborate mummy cults for generations. Each dead ruler had an oracle who served as his spokesperson and caretaker. The oracles sat next to the mummy and spoke for the dead king, claiming that they were fulfilling the latter's desire.

On the main plaza in Cuzco, the royal mummies were seated in the order in which each had reigned. The display of each mummy legitimized the rights of his descendants, his servants, and his caretakers. Sometimes a statue or a bundle of his hair and fingernail clippings could stand in for the dead ruler. "By working through the multiple embodiments of substitutes, statues, and mediums, a ruler extended his influence in space and time and delegated enough power to govern effectively. At the same time, he demonstrated his divinity by 'animating' these far-flung divisions of himself" (Gose 1996:21). For example, when there was a need for water in the agricultural lands, his caretakers brought the mummy of the emperor Inca Roca to visit the fields; his followers were convinced that the mummy's visit caused the rain to come.

Positioning the Body After Death

Nineteenth-century scholars not only commented on the excellent preservation of coastal Peruvian burials, but also noted that a common body position for both men and women was seated or squatting (e.g., Dorsey 1894; Hutchinson 1874).

> The bodies being placed in what may be known as the squatting position—i.e. of thighs flexed on pelvis and legs drawn up perpendicular with thighs. The faces covered over with cotton flock—sometimes with llama wool—the whole body rolled round with cloth, over which is then enshrouded a mat, and a network cording outside. Nuts that may have been talismans, nets for fishing, needles for weaving, heads of Indian corn, agricultural implements (chiefly copper), buttons, sewing-needles, tweezers, and so forth, are included in the rolling. With the men I generally found slings; and with the women almost invariably needles and buttons, frequently some woollen thread and a distaff. (Hutchinson 1874:312)

Other coastal practices included placing pieces of folded or rolled-up metal in the mouth; tying the fingers, wrists, arms, or ankles with string or cord; placing cotton padding over the face; placing food in shallow gourd bowls; tattooing the arms; changing hairstyles based on gender and age; and wrapping the body in layer after layer of cloth to form a large bundle (Allison et al. 1981; Aponte Miranda 2006; Dorsey 1894; Fleming 1986; Frame and Ángeles Falcón 2014; Kaulicke 1997, 2000, 2015; Millaire and Surette 2011; Paul 1990, 1991; Reiss and Stübel 1880–1887; Squier 1967 [1869]; Stothert and Yarberry 1978; Takigami et al. 2014; Tello and Mejía Xesspe 1979; Uhle 1903; van Dalen Luna et al. 2018; Vásquez et al. 2013; Vreeland 1980).

One of the distinct practices of the Andean region was the creation of a multilayer bundle of cloth wrappings around a seated corpse. Among the early examples are the mummy bundles of the Paracas culture, which occupied the Quebrada de Topará and the valleys of Chincha, Pisco, and Ica (Carmichael 2019; Tantaleán et al. 2022; Tello 1929,

1959, 2009; Tello and Mejía Xesspe 1979; Tomasto-Cagigao 2009; Tomasto-Cagigao et al. 2015). In the Paracas phase called Cavernas (850–500 B.C.), funerary bundles were often deposited in pits and bottle-shaped chambers. In the later Paracas phase called Necrópolis, large bundles were placed in groups in underground chambers, accompanied by embroidered textiles and vessels in the shape of fruits.

In the 1920s, Julio C. Tello began excavating mummies on the Paracas Peninsula, 15 kilometers south of the port of Pisco. In the Grande Necrópolis de Wari Kayan, Tello found 429 mummy bundles (Tello and Mejía Xesspe 1979; Yacovleff and Muelle 1934a). Within these bundles, the bodies were often seated in a basket, naked but wrapped in many layers of cloth. To keep the body compact, the arms, wrists, ankles, and fingers were often tied together with string. The two main concentrations of mummy bundles at the Necrópolis were deposited in and around rectangular residences, whose walls were constructed with fieldstone. The excavators concluded that these Paracas mummy bundles had been brought from elsewhere and placed in abandoned houses and domestic middens.

The people buried in the Necrópolis seem to have been important, since there is evidence that their bundles were revisited. Edward and Jane Dwyer (1975:151), as well as Ann Peters (2000, 2014), discovered that the outer wrappings of some bundles featured textiles that were stylistically more recent than those in the inner core of the bundle. Such rewrapping suggests that Paracas mummy bundles do not represent one moment in time, but rather the endproduct of multiple postmortem revisits.

Among the Paracas population, a large number of individuals had endured trephination. Sixty-five percent of men, 30 percent of women, and five percent of children had undergone this procedure. As revealed by bone regrowth, more than 36 percent of the individuals undergoing trephination had survived.

It would appear that the creation of a Paracas mummy bundle involved an enormous amount of time, skill, experience, and repeated handling. The process began with growing cotton and/or procuring camelid wool. Then came the weaving to create the requisite amount of cloth, which could take thousands of hours (Paul 1990:32–33). For example, one Paracas mummy bundle weighing about 200 kilograms required 100 m^2 of cloth just to wrap the body. The spinning and weaving efforts have been estimated at 30,000 hours (DeLeonardis 2012; DeLeonardis and Lau 2004; Tello and Mejía Xesspe 1979). As we have seen, such estimates may include both the initial bundle and any additional textiles added during later ceremonies.

The Late Intermediate witnessed a major investment in creating mummy bundles. According to Vreeland (1978:213):

The greatest emphasis on the production of mortuary wrapping cloths appears to have occurred during the Late Intermediate Period. For example, a 40–60-year-old male dating from the early part of this period had been wrapped in approximately 60 m^2 of plain-weave cloth, woven from over 265 km of single-ply cotton yarn. It is estimated that the production of this amount of yarn required some 4,400 hours of spinning and plying (Vreeland 1976:8).

In another case, an exceptionally large and well-preserved bundle, the body of an 18- to 20-year-old woman had been wrapped in a total of 24 plain weave cotton cloths with a combined surface area of 281.56 m^2, a total weight of more than 150 kg, and an approximate volume of 0.94 m^3.

An 1891 excavation of an undisturbed grave at the coastal site of Ancón provides us with an instructive example of how a mummy bundle and its associated grave goods were arranged. This burial preserved features missing at many other sites, such as the tomb roof, the open space above the mummy bundle, and the original arrangement of bowls, gourds, bags, workbaskets, and other offerings (Figure 1.7). The description of this Ancón grave (Safford 1917:12–14) can be paraphrased as follows:

This Ancón mummy was wrapped in coarse cloth at the bottom of a rectangular pit, three meters deep. The mummy bundle was resting on a cushion filled with *Tillandsia* plants, a species that still grows near Ancón. The tomb roof was composed of two mats supported by six poles of remarkably durable *pacay* wood (*Inga feuillei*). The body, seated with knees under the chin, was inside a cloth bundle that had a false cloth head. Around the neck of the false head was a bag containing coca leaves. In front of the mummy was a workbasket filled with yarn of several colors, as well as tools for spinning and weaving. On top of the basket were loom parts and a *kallwa* or weaving sword. Leaning against each shoulder of the mummy were canes wrapped with brightly colored yarn. In front of the workbasket were pods of *pacay*. On each side of the basket were pottery vessels and gourds. The two largest jars were empty, but Safford surmised that they once contained water or maize beer. The largest jar (at right) was covered with a gourd. In the covered gourd near it were a "number of small fishes." In the wide-mouth vessel (at far right) were ears of dark red maize. Safford says that in the covered dish (to the left of the basket) were "several crabs in a remarkably perfect state of preservation." In the jar behind that covered dish were black beans of two varieties, while another vessel contained peanuts.

Figure 1.7. An 1891 sketch showing a grave at Ancón in Lima, Peru (Safford 1917: Plate 1). Safford describes the grave as nine feet deep, with a roof of mats and canes supported by poles of *pacay* wood. Hanging from the mummy bundle is a bag containing coca leaves. In front of the mummy is a workbasket.

Some of our graves at Cerro Azul shared features with this 1891 excavation of an Ancón burial. One of the burial jars we found contained a matted clump of hair, while another contained a matted layer of coca leaves. In the latter case, we suspected that the jar had contained coca tea, possibly a therapeutic beverage provided to reduce pain in a terminally ill woman. A number of our burials also included pods of *Erythrina* and *pacay*.

One of the potential rewards of opening a mummy bundle is that its contents tell the personal story of an individual. When a woman's workbasket and unfinished textiles are included in her bundle, we learn about her color and style preferences. We also learn about her work habits from the way she arranged and stored the materials in her workbasket. It is even possible that some of the objects kept in her cloth bags were personal heirlooms.

As noted by many who have excavated Peruvian coastal graves, the deceased's head often received special treatment. Cotton padding might be placed over the eyes; a headband, sling, or colored cloth might be wound around the forehead; red pigment might be placed on the face, either at the time of death or later; and metal valuables might be placed in the mouth. In some cases, the mummy bundle was given a substitute head with a painted face. This false head and painted face helped both to personalize the bundle and to orient the bundle when placed in the grave.

In some parts of the world, mummies received ongoing commitments from relatives. In Egypt, for example, wealthy individuals might contract with others before their death to ensure that food and drink be delivered to their graves for several years following the funeral. For example, the tomb of Ramose (ca. 1360 B.C.) had a finely carved scene on its wall showing Ramose and his wife, along with a hieroglyphic text asserting that gifts were to be brought to the tomb daily. As Baines (2014:13) notes,

> This indicates that those depicted are to participate perpetually in the reversion of offerings, an institution in which what was presented to the gods …. was then offered to deceased elites, many of whom would possess statues in the temple, before being consumed by priestly personnel and others. This practice unifies the sacred landscape symbolically, but it is not known whether offerings themselves were brought to the necropolis, as seems to have happened with some consecrated floral bouquets.

Davies (1999:27) adds,

> … the care of the Egyptians for their dead remained the striking and constant feature of their religion. …Several of the old-world customs survive in almost their ancient form. Amongst these are the periodical visitation to the tombs, the feastings and observances on these occasions, the prayers and invocations made almost directly to the dead, the belief of the presence either in or near the tomb of the 'good spirit' or double of the deceased, and the provisioning of the tomb with food.

During burial processions conducted between the Old and Middle Kingdom periods, a cleric, relatives, and well-wishers were expected to sing ceremonial hymns and pray for the deceased. After the hymns and prayers, the mummified body would be transported, first by boat across the Nile and then across the land on a sleigh pulled by oxen. Relatives of the deceased and well-wishers carried gifts, canopic jars, ceremonial oils, vegetation, powders, scarves, belts, pieces of clothing to serve as hair ribbons, and other provisions that were required for the journey to the afterlife (Agai 2015:6; see also El-Shahawy [2005:75–77] and James [1976:157]).

The graves of Andean elites were also periodically supplied with food, but since the Andes lacked a writing system, we have no contemporaneous texts specifying the frequency of delivery. Guaman Poma de Ayala (1980[1615]) notes that some offerings were placed at important highland Peruvian crypts after six months had passed, and again after one year. Food for the afterlife was placed in bowls made from gourds, beverages were poured into jars and other pottery vessels, and stacks of cloth were placed near the body, either in the grave or just outside the mummy bundle. Such items were considered essential to the afterlife of the participants.

Burial Locations: From House Floors to Separate Cemeteries

Many early societies buried their dead below house floors (e.g., Quilter 1989; Tyler 1921). Such people are usually presumed to be family members that resided in that house. While some commoners might continue to be buried that way, there came a time when separate cemeteries were created for elites. In many parts of the world, such burial grounds became sacred places, a destination both for descendants of the elite and for pilgrims. In many cases, descendants came to such a burial ground to make claims to land rights and privileges (Goody 1962).

Typical of an early phase of subfloor burials was Paloma, an Archaic site on Peru's central coast. Quilter (1989) reports that most of the 200 burials at Paloma were associated with houses, having been placed either immediately above or below the house floors. The typical Paloma burial was a cadaver with flexed limbs tied with rope, wrapped and rolled up in mats, buried with a few goods, and placed below the house floor. Quilter (1989:54) suggests that the placement of these burials within the house, rather than in a separate cemetery, indicates that loyalty to the family outweighed any relationship to a larger social unit.

Quilter's data show that as many burials as possible were placed inside each house. At first, burials were placed on the west side of the house; later interments were placed around the interior perimeter, until all the areas against the walls were used. Lastly, an adult male was placed at the very center. This arrangement suggests that the male household head remained at the center of the family even after death, and that other deceased members were arrayed around him.

It is possible that cemeteries were created when societies in which the extended family was the largest permanent unit gave way to societies with larger units such as clans, descent groups or *ayllus*, in the case of the Andes.

Rites Led by Mourners

We expect mourners to perform rituals at the time of the funeral, but in many cultures such rituals continue for days or years (Marcus 2020; Sugiyama 2011). For example, among the Isthmus Zapotec of Mexico there was a forty-day ritual called yoo ba' that united the body and the spirit of the deceased. Anthropologist Anya Royce says that the deceased Zapotec's spirit was "resident in a yoo ba', yes, but still a member of the family and of the lineage, as well as an additional soul strengthening the community with wisdom and knowledge and presence" (Royce 2011:26). What the ritual does is begin the relocation of the deceased from the community of the living to the community of the dead. The transformation is from an individual composed of *guidi ladi* (skin) and *la'dxi'* (insides) first to a *ba'* (body) and then to a *binni gula'sa'* (ancestor). During this process, someone who had once been *nadxe'* (wet) becomes *nabidxi* (dry) (Royce 2011:26).

In Peru, the postmortem manipulation of bodies, especially mummy bundles, has been well documented (Eeckhout and Owens 2008, 2015; Gayoso-Rullier and Uceda-Castillo 2015; Takigami et al. 2014; Tello and Mejía Xesspe 1979; van Dalen Luna et al. 2021). Over time, a bundle could grow impressively in size and weight, because each time it was moved it was necessary to add more cloth, wrapped round and round.

Fleming (1986) and Uhle (1903) illustrate mummy bundles that came to weigh between 100 and 200 kilograms. Some were carried from place to place in a litter and regarded as living participants in the post-funerary rituals; the bundles were fed, clothed, and honored for the deceased's past deeds (Guaman Poma de Ayala 1980[1615], Volume I:230–231; see Figure 1.3 in this volume).

Conclusions

In this chapter we have looked at a variety of burial studies throughout the Andes. In a few cases, we have also shown that some of the patterns seen in the Andes were shared by other regions of the world.

My purpose in discussing these patterns is to prepare the reader for the fact that many of the practices seen in the Late Intermediate burials from Cerro Azul were geographically widespread and had a long history in the Andes (e.g., Aufderheide et al. 1993; Carmichael 1988; Covey 2008; Eeckhout and Owens 2015). Included were the preparation of the body for burial, the creation of a multilayered funerary bundle, the placement of the deceased's personal possessions and the mourners' gifts, and the creation of a venue to which multiple individuals could either be buried together or added over the years.

Chapter 2

Introduction to the Site of Cerro Azul

Cerro Azul was one of several sites in the *señorío* de Huarco, a Late Intermediate polity that covered 140 square kilometers of the lower Cañete Valley (Figure 2.1). Most sites in the polity were devoted to agriculture and craft production, but Cerro Azul focused on fishing. Although the Cerro Azul fisherfolk exploited an array of marine life, their leaders oversaw the capture of small fish that could be dried and stored for export (Marcus 1987b, 2016d). Other Huarco sites included Ungará, a well-defended community overlooking both the Cañete River and a major canal that took off from it, irrigating the lands of farmers whose crops were exchanged for Cerro Azul's fish (Fernandini Parodi 2018; Larrabure y Unanue 1935[1893]; Marcus 1987b, 2016b; Rostworowski 1978–1980; Williams and Merino 1974).

The Pacific Ocean defined the western border of the Huarco polity; its northern and eastern limits were defined by fortification walls and by irrigation canals (Figure 2.2). On three sides, Huarco had autonomous polities as neighbors. To the east was Lunahuaná, which lay upriver in the Cañete Valley (Figures 2.3, 2.4); to the south was Chincha (Menzel and Rowe 1966; Morris and Santillana 2007; Nigra et al. 2014); and to the north was Ychsma (Areche Espinola 2019; Eeckhout 2004, 2010; Rostworowski 1978, 1978–1980, 1989, 1992).

Our original purpose in excavating Cerro Azul was to evaluate the sixteenth-century descriptions of the Cañete Valley, in which fishing communities were said to have only fished and agricultural communities only farmed (Castro and Ortega Morejón 1936[1558]; Marcus 1987b, 2016b, 2019; Rostworowski 1970, 1977b; Sandweiss 1988; Shimada 1982; Slovak and Paytan 2009). We wondered to what extent this degree of occupational specialization had been accurately described.

Site Description

Cerro Azul lies 130 kilometers south of Lima and covers about eight hectares (Kroeber 1937). The Late Intermediate sector of the site occupies a depression protected by the tall sea cliffs of Cerros Centinela and Fraile, which are home to large colonies of Peruvian boobies, Inca terns, and cormorants. Just offshore are rocky outcrops where sea lions and seabirds sun themselves (Figure 2.5).

Set precariously on the summit of the 86-meter-high sea cliffs are the remnants of Inca buildings. The cliffs of Cerro Azul are almost as white as those of Dover, but in this

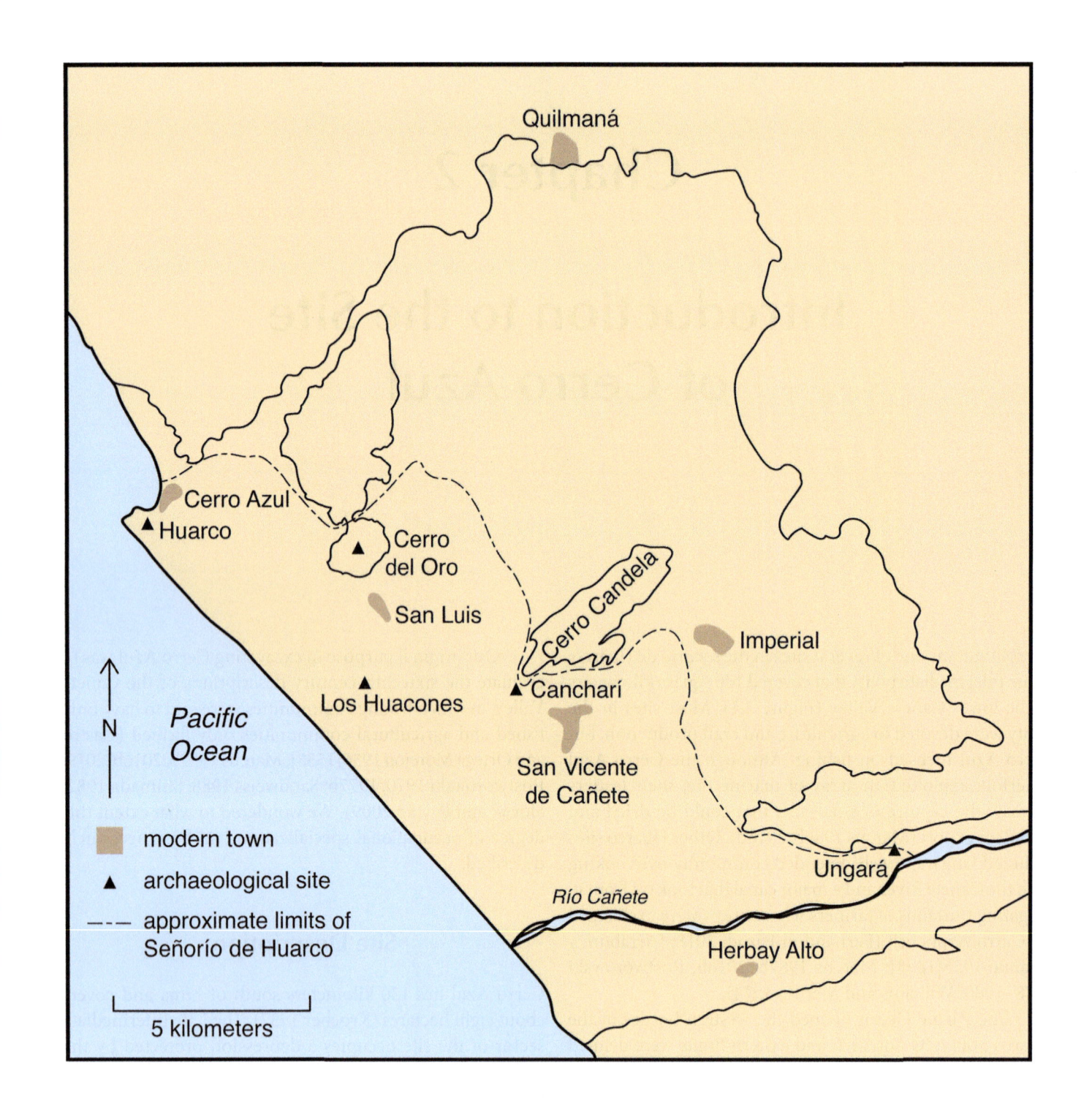

Figure 2.1. On this map, dashed lines show the approximate limits of the *señorío* of Huarco in the lower Cañete Valley. The Río Cañete formed its southern boundary. A defensive wall and a series of irrigation canals formed its eastern border. The site of Cerro Azul lay near its northwestern limits.

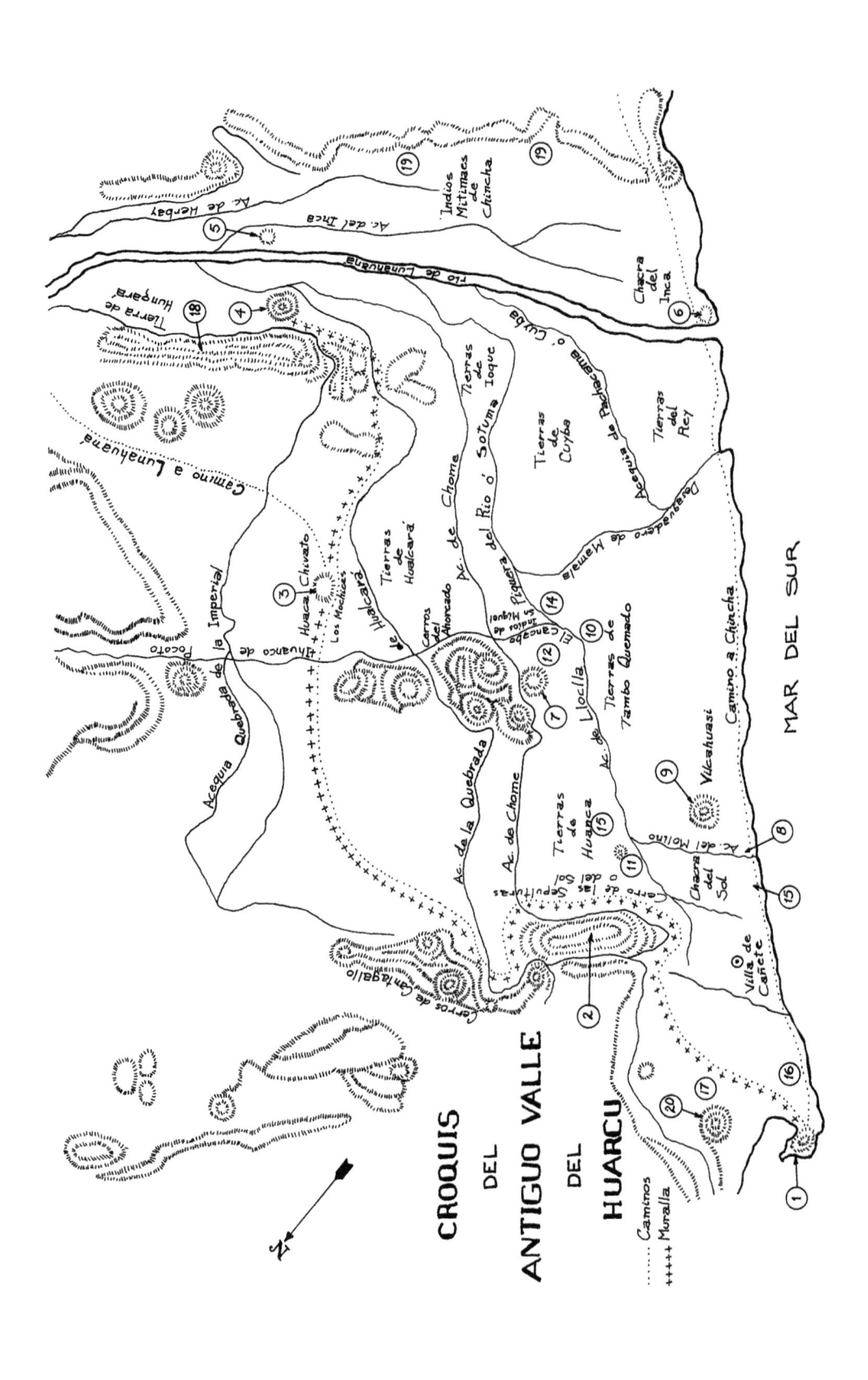

Figure 2.2. This early sketch map of the *señorío* of Huarco uses numbered circles to indicate prominent landmarks: #1 is Cerro Azul, #2 Cerro del Oro, #3 Huaca Chivato, #4 the Fortress of Ungará, #5 Fortaleza de Palo, #6 Palacio de Herbay or Tambo de Locos, #7 Canchari, #8 Colonial *tambo* or Venta de Manta, #9 Templo del Sol, #10 Tambo de Llocila, #11 San Francisco Convent, #12 San Agustín Convent, #13 Cerro de los Celosos, #14 Paso de las Ovejas, #15 hermita de Santa Bárbara, #16 Tierras de la Fortaleza, #17 Tierras de la Rinconada, #18 Ungará cemetery, #19 Herbay cemetery, and #20 Cerro Tinajero. A line of plus signs (+++) indicates the defensive wall delimiting the polity. Lines of dots (.....) indicate roads, such as the route to Lunahuaná and the coastal road to Chincha. Also featured are canals (*acequias*), cornfields (*chacras*), and lands (*tierras*) associated with the King, the Sun, and the Inca (redrawn by Kay Clahassey after Larrabure y Unanue 1935[1893]:270).

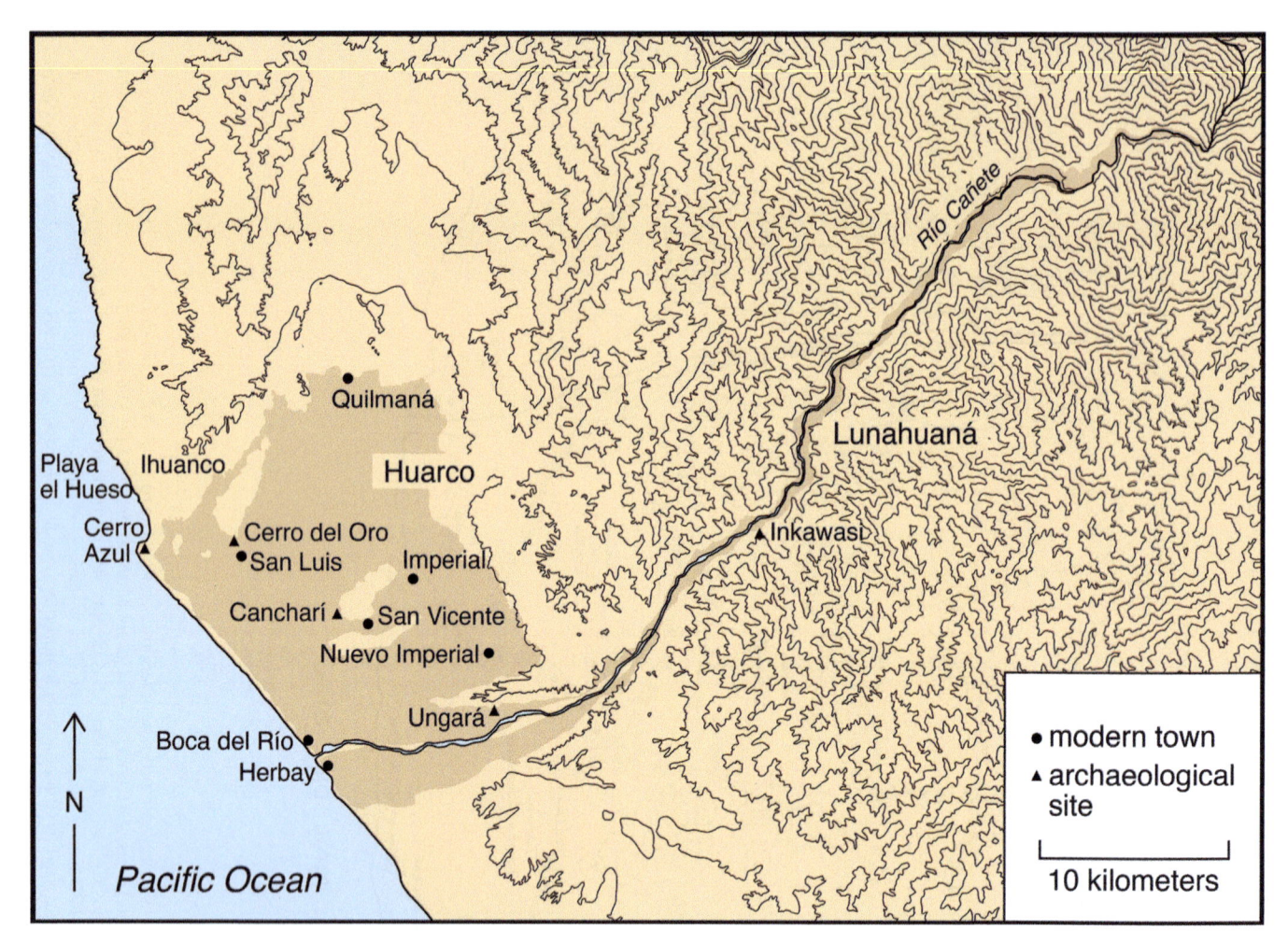

Figure 2.3. This contour map shows the location of two late pre-Conquest polities in the Cañete Valley: Lunahuaná (upriver in the mid-valley or *chaupi yunga*) and Huarco (the shaded area that extends from Cerro Azul to Ungará). (Drawn by John Klausmeyer and Bruce Worden, based on Marcone Flores and Areche Espinola 2015.)

case, the white is caused not by chalk but by thousands of years of accumulated guano from seabirds.

The Inca who conquered Cerro Azul ca. A.D. 1470 wanted their buildings to be highly visible, to make a statement to those on both land and sea. To do so, they placed a building with trapezoidal niches on the summit of Cerro del Fraile, a rocky projection that extends into Cerro Azul Bay. They built a second structure at the very top of nearby Cerro Centinela, but in this case it was an oval platform. From there a spectacular stairway descended the cliff face and led to the sea (Marcus 2017).

The Pre-Inca Occupation at Cerro Azul

In contrast to the highly visible buildings built by the Inca, Cerro Azul's Late Intermediate (A.D. 1000–1470) population wanted privacy. Cerro Azul wanted to hide its constructions from view, and by placing its residential compounds in the depression between Cerro Camacho and the sea cliffs, the Late Intermediate occupants gained that privacy (Figure 2.6).

Ten tapia-walled residential compounds were the most prominent constructions in the depression. Eight of these surrounded an irregular open space. In 1925, Alfred Louis Kroeber assigned the letters A to J to the ten compounds. Structures A through H were probably the residences of high-status families, their staff, and their servants. In the unroofed courts or *canchones* of each compound they dried corn, brewed beer, spun cotton, wove textiles on backstrap looms, stored dried fish, and raised guinea pigs (Marcus 2016c, 2016d; see also Valdez 2019). Outside the tapia compounds were presumably the more modest homes of the Cerro Azul commoners, including fishermen.

Introduction to the Site of Cerro Azul

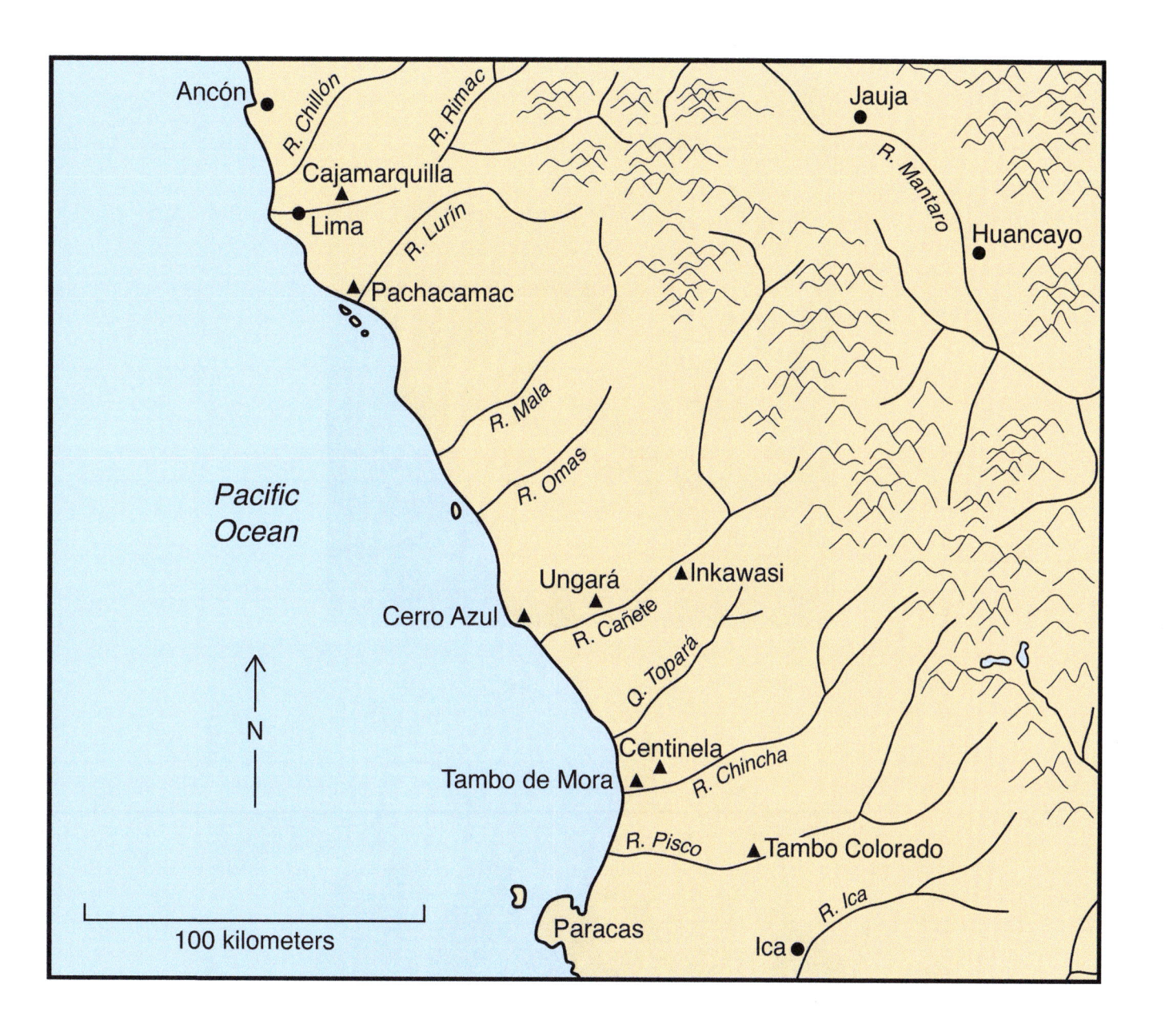

Figure 2.4. A map showing the neighboring valleys that bracket Cañete. To the north are Mala, Lurín, Rímac and Chillón. To the south are the Quebrada de Topará and the valleys of Chincha, Pisco, and Ica. Black triangles indicate archaeological sites; the black circles are modern cities (drawn by Bruce Worden).

Figure 2.5. The archaeological site of Cerro Azul overlooks the Pacific Ocean. (a) Sea cliffs and rocky outcrop. (b) Close-up of a rocky outcrop covered with white guano from the seabirds.

Figure 2.6. This 1920s aerial photo of Cerro Azul shows the bay, Cerro Camacho, the Late Intermediate residential compounds, and the sea cliffs known today as Cerro del Fraile and Cerro Centinela. (Photo taken by Johnson [1930: Fig. 103]; labels added by John Klausmeyer.)

Kroeber's Commoner Burials

Burials at coastal sites often provide important information on fishermen. At some Peruvian sites, fishhooks of shell, metal, and cactus spines, harpoon foreshafts, and other fishing gear have been found in graves (Arriaza 1995b; Arriaza et al. 2005; Rostworowski 1981). We recovered no fishhooks at Cerro Azul, but did find nets of different mesh sizes.

At Cerro Azul, Kroeber excavated what he called "meager burials," including one of 18 individuals and another of 14. Because all of the Late Intermediate individuals in the latter grave had small pieces of copper in their mouths, he came to regard copper as a contribution made by mourners, not a sign of the deceased's status. Kroeber (1937:247) concluded: "copper must have been fairly abundant in order that it could be used as regularly as this; for instance, even in the group burials of relatively poor people at Cerro Azul, who were as a rule put away with at most one or two pottery vessels of rather meager quality and dressed in wrappings of no distinction."

The Quebradas as Burial Sites

Many of the burials at Cerro Azul were placed in artificial terraces in the 12 gullies descending from Cerro Camacho and a single gully from Cerro del Fraile. Kroeber mapped these, labeling them Quebradas 1 to 13 (Figure 2.7). He also noted that three gullies bifurcated as they descended the slopes, and he designated these Quebradas 5/5a, 8/8a, and 9/9a (Kroeber 1937: Plate LXXXI). Kroeber excavated burials in Quebradas 1 and 2, and the entrance to Quebrada 8/8a. Our University of Michigan project recovered burials in Quebradas 5, 5a, and 6, as well as one intrusive secondary burial in Structure 9.

Many of the terraces in the quebradas had resulted from the dumping of midden debris carried from the nearby tapia compounds; others had been created out of beach cobbles so that storage features could be built there. Some terraces eventually accumulated enough debris that burial cists could be inserted.

In the chapter that follows, I will describe the burials found by Kroeber. In later chapters I will describe the multiperson burial cists our Michigan project salvaged, as well as the burials missed by the looters.

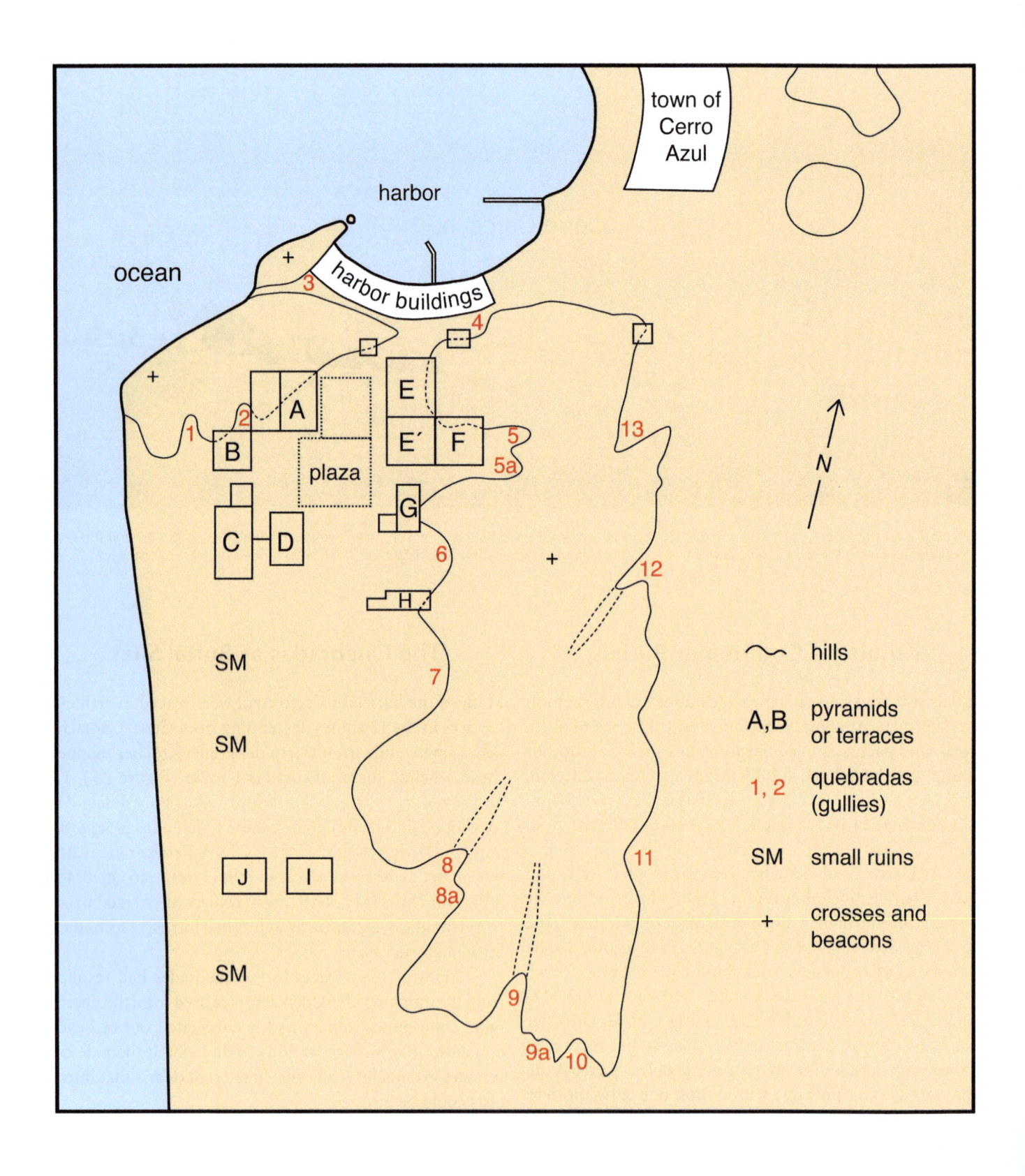

Figure 2.7. Cerro Azul's *quebradas* (1–13) are marked in red on this map, originally prepared by A. L. Kroeber (1937: Plate LXXXI).

Part II

Early Excavations at Cerro Azul

Chapter 3

Burials Excavated at Cerro Azul by Alfred L. Kroeber

Alfred Louis Kroeber (1876–1960) received his PhD under Franz Boas at Columbia University in 1901, the same year he gained employment at the University of California at Berkeley as instructor of anthropology. In the spring of 1925, Kroeber began digging at Cerro del Oro and Cerro Azul. Kroeber's important excavations in the Cañete Valley were truly pioneering, as this was the only place Kroeber worked where Max Uhle had not preceded him.

Kroeber (1937) used the word "tomb" to characterize all the burials he excavated at Cerro Azul, even though some bodies were placed directly in the sand rather than inside a structure. To distinguish Kroeber's burials from those excavated by the University of Michigan, I have added a "K" to his seven burials (that is, changing his designation from Burials 1–7 to Burials K1–K7). For the University of Michigan project, I designated the stone-lined cists "Structures" (4, 5, 6, 7, 10, and 12) and the simple pit graves "Burials" (1–10).

Kroeber's seven "tombs" yielded a total of 37 individuals. Some of these were associated with a modest number of grave goods; others had no offerings at all. Like so many archaeologists, Kroeber based his assessment of social status on the number and kind of grave goods.

Burial K1

Kroeber found his Burial K1 in Quebrada 2 (see Figures 2.7 and 3.1). This proved to be the largest mass grave legally excavated at Cerro Azul (Kroeber 1937: Plate LXXXI; Marcus 2008: Fig. 2.2).

Of the 18 individuals in Burial K1, four were adults and 14 were children or infants. Kroeber (1937:264) described the 18 bodies as being "nested together; more or less cemented together by salt incrustations; all flexed…". He went on to say that this was "a meager burial for eighteen individuals," basing this statement on the paucity of associated offerings.

Kroeber illustrated only five of the nine ceramic vessels he found in Burial K1 (Kroeber 1937: Plate LXXXIII, Figs. 1, 2, 3, 13, and 15) and I reproduce them in Figure 3.2. Kroeber

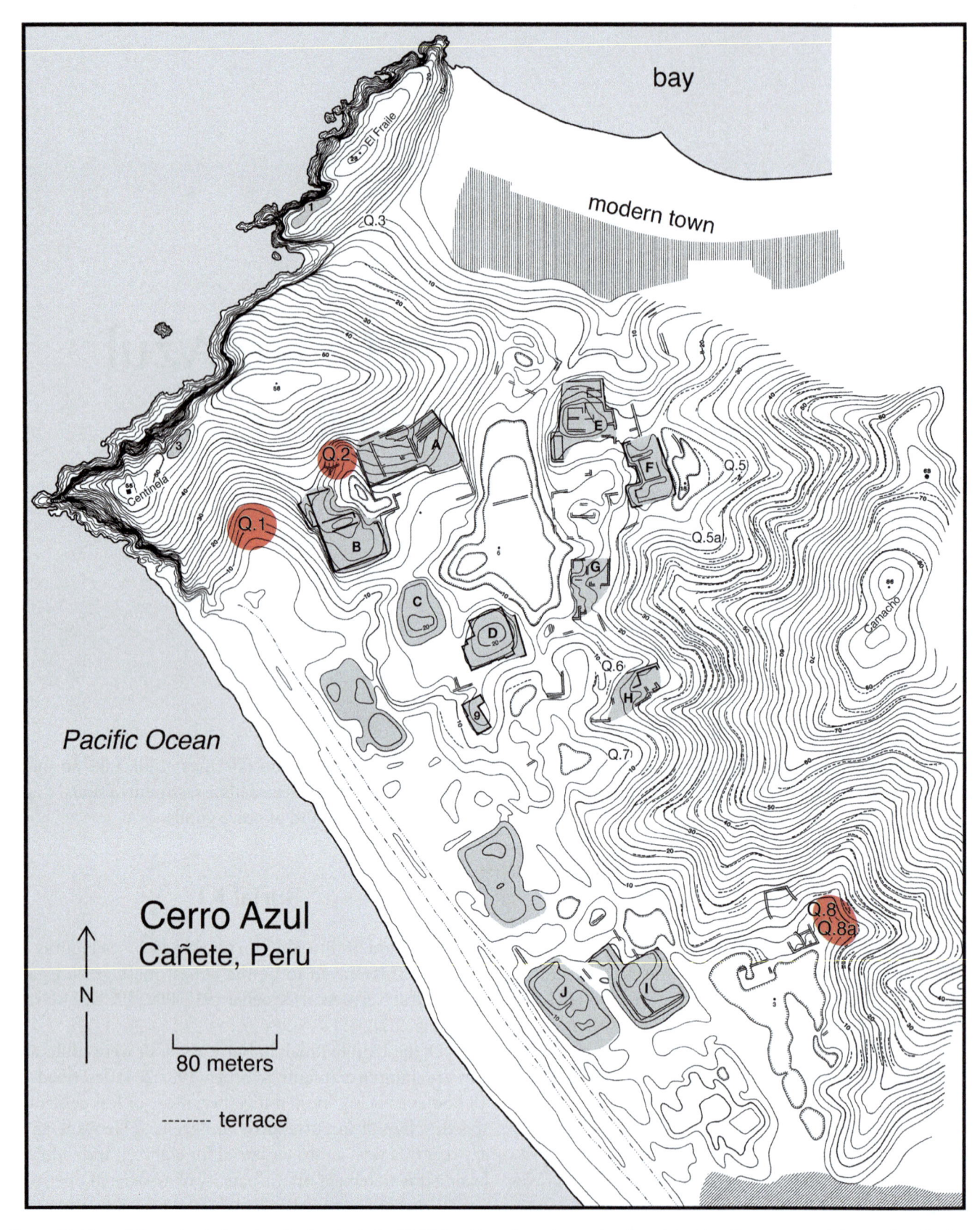

Figure 3.1. Map of Cerro Azul, showing Quebradas 1–8a. Highlighted in red are the quebradas where Kroeber excavated. (Drawn by Charles M. Hastings and Bruce Worden.)

Figure 3.2. Late Intermediate vessels found by Kroeber in Cerro Azul's Burial K1, a grave containing 18 individuals. (Redrawn from Kroeber 1937: Plate LXXXIII, Nos. 1, 2, 3, 13, 15).

Figure 3.3. In Burial K3 at Cerro Azul, Kroeber found sherds from a white-slipped jar with an animal motif (at left) and a strap handle (at right) (redrawn from Kroeber 1937: Plate LXXXIV, No. 1).

indicated that eight of the nine vessels were associated with one adult. Seven were black jars, undecorated, with two handles; of the remaining two, one was red (Kroeber's Specimen 169523) and one bore a design (Specimen 169516). Kroeber (1937:245) notes that "it is a local peculiarity that the small jars are almost invariably found inside the mummy wrappings. Even medium-sized jars are perhaps as often bundled in with the mummy as set beside it."

According to Kroeber, Burial K1 also included the limb bones of a seal, four pink shell beads still strung on a cord, embroidered cloth, fragments of both cotton and woolen cloth, and some red pigment. Kroeber found that pieces of metal had been inserted into the mouths of three individuals. He was unsure whether all these pieces were copper, and suggested that some might prove to be silver.

Given the presence of 18 people in Burial K1, at least two interpretations are possible: either (1) this cist was reopened multiple times, allowing individuals to be added and artifacts rearranged, or else (2) most or all of them had been buried elsewhere, then exhumed and deposited together in one act of mass reburial.

Burial K2

Kroeber found his Burial K2 in the upper part of Quebrada 1, near the southern end of Cerro Centinela; it consisted of two adults. One adult was lying supine, its feet crossed, wrapped in a coarse cloth. The second adult, not wrapped in a cloth, had been decapitated; his head had been placed at his feet. No grave goods were found in association with either adult in Burial K2.

Burial K3

On the western side of Structure B near Quebrada 1, Kroeber discovered an individual who had been buried in a crouching position. No cloth was wrapped around the body, but under the body was a small cloth rag with red and green stains. This individual had been placed in a simple hole in a refuse-filled terrace.

To the south of Burial K3 were 18 fragments of a large white-slipped jar with red-and-black designs (Kroeber 1937:

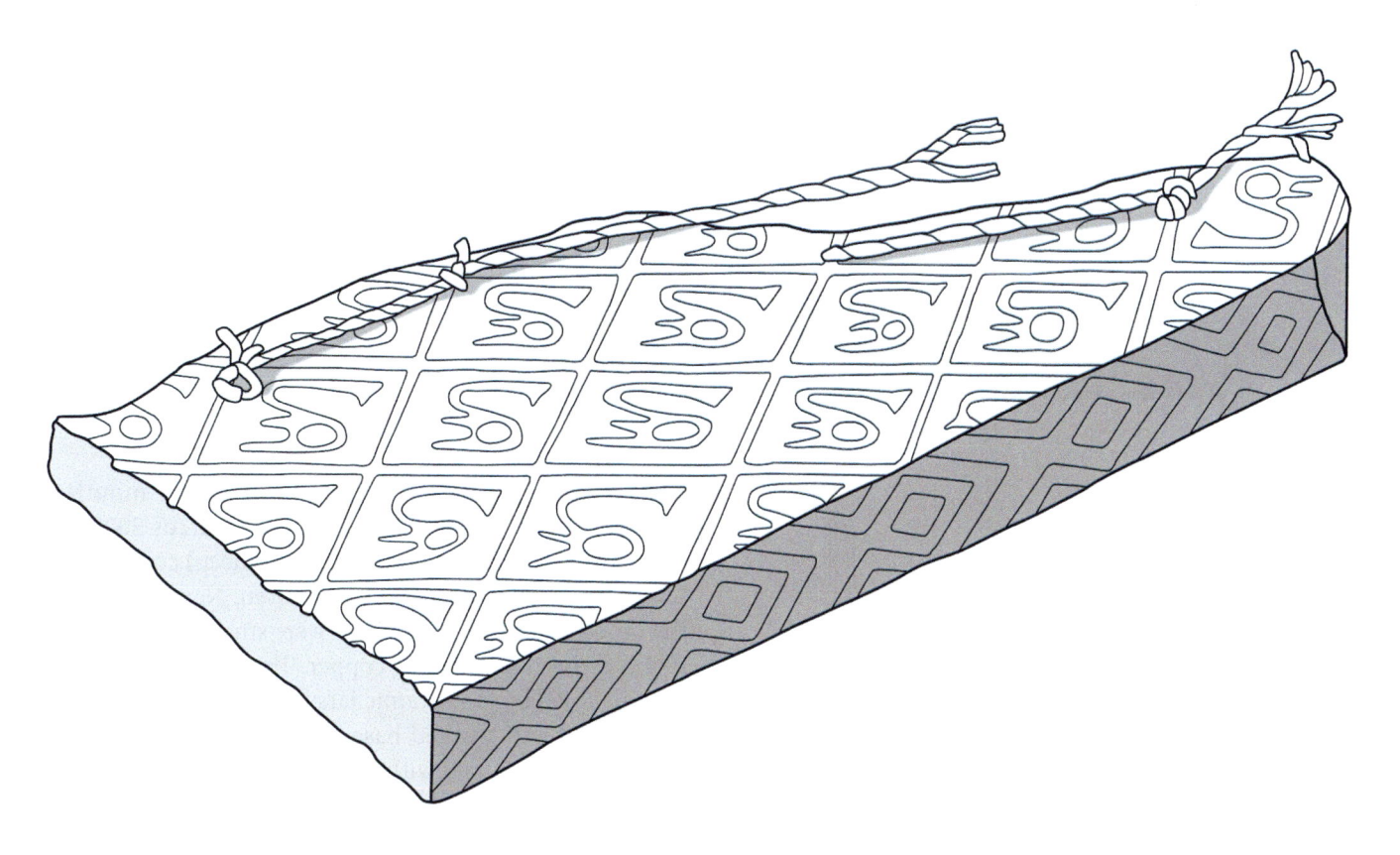

Figure 3.4. In Burial K3 at Cerro Azul, Kroeber found this carved wooden block, decorated with stylized birds; on the edge is a design composed of alternating brown and red diamonds (from Kroeber 1937: Plate LXXXV, No. 4).

Plate LXXXIV, Fig. 1, Specimen 169541). In Figure 3.3, we see the jar's handle and the animal design on it. The vessel wall, which had a coarse paste, was 8 to 10 mm thick.

Three other items were found near Burial K3 (Kroeber 1937:248). The first was a rock crystal. The second was a piece of wood (8.5 cm in length) that had four holes through which cotton string had been passed and lashed from one hole to another (Kroeber 1937: Plate LXXXV, No. 4; Specimen No. 169542). One edge of the wooden item had incised brown and red diamonds (see Figure 3.4), while another surface showed carved birds. This decorated wooden block could have been used as a stamp to apply a painted design to a piece of cloth or to human skin (there is evidence that red paint had been applied to the wooden block). Such a stamp could print out a repetitive pattern of stylized birds, similar to those depicted on textiles at Cerro Azul (Marcus 2015: Figs. 7, 10).

The third item found with Burial K3 was a wooden *balanza* or scale. Other *balanzas* are known from Cerro Azul as well as other coastal sites (Figure 3.5a). Kroeber (1937:248) suggested that the wood used to make this *balanza*'s horizontal beam was *huarango* (*Acacia* sp.). The beam, which measures 16.8 x 2.4 x 1.3 cm, is undecorated and slightly curved (Kroeber's Specimen 169544; see Kroeber 1937: Plate LXXXV, No. 2).

Instead of a pair of metal pans suspended from the horizontal beam, a net sack was attached to each end. These nets were suspended by two strings made from a fine hard fiber that Kroeber described as "probably maguey" (*Agave* sp.). The sturdier cord at the top of the beam appears to be cotton, and has a knot just large enough to prevent the cord from slipping through the hole. For comparison, Figure 3.5b shows a *balanza* that the University of Michigan recovered from Structure D at Cerro Azul.

Figure 3.6 shows *balanzas* from other coastal sites. Some have suspended nets (Figure 3.6a, b) or metal pans (Figure 3.6c). Still another has wooden pans (Figure 3.6d) that were said to have been used to weigh gold (Espinoza Soriano 1987: Fig. 43). Unlike most of the *balanzas* illustrated by Dalton and others (Dalton 2020; Dalton et al. 2022b: Fig. 11; Espinoza Soriano 1987; and Saville 1925), three of the four Cerro Azul scales were undecorated. The

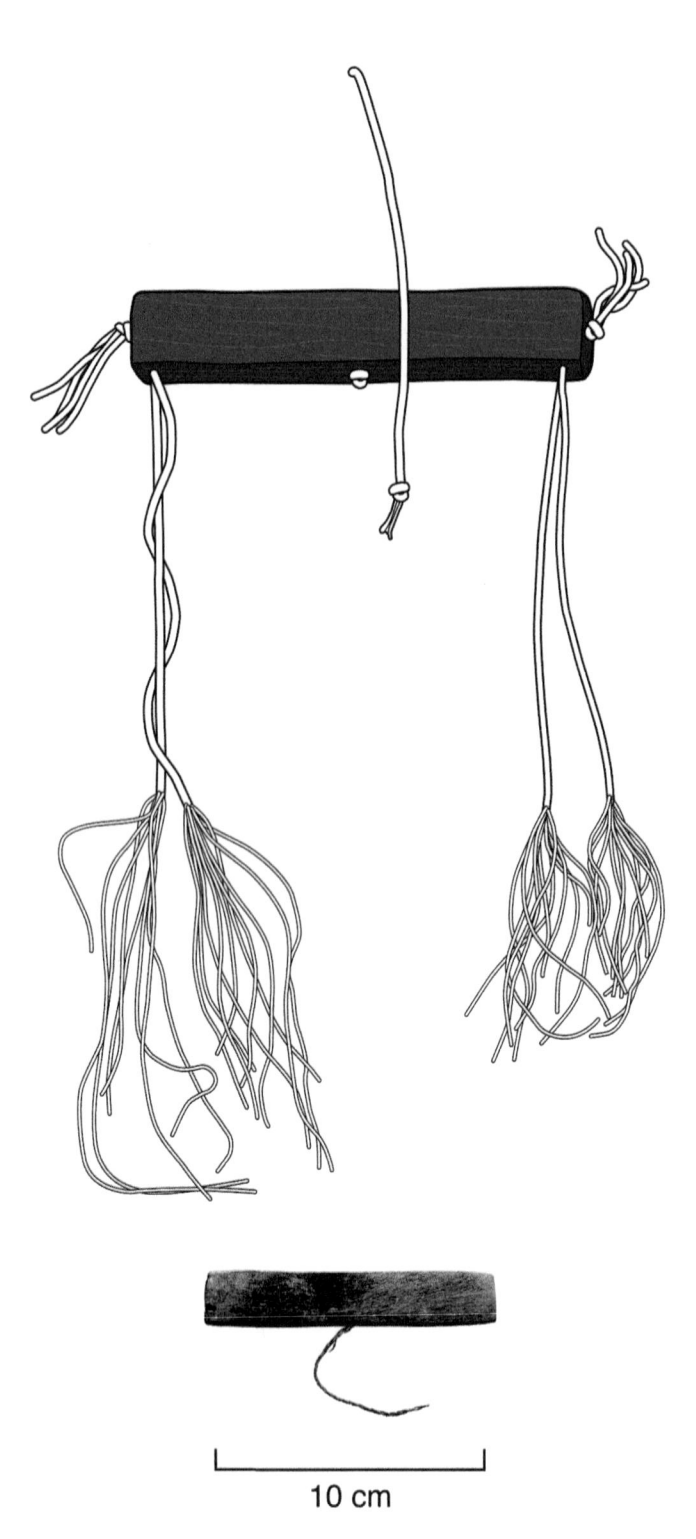

Figure 3.5. Shown here are two of the four *balanzas* found so far at Cerro Azul. (Top) An example found by Kroeber in Burial K3; the items to be weighed were suspended in the nets. (Redrawn from Kroeber 1937: Plate LXXXV, No. 2). (Bottom) An example found by the University of Michigan in a *kincha* house built sometime after Structure D at Cerro Azul was abandoned (Marcus 2008: Figs. 5.5, 5.6, 5.9, and 5.10).

one decorated *balanza* that we found at Cerro Azul was associated with the high-status woman in Burial 4 (see Chapter 10).

Some of the *balanzas* Dalton excavated at Las Huacas in the Chincha Valley were decorated with 10 birds. Donnan (2009) has called attention to the number 10, a recurrent number in coastal offerings and in jewelry as far back as the Moche period (ca. A.D. 100–700), when we see a necklace of 10 gold and 10 silver beads, all depicting peanuts.

Burial K4

Kroeber (1937:265) found Burial K4 at the mouth of Quebrada 8/8a, just east of Structure I (Marcus 2008: Fig. 2.2). This partially lined oval pit (2.0 m deep) contained 12 individuals—six adults and six children. Next to or inside the mouths of all 12 individuals were small pieces of metal that Kroeber identified as copper. These individuals were accompanied by ten ceramic jars (nine black, one red), all with round and pointed bases (Figure 3.7). All the black vessels were equipped with two handles; the red vessel had a painted design. Kroeber illustrated just two of the vessels (1937: Plate LXXXIII, Fig. 7, Specimen No. 169591; Plate LXXXII, Fig. 8, Specimen No. 169585).

Burial K5

Kroeber's Burial K5, adjacent to Burial K4, consisted of a child encased in reeds. The burial pit was circular and 1.0 m deep. The child was accompanied by one black jar with a face modeled on its neck.

Burial K6

Burial K6 was found near Burial K4, and consisted of two adults with no grave goods. The burial pit was circular and 0.70 m deep.

Burial K7

Burial K7 was in the same area as K4, K5, and K6, but slightly closer to Cerro Camacho. It contained one individual with a piece of copper placed on the skull.

Figure 3.6. Four *balanzas* found on the coast of Peru. (a) A specimen from an unknown site. (b) A specimen from Ancón. (c) A specimen with copper pans from the *señorío* of Ychsma, the Late Intermediate polity later renamed "Pachacamac" by the Inca. (d) A specimen with fish-shaped wooden pans, reportedly used to weigh gold; its provenience is uncertain (redrawn from Espinoza Soriano 1987, Tomo I:125–126).

Figure 3.7. Two of the ten pottery vessels found by Kroeber in Cerro Azul's Burial K4, a grave containing six adults and six children, all with pieces of metal in their mouths (redrawn from Kroeber 1937: Plate LXXXII, No. 8; Plate LXXXIII, No. 7).

Summary

All but one of Kroeber's seven burials were multiperson graves; the largest had 18 individuals. In some burials, every individual had a piece of copper in the mouth. Some burials were without grave goods, while others had drab black or red jars.

Because of the modest offerings he found with his burials, Kroeber concluded that Cerro Azul was a community of poor fisherfolk. There was no way for him to know that decades after he finished his excavations, looters at Cerro Azul would expose burials with polychrome textiles, gold, silver, and other signs of high status. By salvaging as many of these looted burials as we could, we were able to bring Cerro Azul's mortuary count to approximately 70 individuals. Furthermore, our excavations left no doubt that Cerro Azul included both high-status individuals and commoners.

Part III

Excavations in Quebrada 5a at Cerro Azul

Chapter 4

The Structure 4 Burial Cist

Chapter 3 provides a summary of the burials excavated by A. L. Kroeber. In this and the following chapters, I report on the burials excavated by our University of Michigan project. As noted earlier, we never intended to excavate burials at Cerro Azul, but we were so appalled by the looters' destruction that we decided to salvage as many data as we could and leave the surface of the site clean.

The first area we tackled was a terrace in Quebrada 5a where several burial cists had been looted (Figures 4.1, 4.2, 4.3). Ultimately, we were able to document the partial contents of four cists (Structures 4, 5, 6, and 8). One other cist, Structure 7, had been emptied completely so there were no contents to record (Figure 4.4).

Even with our small sample of graves, we noted significant diversity in construction materials, burial furniture, and number of individuals in each interment. These differences were seemingly not due to change over time but largely reflected other variables, such as whether a grave was intended to be reopened, the availability of construction materials, the number of individuals to be interred, the relationships among the individuals, and the social status of the deceased.

Quebrada 5a

Three of the gullies that descend from the summit of Cerro Camacho—Quebradas 5a, 5-south, and 6—had been targeted by looters. The first group of burials we salvaged was in Quebrada 5a (Figure 4.1, marked in red). This quebrada is not far from two tapia compounds that Kroeber labeled Structures F and G. In Quebrada 5a (Figures 4.2, 4.3) we saw a line of looters' holes, ugly black gashes in an otherwise peaceful landscape. We first assumed that the looters had taken everything, but soon we learned that they had disdain for many items and left much to salvage.

Terrace 9

The residents of Cerro Azul had selected Terrace 9 of Quebrada 5a as a suitable place to insert burials only after its midden deposits had become sufficiently deep. In its final stages, Terrace 9 came to be densely packed with both simple pit burials and stone-lined cists. Our 5 x 5 m excavation into this terrace ultimately yielded nine pit burials (Burials 1–9) and five cists (Structures 4–8) (see Figures 4.4 and 7.1).

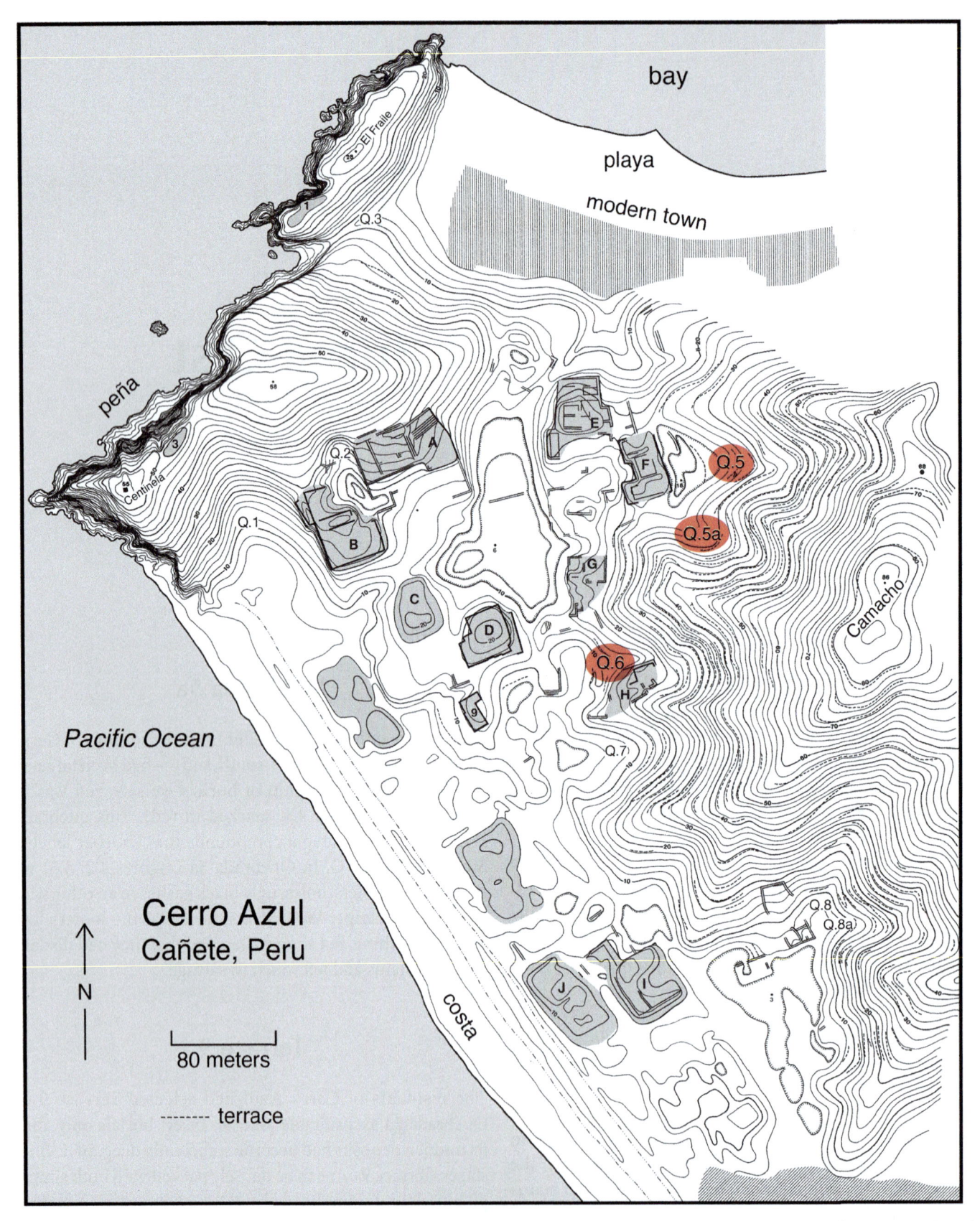

Figure 4.1. Map of Cerro Azul with red ovals marking Quebradas 5, 5a, and 6, three locations where the University of Michigan Project found scattered human remains and set about salvaging looted burials.

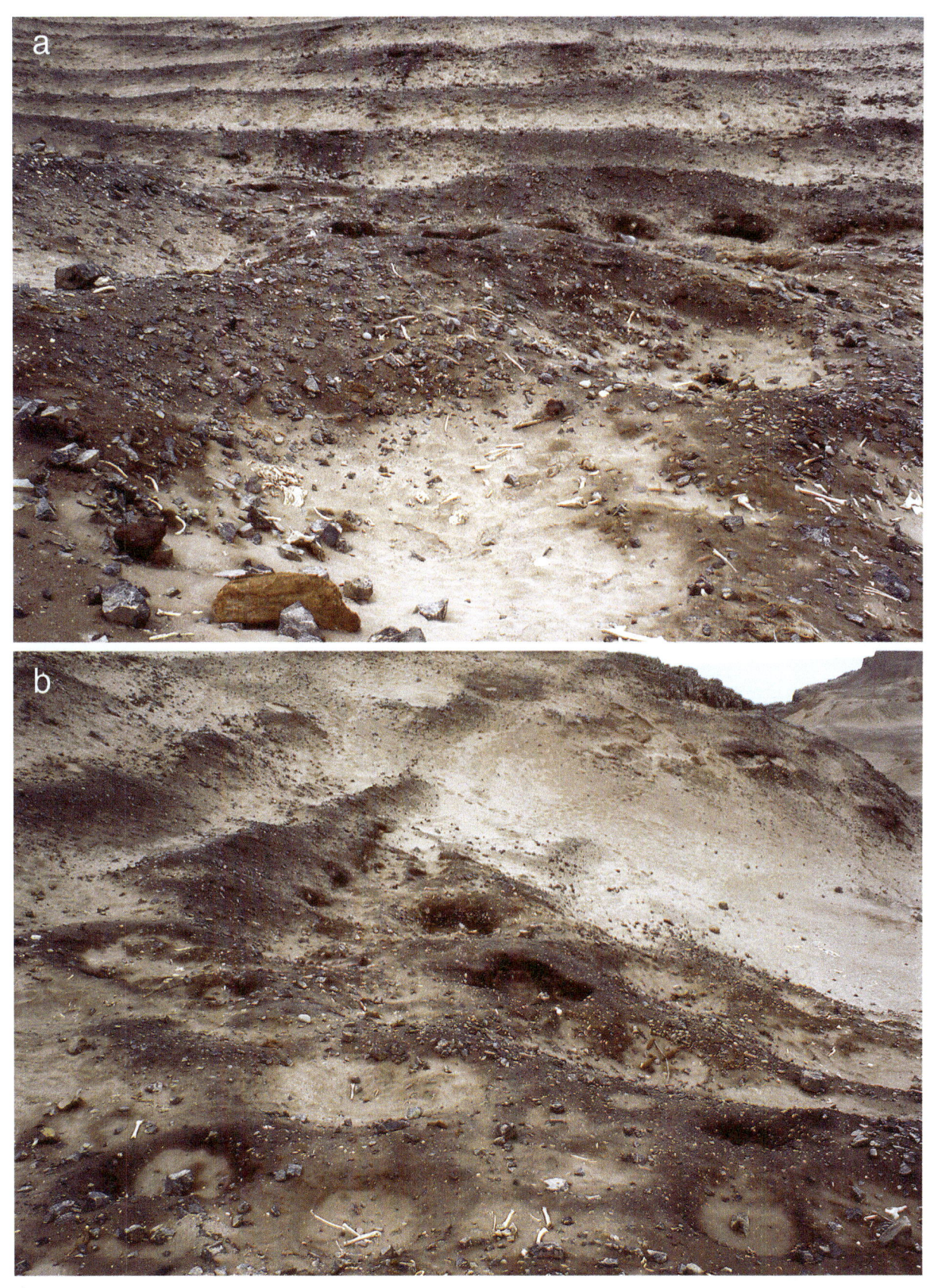

Figure 4.2. Evidence of looting in Quebrada 5a at Cerro Azul. (a) In the foreground we see scattered human bones and artifacts; in the background we see a line of looters' holes. (b) In the foreground we see scattered human bones and several looters' holes.

Figure 4.3. Quebrada 5a at Cerro Azul. (a) A workman sits near the looters' hole where our excavations revealed the burial cist we called Structure 4. (b) Looking down the quebrada toward our 5 x 5 m excavation that included Structure 4; in the background we see Cerro Centinela and the Pacific Ocean.

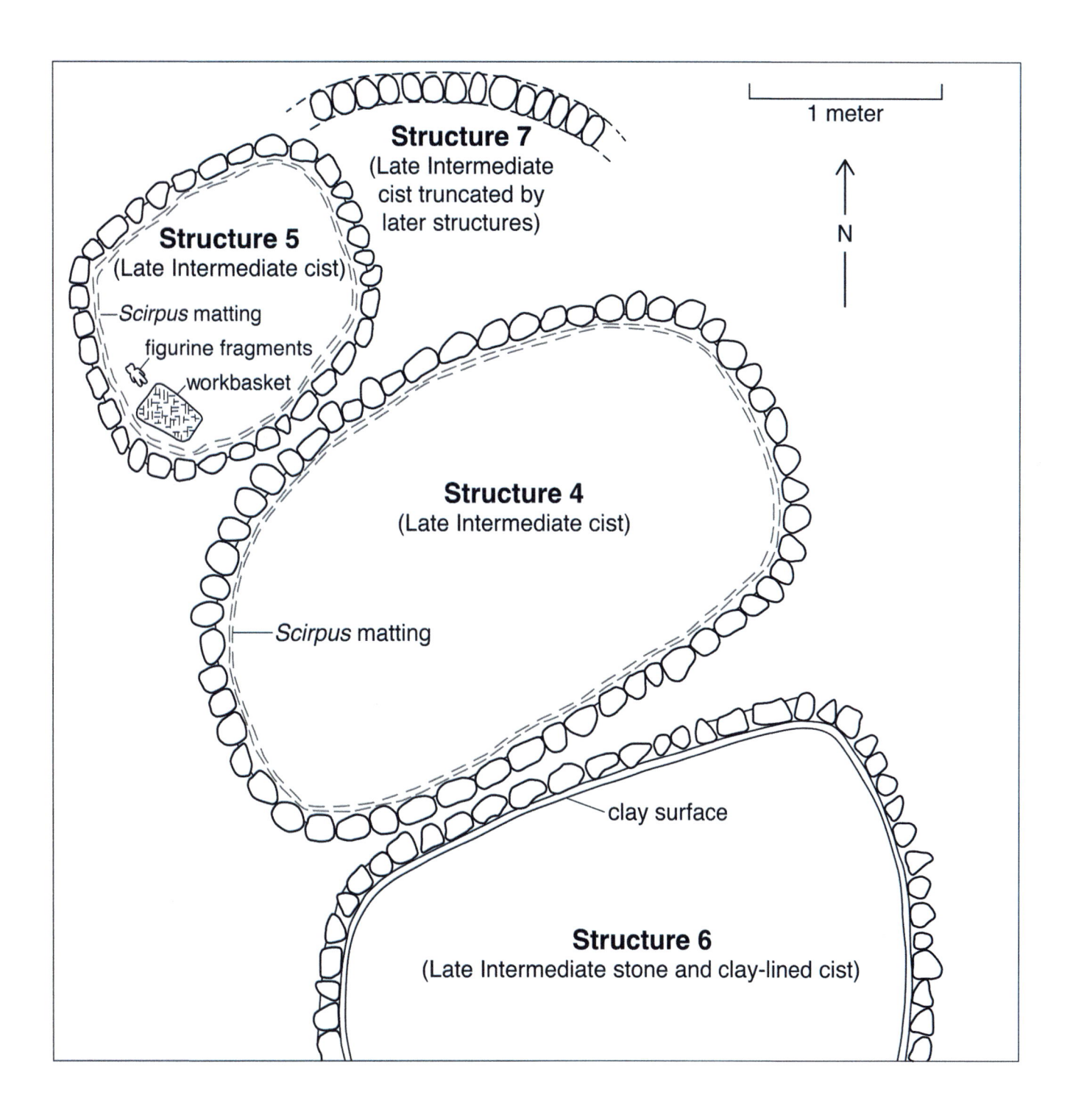

Figure 4.4. Our 5 x 5 m excavation in Quebrada 5a at Cerro Azul revealed Structures 4, 5, 6, and 7.

The first cist we came upon was Structure 4. By sweeping the surface around it, we recovered large ceramic fragments and a few whole vessels, presumably discarded by the looters because the vessels were considered to be of little value. One sherd was from a highly burnished Camacho Black jar with two loop handles (Figure 4.5a). Another was a Pingüino Buff jar neck with a modeled human face, painted black, white, and reddish-brown (Figure 4.5b). Still another sherd was the neck of a miniature Camacho Black jar with a cotton plug still in place (Figure 4.5c).

Other items next to Structure 4 included pieces of well-preserved cloth, mats, slings, nets, and a left ulna robust enough to be that of a male sea lion. The looters had surely taken some items with them, but it was impossible to determine how many.

The Stratigraphy of Terrace 9

Our Terrace 9 excavations revealed three stratigraphic levels (Figure 4.6). **Zone C** (the oldest) was found at a depth of 2.2 m to 2.6 m. It lay directly above the rocky surface of Cerro Camacho, and consisted of basketloads of domestic refuse.

Zone B was a meter-thick midden of gray ash, mixed with marine shell. The most common mollusc in the midden was the coquina clam or *Donax obesulus*. Like Zone C, Zone B was an accumulation of domestic trash, evidently dumped during the transition from an early stage of the Late Intermediate to a later stage within the same period. We reached this conclusion by comparing the Zone B pottery to the types recovered from Structure D (Marcus 2008).

Zone A (the uppermost level) was 1.2 m thick. This was the level into which the stone burial cists had been excavated. Some of these cists lacked mortar; others had their cobblestones cemented together with a mixture of ash and sand (Marcus 2008: Fig. 9.28). Zone A, as well as the burial cists, yielded the same ceramic complex that had characterized Structure D, suggesting that Structure D and the burial cists were broadly contemporaneous.

Figure 4.6 shows the aftermath of multiple episodes of looting, as well as the stratigraphic levels below Structure 4.

Excavating Structure 4

As we began to expose Structure 4, we noticed that its walls consisted both of scree stones from Cerro Camacho and rounded beach cobbles, the latter probably brought from the zone that today's fishermen call "*costa*" (see Figure 4.1).

Lining the walls of Structure 4 were mats; two fragments can be seen in Figures 4.7 and 4.8. Figure 4.7 shows the finished edge and corner of a mat made of bulrushes (*Scirpus californicus*). The plaited elements on the smaller fragment are 4 to 5 mm wide (Figure 4.8).

Based on the human bones scattered on the surface next to Structure 4, this cist probably contained at least four adults and a child. The mummy bundle of the child had a false head made from a wad of cloth. Not far from the false head, we noticed a bundle of bulrushes that may have been used as a pillow (Figure 4.9); such pillows are known from other coastal burials. Items on the surface next to Structure 4 also included dozens of fishing net fragments, part of a sling, a comb, a spindle, and a spindle whorl.

Ceramic Vessels

In addition to the sherds shown in Figure 4.5, we found several complete vessels on the surface next to Structure 4. One was a miniature Camacho Black amphora that had suffered some damage in antiquity; the rim was chipped, and a handle was missing. The remaining handle was 1.5 cm wide. The height of the vessel was 15.5 cm; the rim diameter was ca. 4.0 cm; and the vessel wall was 5 mm thick. The surface color of the vessel varied from black to dark gray to brownish gray (see Figure 4.10).

Figure 4.11 illustrates the two Camacho Black amphorae found next to Structure 4. One amphora (Figure 4.11a) still had a corncob used to plug its neck. The exterior surface was mainly black but in those places where the vessel was most heavily burnished, it was very dark gray; where the surface was least burnished, it was brownish gray. The amphora's height was 16.7 cm; its rim diameter was 4.1 cm; and the wall thickness was 4 to 5 mm.

Figure 4.11b shows an amphora that has a mostly black exterior but is occasionally brownish gray. Its height is 13.4 cm; its rim diameter is 3.7 cm; and its wall is 4 to 5 mm thick.

Figure 4.12 shows a Camacho Black miniature jar that we found in the looters' backdirt next to Structure 4. A cotton plug remained in the jar neck. The vessel height was only 4 cm; its neck diameter was 2 cm; its maximum width was 5.2 cm; and its wall thickness was 3.0 to 3.5 mm.

Figure 4.13 shows a miniature jar found next to Structure 4; a cotton plug is still lodged in its neck. The rim diameter is 3.0 cm; the height is 7.5 cm; and the maximum width is 6.8 cm. The thickness of the vessel wall is 3.5 to 4.0 mm. The Munsell color (Munsell 1954) of the vessel surface varies from 7.5 YR 7/4 ("pink") to 5 YR 5/4 ("reddish

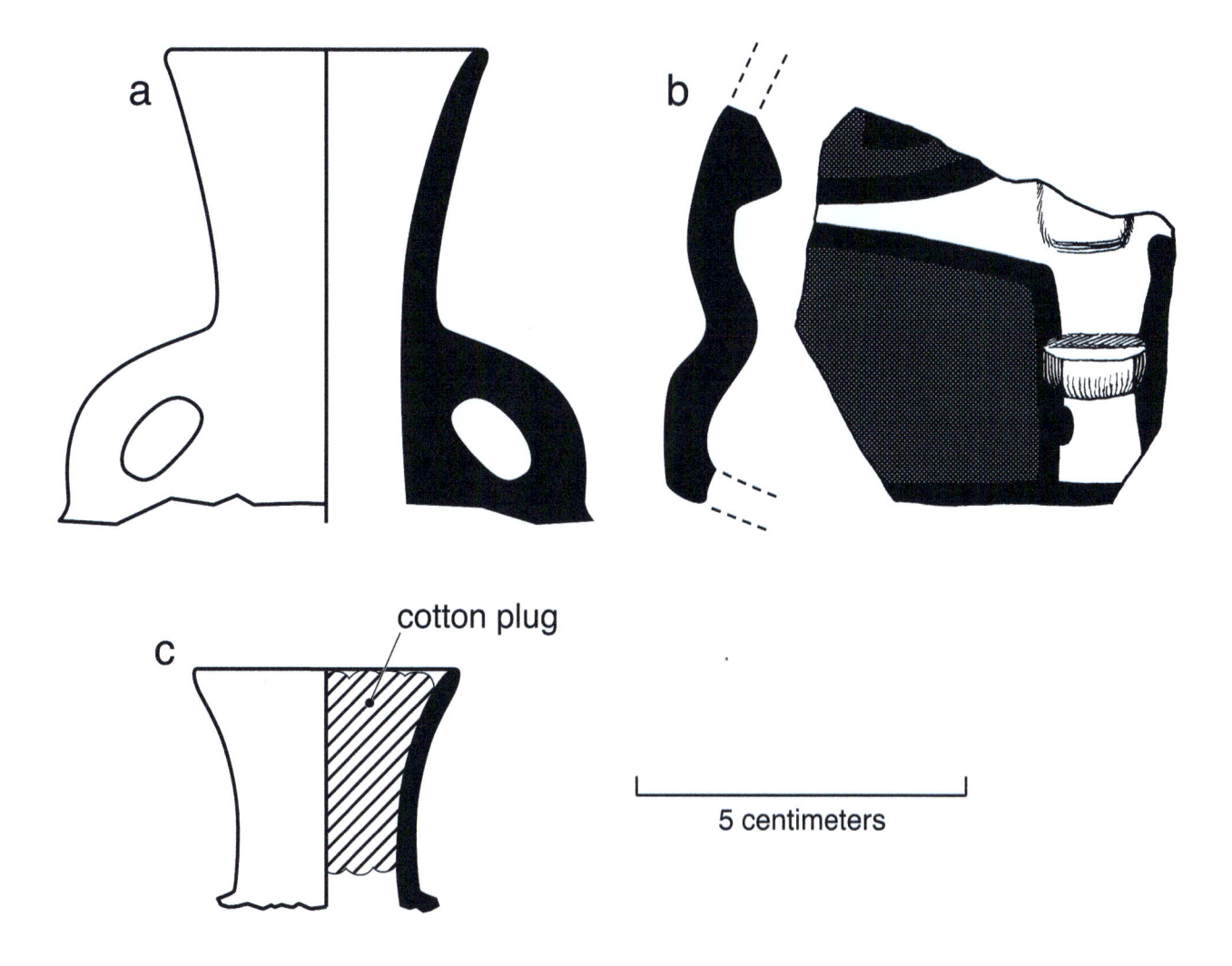

Figure 4.5. Vessels broken by looters found next to Structure 4. (a) Neck of a Camacho Black jar. (b) Neck of a Pingüino Buff jar. (c) Neck of a Camacho Black jar, plugged with cotton.

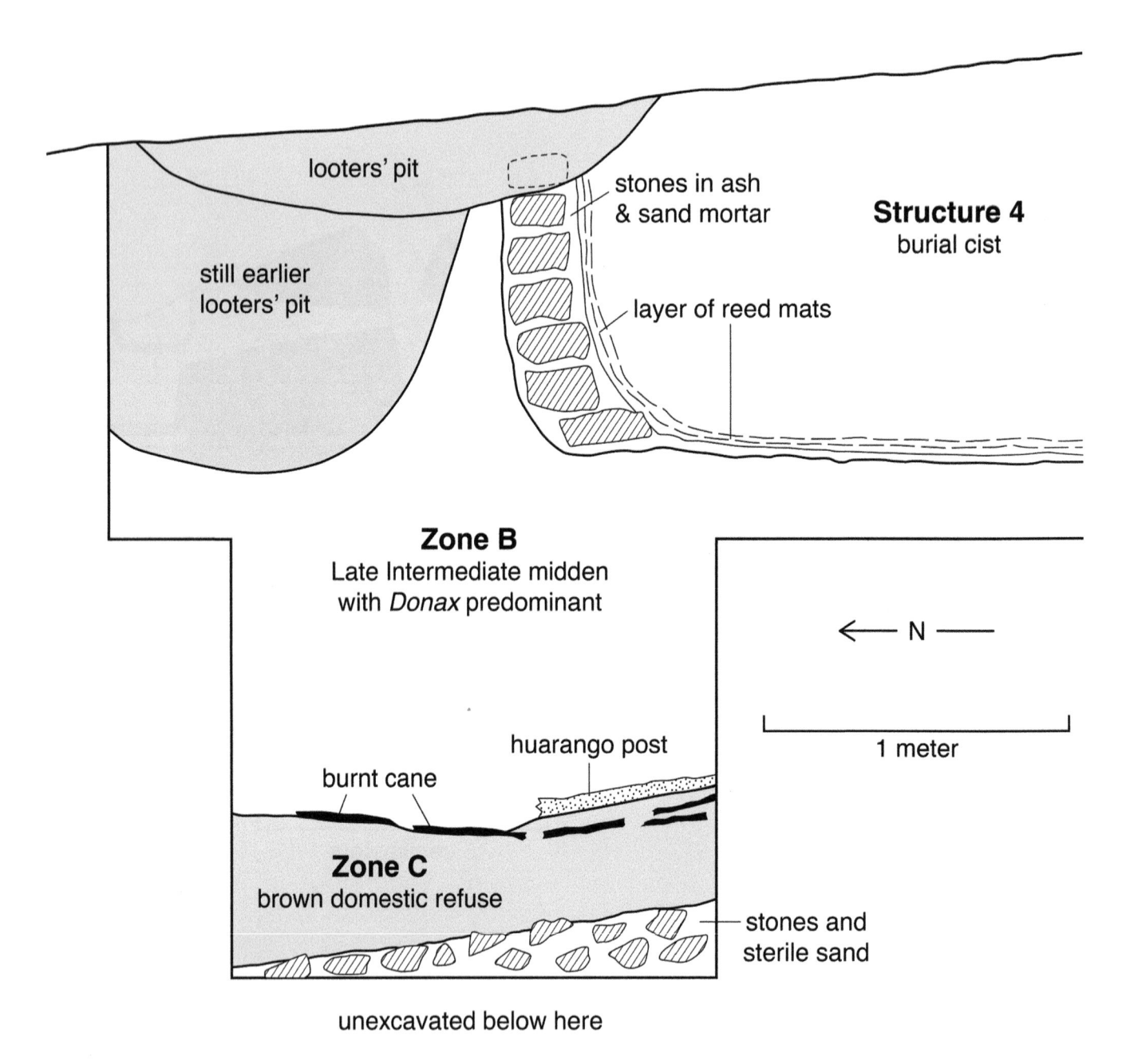

Figure 4.6. This cross section of our 5 x 5 m excavation shows Structure 4 in Stratigraphic Zone A (upper right). Below it are Zones B and C, the middens that accumulated on this terrace before it could be used as a cemetery. Note that we found two generations of looters' pits (upper left).

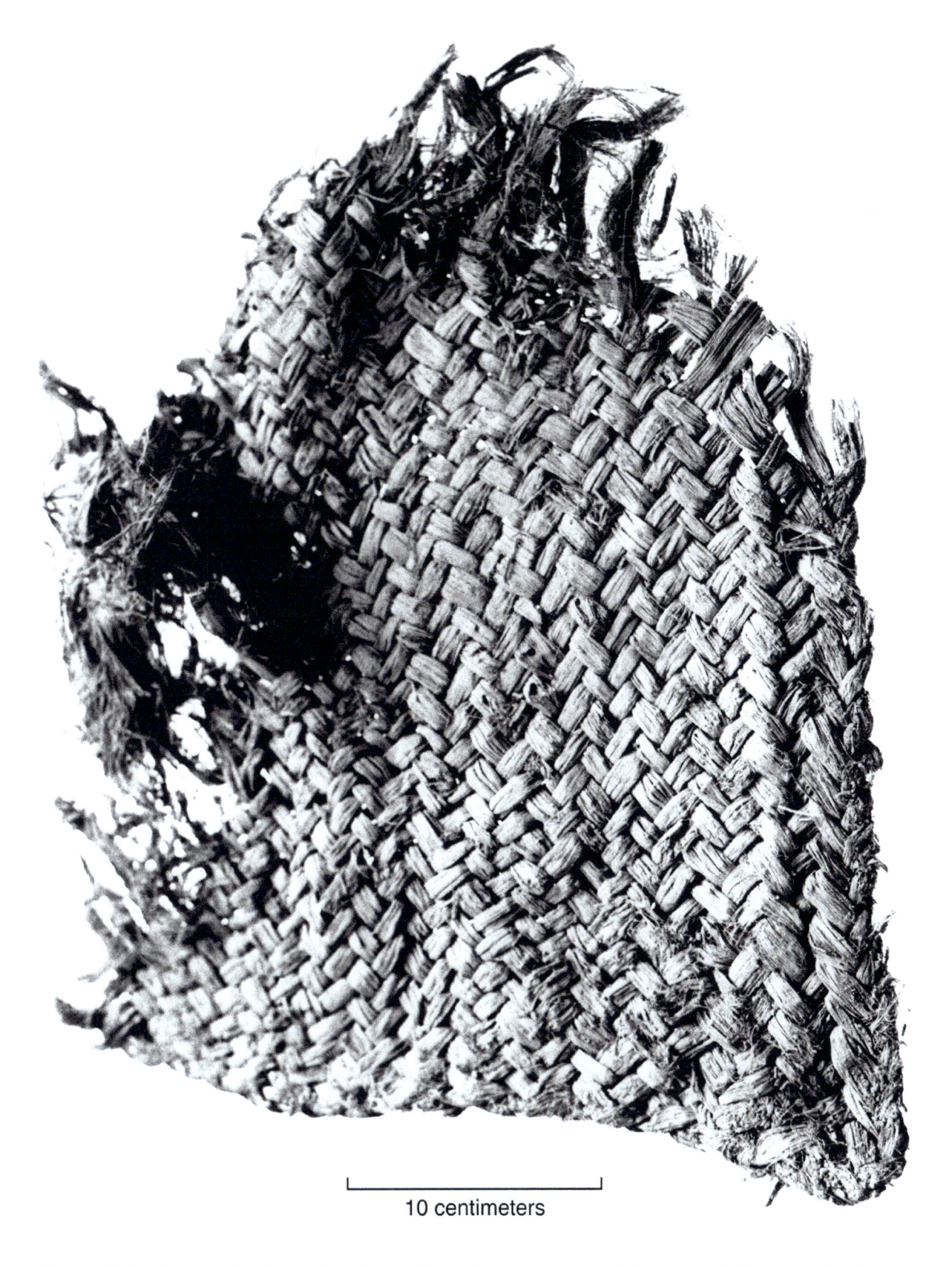

Figure 4.7. This fragment of twill mat—featuring one finished corner—was part of the lining of the Structure 4 burial cist.

Figure 4.8. A second mat fragment from the lining of the Structure 4 burial cist.

Figure 4.9. A bundle of bulrushes, possibly used as a pillow for one of the burials in Structure 4.

5 centimeters

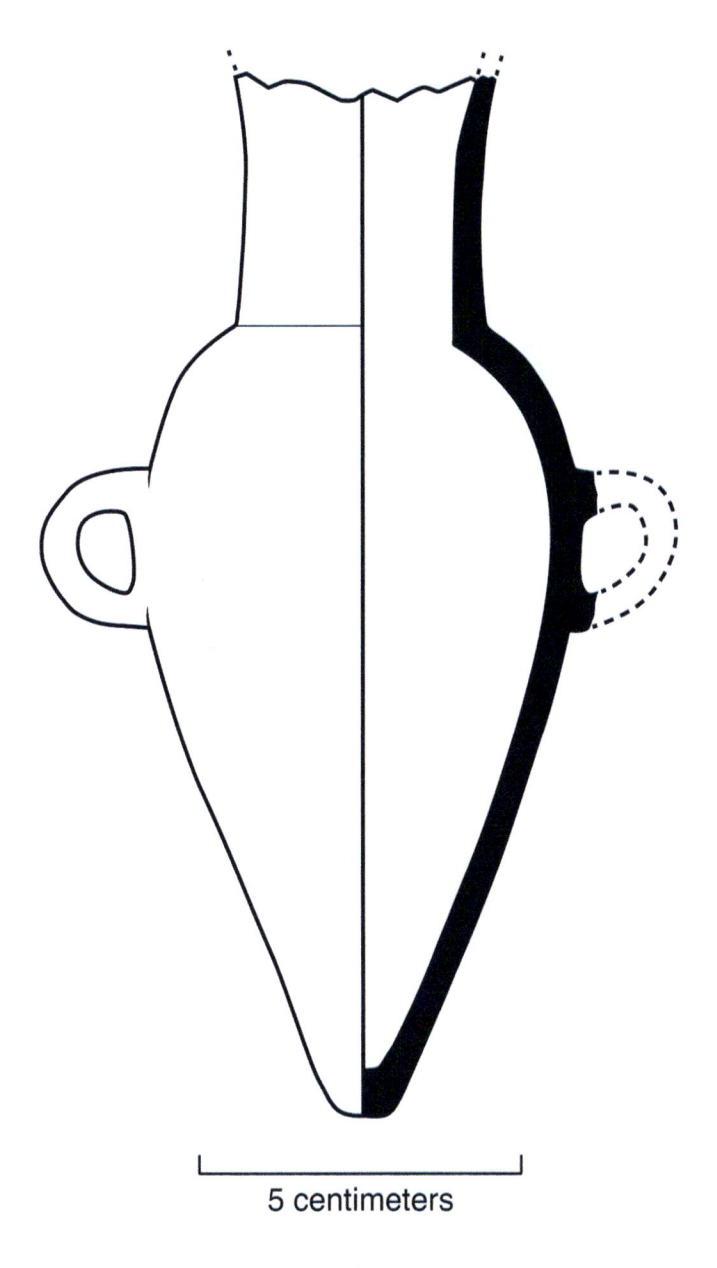

Figure 4.10. A miniature Camacho Black amphora, found next to Structure 4.

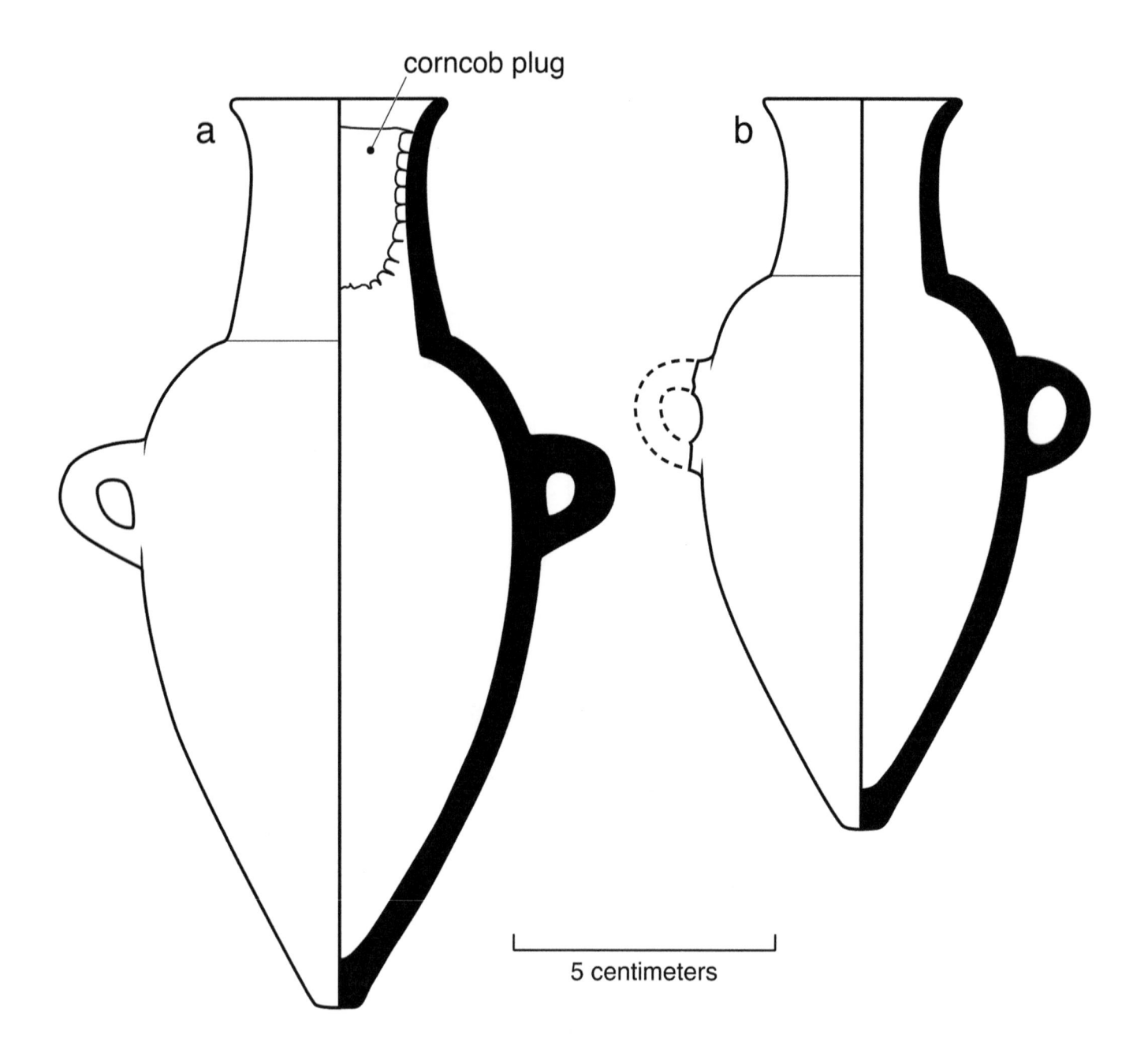

Figure 4.11. Two miniature Camacho Black amphorae, discarded by looters next to Structure 4. Specimen a had a corncob plug in its neck.

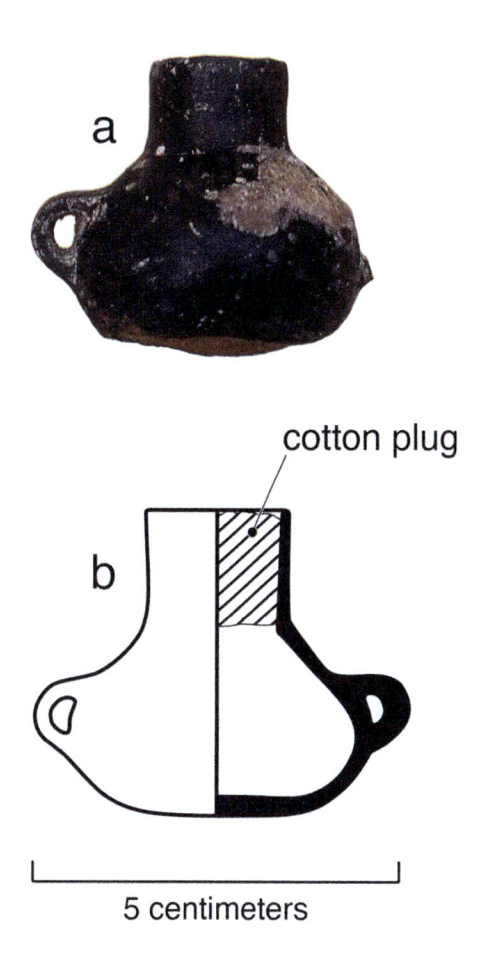

Figure 4.12. Photo and drawing of a Camacho Black miniature jar, found in looters' backdirt next to Structure 4. Its neck had been plugged with cotton.

brown"). There are numerous firing clouds, both brownish gray to dark gray. This vessel appears to have been misfired, resulting in a reddish-brown vessel that was probably the oxidized version of Camacho Black.

Figures 4.14a and 4.14b show a Camacho Reddish Brown amphora left by the looters next to Structure 4. At the bottom of this vessel, we found a mass of coca leaves (*Erythroxylum coca*) that may have been infused in water first, and then heated to make a tea; these coca leaves can be seen in Figure 4.14c. In many Andean societies, coca is chewed to assuage hunger, to help endure cold, and to numb pain (Allen 1988; Bastien 1978; Bolton 1979; Díaz Carranza 2015). In this mortuary context, the mass of coca leaves in the amphora suggests that this vessel may have contained a medicinal tea for the person buried with it. Using coca externally and taking it internally are both reported by Garcilaso de la Vega (1966[1609], Chapter XV, page 509): "Coca protects the body from many ailments… and if it does so much for outward ailments, will not its singular virtue have even greater effect in the entrails of those who eat it?"

This aforementioned amphora is one of the larger vessels associated with this cist. Its height is 34.2 cm; its rim diameter is 8.5 cm; and its vessel wall is 6 to 7 mm thick. It has strap handles 3.0 to 3.5 cm wide. The Munsell color of the vessel surface is mainly 2.5 YR 5/6 ("red") that grades into 2.5 YR 4/6 ("red") and 2.5 YR 4/4 ("reddish brown"). Firing clouds are brownish gray and surrounded by areas that are 7.5 YR 6/4 ("light brown") in color. The clay body is 10 R 6/6 to 2.5 YR 6/8 ("light red").

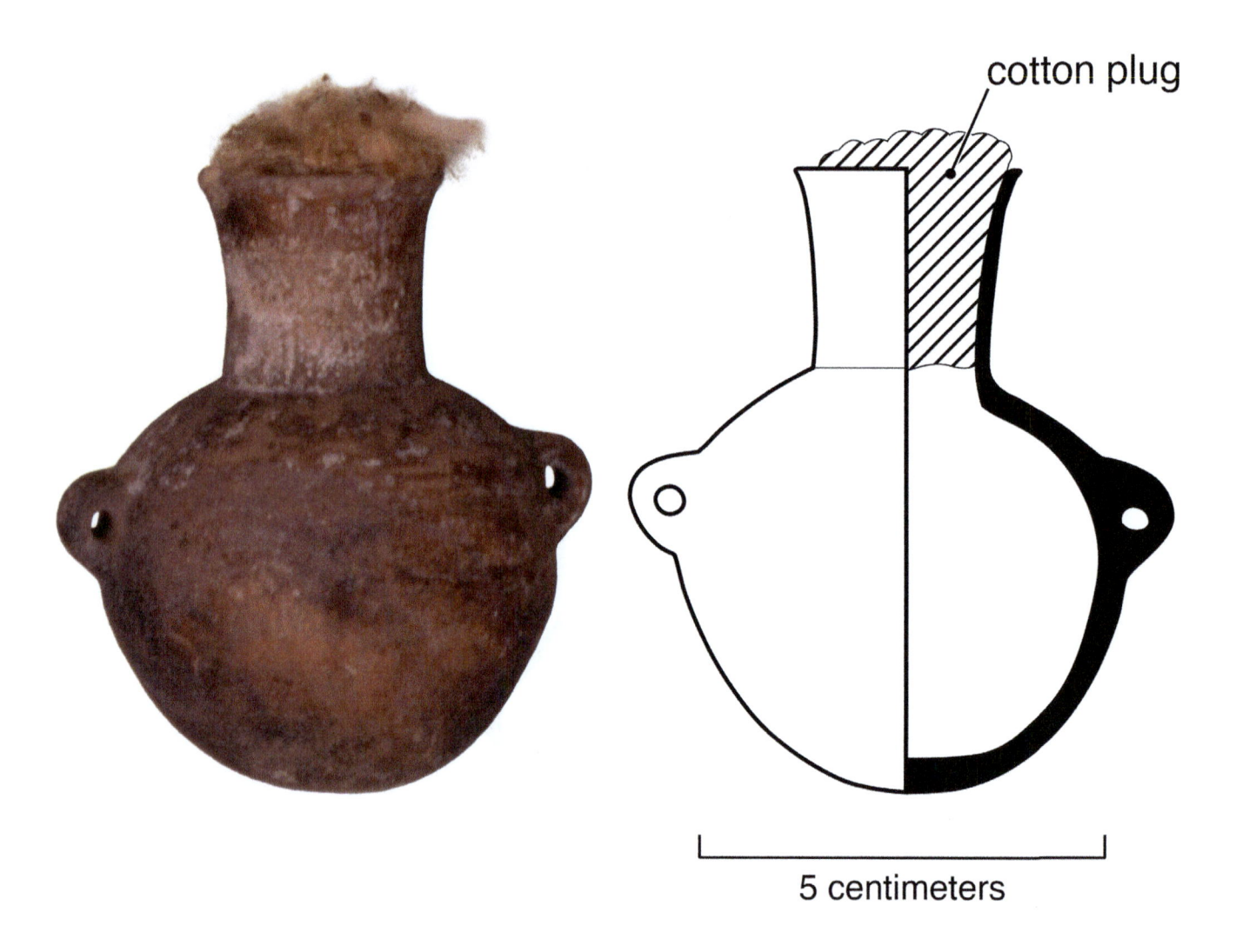

Figure 4.13. A Camacho Reddish Brown miniature jar with a cotton plug still in its neck, found next to Structure 4.

Gourd Vessels

Resting on the floor of Structure 4 was an incomplete gourd bowl (Figure 4.15). We estimate that its original diameter was 15 cm, its height 4 cm, and its wall thickness 5 mm. The surface color of the gourd was not uniform, varying from 2.5 YR 2/2 ("very dusky red") to 2/4 ("dark reddish brown").

We found other gourd fragments just outside the cist. Unfortunately, we cannot be sure that all of them came from the Structure 4 burial cist, since gourd vessels were common in the other burials on this terrace. We illustrate these gourd vessels in Figures 4.16–4.20.

In Figure 4.16, we see fragments of two gourd bowls. One rim suggests that the vessel had a diameter of 20 cm and a wall thickness of 6 mm; its color is 10 R 2/2 ("very dusky red"). The second gourd rim suggests a vessel with a diameter of 15 cm and a wall thickness of 6 mm. The surface color is 2.5 YR 2/4 ("dark red"). We also found the base of a shallow gourd vessel with a wall thickness of 5 mm and a surface color of 2.5 YR 2/4 ("dark red").

The gourd vessel in Figure 4.17 was another example of the shallow bowl type. Its rim diameter was 19.4 cm, its height 4.5 cm, and the thickness of its wall 6 mm. Its color is 10 R 3/4 ("dusky red").

The incomplete gourd in Figure 4.18 had an unusual shape (Specimen 24). It was ca. 17.5 cm in diameter and 5.8 cm high. Its wall was only 4 mm—a bit thinner than other gourd vessels from Structure 4—and its color was 5 YR 3/3 ("dark reddish brown").

We recovered almost half the vessel shown in Figure 4.19. This vessel is one of our rare examples of a pyroengraved gourd. Its rim diameter was ca. 22 cm and its height 4.5 cm.

The Structure 4 Burial Cist 55

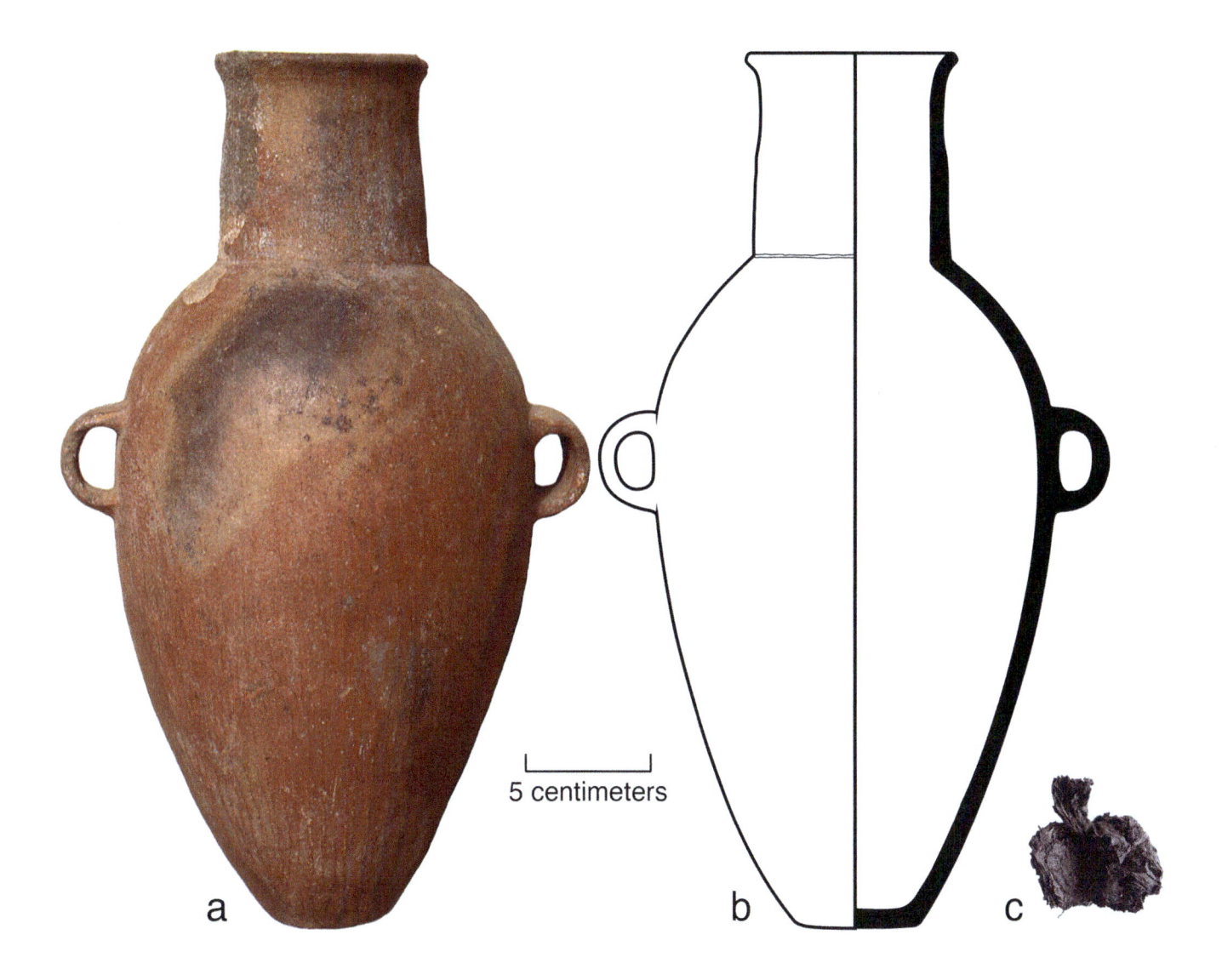

Figure 4.14. Photo and drawing of a Camacho Reddish Brown amphora, found next to Structure 4. In the bottom of this vessel we found a desiccated clump of coca leaves (c), suggesting that the amphora may have contained coca tea.

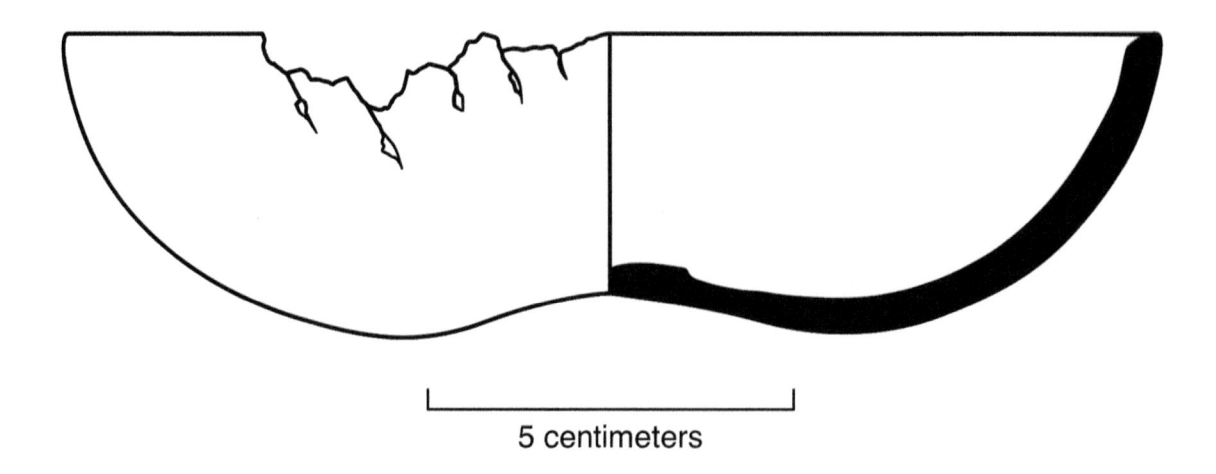

Figure 4.15. One of several *mates* or gourd vessels associated with Structure 4.

The pyroengraved motif consists of a strip of diagonal lines, each bearing triangles with a dot in the center. The surface color of the gourd is 5 YR 3/4 ("dark reddish brown").

The shallow gourd bowl in Figure 4.20 measured 23 x 26 cm, with a height of 7 cm and a wall thickness of 5 mm. The color was 2.5 YR 3/6 ("dark red").

Lúcuma Seed Containers

In addition to the ceramic and gourd vessels, we found two *lúcuma* seeds that had been converted into tiny containers by the drilling of a hole. We found one of these in Structure D (Figure 4.21a), and another in the Structure 4 burial cist (Figure 4.21b). While we do not know the function of these tiny containers, it is interesting that at least one had been included in a burial cist.

Shell Artifacts

We did not find as many marine shell artifacts as we expected, given Cerro Azul's seaside location. Structure 4, however, did produce a handful. One ornament had been made from a clam, probably a beach-worn *Mulinia edulis* (Figure 4.22a). The hole drilled in its umbo was 2.4 mm in diameter, allowing the shell to be worn as a pendant.

In Figure 4.22b we see a bead or pendant made from a possible *Olivella* shell. In Figure 4.22c we see a small piece of *Spondylus*, converted into a bead; its length and width are both 18 mm and it is 10 mm thick. The drill hole is biconical, narrowing from 4 mm to 2 mm inside the bead.

Figure 4.22d shows a *chanque* or false abalone (*Concholepas*), modified for use as a personal cosmetic palette. In this palette, we found traces of two different shades of red paint matching the colors of the fingernail polish on some of the women buried on Terrace 9. The shell, which now measures ca. 5 x 4 cm, had been modified by trimming its edge.

In Figure 4.22e we see a mussel shell that also bears evidence of two different shades of nail polish: 10 R 5/8 ("orangish red") and 7.5 R 3/6 ("dark red"). The latter was the same shade of red used on the fingernails of one woman whose mummified hand was found lying on the surface of the site, where the looters had discarded it.

Metal Artifacts

Only two pieces of metal were associated with Structure 4. One packet of silver foil (Specimen 14) had been folded several times. It measured 3.8 x 3.0 cm and weighed 9 g. The second item (Specimen 16) was a square piece of silver measuring 1 cm on a side and weighing a bit less than 1 g.

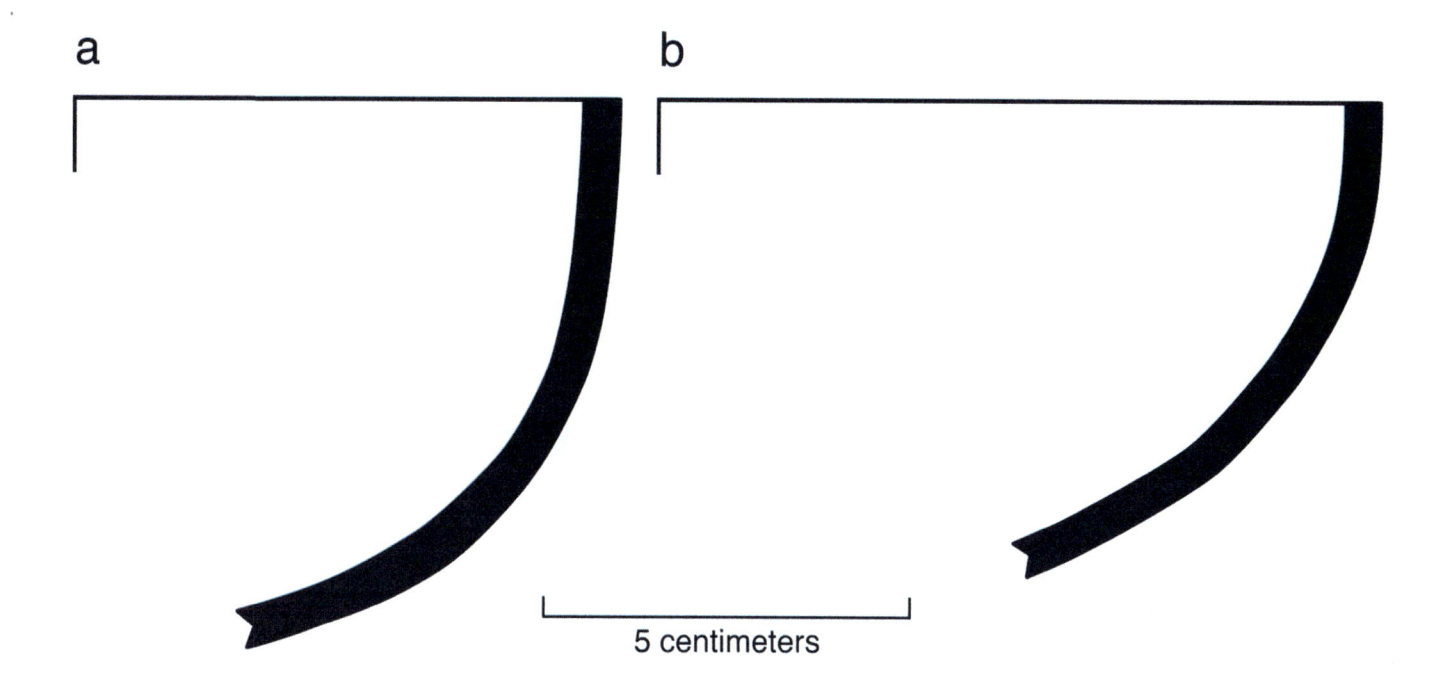

Figure 4.16. Rim profiles of two gourd bowls that were found just outside the opening of Structure 4.

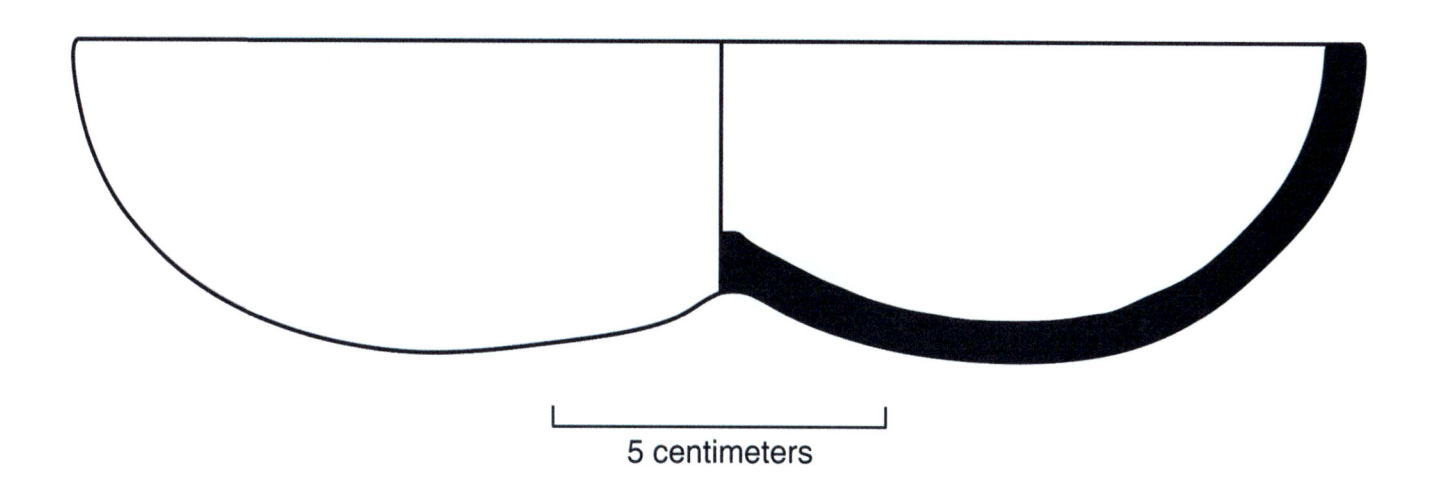

Figure 4.17. Gourd bowl found adjacent to Structure 4.

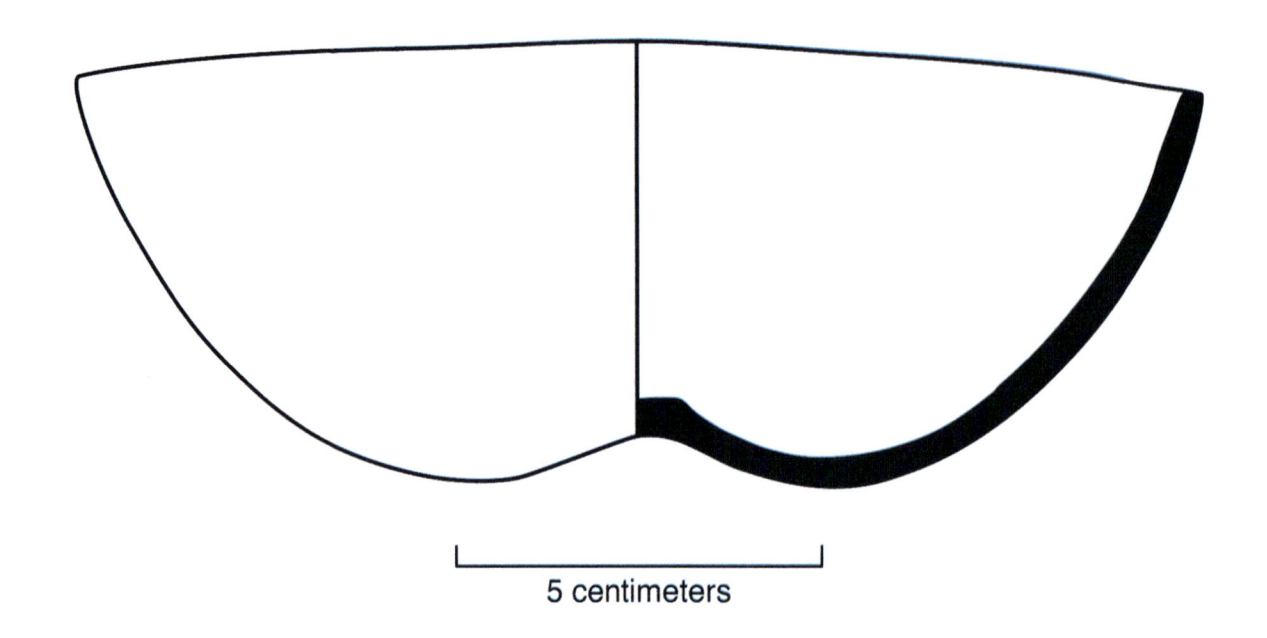

Figure 4.18. A second gourd bowl found adjacent to Structure 4.

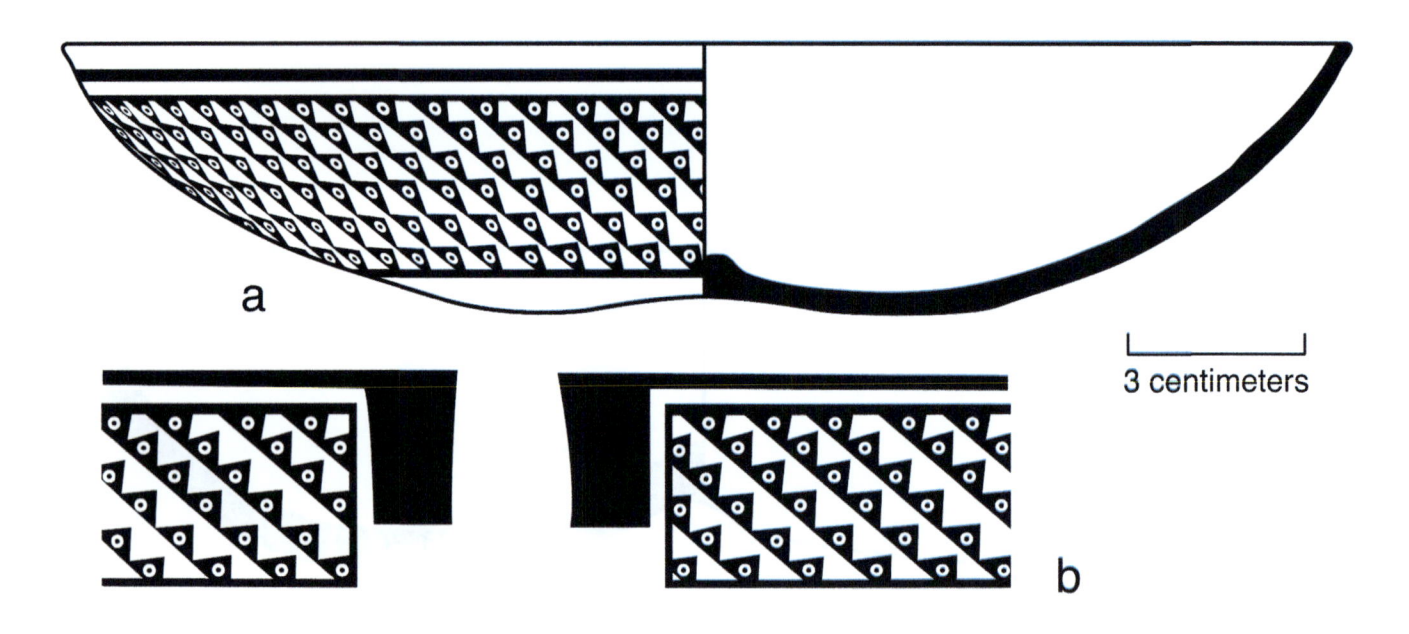

Figure 4.19. A pyroengraved gourd bowl, found on the surface adjacent to Structure 4. (a) The bowl in cross section. (b) A roll-out of the pyroengraved motif.

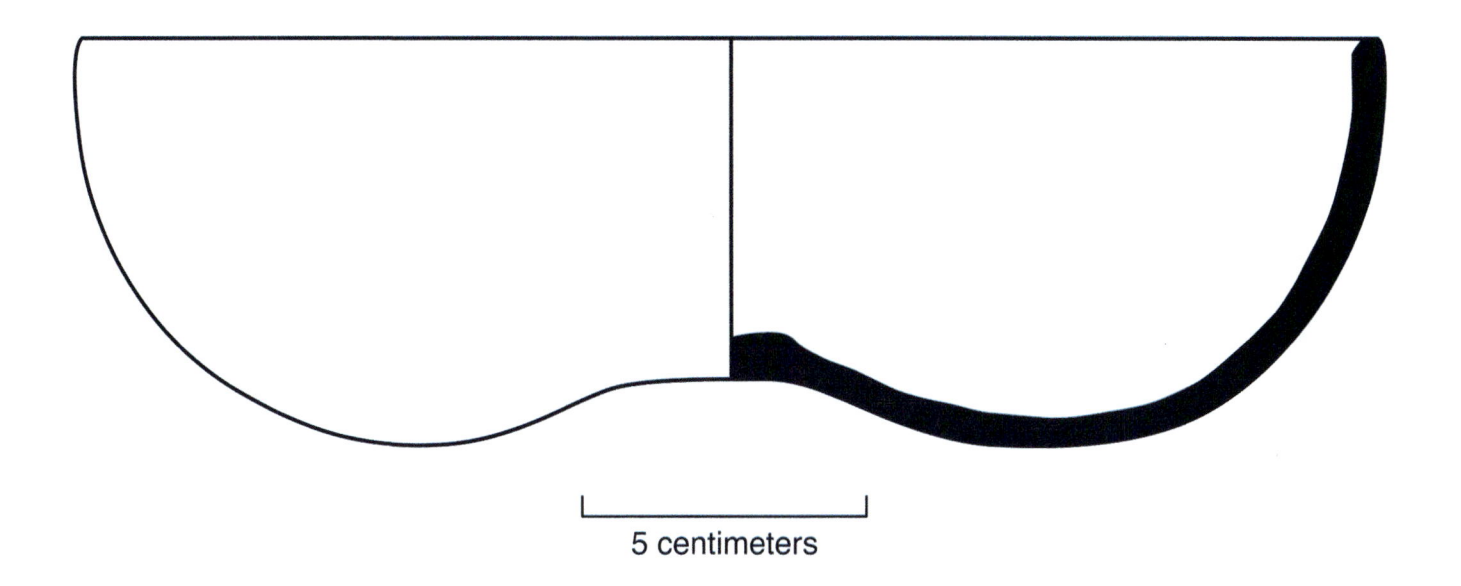

Figure 4.20. A gourd bowl from Structure 4.

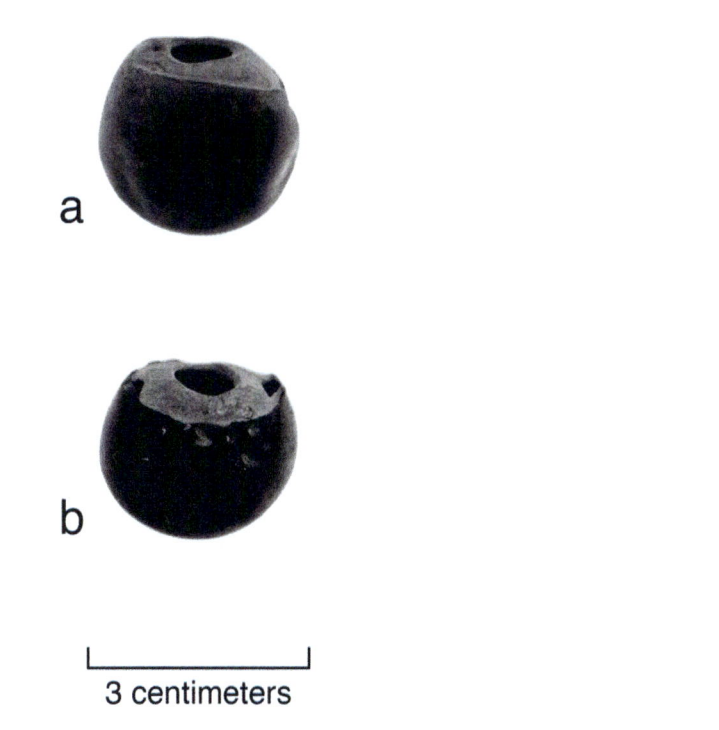

Figure 4.21. Two miniature containers, created by drilling holes in lúcuma seeds. (a) Found in a storage bin in Structure D. (b) Found in the Structure 4 burial cist.

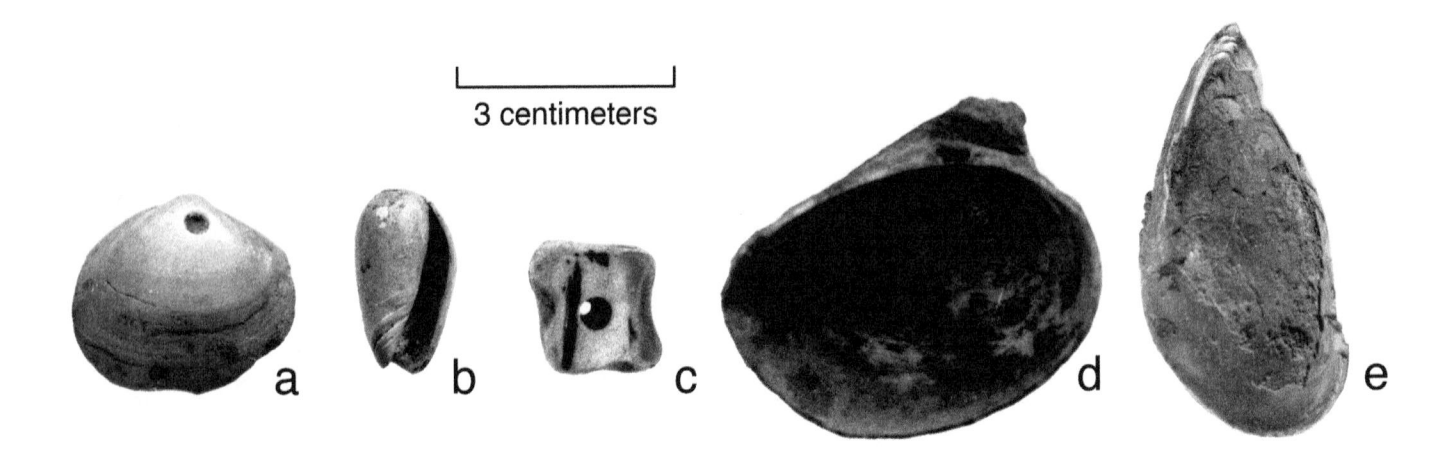

Figure 4.22. Molluscs associated with Structure 4. a–c were ornaments. d–e were used as pigment palettes. (a) Specimen 11, a clam trimmed and drilled for suspension. (b) Specimen 9, a cone shell perforated for suspension. (c) Specimen 6, a rectangular bead cut from *Spondylus* shell. (d) Specimen 5, a false abalone. (e) Specimen 10, a mussel.

Unfortunately, owing to looting we could not associate these bits of metal with specific mummies.

Fishing Nets

Since the fishing nets associated with Structure 4 had deteriorated (and fragmented into 55 pieces), it was impossible to reconstruct how many complete nets they once formed. We can say, however, that there was at least one cast net (*atarraya*) and at least one trammel or curtain net (*red de cortina*) in Structure 4 (both Marcus and Flannery 2010 and Rodríguez Suy Suy 1997 discuss different types of nets). Almost all the Structure 4 net fragments were cotton. A few fragments, however, incorporated slivers of vegetal fibers from a plant other than cotton; one possibility is milkweed (see Bird and Hyslop 1985; Splitstoser 2017).

The Structure 4 net fragments varied in mesh size. Since I suspected that there was a relationship between mesh size and fish species, I decided to show our net fragments to some of Cerro Azul's oldest fishermen—those who had fished and made cotton nets long before nylon nets arrived on the coast. Don José Chumpitaz, an 80-year-old fisherman, agreed to be interviewed on the subject; I was joined in most of these interviews by my colleague Ramiro Matos.

We asked Sr. Chumpitaz how many varieties of nets he had used in his youth. He described three types:

(1) nets with small mesh, which he called "pejerreyeras" and described as having *malla ciega*;

(2) nets with medium-size mesh, which he called "liseras"; and

(3) nets with large mesh, which he called "corvineras" and described as having *malla clara*.

Note that the terms used refer to the fish called pejerrey (silversides), lisa (mullet), and corvina (large drum). (For details and species identifications, see Flannery and Marcus 2016:72–97.)

We then handed Señor Chumpitaz 16 net fragments from Structure 4. After studying each, he declared that only two of his three types were present in our sample: *malla ciega* and *malla clara*, the two extremes. In a later interview, however, Sr. Chumpitaz identified a wooden *mallero* (the template that generated standardized mesh openings) from Cerro Azul as belonging to the size that he had used to make the kind of net he called *lisera*.

In speaking specifically of the fishermen once buried in Structure 4, Sr. Chumpitaz concluded that they had used nets appropriate for sardine-sized fish and large drums, but not fish of intermediate size. However, he said that the wooden *mallero* in Structure 4 suggested that these fishermen also made nets appropriate to catch mullet.

Sr. Chumpitaz then began to discuss knots. He told us about two types—the *medio nudo* (half knot) and the *nudo completo* (full knot). The full knot, he said, was used most often to make small-mesh nets, while the half knot was used mostly for large-mesh nets that had *malla clara*. We asked him whether any dyes had been used to make the cotton nets less visible to the fish. He was only familiar with one kind of vegetal dye that he had used years before, a dye that came from an unidentified tree he called *negrito*.

The 16 net fragments from Structure 4 would be classified as follows:

Net 1: *nudo completo, malla ciega* for pejerrey or anchoveta (Figure 4.23a, b)

Net 2: *medio nudo, malla grande*, dyed for lisa, caballa, bonito, jurel, lenguado (Figure 4.24a, b)

Net 3: *nudo completo*, dyed for small fish (Figure 4.25a–c)

Net 4: *nudo completo, más grande que ciega*, for large anchovies, large pejerrey, mismis, small jurel, small bagres, rayas (Figure 4.26a–d)

Net 5: *nudo completo, malla ciega*, pescado menudo, dyed (Figure 4.27)

Net 6: *nudo completo, malla más grande que ciega* (Figure 4.28)

Net 7: *nudo completo, malla ciega* for small fish (see Net 1) (Figure 4.29)

Net 8: *nudo completo, malla ciega*, undyed, small fish (Figure 4.30)

Net 9: *nudo completo, malla ciega*, dyed, small fish (Figure 4.31)

Net 10: *medio nudo, malla clara*, dyed, for large lisa, zorrito, caballa, big fish (Figure 4.32)

Net 11: *nudo completo, malla ciega*, for small fish (shows evidence of vegetal dye like Nets 1 and 7) (Figure 4.33)

Net 12: *nudo completo, malla ciega*, dyed thin string (Figure 4.34)

Net 13: *nudo completo, malla ciega*, small fish, undyed; for smallest anchovy and pejerrey (Figure 4.35)

Net 14: *nudo completo, malla clara*, undyed, for large adult fish (Figure 4.36)

Net 15: *nudo completo, malla ciega*, undyed, for small fish (Figure 4.37)

Net 16: *medio nudo, malla clara*, undyed, for corvina or larger adult fish (Figure 4.38)

Mallero (net-making template)

The *mallero* in Figure 4.39 (Specimen 31) measures 8.7 x 2.3 cm and is 4 mm thick. According to Sr. Chumpitaz, this *mallero* would have been used to make nets with the medium-size mesh he called *lisera*. It is thus possible that the individuals buried in Structure 4 included fishermen who used all three of Chumpitaz's mesh sizes.

Fishing Net Fragments

To fish in multiple places, a fisherman needed several kinds of nets. A cast net was typically used by a fisherman perched on the sea cliffs overlooking the Pacific. A curtain net was typically used by two or more men wading into Cerro Azul Bay, each holding one end of the net to ensure that it would stay upright and taut, like a volleyball net.

Irene Emery (1966, 1980, 1995), an expert on fabric structure, has noted that fishing nets are usually distinguished by their knots (Figure 4.40). Although Cerro Azul fishermen today can describe each knot, they emphasized to us that it was the mesh or "malla" (the size of the openings in the mesh) that was the essential criterion for them. In our interviews they said that, "If the openings in the mesh are too large, many small fish such as pejerreyes, sardinas, and anchovetas just swim right through."

We found **Net 017** next to Structure 4; it is a fragment (1.38 m x 15 cm) of a trammel net (Figure 4.41a, b). It consists of two yarns (A and B), each a different color; one was white, the other light brown. Botanist C. Earle Smith, Jr. identified both Yarns A and B as natural cotton, i.e. not dyed. The thickness of Yarn A is 2.3 mm, while that of Yarn B is 1.5 mm. Yarn A has a 35 degree spin; Yarn B has a 40 degree spin. Yarn B is attached to Yarn A in some places by a half hitch #2 knot, and in other places by a cow hitch. The mesh openings using Yarn A average 1.25 cm; the mesh openings using Yarn B averaged 1.1 cm. In Dwight Wallace's system, Yarn A would be described as S10 Z2 S and Yarn B as S4 Z2 S.[1]

---

1. In Splitstoser's parenthetical notation method for recording yarn structure, the yarns used in Net 017 would be S (2z(s10)) and S (2z(s4)), respectively. (Splitstoser's method is described in the following source— http://digitalcommons.unl.edu/tsaconf/745). Although I considered converting all of Wallace's descriptions of fabric structures to Splitstoser's effective parenthetical notation, I honor Wallace's request that his notations be retained so that the Cerro Azul textiles could be compared to his previous publications (e.g., Wallace 1960, 1979) as well as to other textile studies (e.g., Aponte Miranda 2000; Bird 1952; Bird and Bellinger 1954; Bruce 1986a, 1986b; Cahlander and Baizerman 1985; Conklin 1975a, 1975b, 1979; Desrosiers 1986; Dwyer 1979; Emery 1966, 1980, 1995; Feldman 1986; Franquemont and Franquemont 1988; Garaventa 1977, 1979; Gayton 1967; Goldberg and Orcutt 1979; King 1958; Medlin 1986; O'Neale 1932, 1936, 1937, 1946, 1949; O'Neale and Clark 1948; O'Neale and Kroeber 1930; O'Neale et al. 1949; Rehl 2002; A. Rowe 1977, 1978, 1986, 1995–1996, 1996a, 1996b, 2011; Skinner 1986; VanStan 1967). Thus, all textile descriptions in this volume are those of Dwight Wallace.

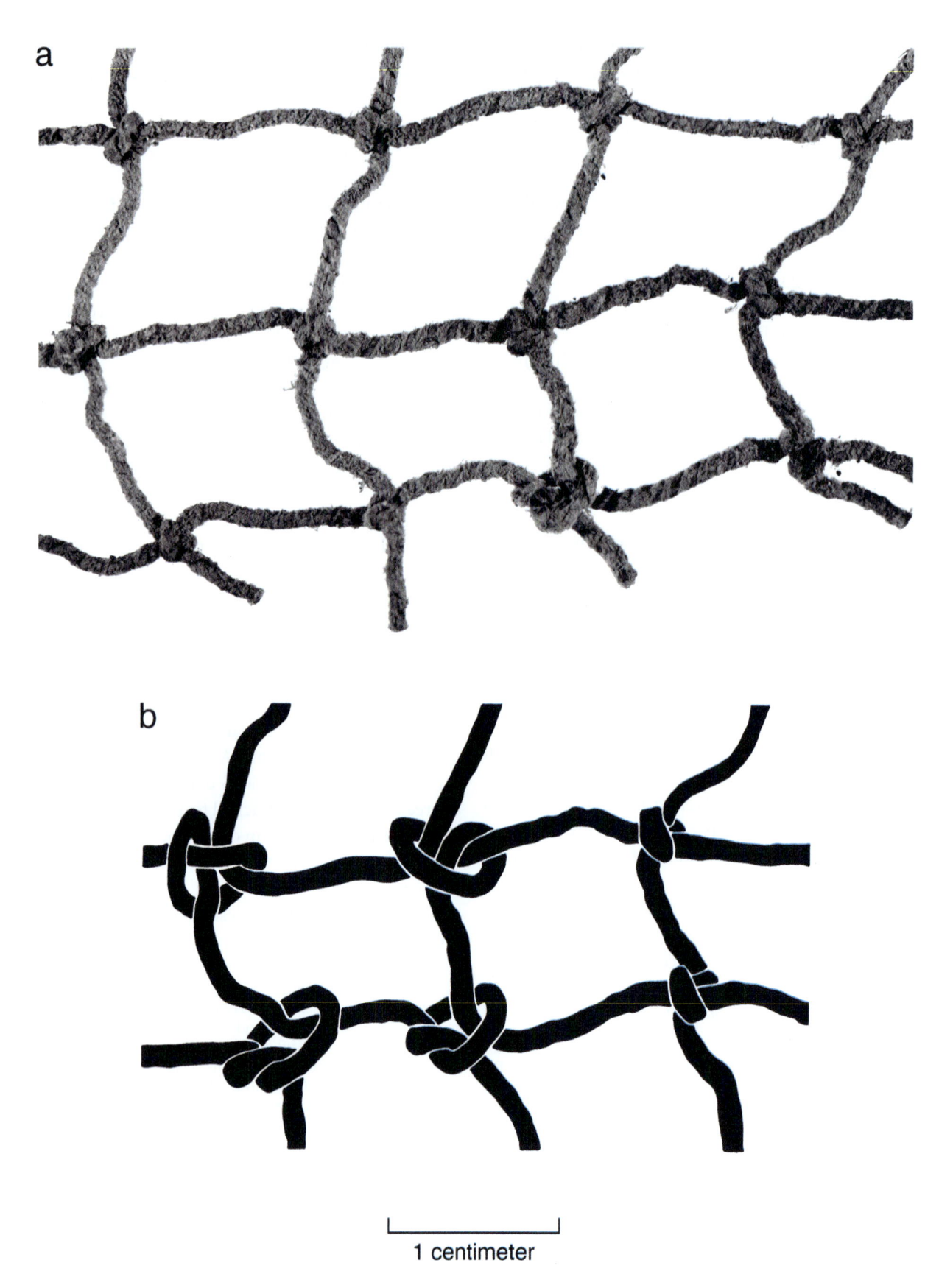

Figure 4.23. Net 1 from Structure 4. (a) photo. (b) drawing.

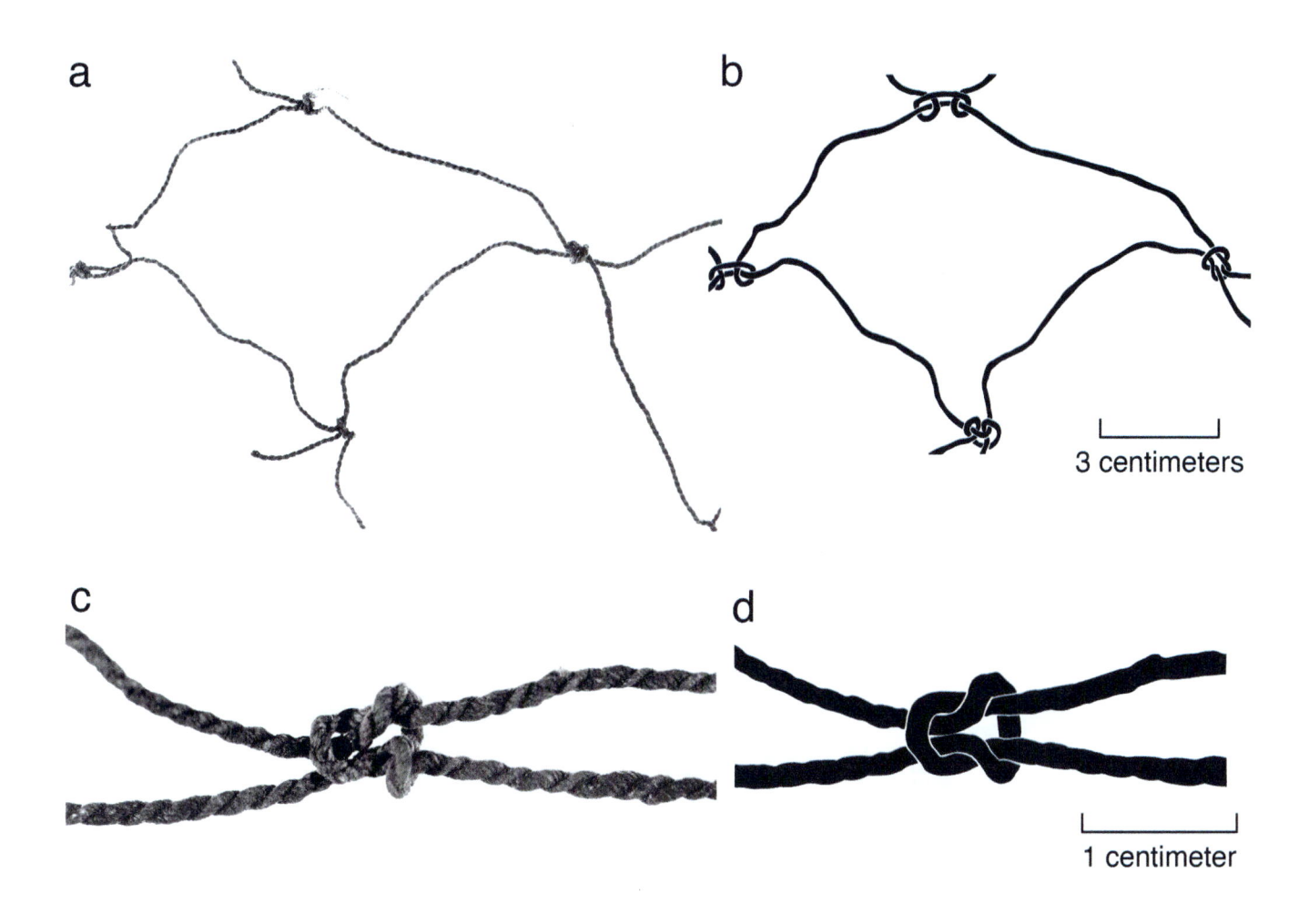

Figure 4.24. Net 2 from Structure 4. (a, b) photo and drawing of net. (c, d) close-up photo and drawing of knot.

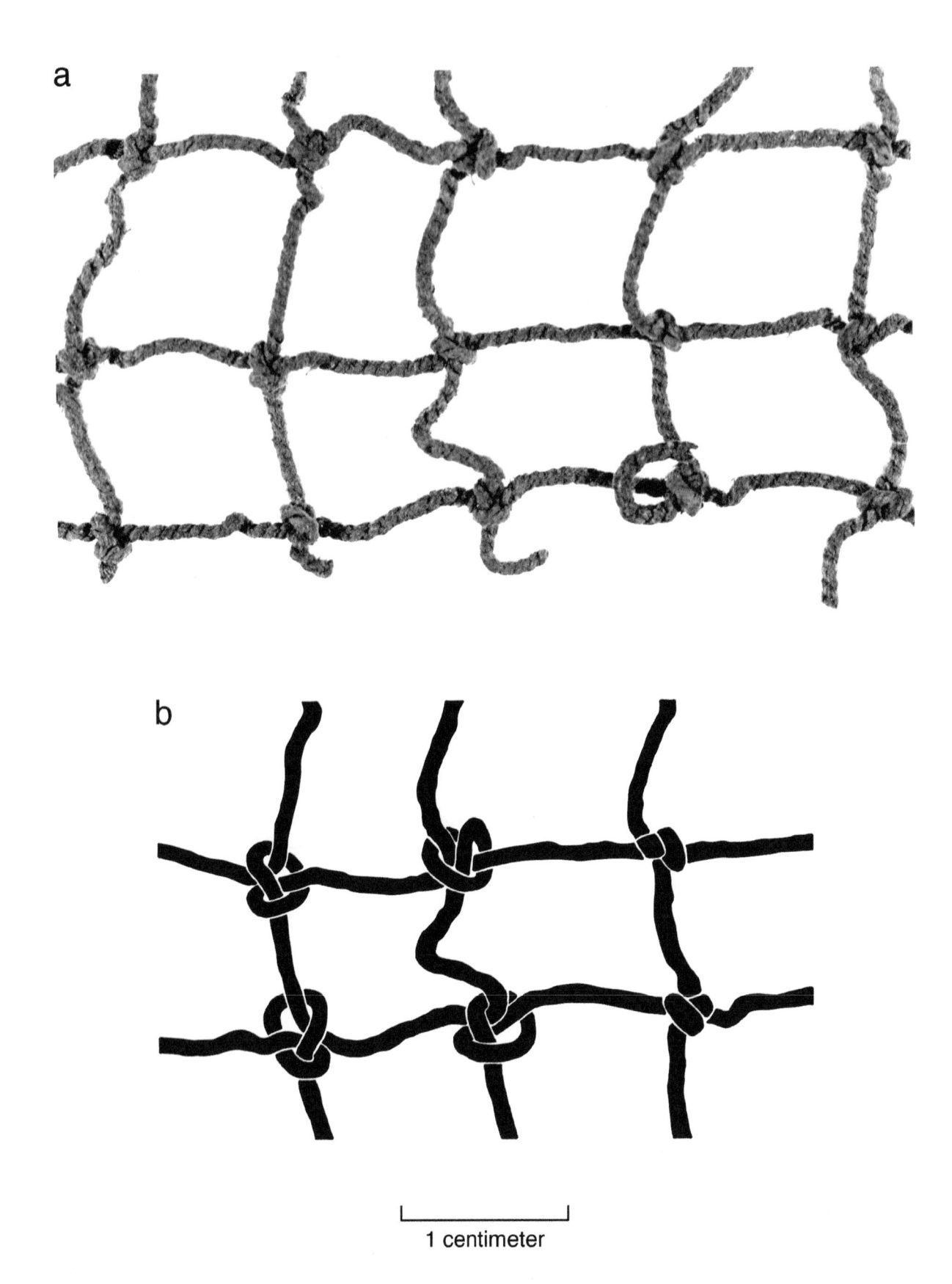

Figure 4.25. Net 3 from Structure 4. (a) photo. (b) drawing.

1 centimeter

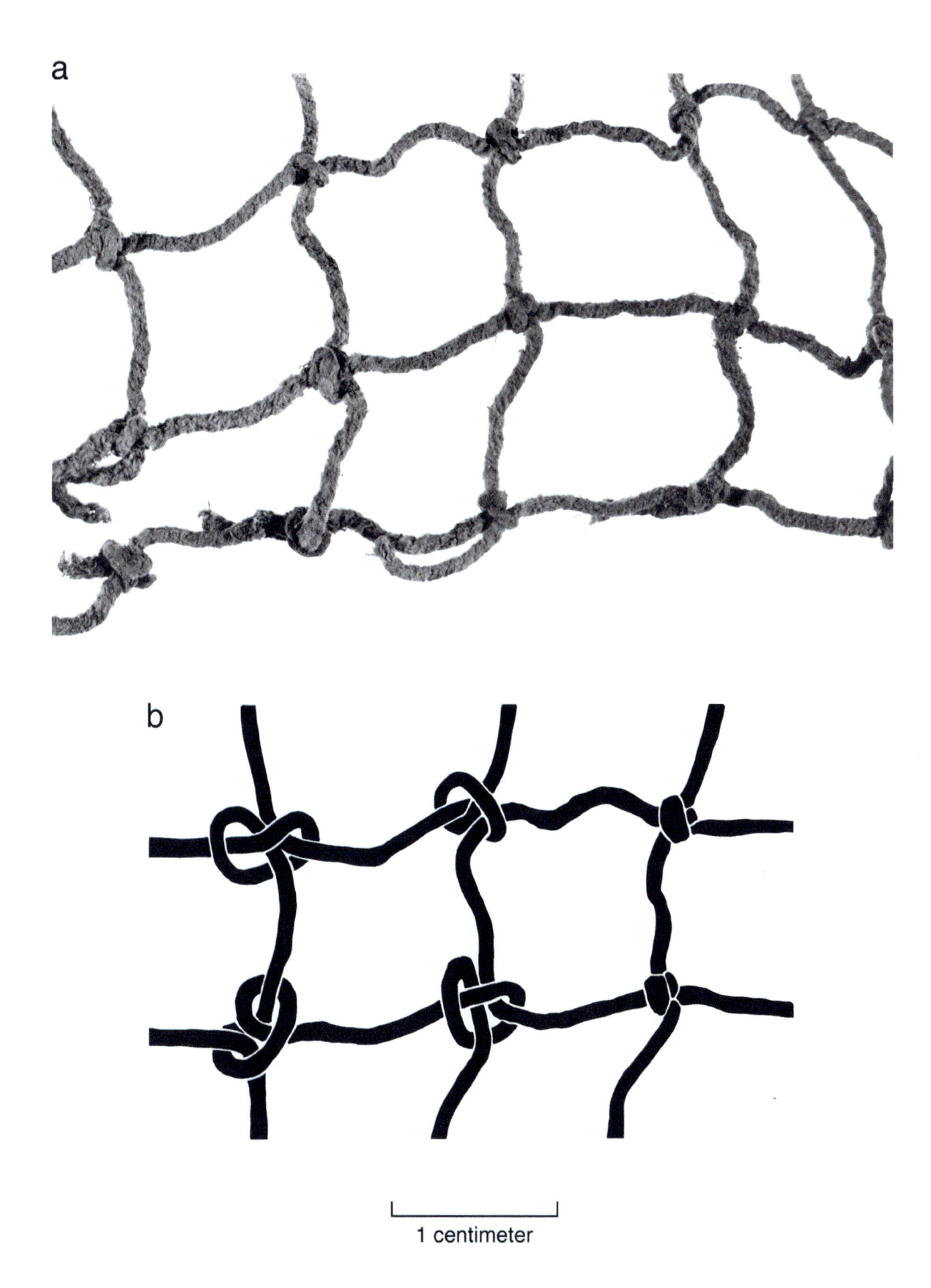

Figure 4.26. Net 4 from Structure 4. (a) photo. (b) drawing.

66　　　　　　　　　　　　　　　　　　　　　Chapter 4

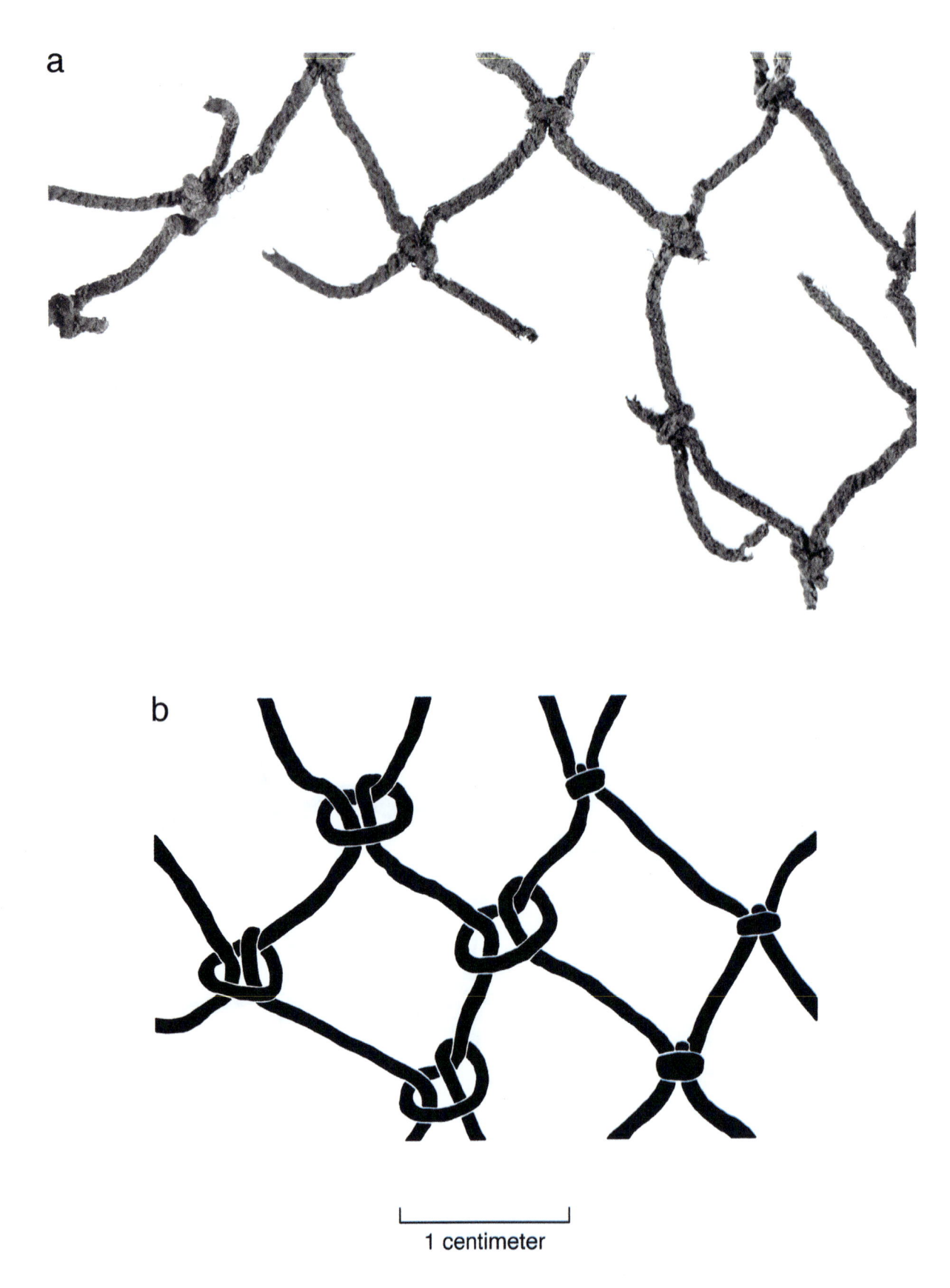

Figure 4.27. Net 5 from Structure 4. (a) photo. (b) drawing.

The Structure 4 Burial Cist

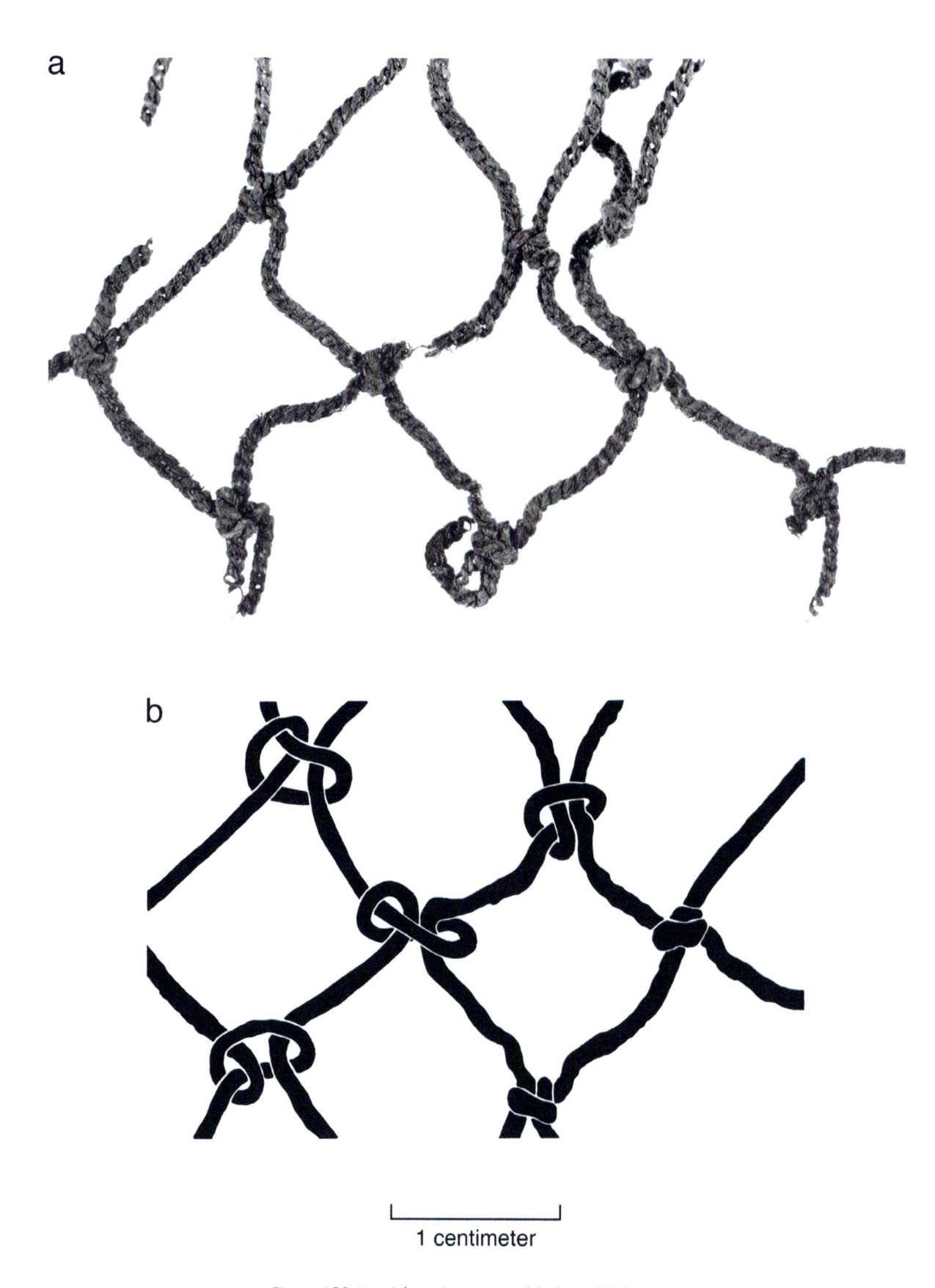

Figure 4.28. Net 6 from Structure 4. (a) photo. (b) drawing.

68   Chapter 4

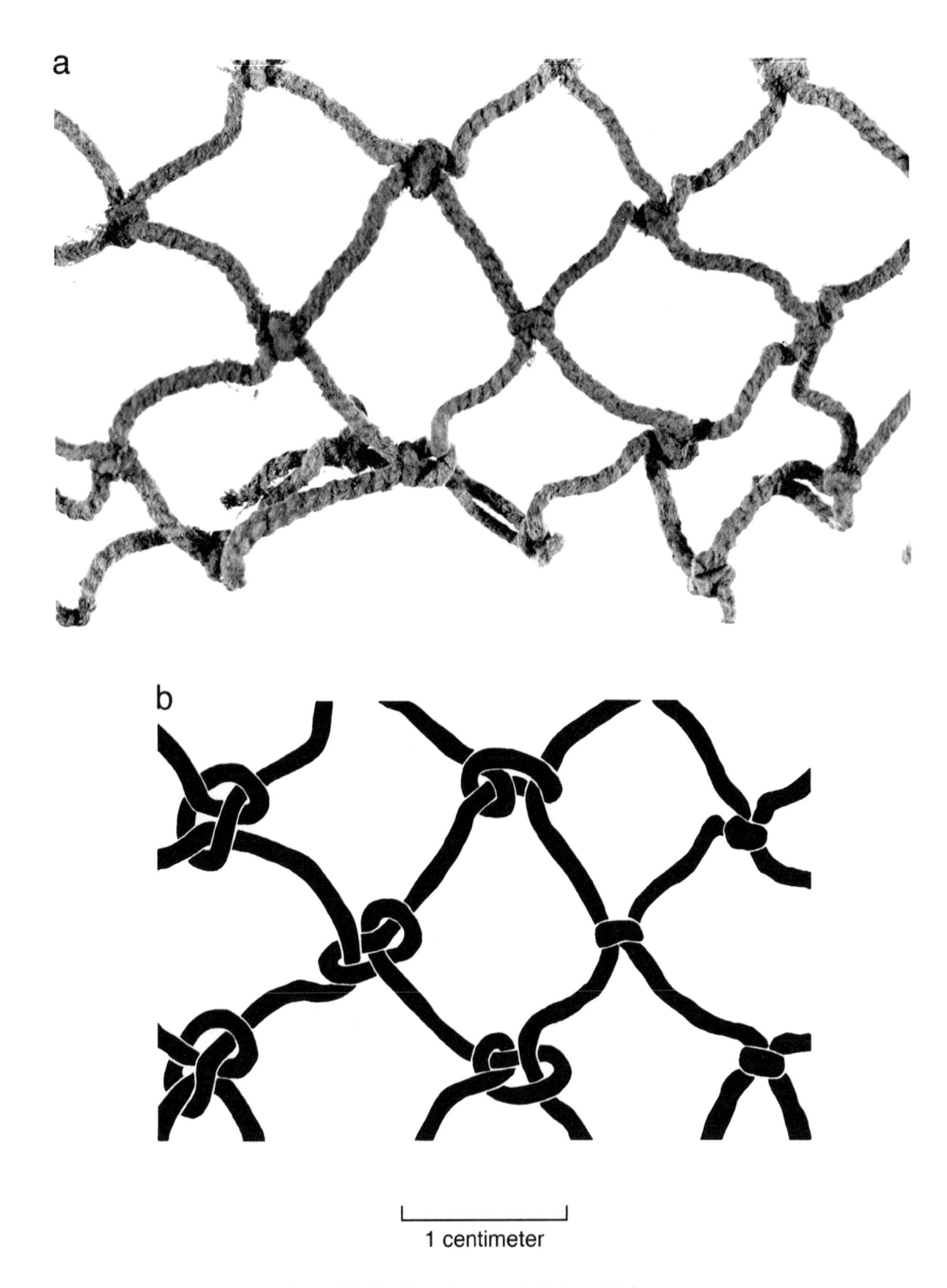

1 centimeter

Figure 4.29. Net 7 from Structure 4. (a) photo. (b) drawing.

The Structure 4 Burial Cist 69

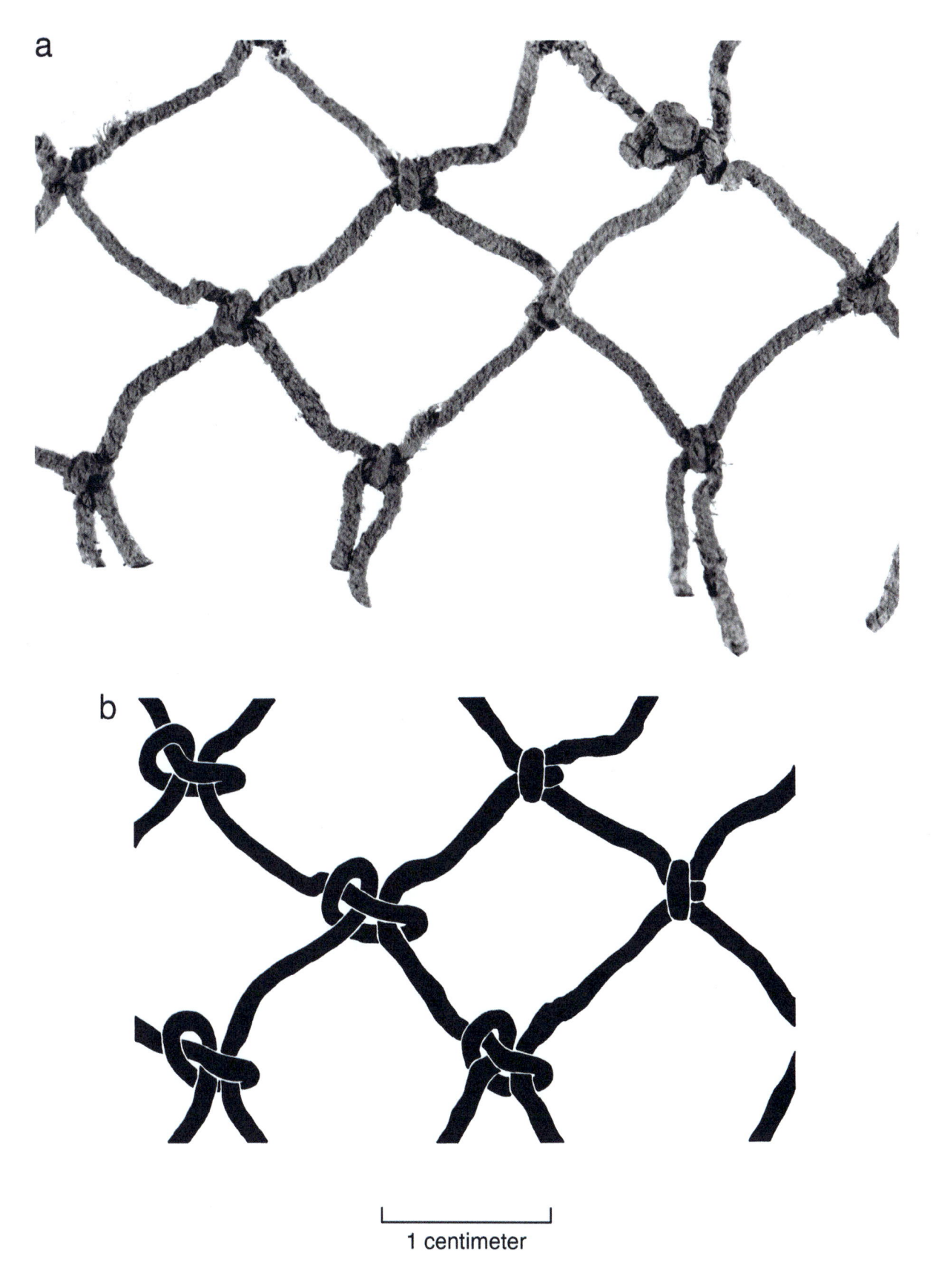

Figure 4.30. Net 8 from Structure 4. (a) photo. (b) drawing.

70 Chapter 4

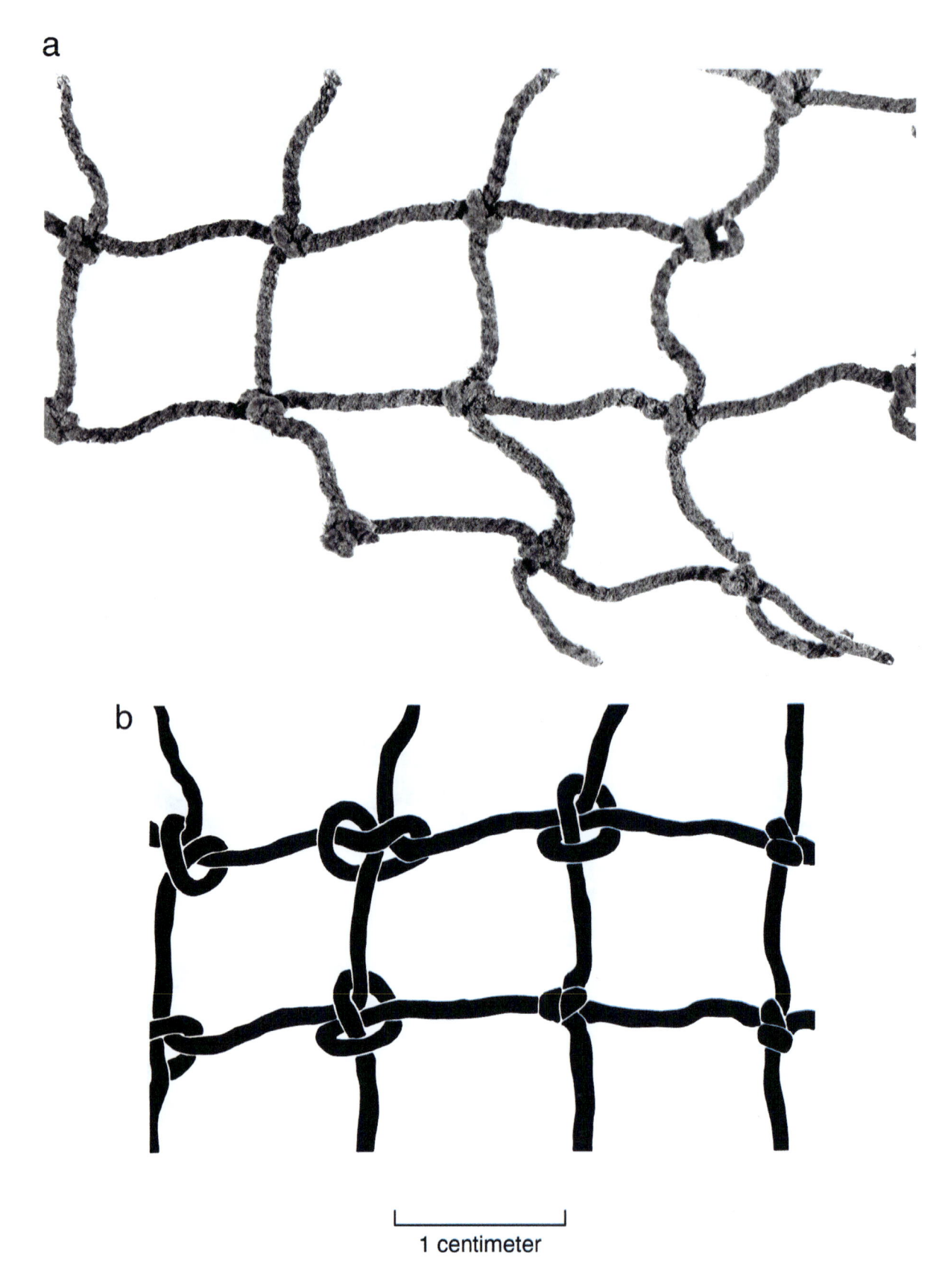

Figure 4.31. Net 9 from Structure 4. (a) photo. (b) drawing.

The Structure 4 Burial Cist 71

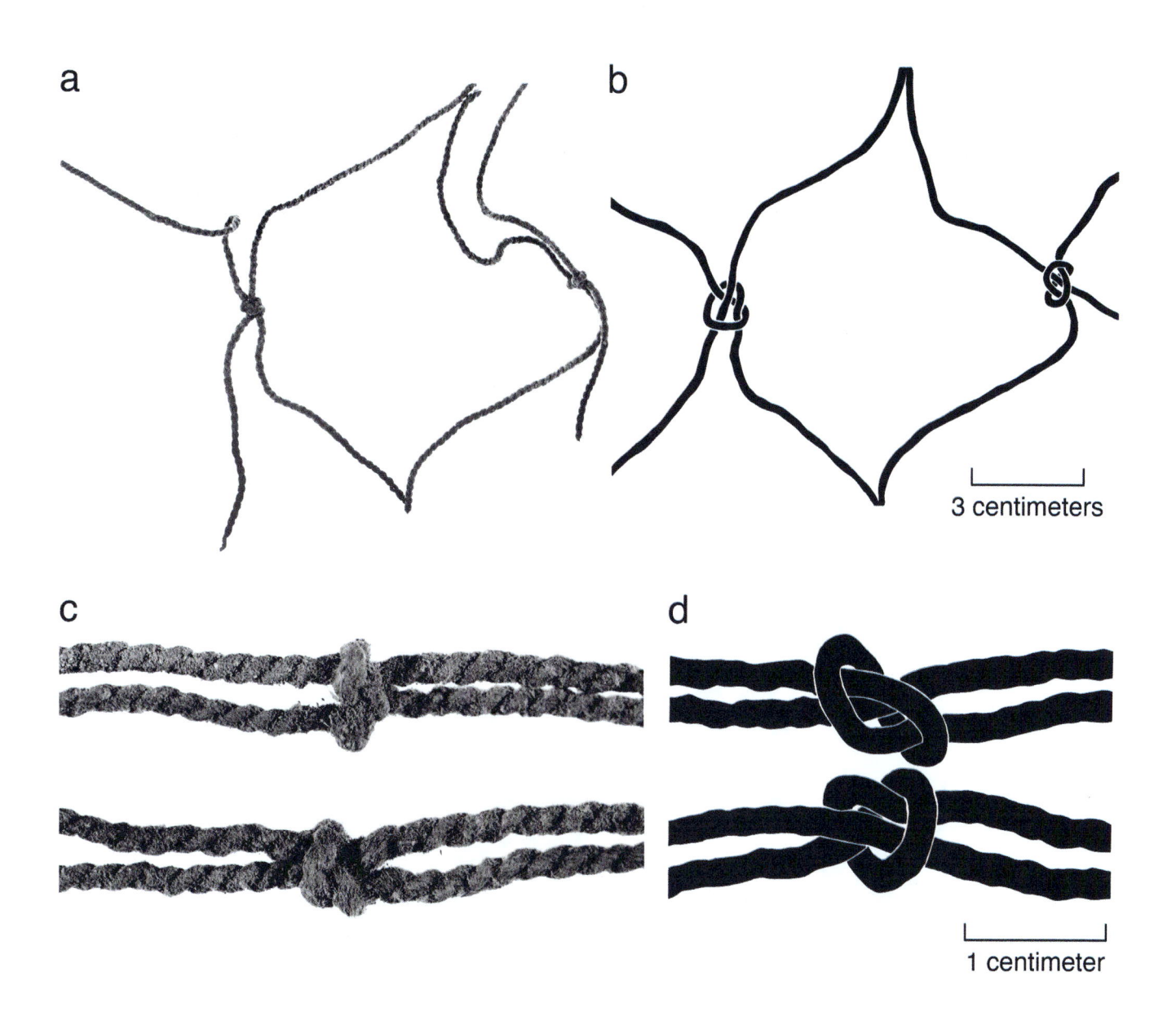

Figure 4.32. Net 10 from Structure 4. (a, b) photo and drawing of net. (c, d) close-up photo and drawing of knots.

72 Chapter 4

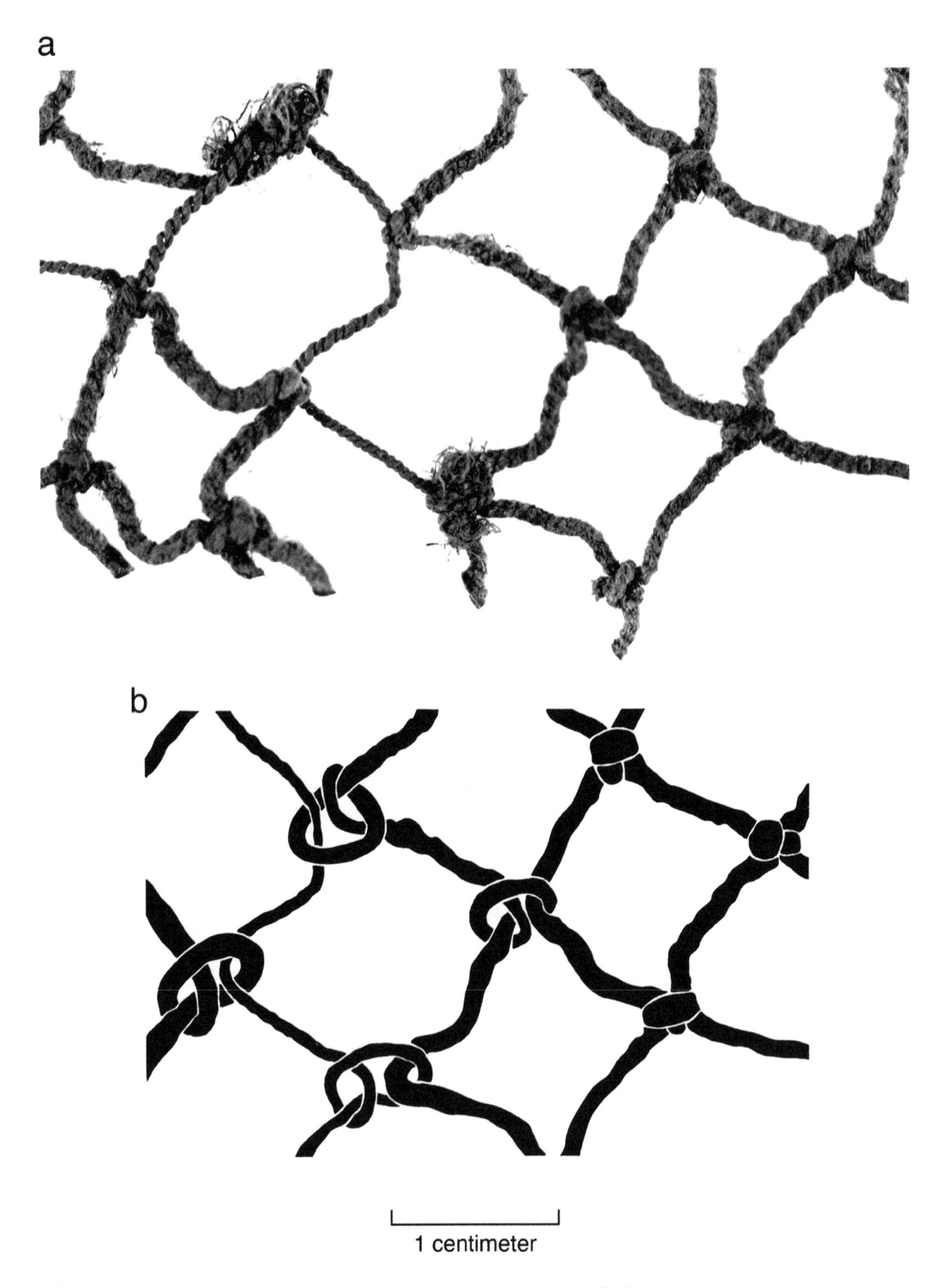

Figure 4.33. Net 11 from Structure 4. (a) photo. (b) drawing.

The Structure 4 Burial Cist 73

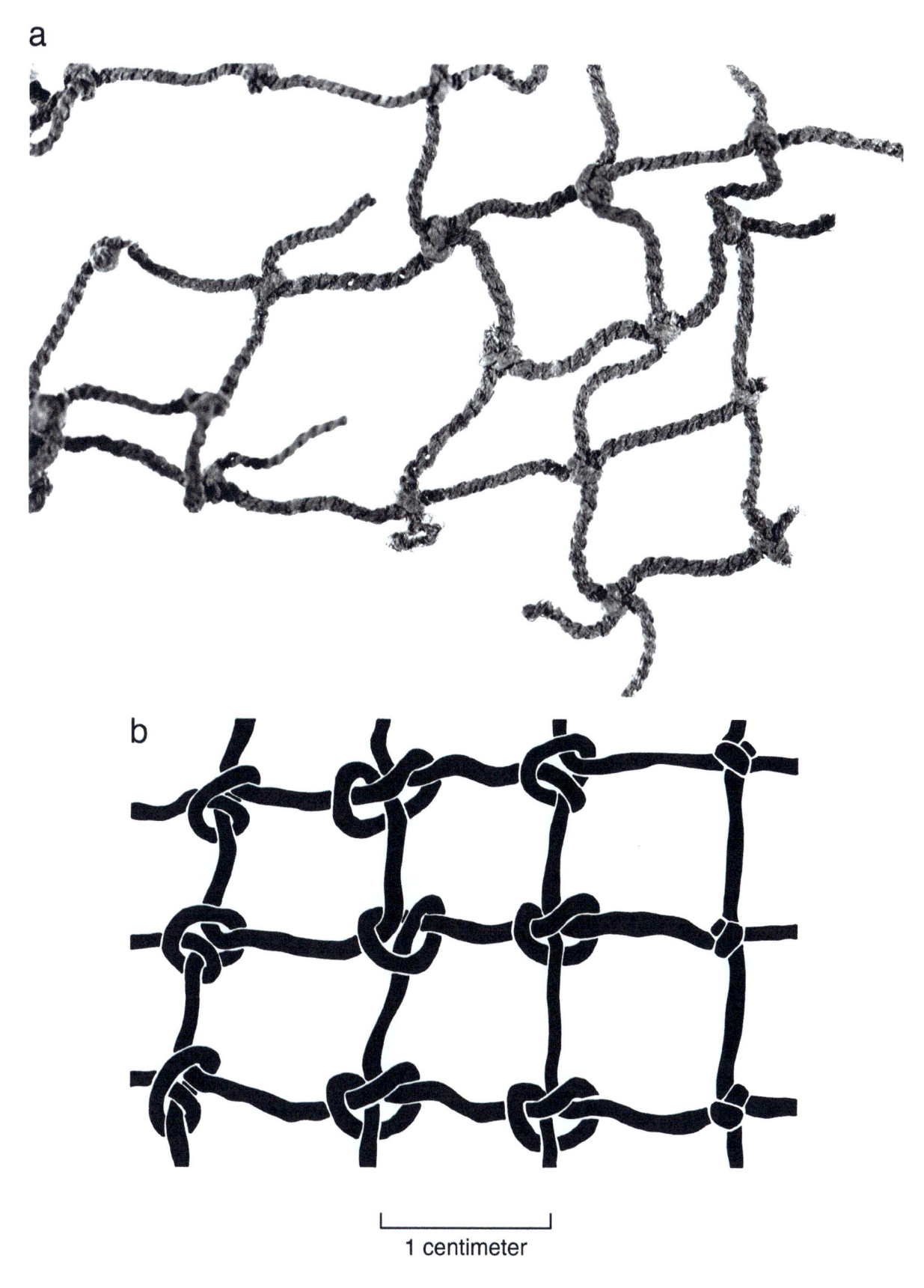

1 centimeter

Figure 4.34. Net 12 from Structure 4. (a) photo. (b) drawing.

74 Chapter 4

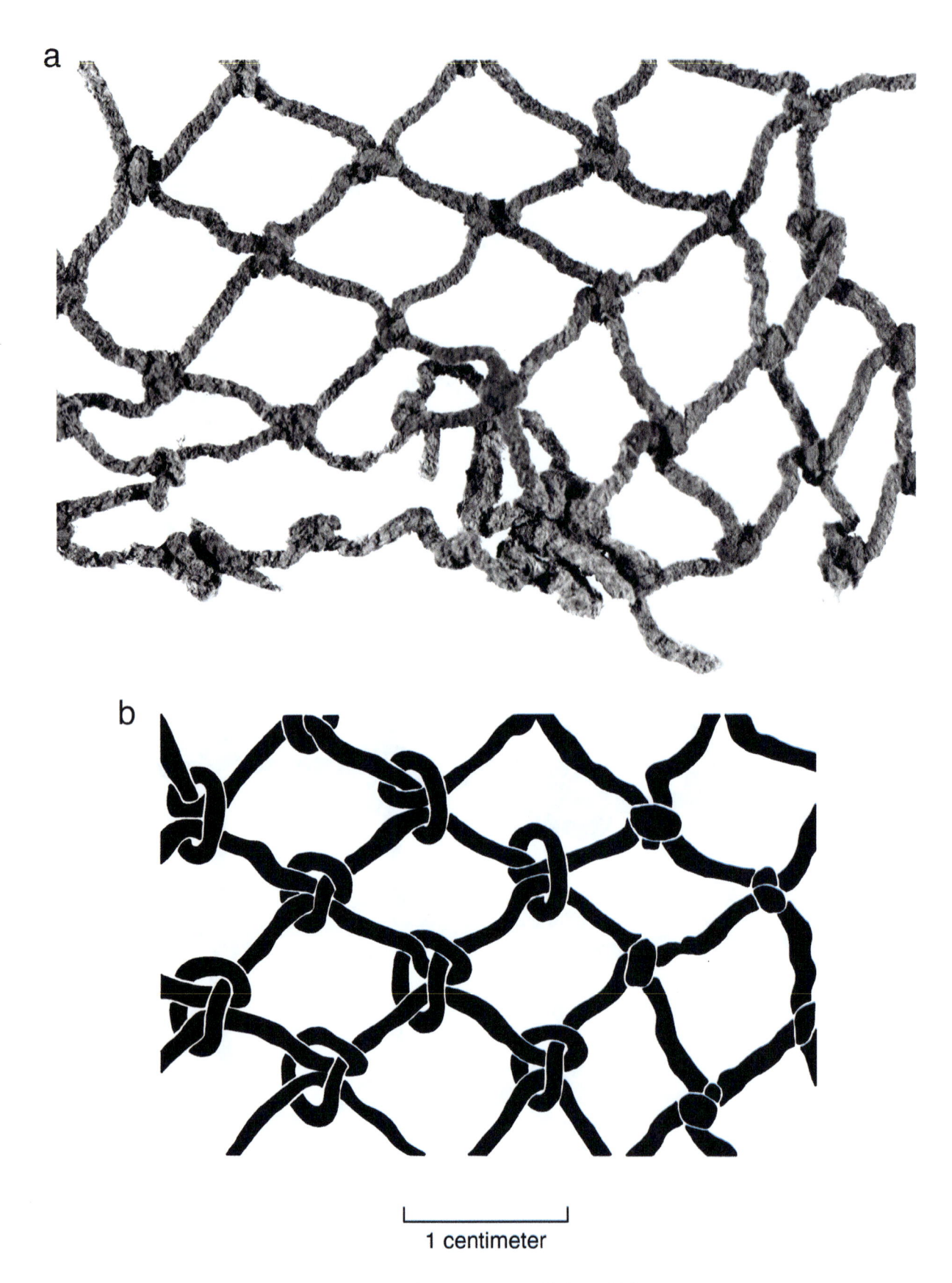

1 centimeter

Figure 4.35. Net 13 from Structure 4. (a) photo. (b) drawing.

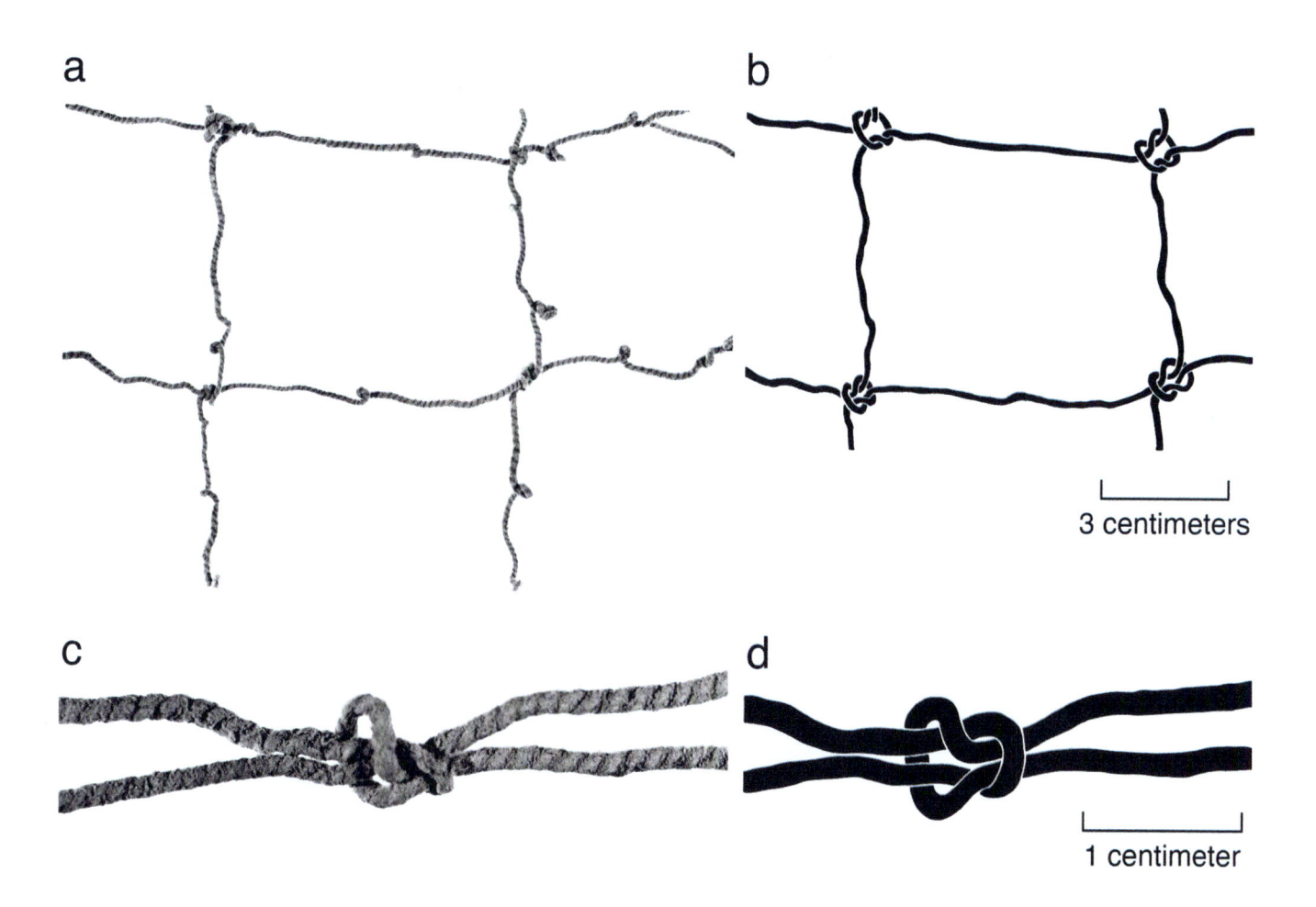

Figure 4.36. Net 14 from Structure 4. (a, b) photo and drawing of net. (c, d) close-up photo and drawing of knot.

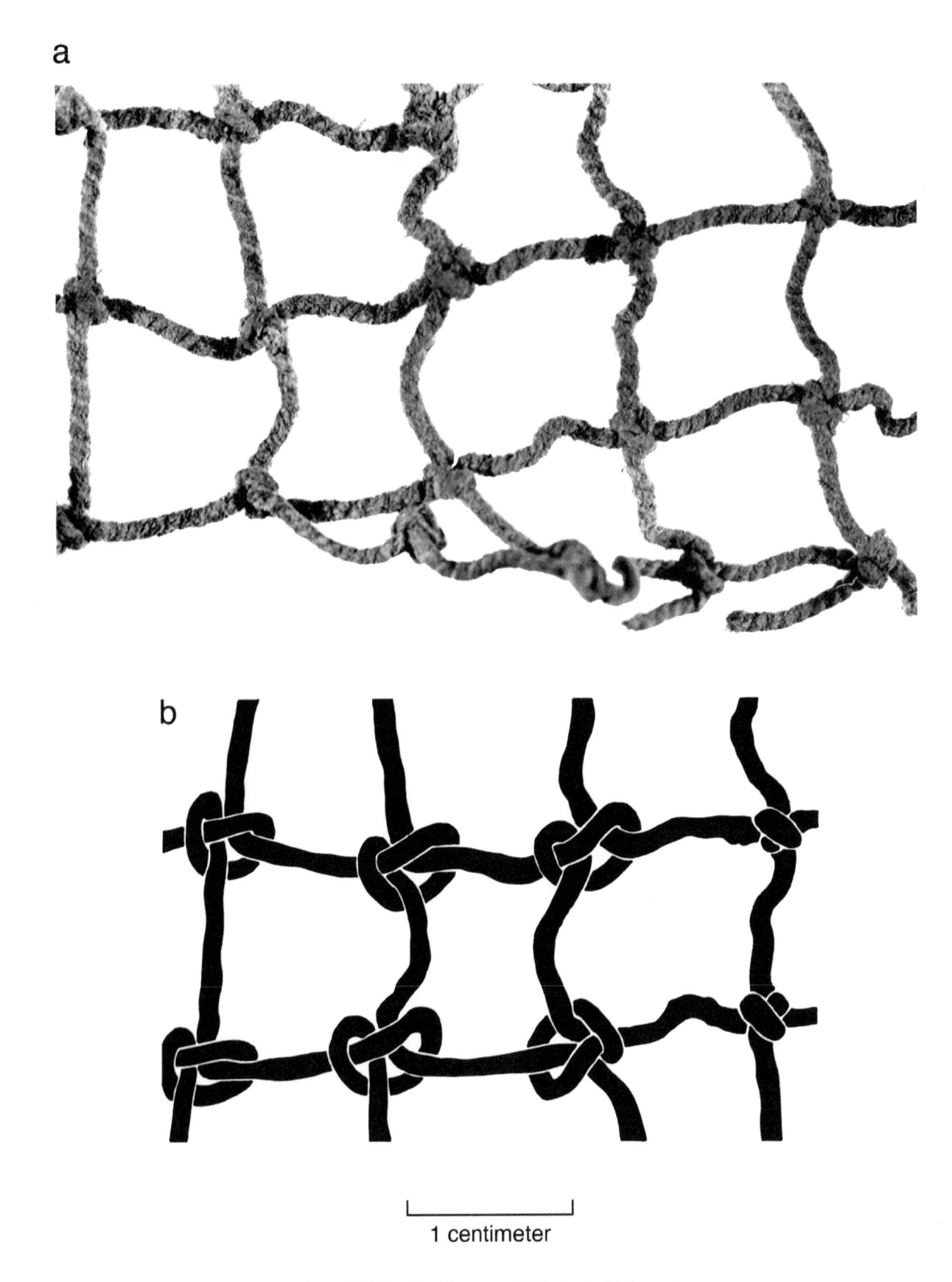

Figure 4.37. Net 15 of Structure 4. (a) photo. (b) drawing.

The Structure 4 Burial Cist

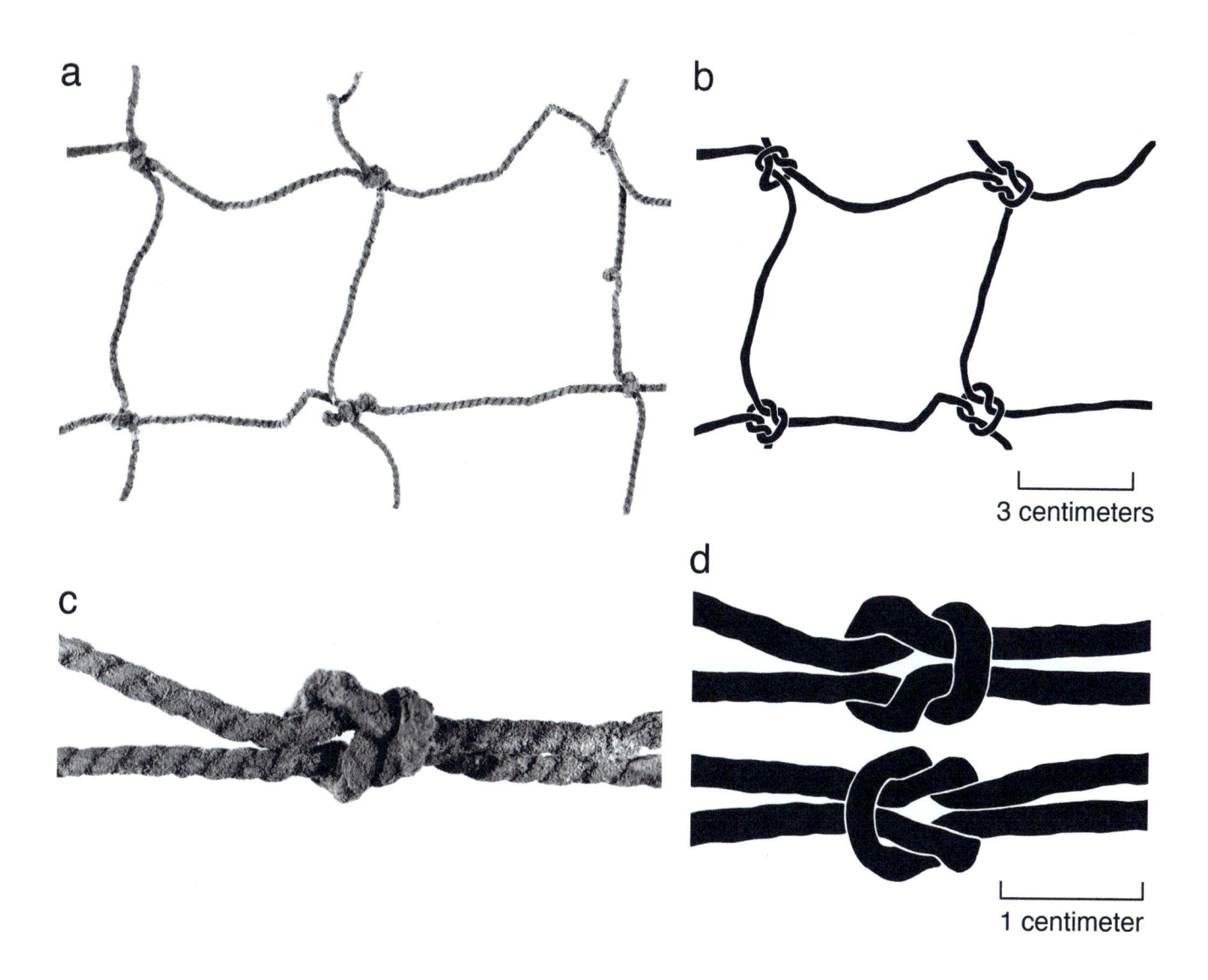

Figure 4.38. Net 16 of Structure 4. (a, b) photo and drawing of net. (c, d) close-up photo and drawing of knots.

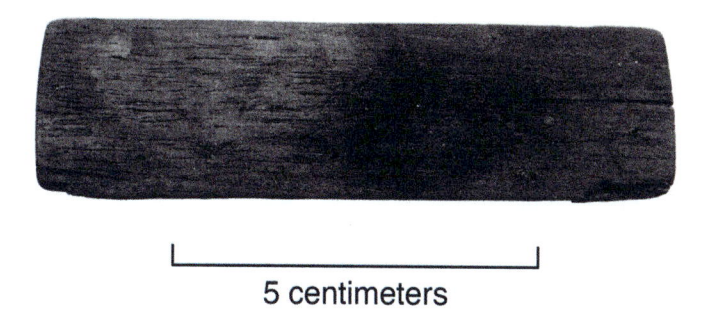

Figure 4.39. A *mallero,* or wooden template used to create uniform mesh openings in a net, found near Structure 4.

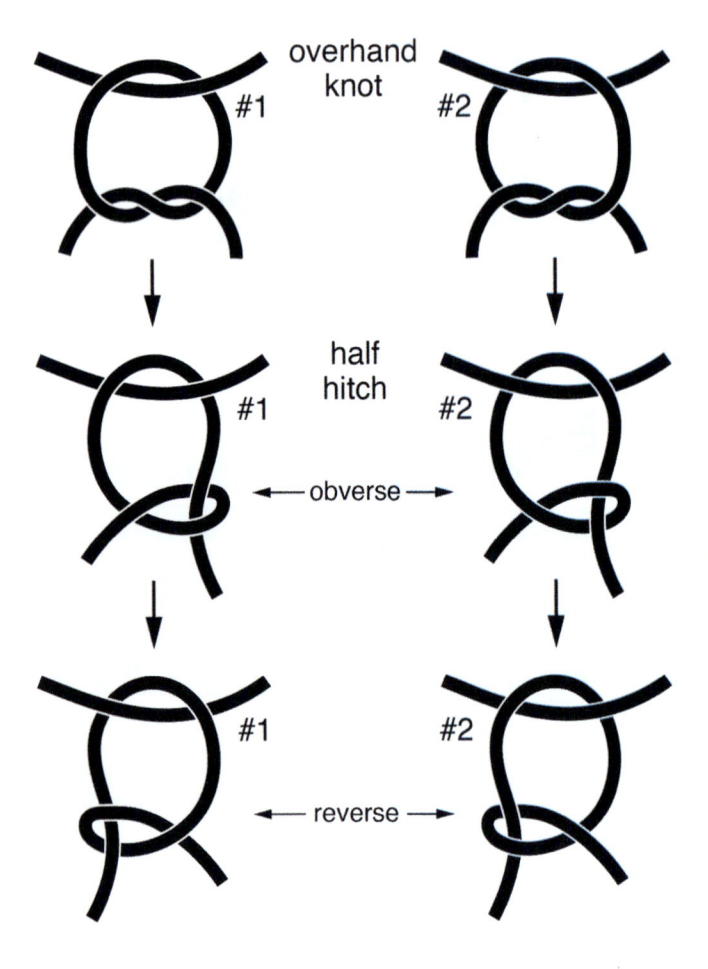

Figure 4.40. Examples of the knots used to make fishing nets at Cerro Azul. Overhand and half hitch knots are different versions of the same knot; one version can be changed to the other without retying. Overhand #1 is the typical overhand knot made by a right-handed person, as is half hitch #2. A left-handed person is more likely to produce overhand #2 or half hitch #1. The vast majority of knots seen in the nets at Cerro Azul are half hitch #2, presumably the work of right-handed fishermen.

Net 022 consists of multiple fragments, with the largest measuring 35 x 10 cm (Figure 4.42). The mesh openings measure 1.7 to 1.9 cm. Three different yarns (A, B, and C) are present. Yarns A and B are dark brown in color. A square knot was used in most places, but one set of knots were cow hitches.

Yarn A: two-ply Z-S; yarn thickness 1.6–1.7 mm; degree of spin is 30 degrees.

Yarn B: two-ply Z-S. In Dwight Wallace's system, the "Z" is the original spin and the "S" is the visible final twist. The Yarn B thickness is 0.9 mm; its degree of spin is 35 degrees in one section and 45 degrees in another.

Yarn C: two-ply Z-S; yarn thickness 0.7 mm; degree of spin is 35 degrees.

One of the more complete fragments has both Yarns B and C as well as direct knotting to heavier yarn (Yarn A).

Net 023a, a fragment measuring 80 x 50 cm, shows evidence of having been repaired. The mesh size varies from 2.3 to 2.5 cm. The knots are half hitch #2. The net is medium brown in color and the yarn is two-ply Z-S. The thickness of the yarn varies from 0.80 mm to 1.0 mm, and its degree of spin is 35 degrees.

Net 023b is a square fragment, measuring 50 x 50 cm. It is medium brown in color. The mesh size is 2.5 to 2.7 cm and the knots are half hitch #2. The yarns are two-ply Z-S and the thickness is 0.9–1.1 mm. The degree of spin is 40 degrees. Note: Nets 023 a, b, e have similar mesh openings (between 2.3 and 2.8 cm).

Net 023c, a fragment measuring 65 x 32 cm, is rectangular with relatively straight sides, but with no original edges. Mesh openings vary from 3.5 cm to 3.64 cm to 3.69 cm. This net fragment is light to medium brown in color. The knot used is a half hitch #2; the yarn is two-ply Z-S. The thickness of the fiber is 0.9 to 1.0 mm and the degree of spin is 40 degrees. Note that Nets 023 c, d, f, g have similar mesh openings (ca. 3.5 cm).

Net 023d is a rectangular fragment (53 x 33 cm) that is straight on two sides. There are no original edges. The mesh size varies from 3.3 to 3.6 cm and the color is dark brown. The knots are half hitch #2. The yarn is two-ply Z-S and its thickness is 0.9 to 1.0 mm. The degree of spin is 45 degrees.

Net 023e is a fragment that measures 120 x 15 cm. Its mesh size varies from 2.5 to 2.8 cm and is similar to that of Nets 023a and 023b. The color is medium to dark brown. The knot used is half hitch #2, and its yarn is two-ply Z-S. Its thickness is 0.8 to 0.9 mm, and its degree of spin is 40 degrees.

Net 023f is a fragment that measures 37 x 25 cm. Its mesh openings measure 3.4 to 3.6 cm, and its color is dark

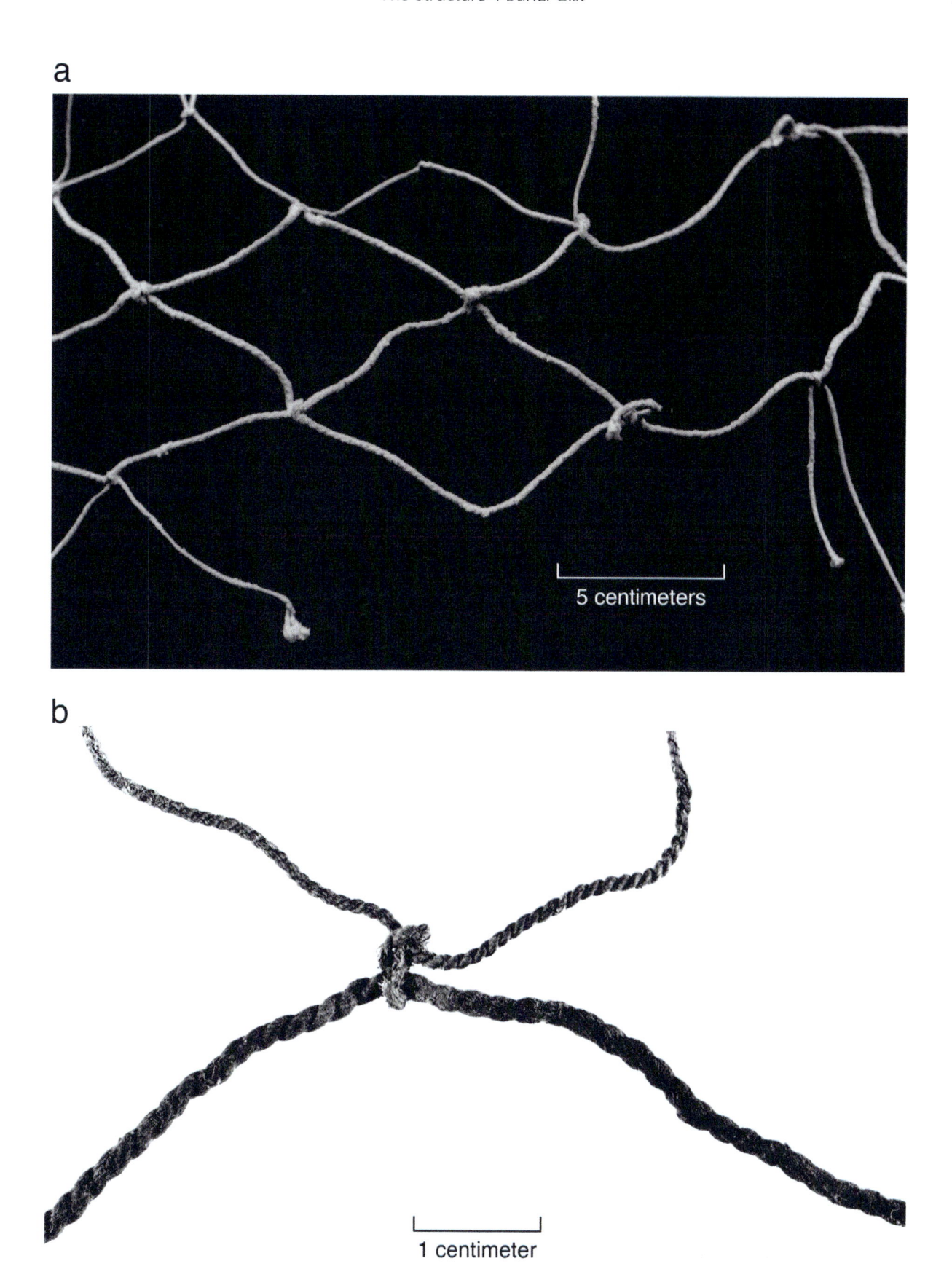

Figure 4.41. Net O17, a fragment of trammel net discarded by looters adjacent to Structure 4. (a) Photo of the net. (b) Close-up photo of a knot.

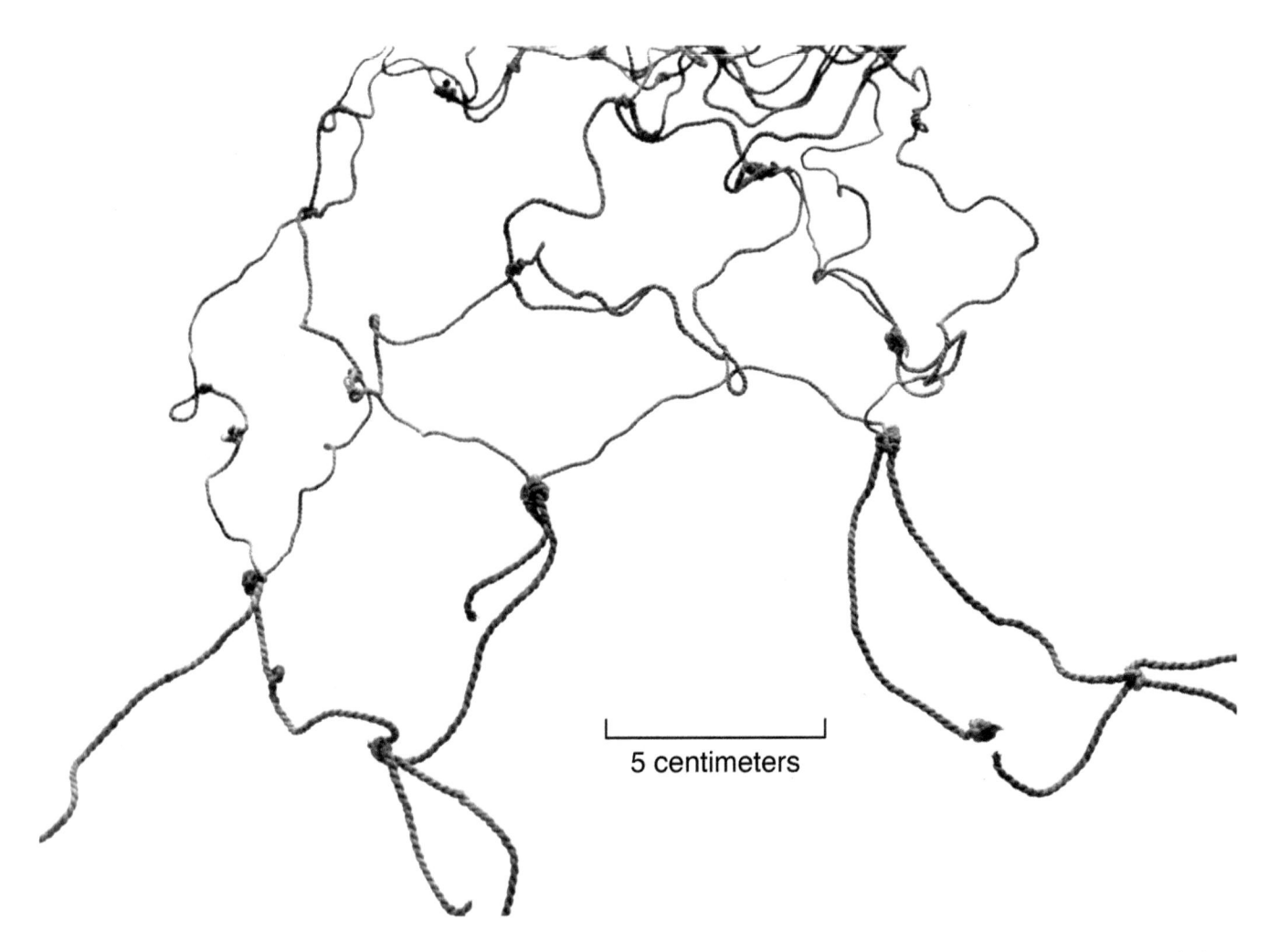

Figure 4.42. Net 022 from Structure 4. This net had fragmented into many pieces, the largest of which measured 35 cm x 10 cm. Made from three different yarns of varying thicknesses, it had endured many repairs.

brown. The knots are half hitch #2, and its yarns are two-ply Z-S. Its thickness is 0.7 to 1.0 mm, and its spin is 40 degrees.

Net 023g consists of several fragments from an entangled mass. Its mesh openings vary from 3.4 cm to 3.6 cm (cf. Nets 023 c, d, and f). Its color is dark brown. The knot used is a half hitch #2, and the yarn is two-ply Z-S. The thickness of the yarn is 0.8 to 0.9 mm, and the degree of spin is 45 degrees.

Net 023h has mesh openings that are at least 1.60 cm. The knot used is a square knot, and the yarns are two-ply Z-S. Its thickness is 1.6 to 1.7 mm, and the degree of spin is 35 degrees.

Net 024 consists of four large fragments, as well as multiple smaller fragments. The four large fragments measure 34 x 32 cm, 60 x 50 cm, 36 x 20 cm, and 36 x 15 cm. Their mesh openings are 2.3 cm; the colors vary from light to medium brown, with most fragments medium dark brown. The knot used was a half hitch #2, and the yarn was two-ply Z-S. Its thickness is 0.8 mm, and its spin is 45 degrees.

Net 025 is a fragment that measures 97 x 120 cm. Its openings measure 2.9 cm and its colors are light and dark brown. The net uses overhand knot #1, and the yarn thickness is 0.8 mm. The yarn is two-ply Z-S, and its degree of spin is 40 degrees.

Net 026 is a fragment about 12 x 12 cm. Its mesh openings are 3.2 cm, and its color is dark brown. The knot is overhand knot #1, and the yarn thickness is 0.9 mm. The yarn is two-ply Z-S, and the degree of spin is 40 degrees.

Net 027a is a fragment measuring 88 x 110 cm. The mesh openings are 2.7 cm, and the color is light to medium brown. The knot used is half hitch #2, and the yarn thickness is 0.9 mm. It is two-ply Z-S, and its degree of spin is 40 degrees.

Net 027b is a fragment measuring 55 x 53 cm. Its mesh openings are 2.4 cm, and its color is light to medium brown.

A half hitch #2 knot is used, and the yarn thickness is 1.0 mm. The yarn is two-ply Z-S, and the spin is 40 degrees. This net has a lacing repair that was poorly done; the repair yarn is the same seen on Net 027c.

Net 027c is a fragment measuring 70 x 40 cm. The mesh opening measures 2.5 cm, and the color is light to medium brown. The knot used is the half hitch #1, and the yarn thickness is 0.9 mm. The yarn is two-ply Z-S, and the spin is 40 degrees. It has been repaired with the same yarn seen on Net 027b.

Net 027d consists of various pieces with mesh openings varying from 2.3 cm to 2.6 cm. The color is light brown, in some cases lighter than Nets 027 a, b, and c. Half hitch #1 and half hitch #2 knots were used. The yarn has a thickness of 0.9 mm and is two-ply Z-S. The spin is 40 degrees.

Net 028 is a fragment measuring 25 x 15 cm. Its mesh openings are 2.6 cm, and its color is light to medium brown. The knot used is a half hitch #2, and the yarn has a thickness of 0.9 mm. The yarn is two-ply Z-S, and its spin is 45 degrees.

Net 029 consists of multiple fragments. The mesh openings vary from 2.4 cm to 2.7 cm, and the color is dark brown. The knot used is a half hitch #2, and the yarn is 0.6 to 0.9 mm thick. The yarn is two-ply Z-S, and the degree of spin is 35 degrees.

Net 030a, believed to be associated with Net 031a, measures 40 x 15 cm. Although this fragment is badly disintegrated, it shows evidence of a repair using a segment of a thinner yarn (1.0 mm thick). The mesh of Net 030a had openings of 1.9 cm. Yarn A (the original) is S10 Z2S, 1.8 mm thick, and has a 30 degree spin. Yarn B (the repair yarn) is S3 Z3S, employs a square knot, is 1.0 mm thick and has a 40 degree spin. (Yarn A of Net 030a matches the construction of Yarn A in Net 017.)

Net 030b features various lengths of yarns wrapped together; one is 66 cm in length and without knots. The yarn is 2.0 mm thick, with a spin of 30 degrees. One bit of yarn (Z3S) has slivers of an unidentified fiber.

Net 031a consists of many fragments forming a large mass. The largest fragment is 90 x 50 cm, with mesh openings of 2.5 to 2.8 cm; its color is light to dark brown. The knot is a half hitch #2, and the yarn thickness is 0.7 mm. It is two-ply Z-S, with a 40 degree spin.

Net 031b appears identical to Net 030b. The mesh opening is 1.60 cm, and the color is medium to dark brown. This net includes both square knots and cow hitches. Yarn A, the original (S8 Z2s), is 1.7 mm thick with a spin of 35 degrees. Yarn B—a thin yarn used for repair—appears to be the same as Yarn B in Net 030b. Some heavy cordage, perhaps a retrieval cord, is wrapped in Net 031b.

Net 031c consists of four fragments, the longest being 85 cm. Two of the fragments are tied together with an overhand knot; these two fragments, in turn, have been tied to another pair. This item includes some lengths of cord identical to those in Net 030b.

Net 032 is a fragment measuring 140 x 120 cm. The mesh opening is 2.6 cm and the color is medium brown. The knots are half hitch #2, and the yarn thickness is 0.7 mm. The yarn is two-ply Z-S, and its spin is 45 degrees.

Net 033 measures 10 x 6 cm. It has mesh openings of 2.5 cm, and its color is medium to dark brown. The knot used is a half hitch #2. The yarn is 0.8 mm thick, two-ply Z-S, with a 35 degree spin.

Net 034 is one fragment of a large trammel net (Figure 4.43). By joining some of the fragments of this net, I was able to conclude that it once measured at least 8.5 m wide and 60 cm high. (For comparison, a standard volleyball net is 9.7 m wide and 99 cm high.) The knots on Net 034 were either square knots or cow hitch #2 knots (Emery 1966: Fig. 20). All the knots were originally classic square knots; later, at least half of the square knots ended up as cow hitches (sometimes intermediate between a square knot and a cow hitch). The mesh openings vary from 1.7 to 1.9 cm.

Many fragments of Net 034 have a distinctive yarn that is now creped; it seems likely that these fragments were the product of the same net maker. Other fragments had newer yarns that were not creped; thus, the creping seems to be characteristic of the older, worn sections of the net.

Most fragments are long narrow strips, the longest being 3.7 m x 60 cm. Net 034 was unusual in that no dirt or salt crystals were evident. All its yarns were two-ply Z-S, and most were made with slivers of a vegetal fiber other than cotton.

Botanist C. Earle Smith, Jr. was the first to note that this cotton net included unidentifiable fibers from a dicotyledonous plant, to which he applied the generic term "bast." Although he could not determine the specific plant fibers used, we know that elsewhere on the Peruvian coast the stem fibers from milkweed were used to create twine and nets. For example, Engel (1960, 1970) found that milkweed was used at Paracas sites and at Asia.

Net 035a. This fragment measured 50 x 30 cm. Mesh openings vary from 2.2 to 2.6 cm, and the color is light to medium brown. The knot used is a half hitch #2, and the yarn is a two-ply Z-S. The yarn thickness varies from 0.8 to 1.1 mm in different areas, and the degree of spin is 40 degrees. This net shows evidence of patching and repair and combines old and new yarn.

Net 037 is a dark brown net fragment identified by C. Earle Smith, Jr. as cotton. This fragment (Figure 4.44) was found in the gray ash just below Structure 4. It is small (6 x 5 cm) and its mesh openings are 1.1 cm; the knot used is a half hitch #2. The yarn thickness is 2.2 mm, and the spin is 45 degrees.

Net 038a measures 80 x 90 cm. Its mesh openings are 2.5 cm, and its color is medium brown. The knots are mostly half hitch #2, although half hitch #1 occurs in one repair yarn found in two different areas of the net. The yarn is a two-ply S-Z, which is unusual for Structure 4. The yarn is 1.0 mm thick and has a 45 degree spin.

Net 038b measures 70 x 60 cm. Its mesh openings are 2.2 cm, and the yarn has a medium brown color. The knots are half hitch #2, and the yarn is a two-ply Z-S. The spin is 45 degrees, and the yarn thickness is 1.0 mm.

Net 038c, which measures 190 cm x 23 cm, has two parallel straight edges. The mesh openings are large, varying from 3.7 to 4.1 cm, and the color is medium brown. The knots are half hitch #1, and the yarn is 0.9 mm thick. The latter is two-ply Z-S, and its spin is 40 degrees.

Net 038d is a fragment measuring 45 x 38 cm. The mesh openings are 2.5 cm, and the color is medium brown. The knots are half hitch #2, and the yarn is 1.0 mm thick. The yarn is two-ply Z-S, with a spin of 40 degrees.

Net 038e measures 52 x 34 cm. It is medium brown in color, with mesh openings of 2.2 cm; it uses half hitch #2 knots. The yarn is 1.0 mm thick and two-ply Z-S, with a 45 degree spin.

Net 038f includes three fragments, each 30 x 20 cm. The mesh openings are 2.3 cm, and the knots are half hitch #2. The net is medium brown in color, with yarn 0.9 mm thick. It is two-ply Z-S, with a spin of 40 degrees.

Net 038g measures 45 x 10 cm; its mesh openings are 2.4 cm. It is medium brown in color, with a half hitch #2 knot; the yarn is 0.9 mm thick. It is a two-ply Z-S, with a 40 degree spin.

Net 038h is a fragment measuring 110 cm x 35 cm. The openings in the mesh are 2.6 cm, and the knots are half hitch #2. The net is medium brown in color, and the yarn is 1.0 mm thick. The yarn is two-ply Z-S, with a 45 degree spin.

Net 038i measures 90 x 40 cm and its mesh openings measure 2.7 cm. It is medium brown in color, and has knots that are half hitch #2. The yarn is two-ply Z-S and 1.1 mm thick, with a 35 degree spin.

Net 038j measures 90 x 70 cm and has one straight edge. The mesh openings are 2.7 cm, and the color is medium brown. The knots are half hitch #2, and the yarn is 1.0 mm thick. It is two-ply Z-S, with a spin of 40 degrees.

Net 038k is a fragment measuring approximately 80 x 50 cm and very irregular in shape. It is medium brown in color, and its mesh openings measure 2.4 cm. The knots are half hitch #2, and the yarn is 0.9 mm thick. It is two-ply Z-S, with a spin of 40 degrees.

Net 038l consists of more than 20 very irregular fragments.

Comment: Nets 038a–038l were probably from two nets featuring small mesh. In contrast, the fragments from Net 038m (see below) seem to be from two nets with large mesh openings.

Net 038m (Figure 4.45) is a fragment of curtain net (210 m x 45 cm), the kind of net usually held between individuals in the bay. The large mesh openings are 1.80 cm. Square knots had been used to create the net, while half hitch knots were used to attach the loops that held weights. The half hitch #1 knot occurs several times on one of the net's repair yarns. The main yarns are two-ply Z-S and 1.6 mm thick, with a spin of 35 degrees. The small loops for weights are all of thinner yarn (1.0 mm). The lower edge of this net has unbroken yarn, indicating that that edge is an original one. Some of the small weight loops appear original, while others seem to have been added on later as replacements. Because the loops were empty when Net 038m was found, we do not know whether stones or potsherds were used as weights.

Net 038n measures 80 x 60 cm. The mesh openings are 1.90 cm, and the color is medium brown. The yarn is 1.5 mm thick and two-ply Z-S, with a spin of 35 degrees. The knots include the square knot and cow hitch; in addition, the half hitch #2 knot was often used on Net 038n for tying straight edge courses to one another and fastening the small loops that held weights.

Net 038o is approximately 130 cm in length and 50 cm wide. It is medium brown in color, and the mesh openings are 1.90 cm. Square knots are common, but half hitch #2 knots were used on the outer loop of one edge. The yarn is usually 1.7 mm thick, but on the edges a thinner yarn (0.9 mm) was used. The thicker yarn is two-ply Z-S with a 40 degree spin; the thinner yarn has a 45 degree spin.

Net 038p measures 90 x 70 cm. The net is medium brown in color and the mesh openings are 2.0 cm. Most knots are square knots, with half hitch #2 reserved for the straight edges. The yarn is 1.9 mm thick (except at the edges, where it is 1.1 mm); it has a 45 degree spin.

Net 038q measures roughly 1.0 m x 35 cm. The mesh openings are 1.90 cm and the color is medium brown. Most knots are square knots, with some half hitch #2 knots on straight edges. One end of the net has been patched. The two-ply Z-S yarn is usually 2.1 mm thick, but in the patched area it is 1.0 mm. The thicker yarn has a spin of 40 degrees, while the thinner yarn has a spin of 45 degrees.

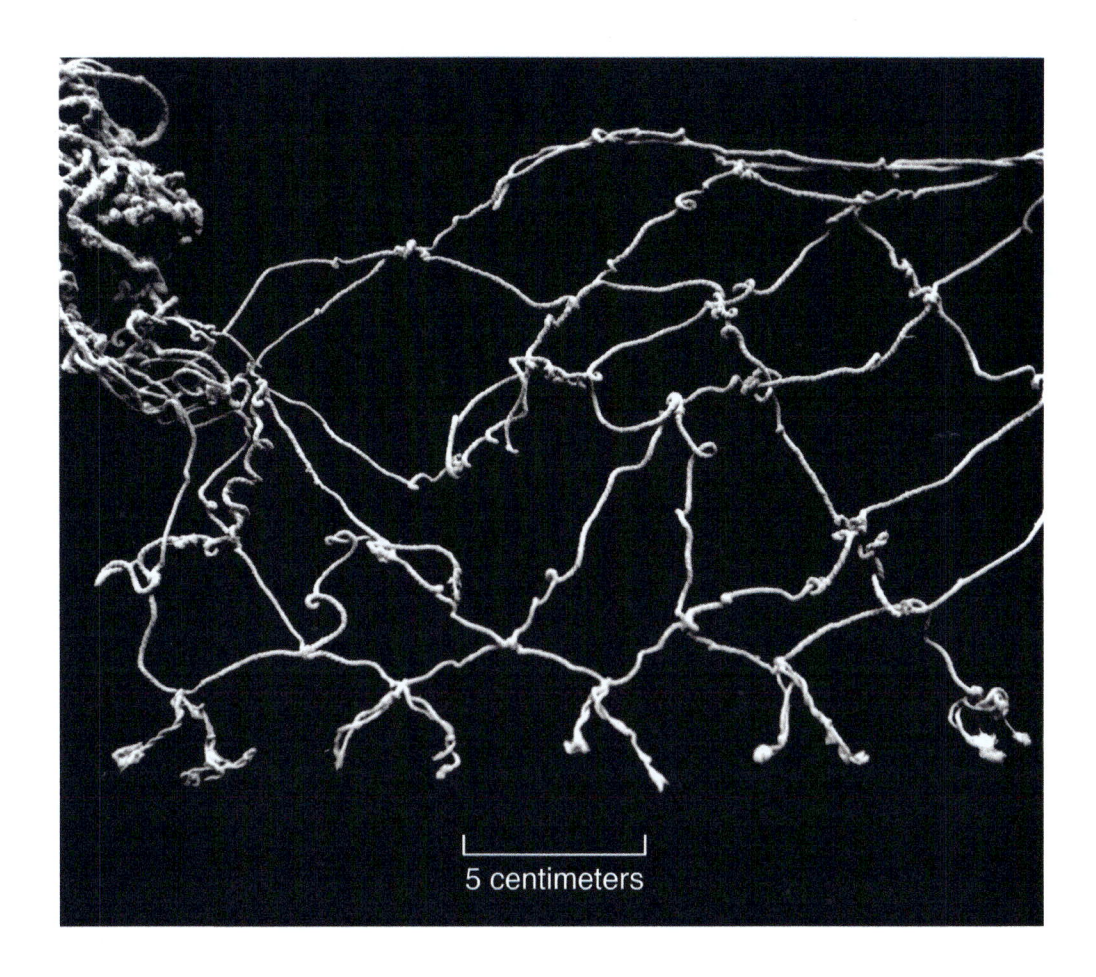

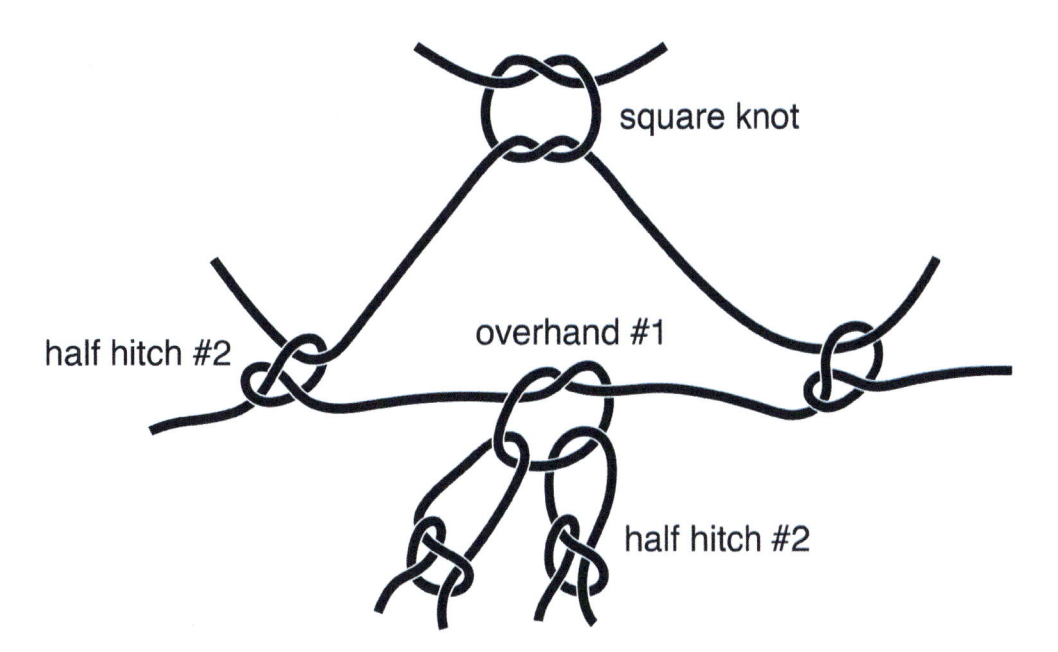

Figure 4.43. Net O34 from Structure 4 was a fragment of a trammel net. Almost all of its knots were square knots. The photo (above) shows five pairs of dangling cords that were likely intended to hold weights. The drawing (below) shows the knots that created each pair of dangling cords.

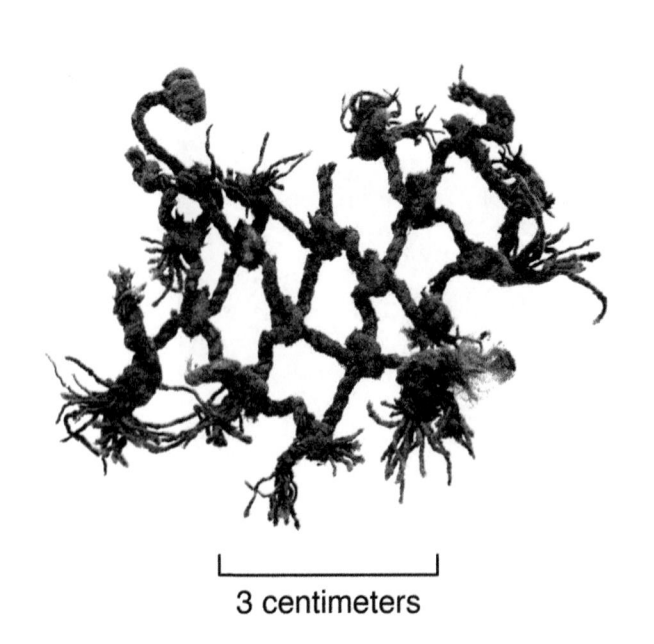

Figure 4.44. Net 037, found just below Structure 4 and likely associated, is a fragment of cotton net with small mesh openings; it was created using a series of half hitch #2 knots.

Net 038r is roughly 1.5 m long x 65 cm (the latter is the original width). It is medium brown in color, and its mesh openings are 1.9 cm. Square and cow hitch knots are present, but half hitch #2 was used at the edges. In two places, the bunched mesh is held together by a simple overhand knot. The main yarn is 1.3 mm thick and two-ply Z-S, with a spin of 40 degrees. In places, 0.9 mm yarn was used for patching.

Net 038s measures ca. 80 x 30 cm. The color is medium to dark brown, and the mesh openings are 1.9 cm. Most knots are square knots, with some half hitch #2 knots at the edges. The main yarn is 1.3 mm thick, while the patching yarn is 0.9 mm thick. The yarn is two-ply Z-S, with a spin of 40 degrees.

Net 038t is a handful of net fragments that vary in color from light to dark brown; the mesh openings are 1.9 cm. Cow hitch and square knots can be seen. The yarns vary from as thin as 1.0 mm to as thick as 2.1 mm. These yarns are two-ply Z-S, with a spin of 40 degrees.

Net 038u is a net fragment with large mesh openings and very worn cords where the net weights were attached.

Net 039a was made of medium gray to buff cotton. The mesh openings are 2.4 cm and the usual knot is half hitch #2. The yarn is two-ply Z-S, 0.9 mm thick, with a 35 degree spin.

Net 039b measures 10 x 5 cm. Like Net 039a, this fragment is also medium gray to buff in color. The mesh openings are 2.3 cm, and the knot is a half hitch #2. The yarn is 0.8 mm thick and two-ply Z-S, with a 40 degree spin.

Net 039c is 12 x 6 cm and dark brown in color; the mesh openings are 2.2 cm. The knots are half hitch #2, and the yarn is two-ply Z-S, 1.1 mm thick, with a 40 degree spin. This piece of cotton net was encrusted with salt and sand.

Net 040a, which measures 30 x 42 cm, has two parallel straight edges. The mesh openings are 2.3 cm, and the color is medium brown. The knot is a half hitch #2, and the cotton yarn is two-ply Z-S, 1.1 mm thick, with a 40 degree spin.

Net 040b is a fragment 35 x 20 cm. The mesh openings are 2.4 cm, and the cotton is dark brown in color. The knot is half hitch #2, and the yarn is a two-ply Z-S, 1.0 mm thick, with a 45 degree spin.

"**Net 040c**" is actually a 24 cm piece of cordage that became intertwined with Net 040b. It was constructed by combining dark brown cotton with slivers of an unidentified fiber. The yarn is two-ply Z-S, 2.4 mm thick, and has a 40 degree spin.

The Structure 4 Nets in Wider Perspective

Cotton nets and textiles have a long history on Peru's south coast (Engel 1957, 1970). At Village 514, a site on the Bay of Paracas, Frédéric Engel (1981:37–38) found cotton nets and fabrics dating to 3940 B.C. Similar fabrics and fibers were found with individuals in a Paracas cemetery associated with the residential site of Cabeza Larga (Engel 1960: Plate 4.3).

Cotton fishing nets appeared by 3750 B.C. at sites near Chilca (Engel 1970:58), as well as Paloma (Quilter 1989:41) and the Tank Site near Ancón (Stephens and Moseley 1973). At Huaca Prieta on Peru's north coast, Junius Bird recovered more than 370 nets. Bird was an experienced sailor with a deep knowledge of knots. His analysis of Huaca Prieta's nets drew on both his knowledge of sailing and the work of Ashley (1944).

At Huaca Prieta, Bird found nets of two types: small mesh and large mesh (Bird and Hyslop 1985:207; see also Petersen et al. 1984). At Asia, Engel (1963) also described two types of netting, but these were of milkweed rather than cotton.

The more recent excavations at Huaca Prieta by Dillehay (2017), as well as analyses by Splitstoser (2017),

The Structure 4 Burial Cist 85

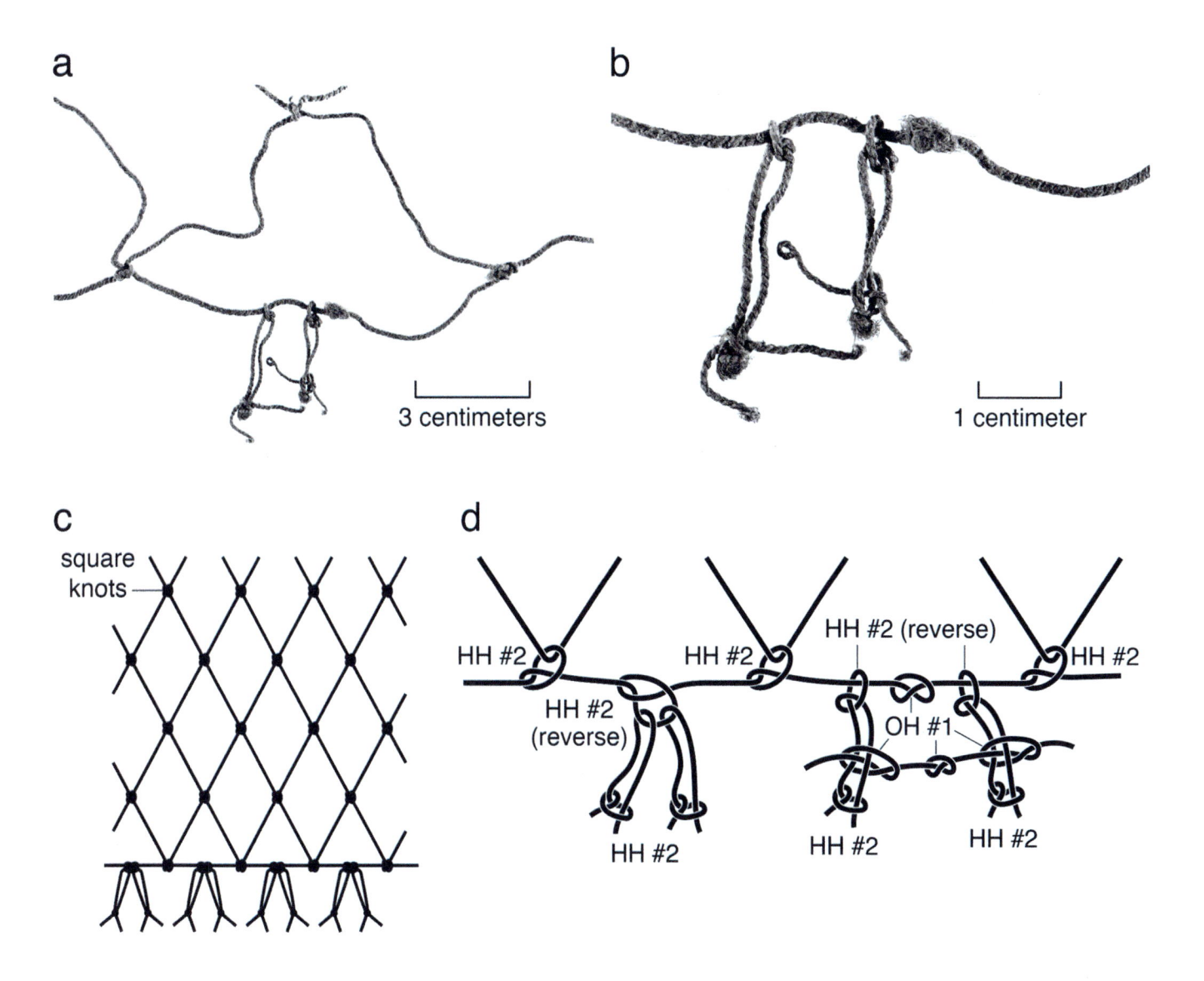

Figure 4.45. Four views of Net O38m from Structure 4, a fragment of trammel net. (a) Photo of one section. (b) Close-up photo of one pair of dangling cords. (c) A simplified drawing of another section of the same net. (d) A drawing of the dangling cords probably used to hold weights.

confirm Bird's classification of his nets into two types. The Type 1 nets at Huaca Prieta had "simple half-hitch knots, thick Z(2s) cotton yarn elements with an average diameter of 1.2 mm ranging from 1.1 mm to 1.4 mm," an average twist of 54 degrees, and a small mesh opening ranging from 0.5 to 0.8 cm. The Type 2 nets have larger mesh openings that range from 1.3 to 5.7 cm (Splitstoser 2017:482). (Z(2s) is how Splitstoser characterizes the net in the "parenthetical notation" he developed [see Splitstoser 2012]; his Z(2S) notation corresponds to S2Z in Dwight Wallace's system.)

Like many earlier central and south coast fishermen, those at Cerro Azul in the Late Intermediate era continued to use cotton to make their nets. The Cerro Azul fishermen, however, made nets with mesh openings of three sizes, and made occasional use of an unidentified plant fiber that might have been milkweed. Ethnobotanist C. Earle Smith, Jr. could not identify these fibers, referring to them simply as "bast." At Cerro Azul such bast was more commonly used in cords, ropes, and slings than in fishing nets. Cahlander (1980) reports that many Andean men still make their slings, ropes, and cords from a range of bast fibers.

Most of the net fragments from Structure 4 at Cerro Azul featured overhand knots of the half hitch #2 variety (see Figure 4.40). We cannot be sure whether this results from an overall preference, or the fact that many fragments in Structure 4 came from the same net.

Late Horizon fishing nets from the site of Lo Demás in the Chincha Valley provide a contrast with our Late Intermediate Cerro Azul nets; most were made of fibers other than cotton. Sandweiss (1992) reports that only four of the Lo Demás nets were made of cotton; they were Z-spun and S-plied and their mesh openings were the size designed to catch pejerrey and óetas.

Leather Pouch (Miscellaneous Specimen 20)

A leather pouch 10.5 cm long and 8.0 cm wide was found inside Structure 4 (Figure 4.46). It may have been made from deer or camelid hide.

Slings (*warak´a*)

At least six slings (or fragments thereof) were found in or near Structure 4. This was an artifact sometimes used to hunt sea lions, seabirds, and other coastal game, and it is tempting to think of slings as part of the local hunting

Figure 4.46. A damaged leather pouch, found inside Structure 4.

equipment. Sea lions were valued not only for their large amount of meat but also for their skin, which could be used to create waterproof rafts inflated with air (Acosta 1954[1590]: Book 3, Chapter 15; Acosta 2002[1590]). Slings are sometimes found wrapped around a deceased's head, perhaps placed there because the person preparing the deceased for burial needed a convenient cord or because it was an item the deceased had used in life (e.g., Aponte Miranda 2006; Bird and Bellinger 1954; Cahlander 1980; Engel 1963; Kroeber and Wallace 1954; Millaire and Surette 2011; Squier 1967[1869]:214).

Andean slings tend to have two contrasting types of cradles, which is the term for the central pouch that holds the projectile to be hurled. These two types are the slit cradle and the webbed cradle; both types were present at Cerro Azul, and it is possible that most hunters possessed one of each.

One sling found next to Structure 4 was complete (Figure 4.47). This sling measures 1.92 m from the finger loop at one end to the beginning of the tassel at the opposite end. The cradle is of the slit type. Color was added by the decorative yarn that appears to one side of the cradle. The decorative wool section differs from one sling to another and may reveal the personal color preferences of the sling's owner.

Figure 4.48a shows a close-up of a webbed cradle from a sling. For a similar webbed cradle, see Cahlander (1980: Plate 1, fifth item from the top).

Figure 4.48b shows a well-made finger loop and one end of a sling that includes edge embroidery (30 cm long).

Figure 4.49 (top) shows a sling whose interior has grass fibers that were tightly wrapped with cotton yarn. To either side of the slit cradle are two remaining strands; wool has been used to decorate one side of the cradle.

Figure 4.49 (bottom) shows a sling with a grass fiber interior that was tightly wrapped with cotton yarn. To one side of the cradle, a design of nested diamonds has been added. The outermost diamond features red yarn, and as we move toward the interior we see white wool, then purple wool, and finally white wool at the center of the innermost diamond.

Figure 4.50 (bottom) shows a band of plain weave with extra-warp patterning. "Plain weave" is a two-element weaving technique in which one element regularly crosses over and then under the other element (see Emery 1966:76). This flat band, of which some 11.5 cm are preserved, is structurally a plain weave but woven with warp ends that are free and active. Both the warp and weft are made of cotton, S-Z, 1.1 mm thick, and white in color. The decorative yarn on the band, however, is wool, Z-S, and 0.8 mm thick; this wool is red and black in color. Only 7 cm of the six parallel foundation elements (at lower left) are preserved; they are wrapped with white, yellow, and brown yarns in a repetitive sequence.

Figure 4.50 (top) shows what may be a fragment of a sling. Three exposed foundation elements can be seen at the lower right, each 1.2 mm thick and consisting of slightly S-twisted bundles that together form a loosely Z-twisted element. This foundation element was tightly wrapped with one-ply S-spun cotton yarn, which in turn was wrapped with Z-S wool. The design on the central strap uses black yarn to create the outer border; inside, red chevrons alternate with off-white chevrons, resulting in a band of nested chevrons. A 4.9 cm section of eight-strand square braid is attached to the above; this attachment was constructed from bast fibers.

Combs

Complete and well-preserved combs were not common at Cerro Azul (Figure 4.51). A comb, however, was evidently the personal possession of someone buried in Structure 4 (Figure 4.51a; Specimen 27); we found it in the looters' backdirt next to the Structure 4 burial cist.

The comb measures 7 cm in length, 4.8 cm in width, and 0.5 cm thick; the teeth run virtually the full 7 cm length of the comb, which was dirty when found and off-white in color. The design on the comb appears to be a geometric design reminiscent of those on some textiles.

In 1925, Kroeber found a comb in a cache on the slopes of Quebrada 1 at Cerro Azul (Kroeber 1937:250, Fig. LXXXVI, 4). Kroeber's comb (Figure 4.51b) was somewhat wider than the one we believe to be associated with Structure 4; his was 6.2 cm high and 10 cm wide. Although Kroeber believed that several spines were missing, he reported that 26 were still in place, a number similar to the 24–25 spines in the Structure 4 comb. The design on Kroeber's comb is also geometric and similar to some textile designs. Kroeber (1937:250) describes his comb as "splints twilled with brown cotton thread; ends, a black, hard gum or pitch. Spines, aver. projection, 20 mm; 26 remain, 13-14 lost."

Cords, Braids, and Bands Associated with Structure 4

As is typical of many looted burial cists from the Late Intermediate, there were numerous fragments of cloth and textiles, as well as rope, cords, and string in the backdirt.

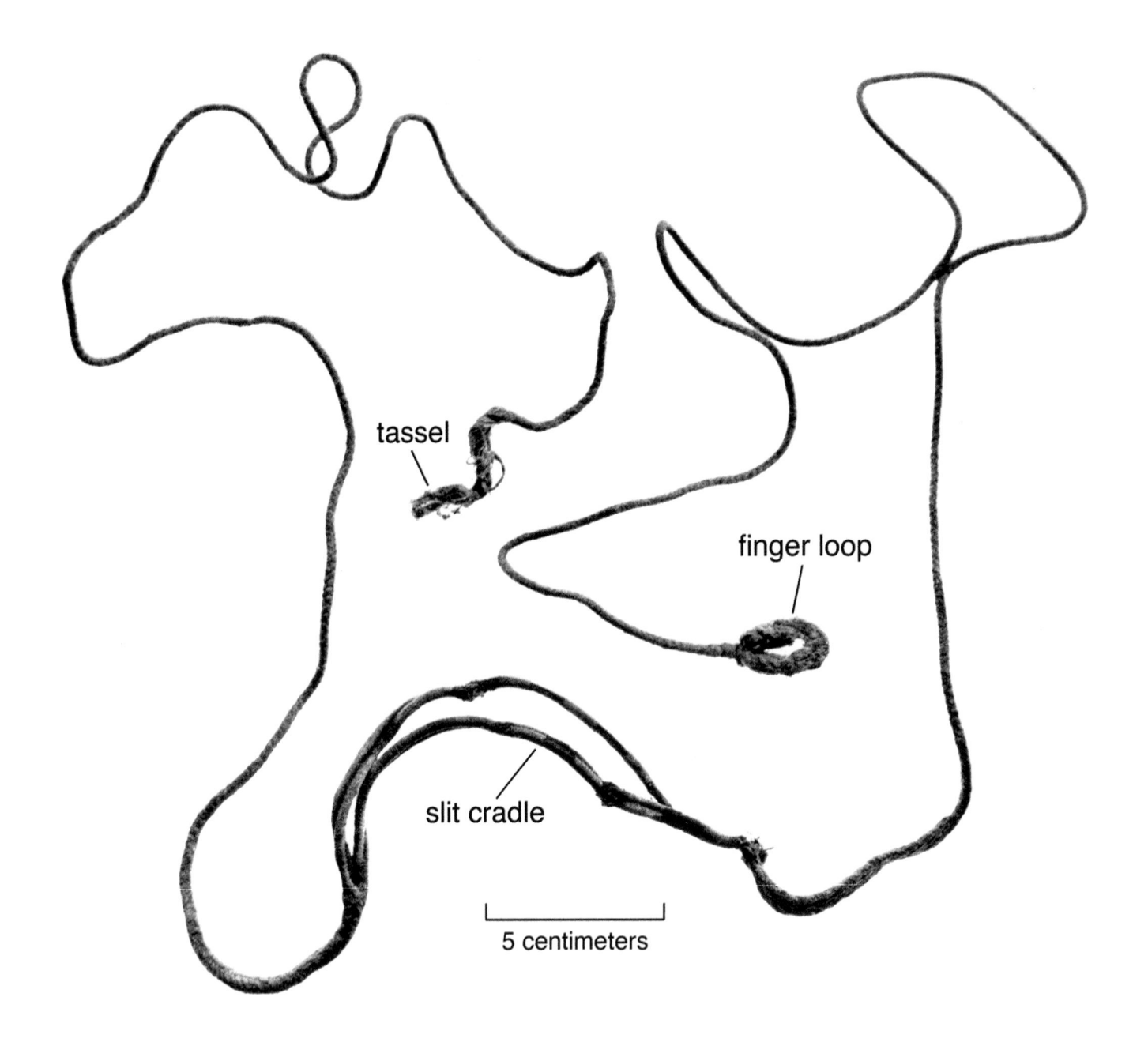

Figure 4.47. A slit-cradle sling, found next to Structure 4.

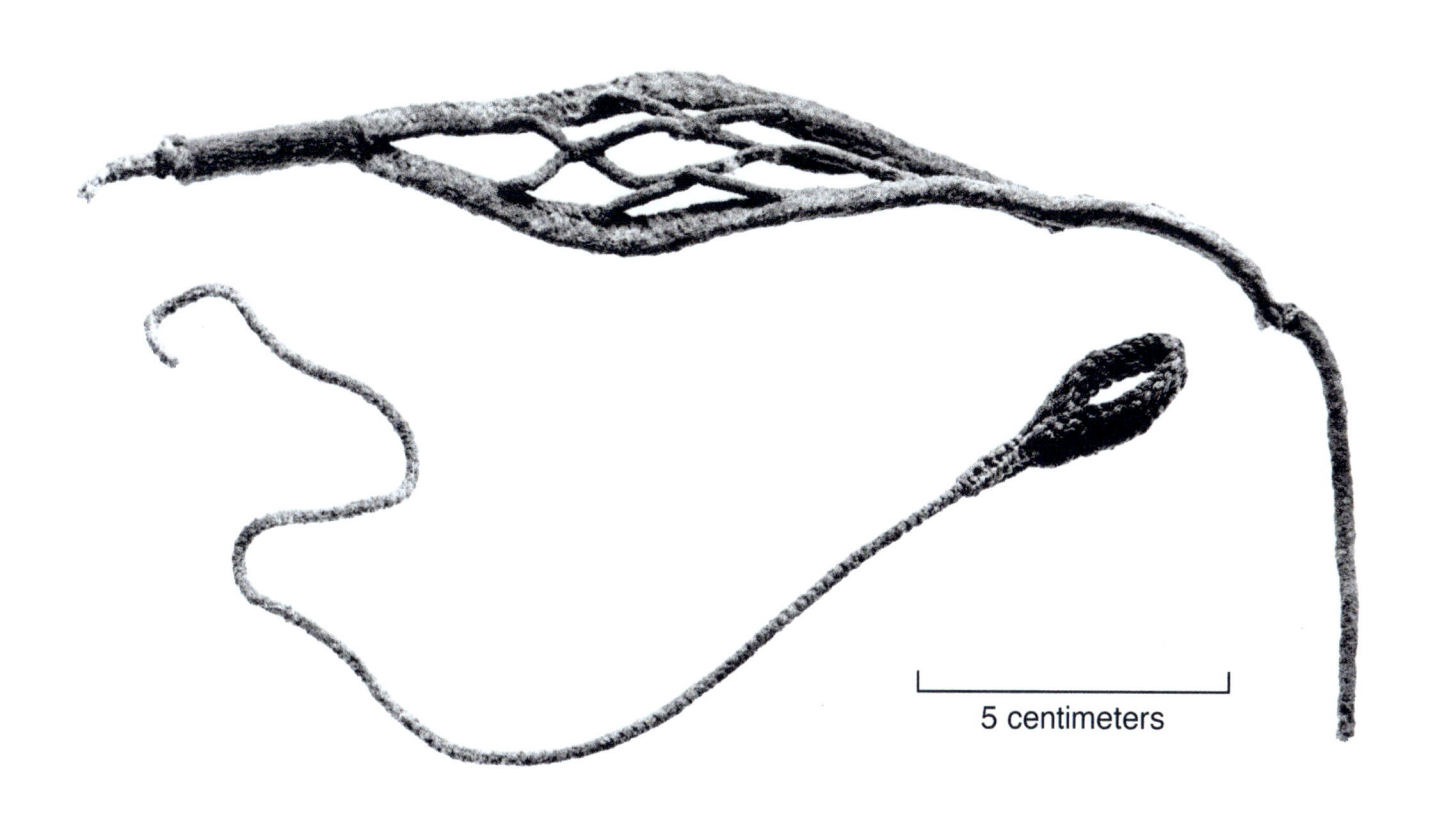

Figure 4.48. Specimens 10 and 11, two sling fragments from Structure 4. (Above) Close-up of Specimen 11, a webbed cradle. (Bottom) Close-up of Specimen 10, a well-made finger loop.

T 209b was a specimen of cordage made from two stems, each twisted S then plied Z; both were 8 mm thick.

T 240a consisted of four strands of cotton, all S18Z. Three strands were 0.98 m long and one measured 1.13 m.

T 240b was a braided cord, 55 cm long.

T 240c was a grass cord, 80 cm long and Z2S.

T 240d was a braided cord, 1.10 m long.

T 240e was a decorative cord 61 cm long, an example of multicolored spiral cross-knit looping (see descriptions by Emery 1966, 1980).

T 240f was a diagonal plaited twill basketry band (7.5 cm wide, 45 cm long) with a 23 cm long braided cotton cord attached.

T 240g was a very thick cord (Z-S) accompanied by *algodón pardo* (a supply of unspun brown cotton).

T 244 consisted of two woolen cords from looters' debris. One cord measured 35 cm in length and the other 21 cm. Both were Z-S and solid red in color.

T 249a was a circular braided cord made of wool, 7 cm long. It was Z-spun and S-plied, 8 mm in diameter, with a chevron pattern. The colors were too faded to identify.

T 251a was a segment of a cord; it is a four-strand round braid, possibly made from a bromeliad (Figure 4.52a).

T 252d is a cord whose unknotted full length is 1.96 m (Figure 4.52b).

T 251b consisted of a narrow woven band, 1.21 m long. The width of the central section measures 5 mm, while the ends taper down to a width of 3 mm. The central section has a simple design of warp stripes at the band's edge and center, with the rest being red. Dwight Wallace adds that the narrower sections have a red border, then a series of short and long floats, resulting in a dot-and-dash design that alternates between white and yellow along the length of the band. The design is identical on the reverse side of the band, except that white substitutes for yellow; these yellow and white figures are outlined in black. The technique used

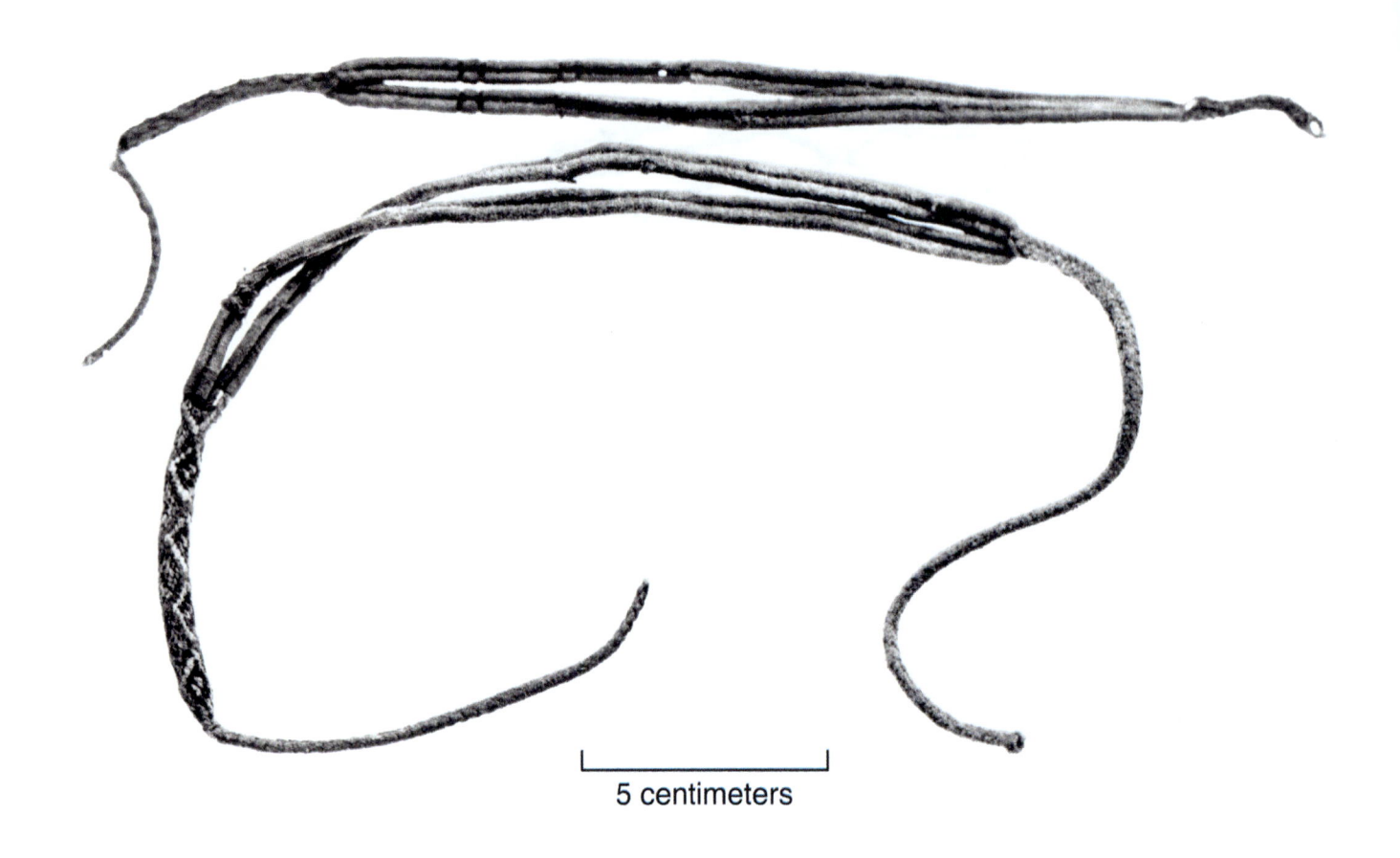

Figure 4.49. Two slit-cradle sling fragments from Structure 4. The lower specimen has a design featuring nested diamonds in colorful woolen yarns.

is a combination of simple warp floating of the white and yellow, plus the use of a complementary warp technique in which yellow or white yarn occupies the same warp course, which is not visible on one face—either because it is floated on the reverse, or because it interlaces with the wefts while the yarn of the other color floats over it. The warp yarns are wool, Z-S, in red, yellow, white, and black; the weft yarns are S-Z bast fiber.

T 251c is a segment of a very narrow woven band, 1.02 m long and 4.5 mm wide. This band is knotted in a clove hitch, forming a loop 32 cm in circumference. Its woolen warps are Z-S, and the yarns are red, yellow, white, and black; the weft is probably the same as that in Textile 251b. The last 14 cm of this narrow band (T251c) are 3 mm wide and solid red, matching other narrow red tape from Structure 4.

The wider section of this tape has a single-face design of complementary warp in which yarn of the desired color is brought to the surface and interlaced, while the yarns not used just float on the reverse side. The design floats over 1, 2, or 3 wefts. To create single diagonal lines, the floats are over two adjacent warps. The design shows upside-down birds alternating with birds right side up; the color of the birds also alternates—red bird, yellow bird, red bird and so on (Figure 4.53).

T 252b is a wool cord measuring 84 cm in length and 4 mm in diameter, with four row cross-knit needle looping. The yarn is Z-S. Many colors are used; they change every 7 mm, with color changes staggered from row to row. The colors are red, white, black, yellow, dark red, dark green and purplish brown, and some of the color changes create chevrons.

T 252c is a cord that has an inner core of cotton yarn, which was in turn tightly wrapped with wool yarn. The cord is 15.5 cm long, and its central cotton section is wrapped with Z-S yellow wool yarn.

The Structure 4 Burial Cist 91

Figure 4.50. Possible sling fragments, found just outside Structure 4.

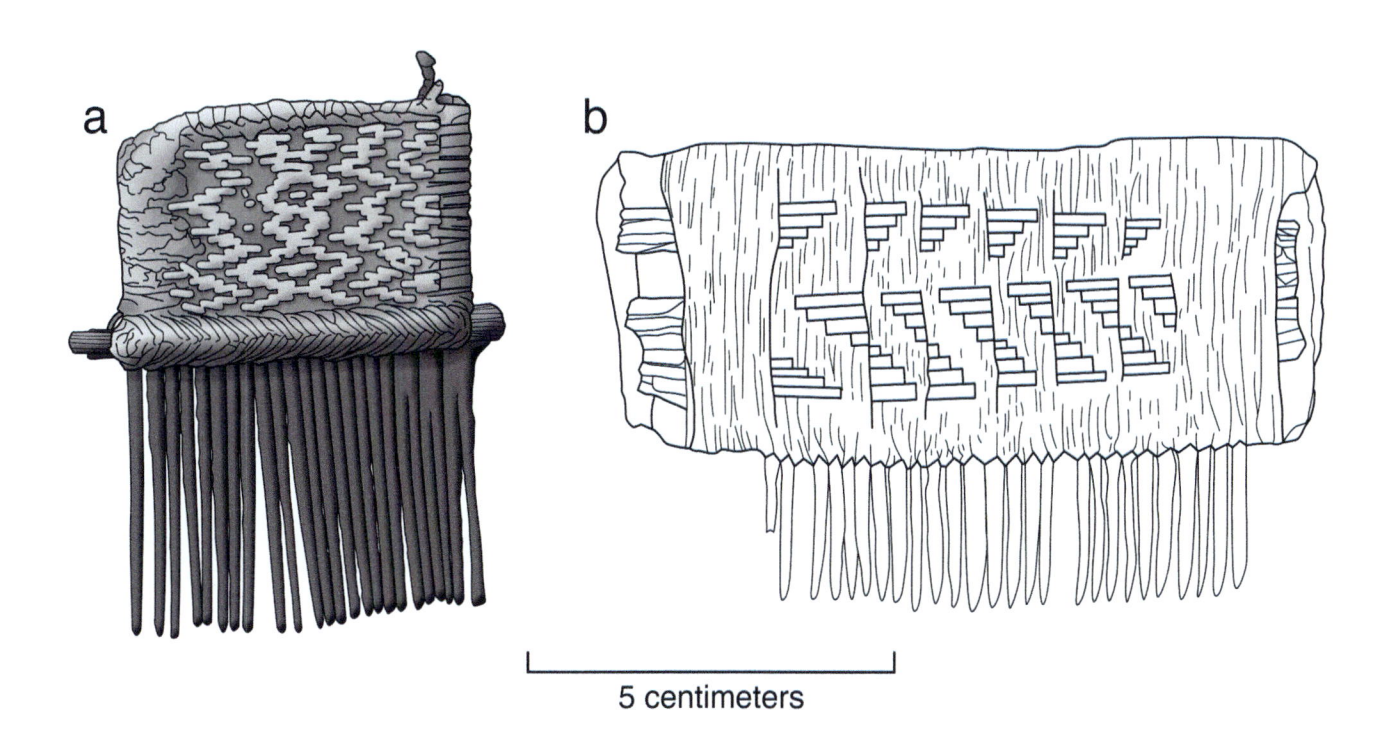

Figure 4.51. Two combs from Cerro Azul. (a) A comb found in looters' backdirt next to Structure 4. (b) A comb found by Kroeber in a cache on the slopes of Quebrada 1.

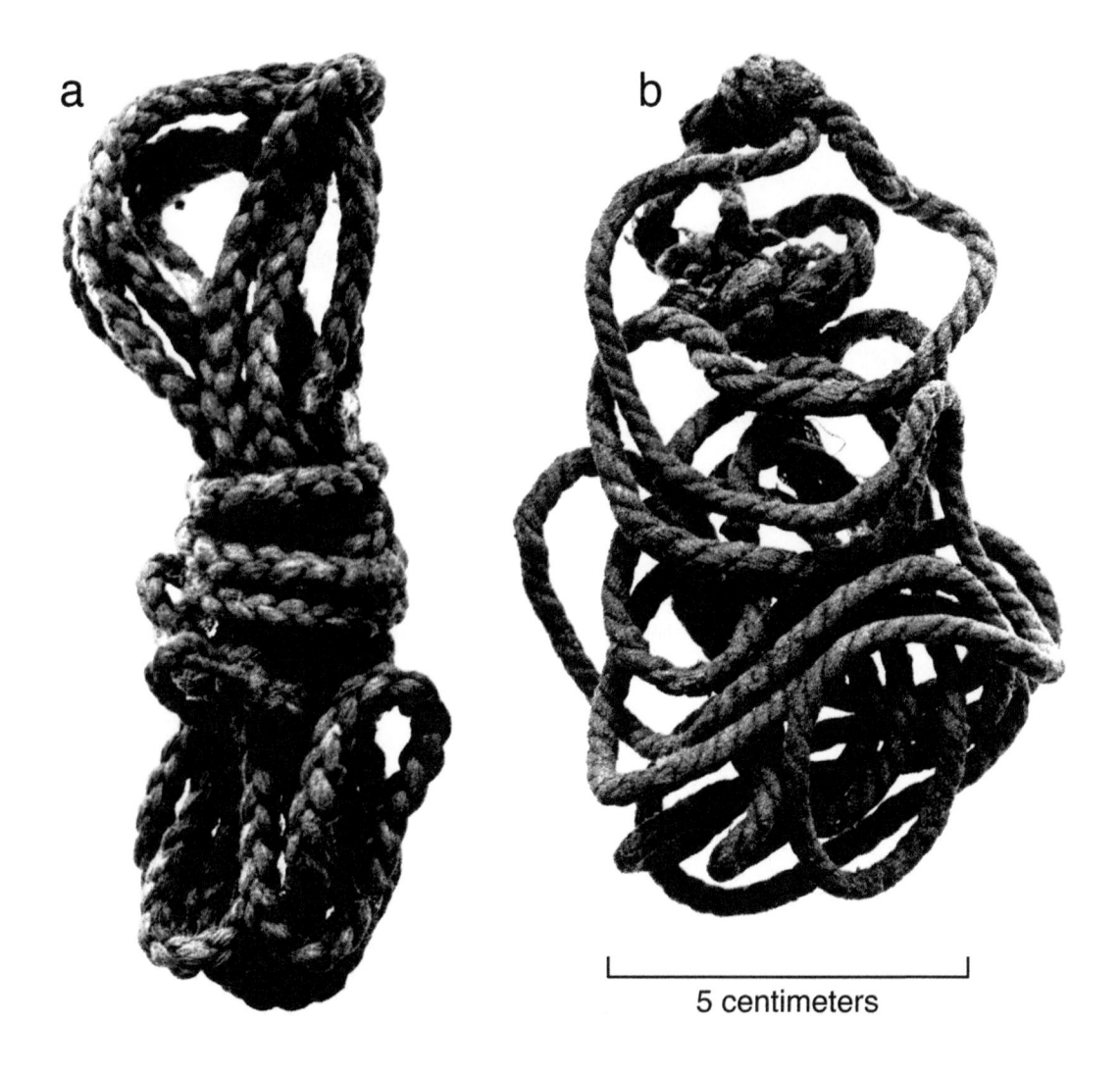

Figure 4.52. Two bundles of cordage found just outside Structure 4.

Figure 4.53. Artist's rendition of a design, consisting of alternating red and yellow birds, on a textile band found next to Structure 4.

Clothing and Other Textiles

The dominant fiber used to make the clothing and other textiles in Structure 4 was cotton, and it occurred in several natural colors—white, tan, light brown, and dark brown. Camelid wool was much less common than cotton, and may have been rationed by those who could acquire it from the highlands (A. Rowe 1984:25, Topic 1982:163). Often red, yellow, and brown wool yarns were used to add color and texture to fabrics made of white cotton.

Bast fibers were commonly used to make sandals, braided cords, thick ropes, and the innermost structural cores of slings. These are examples of "hand processes" in Emery's (1980) terminology. Such hand processes were also used at Cerro Azul to make fishing nets, crayfish traps, slings, bolas, mats, and workbaskets. *Soumak* or weft-wrapping—as well as spiral cross-knit looping, plaiting, and braiding—were also common techniques at Cerro Azul. Such "hand strategies" are often contrasted with "loom strategies" (e.g., Cahlander 1980). Cross-knit loop stitch is usually an edge-finishing stitch that resembles a braid (Emery 1966:243).

One of the common loom strategies at Cerro Azul was plain weave, which is the simplest way to interlace warp and weft elements into a fabric. In plain weave, each weft passes over and under successive warp units. The obverse and reverse of plain weave are structurally identical (Emery 1995:76). When the warp and weft are equally spaced and equal in size, count, and spacing, the plain weave is described as balanced. If the warp hides the weft completely, the cloth is said to be a warp-faced textile (Emery 1980:76). Such warp-faced fabrics were common in the graves of high-status women at Cerro Azul.

In addition to the frequently encountered plain weave was something called "warp-stripe plain weave." This weave may feature alternating stripes of brown and white, blue and white, or even more complex sequences of bands and stripes of different colors.

Textiles Associated with Structure 4

Textile 101, found next to Structure 4, measures 34 x 24 cm (Figure 4.54). It is a warp-stripe, warp-faced plain weave featuring brown stripes alternating with light tan stripes. The brown stripes are 12 mm wide with 20 paired warp yarns, while the light tan stripes are 15 mm wide and comprised of 24 paired warp yarns. The medium-brown cotton fiber of the warp is S-spun; the weft is a light tan cotton fiber that is S-spun. The sewing thread is tan cotton, S-Z, 0.5 mm thick; the warp and weft yarns were 0.25 mm thick. The one remaining side selvage is plain and highly compacted, with a thread density of 95–100. [Although the American spelling is selvage and the British spelling is selvedge, it is the same term.] The term selvage usually refers to the finished edge of a cloth, either at the warp ends or weft ends.

Textile 103, found next to Structure 4, measured 25.5 x 14.5 cm (Figure 4.55). Its edges are turned under on all four sides, with traces of a running stitch. This is a warp-stripe, warp-faced, all-cotton plain weave textile. The warp has stripes of three colors—(a) off-white yarn, 0.2 mm thick, Z-spun; (b) blue yarn, 0.3 mm thick, Z-spun; and (c) medium brown yarn, 0.5 mm thick, Z-S. The weft is Z-spun, off-white, and 0.2 mm thick. The sewing thread is tan cotton, Z3S, and 0.9 mm thick. The sequences of colors are as follows:

Sequence A: wide blue, narrow white, blue, white, wide blue ("wide" is 14–18 yarns; "narrow" is 6 blue yarns).

Sequence B: wide white, narrow brown, blue, brown, wide white.

Sequence C: ten alternating narrow stripes of brown and blue, with white replacing brown in two cases, with no overall pattern noted.

Sequence D: very wide stripe, 30 blue yarns, 24 x 2 white yarns.

The sequence in the textile is as follows: Sequence A, then two brown yarns; Sequence B, then two brown yarns; Sequence A, then two brown yarns; Sequence B, then two brown yarns; then Sequence C; Sequence D; Sequence C, then two brown yarns; and finally, Sequence D.

Textile 112 (85 x 37 cm) is a warp-stripe plain weave cotton textile with alternating stripes (Figure 4.56). Bands measuring 7.5 cm wide alternate with narrower stripes 3 cm wide. The long dimension of 85 cm is the actual loom length, and the main stripes are medium brown, blue, light brown, and salmon. The color sequence often used is buff, turquoise, medium dark brown, dark brown, purple, and pinkish brown. The brown is used to outline stripes of the colors in one set, while the blue is used to outline stripes of the colors in another set. There are 12–16 warps per centimeter and 12 wefts per centimeter.

Textile 121 (59 x 7 cm) is an example of slit tapestry (Figure 4.57). The warp is made of white cotton yarns (S-Z spun with 38 yarns per cm); the weft is comprised of dyed wool (Z-spun S-twisted with 8 yarns per cm). We see red, white, black, yellow-brown, and medium-dark brown yarns. The wool design is seen in the weft face, and consists of opposed bird heads in diagonal interlacing fret; fillers appear

Figure 4.54. A warp-faced plain weave textile, featuring brown stripes alternating with light tan stripes, found next to Structure 4.

The Structure 4 Burial Cist

Figure 4.55. A cloth with faded blue, brown, and off-white stripes, found next to Structure 4. All four of its edges are turned under.

Figure 4.56. A warp-stripe plain weave cotton textile with multicolored stripes, found next to Structure 4.

Figure 4.57. A slit tapestry associated with Structure 4. It features opposed bird heads in a diagonal interlacing fret.

in triangular open spaces. The color sequence for the bands with attached bird heads is medium brown, light brown, white, light brown, red, red, and dark red. The background area in between these bands has a different sequence—red, red, dark red, medium brown, light brown, white, and light brown. There are two side selvages. One has warps turned 90 degrees and woven on themselves to form a short horizontal band 2.5 mm deep; the other side selvage is covered with cross-knit stitch embroidery, using paired two-ply yarns. The bird motif on this slit tapestry appears on other textiles.

Textile 126 (61 x 91 cm) was possibly a shirt or tunic (Figure 4.58). It is a plain weave cotton textile with wool brocading in red, yellow, and brown. This wool is Z-spun and S-plied, with yarn 0.7 mm thick. This garment has six webs, each 61 x 15 cm, stitched together with 5 mm thick yarns in whipping stitches. These six webs have 12 side selvages and eight end selvages (the three-shot cotton heading cord is S6Z). The bands that display bird heads are double-faced, while geometric bands have long floats on the reverse side. The arrangement consists of A, a diagonal band of bird heads, and B, a diagonal geometric band of interlocking units of three triangles. The color sequence is A= yellow; B= yellow + white; A= white; B= white + red; A= red + yellow. Side and end edges (piping) have a simple looped buttonhole stitch of paired light blue cotton yarns (Z-spun and 0.4 mm thick); some are selvage-joining whipping stitches. This garment may well have been worn by someone buried in Structure 4.

Textile 128 is a band or strap measuring 3 x 51 cm, made with 15 warps to the centimeter and 5 wefts to the centimeter. No selvages are present. The warp yarns are wool, Z-S, of medium brown color, and 0.7 mm thick. The weft yarns are also wool, Z-S and 0.7 mm thick. The sewing thread is all cotton, medium brown in color, but of two kinds (S-Z and S4Z). Textile 128 is essentially one length of black warp-faced material, folded lengthwise. The edges on the long side are whipstitched with S-Z yarns, and then folded and whipstitched along the edges again; one end is whipstitched shut. Much of this band had fallen apart (especially the wefts), but it had been crudely darned to keep it usable.

Textile 146 bears a transposed extra-warp float single-face pattern on plain weave (Figure 4.59). It was once approximately 38 x 43 cm, but is now irregular in shape. There are 20 warp yarns per centimeter and 10.5 weft yarns per centimeter. One end selvage bears a three-shot heading cord. The warp and weft yarns are S-spun cotton, and the decorative yarn is S-Z spun wool yarn that is yellow gold in color. The heading cord is cotton, light tan in color, and S4Z.

The design consists of vertical bands, each 9 to 10.5 cm in width, alternating gold and dark brown in color. It is made up of diamonds created by bringing pairs of decorative yarns to the surface; there are also diagonal interlocking frets with bird heads and small triangles.

Textile 179 may consist of a complete blouse (Figure 4.60). This is a plain weave garment, made of brown cotton. Along the top is a central opening (ca. 20 cm) for the neck; flanking that are two apparent armholes. The full loom dimensions of the cloth from which this blouse was made are 60 x 96 cm. To make the blouse, however, the cloth was folded over once, making the dimensions of the blouse 60 x 48 cm. The garment was then loosely stitched with a paired yarn running stitch. Some running stitches in red wool can be seen near one corner; they look like darning, but no tear can be seen.

Textile 180 (Figure 4.61) provides us with an example of warp-stripe plain weave, with wide pink and tan stripes within a brown outline. This fragment measures 27 x 33 cm—probably the actual loom dimensions, since we have two end selvages and two side selvages. Both warp and weft yarns are S-spun cotton fiber.

Textile 181 (Figure 4.62) is a warp-stripe plain weave, with narrow brown stripes alternating with tan stripes. This fragment measures 41 x 38 cm; the warp and weft are cotton, both S-spun.

Textile 182 is a warp-stripe plain weave that has both medium and narrow stripes of blue and white. It is made from two pieces of cloth stitched together, totaling 28 x 41 cm. The cotton yarns for both warp and weft are S-spun.

Textile 184a is a warp-stripe plain weave with alternating brown and white stripes. The warp and weft yarns are cotton, and both are S-spun.

Textile 184b consists of two fragments (one measuring 20 x 12 cm, the other 11 x 6.5 cm). This is a warp-stripe plain weave with alternating wide brown and white stripes. The cotton yarn for both warp and weft is S-spun.

Textile 184c is a plain weave red cotton cloth, measuring 41 x 10 cm. Both the warp and weft are S-spun cotton yarn.

Textile 184d is a plain weave cotton cloth; we have its actual loom dimensions, 77 x 61 cm. Both the warp and weft are cotton, S-spun.

Textile 186 (Figure 4.63) is a warp-stripe plain weave with alternating wide white stripes and medium-wide brown stripes, spaced about 4 cm apart. The dimensions are 81 x 61 cm, with 61 cm being the full loom dimension. Cotton yarn was used for both warp and weft, and both are S-spun.

Figure 4.58. The remains of what may have been a cotton tunic, found next to Structure 4. Red, yellow, and brown camelid wool were used to decorate this garment with a brocaded design.

Textile 187 (Figure 4.64) is a warp-stripe plain weave with alternating wide white stripes and medium-wide brown stripes. This specimen is a square 35 x 35 cm, with both dimensions being actual loom dimensions. Both warp and weft are cotton, S-spun yarns.

Textile 188 (Figure 4.65) consists of two fragments, measuring 35 x 19 cm and 28 x 15 cm. This warp-stripe plain weave has alternating brown and white stripes. Its warp and weft are cotton yarns that were S-spun.

Textile 197a is a red warp-faced strip 2.7 cm wide and 42 cm long with wool warp yarns (Z-S) and paired cotton wefts (S). It is probably a remnant from a padded tapestry belt, similar to the backstrap loom belts associated with elite women at Cerro Azul.

Textile 197b appears to be another warp-faced strip from a backstrap loom belt. It is 23 cm long, and the warp is wool (Z-S); the weft features stripes of red cotton (S-spun) and brown wool (Z-S). The red stripes are 2.3 cm wide, while the brown stripes are 3.1 cm.

Textile 197c is similar to Textile 197a in having paired cotton wefts, but its dark brown wool indicates that it is not from the same belt. The warp has wool yarn, Z-S; the weft has cotton yarn, S-spun.

Textile 197d is an eight-strand square braided cord, made with bundles of single-ply yarns. The braid is made of *algodón pardo*, or naturally dark brown cotton. The length is 23 cm.

Textile 197e is a four-strand round braided cord, made from light brown cotton fibers (S3Z). The braid is 14 cm long.

Textile 200 (Figure 4.66). Given the association of so many fishing nets with Structure 4, it would not be surprising to find articles of men's clothing, such as breechclouts (*wara* in Quechua; *taparrabo* in Spanish). In fact, Textile 200 appears to be such a breechclout, made by sewing two webs of plain weave cotton cloth together. The warps are pulled closer together in the center (higher thread count, higher thread density); the count and density

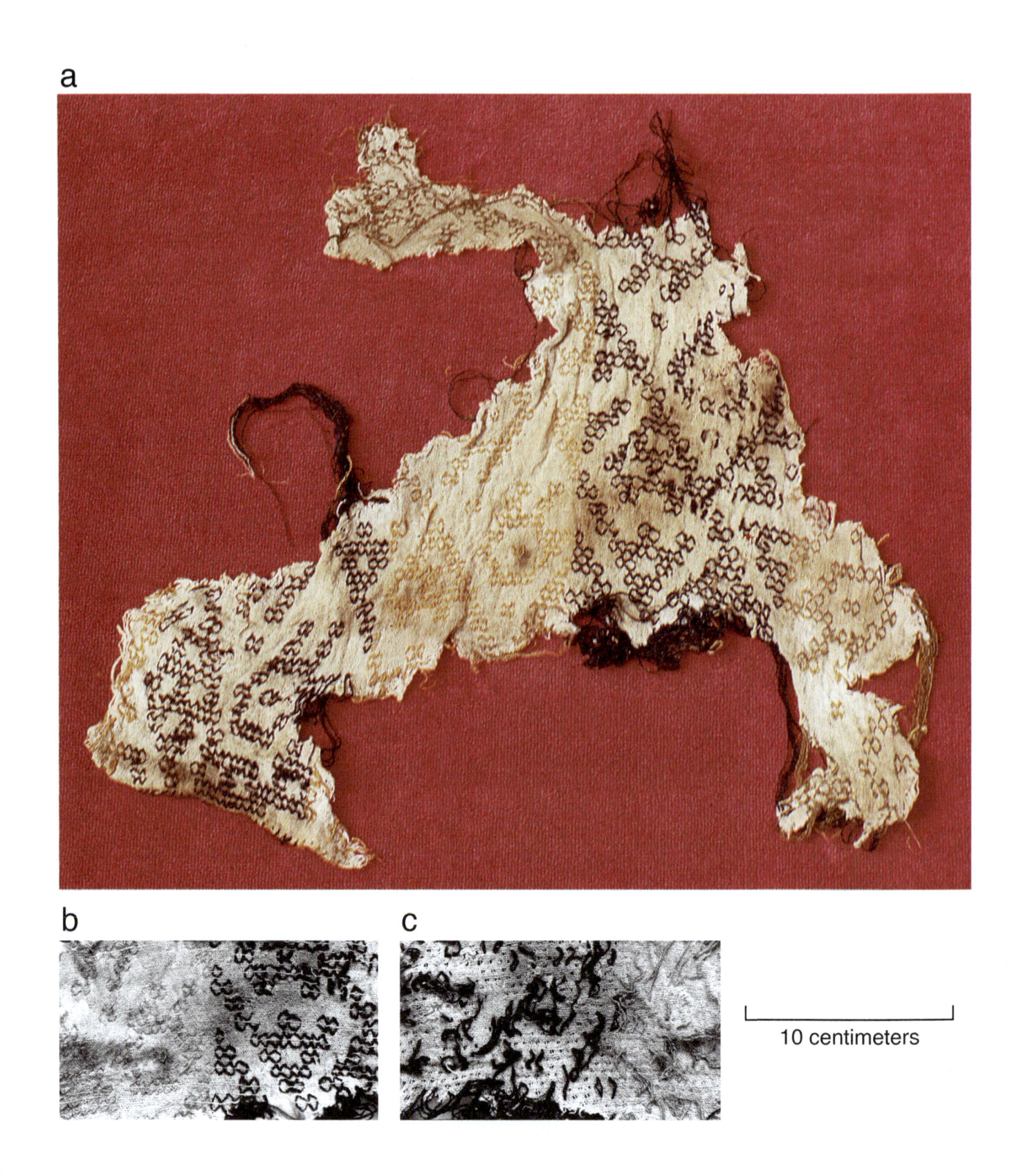

Figure 4.59. A decorated plain weave cloth associated with Structure 4. (a) An overall view. (b) A close-up of the obverse side. (c) A close-up of the reverse side.

Figure 4.60. Remains of a possible blouse or tunic, found inside Structure 4. At top center one can see an opening for the neck; there are also two apparent armholes (not clearly visible in the photo).

Figure 4.61. A warp-stripe plain weave textile with wide pink and tan stripes outlined by thin brown stripes, found next to Structure 4.

Figure 4.62. A textile from Structure 4, featuring narrow brown stripes alternating with tan stripes. Dark areas that resemble burning most likely resulted from contact with a corpse's stomach acid.

Figure 4.63. A warp-stripe plain weave cotton textile, featuring wider white stripes alternating with narrower brown stripes, found inside Structure 4.

Figure 4.64. A warp-stripe plain weave cotton textile with brown and white stripes, found inside Structure 4.

Figure 4.65. An all-cotton plain weave textile with brown and white stripes, associated with Structure 4.

lessen as the breechclout fans out toward both ends. The loom length would have been 81 cm; the breechclout's width is 28 cm at the ends and 15 cm in the center. The webs were tightly whipped at side selvages. The warp was S-spun and the weft was S-plied, while the sewing yarn was S-Z. This Cerro Azul breechclout is similar to other Late Intermediate breechclouts found in the Chincha and Virú valleys (see Garaventa 1979: Fig. 6; Millaire and Surette 2011).

Spindle Whorl

Figure 4.67 presents a whorl still threaded on its spindle (Specimen 21). The whorl is burnished black, undecorated, and resembles a squat teardrop. This whorl is 17.2 mm high and has a maximum diameter of 18.4 mm; its hole is 3.5 mm wide. The end of the spindle is frayed and incomplete.

Yarn Balls

One large yarn ball had very coarse yarn (1 mm thick), a diameter of 6 cm, and weighed 31 g. This yarn ball was discolored, having faded from blue to a dull white (Figure 4.68a). The second yarn ball (Figure 4.68b) has a diameter of 2 cm, weighs 2.5 g, and is 7.5 YR 6/6 ("reddish yellow") in color.

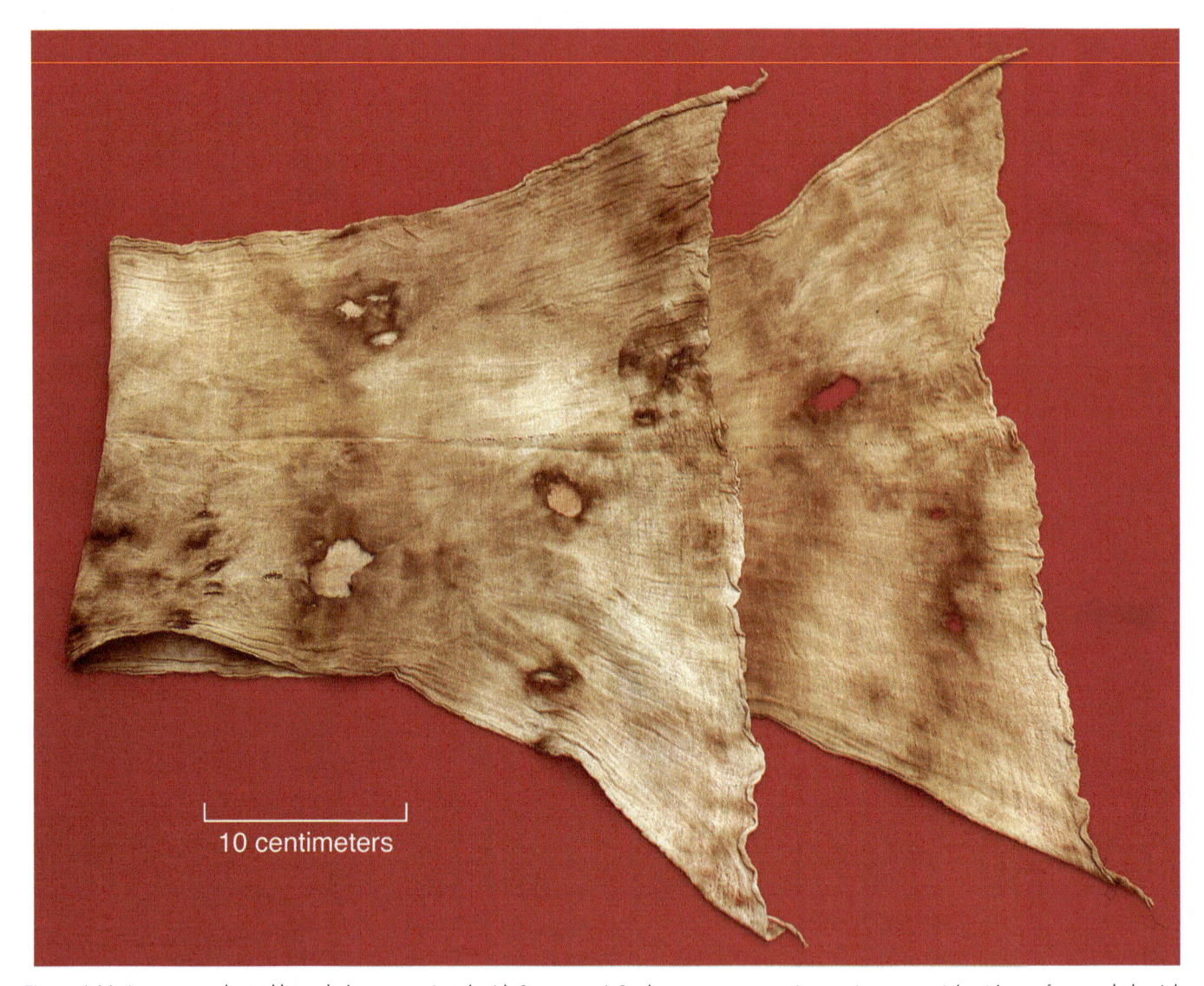

Figure 4.66. A *wara*, or shaped breechclout, associated with Structure 4. Such a garment constitutes circumstantial evidence for a male burial, and the "burn holes" likely resulted from contact with a corpse's stomach acid.

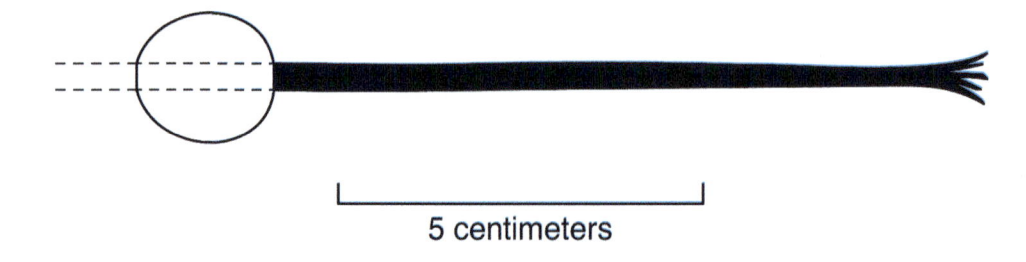

Figure 4.67. A frayed spindle with its whorl still attached, associated with Structure 4.

Needlecase

The needlecase, a hollow cane tube 15.5 cm long and 14.4 mm in diameter, still contained sewing needles made from *Opuntia* spines (Figure 4.68c).

Belt Loom

Just outside Structure 4, we also found part of a belt loom (Figure 4.69) (Specimen 101); the cane at the top was 13 cm long, 9.8 mm in diameter, and wrapped in yellow yarn (10 YR 7/6 "yellow").

Summary of Structure 4

We believe that the Structure 4 cist, like some of the multiperson burials excavated by Kroeber, contained both men and women. Unfortunately, this cannot be confirmed osteologically because the bones from multiple cists had been scattered by looters.

Among the items likely buried with men were fishing nets of several kinds, including both cast nets (*atarrayas*) and trammel nets (*redes de cortina*); we also found a *mallero* for net making. Other artifacts likely associated with men were a breechclout, slings, and bolas.

Items typically associated with women were also present, including a blouse, loom backstraps, spindles and whorls, yarn balls, sewing needles, and belt looms.

Figure 4.70 shows the empty burial cist after we had salvaged every item we could.

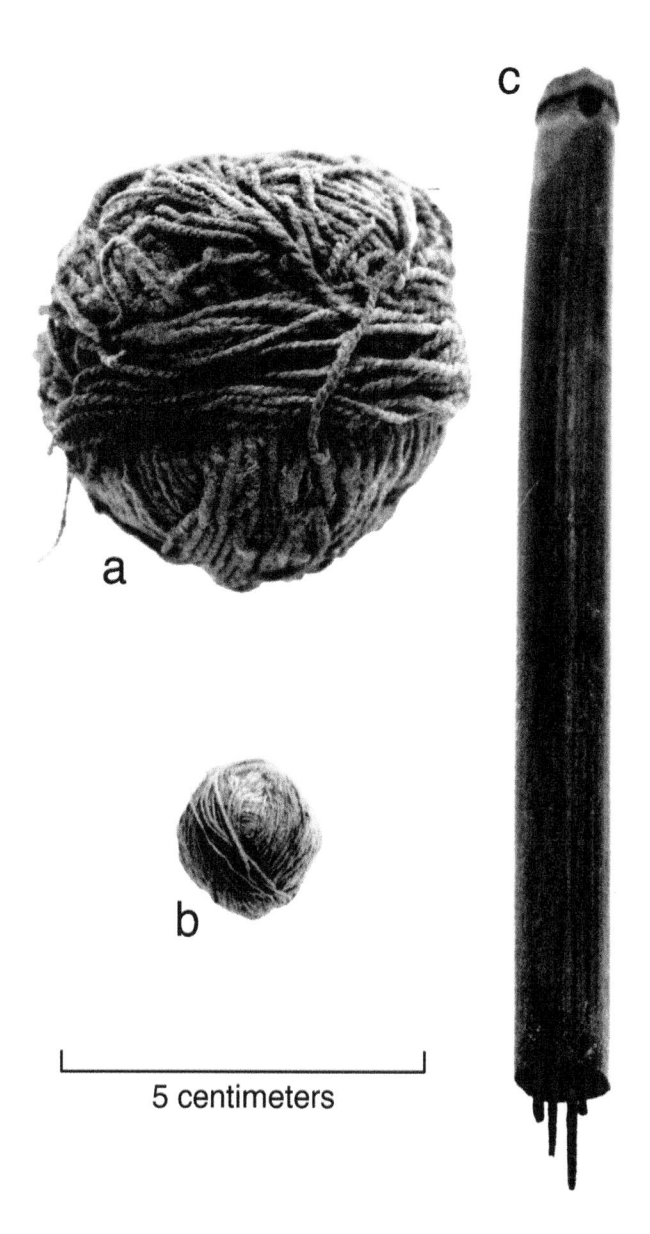

Figure 4.68. Three items found inside Structure 4. (a) Yarn ball weighing 31 g. (b) Yarn ball weighing 2.5 g. (c) Cane tube filled with sewing needles made from *Opuntia* spines.

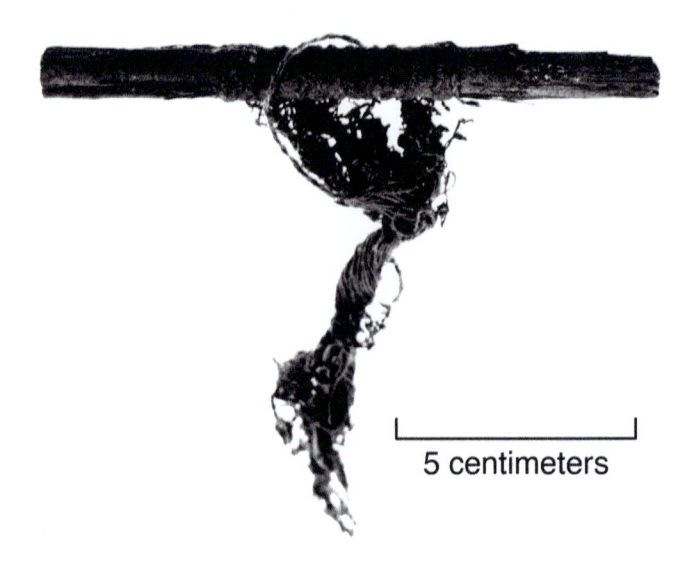

Figure 4.69. A fragment of belt loom with a portion of unfinished textile still attached, associated with Structure 4. This item constitutes circumstantial evidence for a female burial.

Figure 4.70. The Structure 4 burial cist, now empty, after we had salvaged everything we could.

Chapter 5

The Structure 5 Burial Cist

After salvaging Structure 4, we turned our attention to another looted cist on the same terrace. This cist was designated "Structure 5" (see Figures 4.4, 5.1).

Even though the looters had removed most of the skeletal elements from Structure 5, the human remains left behind still provided important information about mortuary practices (Figures 5.2a, b). For example, next to Structure 5 we found two adult skulls whose eye sockets, mouths, and nostrils had been plugged with white cotton balls and dark brown cotton pads. A cloth had been wrapped around one skull, covering the face. The other skull sported a brightly colored headband, still tied in place. One desiccated hand had string tied around each of its fingers (Figure 5.2a). One woman whose mummified remains had been tossed aside had a piece of copper in her mouth; near her desiccated forearm lay a gourd vessel and a workbasket, containing sewing needles and a ball of yarn. Inside the shroud of another looted adult we found corn on the cob.

Excavating Structure 5

In Figure 5.1 we see workman José Manco beginning to investigate Structure 5. We encountered the floor of that cist some 2.6 m below the surface of the terrace; it was uneven, partly resting on sterile sand and partly on the bedrock of Cerro Camacho. The floor had been covered with mats and then given a soft covering of *pacay* leaves (*Inga feuillei*) before the corpses were interred.

Despite the looting, a gourd bowl and two flattened workbaskets remained in the cist. We also found skeins of yarn, fragments of fishing nets, slings, cloth, and grass stems (Smith and Marcus 2016a:275, Fig. 16.21). Skeins consist of finished thread or spun yarn that can be stored by winding it around a stick or spindle.

Figure 5.1. Workman José Manco is shown salvaging items left inside Structure 5, a looted burial cist in Cerro Azul's Quebrada 5a. The line of stones seen on the left was created by our workmen to prevent the collapse of the profile, already weakened by looting.

Ceramic Vessels

Still in the burial cist were five ceramic vessels, probably left behind because the looters saw no commercial value in them. **Vessel 1** was a Camacho Black globular jar with a funnel neck and two loop handles. It was 10.2 cm high and had a rim diameter of 4.2 cm (Figure 5.3a).

Vessel 2, also a Camacho Black globular jar with a funnel neck and two loop handles, was 9.9 cm high and had a rim diameter of 5.2 cm (Figure 5.3b).

Vessel 3, a Camacho Reddish Brown globular jar with looped handles and a cambered rim, was plugged with unspun cotton when discovered (Figure 5.4a). The olla's height was 6 cm and its rim diameter was 3 cm. The clay body is 2.5 YR 6/4 ("light reddish brown"), while the burnished exterior ranges in color from 10 R 5/6 ("red") to 2.5 YR 5/4 ("reddish brown").

Vessel 4 was the broken-off neck of a grayish black globular jar with a rim diameter of 13 cm (Figure 5.4b).

Vessel 5 was a Camacho Black miniature bottle with a cambered rim (Figure 5.5); this vessel had a plug of *algodón pardo* or brown cotton still in place. The bottle's height is 8 cm, its rim diameter is 3 cm, and its wall thickness is 4 to 5 mm. The surface color is mainly black, with firing clouds ranging from dark brownish gray to 5 YR 6/4 ("light reddish brown").

Gourd Vessels

Four *mates* or gourds were still present inside Structure 5. Figure 5.6 shows one of these gourd vessels (Specimen 7), which was filled with dark brown cotton when found. The bowl is 6 cm high; its rim diameter is 5.8 cm, its maximum diameter is ca. 9 cm, and its wall thickness is 5 mm. The surface color varies from 2.5 YR 2/2 ("very dusky red") to 5 YR 2/2 ("dark reddish brown").

Figure 5.7 shows another shallow gourd bowl (Specimen 32), one filled with food for the afterlife when

The Structure 5 Burial Cist

Figure 5.2. The looters, not surprisingly, showed no regard for the human remains in Structure 5, discarding them nearby. (a, b) Two views of a mummy left next to Structure 5. (c) A mummified left hand with red-painted fingernails, clutching a piece of metal. (d) A brown and tan striped cloth found next to Structure 5. (e) A blue striped cloth found next to Structure 5.

5 centimeters

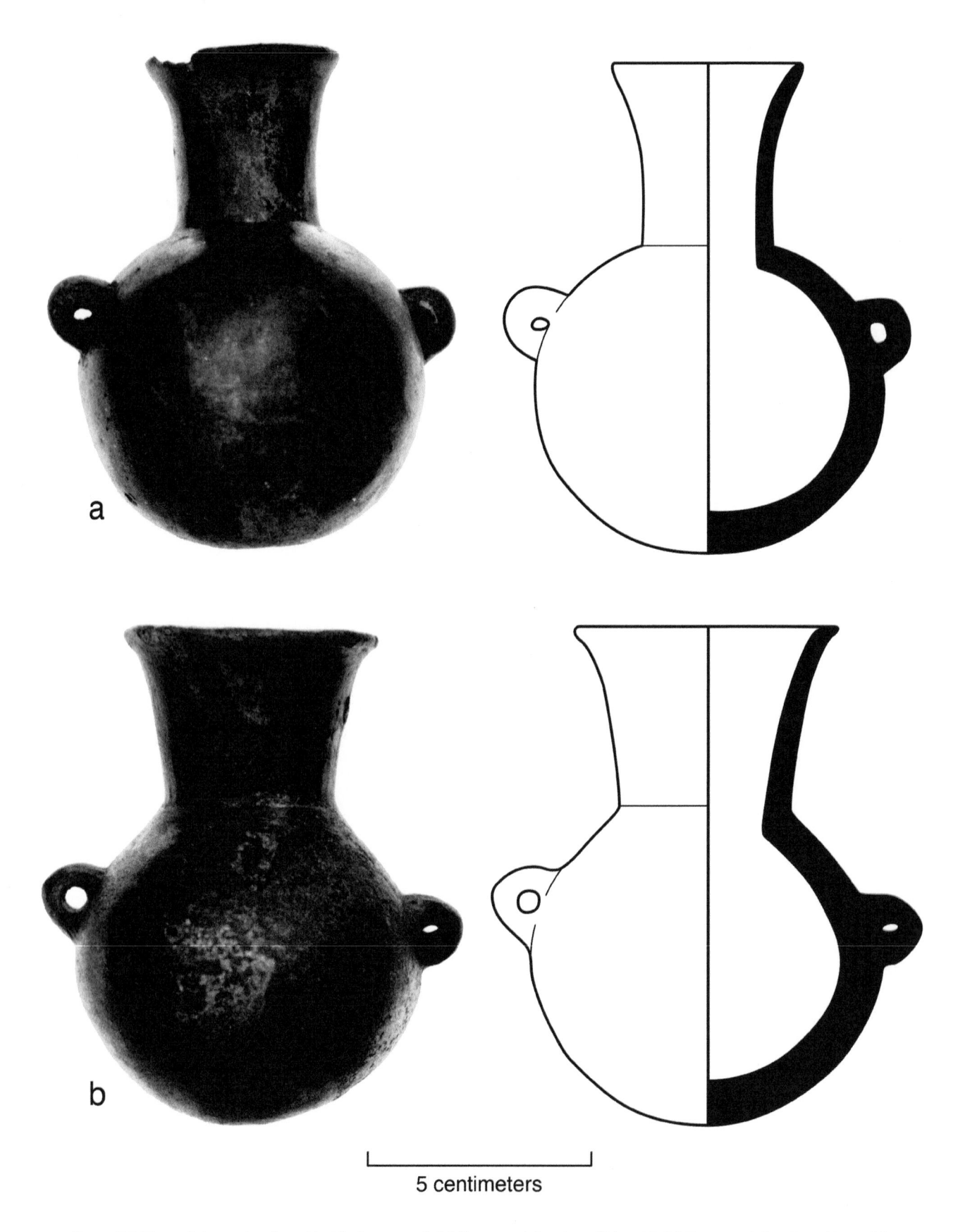

Figure 5.3. Two miniature jars found inside Structure 5. (a) Photo and drawing of Vessel 1. (b) Photo and drawing of Vessel 2.

The Structure 5 Burial Cist 113

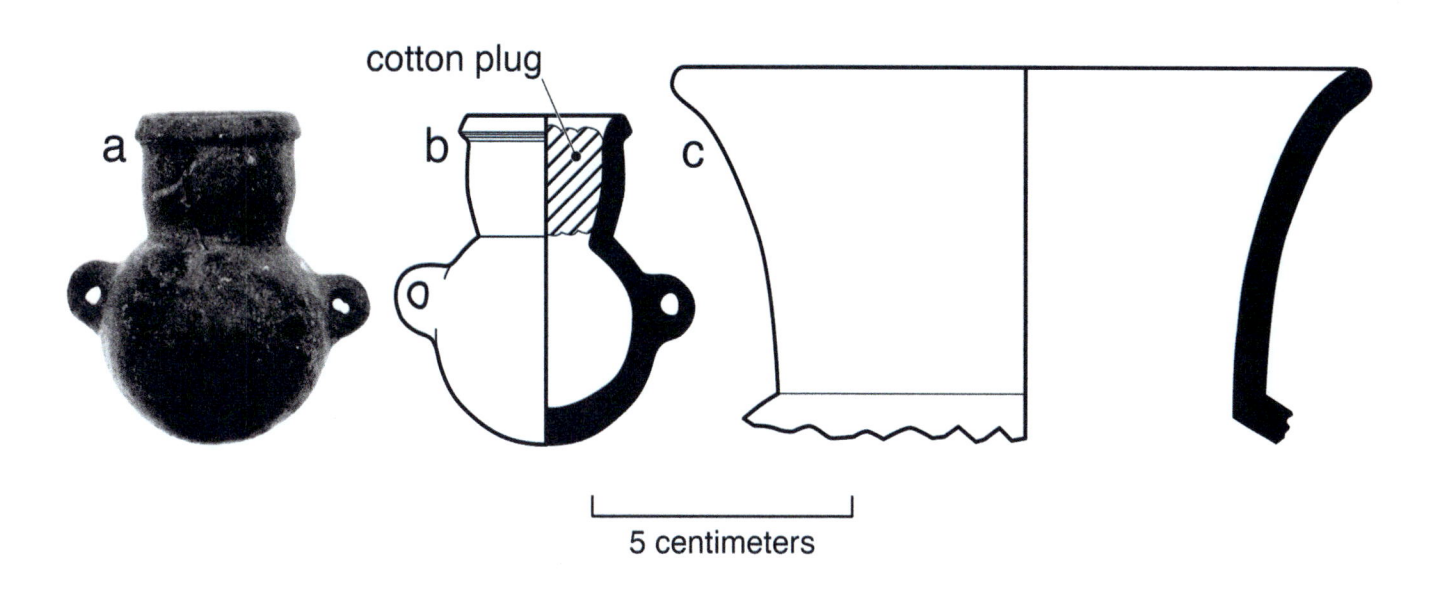

Figure 5.4. Two vessels associated with Structure 5. (a, b) Vessel 3, a Camacho Reddish Brown miniature jar, sealed with a cotton plug. (c) Vessel 4, the neck of a large broken jar.

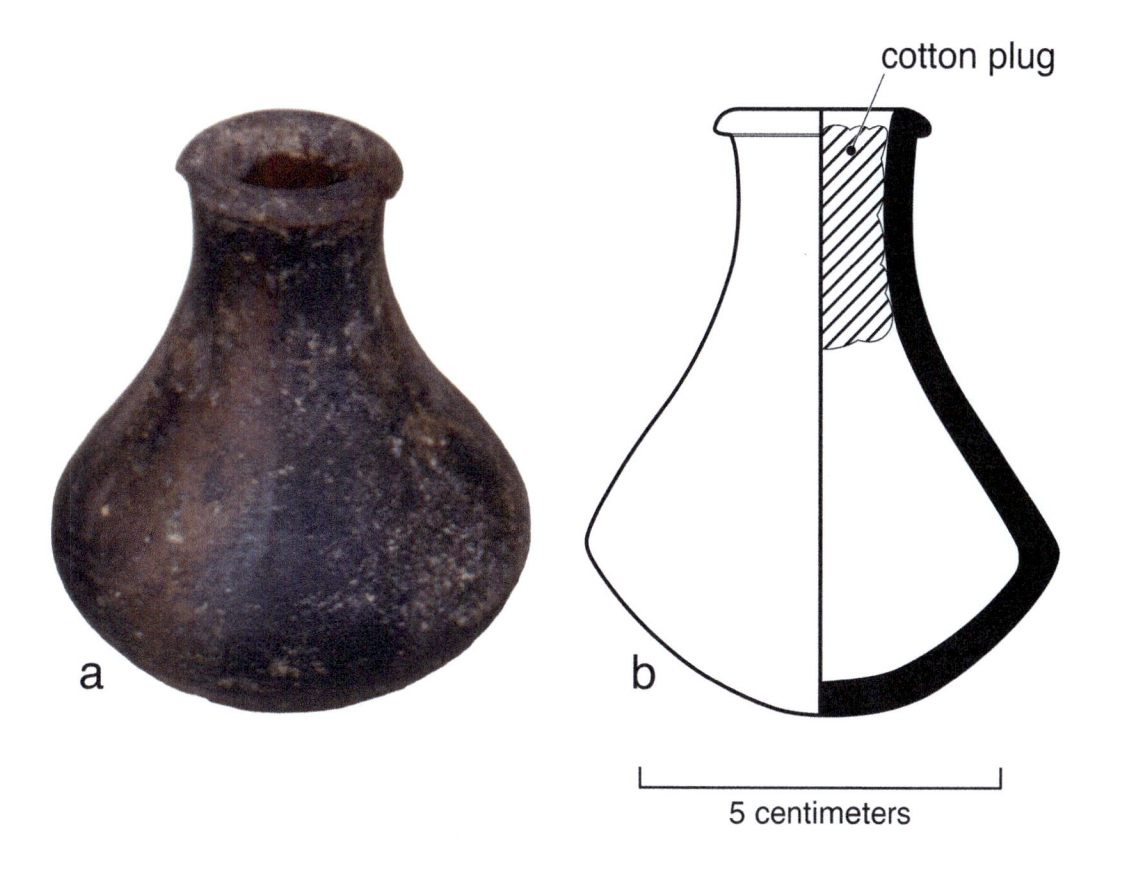

Figure 5.5. Vessel 5 of Structure 5, a Camacho Black miniature vessel sealed with a cotton plug. (a) photo. (b) drawing.

114   Chapter 5

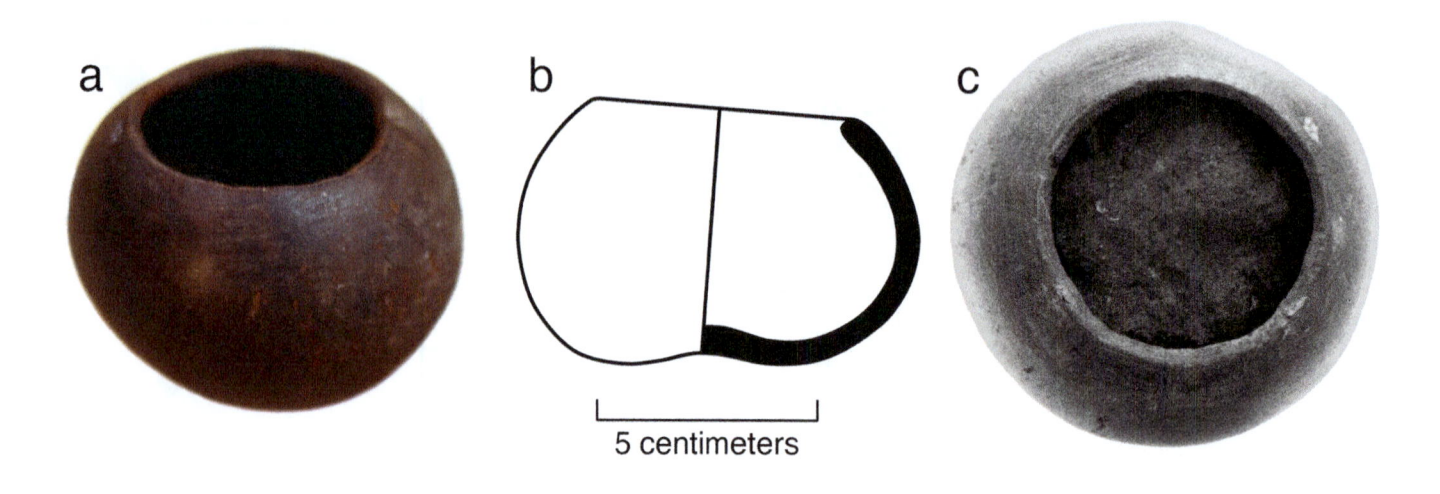

Figure 5.6. Three views of a miniature gourd bowl from Structure 5. (a) color photo. (b) drawing. (c) black-and-white photo showing the wad of *algodón pardo,* or unspun brown cotton, inside the gourd.

Figure 5.7. A gourd bowl from Structure 5 that contained one guinea pig, two molluscs, one anchoveta, and an unidentified second fish.

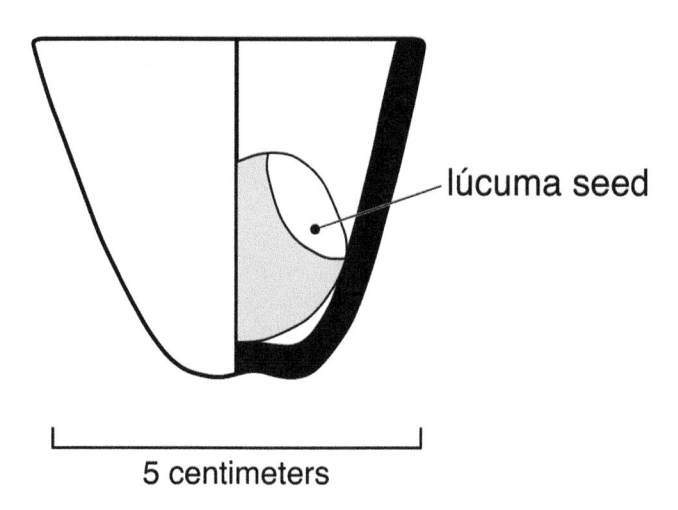

Figure 5.8. A miniature gourd vessel from Structure 5, containing a *lúcuma* seed wrapped in cloth.

found. Its contents included one clam (*Donax*), one mussel (*Perumytilus*), one anchoveta (*Engraulis ringens*), one unidentified fish, and one complete guinea pig (Glew and Flannery 2016b). The guinea pig's coat color varied from 7.5 YR 6/6 ("reddish yellow") to 7.5 YR 5/6 ("strong brown").

The gourd itself had an irregular shape, with a diameter that varied from 19.5 to 20 cm. Its height is 4.5 to 5.5 cm, and its wall thickness is 5 mm. The color of the gourd is 5 YR 3/3 ("dark reddish brown").

We also found a miniature gourd (Specimen 17) that had been fashioned into a cup (Figure 5.8). Inside the cup was a *lúcuma* seed wrapped in cloth. The cup's rim diameter is 5.3 cm, its height is 4.4 cm, and its wall is 4.5 to 5.0 mm thick. The color is 2.5 YR 2/2 ("very dusky red").

The final gourd bowl found inside Structure 5 was slightly crushed. It was unusual in having a 6 mm wide band of black paint encircling the exterior at the rim. The bowl measures 20 cm in diameter (Specimen 13) and its wall is 6 mm thick. Its Munsell color is 2.5 YR 2/4 ("dark red").

Other Food for the Afterlife

Two varieties of maize were found loose in Structure 5—yellow dent and purple imbricated (Figure 5.9). We also recovered an *Erythrina* pod from the cist (Figure 5.10). Adjacent to, and likely associated, was a whole white potato (Figure 5.11).

Coprolite

A human coprolite, found in Structure 5, was analyzed by John Jones (2016). It contained (1) small fragments of *Zea mays* kernels, (2) *Capsicum* (chile pepper) seeds, (3) one Poaceae (grass) caryopsis, (4) a fragment of a mammal bone, (5) a fish bone, (6) fragments of crayfish shell (genus *Cryphiops*), (7) strands of hair, (8) a golden spider beetle, and (9) pollen of several kinds. The presence of maize and crayfish is no surprise, since these items were found in all human coprolites at Cerro Azul. The golden spider beetle (family Ptinnidae) is a coprophagous species, typically found in dry feces.

Figurines

We have previously mentioned the mats at the bottom of Structure 5. When these mats were lifted, we found one nearly complete figurine and the head of another (Figure 5.12a, b, and c). These figurines were lying immediately beneath the mats, which probably explains why the looters failed to see them. The nearly complete figurine is 7.8 cm

Figure 5.9 (above). Structure 5 contained cobs of two maize varieties—the two yellow dent cobs flank the two purple imbricated cobs. The tallest cob in this photo has spiral rows of kernels, one of the diagnostic features of the race Confite Puntiagudo.

Figure 5.10 (right). An *Erythrina* pod found in Structure 5.

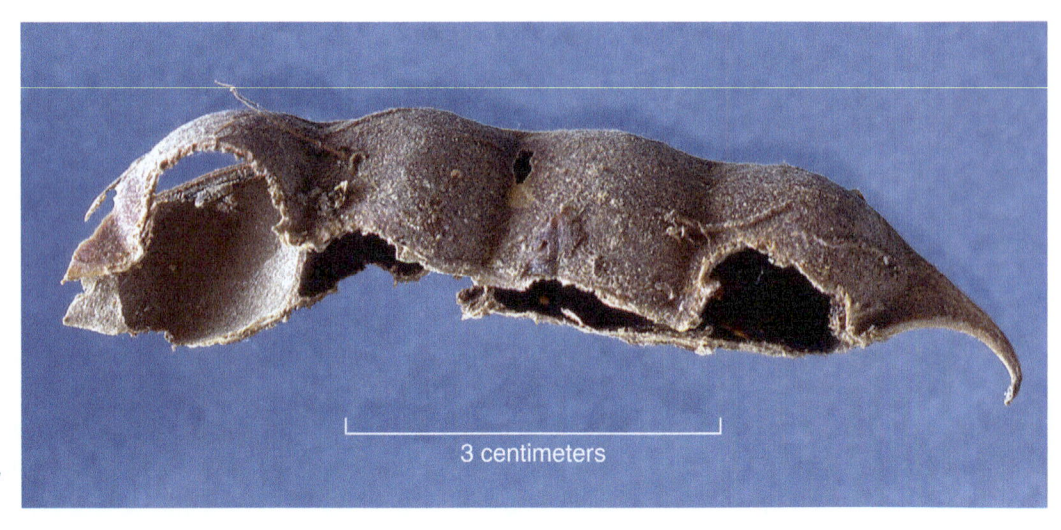

Figure 5.11. A well-preserved potato found beside Structure 5.

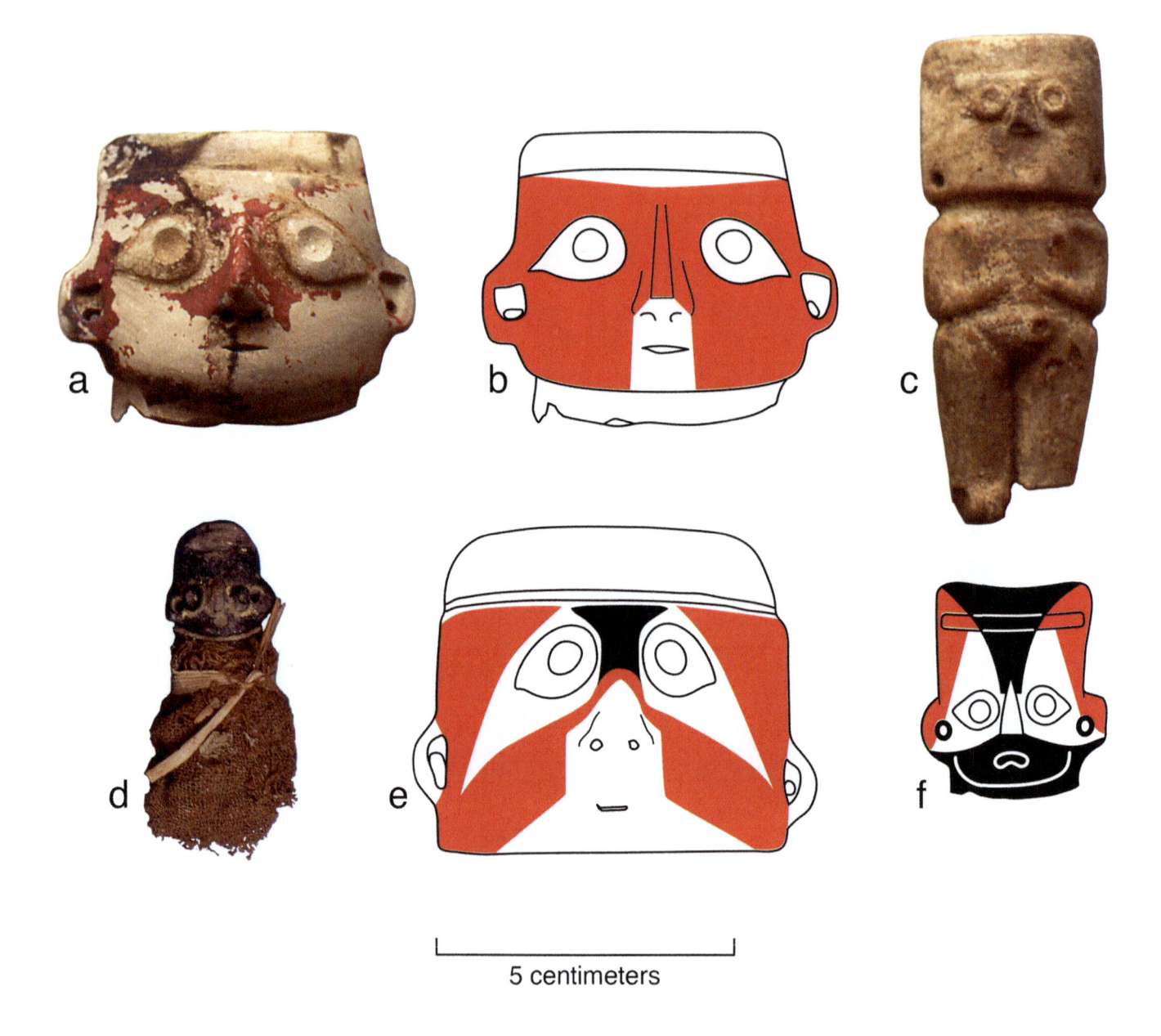

Figure 5.12. A figurine head (a, b) and a nearly complete figurine (c) from Structure 5, compared to those from other contexts at Cerro Azul. (a) A figurine head from Structure 5 with red paint on its nose, cheeks, and ears. (b) An artist's reconstruction of the figurine shown at a. (c) An unpainted figurine found in Structure 5. (d) A figurine, found inside a storage bin or Collca 1 in Structure D, was fully dressed, with a sash around the waist and a string necklace. (e) The head of a complete figurine associated with Individual 3 of Burial 4 (see Chapter 10, Figure 10.32). Its facial paint can be compared to that seen on other figurines from Cerro Azul. (f) A figurine head from Room 5 of Structure 9 at Cerro Azul, featuring well-preserved facial paint.

Figure 5.13. Items of metal associated with Structure 5. (a, b) Packets of silver foil inserted into the mouths of mummies. (c) Silver foil found in the mouth of an individual identified as a woman. (d, e) Packets of silver foil found loose at the bottom of Structure 5. (f) Silver tweezers with a tiny hole at the top for suspension, found in looters' backdirt associated with Structure 5.

high (Figure 5.12c), and its hands are folded on its chest (Specimen 10). Its Munsell color is 10 YR 8/4 to 10 YR 8/6 ("very pale brown").

The detached figurine head is 4.5 cm high and has red paint on its face (Figure 5.12a, b); the shade of red is 5 R 3/8 ("dark red"). This facial paint (Figure 5.12a, b) is similar to that on figurines found in Structure 9 and with Burial 4 (Figure 5.12e, f). Some of these other figurines were discovered wearing a necklace of seeds strung on a thread (Figure 5.12d, e).

Metal Artifacts

Given the evidence of looting, we were surprised to find more than a dozen small items of metal associated with Structure 5. We can only attribute this to the fact that the looters were not using screens. It is also the case that some pieces were concealed in the mouths of corpses. In fact, the most frequently encountered metal item was a piece of silver foil small enough to be inserted into a mouth.

Such pieces of silver were usually folded, bent, or rolled into a disc or tight packet (e.g., Specimen 12). In the case of one skull tossed aside by the looters, the mouth held two packets of silver; one weighed 33 g (Figure 5.13a), while the other weighed 11 g (Figure 5.13b). Both packets appeared to be made from pieces cut from a larger silver disc. A similar piece of folded silver foil was found in the mouth of a discarded middle-aged woman (Specimen 10). When unfolded, its dimensions were 7.7 x 2.8 cm. The foil was 0.7 mm thick, weighing 4 g. This piece clearly had been cut from a larger item of silver foil (Figure 5.13c).

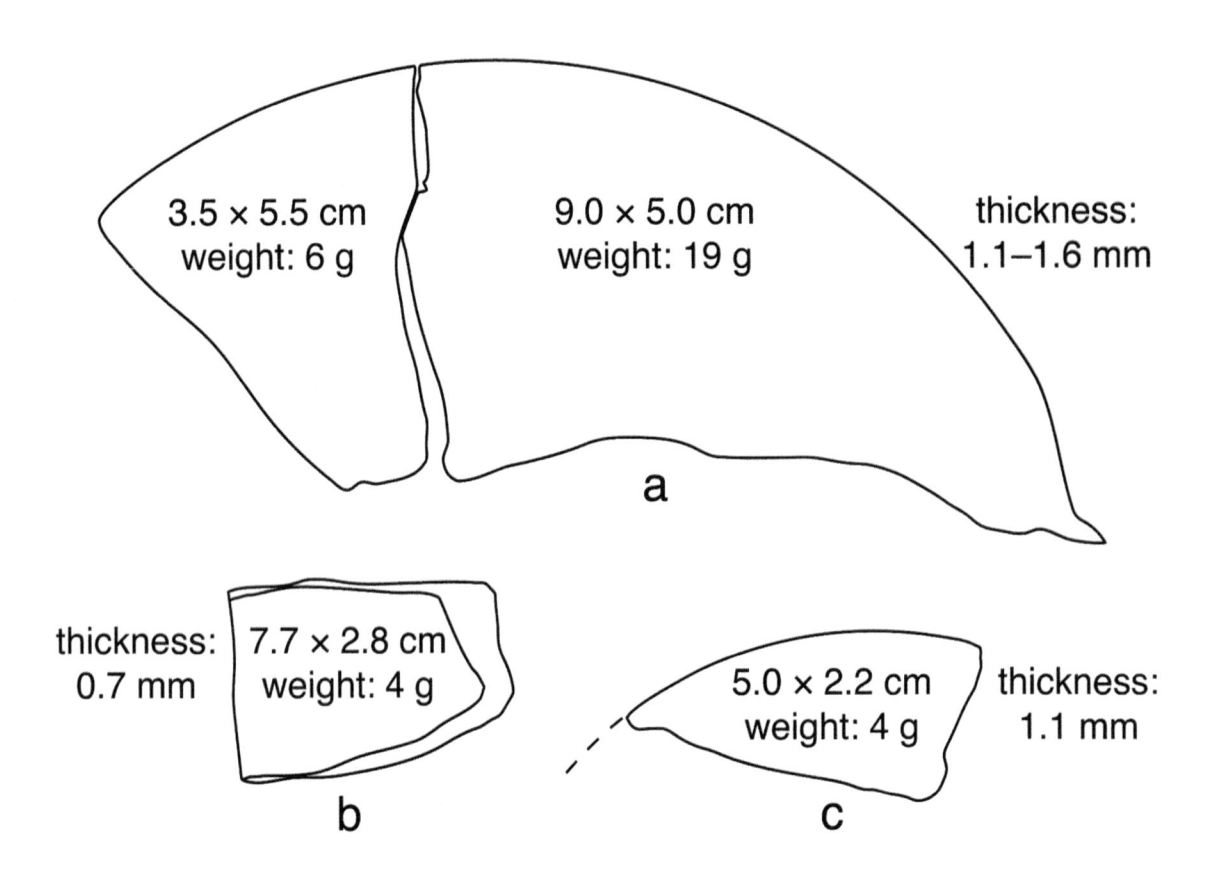

Figure 5.14. Pieces of metal found in Structure 5. (a) Two fragments of copper cut from the same disc. (b) A folded piece of silver from the mouth of a woman (see Figure 5.13c). (c) Triangular piece of metal found clutched in a mummified hand with its fingernails painted red (see Figure 5.2c).

Two other packets of folded silver wedges or sheets were found by screening looters' backdirt. One (Specimen 14) was 3.8 cm long, 3.0 cm wide, and 0.9 cm thick, and weighed 9.0 g (Figure 5.13d).

The other packet (Specimen 8) was 3.5 x 3.0 cm and weighed 2.5 g (Figure 5.13e).

One remarkable item that escaped the looters' hands was a pair of silver tweezers (Specimen 7). These tweezers are 5.1 cm high and 3.9 cm in diameter (see Figure 5.13f). Their weight is 9.5 g and their thickness is 0.7 mm. A hole at the top suggests that these tweezers were suspended from a cord, perhaps to be worn around the owner's neck. There are precedents for this; in the 1860s, Squier (1967[1869]:212) found the "grave of a fisherman" at Ancón in which there were tweezers hanging from a thread around the corpse's neck. Squier suggested that the tweezers were used to pluck hairs from the man's chin. In addition, more than 50 tweezers have been reported from the Chincha Valley (Kroeber and Strong 1924:40).

In addition to silver, we found a few items of copper. Figure 5.14a shows two fragments from a copper disc (Specimen 6). One fragment measures 3.5 x 5.5 cm and weighs 6 g. The second measures 9 x 5 cm and weighs 19 g.

Figure 5.14b shows the folded piece of silver (7.7 x 2.8 cm) found in the mouth of a woman whose head had been discarded by the looters. Figure 5.14c, on the other hand, is a piece of metal that had been placed in the hand of a woman whose fingernails were painted with red nail polish. The ring finger of her discarded hand was still pressed down into her palm. That piece of metal, which appears to have been cut from a large disc, weighs 4 g and measures 5.0 x 2.2 cm (see Figure 5.2c).

Later, we were lucky enough to find confirmation that silver was imported to Cerro Azul in the form of circular discs. From the looters' backdirt, we recovered a complete disc that had escaped their detection because it was wrapped in a dirt-encrusted cloth. This disc, described in Chapter 16, had a diameter of 9.5 cm and weighed 68 g; it was 2.1

to 2.4 mm thick. We believe that some of the silver packets we found were wedges cut from such discs.

Finally, we note that we found no gold with Structure 5. Either none was present, or the looters had made off with it.

Fishing Nets

We found only two net fragments inside Structure 5. **Net 018** measures 81 x 35 cm; it had been repaired with a two-ply Z-S yarn, 1.1 mm thick. That repair yarn is a bit thicker than the principal yarn (0.8–0.9 mm) used to make the net. The mesh openings of Net 018 varied from 1.6 to 1.8 cm; the color of the cotton was light to medium brown. The knots were half hitch #2 and the principal yarn was two-ply Z-S.

Net 019 is a fragment of an *atarraya* or cast net (Figures 5.15, 5.16). The preserved fragment measures only 30 x 28 cm, but when cast into the ocean the complete net would have formed a circle with a diameter of three meters. Descending from the corona (the ring at the top of the net) are 22 paired cords; these led to an apron of 14 extensions (called *ensanches*) that opened when the net was cast. This cotton net has mesh openings varying from 15.6 to 16.6 mm. My local informants claimed that these mesh openings were the appropriate size for anchovetas and other "peces menudos" (small fish). When the net is pulled out of the ocean, weights attached to the bottom all converge, converting the net to a *bolsa* or bag that holds the captured fish. The cotton on this net is dark brown in color, and the knots forming the mesh are half hitch #2. The yarn is two-ply Z-S, 1.2 mm to 1.5 mm thick and showing a spin of 60 degrees.

Slings

A complete sling with a webbed cradle was discovered in Structure 5 (Figure 5.17). It was accompanied by fragments of other slings, some of which still included the cradle. Such fragments often displayed a colorful wool decoration next to the cradle, but present only on one side; examples of such decoration can be seen in Figure 5.18. The motifs include diamonds, checkers, chevrons, zigzags, bands, and dots, and the colors can include red, yellow, lavender, purple, and brown.

The Structure 5 slings whose length could be estimated would have been almost two meters long. They featured a grass fiber interior, tightly wrapped with cotton yarn; at one extreme was a tassel, and at the other a finger loop.

Most of the slings from Structure 5 featured eight-strand braiding. All were the product of "hand processing," as discussed in detail by Cahlander (1980) in her book *Sling Braiding of the Andes*. Cahlander illustrates the way men braid such slings today in various highland communities, and shows that different sections of the sling can be composed of different numbers of strands (anywhere from four to twenty-four). Adele Cahlander (1980), Ann Rowe (1995–1996), and Elayne Zorn (1982) report that the technique used by men to make rope, sandals, and slings was distinct from the technique women used to spin yarn and weave fabrics. The place on the sling that was most often used to display a colorful design was the braided wool section next to the sling's cradle. A few of the pre-Columbian examples illustrated by Cahlander (1980: Plate I) are similar to the slings found at Cerro Azul.

Our Specimen T123 may be part of one additional sling. This fragment is 25.5 cm long and constructed of cotton over some other plant fiber. It has three sections: (1) 10 cm of brown, double square braid, S-spun, 0.8 mm thick; (2) 5.5 cm of red, yellow, and brown wrapping yarns that were Z-spun S-twisted, 1.0 mm thick; and (3) a tassel section 12 cm long made of a vegetal fiber that may be *puya* (bromeliad).

Textiles

Textile 102 from Structure 5 is a brown and white striped cloth measuring 76 x 46 cm (Figure 5.19); the 46 cm dimension is the actual loom width. This is a cotton warp-stripe, plain weave in which both the warp and weft yarn are S-spun. The heading cord is cotton, S6Z, and 1.8 mm thick. The brown stripes (2.5 to 3.4 cm wide, 10 warp pairs) alternate with light tan stripes (2.7 to 3.2 cm wide, 10 warp pairs). There are usually 7 warps per centimeter and 3.5 wefts per centimeter. The density of the weave varies from 60 to 80. This cloth is unusual in the Cerro Azul collection because the weave is less standardized in its construction; it has the look of a textile made by a novice.

Textile 116 may have been part of a woolen backstrap or belt (Figure 5.20). Its total preserved length is 72 cm and consists of three parts: a 12 cm round braid, a 34 cm section, and a deteriorated 38 cm section. The weft-wrapping is bidirectional and diagonal. The 12 cm long round braid is 0.7 cm wide (shown in Figure 5.20a). Both sides of the band are decorated, each with a different design. In Irene Emery's classification, this textile would be an example of *soumak* weft-wrapping. Emery (1966:215) says, "In the simplest and clearly the basic form of *weft-wrapping*, there are only two

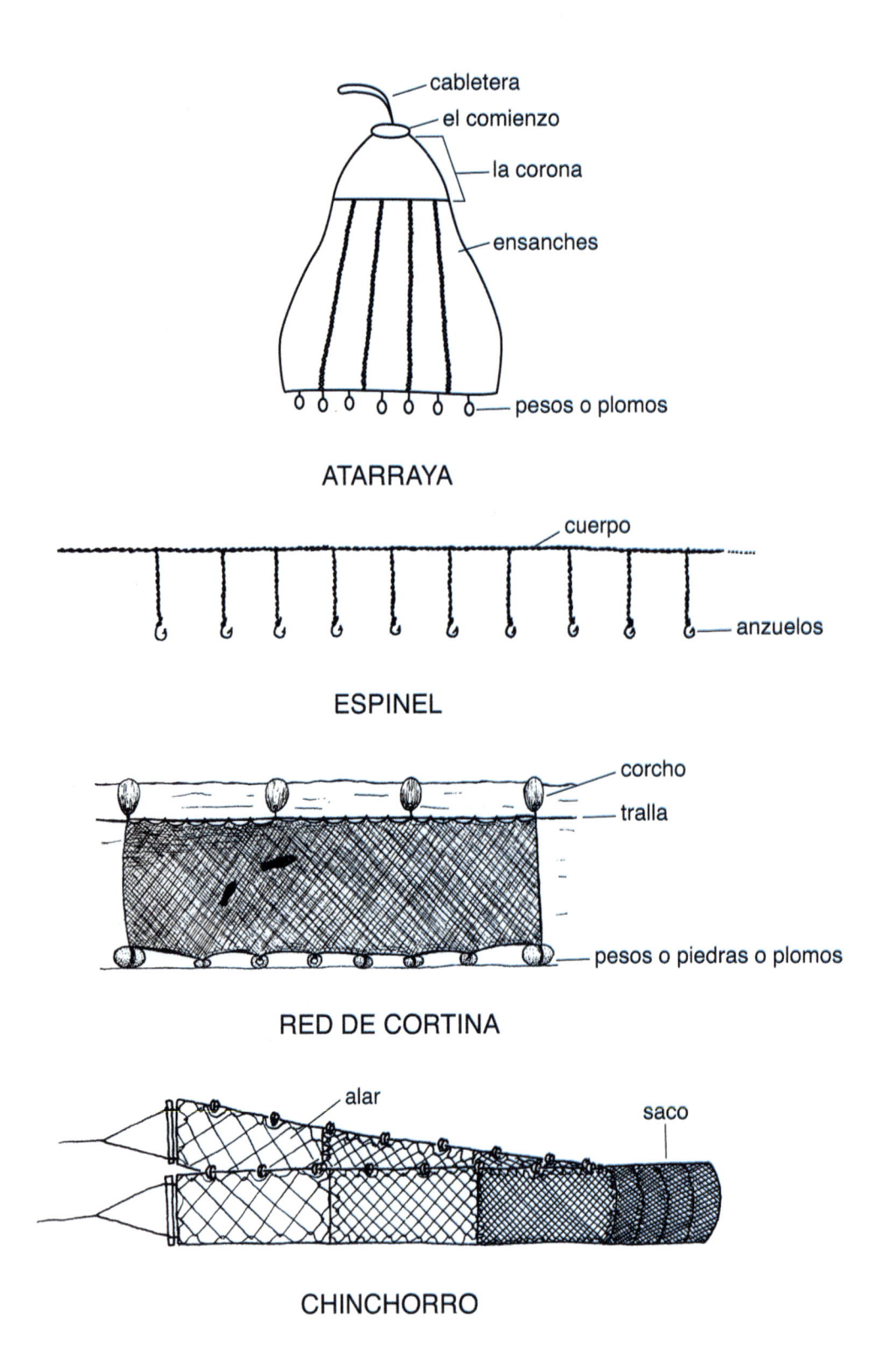

Figure 5.15. Various kinds of nets used today at Cerro Azul, including the *atarraya* or cast net; the *espinel* with its multiple suspended hooks; the *red de cortina* or trammel net, with floats along the top and weights along the bottom; and the *chinchorro*, which has two wings—open at one end and closed at the other to form a pouch (see Marcus and Flannery 2010).

The Structure 5 Burial Cist 123

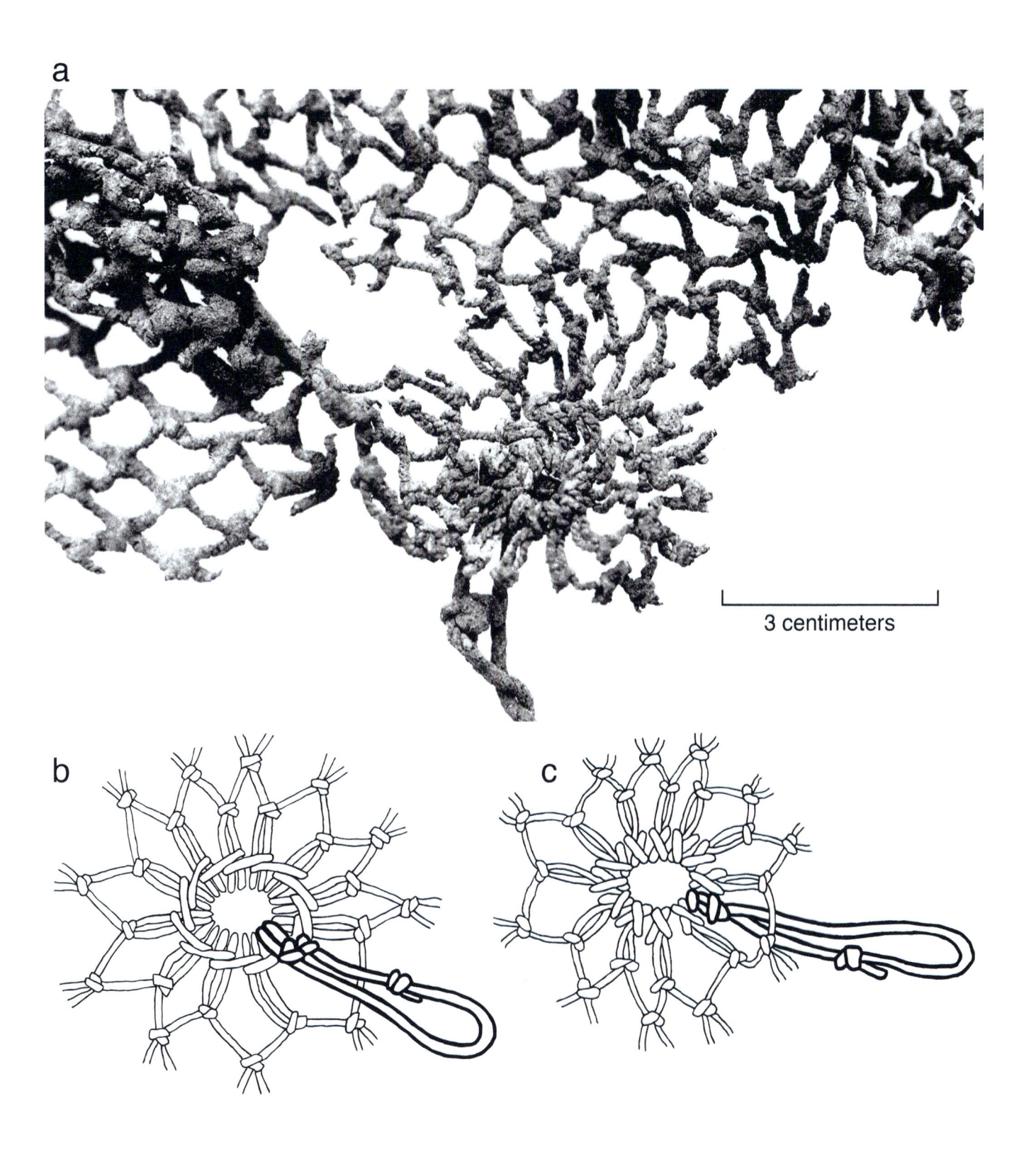

Figure 5.16. Fragments of an *atarraya* or cast net, found in looters' debris next to Structure 5. (a) Photo of the *comienzo* or circular ring at the top of the net. (b, c) Drawings showing the *cabletera* attached to the *comienzo* (see Figure 5.15). (b) The view from above (or outside the net); (c) The view from below (or inside the net).

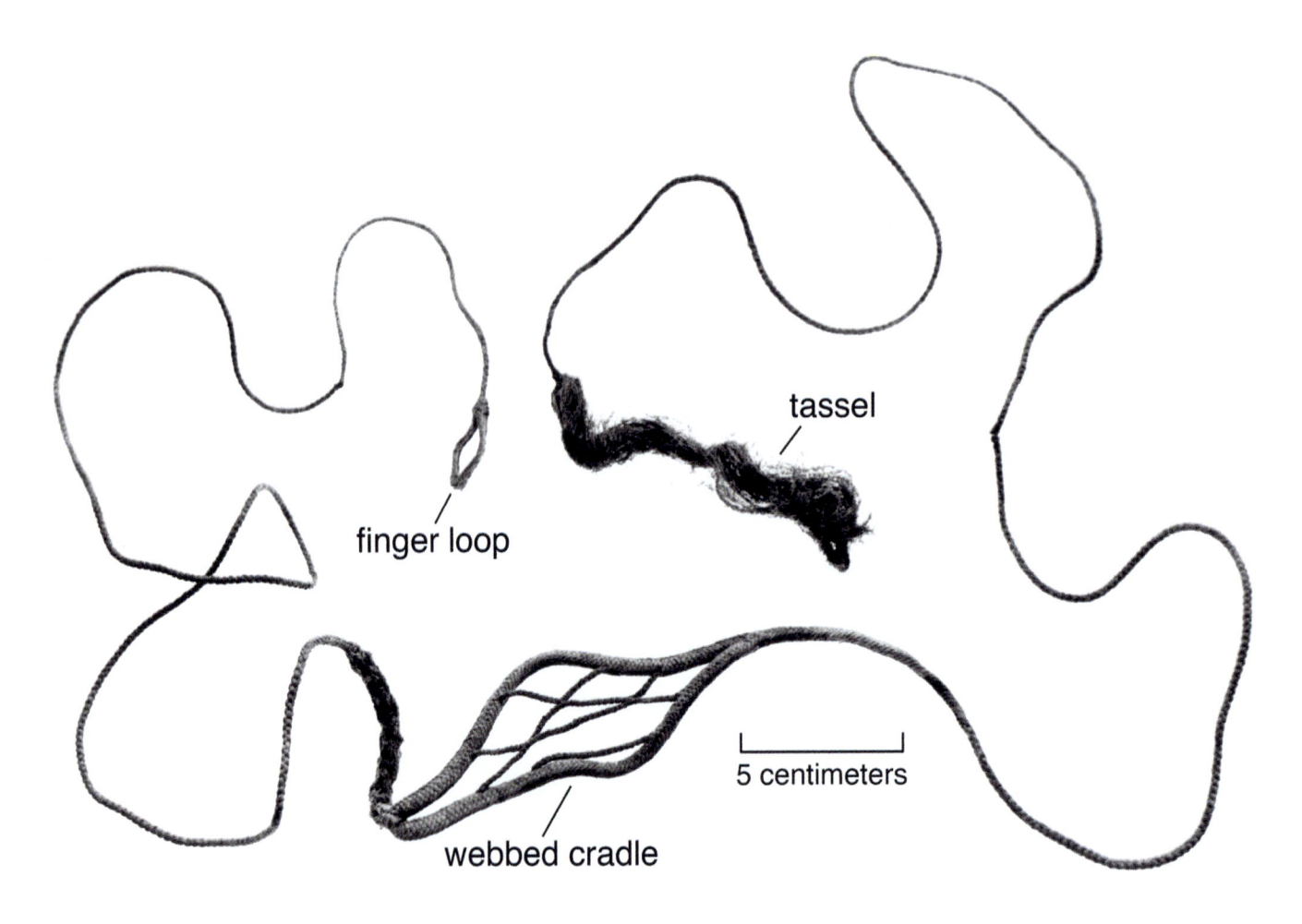

Figure 5.17. A complete sling with webbed cradle from Structure 5. To the immediate left of the cradle is a short section decorated with colorful woolen yarns.

Figure 5.18. Three examples of the decorative wool used on slings; these colorful areas appear next to the cradle, usually on one side. (a, b) Examples from slings associated with Structure 6. (c) Example from a sling associated with Structure 5.

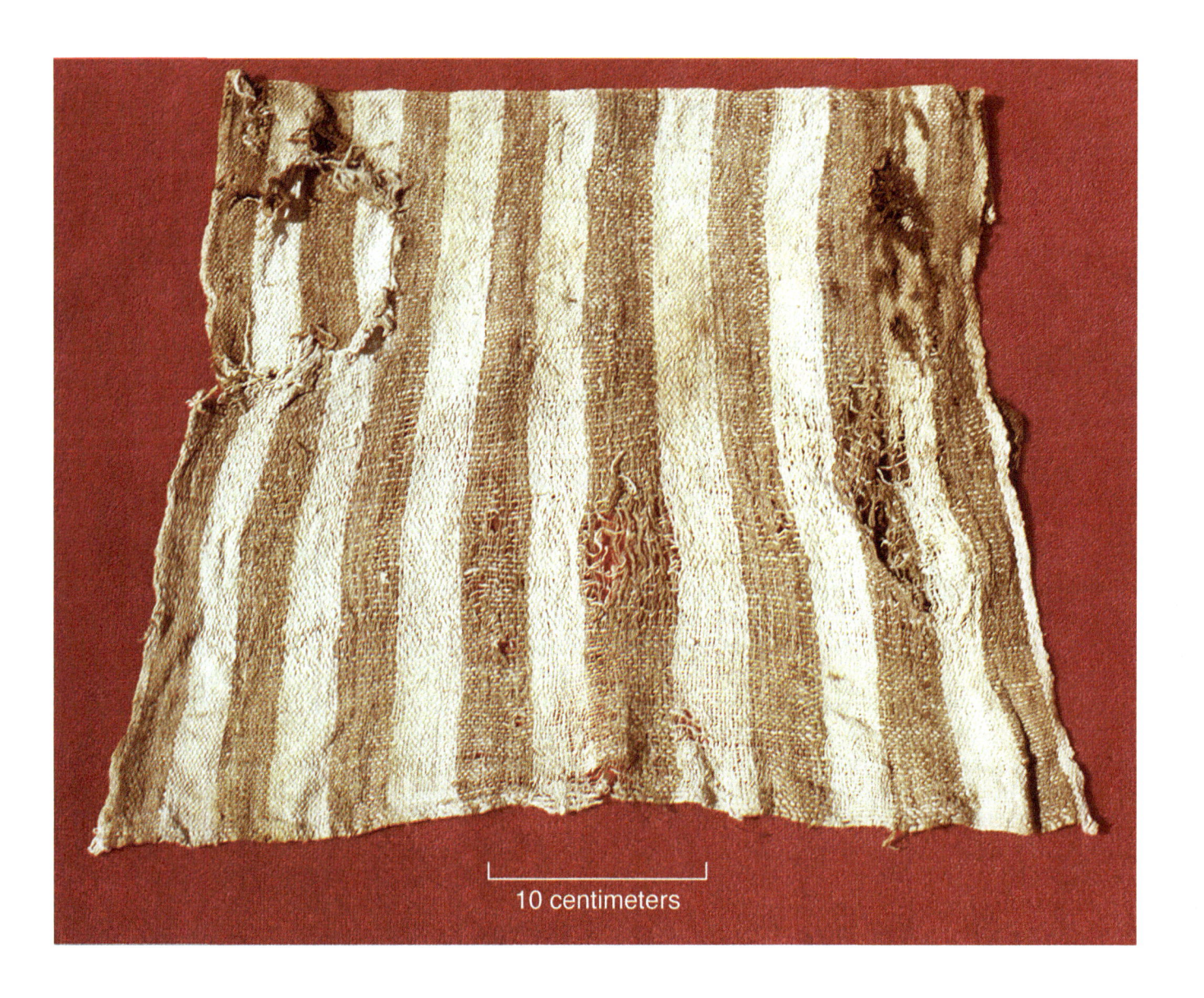

Figure 5.19. A brown and white warp-stripe plain weave textile associated with Structure 5.

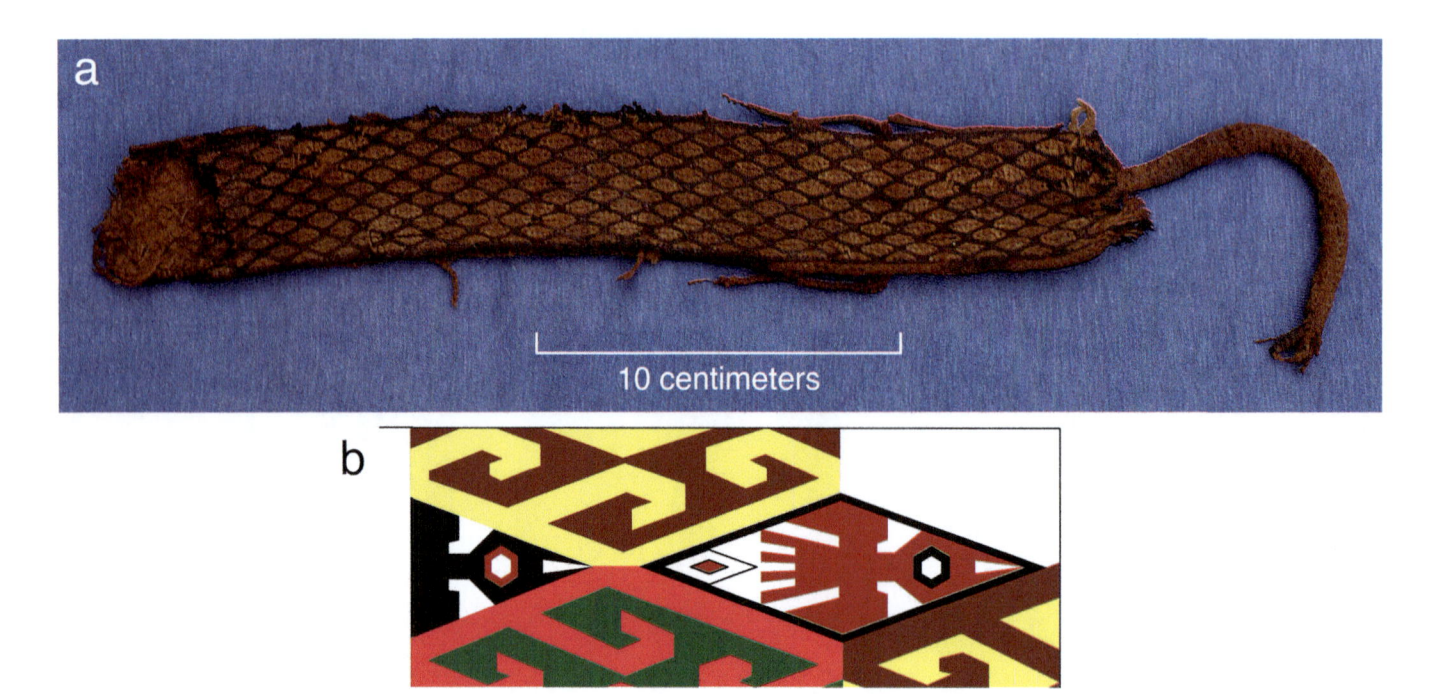

Figure 5.20. A two-sided, reversible loom backstrap found in Structure 5. (a) Photo of one side, with black yarn outlining gold diamonds. (b) A drawing of the opposite side, which features red birds alternating with black birds within diamonds; other spaces are filled either with green and red yarns or brown and yellow woolen yarns.

weft movements. Weft elements repeatedly cross over (or under) two or more warp units, then back under (or over) half the number (one or more), thus progressively encircling, or *wrapping*, all warp elements one or more at a time. … the term *Soumak wrapping* has come to be fairly definitive as a designation of the basic over-2-and-back-under-1 (or over-4-under-2, etc.) use of *wrapping wefts* wherever found."

Textile 116's designs are shown in Figures 5.20a and 5.20b. One side (Figure 5.20a) features a diagonal lattice of diamonds within diamonds (there are five across the width of the band). Black wool is used to outline a yellow-white center. The other side (Figure 5.20b) features colorful birds (a red bird with black eye alternating with a black bird with red eye) inside triangles; the designs are made with green, yellow, red, and brown wool yarns.

The body of Textile 116 is tubular. Its interior reveals many loose yarns, resulting from frequent color changes in the fabric. Some thick yarns (S10 Z) were added as padding, and in the narrowest section some twigs were added as stiffening. The warp is a continuous spiral, passing around the edges from one face to the other.

Textile 138 is a strip of eccentric slit tapestry with edge embroidery (Figure 5.21) that may have been part of a headband or belt. The term "eccentric" is often used to refer to wefts used for curvilinear figures, a thread movement that contrasts with the usual rectilinear relationship of elements. "The structure of a tapestry-woven fabric characterized by the 'eccentric' use of wefts for figuring is sometimes referred to as 'eccentric tapestry' or 'eccentric weave' " (Emery 1966:83). The warp of Textile 138 was apparently constructed from fern stipes, while the weft is wool, Z-spun and S-twisted, with yarn 0.8 mm thick. The weft uses colorful yarns of red, yellow, brown, and dark brown. There are 21 warps per centimeter, five wefts per centimeter, and two side selvages. The embroidery yarn is wool, 0.8 mm thick, and red in color. The three rows of embroidery are made up of two staggered lines of red wool 0.8 mm thick, and the running stitches form a continuous line.

The design on Textile 138 is a series of birds with double hook beaks, and below each beak is a regular hexagon. The background color of the band is brown. Most motifs continue the familiar pattern of alternating red and yellow yarn—when a bird is red, its eye is yellow, and when a bird is yellow, its eye is red. Each eye stands out from the background because it is padded and raised. Hexagons below the birds' beaks alternate in color, such that red

Figure 5.21. A band of slit tapestry from Structure 5, showing birds in faded red wool or yellow wool. The associated hexagons alternate in color—red interior/yellow exterior to yellow interior/red exterior to red interior/yellow exterior.

hexagons have yellow interiors and yellow hexagons have red interiors.

Textile 139 is a 30.5 x 4.5 cm fragment of slit eccentric tapestry with a flat braided double cord (Figure 5.22). It has a wrapped-base tassel that provides an additional 10.5 cm to its length. This tapestry fragment features beautiful fish with raised hemispherical eyes. The weaver seems to have had a preferred color sequence that consisted of a red fish, a yellow-white fish, a gold fish, a red fish, and so on. The eyes of the fish also display a preferred color sequence—in this case, yellow, red, red, and yellow. The background was black, but is now faded.

Textile 140 is a 28 x 5.3 cm fragment of slit eccentric tapestry with edge embroidery and plaited cords (Figure 5.23). It is constructed in the same way as Textiles 138 and 139; its decoration, however, is different. This specimen's design consists of three parallel rows of interlocking hooks or waves. The colors are red and yellow, and they alternate across the width of the specimen.

Textile 141 (Figure 5.24) consists of two slit tapestry bands, reminiscent of the Late Intermediate "neckpiece" known from a cemetery near La Cumbe in the Chincha Valley (Garaventa 1979: Fig. 3). The design on this textile consists of a diagonal series of spirals or waves with a color sequence of yellow/gold, red, dark brown, yellow/gold, red, and brown; the red comes in two shades, dark red and light red.

Textile 141's two tapestry bands measure 31 x 5.1 cm (Band A) and 38 x 3.7 cm (Band B). Both ends of Band B are tightly stitched to one end of A, and the opposite end of Band A splays out to a width of 5.5 cm. Both bands have embroidered edging like that seen on Textiles 138, 139, and 140. The construction of the warp, weft, and other elements of Textile 141 is also similar to those three specimens.

Textile 156 is a coarse, plain cloth, plain weave bag that was found to contain cotton seeds (Figure 5.25). This cotton bag was found inside a tied-up workbasket (Specimen 116) lying on the floor of Structure 5. The bag measured 27 x 19 cm, and its warp and weft were both S-spun. The bag's handle was made of cotton, S4 Z2S and ca. 0.4 mm in places. The sewing thread was S-spun cotton that also displayed uneven thickness, ranging from 0.7 mm to 1.1 mm. The bottom of the bag appeared to be singed, as if it had come into direct contact with stomach acids.

Textile 163 (Figure 5.26) was the coarse weave cotton cloth wrapped around Workbasket #1, which (as mentioned

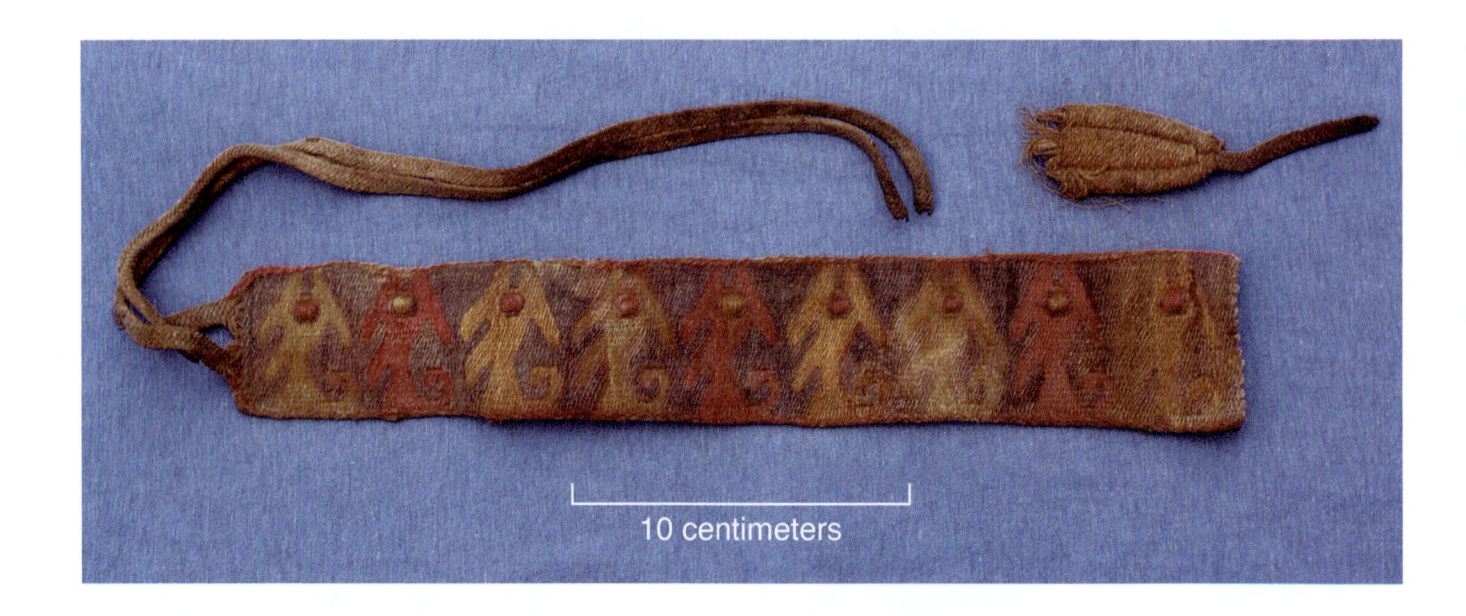

Figure 5.22. A possible headband made of slit tapestry, featuring fish with raised eyeballs, found in Structure 5. The faded colors of the fish seem to show a color sequence of red, yellow-white, gold, then red again.

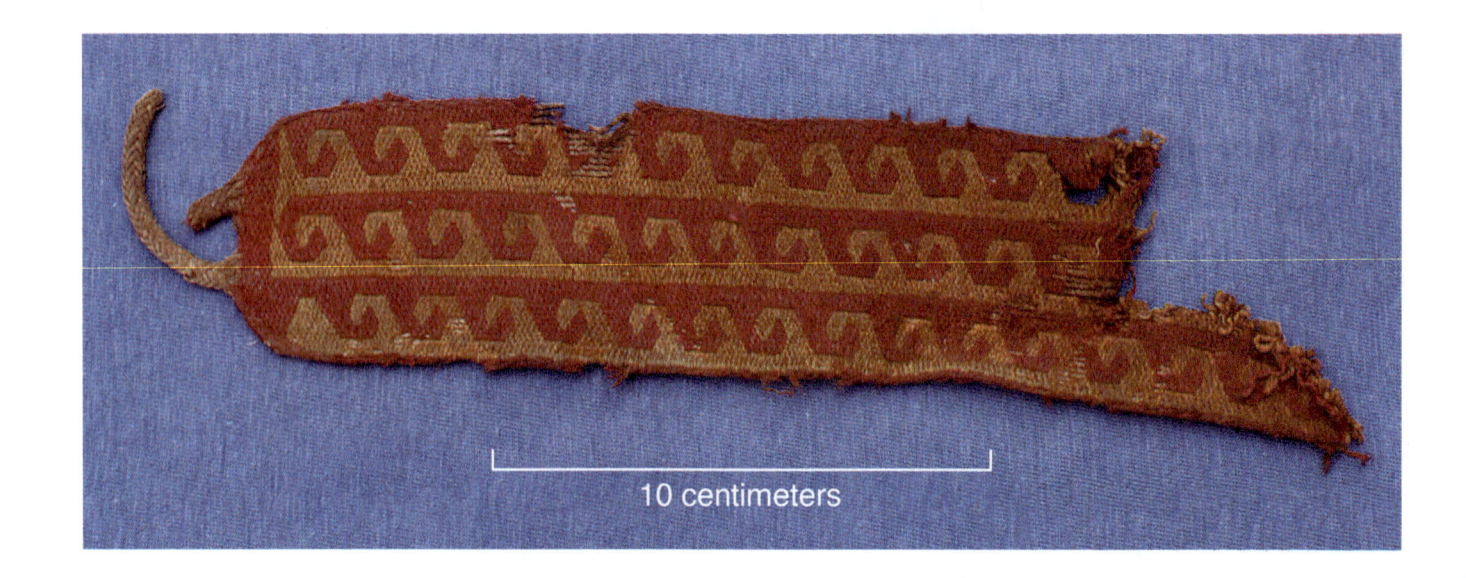

Figure 5.23. A band of eccentric slit tapestry with edge embroidery, found in Structure 5. It features a design of waves or hooked spirals in gold on red.

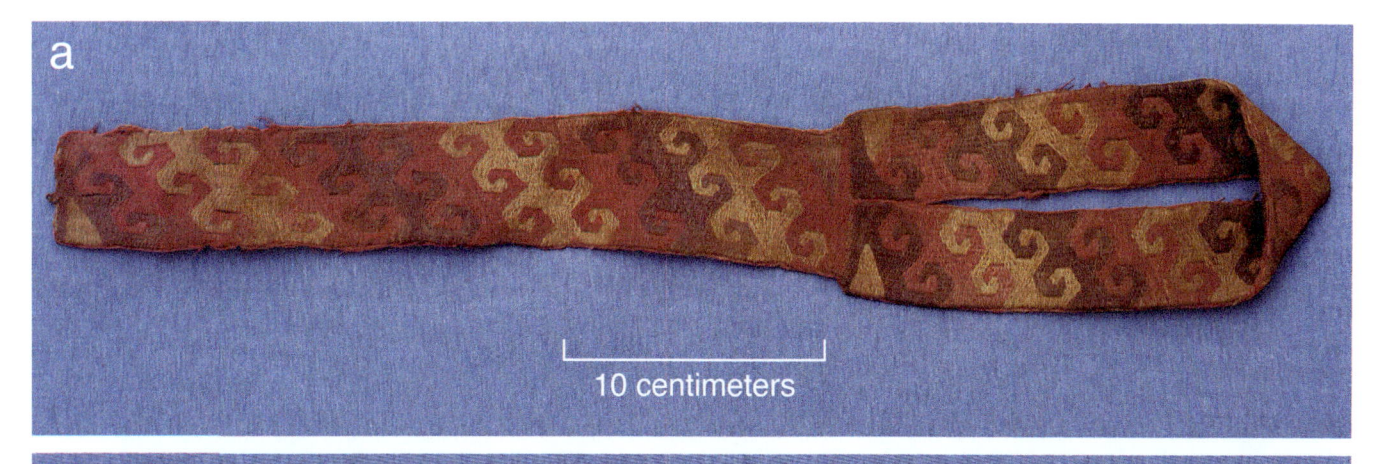

Figure 5.24. A textile consisting of two bands of eccentric slit tapestry found in Structure 5. Both ends of one band are sewn to one end of the other band. (a) The complete textile. (b) Close-up of the joint between bands.

Figure 5.25. A coarse plain weave bag that contained cotton seeds. This bag was found inside Workbasket #1 of Structure 5, which the looters left on the floor of the burial cist.

Figure 5.26. A coarse plain weave cloth, found wrapped around Workbasket #1 of Structure 5.

above) was found lying on the floor of Structure 5. This plain cloth, plain weave measured 80 x 60 cm and had two side selvages; the warp and weft were both of S-spun yarn. The texture of this coarse cloth was very uneven.

Textile 165 is a plain cloth, plain weave bag (Figure 5.27). This bag was found inside a gourd bowl (see Figure 5.7) found near the partial remains of a woman at the bottom of Structure 5. The warp, weft, and heading cord of the bag are cotton; the cloth was a full web, folded in half from side selvage to side selvage. The term "heading cord" refers to the heavy threads at the top and bottom of a web that are tied to the loom bars and serve to reinforce the edge or selvage. At the top of the bag, there is a running stitch of paired yarns, 2 cm apart.

Textile 172a (Figure 5.28a) is a blue and white warp-stripe plain weave (180 x 28.5 cm).

Textile 172c (Figure 5.28b) is a warp-stripe plain weave (49 x 19 cm). Warp and weft are cotton, S-spun, and the yarn is highly variable in thickness. The design consists of a 5 cm wide white stripe followed by a 5 cm brown stripe, an 8.5 cm white stripe, an 11 cm brown stripe, and finally a 13 cm white stripe.

Textile 172b is a plain weave "practice web" featuring embroidered fish (Figure 5.28c). The warp and weft are cotton and S-spun; the decorative yarn is wool, Z-spun and S-twisted. The brocade-like embroidery features two red and two brownish-yellow yarns. Three of the four fish point upward; one (upper left) faces down. The embroidered fish are confined to an area that measures 3 x 2 cm.

Textile 172d (Figure 5.29) is a plain weave cloth with a very thick cord attached (53 x 26 cm). The warp and weft are cotton, S-spun. The cord is 1.9 cm thick and attached through a hole at the selvage corner. The cord (29 cm long) is a four-strand round braid made of very large bundles of white S-spun yarns.

Textile 185 is a warp-stripe plain weave cotton cloth (90 x 48 cm) featuring brown and white stripes (Figure 5.30). The 48 cm width is the actual loom dimension.

Textile 189 (Figure 5.31) is a plain cloth, plain weave textile that was wrapped around a buried infant. The infant was accompanied by 20 *Perumytilus* shells and a glossy *lúcuma* seed, carved into a miniature vessel.

Textile 195 (Figure 5.32) is a band with a warp made of fern stipes; this textile is an example of weft-wrapping or

Figure 5.27. The remains of a possible cotton cloth bag, found inside a gourd vessel associated with a female mummy left in the bottom of Structure 5.

Figure 5.28. Textile remains from Structure 5. (a) A blue and white striped plain weave cotton cloth. (b) A brown striped plain weave cotton cloth. (c) A "practice web" with fish embroidered in woolen yarn on a cotton cloth.

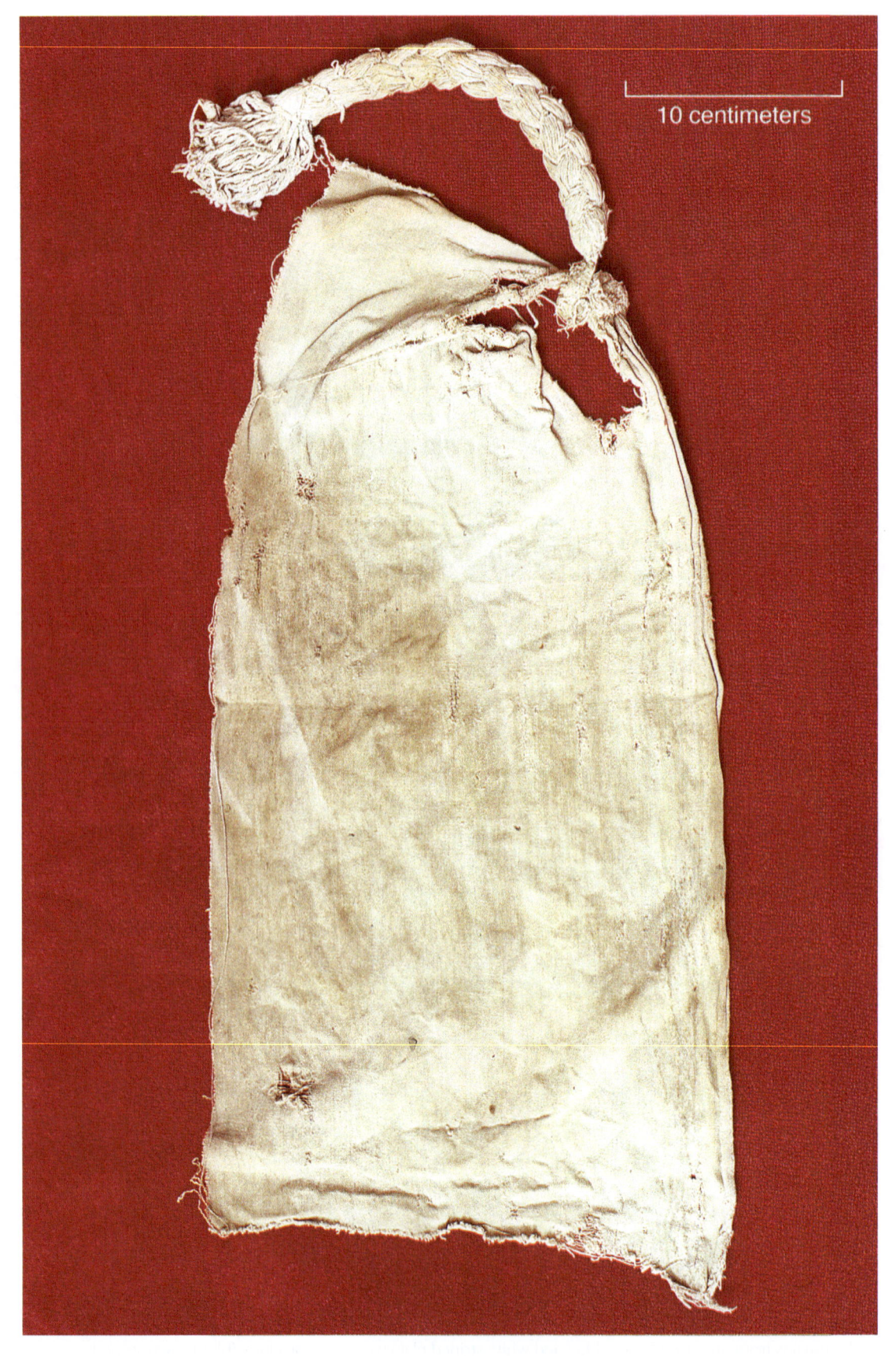

Figure 5.29. A plain weave cotton cloth from Structure 5. A section of thick cord is attached.

Figure 5.30. A warp-stripe plain weave cotton cloth, with alternating brown and white stripes, associated with Structure 5.

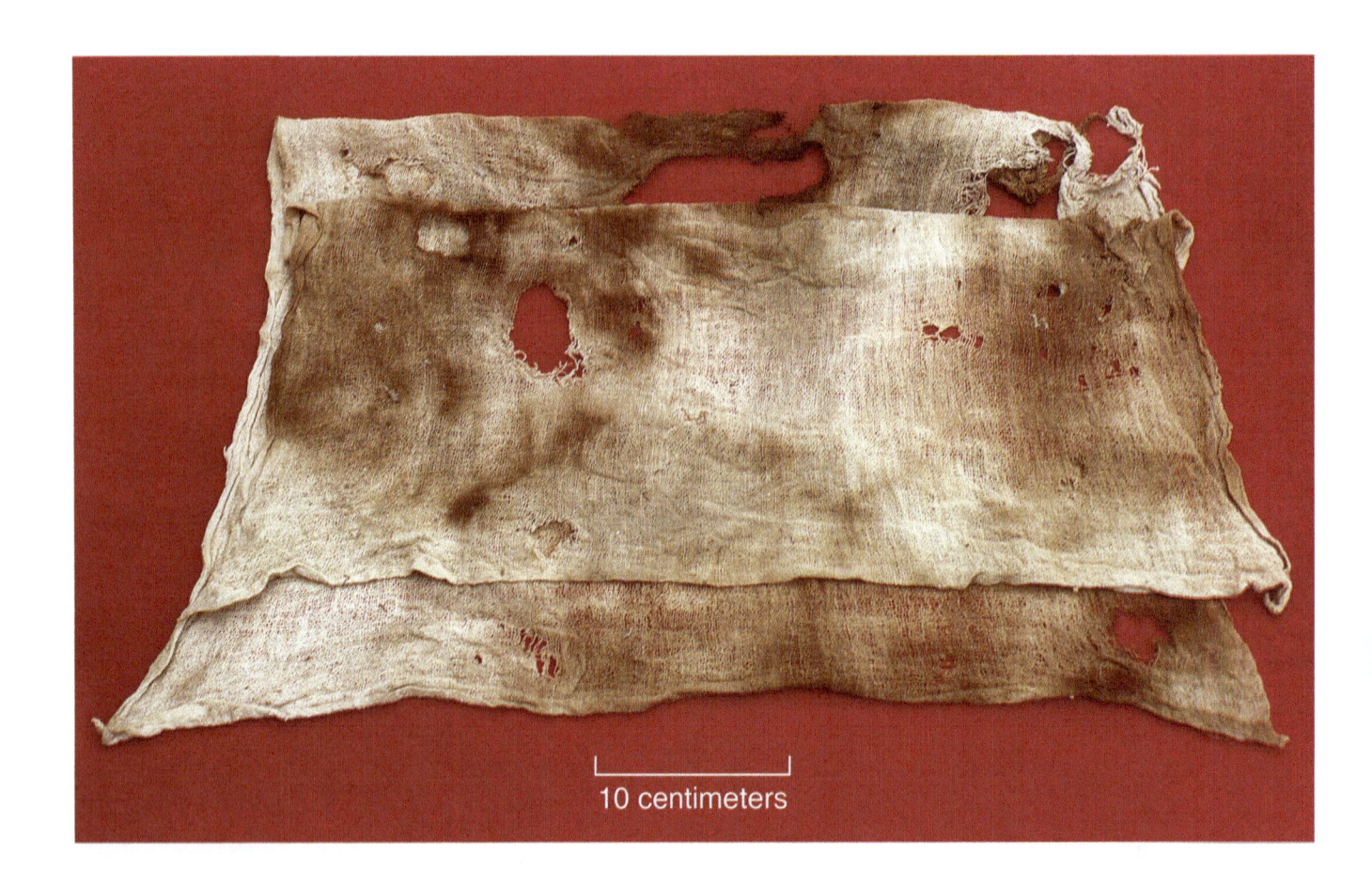

Figure 5.31. A plain weave textile, associated with an infant buried in Structure 5.

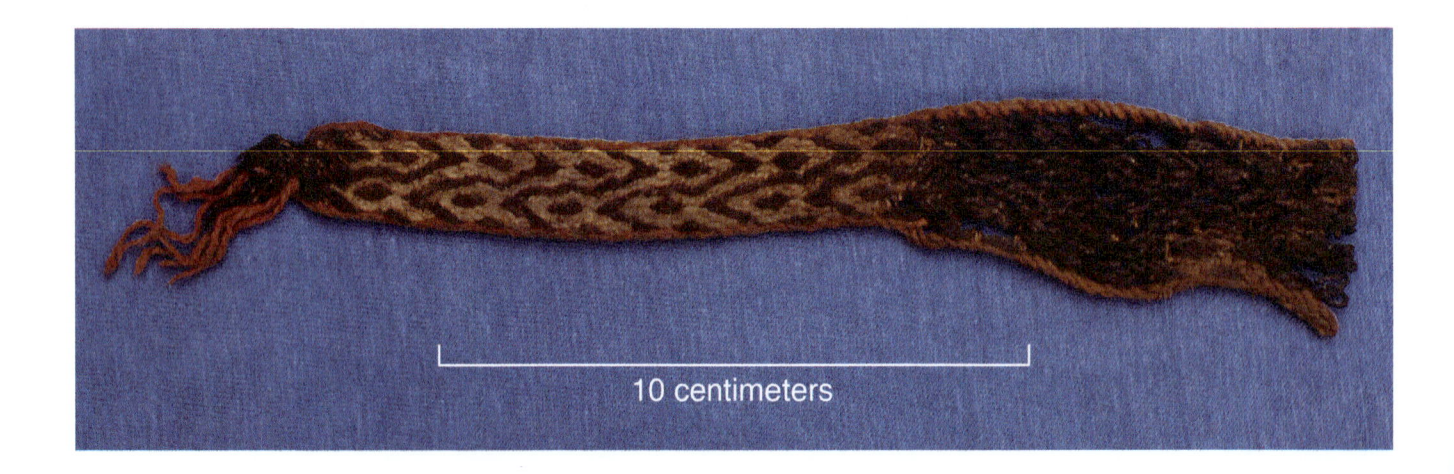

Figure 5.32. A narrow wool band with a warp of fern stipes and weft-wrapping *soumak*, found in Structure 5.

soumak. The weft-wrapping (Z-S) was composed of garnet, yellow, and black wool yarns. The wool yarn design is in black and gold/yellow wool, and there is a red line at the edges. The band narrows at one end, where a cord is attached. The cord is torn off at the other end and the warp is missing, but the weft-wrapping yarns all turn back, leaving a neatly squared-off end that may be original. The design on this band seems to be stylized interlocking elements, possibly swimming fish.

Textile 199 is a plain cloth, plain weave. This is an orange-brown cotton textile, bearing smears of red pigment. The actual loom dimensions would have been 21 x 19 cm (Figure 5.33).

T210 is a fragment of a diagonal twill plaited grass band (11 x 5.8 cm). The flattened grass elements are 3 mm wide. Sets of elements were turned back on opposite sides (two over, two under), then back into the previous weave.

T211 is a 24 cm long grass band, 5.2 cm wide. This is a twill plaited band that used grass elements 2.8 mm wide.

T217a is a diagonal twill plaited basketry band, 57 cm long and 7.5 cm wide. It was made from grass stems 3 mm wide and has simple turn-back edging, with one end torn. The alternate element sets are turned back at 90 degrees on each side; it is woven over two, then under two.

T217b is a diagonal twill plaited basketry band measures 66 x 2.5 cm. It is identical in construction to Specimen T217a.

Workbaskets

For more than a century, Peruvian archaeologists have been finding well-preserved twill workbaskets in the graves of women and girls (e.g., Donnan 1995; Dorsey 1894; Dransart 2020; Hutchinson 1874; Price et al. 2015; and Squier 1967[1869]). As Costin notes (2016:35–36), "Regarding the sex/gender of LIP [Late Intermediate Period] domestic textile producers, we can turn to the burial data. Of sexed adults from a range of cemeteries throughout the empire, only females had tools related to textile production (loom parts, weaving baskets, and/or spindle whorls), although not all female burials contained these items." As noted by Price et al. (2015:82), "There is clear evidence from the baskets and the spindles of use-wear and repair, indicating that workbaskets served practical utilitarian functions and were not made especially and specifically for purposes of burial. It seems reasonable to assume that the majority of workbaskets were indeed the personal possessions of the deceased. Nonetheless, the contents of the baskets must be considered dynamic in that materials may have been added or removed in preparation for burial."

Most of the Cerro Azul twill workbaskets reinforce Costin's, Donnan's, and Price et al.'s conclusions—workbaskets typically contained items for spinning, weaving, and sewing as well as unfinished textiles and cords. The workbaskets that were in poor condition were often tied up in a cloth that kept the basket and its contents together (e.g., Figure 5.34).

Figure 5.34 shows the workbasket found at the bottom of the Structure 5 burial cist near the partial remains of a woman.

Workbasket #1 (Figure 5.34) is 42 cm long, 23 cm wide, and 8.0 cm high. The top panel (or workbasket lid) has five split canes, sometimes called splints or stiffeners; each is 42 cm long and 10 mm wide. The bottom (or floor) of the basket had been constructed the same way; the side panels differ in that each has only three splints.

When found, this workbasket (Figure 5.34a) was wrapped in a coarse cotton cloth, the color of wheat (see Figure 5.26); the cloth had been tied with an overhand knot. Inside we found the following items:

—a cloth bag that contained cotton seeds (Specimen T156; see Figure 5.25)
—a wad of white cotton (14 x 6 cm) weighing 4.5 g
—a wad of brown cotton (5 x 4 cm) weighing 4 g. Its Munsell color was 7.5 YR 5/6 ("strong brown")
—four spindle whorls, as follows (see Figure 5.35a–d).
  · *a teardrop-shaped Camacho Black whorl* with a height of 11.6 mm, a diameter of 15.8 mm, a hole diameter of 3.5 mm, and a weight of 4.5 g (Figure 5.35a).
  · *a whorl with a shape similar to a piece of wood turned on a lathe* (Figure 5.35b). The top of the whorl is unpainted, while the bottom is painted red (7.5 YR 5/8, "weak red"). The whorl's height is 16.5 mm, its diameter 11.7 mm, its hole diameter 3.5 mm, and its weight 2.5 g.
  · *two whorls, carinated, unburnished, and grayish brown in color* (Figure 5.35c, d). Both whorls are 16.2 mm high, their diameter is 14.7 mm, and their hole diameter is 3.5 mm. The weight of each whorl is 3.5 g.
—five painted spindles, three of which are painted with the same "barcode" (i.e. the same sequence of lines and bands) (Figure 5.35)
—two spindles (one 27.7 cm long and 3.3 mm in diameter, the other 28.8 cm long and 3.2 mm in diameter) and three broken spindles (one 25.7 cm

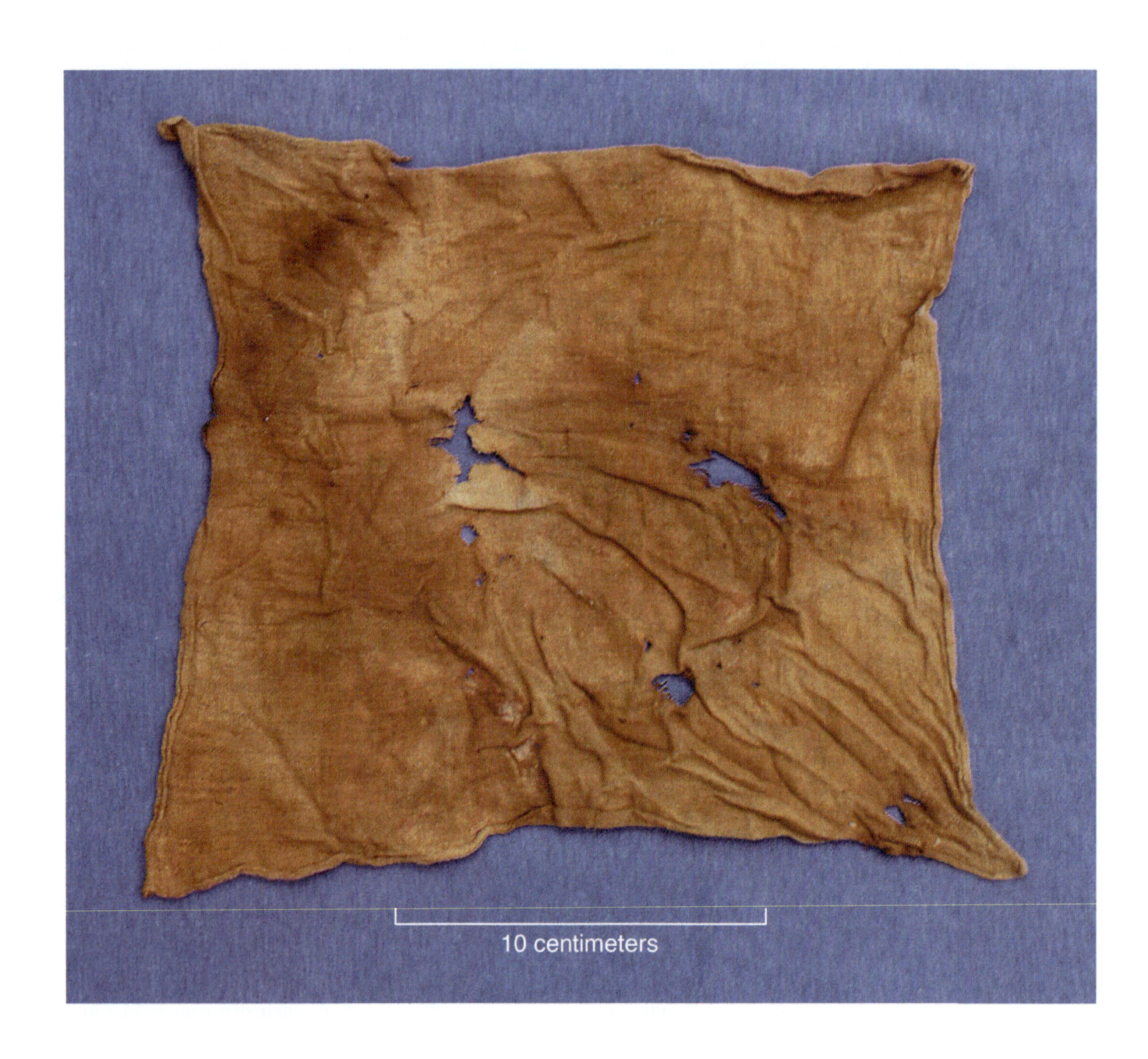

Figure 5.33. A plain weave cotton cloth from Structure 5.

Figure 5.34. Workbasket #1 was found lying at the bottom of the Structure 5 burial cist. (a) The workbasket as we discovered it, wrapped in a cloth (see Figure 5.26). (b) The same basket with the cloth wrapping removed.

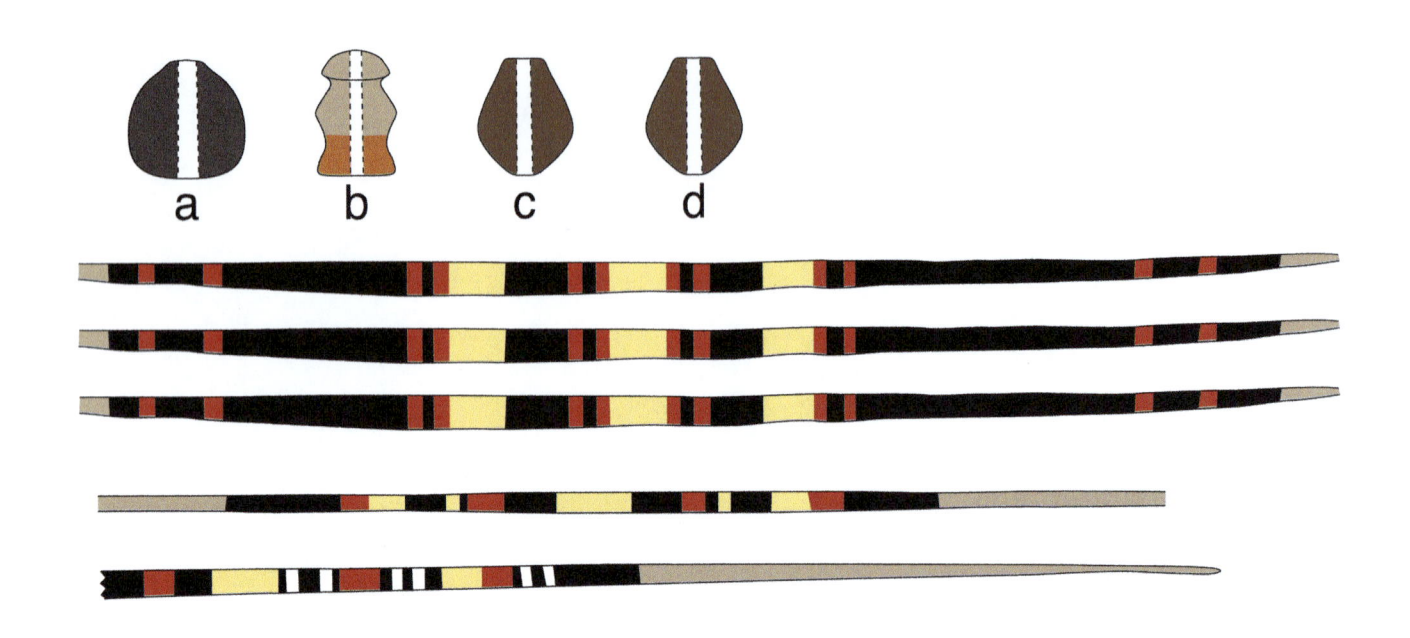

Figure 5.35. Four spindle whorls (a–d) and five spindles, found inside Workbasket #1 of Structure 5. Note that three of the spindles are painted with the same barcode, while the others are similar in their choice of colors.

long and 3.7 mm in diameter, the second 21.5 cm long and 3.1 mm in diameter, and the third 15.8 cm long and 3.4 mm in diameter).

—one *Opuntia* spine, 9.6 cm long and 2.1 mm in diameter

We were struck by the three spindles painted with the identical barcode; it suggested that each woman used such a code to identify her spindles so that she could retain them in settings when multiple women worked together (Marcus 2016a).

Workbasket #2 (Figure 5.36) was found among the looters' debris at the bottom of the Structure 5 cist. This workbasket measures 42 cm in length, 24 cm in width, and 8 cm in height. Like Workbasket #1, this basket's lid had five splints or stiffeners. It differs from Workbasket #1 in that its lid had a string attached with which it could be tied shut.

Workbasket #2 contained very few items, possibly because most of them fell out when the looters disturbed it. Among the contents were three *Opuntia* spines (one complete spine measured 12.8 cm long and was 2 mm in diameter).

Also present in the basket were four balls of camelid wool yarn. One was 3 cm in diameter and weighed 2.5 g; the Munsell color of the yarn was 2.5 YR 2/4 ("dark reddish brown"). The second weighed 2.5 g and was 2 cm in diameter; its Munsell color was 7.5 YR 6/6 ("reddish yellow"). The third was 3 cm in diameter and consisted of off-white, very fine yarn weighing 4 g. The fourth ball was brown wool, 7.5 YR 5/4 ("brown"), and weighed 4 g.

In addition to the four yarn balls that were still inside the workbasket, we found five loose woolen yarn balls nearby. The first was 2.5 YR 2/2 ("very dusky red") and 3.2 cm in diameter, weighing 3.5 g. The second was 2.5 YR 2/2 ("very dusky red") and 3 cm in diameter, weighing 3 g. The third was 2.5 YR 2/2 ("very dusky red") and 2 cm in diameter, weighing 1 g. The fourth ball was 2.5 YR 2/2 ("very dusky red") and 1.5 cm in diameter, weighing < 1 g. The fifth was

Figure 5.36. Workbasket #2, found at the bottom of the Structure 5 burial cist.

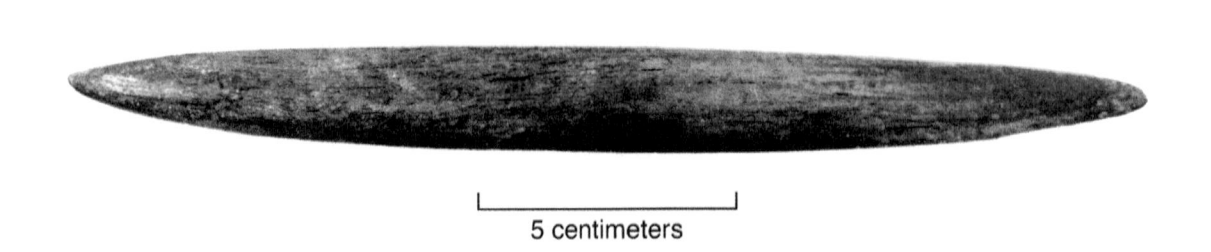

Figure 5.37. A *kallwa*, or weaving sword, found inside Structure 5.

7.5 YR 6/8 ("reddish yellow") and 1 cm in diameter, weighing < 1 g. Since we found no evidence that the occupants of Cerro Azul raised camelids (Glew and Flannery 2016a; Marcus et al. 1999), we presume that these yarn balls were received in trade (A. Rowe 1984:25; Topic 1982:163).

Weaving Sword

We also found a *kallwa* or weaving sword (*espada*) loose in the cist; it was 21.1 cm long and may have been made of chonta wood (Figure 5.37). When weaving was done on a backstrap loom, such *kallwa* were used to press down the weft yarns, allowing for a wider shed to facilitate hand manipulations. Larger weaving tools such as this would usually be left outside a woman's mummy bundle because they would likely bend or break if wrapped inside the multiple layers of a *fardo* (e.g., Cock and Goycochea Díaz 2004; Safford 1917; and Squier 1967[1869]).

Comments on Structure 5

As was the case with Structure 4, we have reason to suspect that Structure 5 once contained both men and women—men with their nets and slings, on the one hand, and women with their spindles, whorls, needles, and yarn balls, on the other hand. Unfortunately, owing to the extensive looting, there were many objects we could not associate with either men or women.

One of the surprising aspects of Structure 5 was the diversity of objects made of metal. There were packets of silver foil lodged in the mouths, silver tweezers, pieces of copper cut from a disc, and a piece of silver held in a woman's hand. Most of the foil packets in Structure 5 seem to have been silver, unlike the exclusive use of copper that Kroeber (1937:264) documented in Burial K4 at Cerro Azul. Because all 12 individuals in his Burial K4 had pieces of copper in their mouths, Kroeber came to regard copper as a contribution made by mourners, rather than a sign of the deceased's status. This makes good sense because it is obvious that the deceased could not place the metal in his or her own mouth. The presence of several silver items in Structure 5 may signal that the deceased and their families might have been of slightly higher status than anyone Kroeber encountered.

Chapter 6

The Structure 6 Burial Cist

The third looted cist we excavated in Quebrada 5a was Structure 6 (Figures 4.4, 6.1). Based on the fragmentary skeletal remains inside the cist and adjacent to it, this cist may have contained as many as eight adults and one child. According to biological anthropologist Sonia Guillén, the cranium of one of the adults—that of a young woman— shows porotic hyperostosis in the occipital bone and possible evidence of trephination.

Given that Structures 4 and 5 had bulrush mats lining their walls and floors, we were expecting the same to be true of Structure 6. Instead, the walls of Structure 6 were lined with white clay coated with a layer of mud plaster. Another difference was that Structure 6 contained large quantities of white sand, which served as an effective matrix for desiccation and preservation.

These construction differences are noteworthy, but our sample is too small to reveal the factors that determined whether a cist would be stone-lined, clay-lined, mat-lined, mud-plastered, or treated in some other way. As early as the nineteenth century, archaeologists were aware of these differences in cist construction. Without attempting to explain such differences, early investigators described the variation in cist construction and documented the number of individuals per cist (Dorsey 1894; Hutchinson 1874; Reiss and Stübel 1880–1887). Many of the differences were synchronic, not diachronic.

As was true of Structure 5, the floor of Structure 6 was covered with a thick layer of *pacay* leaves (Figure 6.2); some of these leaves were found above the floor mats and some below. Together, the leaves and mats provided a clean and soft surface for the mummy bundles.

Even though looters had greatly disturbed the contents of Structure 6, there was still much to salvage and document. Among the items were loose cords, textiles, half a mace head, several slings and bolas, grinding stones, a workbasket with items for both sewing and weaving, and pottery vessels.

Most of the human remains had been tossed unceremoniously to one side of the cist (Figures 6.3, 6.4, 6.5). These scattered remains were from several mummy bundles, making it impossible to link specific items to the

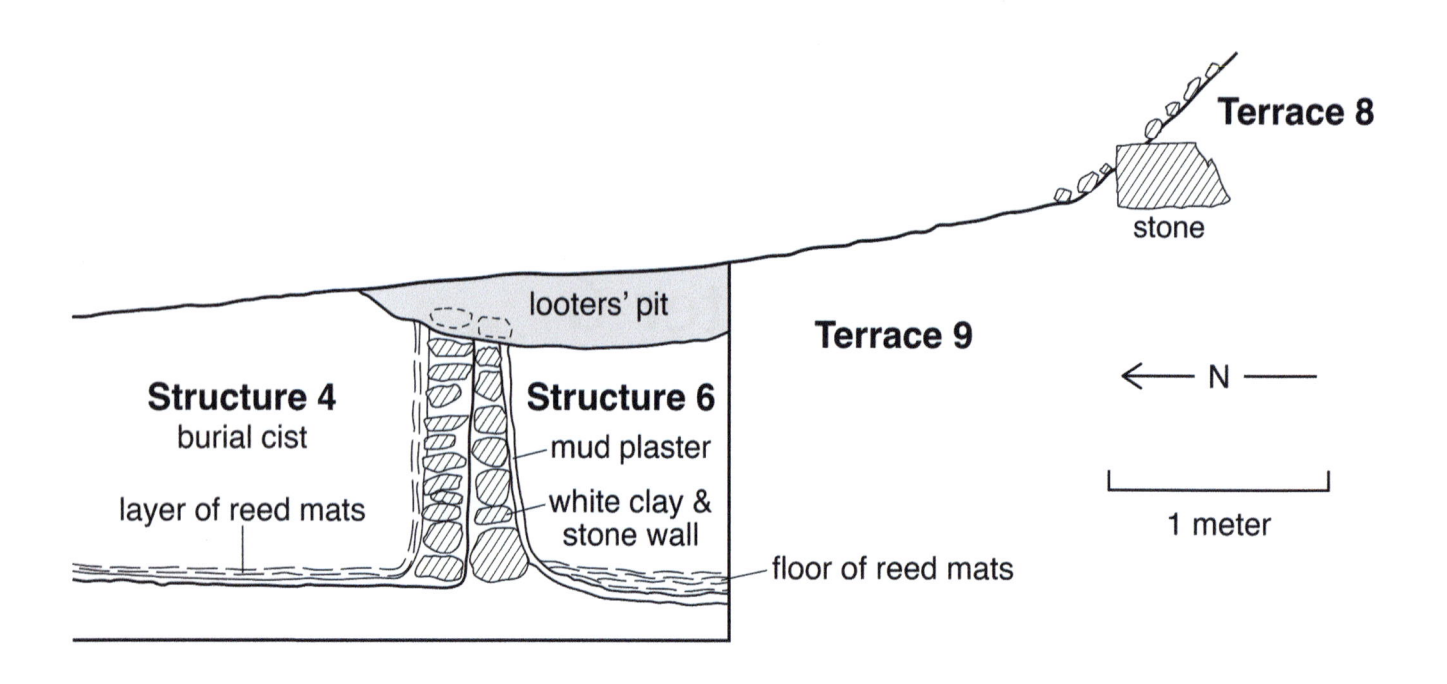

Figure 6.1. A north-south cross section of Terrace 9 in Quebrada 5a at Cerro Azul. Shown are Structure 4, a looters' pit, Structure 6, and the base of Terrace 8.

Figure 6.2. Leaves of *pacay* (*Inga* sp.) from the floor of the Structure 6 burial cist.

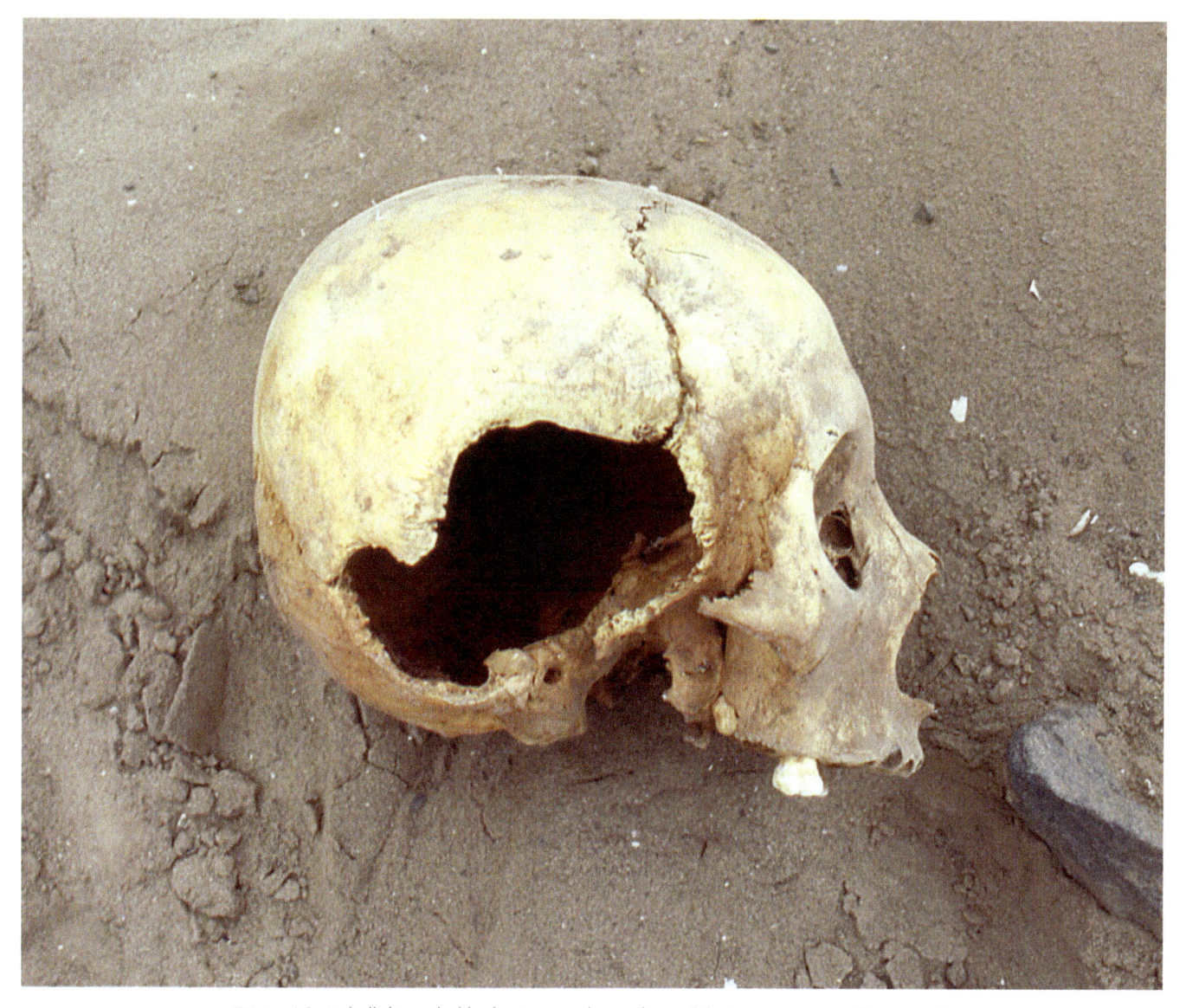

Figure 6.3. A skull discarded by looters on the surface of the terrace next to Structure 6.

remaining collection of bones still in the cist. On the surface of the terrace we recovered a skull, some lower limbs with the ankles tied together, and a forearm with fabric tied around the wrist. We also found hands that had string tied around each finger. It appears that individuals tightly wrapped in *fardos* (cloth bundles) were more likely to have been treated in this way.

Discarded on the surface near Structure 6 was an item constructed of wood and *caña brava* (*Gynerium sagittatum*). It appeared that this item was either the roof of the cist or part of a litter that had supported one of the burials (Figure 6.6a, b). It is worth noting that at Pachacamac and Ancón, items with similar construction were used as roofs (e.g., Dorsey 1894; Safford 1917; and Shimada et al. 2022). In addition, mats were associated with some of the burials at Cerro Azul (e.g., Figures 4.7, 4.8, and 6.7).

We also found a possible "pillow," identified by botanist C. Earle Smith, Jr. as having been made from bundles of willow twigs and *pacay* rachises (Figure 6.8).

Ceramic Vessels

We found two ceramic vessels in Structure 6. The miniature jar shown in Figure 6.9 was broken when discovered. It is a Camacho Black vessel with loop handles. The height is ca. 8 cm and the rim diameter ca. 2 cm. The exterior surface was burnished, and in those burnished areas the surface varies

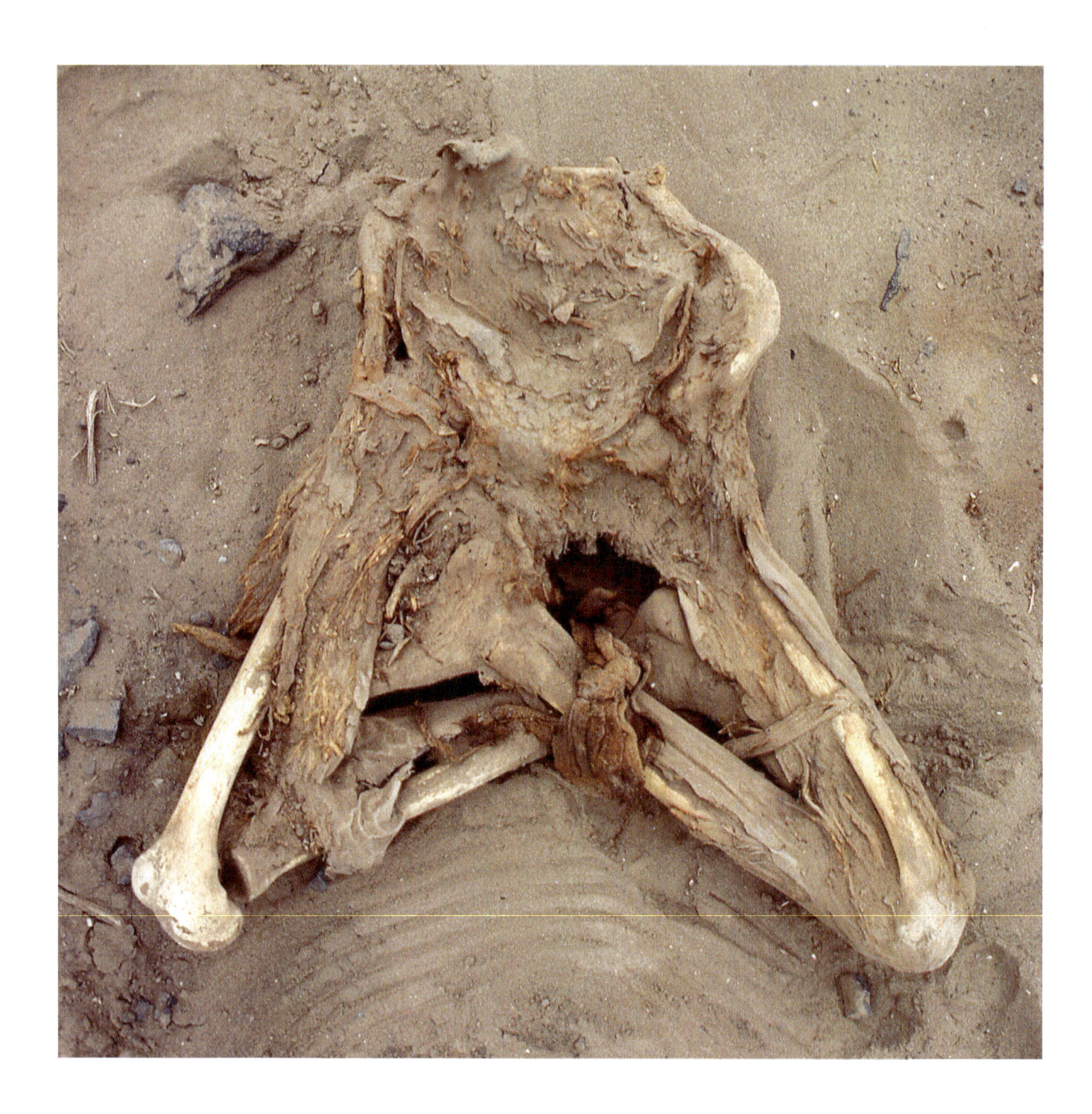

Figure 6.4. The lower half of a partially mummified individual whose ankles had been tied together with a cloth, discarded by looters next to Structure 6.

Figure 6.5. Remains of a second individual discarded by looters next to Structure 6. Evidently the wrists had been tied together with a cloth.

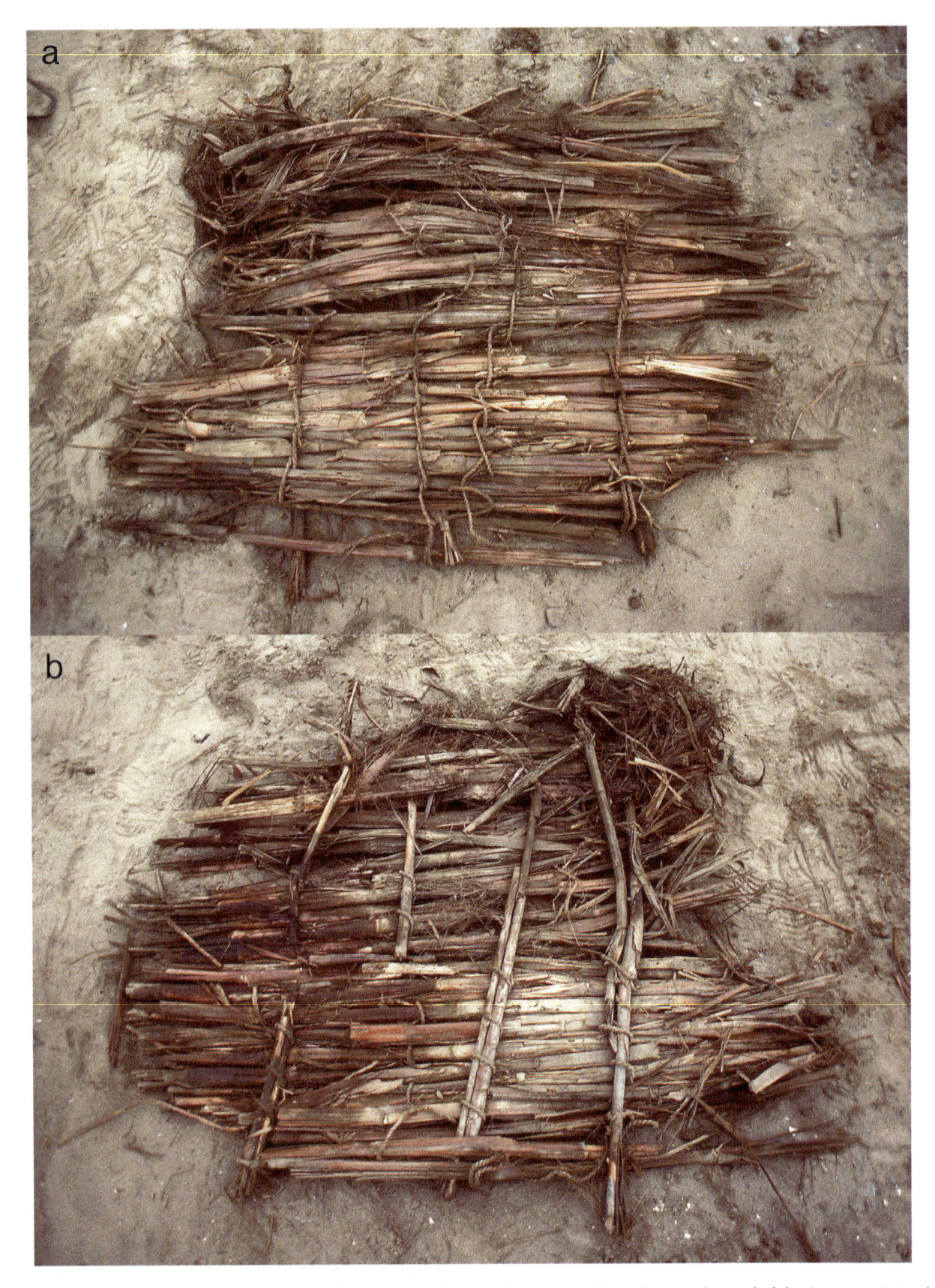

Figure 6.6. Two views of a damaged cane and wood construction that may have been either a litter or the roof of the Structure 6 cist. (a) the upper surface (or top). (b) the under surface (or bottom).

Figure 6.7. Remains of a mat found inside Structure 6.

Figure 6.8. This bundle of willow twigs, found lying on the floor of Structure 6, may have served as a pillow for one of the deceased.

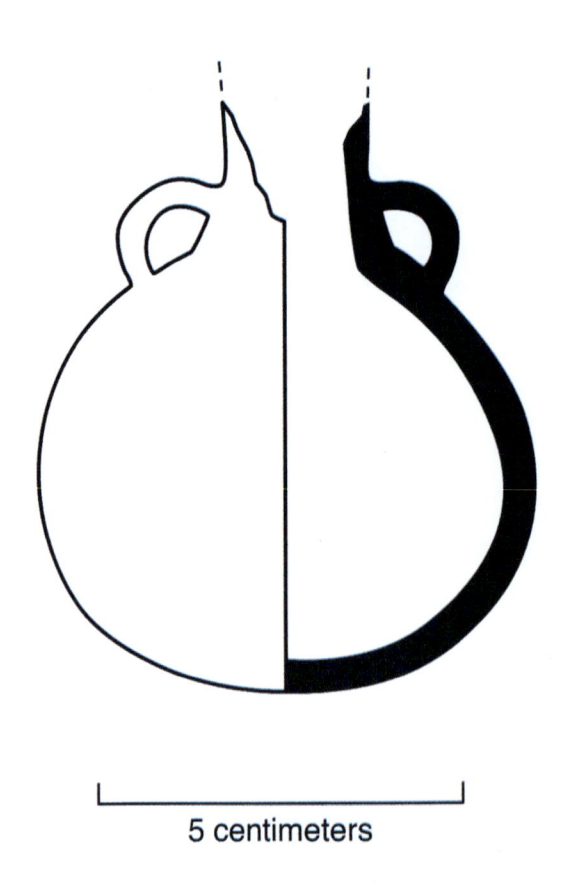

Figure 6.9. A Camacho Black miniature jar, one of two vessels found inside Structure 6.

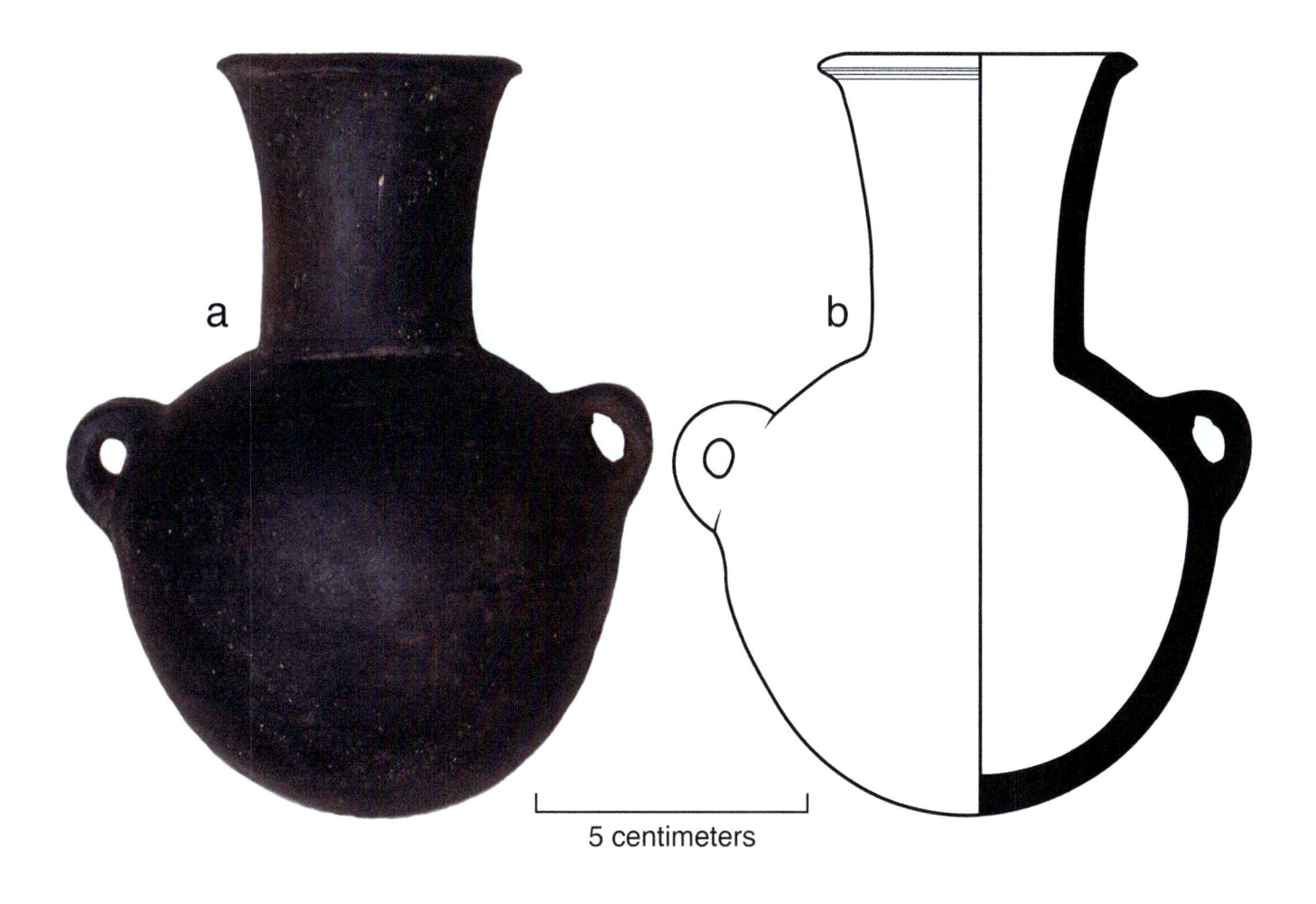

Figure 6.10. Photo and drawing of a Camacho Black miniature jar, the second of two vessels found inside Structure 6.

in color from 2.5 YN 2/0 ("black") to 2.5 YN 3/0 ("very dark gray") to 2.5 YN 4/0 ("dark gray"). It appears likely that 2.5 YN 2/0 ("black") was the intended color. The clay body displays different shades of gray, 10 YR 6/1 ("light gray") to 10 YR 5/1 ("gray").

The second vessel in Structure 6 was a Camacho Black miniature jar with a tall funnel neck and two handles (Figure 6.10a, b). Its height is 13.5 cm, and its rim diameter 5.7 cm. Its wall thickness is 5–6 mm, and its handles are 1.0 cm wide. The surface color is mostly jet black, with an occasional firing cloud of dark reddish brown or brownish gray.

Metal Artifacts

Six pieces of metal were found loose in Structure 6. Figure 6.11a shows a rectangular piece of a silver sheet measuring 6.2 x 3 cm. Figure 6.11b is a 6.2 x 1.8 cm piece of silver foil. Figure 6.11c, also silver foil, is 0.33 mm thick and measures 3.1 x 1.2 cm. Together, 6.11b and 6.11c weigh 3 g. At 6.11d, e, and f we see three silver pieces that may have been cut from the same disc. The piece at 6.11d is folded over, measures 3 x 2 cm, and is 1.0 mm thick; the piece at 6.11e measures 2.5 x 2 cm, and the item at 6.11f measures 2.5 x 1.5 cm. These last two pieces combined have a total weight of 4.0 g (Specimen 26).

Mace Head

We found a broken mace head inside Structure 6. Had it been complete, it would likely have measured 7.5 cm in diameter (Figure 6.12a). The mace was 4 cm thick and made of a bluish black stone. The hole for its handle had a diameter

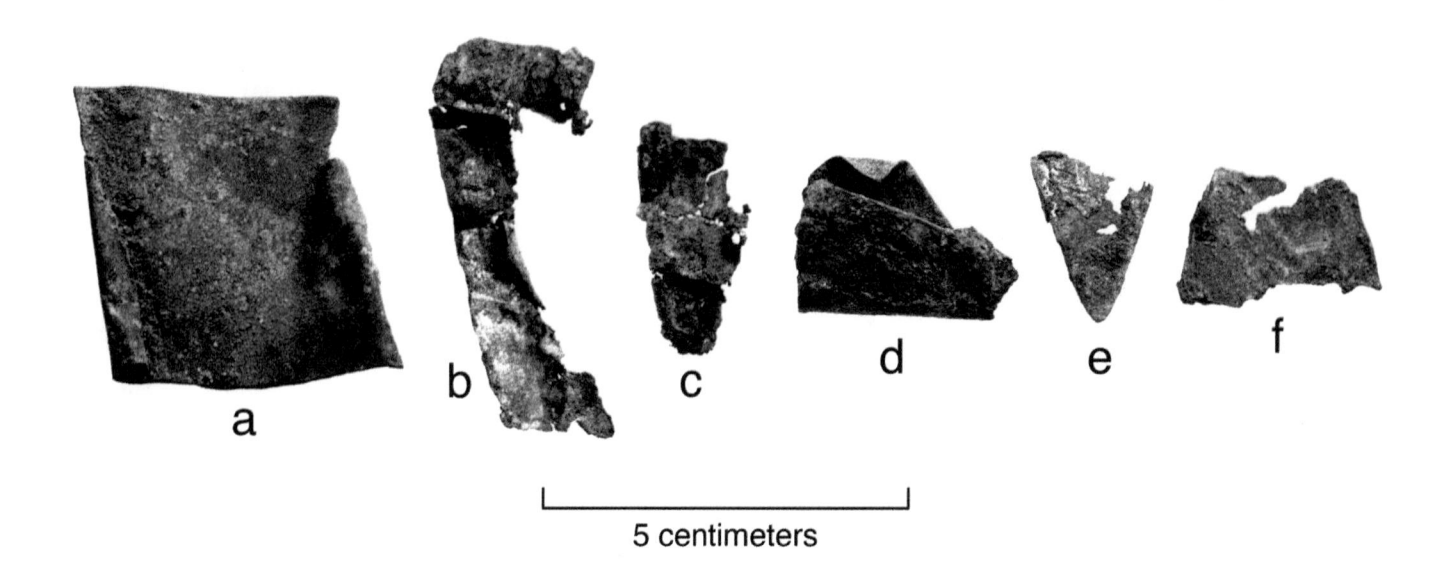

Figure 6.11. Six pieces of silver or silver foil, found loose in the Structure 6 burial cist. It is possible that some or all of these pieces had been inserted into the mouths of the deceased, and were somehow overlooked by the looters.

of ca. 3 cm and was biconically drilled. This mace head is the only one known so far from Cerro Azul. John Hyslop (1985) discovered a complete mace head in the piedmont of the Cañete Valley, some six kilometers from Inkawasi (Figure 6.12b).

Slings

A number of slings were found in and around Structure 6. See Figure 5.18a for an example of a colorful design on a sling; it consists of diamonds in red, beige, yellowish brown, and dark brown wool. Another sling features a 6.5 cm long decoration of black diamonds inside red diamonds (Figure 5.18b); this particular sling is made of a tough plant fiber with cotton fibers wrapped around it. Still another sling had a slit cradle for launching large projectiles.

Figure 6.13 shows an example of a webbed cradle. In addition to slings, we recovered a few stones that could have been used either as slingstones (Figure 6.14a) or inserted into the stone-carrying loops of bolas (Figure 6.14b).

Bolas

Structure 6 yielded two varieties of bolas: two-stone and three-stone. The bolas illustrated in Figure 6.15 seems to be of the former variety, given the presence of two loops. Note that one of the two loops (on the right) has been repaired with a Z-twisted plant fiber; a close-up of that repair can be seen in Figure 6.16. The fiber used to make this particular bolas was called *cabuya* by our workmen. Each of the two cords leading to a loop runs for ca. 1.03 m.

When we first examined the bolas shown in Figure 6.17, we thought that it might originally have had three loops, with the third loop pulled out of place by the looters. Further analysis convinced us that the apparent loop on the long cord more likely resulted from tying the bolas around a burial; it was, in other words, a two-stone bolas. Each loop cord was 6 mm in diameter and 50 cm long, and each loop could have held a stone approximately 8–10 cm in diameter.

Figure 6.18 shows two more examples of bolas; the fragment in Figure 6.18a could have held stones 7.5 cm in diameter.

Camelid Bone

Camelid bones were included with some of the Cerro Azul burials. In Structure 6 we found one camelid first phalanx in the looters' debris (Glew and Flannery 2016a:300).

Grinding Stones

Figure 6.19 shows two grinding stones. We do not know whether these stones were used by one of the deceased individuals while alive, or used by mourners to prepare a funerary meal.

Loom

In the Structure 6 burial cist we found all the parts composing an *awana* or loom (Specimen 127). These loom parts had been carefully stored together, tied up with a cotton cord that had been wrapped around them some nine times (Figure 6.20). Included were the following:
— one *oceana kallwa*, 51.6 cm long, with a maximum width of 2.7 cm; it was 9 mm thick and tapered at both ends.
— one mini *qumacha* or *quma*, 63.4 cm long and 6.5 mm in diameter.
— one possible *machana* made of *caña brava*, 60.5 cm long and 14 mm diameter.
— four *akllana caspi* (or *mini quma*), whose dimesions were:
    48.2 cm long, 10.6 mm in diameter;
    51.2 cm long, 12.7 mm in diameter;
    57.8 cm long, 14.1 mm in diameter; and
    60.0 cm long, 12.0 mm in diameter.

To learn more about this prehistoric loom and its component parts, I decided to show it to a local woman who was a monolingual Quechua speaker. On the day I approached her she was sitting on the dusty, vegetationless soil in her dooryard, weaving on her backstrap loom. I watched her for several minutes as she leaned forward, then backward, all the while working on a narrow textile. She referred to the small portable loom she was using as a *chumpi awana* or "belt loom."

I then asked her to identify the parts of the loom found inside Structure 6 (see Figure 6.21a, b). She identified Item #1 as the *aparina* or backstrap that rests on the weaver's lower back (see Bennett and Bird [1949:266] for their original illustration of an Andean loom). The backstrap, she said,

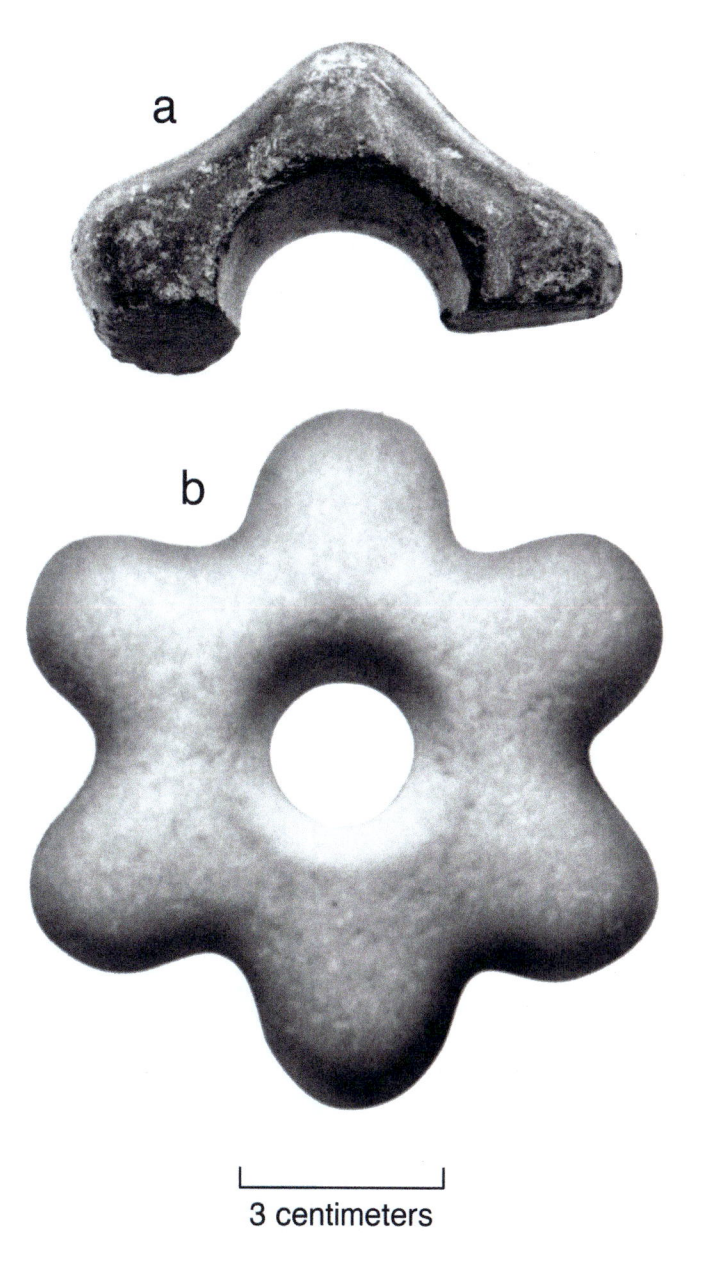

Figure 6.12. Two stone mace heads from the Cañete Valley. (a) Half of a broken mace head from Structure 6, Terrace 9, Quebrada 5a, Cerro Azul. (b) A complete mace head, found by John Hyslop (1985: Fig. 19) some six kilometers from Inkawasi, a site upriver in the Lunahuaná polity.

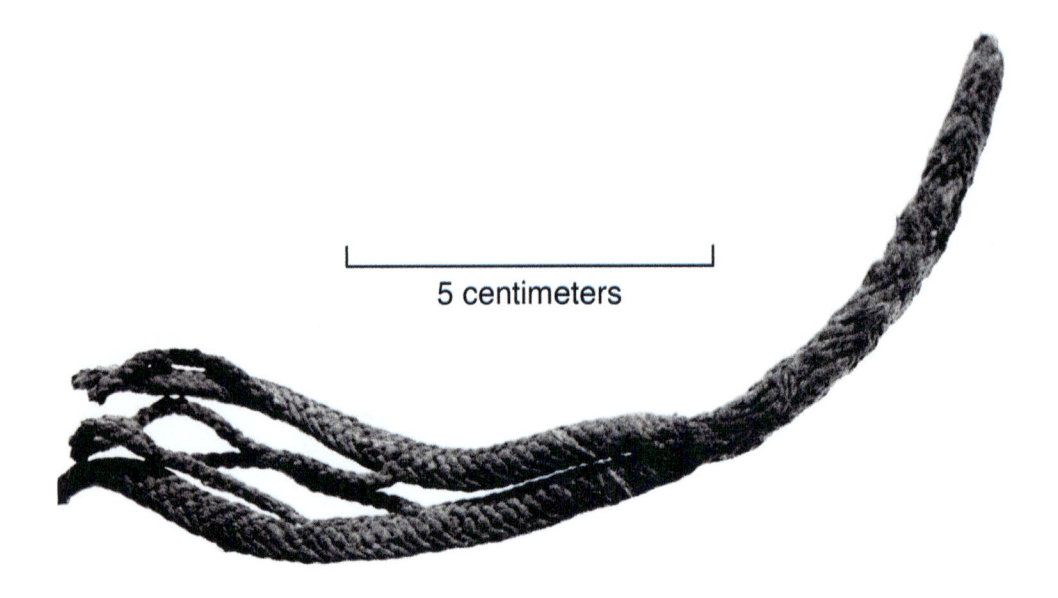

Figure 6.13. Webbed cradle from a sling found in Structure 6.

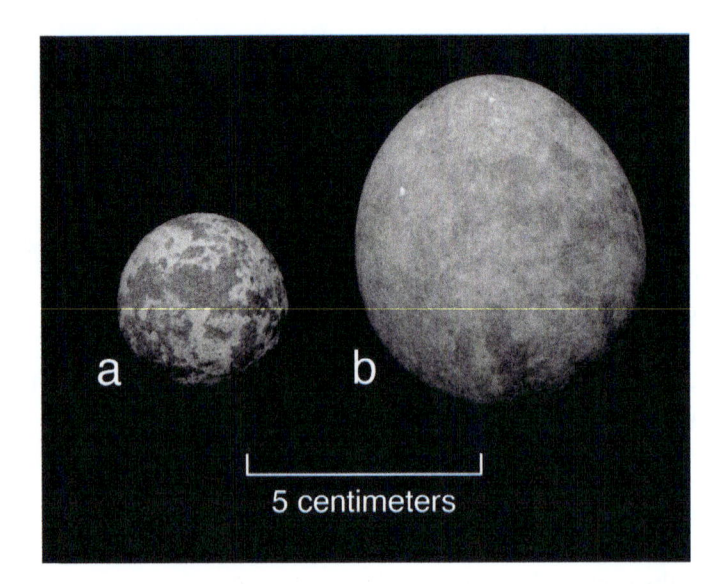

Figure 6.14. Two smooth, spherical stones from Cerro Azul. (a) A possible slingstone. (b) A larger stone, suitable for insertion into the loop of a bolas.

The Structure 6 Burial Cist 155

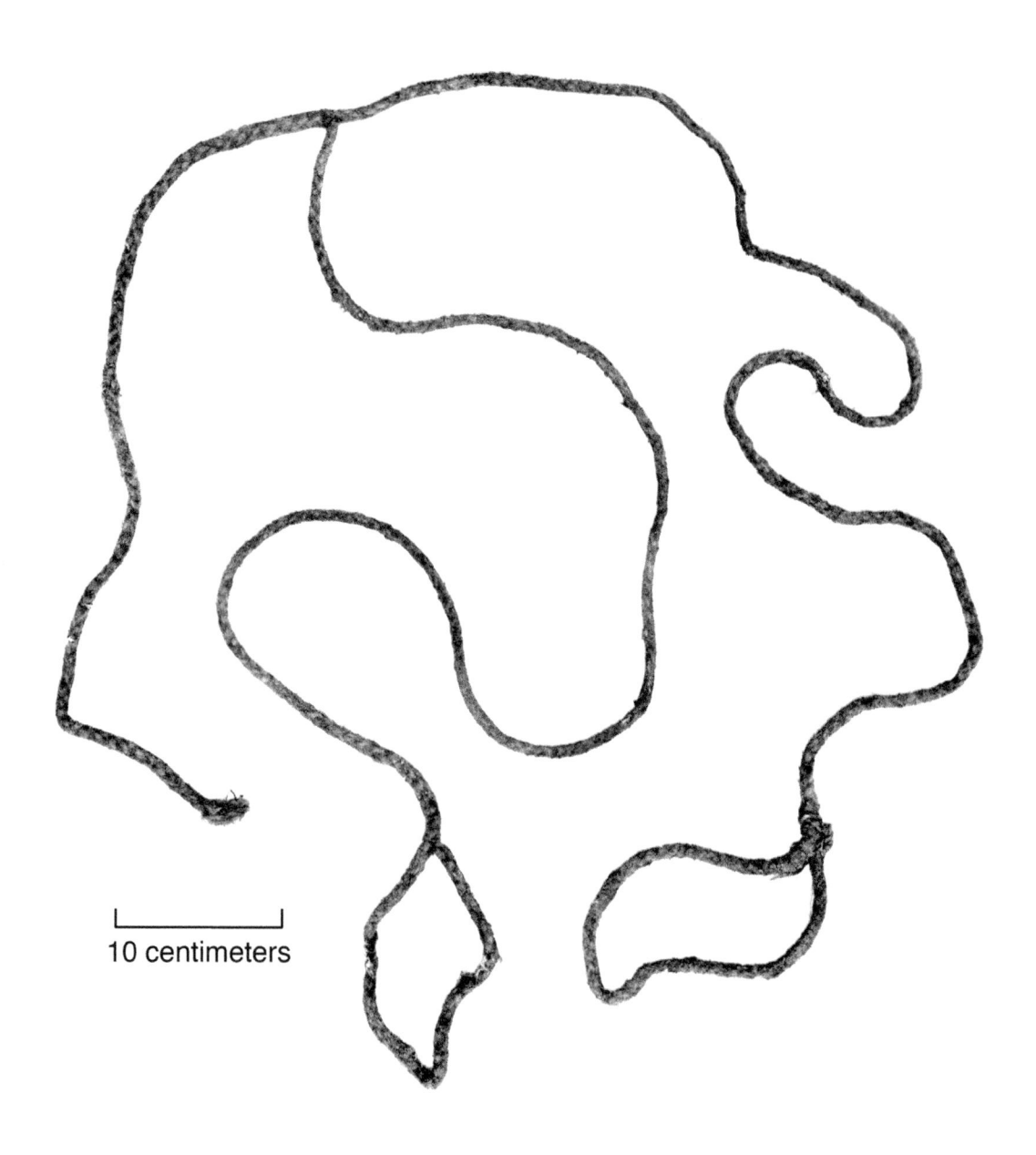

Figure 6.15. A two-stone bolas, found in Structure 6.

could be made of various materials—animal hide, *cabuya*, cotton, or wool braided fibers that provided "padding that is soft, durable, supportive, and comfortable." The strap must be strong and thick, because it supports her while she leans forward and backward in the process of weaving. She said that formerly only women used this kind of backstrap, but today it could be used by either gender. The nature of the *aparina* can vary, according to the type of cloth to be created. "For example," she said, "making a thick cloth on the loom will require a thicker and heavier *aparina*."

Item #2 is a *waska* or *watana*, a thick rope. The width of the rope depends on the coarseness of the weaving.

Item #3 is a *tuklla watu*. My informant said that this knot is the same kind she used on a trap, i.e. the type of knot that gets tighter as you work against it.

Item #4 is a *machana hurin* (lower *machana*), the *machana* closest to the waist of the weaver.

Item #5 is the *machana qaytu*, "the thread of the machana." Not shown in Figure 6.21b is the *allwi watu* or *allwi qaytu*, the piece of string used to tie the loom to the wooden stakes or upright post. The *machana qaytu* stays tied to the *allwi qaytu* even after the stakes or posts are removed.

Item #6 is the *chichi*, the strands that begin the fabric. These strands are typically uneven and unequal.

Item #7 is the *mini*, the trama or weft, the "hilo en movimiento," which passes from one side of the fabric to the other—often not changing the color of the fabric, but varying in thickness. The final texture of the textile is determined by the *mini*.

Item #8 is the *mini quma* or bobbin. This item was also called a *lanzadera* by some informants. This wooden stick holds the weft or *mini*.

Item #9 is the *mini qumasqa*, the yarn stored or rolled up on the wooden stick.

Item #10 is the *kallwa*, the large batten or sword that serves as a *tinglador* or adjuster. Examples of this artifact were found both in the burials of women and in a storage bin in Structure D.

Item #11 is the *awan qaytu*, the upper string or face of the fabric.

Item #12 is the *illyaw urqu*, the wooden artifact that lifts the warp or *urdimbre*. Not illustrated are the *choqchi*, tools made from camelid bones used with the *illyaw urquna* to distribute the strings. These *choqchi* are also called *tullu*, or bones.

Item #13 is the *ukuy qaytu*, the lower inside string on the reverse face of the fabric.

Item #14 is the shed rod or *qansa allwi sujetacc*, which always stays in place. This shed rod keeps the weft and warp

Figure 6.16. Close-up photo of the bolas seen in Figure 6.15, showing the way that coarse fiber was used to reattach one of the loops to the main cord. It is possible that that location was often in need of repair, given the weight of the stones used in the bolas.

The Structure 6 Burial Cist

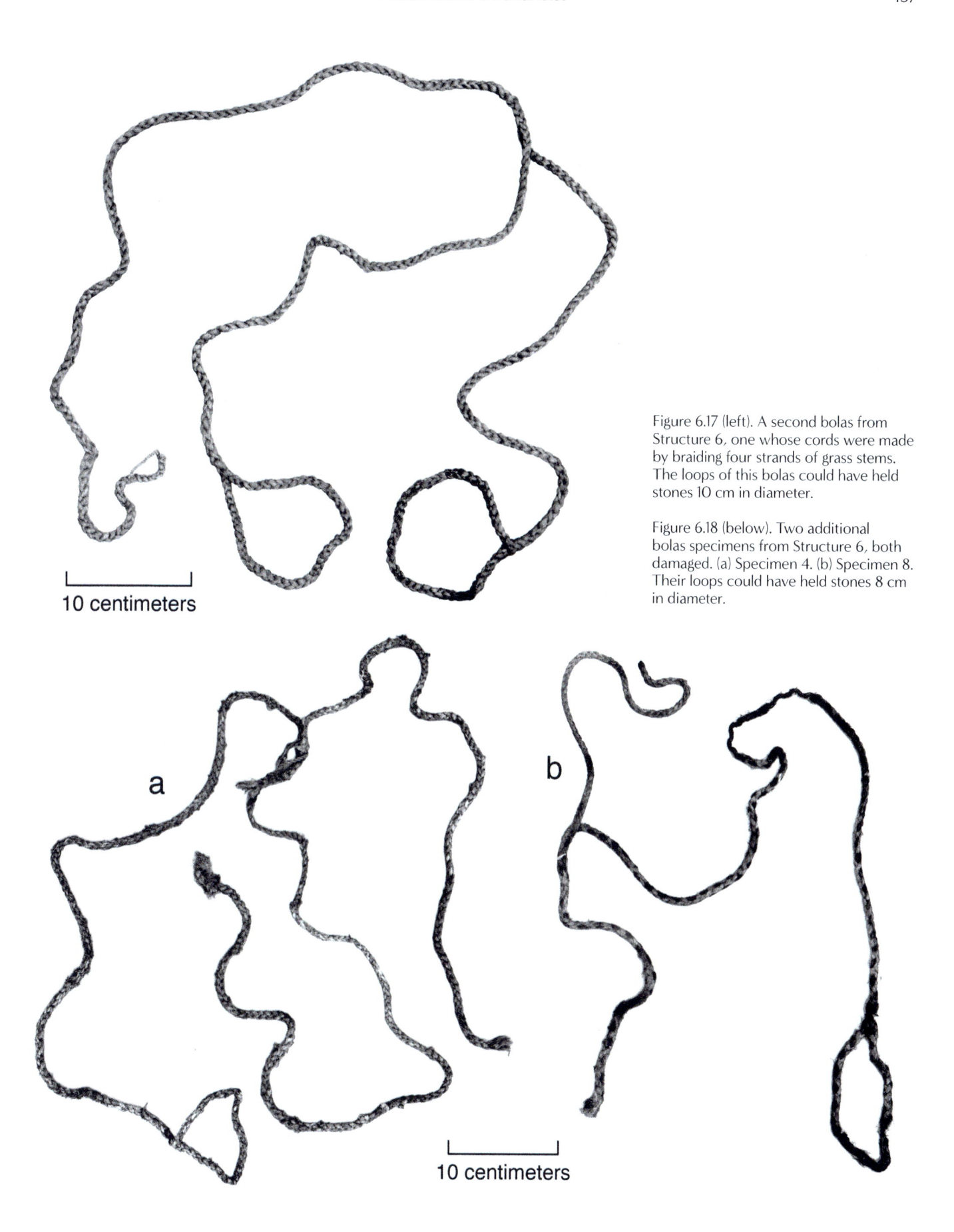

Figure 6.17 (left). A second bolas from Structure 6, one whose cords were made by braiding four strands of grass stems. The loops of this bolas could have held stones 10 cm in diameter.

Figure 6.18 (below). Two additional bolas specimens from Structure 6, both damaged. (a) Specimen 4. (b) Specimen 8. Their loops could have held stones 8 cm in diameter.

Figure 6.19. Two grinding stones associated with Structure 6. The stone on the left was from the looters' backdirt; the one on the right was found inside the burial cist.

Figure 6.20. A tied bundle of loom parts, found inside Structure 6.

open and separated from each other. The *qansa* is generally made of agave and is light in weight.

Item #15 is the *sunqun*, considered the heart or essence of the fabric because it is the last line of defense. My informant said that Item #12 was the first line of defense; and that if Item #12 were to break, there is Item #14. However, if Item #14 breaks, there is only Item #15.

Item #16 is the *machana hanan*, the term for the upper loom bar, the one farthest from the weaver. The *machana hanan* contrasts with the *machana hurin*, the term for the lower bar, the one nearest the weaver.

Item #17 is the *machana qaytu*, the *amarre* or knot of the *machana*.

Item #18 is the *chikyaq waska*, the cord used to tie the loom to a tree. This cord needs to be very strong to withstand the back and forth movement of tightening and loosening the textile on a backstrap loom.

Not illustrated is the *allwi watu* or *allwi qaytu*, the piece of string used to tie the loom to a post.

Both *machanas* (see Items #4 and #16) are the same size and thickness. The warp is called *allwi qaytu*, the weft *mini*. (Bird and Mendizábal Losack [1986:342–345] also recorded the terms for loom parts in the central highlands.)

According to my informant, to make large cloths or *mantas* one may need to use three or more *kallwas*. She said that the color of any garment she was making would be determined by the yarns of the warp. She estimated that four kilos of cotton (cleaned, without seeds) would be needed to weave one *manta*, and six kilos would be needed to weave one large *poncho*.

Textiles, Cords, and Bands

Textile 100 (98 x 76 cm) was a warp-stripe, warp-faced plain weave associated with Structure 6 (Figure 6.22). The warp and weft of this fragment are cotton. The warp has both dark brown cotton yarn and tan cotton yarn; the weft is made of cotton that is medium brown in color and Z-spun. The end selvage has a three-shot heading cord (S14Z), with the third shot (S9Z) made of thinner yarn. The side selvage is plain and compacted. The dark brown stripes (9.5 mm wide) alternate with light tan stripes (14 mm wide). There are 17 warp pairs of tan yarn per centimeter and 9 wefts per centimeter. There are 17 warps of brown yarn per centimeter and nine wefts per centimeter. This is high density cloth, with a score of 95–100.

Textile 104 is a poorly preserved cloth that was found loosely wrapped around one of the workbaskets (Specimen 125) at the bottom of Structure 6 (Figure 6.23). Direct contact with the stomach acids of one individual appears to have contributed to its deterioration. This plain cloth, plain weave measures 66 x 32 cm, which are the actual loom dimensions. The warp and weft are cotton, and both are S-spun. All the yarn is natural cotton, light brown in color. This cloth has four heading cords; the first two are Z9S and

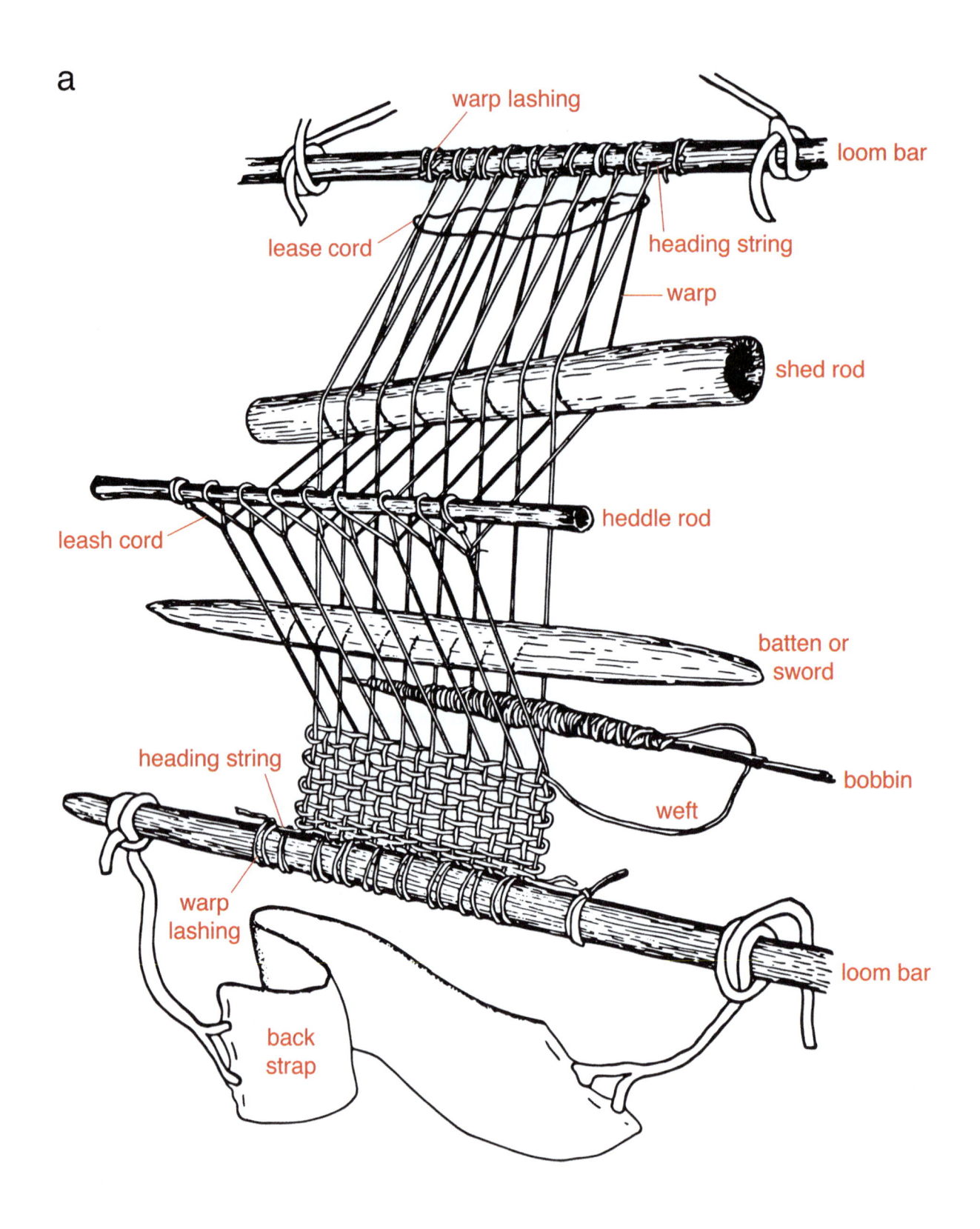

Figure 6.21 (a). The parts of a backstrap loom. This illustration gives the terms for each loom part in English. (Both illustrations were redrawn by Bruce Worden from Bennett and Bird [1949:266]).

The Structure 6 Burial Cist 161

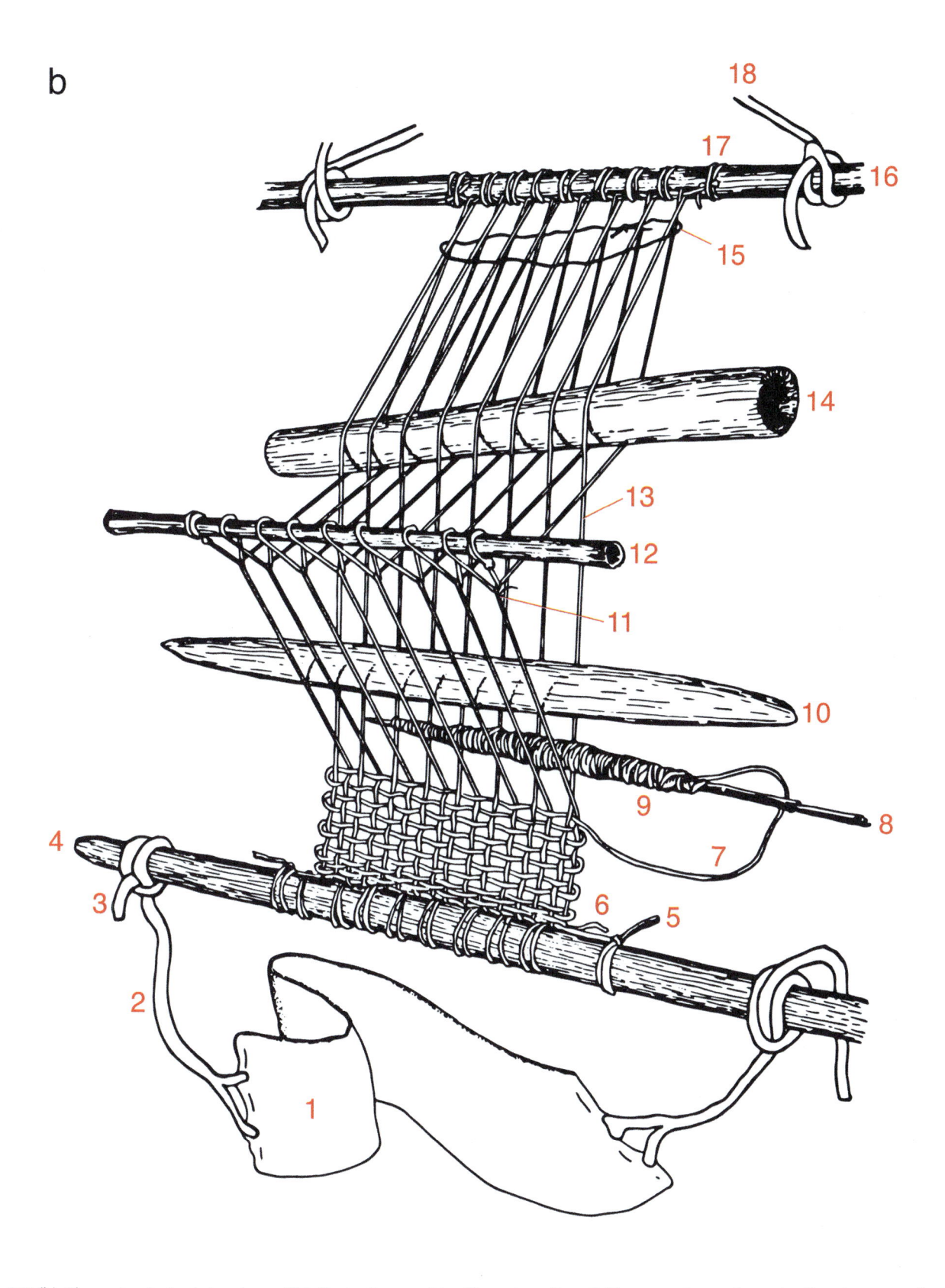

Figure 6.21 (b). The parts of a backstrap loom. This illustration provides 18 numbers (in red). These numbers refer to the Quechua terms for loom parts, which are given in the main text of this chapter (see pages 153, 156, and 159).

Figure 6.22. A brown and white striped textile found inside Structure 6.

the next two are Z3S. The warp yarn is 0.2 mm thick, while the weft is 0.35 mm thick.

Textile 117 constitutes the remains of a woolen bag that contained balls of camelid wool. This bag measures 35 x 40 cm (Figure 6.24); the measurement of 35 cm is the distance from the top of the bag to the bottom, and the 40 cm measurement is the width. The bag had 22 warps per cm and 3.2 wefts per cm; both sides and the bottom had piping. The warp and weft are both Z-S two-ply. Where it has been repaired, the repair yarn is also wool, Z-S two-ply.

This bag is a plain weave, with warp stripes and patterning. Since it is all camelid wool, one might speculate that this bag was made in the highlands; however, it could have been made right at Cerro Azul, because the yarn balls we found included all the colors of yarn necessary both to make it and repair it.

This bag features warp stripes and patterning. The top displays a side selvage; the left and right sides of the bag are end selvages, and the bottom is another side selvage. The edging or piping on the three closed sides is an example of weft-wrapping (*soumak*). The design features decorative yarns that form a diamond pattern in white, tan, and dark brown. The side selvages at the mouth of the bag are reinforced by tan yarns that are Z-S, tightly spun, and 3.1 mm thick; they are done in a very tight overcast stitch (4 stitches to 1 cm) and then plaited (tan and dark brown).

Textile 175, a coarse cotton cloth used as the outermost wrapping of a mummy bundle, has disintegrated into two pieces (Figure 6.25). The larger piece measures 1.07 x 0.57 m; it is a plain cloth, plain weave fragment with three side selvages; the end selvage has a three-shot heading cord. The smaller piece seems to have been part of another web, but

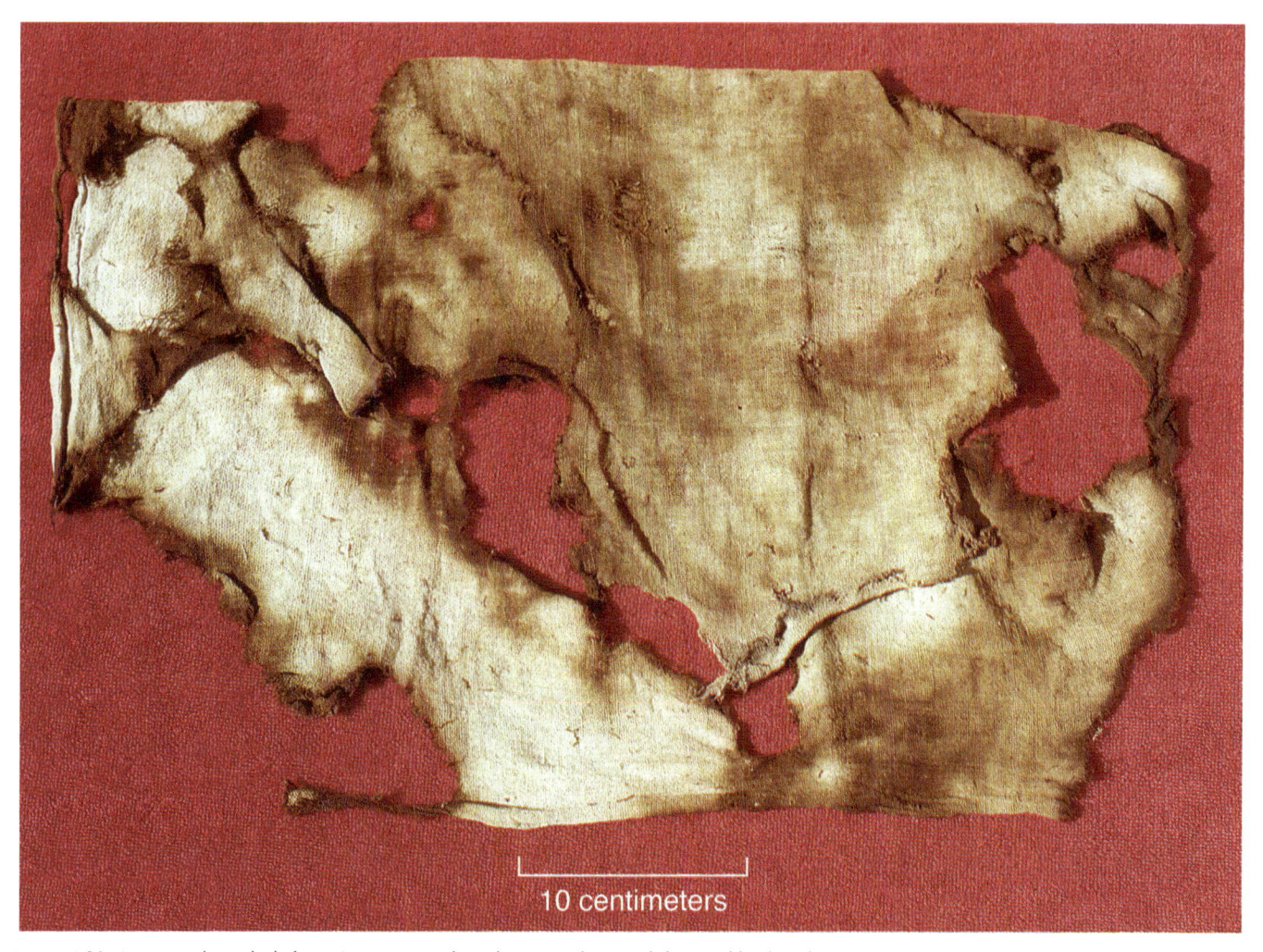

Figure 6.23. A once-white cloth from Structure 6, found wrapped around the workbasket shown in Figure 6.30. Its burned appearance may be the result of exposure to stomach acids from one of the decomposing corpses in Structure 6.

both pieces have a cotton warp and weft that are S-spun. The sewing thread is S4Z, and the lace stitches of the side selvages (2 x 2) are unusual.

Textile 190 (52 x 26 cm) is a plain cloth, plain weave of blue cotton (Figure 6.26). The warp and weft are S-spun.

Bands and Cords

T 167a is a twill basketry band 70 cm long (Figure 6.27). The elements are 2.5 mm wide, and consist of unbroken plant stems that have been flattened but not twisted. The band is 6 cm wide and consists of diagonal 2/2 twill plait. One end is torn; the other was finished by (1) chaining the ends of one set back at 90 degrees behind two others out to the surface, and (2) then back again at 90 degrees and weaving with 2/1, and finally (3) turning a last time, interlacing and passing the ends into flat braids which form a ridge with four finished edges at the end. Botanist C. Earle Smith, Jr. found it impossible to identify the grass to the species level because so many of the diagnostic elements had been modified.

T 167b is a twill basketry band with a round braided cord attached (Figure 6.28, top). Its grass elements are identical to those seen in T167a. The round braid is mixed S and Z cotton fibers that are from 0.3 mm to 0.5 mm thick. The twill band is 14 cm long and very likely a continuation of it (T 167, top); if so, the length of the original band would have been 84 cm. This band has two bundles of 20–30 cotton yarns, put through two holes 1.8 cm apart, then braided (2.5 cm thick).

T 167c (Figure 6.28, bottom) is a twill basketry band with a cord attached; the grass elements are identical to those

Figure 6.24. Two views of a striped textile fragment from Structure 6. (a) Obverse side. (b) Reverse side.

Figure 6.25. One of the textiles used as the outermost wrapping of a mummy bundle in Structure 6.

Figure 6.26. A fragment of blue cotton textile found in Structure 6.

used in T 167a and T 167b. One end of the band is torn, while the other is finished and square. It features a single turn back like that described for T 167a and T 167b. Two lengths of twisted grass stem have been looped through a hole behind the end ridge, then braided.

T167d is an example of 2/2 twill basketry with needlework looped edging and a round cotton cord attached (Figure 6.29). It forms a rectangle measuring 22 x 11 cm and has two finished edges. The plaited grass elements are identical to those used in T 167 a–c. The 2/2 twill is reversed along a diagonal marked by one 3/1 element. The twill diagonals are parallel to the edge, and the twill direction of 80 degrees changes in a line perpendicular to the edge. One edge—the shorter one—is covered with eight-row cross-knit looping that forms a 13 cm thick round edging. The braided cord is an eight-strand circular cord (four bundles of S12 Z single-strand cotton) that is attached to the looped edging; it extends for 11 cm before it divides into two units, each of which is tied into the basketry.

T 168 is an example of heavy cordage. It is 6.11 mm thick and made of grass elements that are Z-spun and then S-twisted. The cord is stiff, and was once perhaps 8–11 m in total length. One fragment (now 3.25 m long) features a 25 cm loop, tied with a granny knot. Elsewhere there are two cases of asymmetrical overhand knots (half hitch #2). One end of the cord is finished with an overhand knot.

T 205a is a 9 cm wide strip, tied into a ring 10 cm in diameter with a square knot.

T 205b is a fragile specimen of cordage, loosely tied with an overhand knot. The approximate length of this fragment is 50 cm.

The Structure 6 Burial Cist

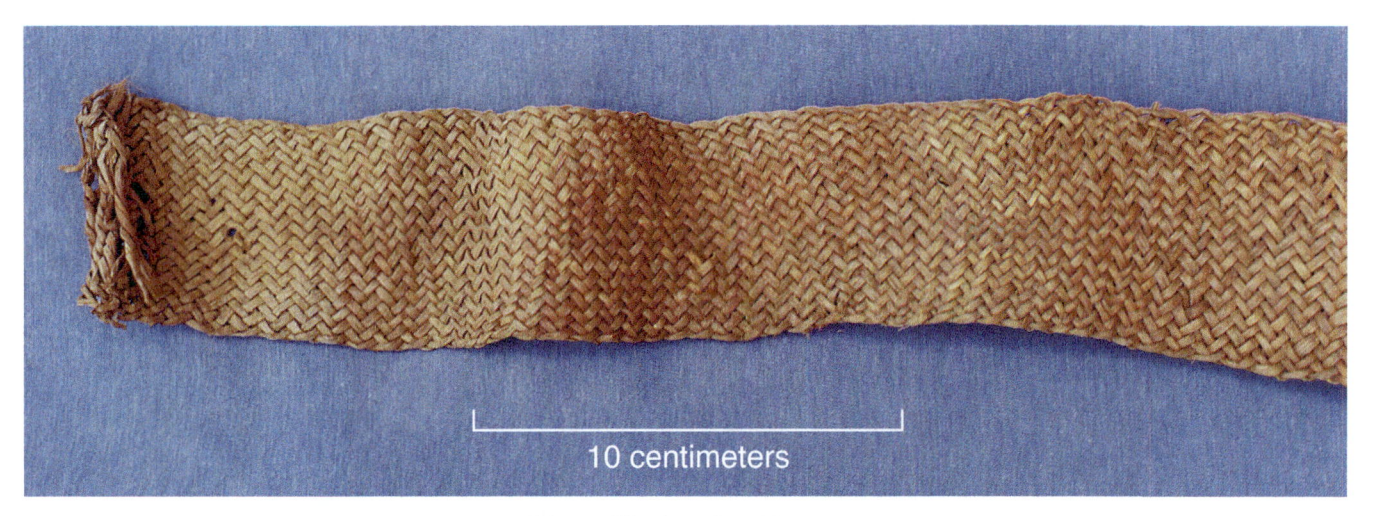

Figure 6.27. A twill basketry band from Structure 6.

Figure 6.28. Two twill basketry bands, possibly the interior components of backstraps, found in Structure 6.

Figure 6.29. A fragment of twill basketry found in Structure 6.

T 219a is a skein of S-spun white cotton yarn, 164 cm long.

T 219b is a small hank of red wool, Z-spun S-twisted; it has been wrapped with a grass fiber bundle.

T 219c is an S18Z cotton cord, 76 cm long.

T 219d consists of four lengths of grass cordage, Z-spun S-twisted. It is 5.5 mm thick and tied with overhand knots. The length of the longest cord is approximately 50 cm.

T 219e is an 18 cm length of thick sedge, tied with two half hitches at one end and wrapped with a short length of sedge at the other.

T 219f and **T 219g** are thick wool fibers, forming eight-strand ovate braids.

T 220 consists of segments of a Z2S grass cord with a total length of 13.3 m. Its longest segment is 3.6 m and 6 mm thick.

T 224a is a cotton cord 6.8 m long and 8.5 mm thick. It is made of loosely twisted S48 Z yarn.

T 224b is a three-strand grass braid, 1.06 m long and 6 mm thick.

Workbasket

Associated with Structure 6 was a workbasket, tied up in a cloth (Figure 6.30). This basket measures 38 x 19 cm and has a height of 8 cm. The lid panel has four splints or stiffeners, each of which is a split cane 1.7 cm wide; these splints are spaced 2.5 cm apart. The floor of the basket is constructed the same way, whereas each end panel has three splints (Figure 6.31). The side panels also have three splints, plus a slight flap that folds over in such a way that it makes a good seal with the lid.

The contents of this workbasket included (see Figures 6.32, 6.33, and 6.34):

—20 grams of unspun *algodón blanco*, with two spindles still attached (Figure 6.32). This discovery suggests that the owner of this basket had been spinning thread and storing it on these two spindles and that at the time of her death, she had produced about 20 cm of spun yarn. The *puschan* (first stage) cotton pad measures 20 x 14 cm and is approximately 2 cm thick.

Figure 6.30. Two views of a workbasket from Structure 6. (a) The workbasket as found, wrapped in the cloth shown in Figure 6.23. (b) The workbasket without its cloth wrapping.

Figure 6.31. The same workbasket seen in Figure 6.30, with its lid open and its contents removed.

—One spindle, 28.4 cm long, still bearing a Camacho Black whorl with a complicated dentate design in black and white paint. The whorl's height is 13.6 mm, its diameter is 16.3 mm, and the diameter of its hole is 3.6 mm (Figure 6.33a).
—A second spindle, 24.5 cm long, with a maximum diameter of 3.6 mm. Still threaded on this spindle is a burnished red biconical whorl with a height of 15.6 mm, a diameter of 13.6 mm, and a hole 3.4 mm in diameter. This whorl is painted 5 R 3/3 ("dusky red") (Figure 6.33b).
—A third whorl in the basket, not found on a spindle, had a teardrop shape. Its height is 13.7 mm, its diameter 14.9 mm, and its hole 3.5 mm in diameter. This 3 g whorl is painted red, with an additional white band and yellow spirals. The red color is 5 R 3/3 ("dusky red") (Figure 6.33c). It is worth mentioning that this painted whorl with its yellow spirals is similar to whorls found in the Structure 12 burial cist.
—A piece of stone that may have served as a polisher or smoother (Figure 6.34a). The stone is white with pink veins (3 x 2 x 1.6 cm), and weighs 23 g; it is not of locally occurring raw material.
—Four yarn balls (*kururkuna*) were also in the workbasket (Figure 6.34b–e):
 one weighing 2.0 g; 7.5 YR 6/6 ("reddish yellow")
 one weighing 7.0 g; 5 YR 3/3 ("dark reddish brown")
 one weighing 1.5 g; 5 YR 4/4 ("reddish brown") and
 one weighing 1.5 g; 5 YR 3/3 ("dark reddish brown")
—A fragment from an unpainted spindle, 16 cm long and 3.7 mm in diameter (Figure 6.34f).

The Structure 6 Burial Cist

5 centimeters

Figure 6.32. Twenty grams of cotton from the Figure 6.30 workbasket. Note that this cotton was being spun onto two spindles: the one on the left is a dentate black whorl (see Fig. 6.33a) and the one on the right with a biconical red-painted whorl (see Fig. 6.33b). There is also a loose whorl (top center).

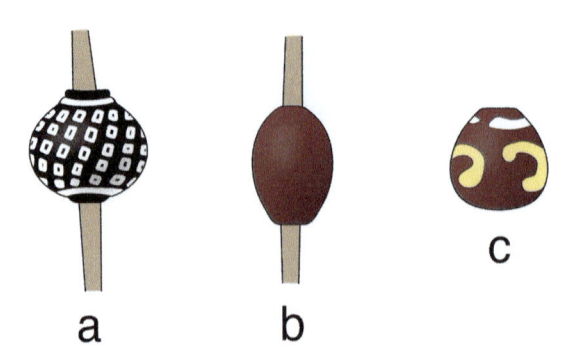

Figure 6.33. Color views of the three spindle whorls shown in Figure 6.32. (a) Black dentate whorl. (b) Red biconical whorl. (c) The loose whorl, painted red with yellow spirals.

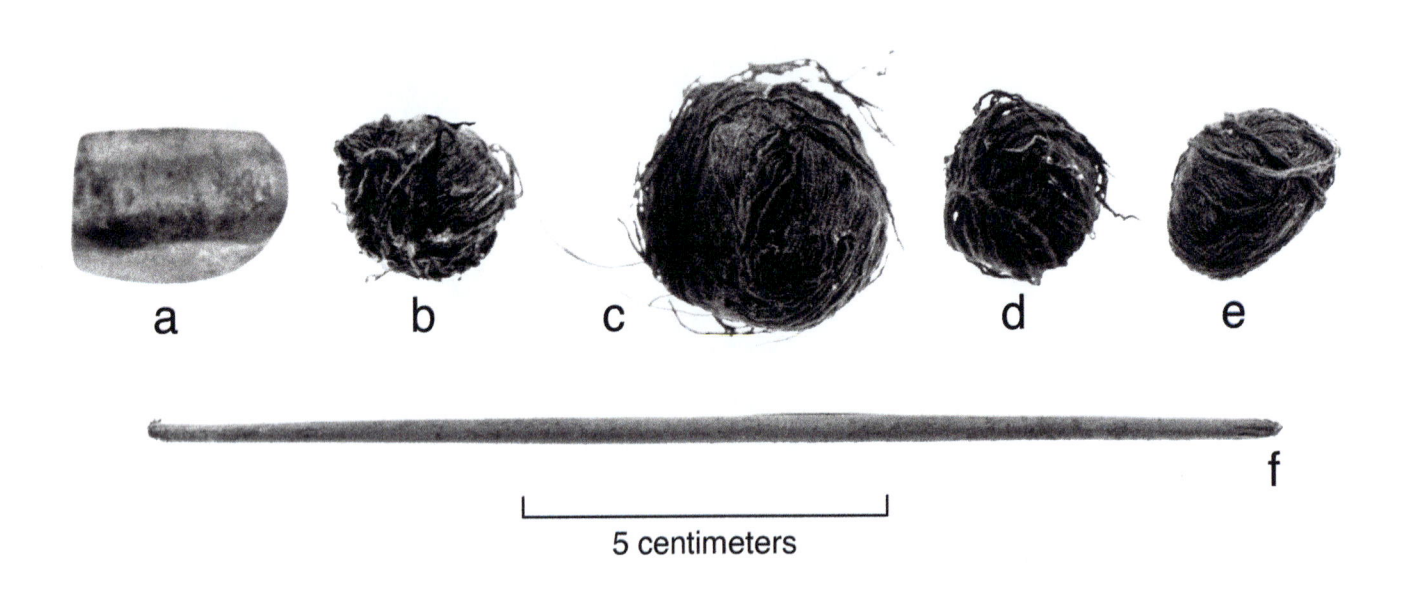

Figure 6.34. More items from the workbasket seen in Figure 6.30. (a) A stone polisher. (b-e) Four yarn balls; the largest weighed 7 g. (f) A spindle found loose in Structure 6, which may have fallen from the deteriorating workbasket.

Yarn Balls

In addition to the yarn balls found in the workbasket, we found one in the hand of a mummy. Although this hand was tossed aside by the looters, it still continued to clutch a yarn ball between its thumb and third and fourth fingers (Figure 6.35). This yarn ball had a diameter of ca. 2 cm, weighed 1.0 g, and was 2.5 YR 2/2 ("very dusky red").

Comments on Structure 6

Like Structure 5, Structure 6 seems to have held the remains of both men and women before it was looted (Figure 6.36). Among the items likely to have belonged to men were bolas and slings, while probable women's possessions included workbaskets with spindles and yarn balls.

Figure 6.35. A mummified hand holding a yarn ball, discarded by looters near Structure 6.

Figure 6.36. Workman Víctor Cubillas sweeps the floor of the looted burial cist designated Structure 6.

Chapter 7

Burial 1

In this chapter we look at secondary burials found in a pit, rather than a stone-lined cist. Burial 1 contained the partial remains of several people. Although the pit was not large, it somehow accommodated six people, a dog, six vessels, two unmodified shells, textiles, spindles, whorls, and two grinding stones.

We found this burial immediately below the string that marked the western limit of our original 5 x 5 m excavation (Figure 7.1). Burial 1 was almost entirely contained within our excavation unit, with only about 20 cm of the burial pit extending to the west of the string.

The pit, approximately one meter deep, had penetrated alternating layers of sand and loose stones. The bottom of the pit and its side walls had been lined with mats. The burial crew then added a layer of soft materials in the form of several squares of cloth; each cloth was in a different state of disintegration by the time we salvaged the burial. In addition to the cloth, we found some plant material that was too decomposed to identify. Our suspicion, which remains unconfirmed, is that this may have been a layer of *pacay* leaves.

The Excavation of Burial 1

The first stage of our excavation involved brushing away the loose dirt that covered the uppermost level of the burial pit. At first, we could only see two grinding stones, three of the six vessels, and some human skulls (Figure 7.2). On that particular day, photography was rendered even more difficult than usual by the swirling dust from strong coastal winds.

Although numerous bones from each secondary individual were missing, six skulls were present. From the skeletal remains, biological anthropologist Sonia Guillén was able to determine that four were adults and two were children:

1 adult, some of whose teeth had been resorbed
1 mature adult
1 adult 30+ years old
1 adult ca. 25 years old
1 child 10–12 years old
1 child 8–10 years old

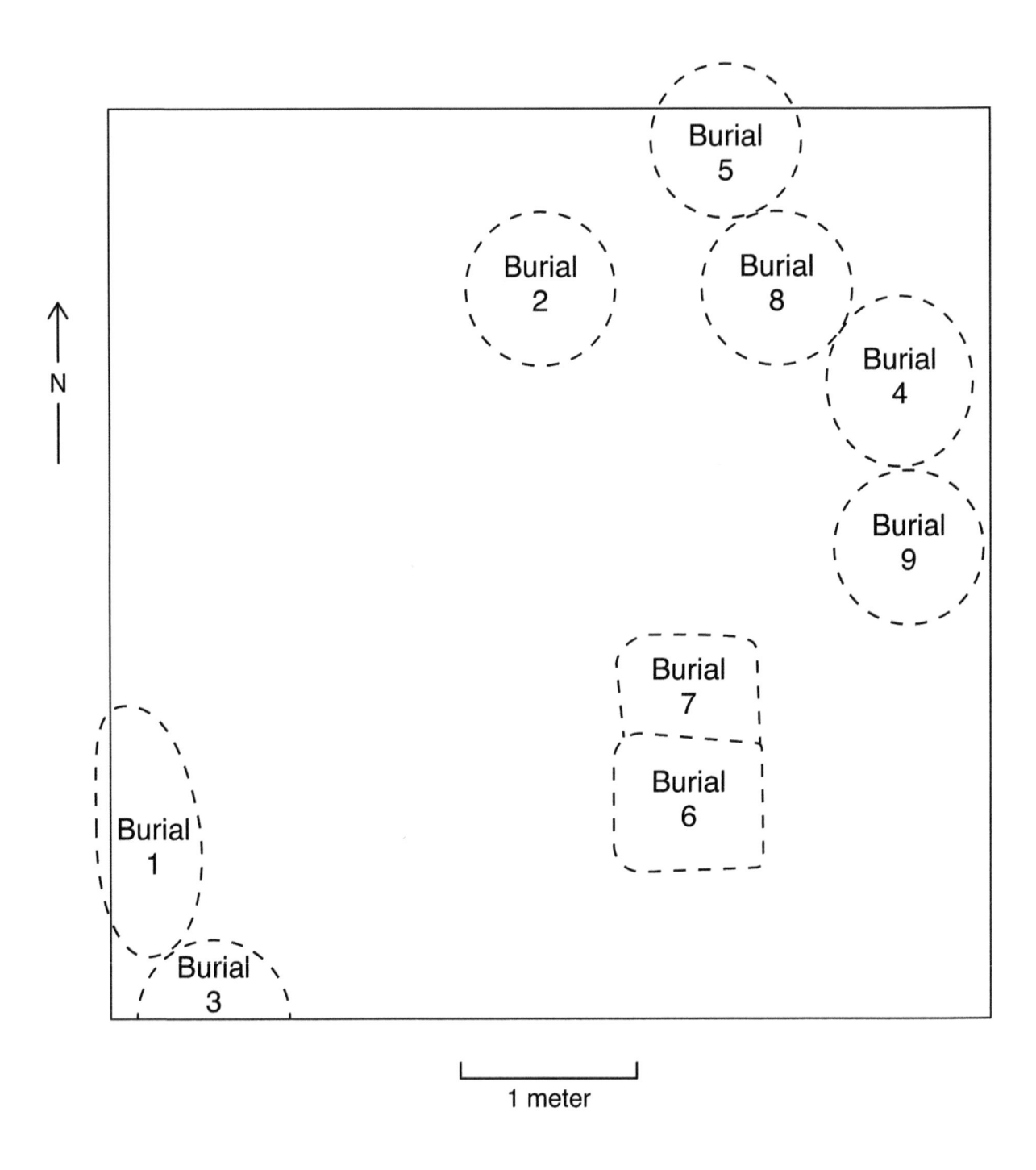

Figure 7.1. The location of Burials 1–9 within our 5 x 5 m salvage excavation unit in Quebrada 5a.

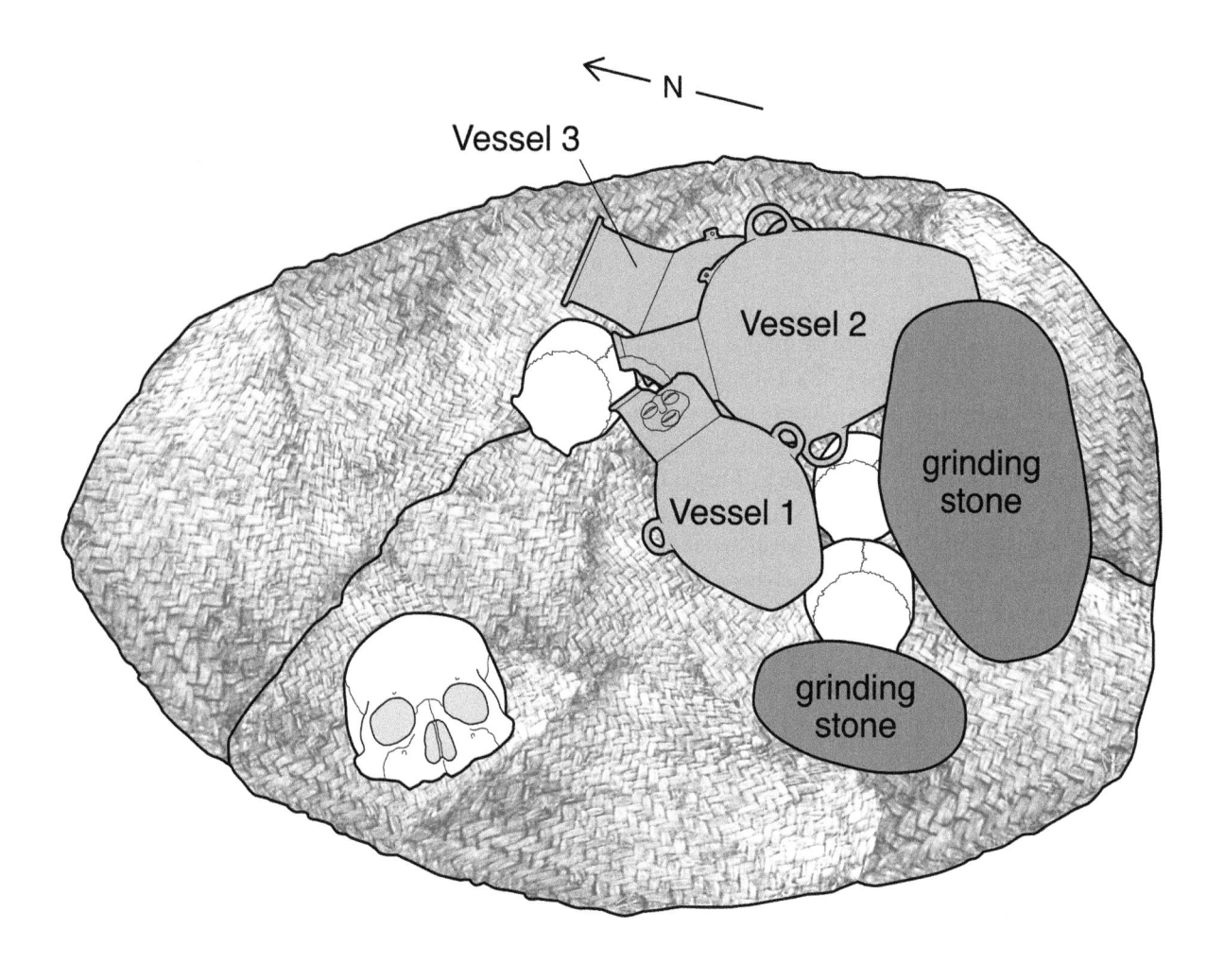

Figure 7.2. Visible in the uppermost level of Burial 1 were two grinding stones, three pottery vessels, and four human crania.

Stratigraphy

This burial pit had three levels. The uppermost level yielded the grinding stones and three large amphorae (Vessels 1–3); the middle level contained the skulls of two children; and the lowest level yielded the partial remains of four adults whose bones were commingled. The custom of placing the remains of children above the bodies of adults is known from other Cerro Azul burials as well as burials at other coastal sites.

Ceramic Vessels

Burial 1 contained five ceramic vessels and one gourd bowl. The five ceramic vessels were as follows:

Vessel 1

Vessel 1 is a Camacho Reddish Brown amphora with an effigy face modeled on the neck (Figure 7.3). The vessel base is slightly concave. The vessel has a cambered rim and two strap handles. The vessel's height is 24.6 cm; its rim diameter is 8.7 cm; and its wall thickness varies from 6 to 7 mm. The strap handles are 2.0 to 2.5 cm wide. The Munsell color of the vessel surface is largely 2.5 YR 4/4 ("reddish brown"), a color that grades into 2.5 YR 3/4 ("dark reddish brown") and 5 YR 3/3 ("dark reddish brown"). There are some blotchy gray firing clouds. The surface is lightly burnished (Marcus 2008: Fig. 3.6b).

In the bottom of Vessel 1 we found a wad of human hair, weighing 6 g (Figure 7.4; Miscellaneous Item 40).

Vessel 2

Vessel 2, a Camacho Black amphora with two strap handles, has two animal effigy lugs on its shoulder (Figure 7.5). This vessel became chipped in antiquity. The vessel's height is 35.5 cm; its rim diameter is 9 cm; and its wall thickness varies from 6 to 7 mm. The strap handles are 3.5 to 4.0 cm wide. The color of the surface is mainly jet black and well burnished, with occasional firing clouds that are 10 YR 4/1 ("dark gray") in the Munsell color system. The color of the clay body is gray to light gray.

Vessel 3

Vessel 3 is a misfired Camacho Black amphora with two strap handles and two effigy lugs on its shoulder (Figure 7.6). Since the vessel is broken it is impossible to determine its original height, but it was probably taller than 30 cm. The rim diameter is 9.2 cm, and the amphora's maximum diameter is 18 cm. Its wall thickness is 6 to 7 mm and its strap handles measure 3.7 cm in width. The color of the vessel ranges from dark gray to dark brownish gray to black.

Vessel 4

Vessel 4 is a Camacho Black amphora with two strap handles and two animal effigy lugs on its shoulder (Figure 7.7). As with other Camacho Black vessels, this amphora is primarily black, but its firing clouds grade from black to dark grayish brown to brownish gray. The damaged vessel's original height is unknown; its rim diameter is 9.4 cm, and its wall thickness is 6 to 7 mm. The strap handles are 4 to 5 cm wide.

Vessel 5

Vessel 5, which bears the shape of a miniature drum with strap handles, is metallic black in color (Figure 7.8). This is an example of the highly burnished variety of Camacho Black, which often occurs in miniature vessels. This specimen is only 6.7 cm tall; its rim diameter is 3.2 cm, and its wall thickness is 4 to 5 mm. The strap handles are 1.4 cm wide.

Gourd Vessel

The weight of the earth partially crushed Vessel 6, a miniature gourd vessel that is unusual in two ways: its exterior has been painted black, and its stem scar is evident in the middle of its side wall (Figure 7.9). Vessel 6 is 7.5 cm tall, with a rim diameter of 2.8 cm; its maximum diameter is ca. 4.5 cm, and its wall thickness is 3 mm.

This gourd vessel may have been a valued personal possession, since it was found carefully stored in a cloth bag. Unfortunately, the bag had nearly disintegrated.

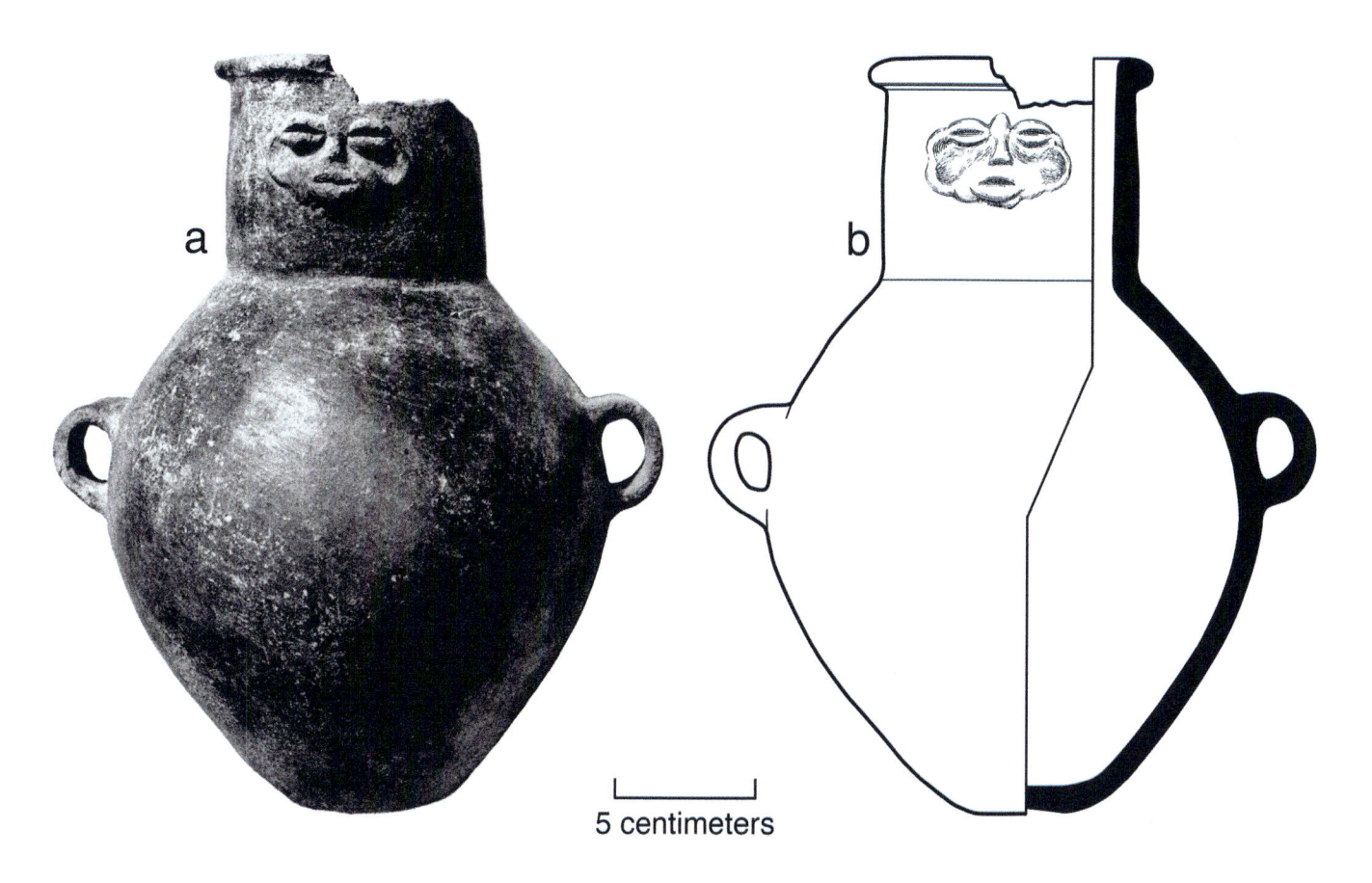

Figure 7.3. Vessel 1 of Burial 1, a Camacho Reddish Brown amphora with a face modeled on its neck.

Figure 7.4. A wad of human hair was found at the bottom of Vessel 1 of Burial 1.

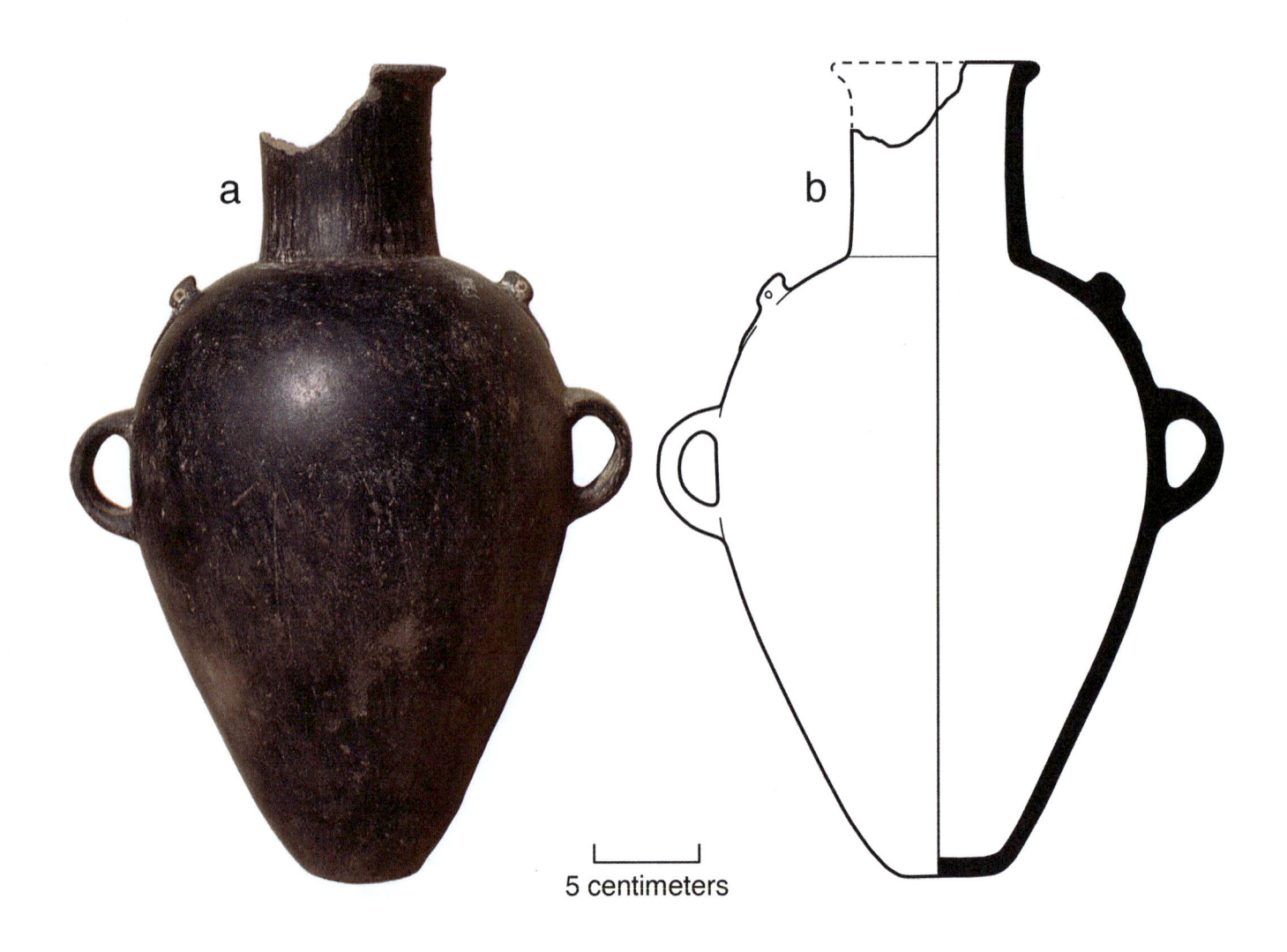

Figure 7.5. Vessel 2 of Burial 1 was a Camacho Black amphora with two small animal effigy lugs on its shoulder.

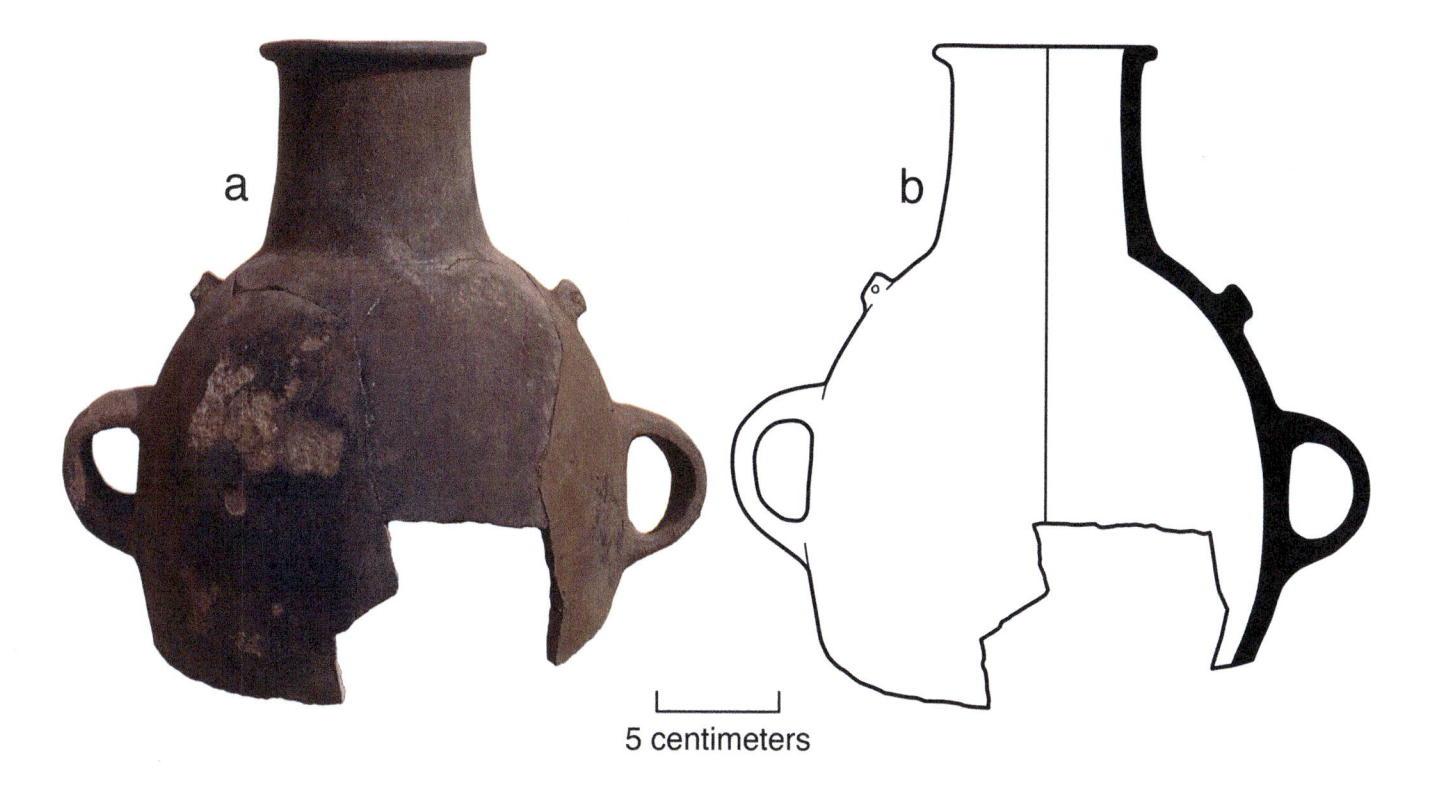

Figure 7.6. Vessel 3 of Burial 1, already broken when found, was a misfired Camacho Black amphora with two effigy lugs on its shoulder.

Figure 7.7. Vessel 4 of Burial 1, already broken when found, was a Camacho Black amphora with two animal effigy lugs on its shoulder.

Grinding Stones

This burial was accompanied by two grinding stones (Figure 7.10). One grinding stone (Figure 7.10a) is a possible *batán* (metate). It is a gray igneous beach cobble, 34 cm long, 20 cm wide, and 9 cm thick. Its worked upper surface (used for grinding) is smooth. This worked surface had been on the receiving end of rockering, presumably done by the smaller stone discussed next.

The second grinding stone is also a gray igneous beach cobble, possibly used as a *mano de batán* of the rocker type (Figure 7.10b). The cobble is 21 cm long, 12 cm wide, and 7 cm thick. One edge is worn from use.

Marine Shells

Also included in the burial were two marine shells, one *macha* (*Mesodesma*) and one false abalone (*Concholepas concholepas*).

Dog

At least five dogs had been associated with the burials we salvaged from Quebrada 5a; one of those dogs was found in Burial 1. Its measurements suggest a dog 75 to 80 percent the size of a golden retriever (Flannery and Glew 2016:319). Its cranium (Figure 7.11) had a maximal basioccipital length of 15.3 cm. The maximum width of its zygomatic arches could not be determined, owing to damage that the skull suffered at the hands of the looters.

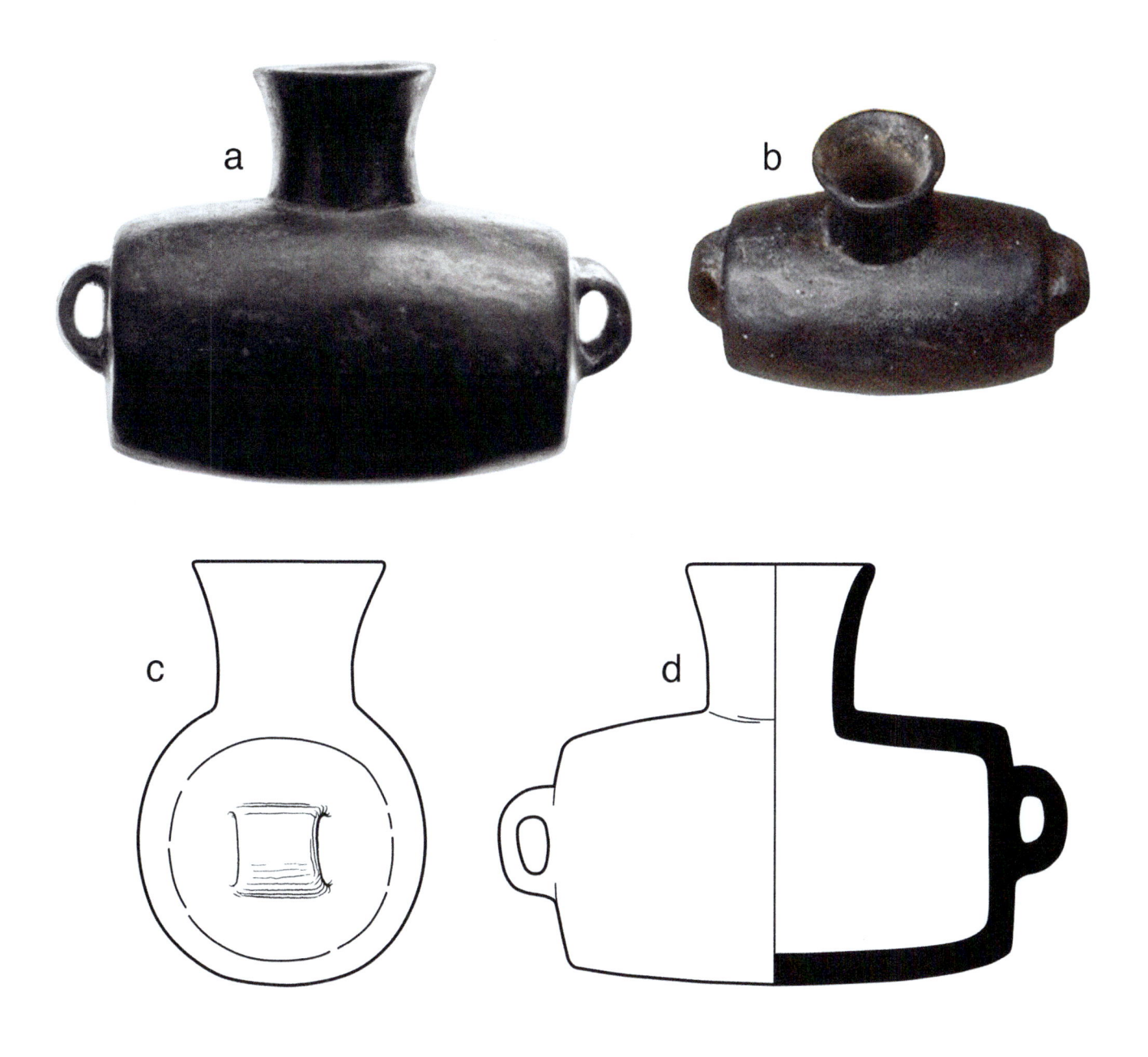

Figure 7.8. Four views of Vessel 5 from Burial 1. This drum-shaped miniature vessel had a metallic black surface, which corresponds to the highly burnished variant of Camacho Black. Views a, c, and d are life-size.

edging in dark brown cotton thread, in three rows of cross-knit needlework; this edging had become the most fragile part of the textile. A whipping stitch of single S-spun cotton yarn was used to close the sides of the garment; to create the armholes, the maker left 13 cm open on each side. At the top was a 17 cm wide opening for the neck.

Textile 201a is what is left of a two-sided wool belt. Brown warp-faced bands flank a central panel of complementary warp weave; the warp float forms a design on one side of the belt. All the wefts had disintegrated, so what is left is mainly a nonphotogenic mass of yarns. In the remaining fragment one sees a diagonal line of interlocking frets, made up of stepped triangles with central dots in red and green. It is notable that one of the loom backstraps associated with Individual 3 of Burial 4 (see Chapter 10) had a similar design.

T 201b consisted of various pieces of braided cord made of dark brown cotton. The pieces are from a six-strand circular braid that once had a diameter of 1.8 mm. The braid elements are made up of bundles of single-ply yarns, the longest fragment of which is 1.37 m. Two of the pieces had been tied together with a clove hitch.

T 201c is a cotton plain weave cloth, measuring 2.25 cm wide and 38 cm long. It is white, with 5 mm bands at each edge of one brown stripe. One end is tied to a 20 cm long, three-strand flat braid, 5.5 mm wide.

T 201d, a 3 cm wide plain weave bast band, is 36 cm long. The warp is Z-spun and the weft is S-spun. The bast, which has a rather rough and uneven texture, is dark brown and has spots of red pigment on it.

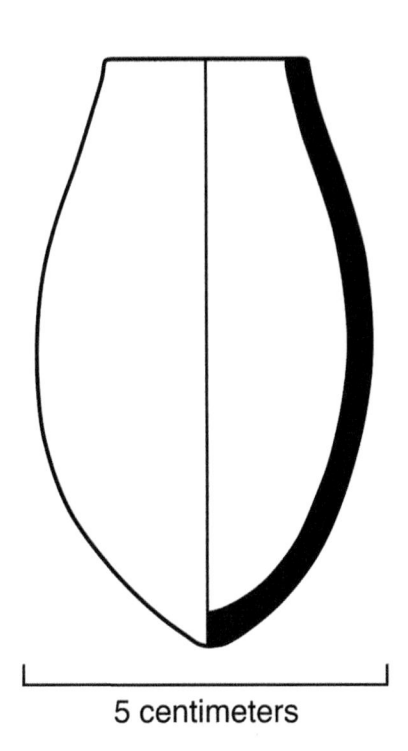

Figure 7.9. Vessel 6 from Burial 1. This miniature gourd vessel, painted black to resemble pottery, was found inside a cloth bag.

It is worth noting that at Cerro Azul, dogs were more likely to be included in burials than in any other context. For example, Structure D (a residential compound that we excavated in its entirety) yielded only one dog bone, and Structure 9 (a residence and fish storage structure excavated in its entirety) produced no dog bones at all.

Spindle and Spindle Whorl

We found one broken spindle (length, 13.5 cm; maximum diameter, 3.8 mm; Specimen 24). This spindle still held a few threads of very fine brown yarn that was 5 YR 3/4 ("dark reddish brown").

Burial 1 also included a Camacho Black globular whorl. Its height is 18.5 mm, its diameter is 20.5 mm, and its hole diameter is 3.5 mm. The whorl weighs 7 g.

Textiles

We found five textile fragments with Burial 1.

Textile 162, an orange cotton garment, was made by sewing together two plain weave webs (Figure 7.12). This garment may be a tunic or blouse (1.26 m x 0.63 m). It has

Comments on Burial 1

Owing to looting, we cannot provide a definitive description of the individuals in Burial 1. The spinning, weaving, and grinding implements suggest that at least one woman may have been present.

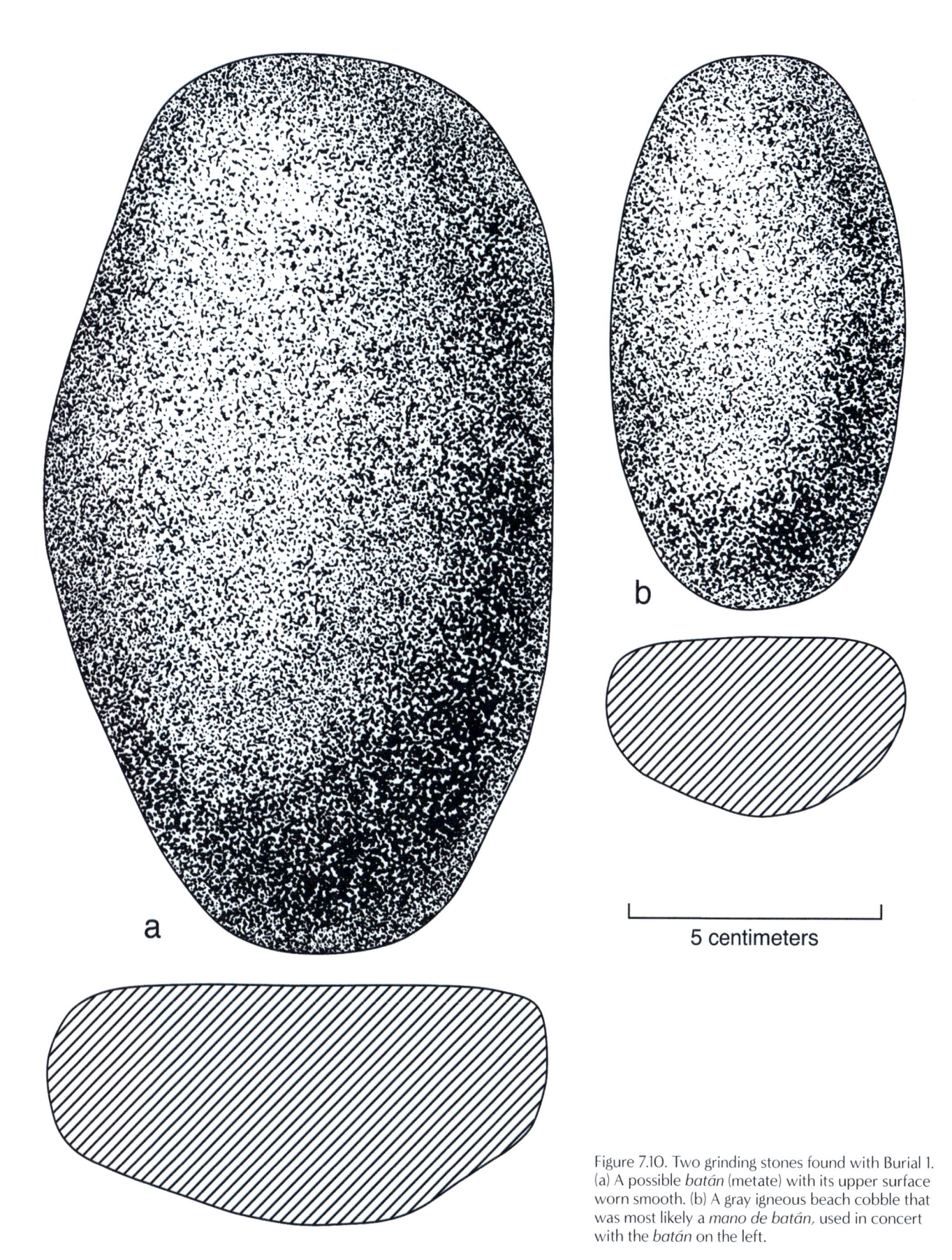

Burial 1

Figure 7.10. Two grinding stones found with Burial 1. (a) A possible *batán* (metate) with its upper surface worn smooth. (b) A gray igneous beach cobble that was most likely a *mano de batán,* used in concert with the *batán* on the left.

Chapter 7

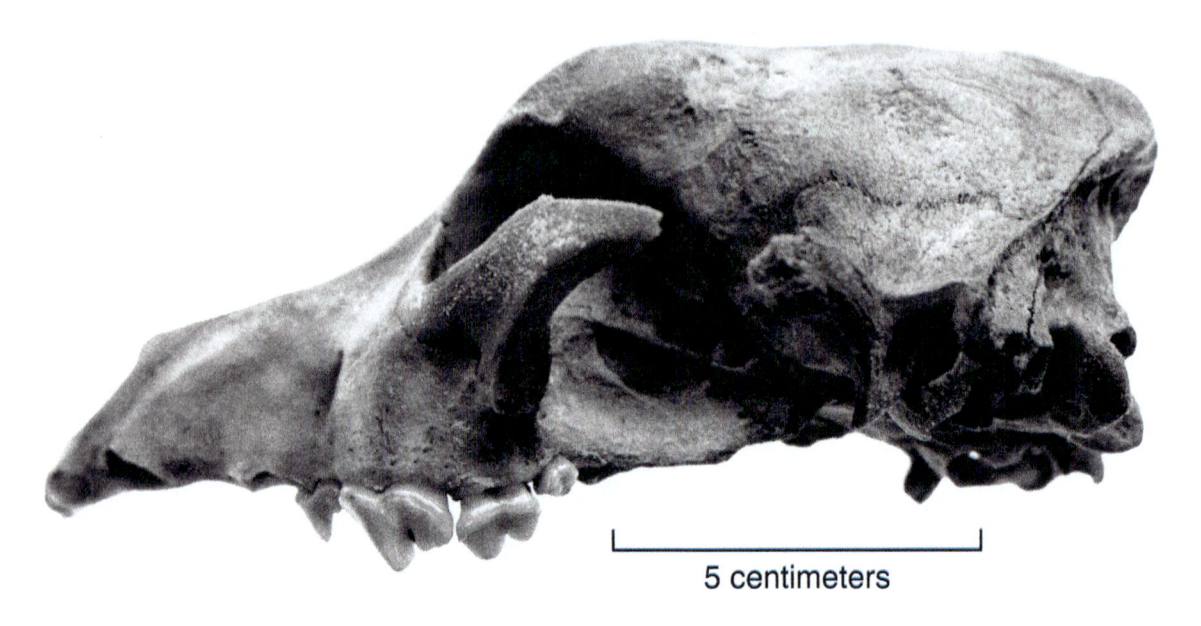

5 centimeters

Figure 7.11. The cranium of a dog whose complete remains accompanied Burial 1.

10 centimeters

Figure 7.12. An orange garment from Burial 1, possibly a tunic or blouse. It was made by sewing together two identical webs, leaving openings for the arms and head.

Chapter 8

Burial 2

We found Burial 2 in the northern half of our 5 x 5 m excavation unit in Quebrada 5a (see Figure 7.1). Its burial pit lay in Stratigraphic Zone B, a one-meter-thick midden of gray ash and coquina clams (*Donax obesulus*). The Zone B midden represented the accumulation of thousands of basketloads of residential garbage, creating a matrix into which burials could be inserted.

Even though Burial 2 had been disturbed by looters, we were able to recover the skull of a child six to eight years of age; this small skull had been placed in an empty gourd of the shallow bowl type (Figure 8.1a, b). The gourd vessel's diameter varied from 16.0 to 17.8 cm; its height varied from 5.0 to 5.8 cm, and its wall was 5 mm thick. The color of this gourd in the Munsell system was 2.5 YR 2/2 ("very dusky red"). Most of the gourd bowls we had recovered with burials contained food for the afterlife, so finding a child's skull in a gourd bowl was unusual.

Near the gourd bowl was a Camacho Black jar with two holes penetrating its body (Figure 8.2a, b). These might be considered deliberate "kill" holes, although we cannot rule out the possibility that they were made by a looter's metal probe, since the jar's neck is also damaged. The surface of the vessel is burnished, and its Munsell color varies from pure black to 10 YR 5/2 ("grayish brown"), 10 YR 5/3 ("brown"), and 10 YR 4/1 ("dark gray"). The vessel's handles are 2.3 cm wide; its height was originally greater than 20 cm, its maximum diameter is 18 cm, and its wall thickness varies from 4.0 to 4.5 mm.

Llama Bone

Burial 2 produced one llama bone, a cervical vertebra that might once have been part of a parcel of *ch'arki* or dried meat (Glew and Flannery 2016a:300). We can only assume that this was food for the afterlife.

188 Chapter 8

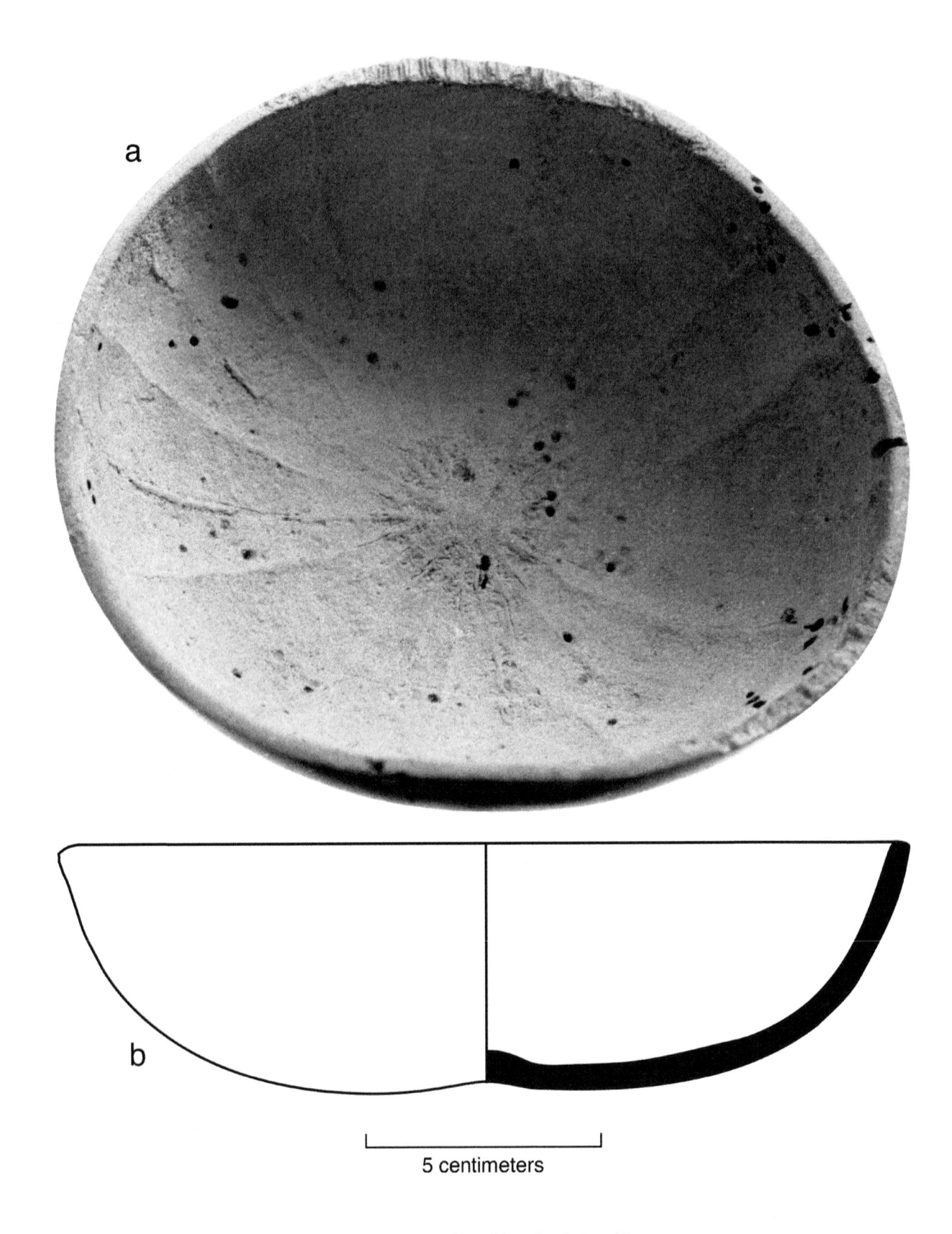

Figure 8.1. A gourd bowl found with Burial 2.

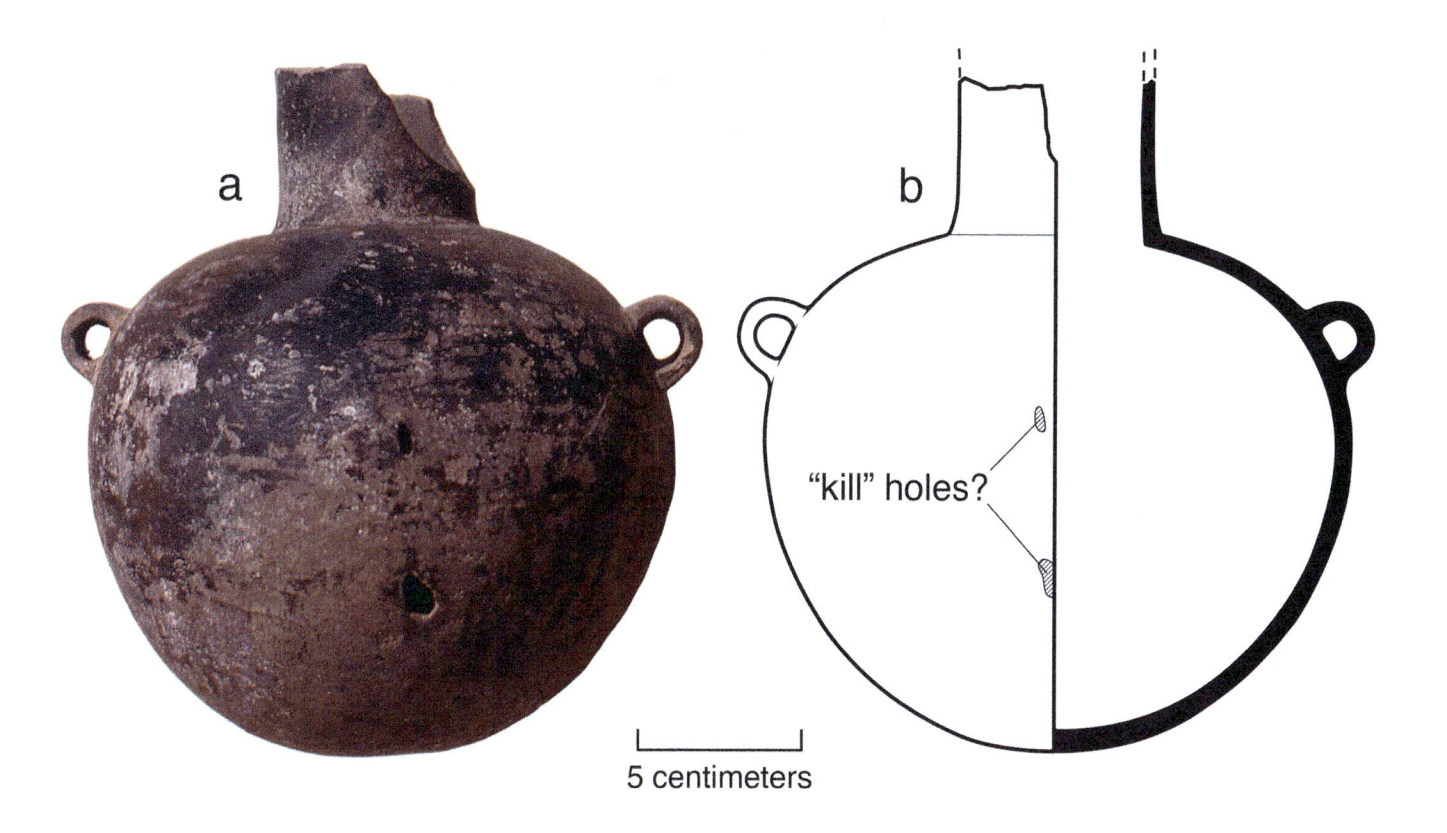

Figure 8.2. A Camacho Black jar from Burial 2, featuring two small holes that might be deliberate "kill" holes.

Chapter 9

Burial 3

Burial 3 was found in a circular pit at a depth of 1.2 m in the southwest corner of our excavation in Quebrada 5a (see Figure 7.1); part of the pit lay outside our excavation unit. All skeletal material had been discarded by the looters, but we managed to salvage two pottery vessels and two gourd bowls.

Vessel 1

Vessel 1 is a Camacho Black amphora with strap handles and shoulder lugs. When found, this amphora still had a long grass rope (Z-spun, S-twisted) inserted through its handles and wound around its lugs (Figure 9.1). Our workmen referred to this type of rope as a *soga de cabuya*. Although largely preserved, it had broken into pieces, with the largest segment measuring 1.23 m long and 6.2 mm thick.

The height of Vessel 1 is 37 cm; its rim diameter is 10.5 cm, and its maximum diameter is 16.8 cm. The width of each strap handle is 4 cm. The Munsell color of the vessel's surface varies from pure black to 10 YR 3/1 ("very dark gray"). The vessel has occasional firing clouds as light as 10 YR 6/2 ("light brownish gray"), and the clay body varies from 2.5 Y 7/0 ("light gray") to 2.5 Y 6/0 ("gray").

Vessel 2

Vessel 2 is a Camacho Black amphora with two strap handles (Figure 9.2a, b). These handles had been set at different heights, making this vessel asymmetrical. The amphora is 19 cm tall, its rim diameter is 6.6 cm, and its wall thickness is 5 mm.

Sixty percent of the vessel's exterior surface is black; the rest has firing clouds which vary from 2.5 Y 5/2 ("light olive brown") to 2.5 Y 4/0 ("dark gray") to 10 YR 3/1 ("very dark gray"). The clay body varies from 2.5 Y 7/0 to 5 Y 7/1 (both considered "light gray").

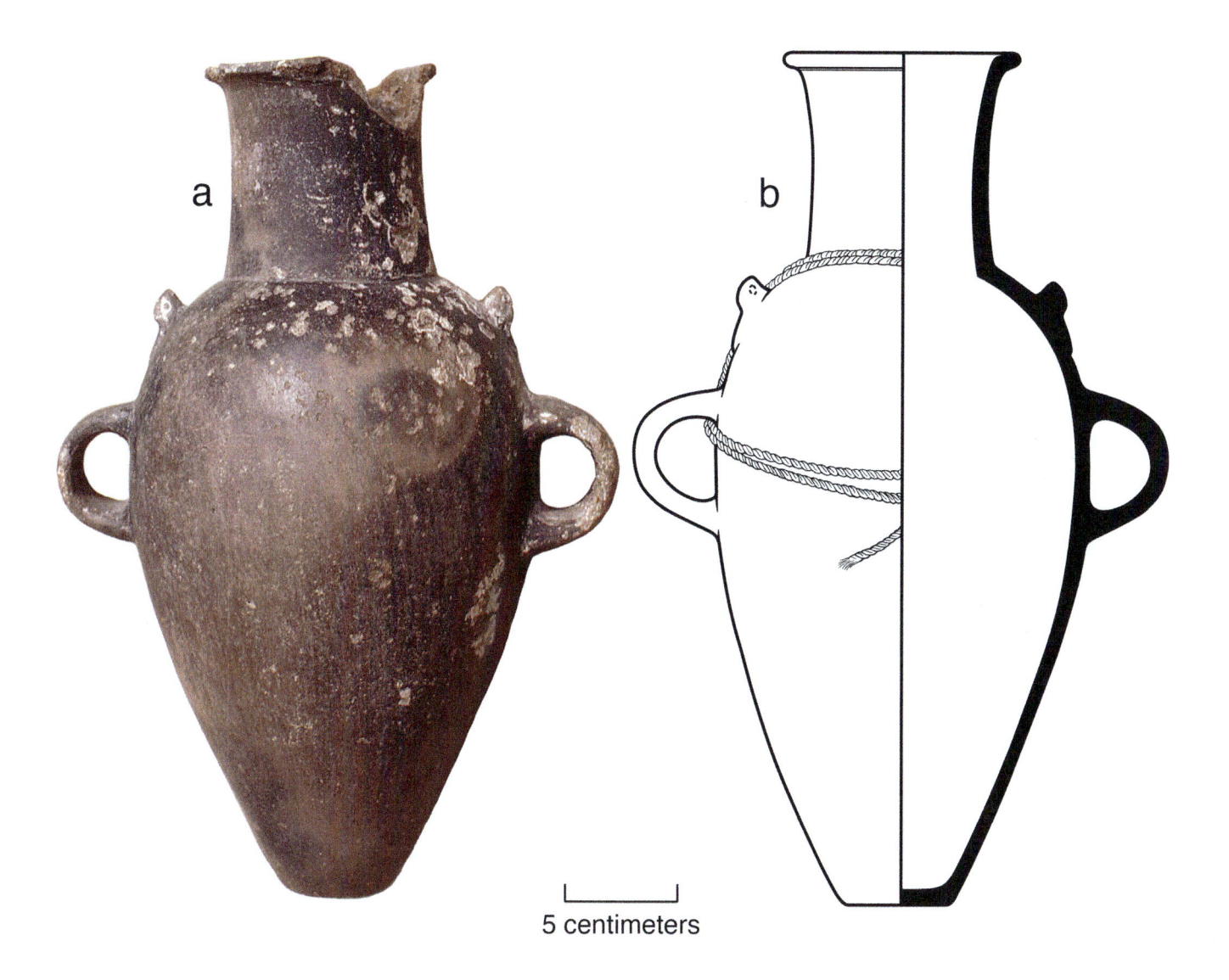

Figure 9.1. Vessel 1 from Burial 3, a Camacho Black amphora with small lugs on its shoulder. When discovered, this vessel still wore a harness of grass rope that passed through the handles and wound around the lugs (see b).

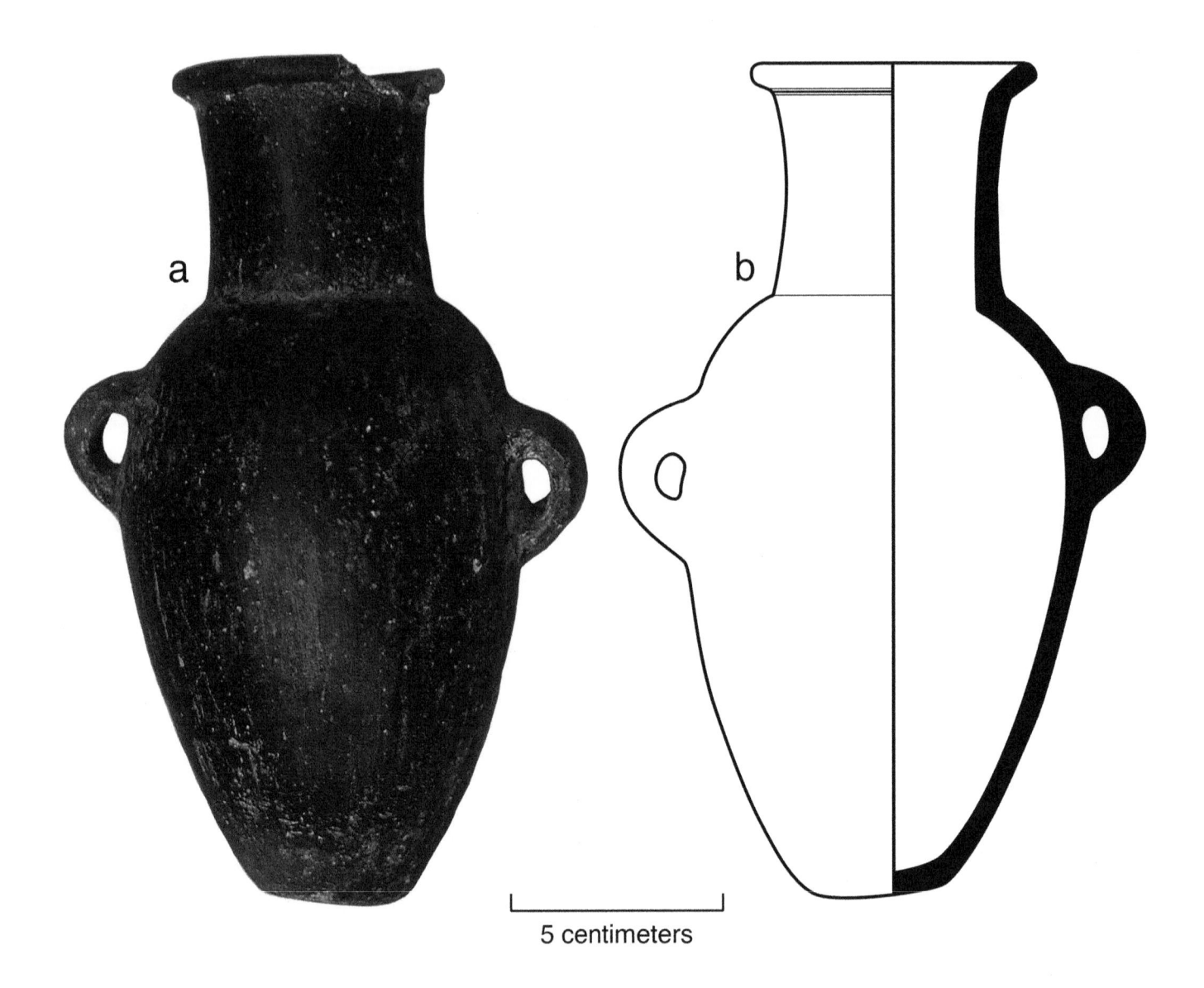

Figure 9.2. Two views of Vessel 2 from Burial 3. This Camacho Black amphora featured two loop handles, each set at a different height. The photograph (a) shows one side; the drawing (b) shows the opposite side of the vessel.

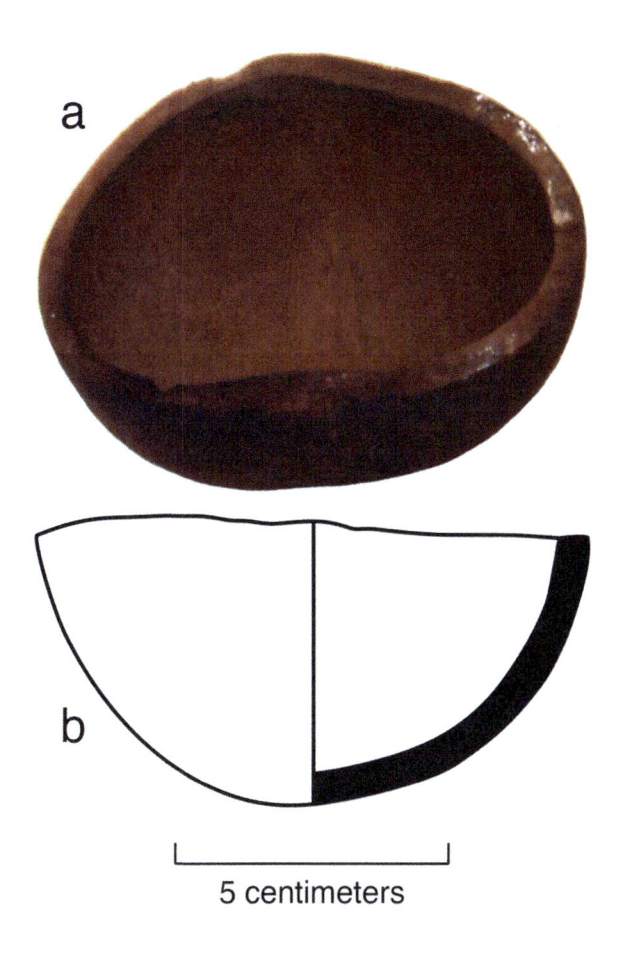

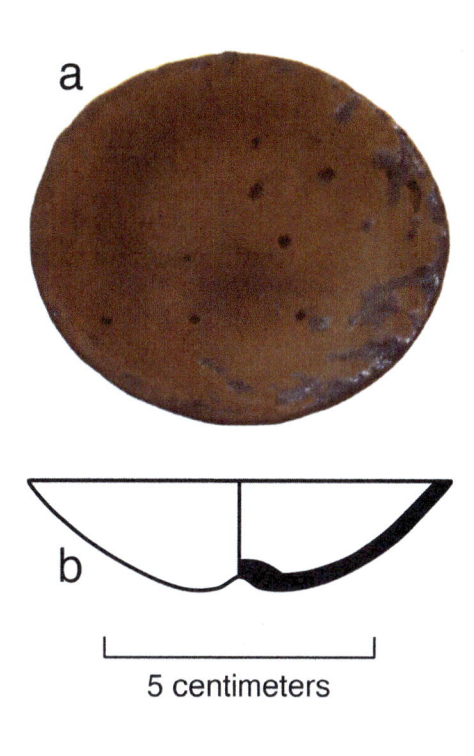

Figure 9.3. Vessel 3 from Burial 3, a gourd bowl.

Figure 9.4. Vessel 4 of Burial 3, a miniature gourd bowl.

Gourd Vessels

By cutting through its stem scars, this gourd (Specimen 27) was converted into a bowl 5 cm high, ca. 10.2 cm in length, and 8.2 cm in width (Figure 9.3a and b). The gourd wall is 6 mm thick. Its color ranges from 2.5 YR 3/2 ("dusky red") to 2.5 YR 2/2 ("very dusky red").

The second gourd bowl from Burial 3 is shown in Figure 9.4 (Specimen 28). This gourd vessel is 7.9 cm in diameter, 2 cm high, and 3 mm thick. Its color is 2.5 YR 2/2 ("very dusky red").

Animal Offering

The lower leg of a llama seems to have been associated with this burial (Glew and Flannery 2016a:300). The right tibia, right astragalus, right fourth tarsal, and right metatarsal were still articulated, and a patch of llama hide with white hair was present. In the fill around the burial were bones from a possible second leg—a left astragalus, left calcaneum, left central tarsal, left second + third tarsal, and left fourth tarsal. All these bones appeared to be from a young animal (or animals).

Comments on Burial 3

Unfortunately, the looters who beat us to this burial had disturbed it so badly that we could not even determine how many individuals were involved.

Chapter 10

Burial 4

Burial 4, which occupied a clay-lined pit, lay to the north of Burial 9 (see Figure 7.1). The Burial 4 pit had two compartments, an upper and a lower (Figure 10.1). At a depth of 30 cm below the surface we encountered a partially preserved clay cap that our workmen called a *torta de barro*. This clay seal was designed to close off the upper compartment.

At a depth of 90 cm we encountered a second clay surface that had been partially broken; this surface was evidently designed to close off the lower compartment. Immediately below the clay, we found a fragment of a gourd and a wooden "grave marker." Similar markers have been reported from valleys to the north and south of Cerro Azul (Frame and Ángeles Falcón 2014:29; Lothrop and Mahler 1957a: Plate 15); such markers may have been created to deter individuals from disturbing the mummy bundles below.

Excavating Burial 4

Burial 4's upper compartment held seven skulls. Its lower compartment contained three mummy bundles and one isolated human skull; the arrangement of the three mummy bundles can be seen in Figure 10.1. Each mummy bundle featured a false head, made of cloth and reeds. Outside the uppermost bundle—that of Individual 2—was a piece of wood that we submitted for ^{14}C dating; it yielded a conventional date of 610 ± 70 years BP or A.D. 1340. When calibrated, the two-sigma range of this date would be A.D. 1276–1431, roughly the latter half of the Late Intermediate.

All three mummy bundles (Individuals 1a, 2, and 3) contained women, and each bundle reflected a different state of preservation. The outer layers of cloth had become loose on all three bundles, and the inner layers had largely disintegrated on the upper two bundles. The deterioration of the outermost layer of cloth allowed some burial objects to fall out of each bundle. Some of these objects made their way to the sides of the pit, while others fell all the way to the bottom. We also found one workbasket that had been damaged by body acids; as a result, the contents of that workbasket had fallen to the bottom of the pit.

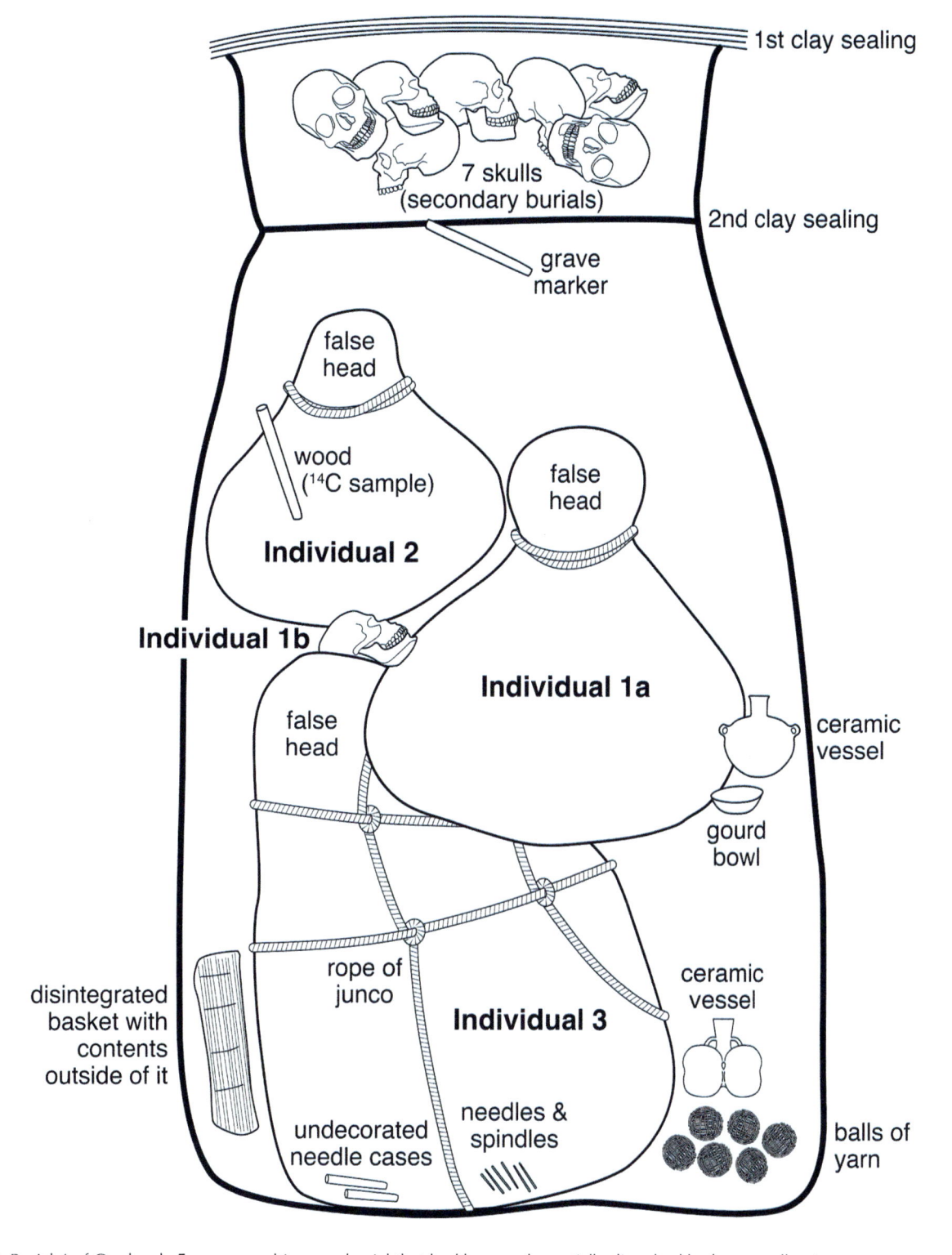

Figure 10.1. Burial 4 of Quebrada 5a was a multiperson burial that had been only partially disturbed by looters, allowing us to recover more information than usual about each individual (redrawn by Bruce Worden from in-the-field sketches made by Ramiro Matos and Joyce Marcus).

Individual 1a

The outermost layer of Individual 1a's bundle was a poorly preserved coarse cloth. Between this outermost cloth and the 12 brown and white striped cloths wrapped around the body we found four *chumpis* (the generic Quechua term for belts or loom backstraps), three of which were well preserved.

Inside the mummy bundle was a woman whose arms were crossed on her chest; her wrists were tied together with a piece of fabric and her fingers tied with string. She was wearing a bracelet of black seeds, similar to the miniature seed necklace worn by the figurine accompanying Individual 3 in this same burial pit (see below). Such seed necklaces are associated with women at other coastal sites such as Pachacamac, Armatambo, and Pampa Flores (e.g., Chan 2011; Díaz Arriola 2015:195; Eeckhout and Owens 2015).

Individual 1a's bundle had a false head, made from rolled-up cloth and bulrushes. This false head presumably enabled those who transported the mummy bundle to determine which end of the bundle was the top; it may also have served to "humanize" the bundle. The Cerro Azul false heads were much simpler than those found at Pachacamac, some of which were given wigs and wooden masks (e.g., Fleming 1986; Shimada et al. 2015; Uhle 1903).

Ceramic Vessel Inside the Mummy Bundle of Individual 1a

Inside the cloth wrappings of Individual 1a's bundle was a miniature Camacho Black amphora with a cotton plug (Figure 10.2a, b). This vessel had just one handle and was 13.4 cm high, with a rim diameter of 2.7 cm. When we opened Individual 1a's bundle, we found that this miniature amphora and some hanks of hair were adhering to one of the 12 brown and white striped cloths (Figure 10.2c, Textile 203).

Ceramic Vessels Outside the Mummy Bundles

Along the sides of the Burial 4 pit, and no longer directly associated with a specific mummy bundle, were a few ceramic vessels. One was a globular jar with two strap handles. This jar is an example of the highly burnished variety of Camacho Black, which has a characteristically metallic sheen (Figure 10.3). The jar is 15.8 cm high, with a rim diameter of 4.5 cm, and a maximum vessel diameter of 14.6 cm. Its wall thickness is 4 to 6 mm, and its strap handles are 2 cm wide. We found vessels of this highly burnished variety of Camacho Black to be more common in miniature form and more likely to appear in burials than in general refuse.

Below Individuals 1a and 1b we found a large amphora with two strap handles and two effigy lugs on the shoulder (Figure 10.4). Most of this amphora's black burnished surface had been eaten away by *salitre*, or salt incrustations. Horizontal striations could be seen inside the neck and on the exterior, presumably made during manufacture when a cloth was wiped over the moist clay. This vessel is 29 cm high, with a rim diameter of 11 cm, and a wall thickness of 6 to 8 mm. The strap handles are 3.5 cm wide. The Munsell color of the exterior surface varies from 10 YR 4/1 ("dark gray") to 10 YR 5/2 ("grayish brown") to 2.5 Y 6/2 ("light brownish gray"); the interior of the clay body is light gray.

Gourd Vessels

We found two gourd bowls below the mummy bundle associated with Individuals 1a and 1b. One of these gourd vessels (Figure 10.5a) lay directly below Individual 1a; it contained two complete specimens of guinea pig (*Cavia porcellus*), whose skeletons were partially decomposed and therefore incomplete. Guinea Pig #1 was represented by its cranium, its right and left mandibles, its right scapula, its right and left humeri, and its right ulna (NISP = 7, MNI = 1). Guinea Pig #2 was represented by its cranium, its right mandible, its right and left scapulae, its right and left humeri, its left radius, its left ulna, its sacrum, its right innominate, and patches of its brownish yellow hair (NISP = 11, MNI = 1). In addition, the gourd contained 21 loose bones or teeth that could have been from either Guinea Pig #1 or Guinea Pig #2. Included were three loose incisors, nine vertebrae, seven ribs, and two complete axes (NISP = 21). Both of the guinea pigs were adults (Glew and Flannery 2016b:329).

This gourd (Figure 10.5a, Specimen 35) is of the shallow bowl type. Its rim diameter varies from 18.5 to 20 cm, its height is 5.0 to 5.6 cm, and its wall thickness is 5.5 mm. The color of the gourd ranges from 5 YR 3/1 ("very dark gray") to 5 YR 2/1 ("black").

The second gourd bowl (Figure 10.5b) had been perforated for suspension, and fragments of a cord were still present in holes found on opposite sides of the bowl. This bowl (Specimen 21) appears to have been modified into a kidney shape for suspension. The gourd is 19 x 15 cm, with

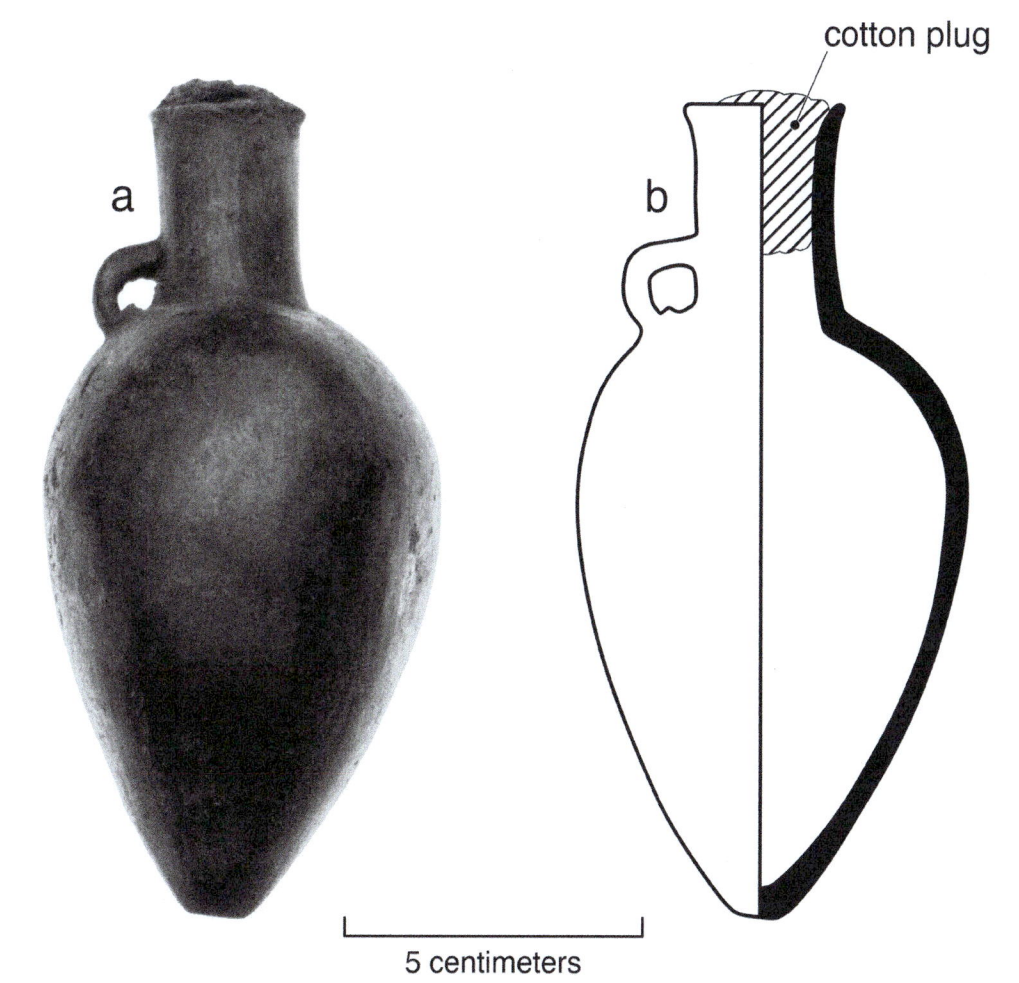

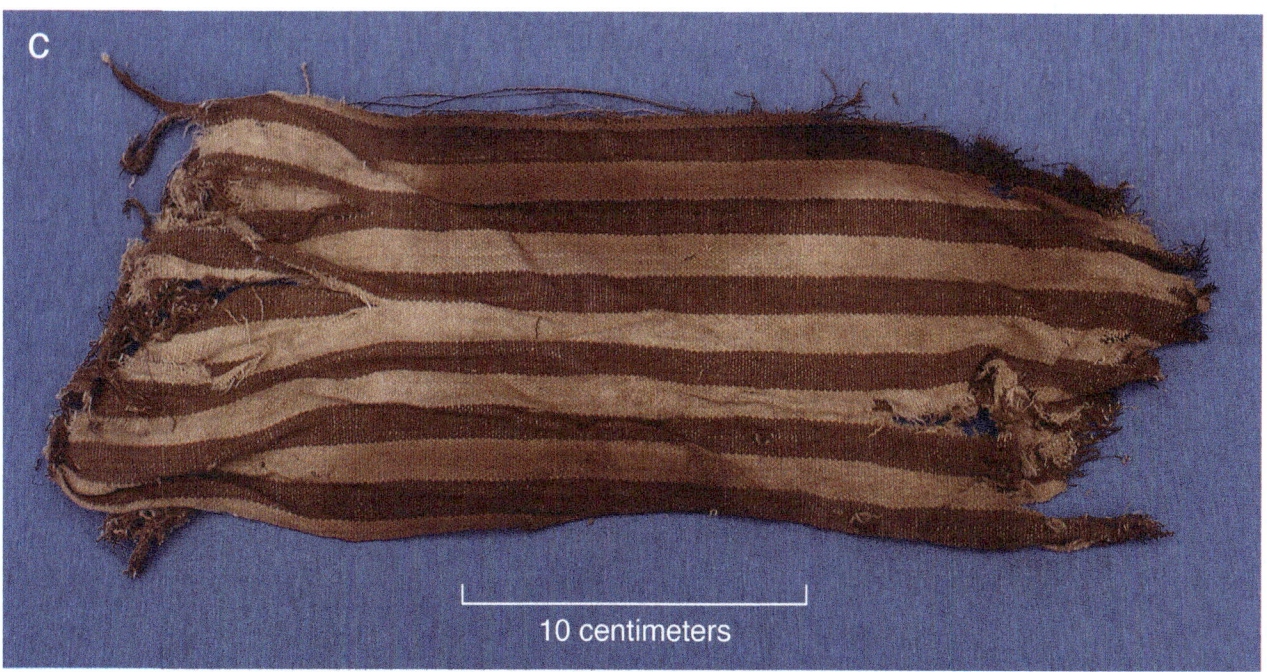

Figure 10.2. Items from Burial 4. (a) Photo of a Camacho Black miniature amphora, found inside Individual 1a's mummy bundle. (b) Drawing of the same amphora, showing its cotton plug. (c) One of a dozen brown and white striped cloths associated with Individual 1a.

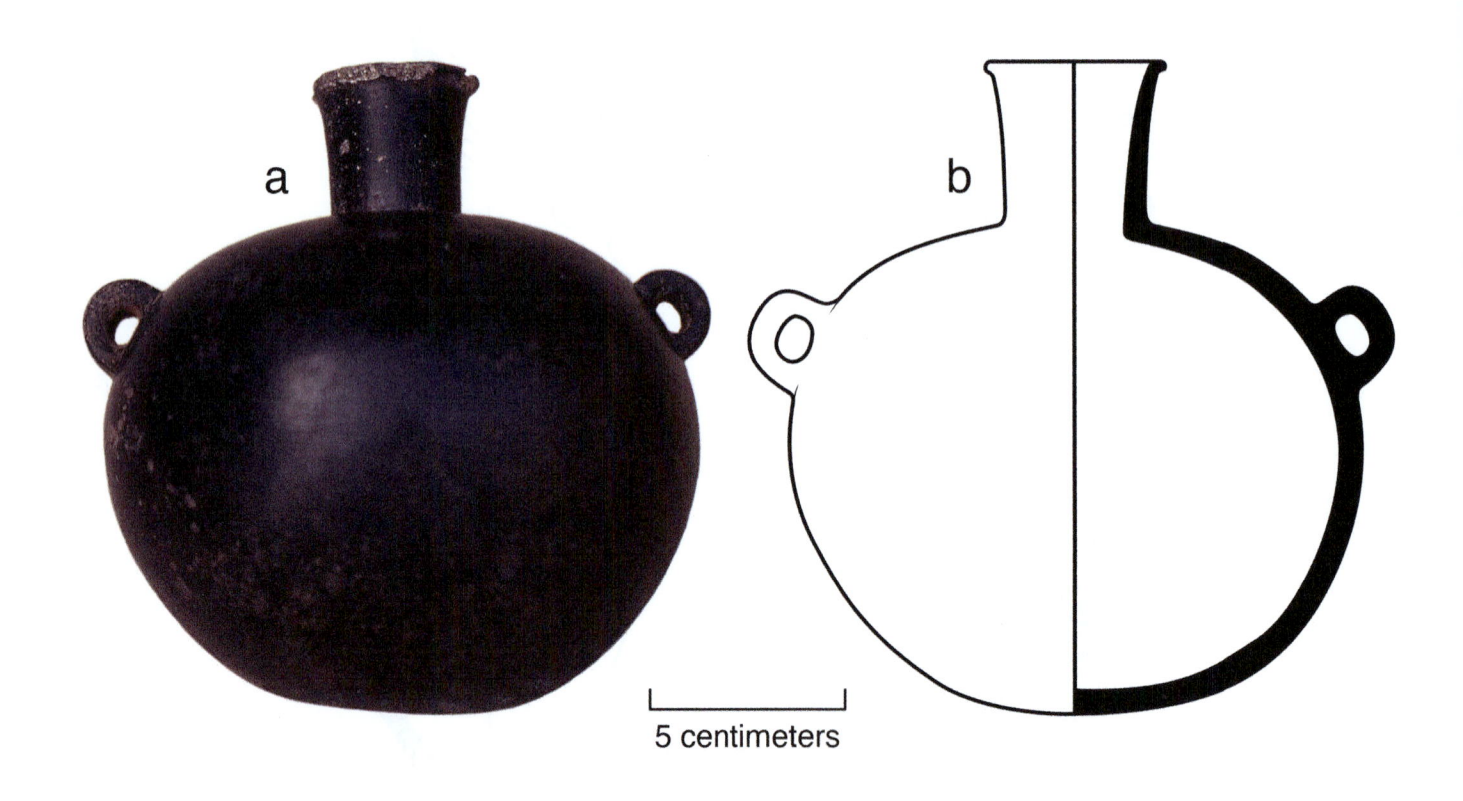

Figure 10.3. A globular jar from Burial 4 (Camacho Black type, highly burnished variant).

a height between 4.5 and 6.5 cm and a wall thickness of 5 mm. Its exterior color is 2.5 YR 3/2 ("dusky red"). There is some evidence of scorching on the inside and at the center of the gourd.

Metal

Items of both gold and silver were associated with the three women in this burial pit, but it was not always clear with which individual they were associated. For example, the gold item in Figure 10.6 had fallen between the mummy bundles of Individuals 1a and 2, along with the silver foil discussed next. The piece of gold foil was 0.6 mm thick, weighing 3 g, and embossed with the sun-shaped motifs called *intis*.

Wrapped inside that gold foil was a thin sheet of silver foil, also embossed with *intis*. This foil had broken into several pieces; the two largest (Figure 10.7) measured 7 x 7 cm and 7 x 8 cm, respectively. Together these two pieces have a total weight of 7 g. At least four smaller silver fragments, evidently with the same shape as the item in Figure 10.6, were also present. One of these smaller silver fragments had been inserted into the mouth of Individual 1a.

Figure 10.8 shows a packet of embossed silver foil (0.15 mm thick) that had been clutched in a woman's hand. Unfortunately, this hand had been jostled free by looters, so we do not know to which individual it belonged. One of her red-painted fingernails (Figure 10.8, lower right) was adhering to one side of the foil, while the skin of her palm was stuck to the other side.

These pieces of silver foil had once formed a larger item, measuring 7 x 6 cm. They had been folded into a packet 3 x 4 cm in size so that it would fit more easily into the palm of a hand. The three largest pieces had once measured 5 x 4 cm, 3.5 x 6 cm, and 4 x 7 cm. The total weight of the packet was 4.5 g.

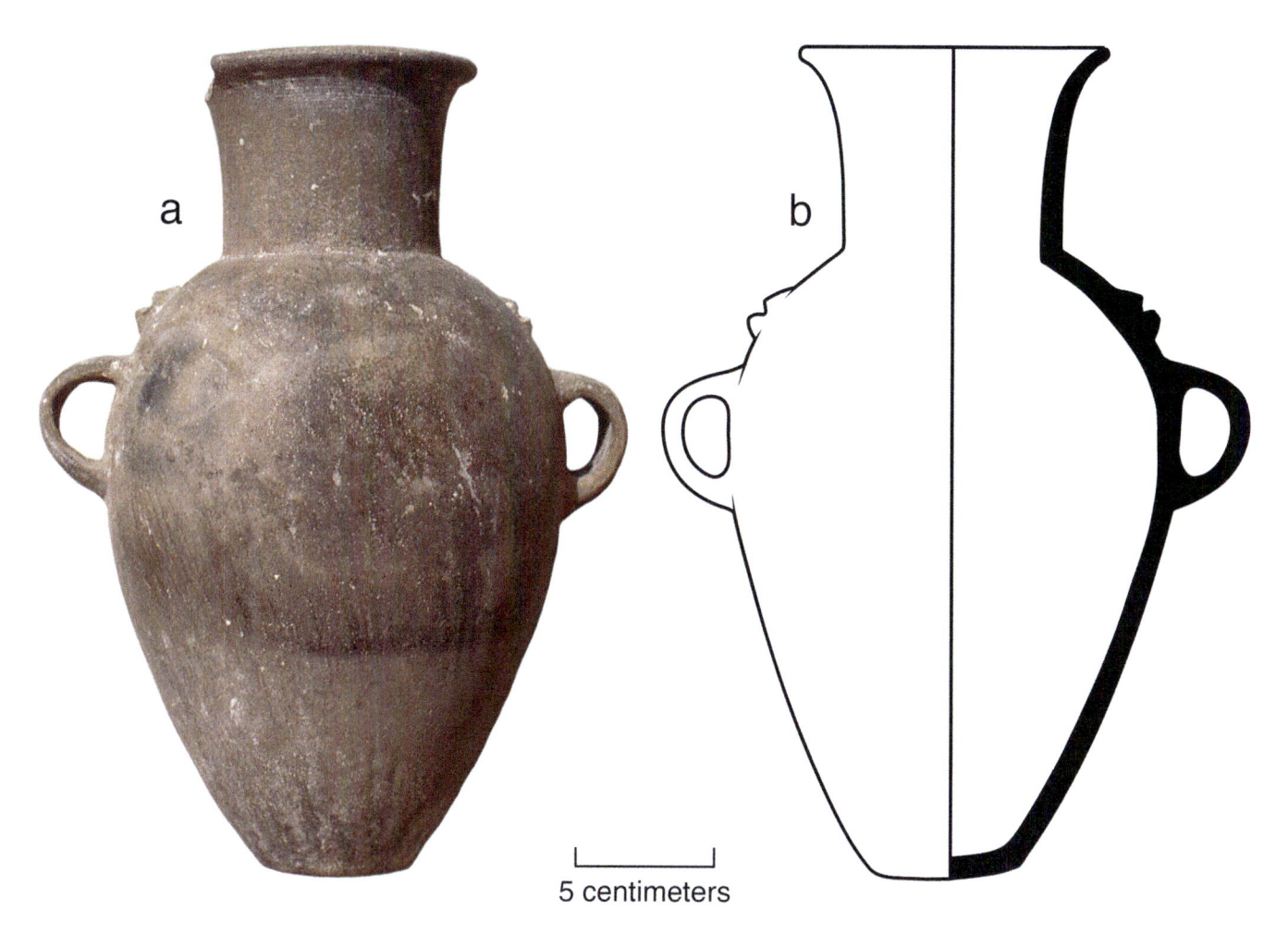

Figure 10.4. An amphora from Burial 4. Originally Camacho Black, its burnished exterior had been eaten away by *salitre*, leaving its surface color grayish brown.

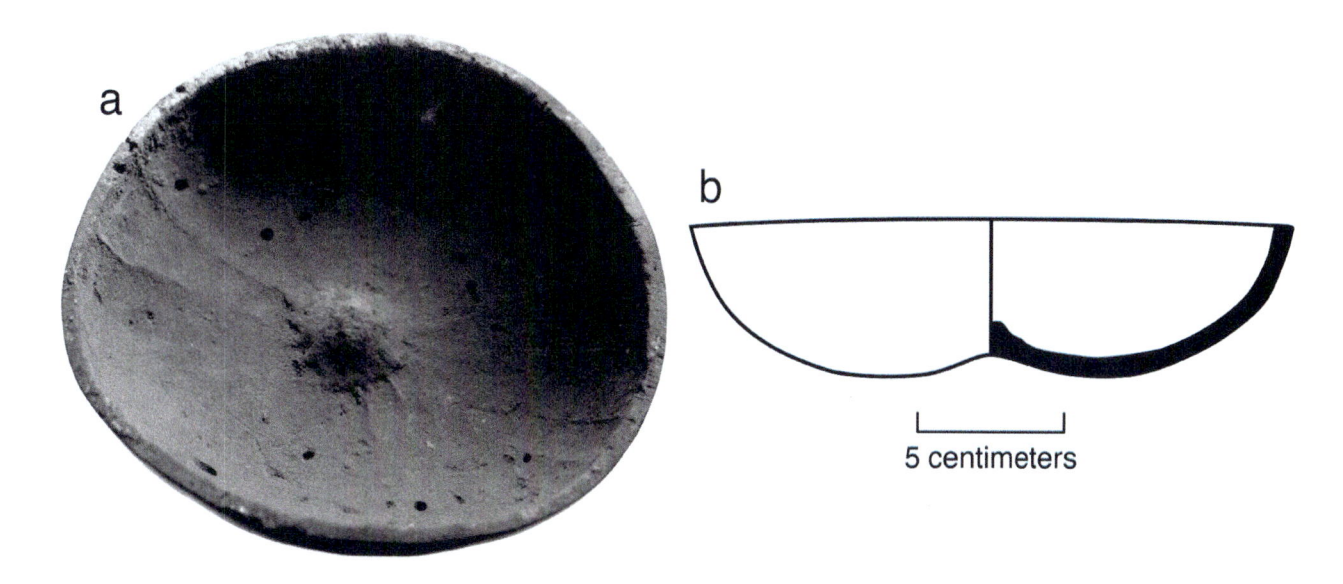

Figure 10.5. A gourd vessel from Burial 4. When discovered, it contained two guinea pigs.

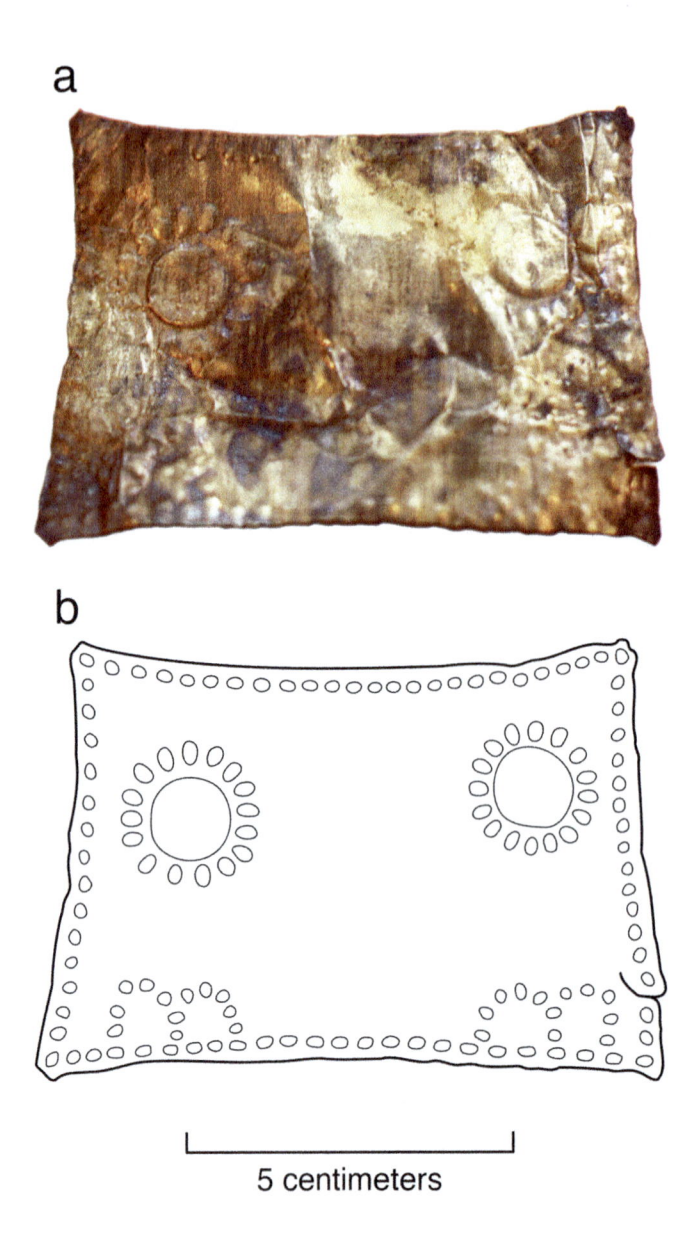

Figure 10.6. Photo and drawing of a gold foil rectangle from Burial 4, embossed with sun-shaped *intis*. When discovered, it was folded over the silver foil shown in Figure 10.7; both had fallen between Individuals 1a and 2.

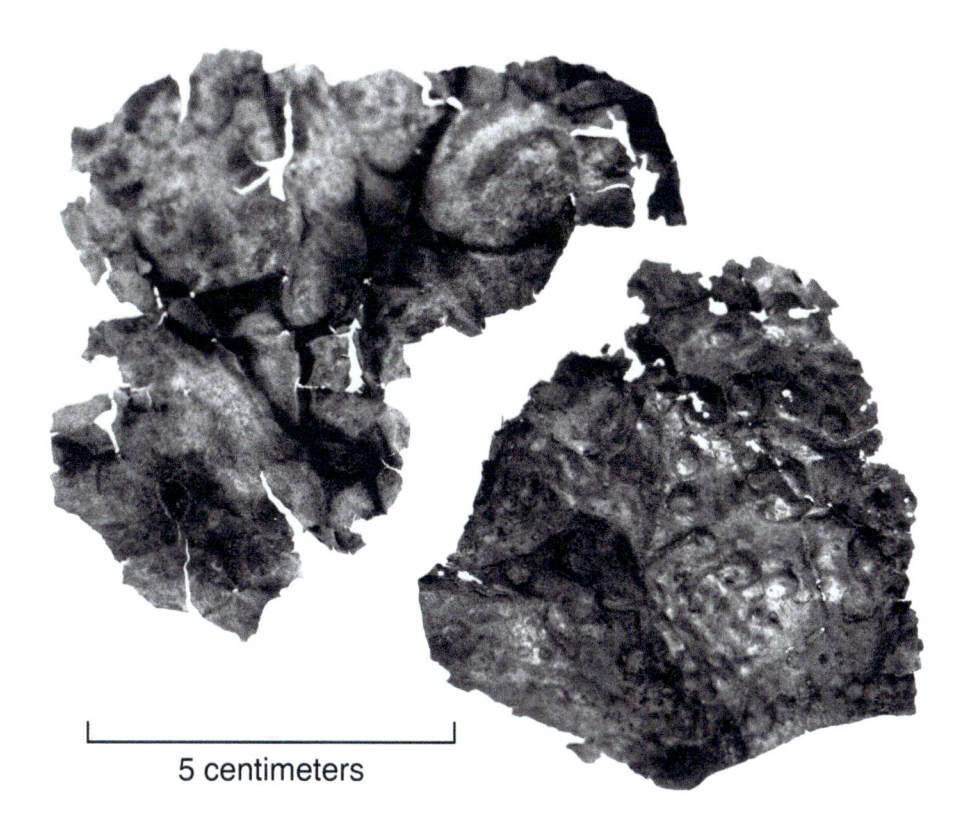

Figure 10.7. Pieces of silver foil, found folded inside the gold foil rectangle shown in Figure 10.6.

Figure 10.8. Four items associated with Individual 1a of Burial 4. (a) Three pieces of silver foil, found folded into a packet clutched in a woman's hand that had been dislodged from her mummy. Her red-painted fingernail is shown at (b).

Pigment Pouches and Yarn Balls Stored in Individual 1a's Bag

Inside Individual 1a's mummy bundle was a bag (T208b) that contained two pigment pouches and eight yarn balls. This brown and gold checkered bag is warp-striped, with nine warps per centimeter and four wefts per centimeter (Figure 10.9a). The bag was made from one woolen textile measuring 20 x 13 cm. The bag was divided into three design sections: (1) a 5.5 cm band or section of dark brown and gold yarn in a checkered pattern that resulted in 13 lines; (2) a 2 cm band of solid gold yarn; and (3) a 5.5 cm section of dark brown and gold yarn in a checkered pattern, resulting in another 13 lines.

The 20 cm long textile had been folded in half to form a 10 cm wide bag. After folding, the base and the open side were closed by sewing them with two Z-spun wool fibers, plied in the S direction.

Inside the bag were eight yarn balls, all of wool: (1) a yarn ball weighing 6 g (Munsell color 7.5 YR 5/8), (2) a yarn ball weighing less than 1 g (5 YR 4/6), (3) a yarn ball weighing 1 g (7.5 YR 3/8), (4) a yarn ball weighing less than 1 g (7.5 YR 5/6), (5) a yarn ball weighing 1 g (7.5 YR 5/6), (6) a yarn ball weighing less than 1 g (7.5 YR 5/6), (7) loose pieces of a yarn ball (5 YR 4/6), and (8) disintegrated pieces of a yarn ball (5 R 2/1).

In addition to the yarn balls, this woman had stored two pigment pouches in her bag (Figure 10.9b). One of these pouches contained a blue pigment which chemist James Burton has identified as azurite. The second pouch contained a red powder that Burton has identified as cinnabar plus anhydrite. Burton noted that the cinnabar + anhydrite mixture had a sticky, tar-like texture that may have resulted from the addition of an organic material that he was unable to identify.

The colors of these pigments—vermilion and blue—were highly valued and perhaps used in more than one kind of ritual. For example, Arriaga (1968[1621]:45–46) mentions that the Inca blew powders of different colors in the direction of sacred huacas as offerings, pointing "to the conopas and huacas to attract their attention before they blow." Other sources mention the importance of red pigment in painting the face and body (Bongers et al. 2022). According to Acosta (1954[1590]), cinnabar was used to paint peoples' faces and bodies, especially those of warriors.

The vermilion-colored powder, called *paria* in Quechua, was said to have been brought from the mines of Huancavelica; mercury and mercury sulfide were also obtained there (Arriaga 1968[1621]:45). Arriaga also mentions *binços*, a fine blue powder.

Red pigments and powders are mentioned elsewhere in the ethnohistoric record. For example, cinnabar is mentioned by Bernabé Cobo, who says that *llimpi*, "es el mismo de que sacan el bermellón." The *Relaciones geográficas* (Carbajal [1586] in Jiménez de la Espada [1965]) state: "in the town of Páras two colors, red and yellow, were obtained from a stone called *llimpi*, from which the metal quicksilver is derived; [these mineral powders] were used to paint themselves…". According to González Holguín ([1608]1952), the word *llimpi* actually means "color," and *llimppikuni* means "pintarse la cara con bermellón."

These pigments were clearly valued by the Late Intermediate women at Cerro Azul; several of them, including Individual 1a of Burial 4, stored these colorful mineral powders in waterproof pouches placed inside woolen bags. These waterproof pouches appear membranous and translucent; zooarchaeologist Kent Flannery says that they look like camelid bladders, but he stresses that this tentative identification would have to be confirmed by microscopic analysis.

Bracelet

Individual 1a was found wearing a tiny bracelet of black seeds (Figure 10.9c). Significantly, this bracelet is similar to the necklace of black seeds worn by a ceramic figurine stored in a bag associated with Individual 3 of this same burial (see below). Such seed necklaces have been found with other female burials at coastal sites (Díaz Arriola 2015:195). Donnan (1995:149) states that on Peru's north coast, a bracelet or necklace was the second most common artifact found in the burials of Moche infants and children.

Textiles

Textile 124 (Figure 10.10) is an example of a brocaded textile (called discontinuous extra-weft patterning). This fragment, which measures 28 x 41 cm, was partly lodged in a looters' hole that penetrated the side of Burial 4.

The area with the design measures 14 x 41 cm. The warp is dark brown wool, S-spun, 0.15–0.30 mm in width; the weft is cotton, S-spun, and dark brown in color. Some extra wefts are wool, Z-S, 0.7 mm thick with a 15 degree spin, and they come in a variety of colors (red, yellow, white, and green).

The extra weft courses create the design. The design elements are separated by bands of background weave that

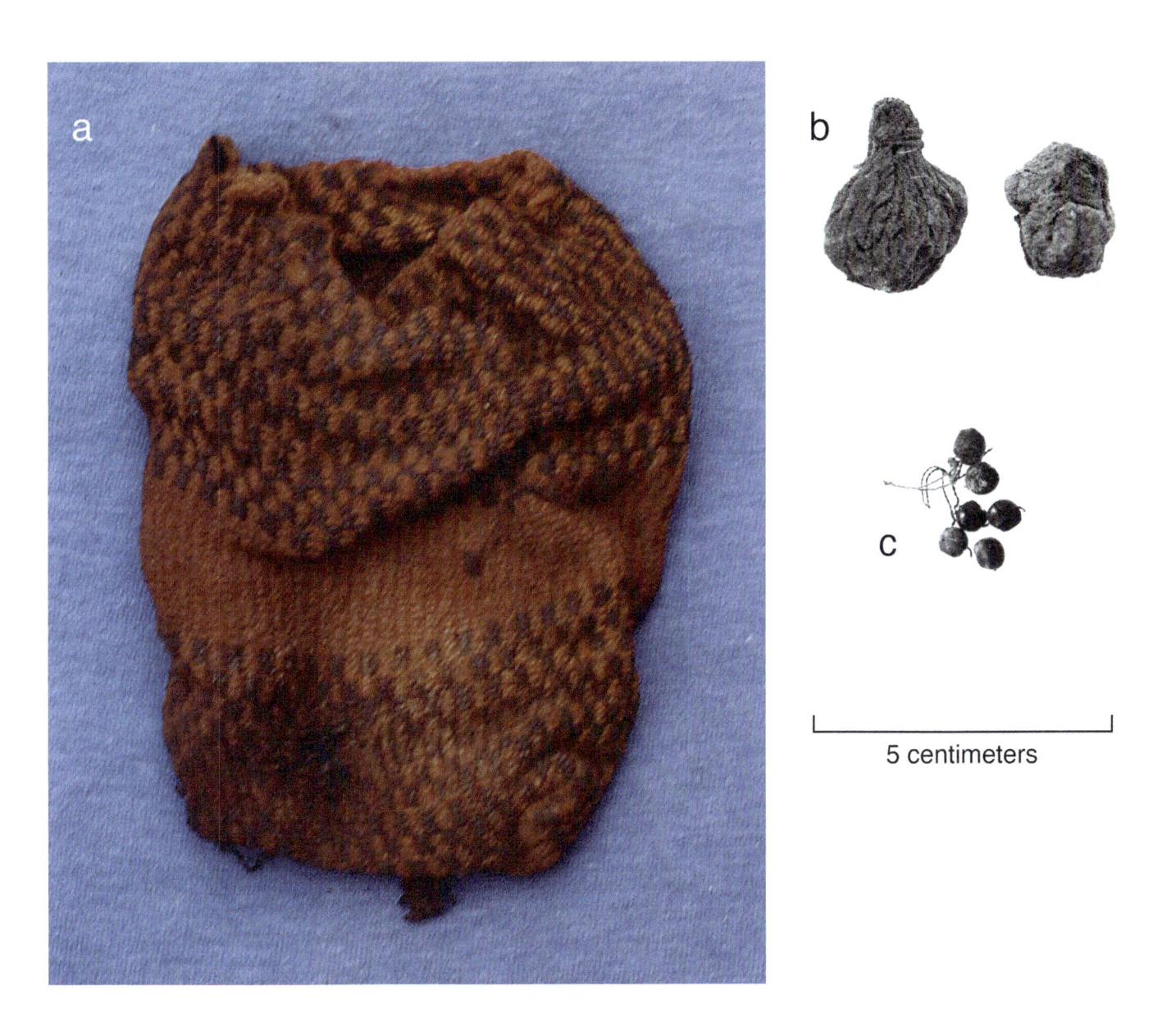

Figure 10.9. More items associated with Individual 1a of Burial 4. (a) A woolen bag that held two pigment pouches and eight yarn balls. (b) Two pigment pouches. (c) A seed bracelet found on Individual 1a's wrist.

Figure 10.10. A portion of brocaded textile, found in a hole made by looters when they penetrated the side of the Burial 4 pit.

have a consistent width and color. The design yarns are floated on the reverse side. This technique could be called "ground checkered patterning." The design is contained in a rectangular band with a height of 14 cm (starting at one end selvage), and a width of 41 cm from one non-loom end to another. The 2 x 2 dark brown plain weave continues as plain cloth below the design band until it reaches an incomplete lower edge. Two centimeters of the design band and of the plain area are turned under and sewn to the band at one end.

The design of Textile 124 is a series of diagonal lines, made up of interlocking pairs of frets forming vertical bands four centimeters wide. One set of interlocking pairs is red across the whole band; the others follow a sequence of yellow, white, green, and then repeat.

Textile 206 is a warp-stripe plain weave cotton cloth, with alternating brown and tan stripes.

Textile 208a is a fragment of a plain weave cloth that has been rolled into a rope-like segment, tied with a large overhand knot. The warp and weft are cotton. This cloth was wrapped around the woolen bag (Figure 10.9a), which contained two pigment pouches and eight yarn balls.

T 208c consists of two cord segments measuring 28 cm and 32 cm in length. Each cord was made with cross-knit looping. This cord has an asymmetric cross section, generally ovate, with one side nearly flat.

T 208d consists of small wads and skeins of wool of different colors, including red, yellow, and several shades of brown. The skein yarns are wool, Z-spun, S-twisted.

Belts Associated with Individual 1a

Among the more elaborate textiles associated with Individual 1a were her four *chumpis*. Three of the four (Chumpis 7, 8, and 9) were well preserved. The fourth *chumpi* is known only from its partial remains; its wefts are so deteriorated that little remains except for a mass of yarns. The one intact area of this fourth specimen displays diagonal interlocking frets, each consisting of a stepped triangle with central dots in red and green wool. Associated with this *chumpi* were various lengths of dark brown six-strand circular braid (1.8 mm in diameter) with a total length of 1.37 m.

Chumpi 7 (65 x 10.5 cm) is a two-sided backstrap (Sides A and B) with a central panel of slit tapestry and flanking bands of complementary warp-faced plain weave (see Cahlander and Baizerman 1985; D'Harcourt 1934; Emery 1966; Kula 1988; A. Rowe 1977; and Stone-Miller 1992a and 1992b for lengthier discussions of these weaving techniques).

Side A of Chumpi 7 (Figure 10.11a) has diagonal rows of diamond-shaped units, each containing intertwined bird heads with two floating small triangles and two floating squares with dots inside them. Every other row on Side A of Chumpi 7 uses a white background inside the diamond-shaped units to substitute for the yellow background.

It is notable that the woman in Burial 9 had a *chumpi* with the identical design seen on Side A of Chumpi 7 (see Chapter 15). However, each woman chose different colors to execute the identical design; Individual 1a of Burial 4 chose red, yellow, and white, while the woman in Burial 9 chose dark green, gold, and brown. This is one of the few archaeological cases in which we learn the individual color preferences of different women.

Side B of Chumpi 7 (Figure 10.11b) also has diagonal rows of diamond-shaped units. Each unit contains two birds with triangular bodies, with one large dot and three small dots inside each bird's body and one small dot next to each bird's tail. Colors repeat in every other diagonal row. The dominant colors are forest green, yellows, and browns.

Chumpi 8 (60 × 13 cm) is a two-sided belt with a slit tapestry panel, flanked by two warp-faced plain weave bands. Only one side (Side A) was sufficiently preserved to show the whole design.

Side A (Figure 10.12) has a 6.5 cm wide tapestry panel made up of five thin strips of motifs, each 1.3 cm high. The design was continuously interlocked in a step fret and rectangular hook pattern. The same color forms a chevron across the five strips of tapestry.

Side B of Chumpi 8 (too poorly preserved to illustrate here) had a 6 cm wide tapestry panel bordered by 3.5 cm wide bands of warp-faced weave. The design is similar to one used on the *chumpis* found with Individual 3 of Burial 4 (see below). The Side B design is an interlocking step fret and volute pattern.

Chumpi 9 is a two-sided backstrap with slit tapestry flanked by warp-faced plain weave bands (Figure 10.13). Some of the *chumpi's* straps were still fastened at one end.

Side A has an 8.5 cm wide tapestry panel. Its design resembles a geometric bird, with interlocking frets and floating rectangular elements as fillers. Each bird is set within a diamond-shaped unit, with white birds alternating with black birds.

Side B of Chumpi 9 has an 8.5 cm wide tapestry panel in the center. The design is a so-called double diamond set in a diamond. The diamond units are arranged in diagonal rows, with five to seven diamond-shaped units on each row. Colors repeat such that diagonal rows 1, 4, 7, 10, are identical, as are rows 2, 5, 8, and 11.

We know little about Individual 1b, an adult woman in her 30s, who was part of a secondary interment placed outside the three wrapped mummy bundles in Burial 4.

We will now look at the sewing and weaving items in a workbasket that lay immediately below the mummy bundles of Individuals 1a and 2; the contents could not be associated directly with either woman.

Workbasket Contents Found Lying Below Individuals 1a and 2 (Specimen 113)

Two weaving implements (Figure 10.14a) made from ungulate long bones (deer or camelid); they are mirror images, and each has a slightly convex side and a flat side. The smaller bone is 21 cm long, 18 mm maximum width, and 3.8 mm thick. The larger bone measures 24.9 cm long, 22 mm wide, and 4.4 mm thick.

Two *kallwas*, or weaving swords, possibly chonta wood (Figure 10.14b). One is 20.6 cm long, 11 mm wide, and 4.5 mm thick. The other is 18.6 cm long, 15 mm wide, and 3.5 mm thick.

Two bone artifacts (Figure 10.14c). One is 15.7 cm long, the other 15.2 cm. Diameters of both are 3.0 to 3.5 mm. Each "skewer" was serving as a core for the *cordoncillo* or piping that the weaver was creating.

Two spindles with whorls (Figure 10.14d). One spindle is 21.3 cm long and has a diameter of 4.0 mm; it bears a globular Camacho Black whorl 15.2 mm in height and 19.3 mm in diameter. The other spindle is 12.5 cm long and has a diameter of 3.2 mm; it bears a spherical Camacho Black whorl 17.0 mm in height and 18.5 mm in diameter (see the lower whorl in Figure 10.14d; the same whorl is shown in Figure 10.16a).

Four knob-headed spindles, two of which still hold yarn (Figure 10.14e). Of the two holding yarn, one is 13.3 cm long and 3.0 mm in diameter; the other is 2.6 mm in diameter and 13.1 cm long. Both feature the same color yarn, 10 YR 6/8 ("brownish yellow"). The two empty spindles are approximately the same size.

Fifty-eight *Opuntia* spines, presumably saved to be made into needles (Figure 10.15a).

Thirty-two needles, all apparently made from *Opuntia* spines (Figure 10.15b). Most needles are between 6.5 and 9.5

Figure 10.11. Artist's rendering of Chumpi 7, a two-sided loom backstrap found with Individual 1a of Burial 4. Painting by Kay Clahassey.

Figure 10.12. Artist's rendering of Chumpi 8, a two-sided loom backstrap found with Individual 1a of Burial 4. Only one side was preserved well enough to record. Painting by Kay Clahassey.

cm in length and 1.2 mm in diameter, but the three largest range from 11.0 to 14.5 cm in length.

One needle measuring 12.8 cm long and 2 mm in diameter (Figure 10.15c).

Fifteen spindles without whorls or yarn, ranging from 16.5 to 23.5 cm in length (Figure 10.15d).

Three spindle fragments bearing yarn (Figure 10.15e). Two have yarn that is 7.5 YR 4/4 ("brown"); the third has yarn that is 7.5 YR 5/8 ("strong brown").

In addition to the whorl with incised lines (Figure 10.16a), there were **four undecorated Camacho Black spindle whorls** of the highly burnished variety. Three different shapes occur: teardrop, squat teardrop, and globular. The teardrop-shaped whorl is 14.9 mm high and 16.5 mm in diameter, weighing 4 g (Figure 10.16b). The squat teardrop is 15.5 mm high and 19.7 mm in diameter, weighing 5.5 g (Figure 10.16c). The two globular whorls are 12.4 mm high and 13.1 mm in diameter, weighing 4.5 g each (Figure 10.16d, e).

Three decorated gear-shaped spindle whorls (Figure 10.16f, g, and h). The first is black, with 11 tiers painted red and white; only traces of this paint exist (Figure 10.16f). The whorl's height is 16.1 mm, its diameter is 18.6 mm, and its weight is 5 g. The second whorl is black, with three tiers above and below a center band with incised fine lines set close together (Figure 10.16g). The whorl's height is 14.5 mm, its diameter is 18.9 mm, and its weight is 5.5 g. The third whorl is gray with three tiers above and below a central band incised with dots and slanted lines (see Figure 10.16h). This whorl's height is 16.9 mm, its diameter is 18.2 mm, and its weight could not be determined because it is broken and incomplete.

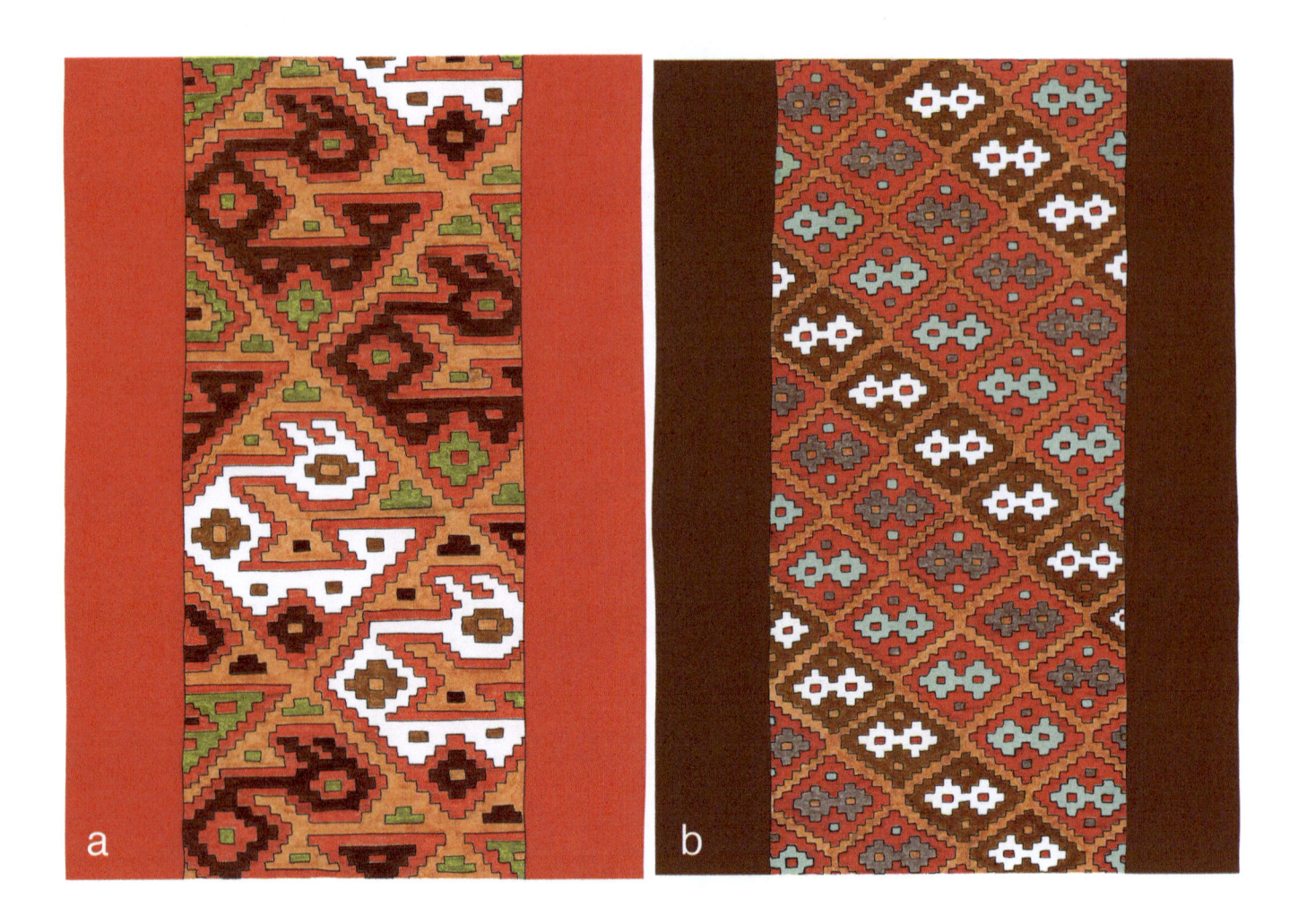

Figure 10.13. Artist's rendering of Chumpi 9, a two-sided loom backstrap found with Individual 1a of Burial 4. Painting by Kay Clahassey.

Two worn stream pebbles (each 1.5 cm in diameter and weighing ca. 5 g). These two stones may have been amulets of some sort kept in the workbasket.

Miscellaneous, Possibly Associated Items

Figure 10.17 shows miscellaneous items (Specimen 124) found near Individual 1a, but not definitively associated with her. Included was a spindle broken at both ends, bearing less than 1 g of dirty white yarn (Figure 10.17a). Also present was a spindle bearing a whorl (Figure 10.17b). The broken spindle is 15.8 cm long, 3 mm in diameter, and painted with a barcode too faded to identify. The teardrop-shaped whorl is Camacho Black, 16 mm high, and 18.3 mm in diameter.

Also present was a broken and bent spindle 21.7 cm long, bearing 13 g of dirty white yarn (Figure 10.17c). Finally, we found a yarn ball 5.5 cm in diameter with a weight of 33 g (Figure 10.17d); its color is 7.5 YR 5/6 ("strong brown"). There were also a number of unmodified *Opuntia* spines.

Other Weaving Implements Found Beneath Individuals 1a, 1b, and 2

Figure 10.18 shows the following items:
— two ungulate long bones (Figure 10.18a). One is 22 cm long; the other, 19.5 cm long.
— three pins with hard fruits still attached (14.5 cm long, 13.8 cm long, 14 cm long) and one *Opuntia* spine with a wrinkled black fruit or seed attached

Burial 4

a

b

c

1 centimeter

d

e

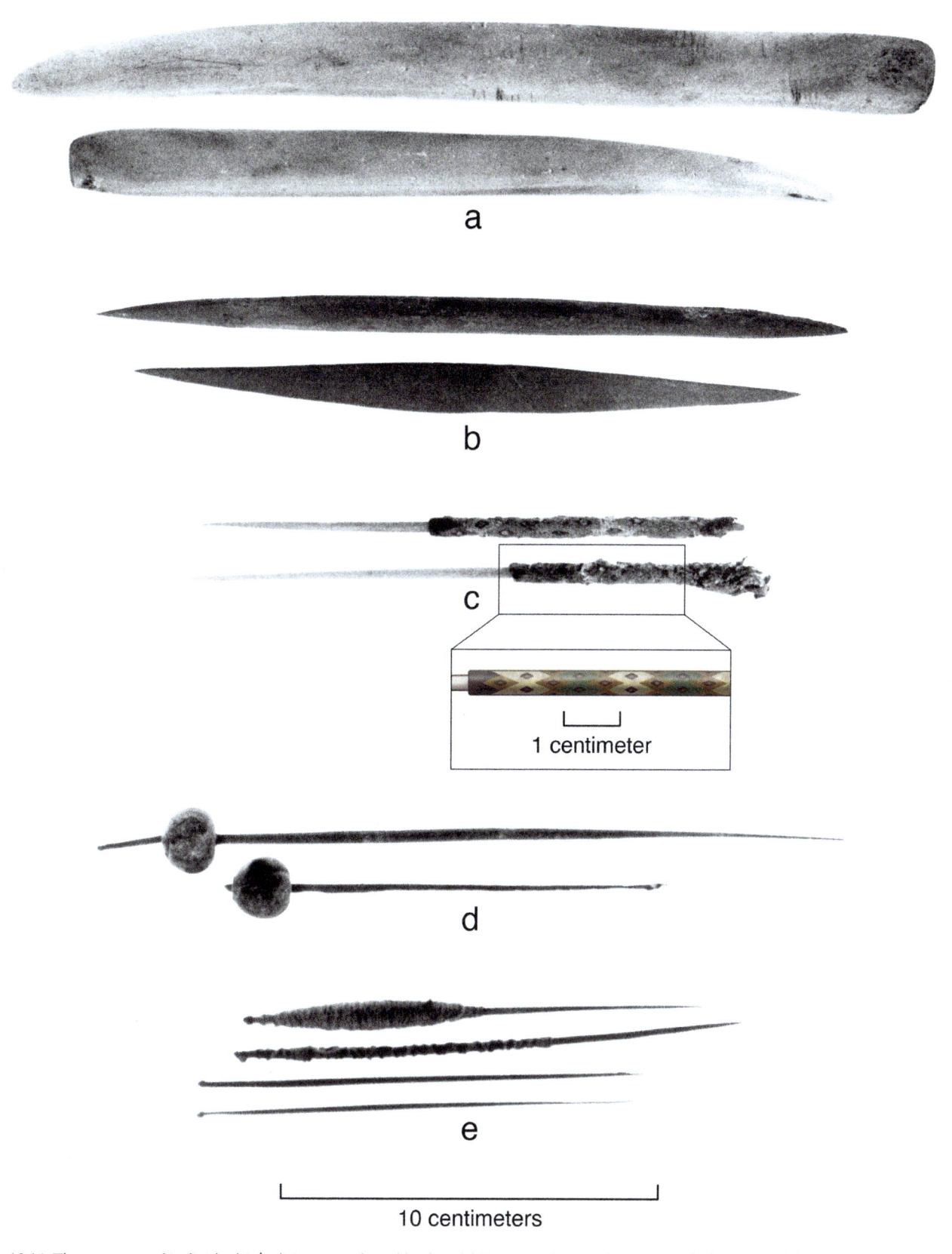

10 centimeters

Figure 10.14. The contents of Individual 1a's disintegrated workbasket. (a) Two weaving implements made from camelid or deer bones. (b) Two wooden *kallwa* or weaving swords. (c) Two bone skewers that served as the cores used to create *cordoncillo* or edge piping (lower skewer, detail drawn in color). (d) Two spindles with whorls. (e) Four knob-headed bobbins, two still holding yarn.

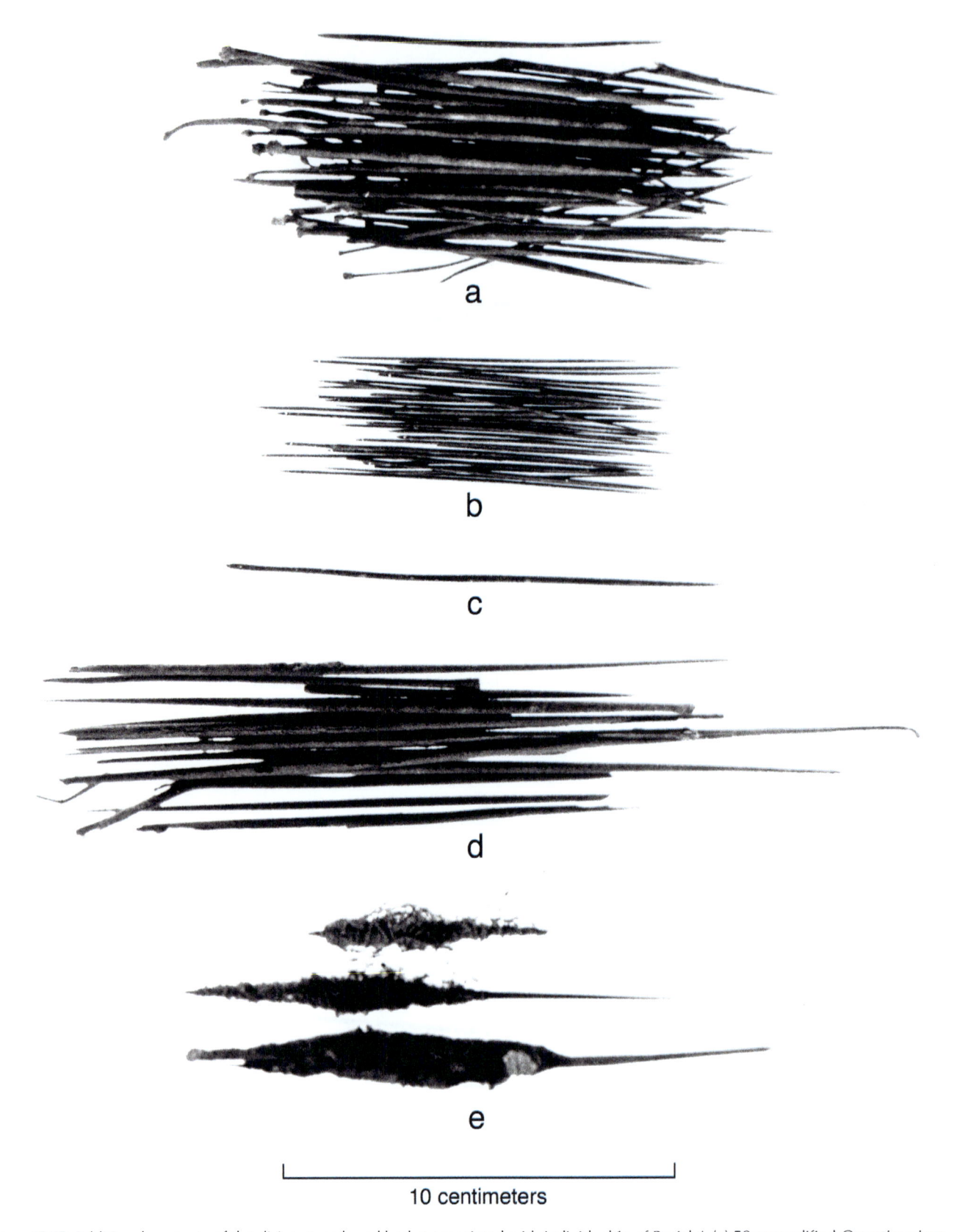

Figure 10.15. Additional contents of the disintegrated workbasket associated with Individual 1a of Burial 4. (a) 58 unmodified *Opuntia* spines, presumably saved to be made into needles. (b) 32 needles with eyes. (c) An unusually long needle. (d) 15 spindles or fragments thereof. (e) Three spindle fragments, still holding yarn.

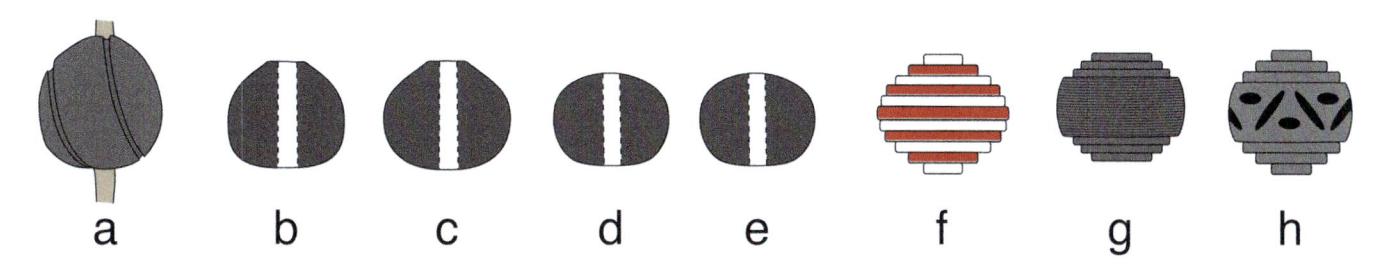

Figure 10.16. Drawings of eight spindle whorls, found in the workbasket associated with Individual 1a of Burial 4. b and c are a matching pair; so are d and e. No matching whorls were found for a, f, g, and h.

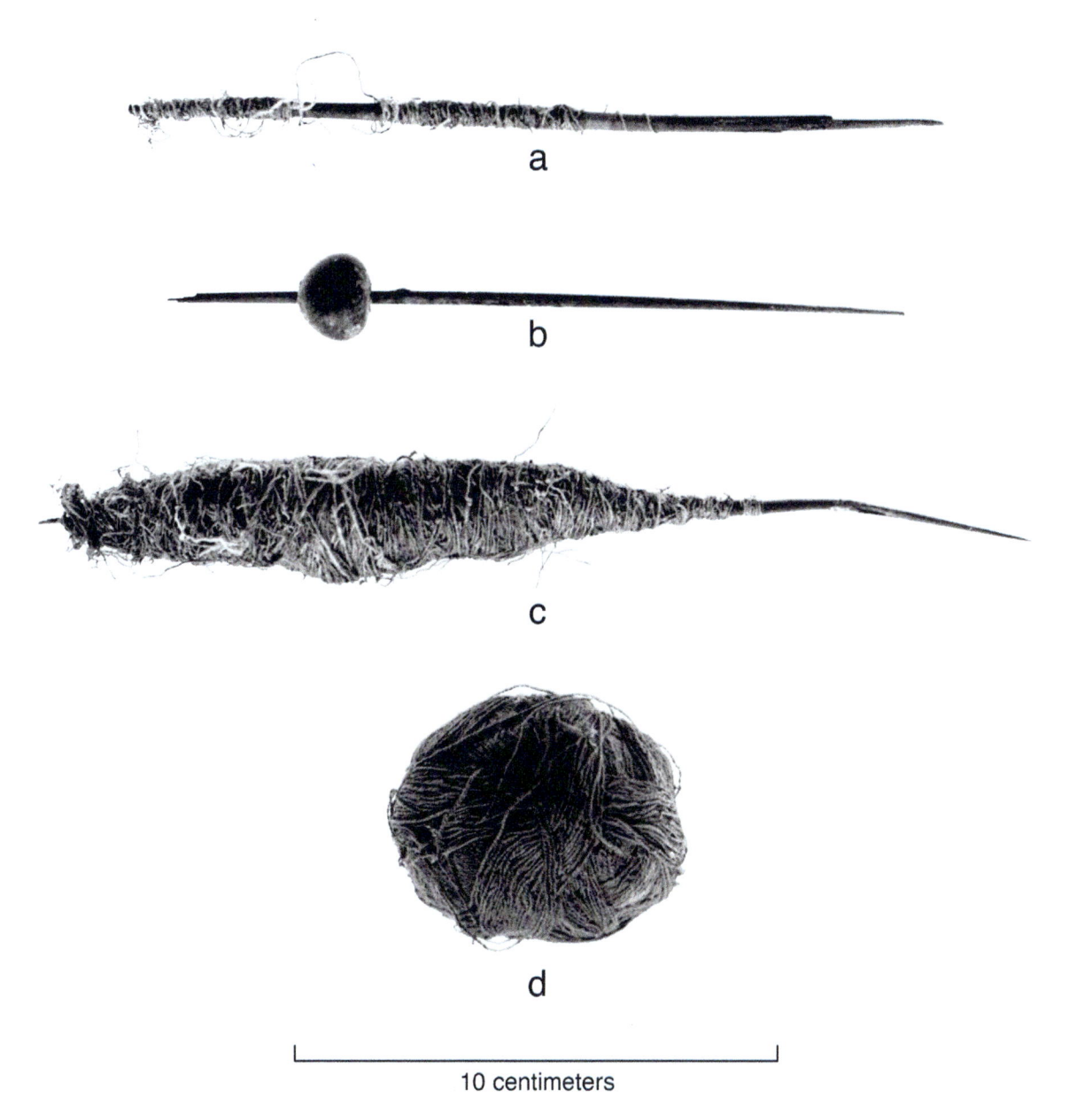

Figure 10.17. Items found loose near Individual 1a's disintegrated workbasket. (a) A broken spindle used to store yarn. (b) A spindle with a whorl. (c) A bent spindle with 13 g of white yarn. (d) A yarn ball weighing 33 g.

to the end (length of spine is 10.8 cm) (Figure 10.18b), and
— twenty knobbed pins that vary in length from 10.7 to 13.7 cm (Figure 10.18c).

Figure 10.19 shows the following items:
— four needles made from *Opuntia* spines (11–13 cm length; diameter 1.3 mm) (Figure 10.19a)
— one giant needle 13.8 cm long and 2.8 mm diameter, possibly made from *Acacia* spine (Figure 10.19b)
— 12 needles with traces of reddish-yellow thread (the needles were 10–13 cm in length); a piece of yarn tied all 12 needles together (Figure 10.19c)
— one *Opuntia* spine, probably for making needles; 7.8 cm long (Figure 10.19d), and
— four *Acacia* spines, varying in length from 12.0 to 13.5 cm (Figure 10.19e).

Yarn Balls

Nine yarn balls and four skeins of yarn were found near Individuals 1a, 1b, and 2, but could not be directly associated with a specific individual. They were as follows (Figure 10.20):
— one yarn ball 9.0 cm in diameter, 2.5 YR 2/2 ("very dusky red"), weighing 127 g
— one yarn ball 8.0 cm in diameter, 2.5 YR 2/2 ("very dusky red"), weighing 106 g
— one yarn ball 6.0 cm in diameter, 10 R 4/8 ("red") (fading to 2.5 YR 4/8), weighing 30 g
— one yarn ball 4.5 cm in diameter, 10 YR 5/6 ("yellowish brown"), weighing 12 g
— one yarn ball 4.5 cm in diameter, 10 YR 6/8 ("brownish yellow"), weighing 17.5 g
— one yarn ball 6.0 cm in diameter, 10 YR 7/6 ("yellow"), weighing 15 g
— one yarn ball 4.0 cm in diameter, 10 YR 7/6 ("yellow"), weighing 8 g
— one yarn ball 4.0 cm in diameter, 10 YR 7/6 ("yellow"), weighing 6 g
— one yarn ball 3.0 cm in diameter, 10 YR 6/4 ("light yellowish brown"), weighing 2 g
— one skein 6.0 cm long, 10 YR 7/6 ("yellow"), weighing less than 1 g
— one skein 4.0 cm long, 10 YR 5/6 ("yellowish brown"), weighing 2 g
— one skein 7.0 cm long, 5 YR 5/8 ("yellowish red"), weighing 8 g
— one skein 7.0 cm long (folded), 5 YR 5/8 ("yellowish red"), weighing 2.5 g, and
— one skein 7.0 cm long 10 YR 6/6 ("brownish yellow"), weighing 6.5 g.

"Individual" 1b

In addition to the three women in their mummy bundles, there was "Individual" 1b, which merely consisted of a skull lodged below Individual 2 (the uppermost bundle) and above Individual 3 (the mummy bundle at the bottom of the pit) (see Figure 10.1). Suspecting that more of this individual's bones might be discovered elsewhere in this burial pit, we classified it as an "Individual," even though it turned out to be an isolated cranium.

Individual 2

Individual 2's mummy bundle was the last to be inserted in the burial pit; it had been placed above Individuals 1a and 3 (see Figure 10.1). Its outermost wrapping had been reused, showing clear evidence of having been repaired and patched. This woman's body had been wrapped in four additional cloths. Her face was covered with a cotton pad, and she had a piece of copper in her mouth. Outside her mummy bundle was a piece of wood, which was submitted for ^{14}C dating (Beta-7797). The wood yielded a conventional date of 610 ± 70 years BP or A.D. 1340; when calibrated, its two-sigma range was A.D. 1276–1431.

A false head, formed of cloth and reeds, had been placed at the top of Individual 2's mummy bundle. Such false heads may have helped the mourners determine which end of the bundle was the top and which was the bottom; this would have been useful when transporting the bundle and placing it in the burial pit. Such practices may have served to humanize the bundle, giving it a symbolic head and allowing the rest of the bundle to represent the deceased's body.

Individual 3

Individual 3 was found at the bottom of the Burial 4 pit. Her mummy bundle was the heaviest and measured a meter high and 0.80 m wide. The bundle had a false head made of cloth, rolled up and linked to the cloth in the bundle below. Both the false head and the rest of the bundle were incorporated into the final rope lashing that held everything together.

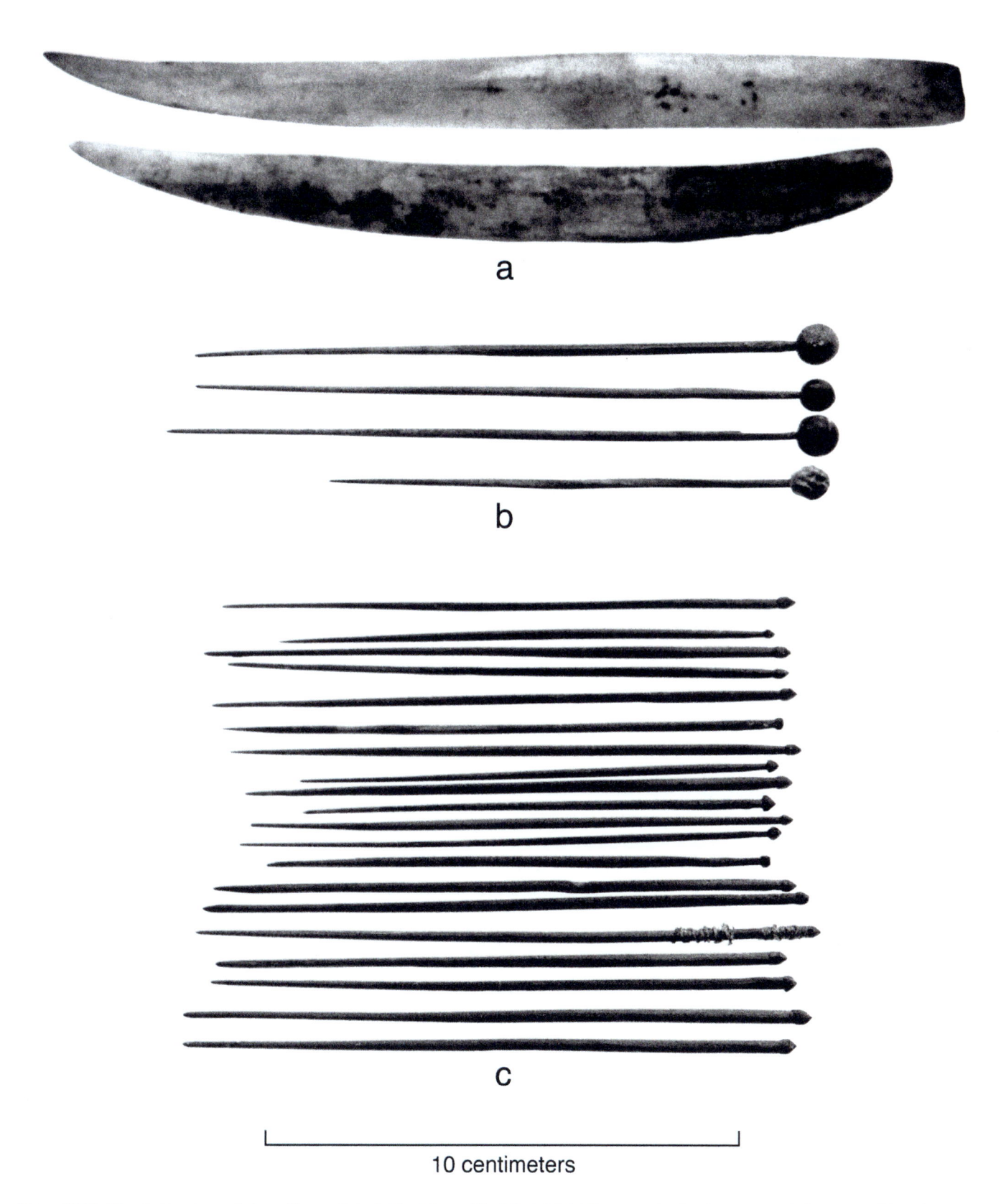

Figure 10.18. Weaving implements found beneath Individuals 1a and 2 of Burial 4. (a) Two weaving implements made from camelid or deer bone. (b) Three pins with hard fruits attached, and a fourth capped by a wrinkled black fruit or seed. (c) 20 bobbins, one of which still displays a small quantity of yarn.

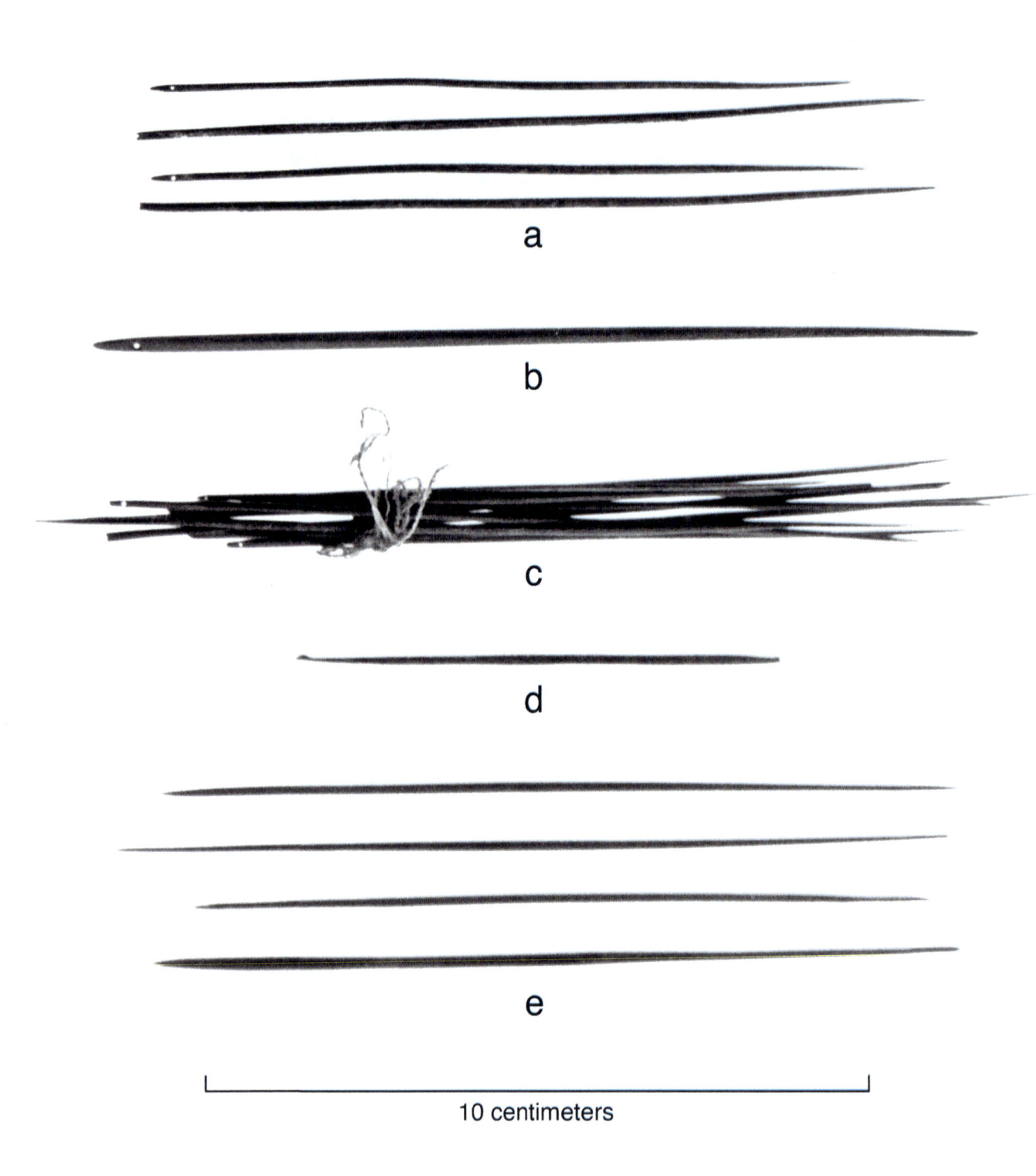

Figure 10.19. Needles found beneath Individuals 1a and 2 of Burial 4. (a) Four needles. (b) One unusually long, sturdy needle. (c) A bundle of 12 needles, tied together with reddish-yellow thread. (d) One unmodified *Opuntia* spine. (e) Four long *Opuntia* spines.

Figure 10.20. A sample of yarn balls and skeins of yarns, found loose near Individuals 1a and 2 of Burial 4. Illustrated here are seven of the nine balls and one of the four skeins (in the middle of the column at far right).

Individual 3 was relatively intact within her tied-up bundle (see Figure 10.2). Based on the number of gold and silver objects found with her, including gold foil and silver *tupus*—as well as a necklace of 230+ beads, six reversible tapestry textiles, a double-chambered effigy bridgespout vessel, miniature flasks, a decorated bone balance, decorated needlecases, many wool bags, and 11 pigment pouches—it is possible that Individual 3 was one of the most highly ranked that we salvaged. Although pigment pouches have been reported in Paracas *fardos* (Fester 1940; Fester and Cruellas 1934; Yacovleff and Muelle 1934b), I know of no other instance in which an individual had 11 pigment pouches.

This mummy bundle was wrapped in at least two pieces of cloth. The outermost layer was a coarse cotton cloth, coated with a slip of fine clay. Inside that piece was another cloth combining *algodón pardo* and *algodón blanco* in the form of alternating white and brown stripes. This striped cloth had been wrapped around the body a total of 30 times. The woman's fingers were tied together with string, and her wrists by a cloth. Such practices are known from earlier times, in the Asia Valley and elsewhere (Frame and Ángeles Falcón 2014: Fig. 31; Owens and Eeckhout 2015).

Individual 3 bore two tattoos (Figure 10.21) and elegant fingernails, 1.4 cm long, that were beautifully trimmed and painted red (Figure 10.22). Buried with her were mussel shell pigment palettes, in which she had mixed her red fingernail polish.

The two tattoos on her left forearm (on the medial surface midway between her wrist and elbow) resemble textile designs (Figure 10.21). We note the presence of tattoos on other coastal women; for example, at the Late Intermediate site of Cerro Colorado in the Huaura Valley, at least 63.3 percent of the female burials had tattoos, and 72 percent of the women with tattoos were older than 30 years of age.

The Cerro Colorado women were usually tattooed on the backs of their left hands and arms (van Dalen Luna et al. 2018); other women, including those of the Chancay culture, are known to have filed and painted their fingernails. Tattooed women were also found in Grave Y at Zapallán near Ancón, as well as in the Asia Valley (Frame and Ángeles Falcón 2014:43; Lothrop and Maler 1957b:4). In addition, Díaz Arriola (2015:198) illustrates tattooed diamonds on the left leg of a woman buried at Armatambo in Chorrillos (Rímac Valley); her tattoos resemble the diamond-shaped elements tattooed on the forearm of Cerro Azul's Individual 3 in Burial 4.

Although such tattooing was certainly not restricted to women, it seems to have been more common among women, in particular elite women. For example, the tattooed women at the site of Armatambo were considered elite individuals. Another woman considered to be noble—perhaps even royal—was the Señora de Cao, found in a tomb at Huaca Cao Viejo near El Brujo in the Chicama Valley (Vásquez Sánchez et al. 2013); the well-preserved tattoos on her arms are very elaborate, as are her burial offerings, which included more than 1,000 items of gold.

Items Held in Individual 3's Hand

It was not unusual at Cerro Azul to find an item still held in a woman's hand; however, Individual 3 of Burial 4 was the only woman that we found who was buried holding something in both hands. In her right hand she held a small piece of gold foil; in her left hand she held ornamental cords that had been tied around the base of her left thumb and first two fingers (Figure 10.22 a, b). The yarn colors of these cords were yellow, red, black, and very dark brown. A second group of cords—almost certainly piping or edging for a bag or something similar—was found wadded up in the palm of her hand. These cords (which were yellow, dull red, and very dark brown) may have been items she was working on when she died, giving mourners the idea that they should place them in her hand so that she could finish them in the afterlife.

One of these cords would be classified as spiral cross-knit looping constructed around bundles of parallel cotton strands (Figure 10.22c). The core foundation is cotton, S-spun and 0.5 mm thick; the decorative wool yarn on the exterior of the cords is Z-S and 0.8 mm thick. Four of the five lengths are 54 cm long and 6.5 mm thick. In Individual 3's hand are examples of what appear to be *cordoncillo*, or edge piping. The design has multiple colors—2.5 Y 8/6 ("yellow"), 5 R 3/8 ("dark red"), and 2.5 YR 2/2 ("very dusky red"). The cord that was simply wadded up in the palm of her hand had a design that used different colors—7.5 YR 6/8 ("reddish yellow"), very dark brown 2.5 YR 2/2 ("very dusky red"), and 5 R 3/8 ("dark red").

Ceramic Vessels

Among the folds of Individual 3's cloth wrappings we found a pair of matching miniature flasks (Figure 10.23). Flask #1 has a tube-shaped neck. Decorating the surface of this Camacho Black flask were small diamonds painted 7.5 YR 4/4 ("weak red"). This pigment had been mixed with resin

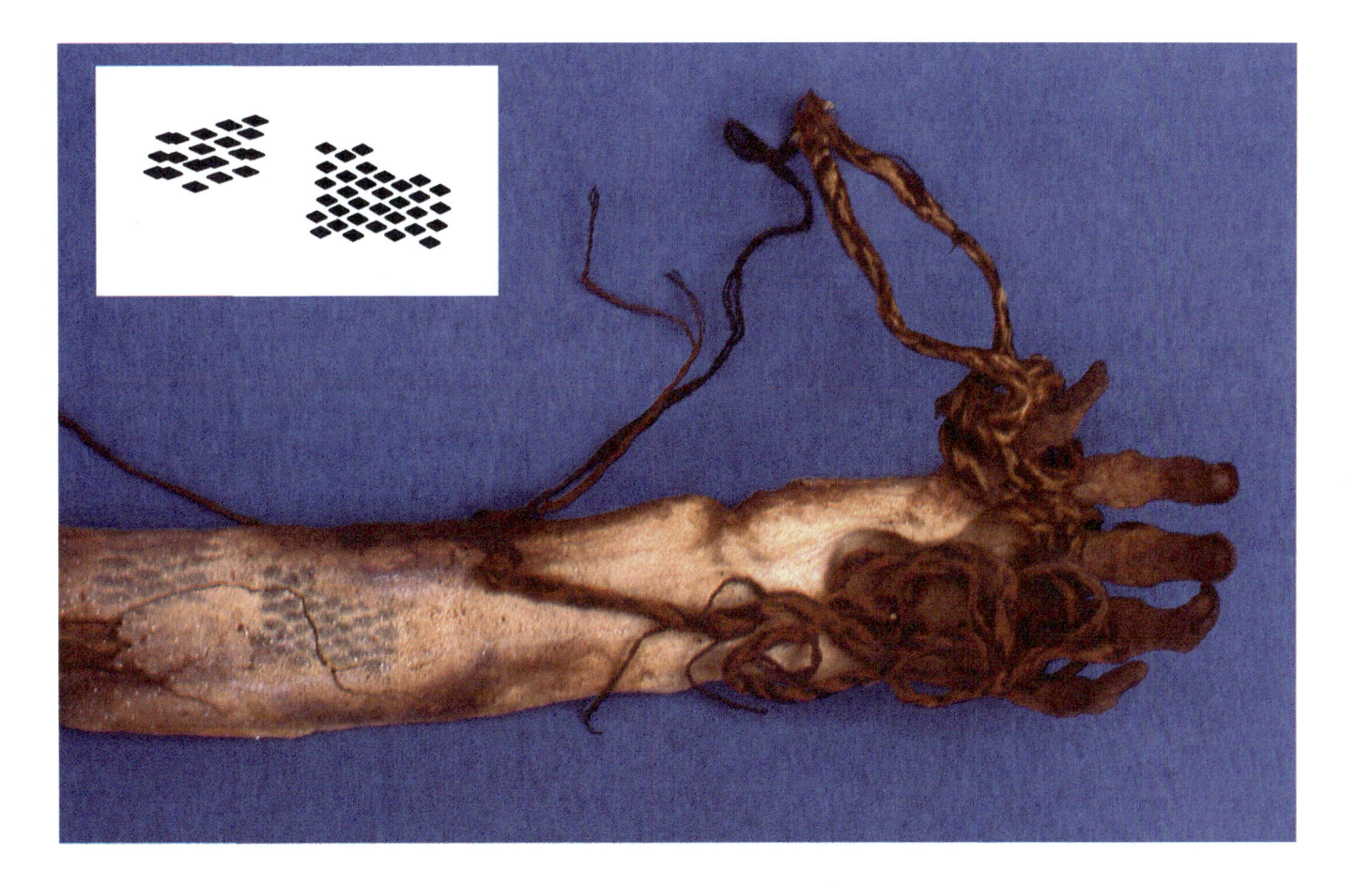

Figure 10.21. Individual 3 of Burial 4, a woman, bore two tattoos on her left arm. The inset at upper left shows a drawing of those tattoos.

218　Chapter 10

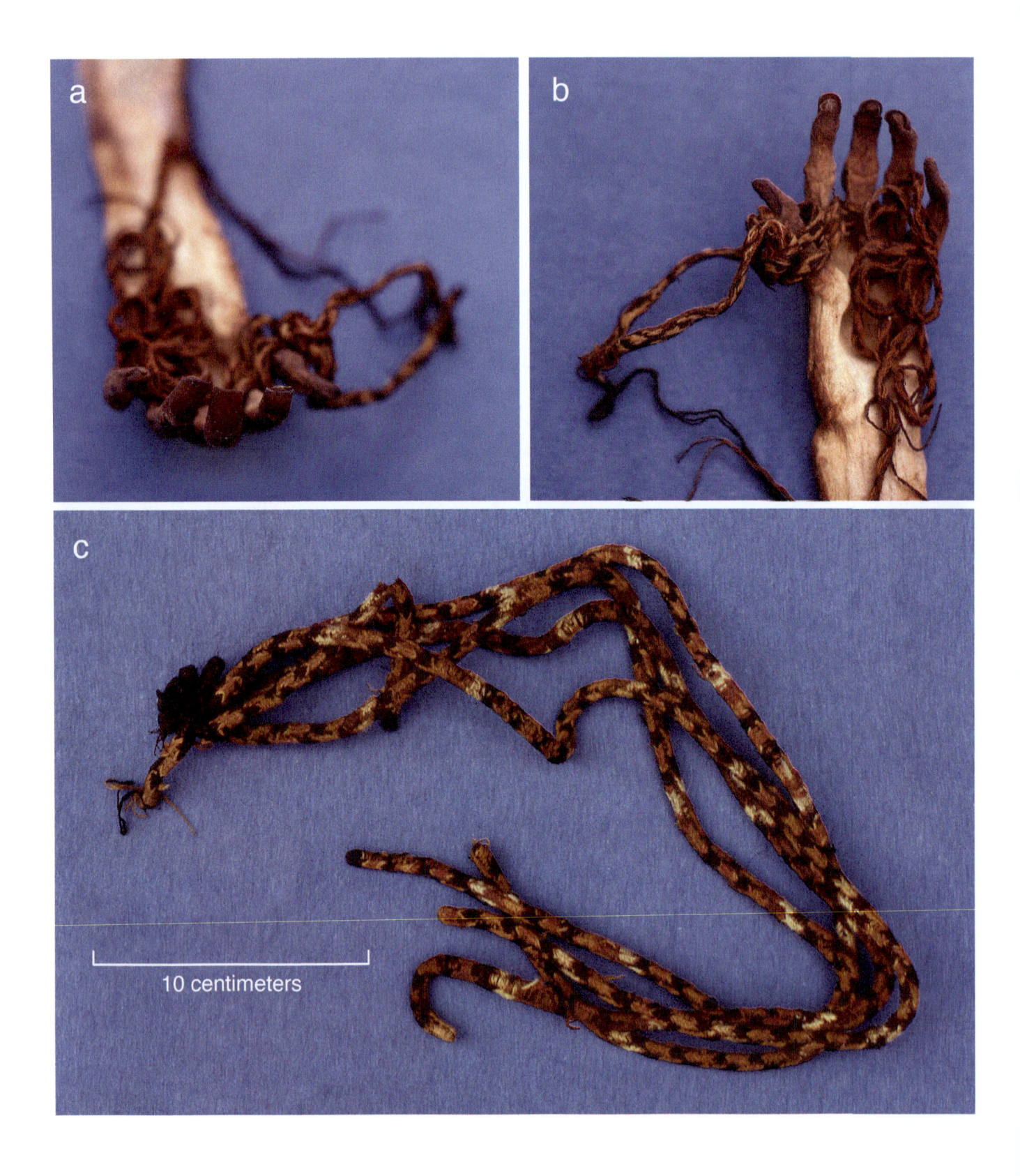

Figure 10.22. Three views of the decorative cords held in the left hand of Individual 3. (a) Her red-painted fingernails are visible in a and b. One decorative cord was tied around the base of her left thumb and first two fingers (b). The cords are shown in c.

or some other sticky substance, still adhering to the flask. According to chemist James Burton, the pigment used resembles the red powder in one of her pigment pouches. After this flask had been placed in the mummy bundle, the cloth stuck to the painted diamonds. Flask #1 is 6.8 cm high and has a rim diameter of 1.5 cm, a frontal width of 4.4 cm, and a side width of 3.4 cm.

Flask #2, also a Camacho Black miniature, has a tubular neck; it has small crosses painted on it with red pigment, 7.5 YR 4/4 ("weak red"). These crosses were applied in the same way as the diamonds on Flask #1.

We suspect that these flasks were painted with diamonds (Flask #1) or crosses (Flask #2) by Individual 3 herself, since she both possessed the same pigment and was found with a mussel shell palette (*Choromytilus*) in which "weak red" paint had been mixed.

A third vessel, which rested on a mat next to Individual 3, had two chambers (Figure 10.24). It was metallic black and featured a bridgespout. The surface of this unusual vessel is similar to what Mesoamerican ceramicists have called "double-burnished graphite." Significantly, each of the vessel's chambers appears to be an effigy potato. Its height is 14.9 cm, its rim diameter is 4.1 cm, its maximum diameter is 15.8 cm, and its wall thickness is 4–5 mm. The color of the clay body is 10 YR 5/1 ("gray"). Similar two-chambered vessels are known from the Chincha Valley to the south (Kroeber and Strong 1924:24).

Gourd Vessels

Individual 3 was also associated with the rim fragment of a gourd vessel resembling a neckless jar (Figure 10.25); this fragment had been mixed in among the loose yarn balls at the bottom of the burial pit. Its reconstructed diameter would be 15 cm, with a wall thickness of 5.0 mm. The gourd's color was 10 YR 3/3 ("dark brown").

Necklace

Rather than a string of simple black seeds like those worn by some of the other Cerro Azul women, Individual 3 had a necklace of stone beads. Included were 14 possible turquoise beads, nine greenstone beads, and more than 210 white-to-orange stone beads (Figure 10.26) (Miscellaneous Specimen 7). The 14 possible turquoise beads were small (1–2 mm in diameter); the nine greenstone beads were larger (5 mm in diameter). This necklace's clasp was metal.

Metal Artifacts

There were metal items hidden among the folds of Individual 3's cloth wrappings. Included were two silver *tupus*, or cloak pins, each of which had a small hole at the top. Each *tupu* weighed 8 g (Figure 10.27a, b); its circular head was 5.2 cm high and 6.3 cm wide. Individual 3 was one of only two women at the site possessing silver *tupus*; the other woman was in Burial 8 (see Chapter 14). Fray Bernabé Cobo (1990:188) says, "these pins are by far the most decorative ornament that they wear." Vetter Parodi and Carcedo de Mufarech (2009) show that *tupus* are a symbol of women's identity.

Individual 3 in Burial 4 was also associated with two pieces of silver foil, each with a hole drilled in it (Figure 10.28). Both pieces seem to have been torn from a larger piece of foil; one piece is 5.4 x 2.1 cm, the other 5.2 x 2.0 cm. The total weight of the two pieces is 1 g, and the foil itself is 0.2 mm thick.

In one of her cloth bags (Bag 5c) Individual 3 had another piece of gold foil, this one decorated with the same *inti* motif seen previously on the gold and silver foil buried with Individual 1a. The same bag also held two pieces of silver, one cut from a disc and one a fragment of foil. These items will be discussed later, along with Bag 5c.

Needlecases

We found five needlecases with Burial 4. Each was a segment of hollow cane (*caña hueca* or *Phragmites* sp.), carefully cut into a tube that held needles made from *Opuntia* spines. Two of the needlecases were plain; three were incised with marine motifs, including the Pacific bonito, a possible school of fish, and possible shark teeth. The decorated cases still contained needles.

Needlecase #1 (Figure 10.29) is the longest of the decorated cane tubes, 17 cm in length and 16.1 mm in diameter. Originally, this tube must have had a stopper closing each end, but only one remained in place; it was decorated with geometric incisions. Its exterior decoration consisted of images of the Pacific bonito (*Sarda sarda chiliensis*), identifiable by the serrated fins on the rear half of its body. The needlecase was long enough to show five and a half bonitos, shown in profile view.

Inside Needlecase #1 were two groups of *Opuntia* spine needles. One group had dark reddish-brown thread wound around them to keep them together. Nine of these needles had eyes, and the group ranged in length from 7.0 to 12 cm.

220 Chapter 10

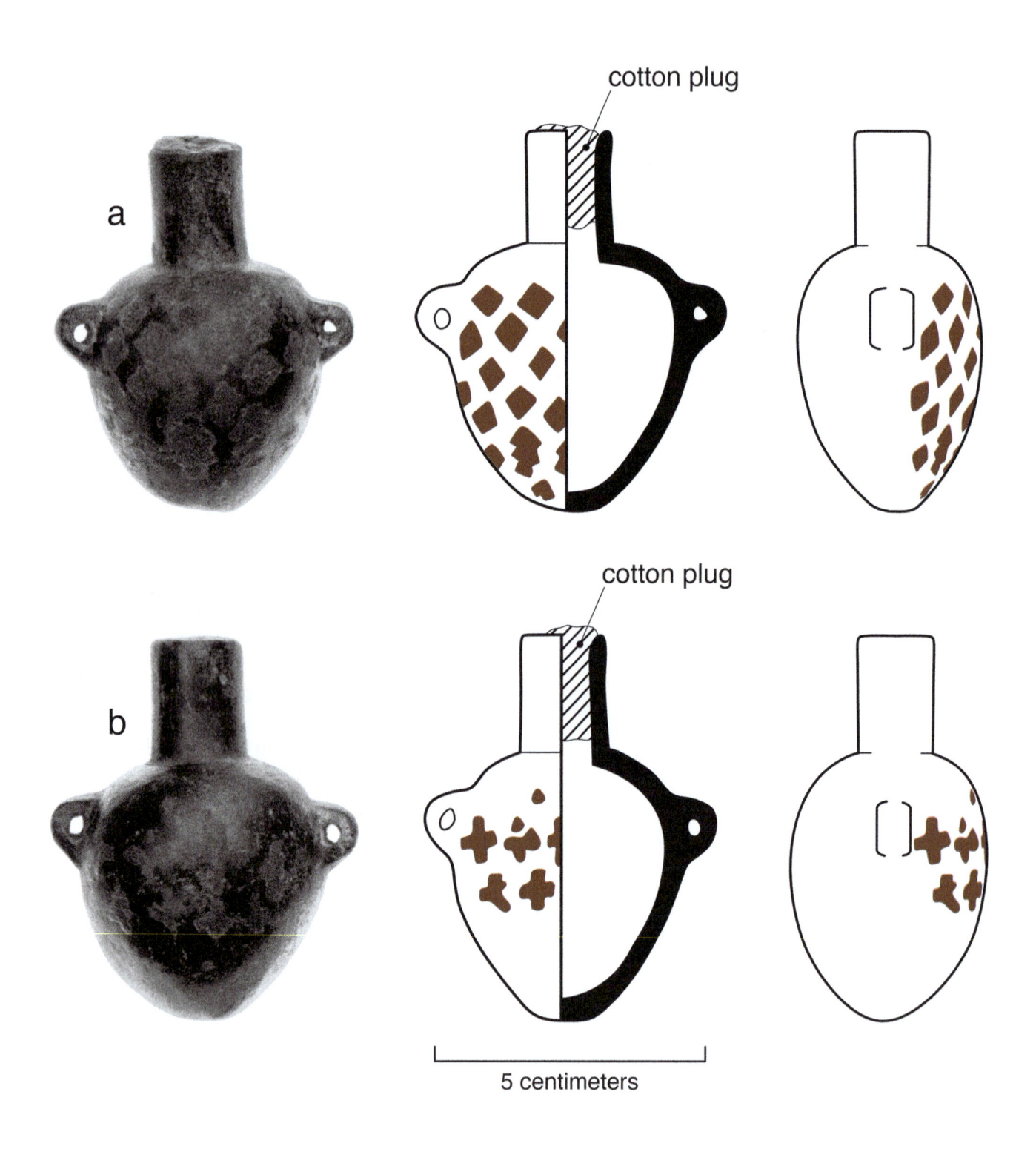

Figure 10.23. Two miniature flasks, hidden in the folds of the cloth wrappings surrounding the body of Individual 3 of Burial 4. (a) A photo and two drawings of one flask, decorated with reddish-brown diamonds. (b) A photo and two drawings of the second flask, decorated with reddish-brown crosses.

Burial 4

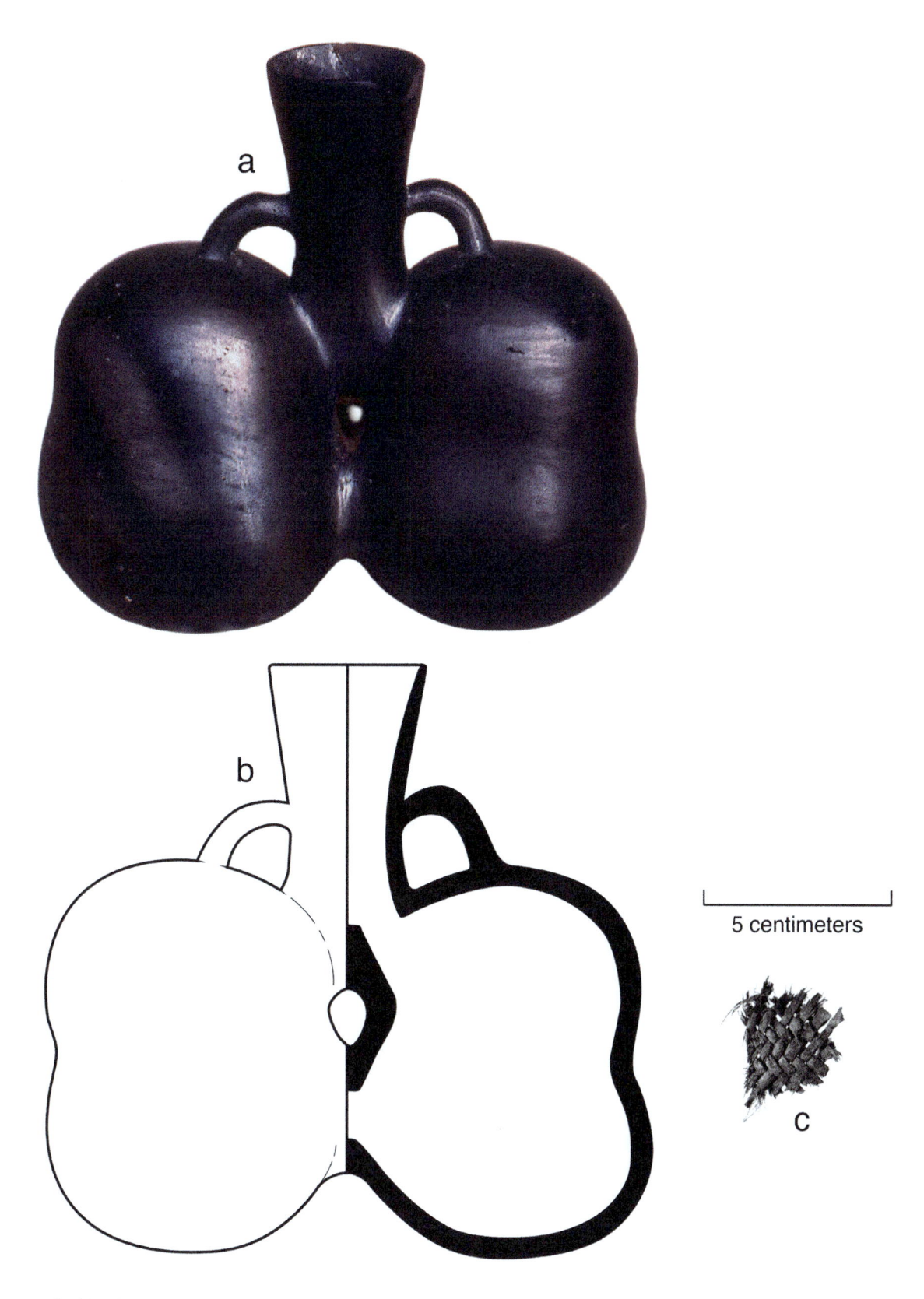

Figure 10.24. A double-chambered bridgespout vessel, associated with Individual 3. This vessel (a, b) was an example of the highly burnished variant of Camacho Black. (c) Fragment of a mat on which the vessel rested, found near the bottom of the Burial 4 pit.

222 Chapter 10

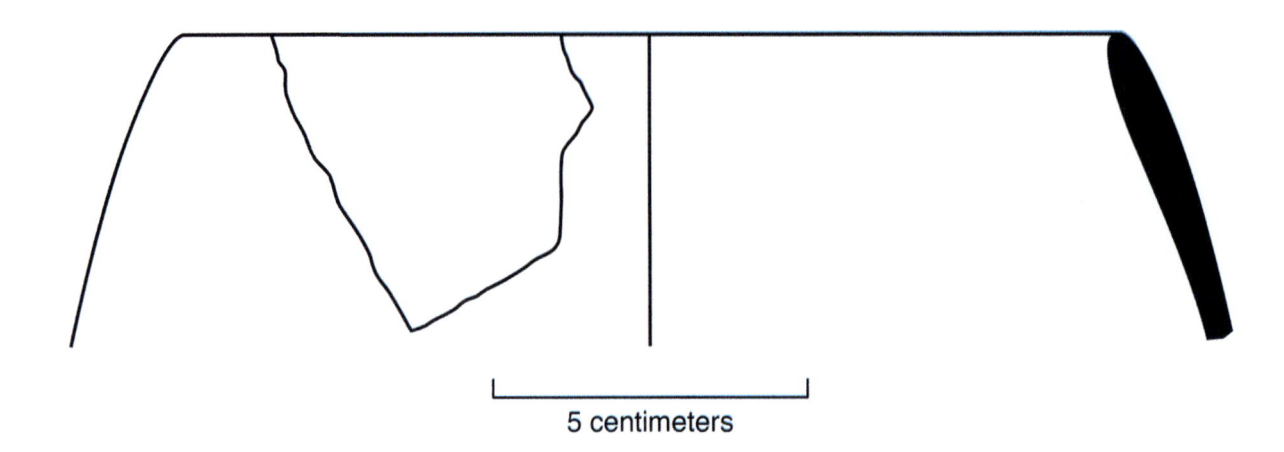

Figure 10.25. A rim fragment from a gourd vessel, found mixed in with the yarn balls at the bottom of the Burial 4 pit.

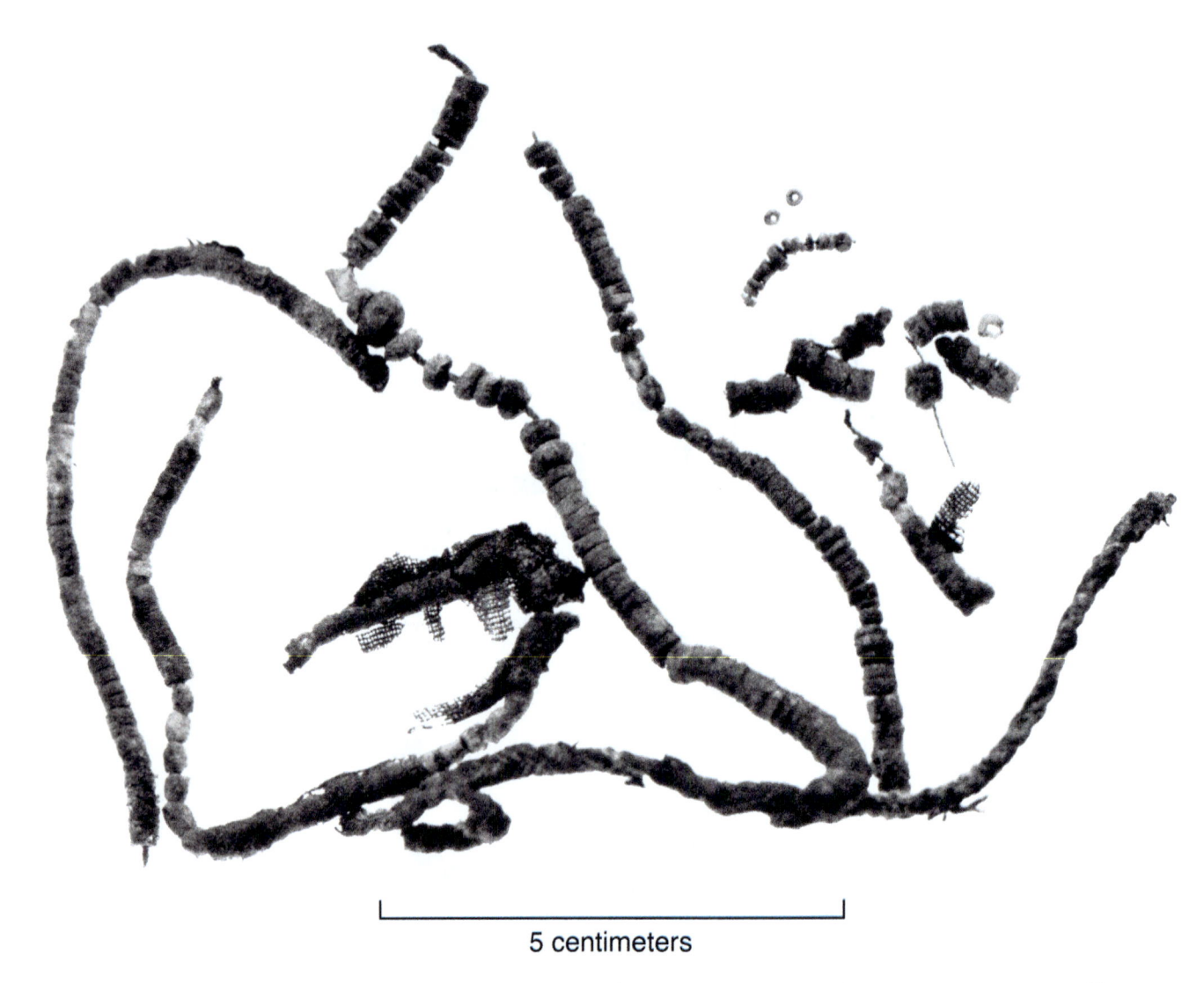

Figure 10.26. A stone bead necklace, found in place around Individual 3's neck when her mummy bundle was opened. This necklace included 210 beads that were white-to-orange in color, as well as 9 greenstone beads, and 14 tiny beads that might be turquoise.

a

b

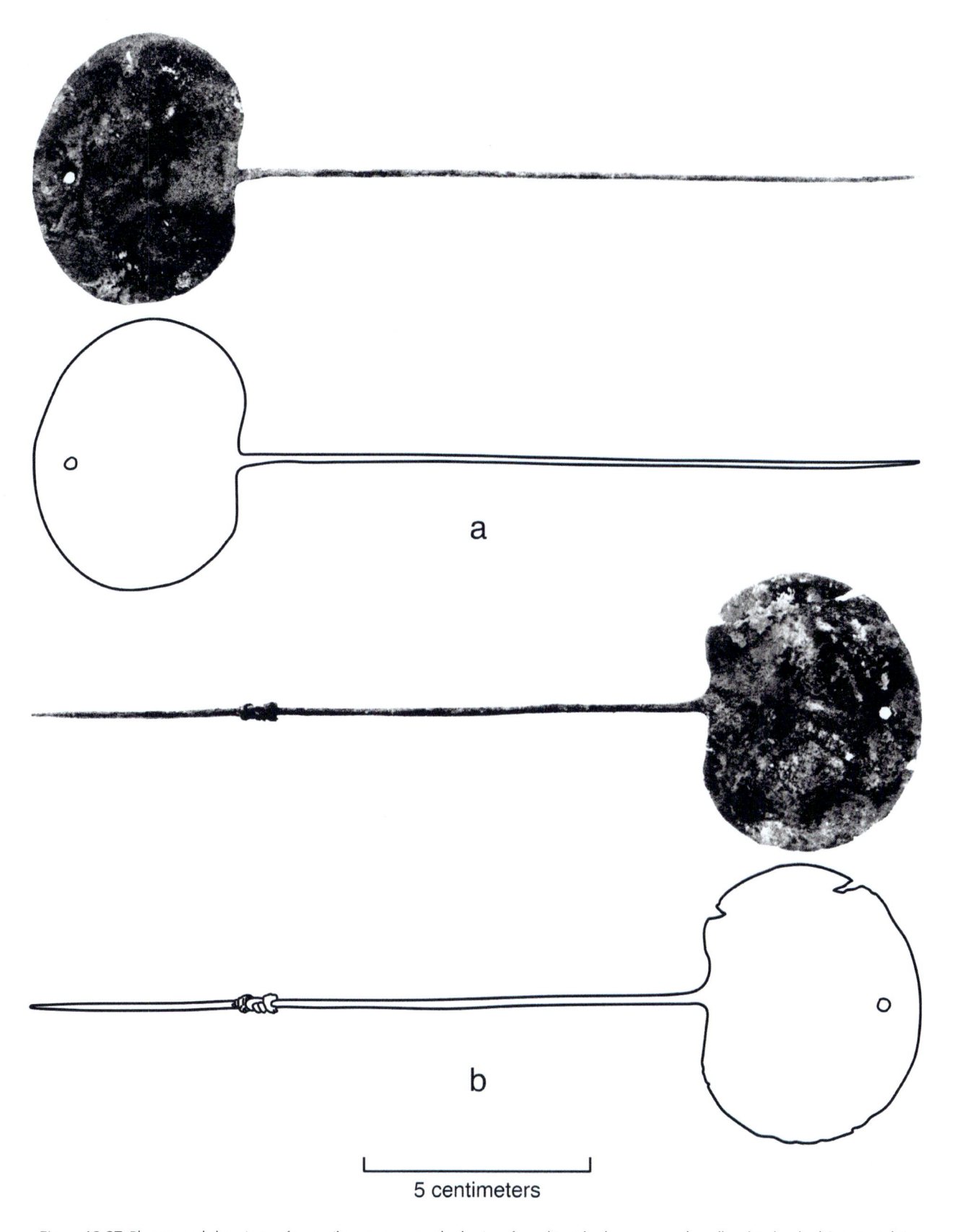

Figure 10.27. Photos and drawings of two silver *tupus*, or cloak pins, found inside the mummy bundle of Individual 3 in Burial 4.

Figure 10.28. Two pieces of silver foil decorated with the *inti* or sun motif, associated with Individual 3 of Burial 4. Each piece had been perforated.

The second group also had thread wound around it, but that thread had largely disintegrated; the three needles in this group ranged in length from 7.5 to 11 cm.

Needlecase #2 (Figure 10.30) was the second longest, at 15.7 cm in length and 15.5 mm in diameter. This needlecase retained both its stoppers or end plugs. It was decorated with multiple arrow-shaped elements, probably representing a school of fish, all swimming in one direction.

Like Needlecase #1, Needlecase #2 also contained two groups of *Opuntia* spine needles. One group consisted of four needles ranging in length from 7.0 to 9.5 cm. All of these needles had eyes, and were held together by golden brown yarn, 7.5 YR 5/6 ("strong brown"). The second group contained seven needles, ranging in length from 9.0 to 11 cm. This packet was tied with dark reddish-brown yarn that had almost completely disintegrated.

Needlecase #3 (Figure 10.31) was 14.9 cm long and 17.2 mm in diameter. The incised decoration on the exterior consists of elements that resemble shark teeth. This needlecase had both stoppers still in place, each 8 mm thick. Its contents consisted of three needles with eyes, ranging in length from 10.7 cm to 14.1 cm. A small amount of dark brown thread was still wrapped around the needles.

Needlecases #4 and #5 were both empty and undecorated. Cane #4 was 17.4 cm long and 12.2 mm in diameter. Cane #5 was 14 cm long and 13 mm in diameter.

Individual 3's Bags

Individual 3a was accompanied by nine bags, more than were found with any other woman. One of these bags contained mussel shells used as palettes for mixing fingernail polish; one contained a fully clothed ceramic figurine and dozens of yarn balls; another held colorful mineral powders, tied up in small pouches; another had a polished bone *balanza*; and still another had pieces of gold and silver.

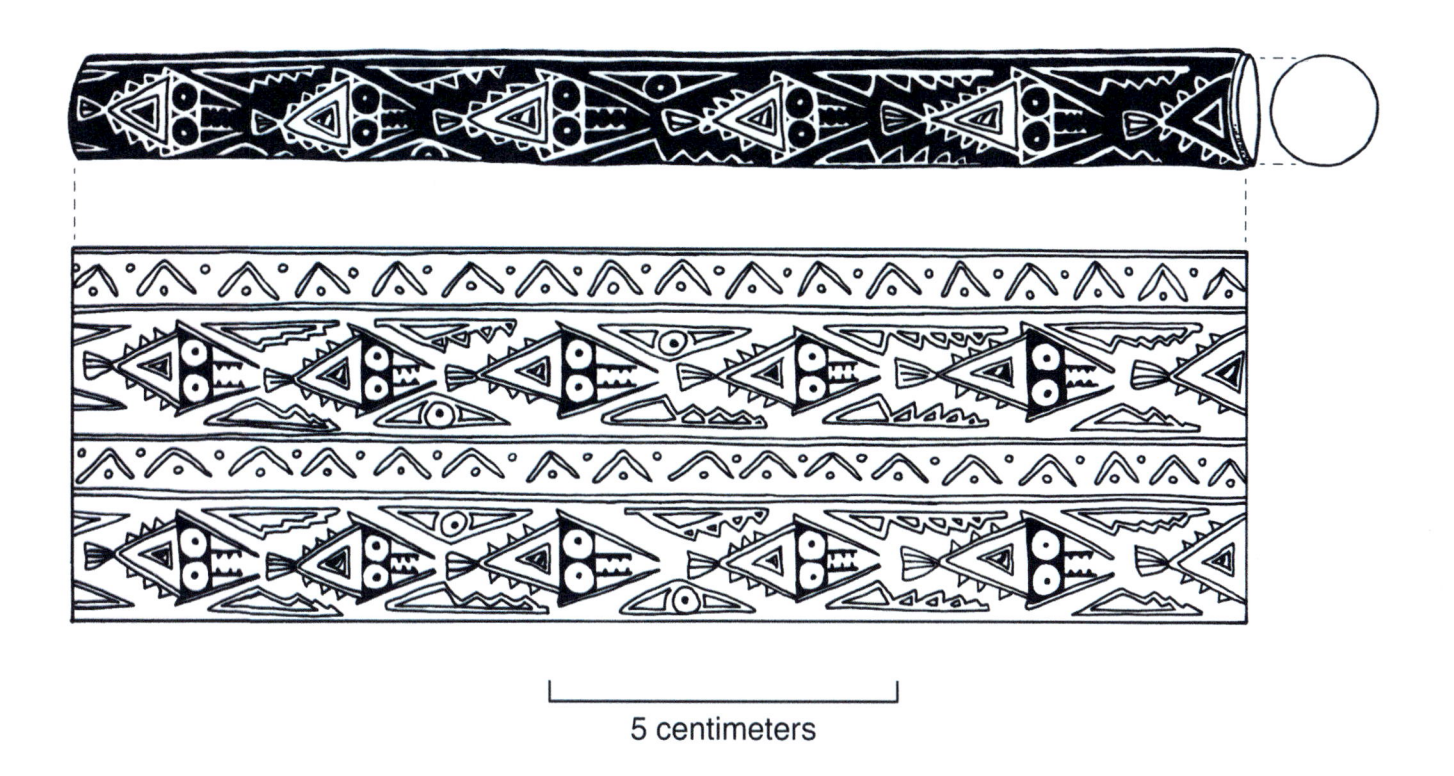

Figure 10.29. Needlecase #1, decorated with incised Pacific bonitos, was associated with Individual 3 of Burial 4. Only one of its two stoppers (or end plugs) was still present when found.

Interestingly, some of these bags were stored inside other bags, a fact we would not have known were it not for the extraordinary preservation of the desert coast.

The Contents of Bag 1

Bag 1 had largely disintegrated but its contents were well preserved; included were 58 items of yarn and a ceramic figurine. The figurine had been painted white; later, over that white surface, red and black paint had been applied to its face. The red paint was used to make diagonal bands on the cheek and it was also applied to triangular sections above the ears; its Munsell color was 5 R 4/8 ("red"). The black paint had been applied to the bridge of the nose.

The figurine is 15.4 cm high and 4 cm thick (Figure 10.32). It wore a cotton string necklace holding more than 20 black seeds that averaged 4 mm in diameter. In addition to the seeds found in place on the string, several more (identified as belonging to the family Leguminosae by C. Earle Smith, Jr.) were found in the bottom of the bag (Figure 10.33). The figurine's garment was a plain weave fabric whose Munsell color was 2.5 YR 3/4 ("dark reddish brown").

Accompanying the figurine in Bag 1 were 58 separate items of yarn (Specimen 31); included were 18 yarn balls, 39 skeins, and one unfinished cord. The 7 cm long cord was clearly a work in progress; the four yarn colors being used to make it were 2.5 YR 2/2 ("very dusky red"), 5 Y 8/4 ("pale yellow"), 10 YR 6/8 ("brownish yellow"), and 5 R 4/8 ("red"). Those four colors were an exact match to the yarn balls stored in the bag. In other words, it is likely that Individual 3 was working on the cord when she died.

Nearly all of the yarn balls were camelid wool; in contrast, most of the skeins were cotton (Figure 10.34). Chemist Max Saltzman of UCLA, who analyzed the dyed yarn from Bag 1, reports that almost all of the red yarn balls had been dyed with cochineal; furthermore, even the yarn balls that today appear brown, brownish red, dusky red, or

226	Chapter 10

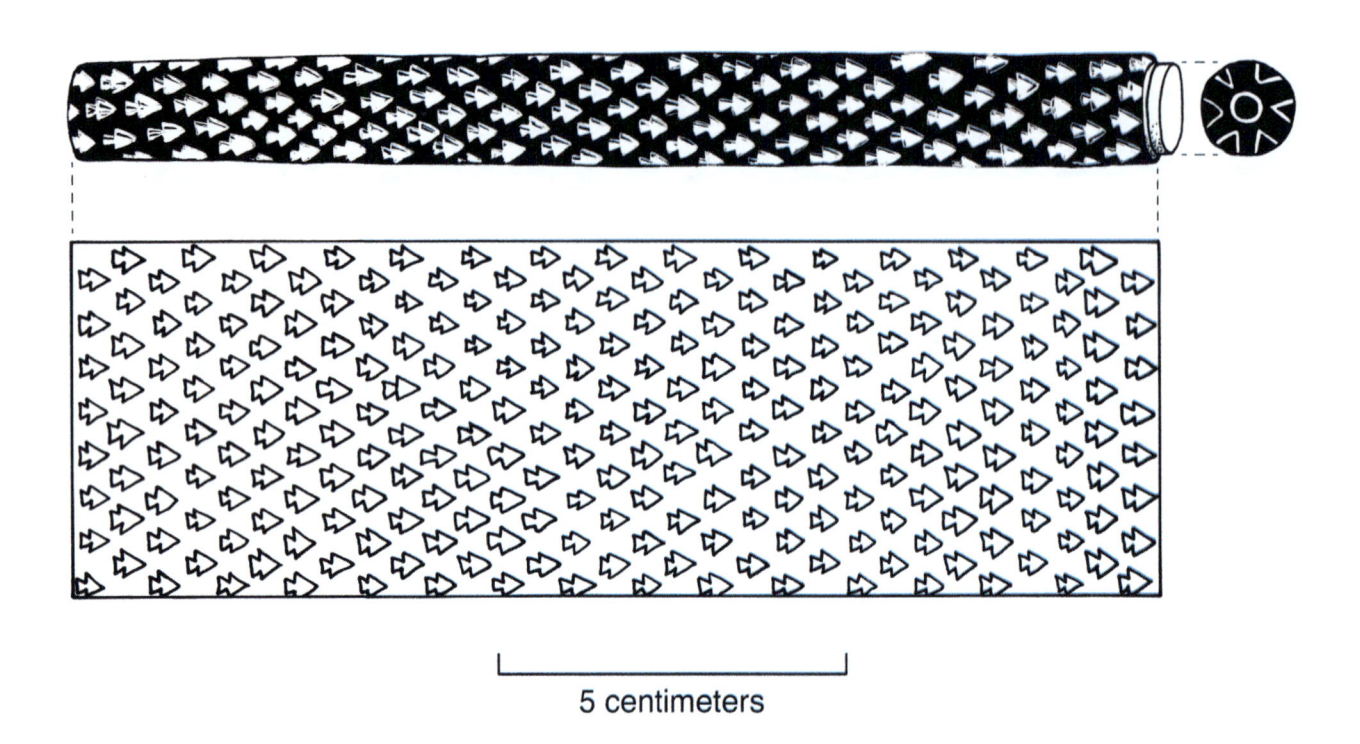

Figure 10.30. Needlecase #2, decorated with what appears to be a school of fish, was also associated with Individual 3. Its stopper was incised with a geometric design.

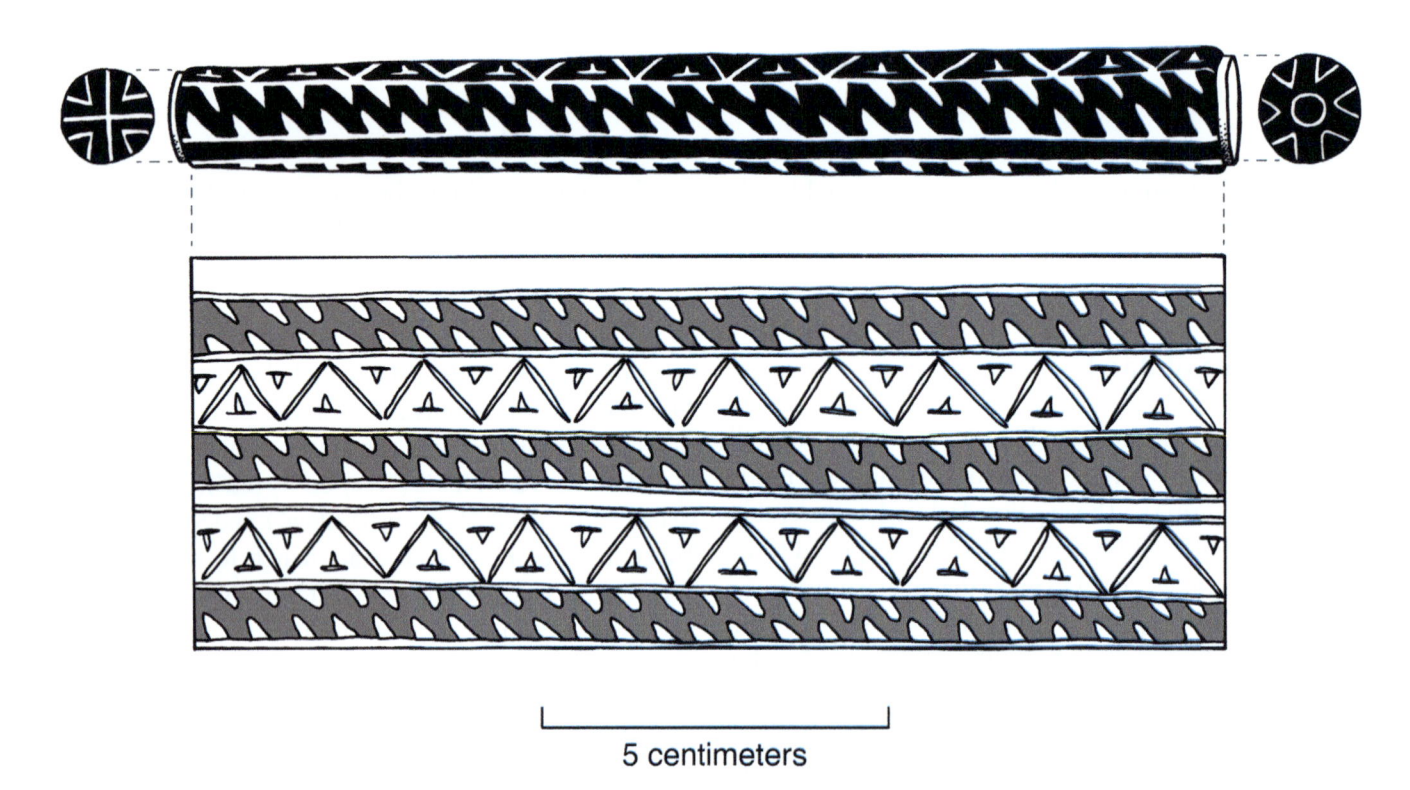

Figure 10.31. Needlecase #3, decorated with possible shark's teeth, was also associated with Individual 3. Its two stoppers were decorated with the same design as Needlecase #2's.

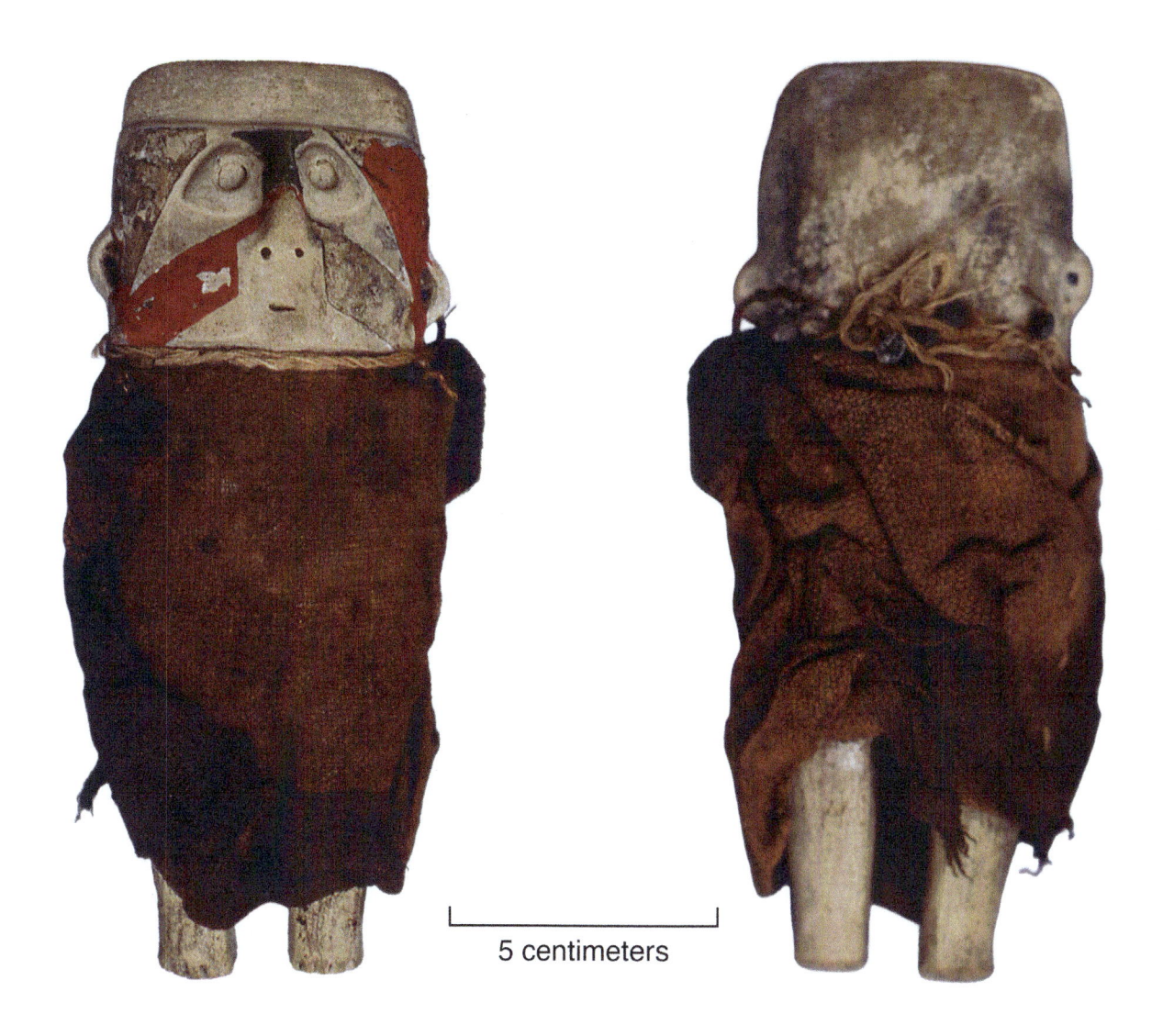

Figure 10.32. A figurine found inside Bag 1 of Individual 3, Burial 4: (left) frontal view and (right) rear view. (To see a reconstruction of this figurine's facial paint, see Figure 5.12e.)

Figure 10.33. Black seeds, perforated for suspension, found in the bottom of Individual 3's Bag 1. The seeds had almost certainly fallen from the necklace found on the figurine shown in Figure 10.32.

dark red proved also to contain cochineal. Cochineal is the red dye obtained from a beetle that lives on the prickly pear cactus. Saltzman could not determine which dye had been used to create the yellowish brown color of the yarn skeins, most of which were cotton.

The Contents of Bag 2

Bag 2, found lying just below the mummy bundle of Individual 3, contained what appeared to be a painting kit. It held three large mussel shells used as pigment palettes (Figure 10.35), plus three pouches of dried pigment (Figure 10.36).

The mussel shells, all of which bear traces of pigment, belong to the genus *Choromytilus*; the largest measures 16 x 6.3 cm. This is the only one of the three shells that has two holes drilled in it. This shell was evidently suspended by a cord, since we found a short piece of cord still in the holes. The second largest *Choromytilus* shell is 15.5 x 6.7 cm, and the smallest measures 9.5 x 4.75 cm.

Individual 3 also stored her pigment in this bag; it was kept in three small pouches of the usual translucent type.

In one of the three pouches, we found a red pigment which chemist James Burton identified as cinnabar + anhydrite. This was the same red pigment seen on the face of the figurine in Bag 1, as well as on Individual 3's fingernails and the miniature flasks mentioned earlier (see Figure 10.23).

The second pouch contained a blue pigment which, according to Burton, turned out to be azurite. Because this pouch was no longer as securely tied as the others, a bit of its contents had spilled out and damaged the embroidered cloth wrapped around it (Figure 10.37).

The third pouch contained an orange pigment that Burton identified as realgar + sulfur (Figure 10.36). Since realgar is normally red, Burton concludes that the orange color might have resulted from some other material mixed into the powder.

Bag 2 was a plain weave warp-faced textile with decorative stripes of complementary warp patterning (Figure 10.38). The actual loom dimensions of the whole textile would have been 74 x 30 cm; that cloth was then folded over to form a bag 37 x 30 cm in size. The bag has a wool warp and wool weft; the decorative yarn, heading cord, and repair edging are also wool. The warp is dark

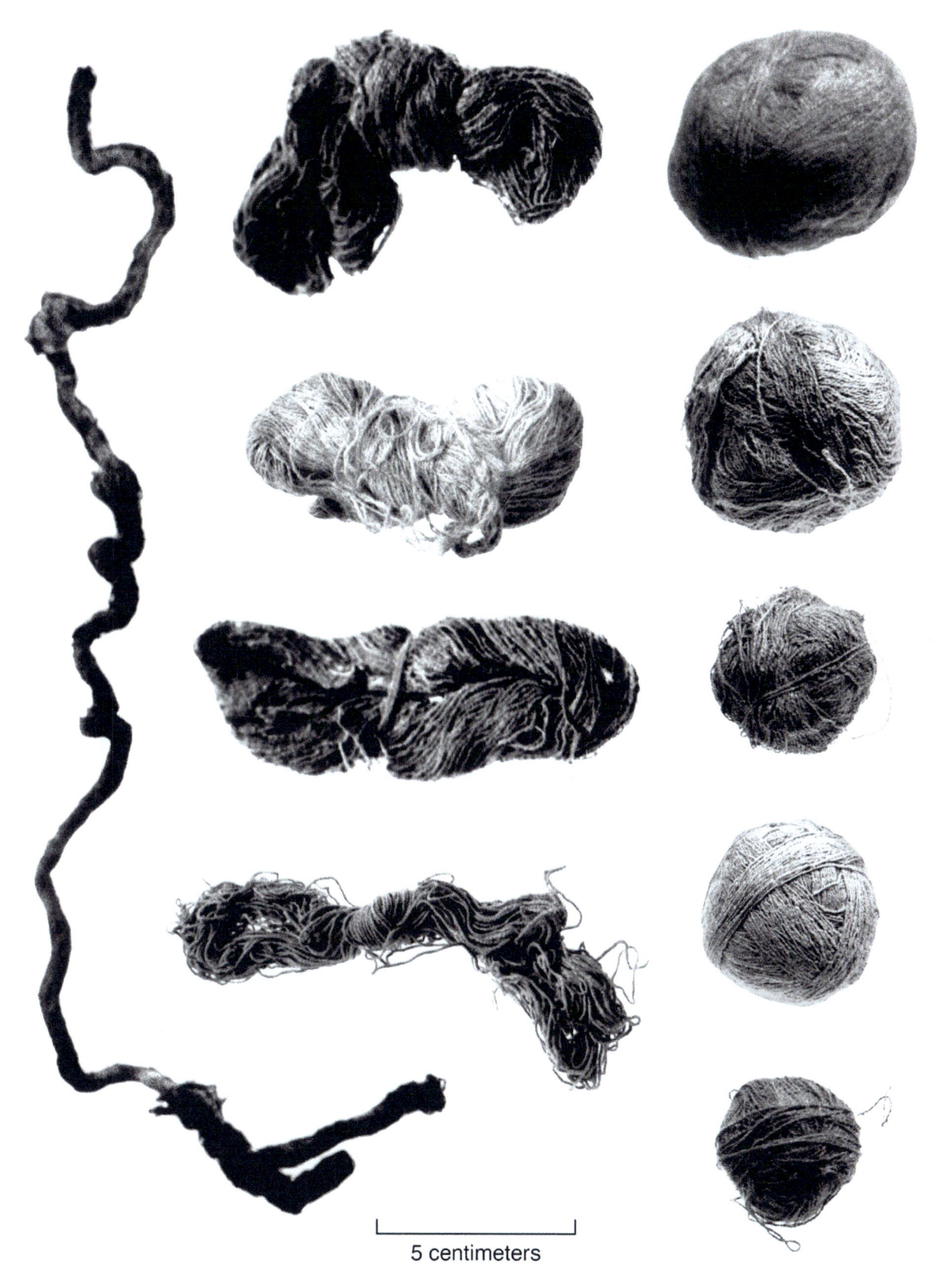

Figure 10.34 (this page and following page). Some of the 58 items found in Bag 1 of Individual 3, Burial 4: yarn balls, skeins of yarn, and unfinished cords and piping.

230　　　　　　　　　　　　　　　　　　　　　Chapter 10

Figure 10.34 (this page and previous page). Some of the 58 items found in Bag 1 of Individual 3, Burial 4: yarn balls, skeins of yarn, and unfinished cords and piping.

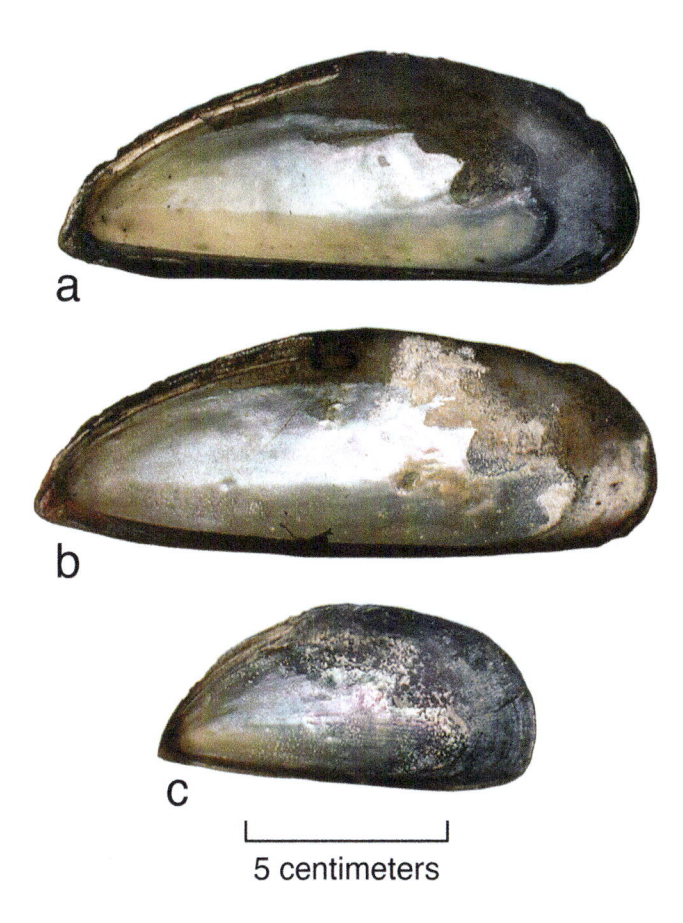

Figure 10.35. Three large mussel shells (*Choromytilus*), found inside Bag 2 of Individual 3, Burial 4. They were used as pigment palettes and still show traces of the red paint applied to her fingernails, her miniature flasks, and the face of the figurine found in her Bag 1.

Figure 10.36. One of the better-preserved pigment pouches found in Bag 2 of Individual 3, Burial 4. These pouches were wrapped in the embroidered cloth shown in Figure 10.37. The pouch illustrated here contained an orange pigment, identified as realgar and sulfur.

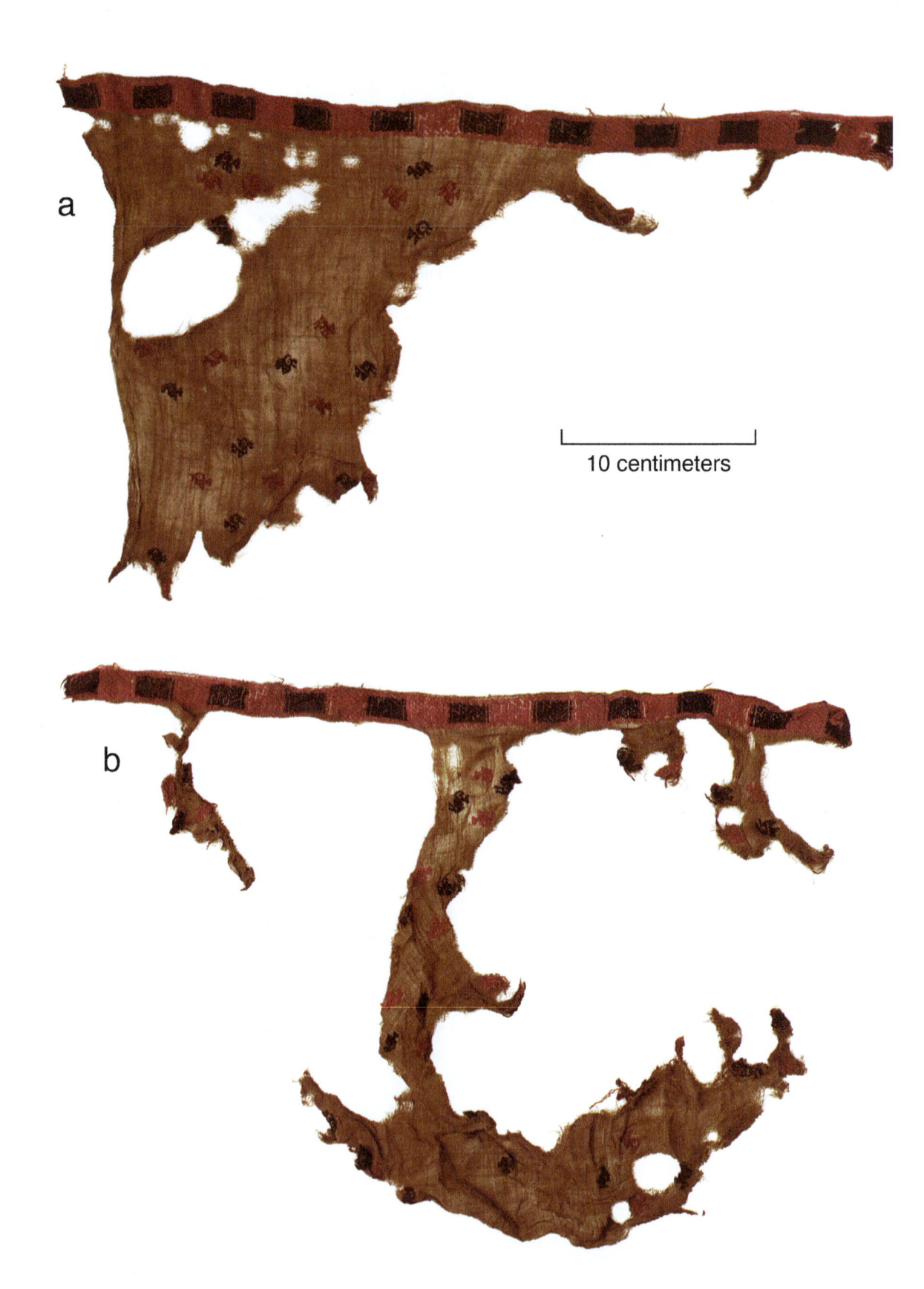

Figure 10.37. This badly disintegrated cloth, found inside Bag 2 of Individual 3, featured embroidered birds in red and black yarn. This cloth had been wrapped around pigment pouches, whose mineral content may have contributed to the cloth's disintegration.

Figure 10.38. Bag 2, a wool bag with decorative stripes of complementary warp patterning, was associated with Individual 3 of Burial 4. Its contents have been shown in Figures 10.35–10.37.

Figure 10.39 (left). Bag 3a, a slit eccentric tapestry bag, was found inside Bag 2 of Individual 3, Burial 4.
Figure 10.40 (right). Two of the eight pigment pouches found in Bag 3b (inside Bag 3a), associated with Individual 3 of Burial 4 (see Figure 10.41).

brown, S-spun, and 0.7 mm wide. The weft is dark brown and S-spun.

The decorative yarn is Z-S and composed of three colors—yellow, red, and blue-green. The heading cord is wool, Z-S, and consists of a group of six one-ply strands. The repair edging is also wool, S-Z, 3.0 mm thick, and yellow in color. The design bands are 12 alternating yellow and red yarns (six each), then 12 alternating blue-green and red yarns (six each) over two one-ply yarns (with a splitting weft of plain dark brown).

We know of other cases where women were buried with shell palettes and pigment pouches. For example, at the site of San Juanito in the lower Santa Valley, Chapdelaine and Gagné (2015:48–49) report a woman buried with *Choromytilus* and a pouch containing pigment; the authors suggest that the pigment was red ochre.

The Contents of Bag 3a

Welcome now to a complicated situation: Bag 3a was found inside Bag 2, and Bag 3b was found inside Bag 3a. Unfortunately, the dusky red cloth wrapped around Bag 3a had largely disintegrated.

Bag 3a (Textile 153) had been made from three strips of slit eccentric tapestry (Figure 10.39); each strip measured 25 x 4 cm. We were able to reassemble Bag 3a because we could see the threads of the whipping stitch that had been used to hold the three strips together.

The reassembled bag measured 12.5 x 12 cm. Its warp and weft were wool, Z-spun and S-twisted, and there were 36 warps and 9 wefts per cm. The sewing thread was cotton, S-spun. Each strip has six design squares, measuring 4 x 4 cm, and the design consists of one bird per design square. Each square on a strip differs in color, and the order of squares varies from strip to strip. Diagonal rows featuring the same color are reminiscent of the sequences seen on the reversible loom backstraps also buried with Individual 3.

The Contents of Bag 3b

Bag 3b was unique in containing eight pigment pouches (Figure 10.40 shows two pouches). These pouches were not loose in the bag, but tied up in a plain weave cloth that had fragmented into multiple pieces.

If one adds to these eight pouches the three found in Bag 2, the total found with Individual 3 is 11. This is the

Figure 10.41. Bag 3b of Individual 3, which was found inside Bag 3a. This was a checkered woolen bag with netting and drawstring; it is similar to a bag found with Individual 1a of Burial 4 (see Figure 10.9).

Figure 10.42. Two views of Bag 4, found with Individual 3 of Burial 4. (a) The bag as discovered, filled with yarn balls. (b) The empty bag.

largest number of pigment pouches associated with any individual, and Individual 3 thus had access to an array of colors. Five of the pouches contained red powder, while the other three held orange, green, or buff.

Although the five red powders look superficially the same, not all proved to be identical in composition. Analyses by chemist James Burton of the University of Wisconsin revealed that two of the red pigments were cinnabar + anhydrite. A third was cinnabar, realgar, and salts. The fourth was cinnabar + orpiment. The last was a mixture of cinnabar + realgar + gypsum.

According to Burton, the orange powder proved to be realgar and sulfur, while the green was copper arsenate hydrate. Finally, the buff-colored pigment proved to be sulfur with orpiment. This powder had a strong sulfur smell when it was ground by Burton; the powder left a red-yellow sublimate in the test tube. Trace amounts of As, Ca, K, and Fe were found in this buff-colored pigment.

Bag 3b itself was a warp-stripe checkered woolen bag, measuring 13.5 x 11 cm (Figure 10.41); its netting and drawstring were made of bast. In addition to the pigment pouches, it contained a length of cotton cord. This bag can be compared to that in Figure 10.9, which was also used to hold pigment pouches.

The Contents of Bag 4

Bag 4 (T145) contained 127.5 g of yarn, consisting of six yarn balls and one skein (Figure 10.42a, b and Figure 10.43). Two of the yarn balls were pea green in color; one had a diameter of 5.5 cm and weighed 28 g, while the other had a diameter of 5 cm and weighed 6 g. The third yarn ball, 5 cm in diameter, weighed 20 g and was 10 YR 6/6 ("brownish yellow"). The fourth ball, 3 cm in diameter, weighed 6.5 g and was 7.5 YR 5/6 ("strong brown"). The fifth ball, 3 cm

Figure 10.43. The contents of Bag 4, Individual 3: six yarn balls and one skein of yarn.

in diameter, weighed 6.5 g and was 10 YR 5/6 ("yellowish brown"). The sixth and last yarn ball, 4.5 cm in diameter, weighed 19 g and was 2.5 Y 8/4 ("pale yellow"). The final item in Bag 4 was a skein 7 cm long, weighing 5 g; its color matched that of the sixth (pale yellow) yarn ball.

Bag 4 itself was a warp-stripe plain weave bag with embroidered edging in red and yellow; its overall dimensions were 19 x 16 cm. There were 30 warp yarns per cm and 3 weft yarns per cm, and the design was a complicated series of narrow stripes and checkerboard bands.

The Contents of Bag 5a

Bag 5a contained yarn balls and a bone *balanza*, suitable for weighing light items such as mineral powders, coca leaves, yarn, or something else (Figure 10.44). Both sides of the *balanza* are decorated. One side (Figure 10.44a, b) of the *balanza* was incised with 78 circles arranged in rows of three or four. The other side of the *balanza* has 84 circles arranged in rows of four (Figure 10.44c). The use of circles on bone artifacts is not unique. An early bone *balanza* with two rows of incised circles was found near Callao (Baessler 1902–1903; Saville 1925:278–279). Other examples of incised circles are known from Andean weaving swords (unfortunately unprovenienced), now housed in New York's Metropolitan Museum of Art. The dozen or so known *balanzas* with similar circles from the Chincha Valley are those geographically closest to Cerro Azul; some of those date to the Late Intermediate and display incised circles arranged in clusters or rows (Kroeber and Strong 1924: Fig. 20). The *balanzas* from a Late Horizon mortuary context at Las Huacas have circles, too, but they are not arranged in regular rows; they are instead dispersed (Dalton 2020).

Given that the earliest *balanza* seems to date to A.D. 1200 (Dalton, personal communication), we wonder what prompted their initial appearance and subsequent use in the Late Intermediate political economy. Kroeber and Strong (1924) indicate that most of the *balanzas* they found dated to the Late Intermediate (their "Late Chincha" era), while few dated to the Late Horizon. One additional south coast grave that contained a *balanza* is that known from the Ica Valley, where Uhle found a bone *balanza* in a workbasket (Menzel 1977:14).

While we do not know what the Late Intermediate woman (Individual 3) in Burial 4 was weighing, it is interesting that two early sources (Bartolomé Ruiz and Miguel de Estete) say that scales were used to weigh gold

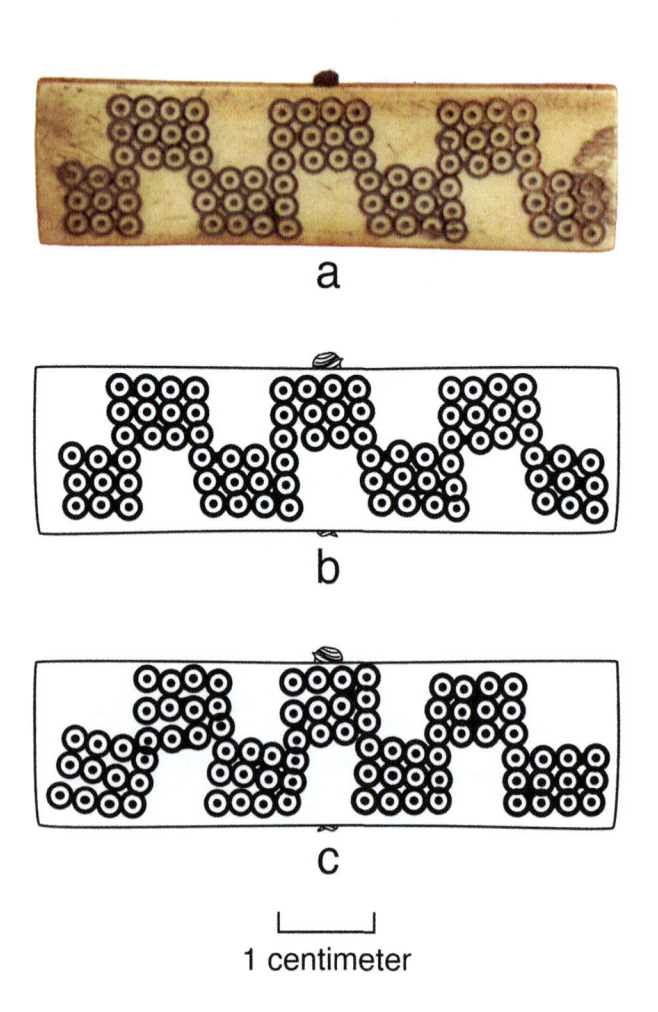

Figure 10.44. A bone *balanza*, found inside Bag 5a of Individual 3, Burial 4. (a, b) Photo and drawing of the *balanza's* obverse side, decorated with 78 incised circles. (c) The *balanza's* reverse side, decorated with 84 incised circles.

Burial 4 239

Figure 10.45. Bag 5a, made from a folded-over slit tapestry textile, had knotted netting at its mouth. This bag, found with Individual 3 of Burial 4, contained the bone *balanza* shown in Figure 10.44, as well as two smaller bags (Bags 5b and 5c).

(see Saville 1925). Other plausible items that might have been weighed include cotton, camelid wool, and coca leaves.

Bag 5a itself (T143a) is a slit tapestry textile (Figure 10.45), with embroidered edging and knotted netting at the mouth. The bag, which measures 14 x 7 cm, consists of a continuous diagonal band of geometric elements. Bag 5a has a step fret design and a drawstring of six-ply, S-Z, dark brown cotton. The term "step fret" (or "stepped fret") refers to a design composed of three or more steps connected to a rectangular hook or a spiral.

Inside Bag 5a we found two smaller bags, which we designated Bags 5b and 5c.

Bag 5b

Bag 5b (6 x 7 cm) displays contiguous zigzag bands that form interlocking triangles (Figure 10.46). The knotted netting at the mouth of this bag is similar to that of Bag 5a, but torn. Bag 5b was empty when discovered.

The Contents of Bag 5c

Bag 5c contained three pieces of metal, designated Items 5d-1 (gold), 5d-2 (silver), and 5d-3 (silver) (Figure 10.47a, b, and c). These items had been combined to form a packet of gold and silver of the type usually placed in a corpse's mouth. Perhaps because Individual 3 already had an even bigger piece of metal in her mouth, this packet had never been used.

Item 5d-1 (Figure 10.47a) was a rectangle of gold foil, 5.3 x 3.0 cm in size and 0.1 mm thick, weighing about 1 g; it appeared to have been cut from a larger piece of thin foil. This foil had been embossed with one complete *inti* (or sun motif) and part of a second.

The two silver pieces (5d-2 and 5d-3) had a total weight of 8.5 g. Item 5d-2 (Figure 10.47b) was a piece of silver sheet, apparently cut from the edge of a disc; it weighed 5.5 g and measured 3.0 x 4.4 cm. The thickness of the piece was 2.2 mm near the center.

Item 5d-3 (Figure 10.47c) was a tightly folded packet of silver foil, too fragile to unfold. The packet measured 2.0 cm x 3.0 cm, was 0.1 mm thick, and weighed 3 g.

Bag 5c itself (T143c) had been made from a textile whose original loom dimensions were 19 x 8.5 cm. That textile had been folded in half to create the bag, which was 9.5 cm high and 8.5 cm wide (Figure 10.48). This bag was similar in construction to Bag 5b, the main difference being that black Z-S wool yarn had been used to whip the sides shut.

Figure 10.46. Bag 5b was found inside Individual 3's Bag 5a (see Figure 10.45). This bag displays contiguous zigzag bands that form interlocking triangles; the knotted netting at the mouth is similar to that seen on Bag 5a.

Figure 10.48. Bag 5c, found inside Bag 5a, held the pieces of silver shown in Figure 10.47.

The Contents of Bag 6

Bag 6 (Figure 10.49) was unusual in that it was divided into six squares or pockets; one of these pockets contained cords (shown below). This bag had the appearance of a wallet featuring alternating gold and black squares; its warp was wool, while its weft was dark brown cotton.

Bag 6 is made from a slit eccentric tapestry with loom dimensions of 25 x 16 cm; when this textile was folded in half, a bag measuring 12.5 cm high and 16 cm wide was created. Each side of the bag had been divided into three squares (vertically) and two (horizontally), resulting in six squares per side. One 4 mm red stripe had been placed in the center of the web to mark the fold.

The decorative motif consisted of diagonal lines of triangular elements with semi-interlocking hooks, one set with bird heads and the other with triangular fillers.

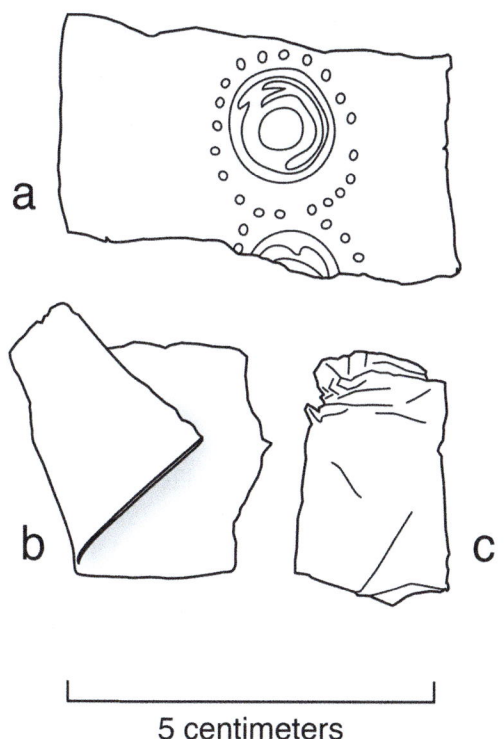

Figure 10.47. Bag 5c, also found inside Individual 3's Bag 5a, contained three pieces of metal (see photo at top). (a) Specimen 5d-1, gold foil with embossed suns or *intis*. (b) Specimen 5d-2, a folded piece of silver. (c) Specimen 5d-3, a packet of silver foil.

Figure 10.49. Bag 6, associated with Individual 3 of Burial 4, contained the cords shown at the bottom of the photo.

As mentioned above, one square or "pocket" contained cords. This cordage had flat sections of compound weave with complementary warp patterning, and an ovate section of single-faced warp patterning.

Many loose yarn balls had fallen to the bottom of the burial pit; if we combine them with those still stored inside Individual 3's yarn bags, the number of yarn balls is more than 100. This woman definitely had a good supply of yarn for weaving in the afterlife.

Portable Loom

Included with Individual 3 was a small loom (Specimen 118) of the type presumably used to make the narrow tapestry panels and loom backstraps found with her. This loom is illustrated in Figures 10.50 and 10.51. The first of those figures shows how the loom was found, wrapped up with cloth made from *algodón pardo* (T130); the second shows all the elements revealed when the loom was unwrapped, as follows:

—two ungulate long bones, called *choqchi* in Quechua. One is 26.3 cm long, with a maximum width of 2.2 cm; the second measures 23.5 cm long, with a maximum width of 2.25 cm. Both examples are shown with their convex sides up. Unlike the usual pair of ungulate long bones, which has a left and a right, my weaver informants concluded that both bones are left-handed implements.

—eight sections of cane that formed the heart of the *chumpi awana*
  · 26.4 cm long, 19 mm in diameter, a hard cane with internodes at intervals of 6–8 cm apart
  · 22.5 cm long, 14 mm in diameter; no visible internodes, smooth cane

Figure 10.50. This belt loom, wrapped up in a dark brown cotton cloth and tied with a cord, was found inside the mummy bundle of Individual 3, Burial 4. (To see the items in this loom, see Figure 10.51.)

- 18.5 cm long, 12.5 mm in diameter; smooth cane, no visible internodes
- 18.3 cm long, 16.3 mm in diameter; hard cane with internodes at intervals of 9 cm
- 17.7 cm long, 13.5 mm in diameter; smooth cane
- 15.3 cm long, 8.4 mm in diameter; completely smooth, no internodes
- 14.6 cm long, 12 mm in diameter; completely smooth, no internodes
- 13.6 cm long, 15 mm in diameter; completely smooth, no internodes

Two of my informants said that four canes are usually sufficient for one such loom. They therefore suggested that this woman either had a second loom, or kept extra canes as replacements in case one or more broke.

Chumpis

Individual 3 was buried with six *chumpis*, all similar in construction and layout but different in decoration. Each featured a central tapestry panel that bore the decorative motif; flanking that panel were two bands of solid color.

All *chumpis* were two-sided, with a different motif on each side. One side typically featured red flanking bands, while the other side had dark brown to black flanking bands. The decorated tapestry panels gave us a glimpse into Individual 3's motif and color preferences (Marcus 2015).

Chumpi 1

Chumpi 1 measures 75.5 x 12 cm. Side A is the one with red flanking bands, while Side B features dark brown flanking bands.

Side A has two red wool, warp-faced plain weave bands, each 3.25 cm wide (Figure 10.52a). The design on the central slit tapestry panel is geometric, featuring multiple triangles or stepped pyramids in a diagonal, with one stepped pyramid branching off at the top and two pyramids branching off from the middle. Surrounding these design elements is a red background with green dots.

Side B has warp-faced dark brown wool bands (3.25 cm wide) that flank the central slit tapestry (Figure 10.52b). The central tapestry features diagonal rows of interlocking step frets with rectangular hooks. Six rows differ in color; then, the seventh row repeats the colors of the first row. The color sequence is gold, dark brown, red, green, red, white, light brown, and then gold again.

Figure 10.51. The belt loom shown in Figure 10.50 consisted of eight sections of cane that presumably served as loom bars (*machanas*), shed rods, and heddle rods (see Figures 6.20, 6.21). Also included were two ungulate long bones (*choqchi*).

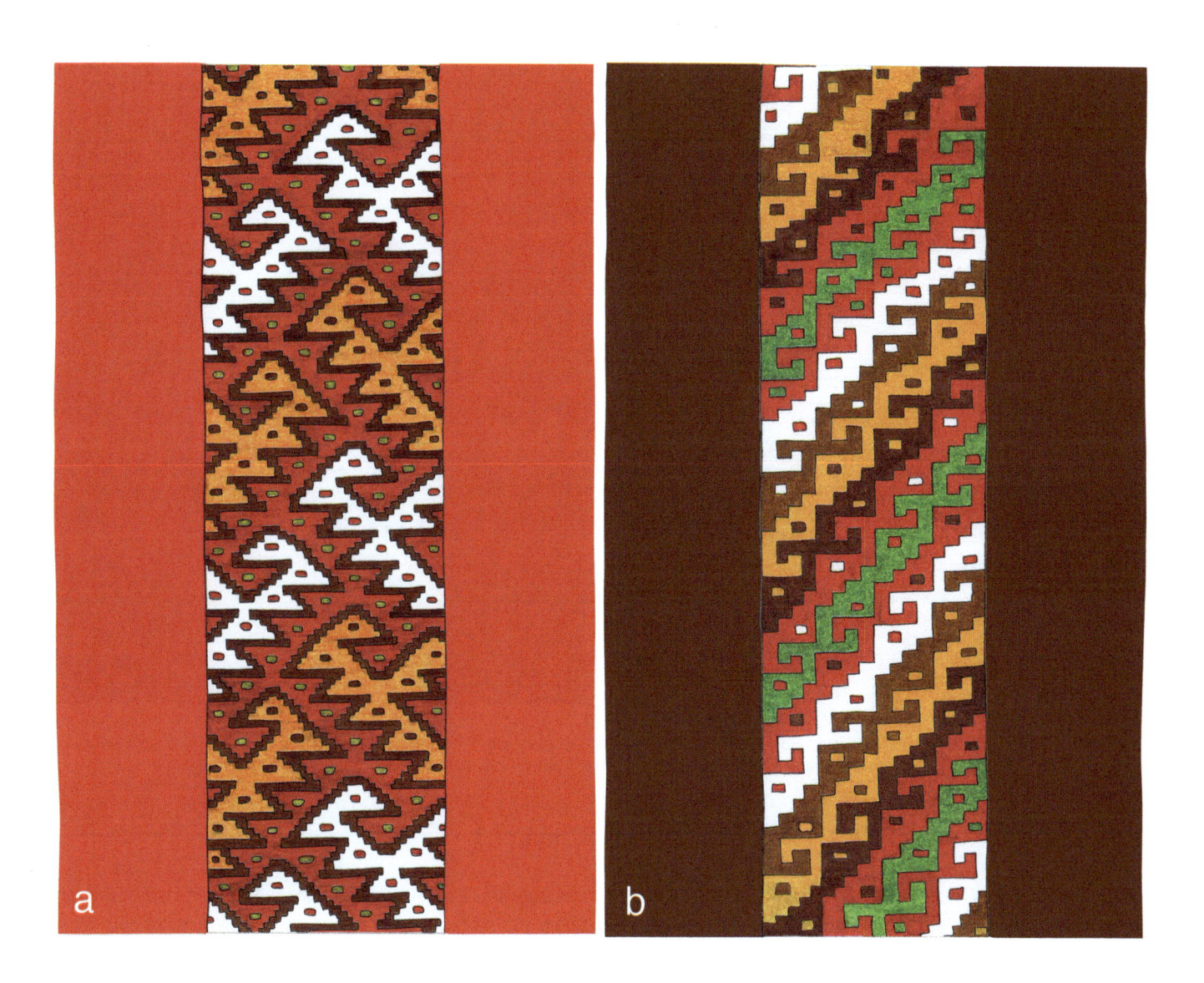

Figure 10.52. Artist's rendering of Chumpi 1, a reversible double-sided loom backstrap associated with Individual 3 of Burial 4. Side A has a geometric design on its tapestry panel, and red flanking bands. Side B features rows of interlocking step frets, with six diagonal rows of different colors before the color sequence repeats; its flanking bands are brown. Painting by Kay Clahassey.

Figure 10.53. Artist's rendering of Chumpi 2, a double-sided loom backstrap associated with Individual 3 of Burial 4. Side A has geometric step frets, flanked by red bands. Side B features a rectangle and hook motif, flanked by black bands. Painting by Kay Clahassey.

Chumpi 2

Chumpi 2 measures 79 x 12 cm, and like Chumpi 1, has red flanking bands on its Side A. Side A of Chumpi 2 (Figure 10.53a) has a central tapestry panel featuring interlocking step frets with rectangular hooks. The tapestry uses red, yellow, brown, red, and white yarns.

Side B (Figure 10.53b) has black flanking bands. The central tapestry design is a repetitive rectangle and hook motif, with the changes in hook directions taking place each time the color sequence repeats. It should be noted that this woman's decision to create a rectangle and hook motif makes Side B of Chumpi 2 similar to Side B of her Chumpi 6 (see below in Figure 10.57). The color scheme was red, white, brown, gold, gray, red, green, then red and white again.

Chumpi 3

Chumpi 3 is a two-sided backstrap (60 x 14 cm) with warp-faced plain weave bands flanking the central panel.

Side A (Figure 10.54a) has solid red woolen bands 3.2 cm wide. The central tapestry panel has step fret triangles that look similar to those on Side A of Chumpi 1, except for the choice of colors. The background color of Chumpi 3 is black with orange dots; red yarn is used to outline the motifs, which is an unusual practice. The fret-dot sequence of the central panel uses an orange stepped platform with black dots inside and a white stepped platform with red dots inside. Five colors in all were used to create this design. Another similarity between Chumpi 3 and Chumpi 1 lies in the sewing and stitching.

Figure 10.54. Artist's rendering of Chumpi 3, a double-sided loom backstrap associated with Individual 3 of Burial 4. Side A has step fret triangles in its tapestry panel, and red flanking bands. Side B has black flanking bands. Painting by Kay Clahassey.

Side B of Chumpi 3 (Figure 10.54b) has a tapestry panel with a color sequence similar to that on Side B of Chumpi 2 (Figure 10.53b). The similarities include the choice of color sequencing and the use of curvilinear elements (possible animal heads) that contrast with the geometric constraints of the overall tapestry design. The flanking bands on Side B are black, as we saw on Side B of Chumpi 2.

Chumpi 4

Chumpi 4 (63 x 17 cm) is a two-sided backstrap. Sides A and B of Chumpi 4 (Figure 10.55) both have step fret designs with interior rectangular dots on their tapestry panels.

Side A of Chumpi 4 (Figure 10.55a) features a slit tapestry panel 8 cm wide, with red flanking bands 4.5 cm wide; the tapestry's step fret decoration is reminiscent of that on Side B of Chumpi 1 (Figure 10.52b). Side A uses two shades of red (dark red and cherry red) in its central tapestry.

The flanking warp-faced bands on Side B of Chumpi 4 (Figure 10.55b) have largely deteriorated, but the few surviving threads appear to be black rather than brown. The color sequence on the tapestry panel is red, green, brown, white, brown, gold, gray, red, light green, brown, and then white again; the motif is a step fret design that features more grays and greens than Side A.

248   Chapter 10

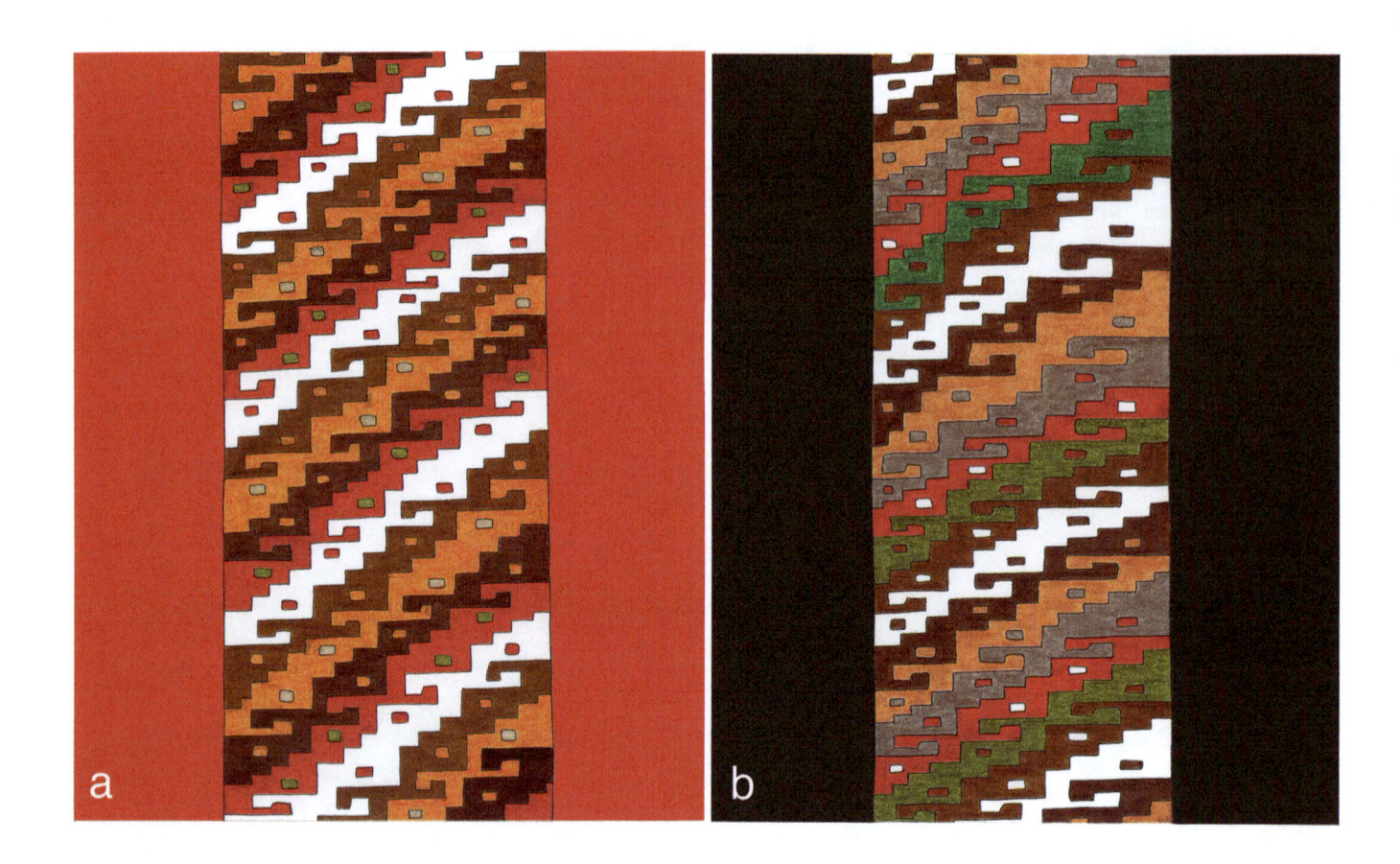

Figure 10.55. Artist's rendering of Chumpi 4, a double-sided loom backstrap associated with Individual 3 of Burial 4. While the motifs on its tapestry panels are similar, Side A has red flanking bands and Side B has black flanking bands. Painting by Kay Clahassey.

Chumpi 5

Chumpi 5 (54 x 16.5 cm) is a two-sided backstrap with two flanking warp-faced plain weave bands (6.5 cm wide); these bands have deteriorated, allowing us to see that the basketry interior of the strap is the same as that inside Chumpis 2 and 4.

Side A (Figure 10.56a) features a slit tapestry panel flanked by red bands. The tapestry design consists of step frets with projections of small stepped triangles and rectangular dots. The color sequence is white, red, brown, gold, light brown, and then white again.

Side B (Figure 10.56b) has a tapestry panel 5.5 cm wide. It bears large interlocking step frets similar to those on Side A of Chumpi 2, except that in this case they have interior rectangular dots and multiple steps, not three ascending steps like those on Side A of Chumpi 2. The flanking bands are dark brown. The colorful panel uses green, red, dark brown, gold, light brown, light brown, white, red, and yellow.

Chumpi 6

Chumpi 6 (72 x 17 cm) is a two-sided backstrap with a central slit tapestry panel, flanked by warp-faced plain weave bands. Its internal padding is quite thick.

Side A of Chumpi 6 (Figure 10.57a) includes a central panel 7.5 cm wide, with red flanking bands 4.75 cm wide. The design on the central panel features step frets similar to those on Side A of Chumpi 5. (Side A of Chumpi 5 has

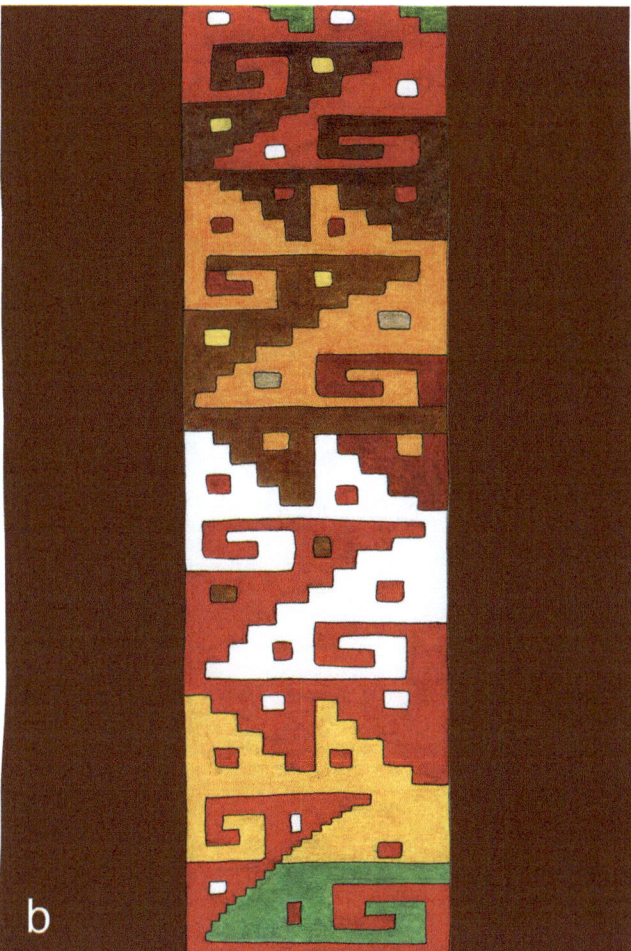

Figure 10.56. Artist's rendering of Chumpi 5, a double-sided loom backstrap associated with Individual 3 of Burial 4. Side A has a geometric design that includes step frets; its flanking bands are red. Side B has a different geometric design, and its flanking bands are dark brown. Painting by Kay Clahassey.

rounder, smaller triangles with smaller delicate dots, but the overall concept is similar in both cases.) The dominant colors are orange, red, white, and black.

Side B of Chumpi 6 (Figure 10.57b) bears a slit tapestry 7.0 cm wide, consisting of three strips or columns. This side features a rectangle and hook motif similar to the one seen on Side B of Chumpi 2; a minor difference is that Side B of Chumpi 6 has one dot per motif rather than two. The hook motifs in the central column extend in the opposite direction from those on the outer columns. The color sequence is the same for all columns, but the sequence of colors on the central column is offset by one which creates a chevron effect; that color sequence is gray, gold, brown, white, gold, gray, red, and then the sequence repeats. The flanking bands are dark brown in color.

Fragments of other textiles and cords found with Individual 3

Textile 193 was the remains of a stray yarn ball bag found below Individual 3; it was a warp-stripe plain weave cloth of brown, black, and white yarn. This wool bag had largely disintegrated, but we were able to see that it contained yarn balls.

T 204a are segments of eight-strand square braid, tied together and folded over. These cords are made of noncotton fibers, Z-spun; one cord has an estimated length of one meter.

T 204b is a cotton cord, S-spun, 24 cm long, 5 cm wide, with a 35 degree twist.

T 130 is one of the cotton bands used to wrap up the beltmaking loom. It consists of an extra weft-patterned plain weave.

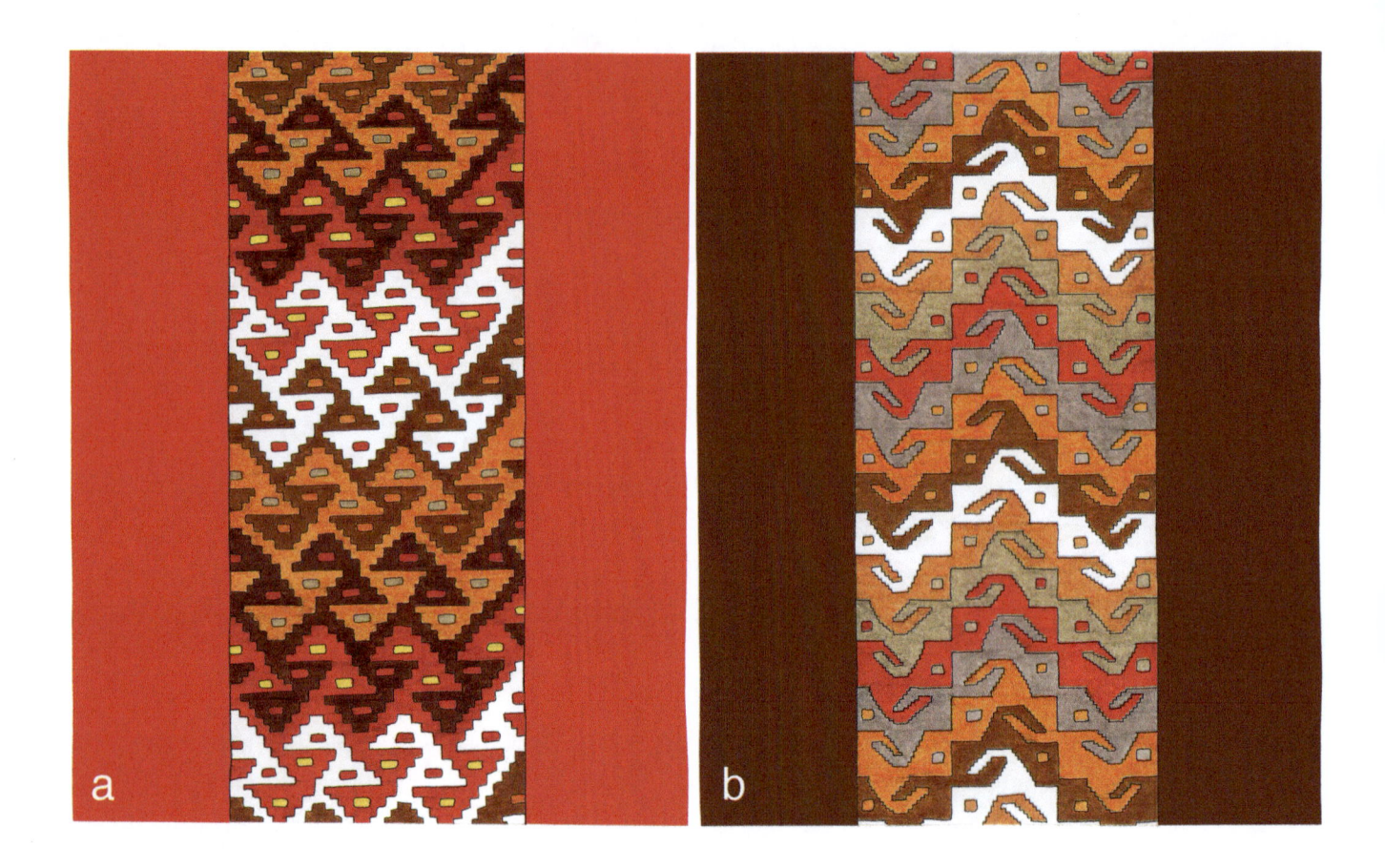

Figure 10.57. Artist's rendering of Chumpi 6, a double-sided loom backstrap associated with Individual 3 of Burial 4. Side A has step frets in its tapestry panel, and red flanking bands. Side B features a rectangle and hook motif flanked by brown bands. Painting by Kay Clahassey.

T 142 is a set of round decorative braids, made by spiral cross-knit looping.

T 207a, made of dyed red wool, was a warp-faced strip from a two-sided belt.

T 207b, largely disintegrated, had been a dark brown cotton plain weave cloth.

T 215a was a fragment of woolen cord, 6.5 mm in diameter, a cross-knit needle looping on the core. It has three-row asymmetrical stitching that formed a flattened ovate cross section. It has a multicolor chevron design. There are seven lengths of cord, tied with yarn 57 cm from finished tips. On the other side of the knot, all torn, the longest distance from the knot is a 31 cm cord. The remaining fragments make up seven lengths of cord.

T 215b consisted of several fragments of four-strand square braid, 2.5 mm in diameter, Z-twisted. The longest section measured 37 cm long.

Textile 215c was a piece of woolen cloth (Z-S), a warp-faced plain weave with additional warps in complementary pairs of contrasting color, floating to create a simple design of dots and dashes in two parallel bands outlined in black; the design is in red and yellow.

Textile 215d was a piece of warp-stripe plain weave cloth combining red, tan, and black yarn.

Textile 216 was a piece of wool and cotton cloth. The basic warp course is over 2 under 1, over 1 under 1; the adjacent course is under 2 over 1, under 1 over 1. The outer courses are all red, forming solid red borders. The central area has alternating red wool and groups of four dark brown cotton single-strand yarns, creating a horizontal line of brown when combined with dark brown wefts. To create a simple geometric design, red warps are floated over 3 in place of over 1 under 1 over 1. The brown weft was largely unraveled, leaving little of the design. A red hank of yarn is 24 cm long.

Textile 231a measured 18 x 16 cm, with 1.5 cm wide bands of plain weave alternating with 1 cm wide bands of 2/2 single gauze weave along warps.

Textile 231b measured 24 x 18 cm; a plain weave cloth with one small figure in red wool, an extra-weft float pattern.

Textiles 198 a, b, c, and **d** were four pieces of the same cotton cloth, all warp-stripe plain weaves displaying brown and white stripes.

Workbasket

Individual 3 was buried with a twill workbasket (Specimen 115), which had luckily not been opened by looters (Figure 10.58a, b). This basket is rectangular, measuring 26 x 13 x 8 cm; it had been made by stitching together six separate pieces (the top, the bottom, and four sides). Its lid closed like a flap.

The panels that formed the lid and floor of the basket measured 13 x 26 cm each. The two longer side panels measured 8 x 26 cm, while the two shorter end panels were 8 x 13 cm. The lid and floor panels each had four cane splints 26 cm long, 8–9 mm wide, 2–3 mm thick, and spaced 2.5 to 3 cm apart. In between the splints were strips of bulrush (*Scirpus* sp.), tightly woven to hold them in place. Each side panel had four splints, 1.0 to 1.5 cm apart.

The contents (Figure 10.59) of the workbasket were as follows:

A wad of raw, unspun *algodón pardo* or dark brown cotton weighing 4 g. The wad measures 15 x 4 x 2 cm and its color ranges from 5 YR 4/4 ("reddish brown") to 5 YR 3/4 ("dark reddish brown").

A piece of chalk-like material measuring 9 x 7 x 1.5 cm and weighing 54 g. Its color is 5 YR 8/2 ("pinkish white") (Figure 10.59, lower right).

Two knob-headed spindles whittled to a point, both 12.9 cm long with a diameter of 2.8 mm.

Twenty-nine knob-headed spindles whose knobs consist of black seeds called *suirucus* in Quechua. The 29 spindles range in length from 13 to 16.5 cm. Their diameters range from 2.5 to 3.5 mm, and the diameters of the black seeds are 9.0 to 10 mm.

A packet of five *Opuntia* spine needles 9.5 to 12 cm in length, wrapped in very dark reddish-brown thread; all the needles have eyes.

Seventeen loose needles, all with eyes, ranging from 8 to 12 cm in length and 1.2 to 2.0 mm in diameter.

Two painted spindles whose barcode has faded, but appears to consist of wide yellow bands and thin black bands flanking red bands (Figure 10.60, left). Both of these spindles have squat, teardrop-shaped Camacho Black whorls. One spindle measures 22 cm long and 3.3 mm in diameter, with a whorl 11.1 mm high and 18.8 mm in diameter. The second is 21.5 cm long and 3.3 mm in diameter, with a whorl 15.8 mm high and 19.6 mm in diameter.

Two painted spindles with whorls that display black, white, and red colors and have crosshatching in the central band. One spindle is 23.9 cm long, with a diameter of ca. 2.6 mm; its whorl is 13.7 mm high, with a diameter of 17.2 mm. The second spindle is 22.8 cm long, with a diameter of ca. 2.9 mm; its whorl is 14.2 mm high with a diameter of 16.7 mm. The spindles feature a band of white Xs (Figure 10.59, middle left; Figure 10.60, right).

A woven drawstring for a bag, tied up with a group of unfinished needles, each 12 cm long, flattened but with no eyehole. The drawstring is a woven ribbon, 7 mm wide and bearing a garnet dot and dash motif.

An unfinished segment of piping that might eventually have exceeded 30 cm; only 6 cm had been finished, presumably because the woman died. The diameter of the piping is 3.3 mm. It would have had a diamond and chevron pattern in dark brown, forest green, and gold.

Fourteen skeins of yarn, as follows:
—forest green yarn, weighing 4 g
—yellowish-brown yarn (10 YR 5/6), discolored, weighing 2 g
—golden brown yarn, discolored, weighing 1 g
—golden brown yarn, discolored, weighing 1 g
—strong brown yarn (7.5 YR 5/8), weighing 4 g
—light yellowish brown yarn (10 YR 6/4), weighing 2 g
—light yellowish brown yarn (10 YR 6/4), weighing 3 g
—light yellowish brown yarn (10 YR 6/4), weighing 2 g
—light yellowish brown yarn (10 YR 6/4), weighing 4 g
—light yellowish brown yarn (10 YR 6/4), weighing 3 g
—light yellowish brown yarn (10 YR 6/4), weighing 3 g
—light yellowish brown yarn (10 YR 6/4), weighing 1 g
—yellow yarn (10 YR 7/8), weighing 1 g
—yellow yarn (10 YR 7/8), weighing 2.5 g

Fifteen segments of yarn, including all the colors listed above plus the following three:
—2.5 YR 3/2 ("dusky red")
—7.5 YR 4/6 ("red")
—2.5 Y 8/4 ("pale yellow")

252   Chapter 10

Figure 10.58. A twill workbasket associated with Individual 3 of Burial 4. (a) The closed workbasket, just as it was found. (b) The open workbasket, with its matching spindle whorls, brown cotton, possible piece of chalk, and skeins of yarn (see Figure 10.59).

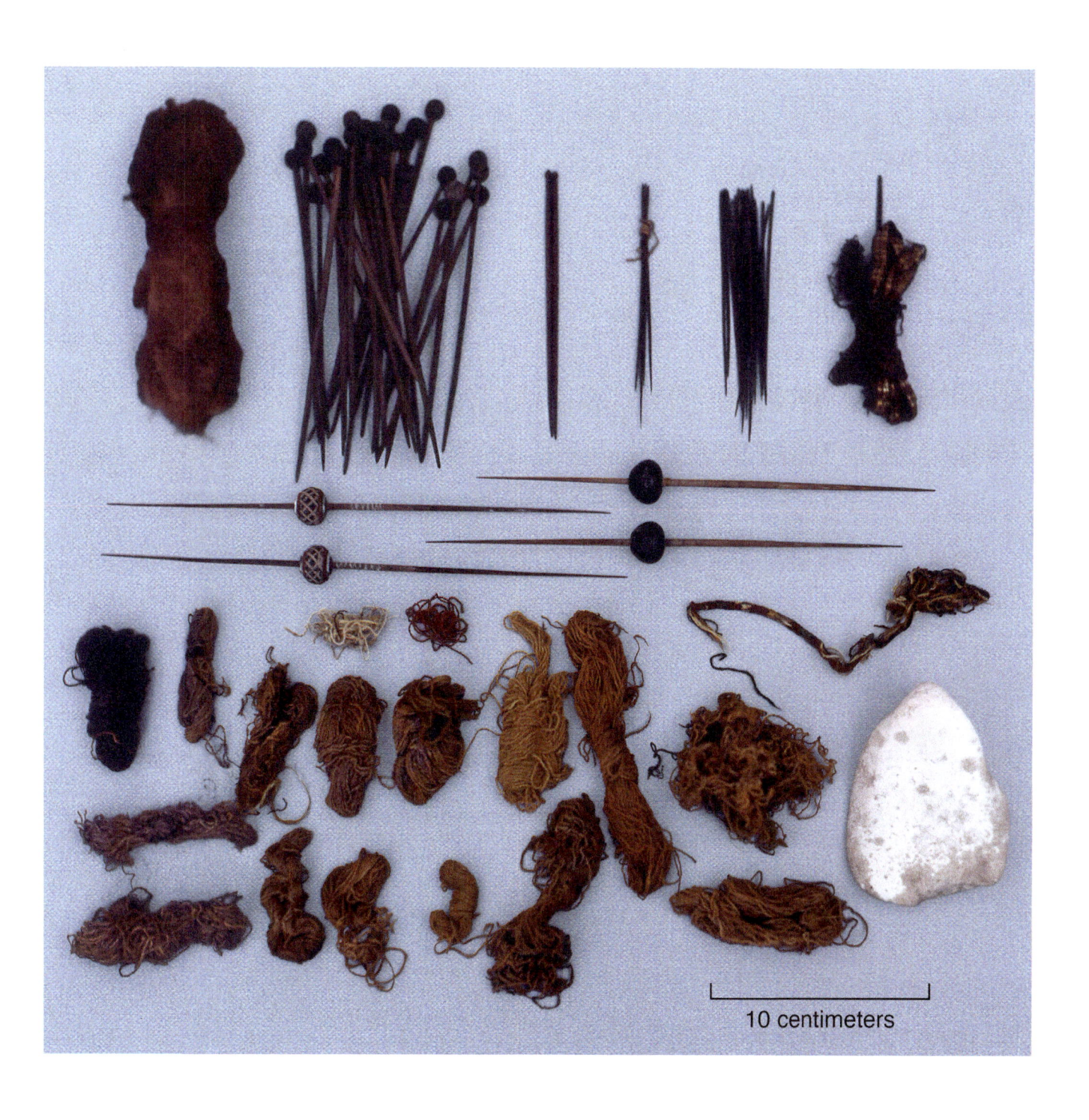

Figure 10.59. The contents of the workbasket shown in Figure 10.58. Included are two pairs of spindles with matching whorls (see Figure 10.60), a packet of needles, a possible piece of chalk, *cordoncillo* or piping, and nearly 20 skeins of yarn.

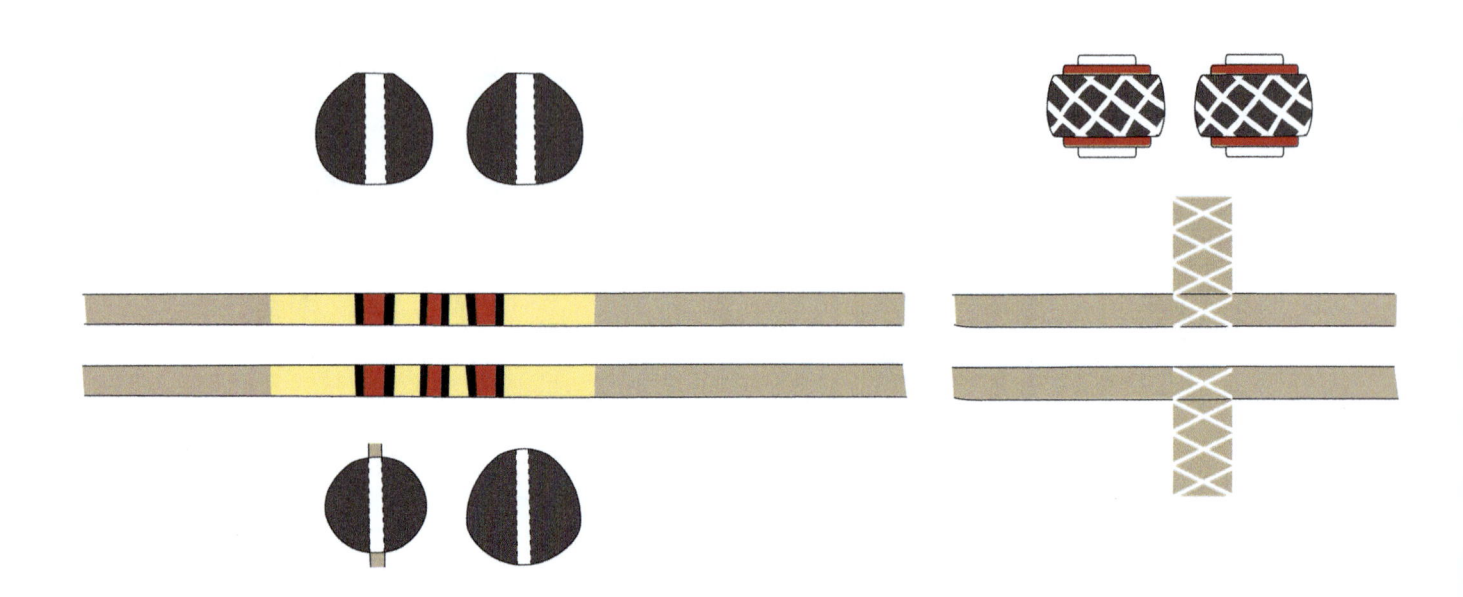

Figure 10.60. Two pairs of barcoded spindles with identical whorls, found inside the workbasket belonging to Individual 3 of Burial 4. One pair of spindles was painted with black and red stripes on a yellow background. The second pair of spindles featured crosshatching, which was also found on their whorls.

Fragments of a disintegrated bag were found loose at the bottom of Individual 3's bundle (Figure 10.61). It appeared that some 33 yarn balls and skeins, totaling 400 g, had escaped from this bag, along with a 2 g lump of pigment with a Munsell color designation of 7.5 R 5/8 ("red"). Four of the yarn balls were dyed red with cochineal, one was forest green, and more than 20 were yellowish brown to dark brown (Specimen 27) (see Figure 10.59).

Comment on Burial 4

Of all the burials we salvaged, Burial 4 was the richest in artifacts. The women in this burial pit may have been somewhat higher in status than the other women salvaged, since they were associated with gold foil, silver *tupus*, and more elegant loom backstraps than the others. To be sure, some of their apparent richness might result from their having suffered less looting.

Figure 10.61. A sample of the yarn balls and skeins that had fallen to the bottom of the Burial 4 pit.

Chapter 11

Burial 5

While shaving the north profile of our 5 x 5 m salvage excavation to a vertical position, we discovered Burial 5 (see Figure 7.1). This burial, disturbed by looters, extended partly outside the 5 x 5. Unwilling to leave it for future looters, we carefully exposed Burial 5 while leaving the rest of the profile intact.

Ceramic Vessel

Accompanying Burial 5 was a Camacho Black globular jar with two handles (Figure 11.1). A plug of unspun *algodón blanco*, or white cotton, was still *in situ* in the mouth of the vessel. The jar's height was 10.8 cm, its rim diameter was 3.9 cm, and its wall was 4 to 5 mm thick; its maximum diameter was 7.6 cm, and its strap handles were 1.2 to 1.5 cm wide. The surface of the jar was black with gray to dark brown firing clouds, and its clay body was light gray.

Belt Loom

The most interesting item found with Burial 5 was a small loom, still bearing a partially completed textile. This loom had been rolled up and tied with a cord, presumably so that the person in Burial 5, a woman, could complete her work in the afterlife (Figure 11.2).

The loom featured three pieces of cane. The piece that would have been farthest from the weaver was 18.2 cm long and 15.1 mm in diameter (Figure 11.3); the piece closest to the weaver was 15.8 cm long and 12 mm in diameter and held yarns. On the central piece of cane was a tan string, attached to one of the 61 cm long cords.

It appeared that at the time of her death, this woman had completed about 6 cm of a polychrome textile 5.5 cm wide; this band would have been at least 60 cm long when completed. Its decoration consisted of long-necked birds and their mirror images, repeated several times. The six colors of yarn used to weave this textile were garnet, orange, white, dark brown, yellow, and lavender (Figure 11.4).

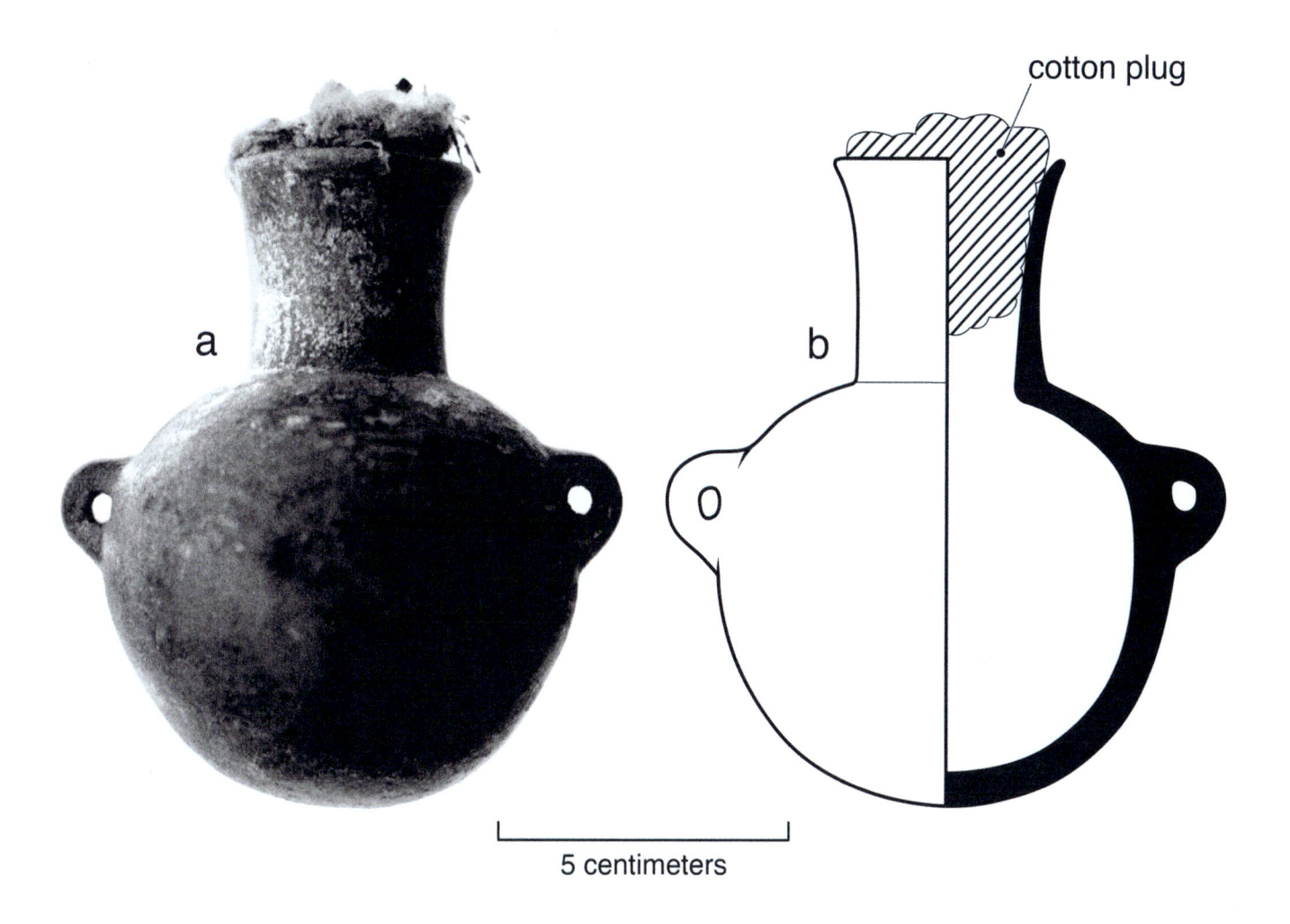

Figure 11.1. Photo and drawing of Vessel 1 of Burial 5, a Camacho Black jar plugged with *algodón blanco*.

Figure 11.2. A rolled-up loom and weaving tool from Burial 5. Note the flint flake attached to the loom by a string.

Figure 11.3. The loom from Burial 5, unrolled to show a textile in its early stages of weaving.

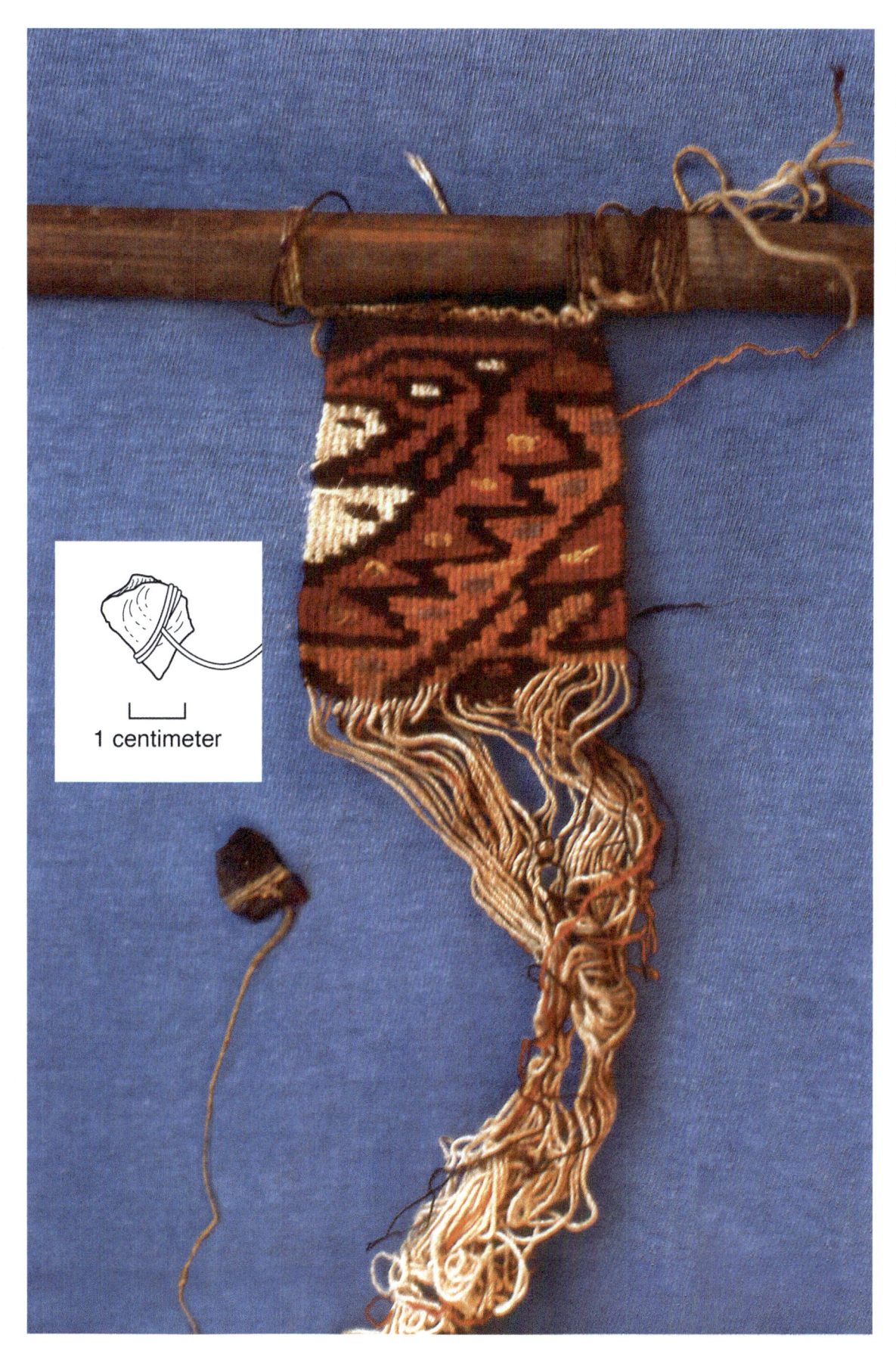

Figure 11.4. A close-up of the unfinished textile shown in Figure 11.3. The inset shows a drawing of the flint flake attached to the loom by a string; it was presumably used to cut yarn.

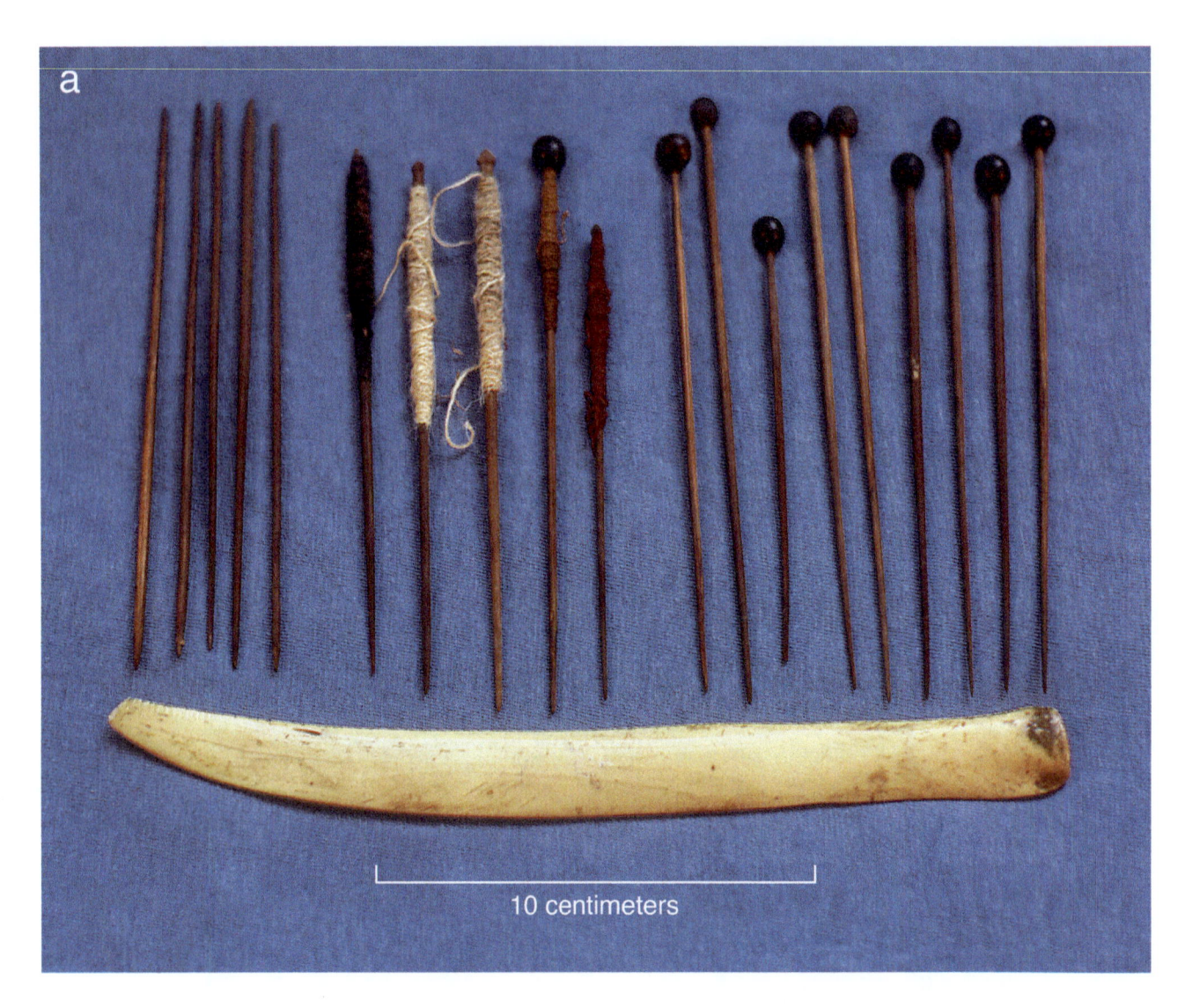

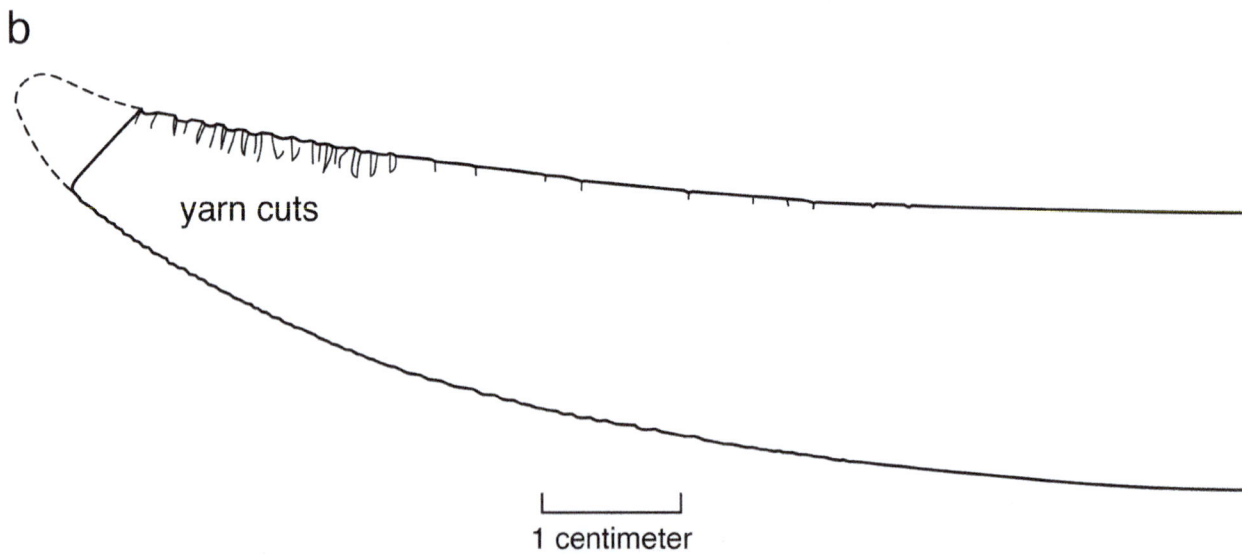

Figure 11.5. Other components rolled up with the loom from Burial 5 included spindles and bobbins. Alongside the loom was an ungulate long bone; it displayed cut marks (b) that probably had been made by taut yarn.

Of special note was a small piece of flint, still attached to the loom by a string (Figure 11.4). This sharp flint flake had presumably been used to cut the yarn as the weaving proceeded, and the weaver had tied it to the loom to prevent losing it. This is not surprising, since we found fewer than half a dozen flakes at Cerro Azul. There was nothing distinctive about this unretouched flake, and had it not been attached to the loom, we would never have guessed its function. The flake was carefully tied over its striking platform (upper right) and a dull edge (lower left), leaving the sharpest edge (lower right) free to cut yarn. The flake measured 14 x 12 mm, and the string to which it was tied was 13 cm long.

Bone Weaving Implement

Associated with the loom was a bone weaving implement (*choqchi*) 22.2 cm long and 2 cm wide. Its convex side, near the point (at left), revealed a clear series of incisions; presumably, these cuts had been made by taut yarns.

Items Rolled Up With the Loom

Figure 11.5 shows the items that were found rolled up with the belt loom.

Nine knob-headed spindles. All these spindles had small, hard black seeds attached to one end. Some of these seeds were shiny, while others resembled wrinkled peppercorns. The spindles themselves ranged in length from 10.3 to 14.5 cm, while their diameters were 2.4 to 2.8 mm.

Five plain spindles. These spindles were found without heads, although they belong to the type that usually have hard seeds on the top. They range in length from 13.7 to 14.3 cm and from 2.5 to 2.7 mm in diameter.

Five spindles wrapped in yarn. The yarn on each spindle weighs 1 g or less.

Spindle with a black seed on top. The spindle is 13.5 cm long, and the Munsell color of its yarn is 7.5 YR 5/4 ("brown").

Knob-headed spindle with no seed. This item is 11.4 cm long, and the Munsell color of its yarn is 5 R 3/8 ("dark red").

Knob-headed spindle with no seed. This item is 12.9 cm long, and the Munsell color of its yarn is 5 Y 8/3 ("pale yellow").

Knob-headed spindle. This item is 13.6 cm long, and the Munsell color of its yarn is 5 Y 8/3 ("pale yellow").

Spindle, apparently plain. This spindle is 12.8 cm long, and the Munsell color of its yarn is 2.5 YR 2/2 ("very dusky red").

Five to seven yarn clippings. These short pieces of yarn may have been cut by the flint flake attached to the loom. Their colors include garnet, off-white, dark brown, and orange.

String. The piece of string used to tie up the loom was 50 cm long.

Chapter 12

Burial 6

In the south half of our 5 x 5 m excavation unit in Quebrada 5a, the looters' pits reached a depth of 1.6 m and had penetrated the floor of the Structure 6 burial cist. This looters' pit damaged the upper part of Burials 6 and 7, each of which consisted of one adult man and one child. Unfortunately, the looters had clipped off the skulls of both adults; from the neck down, however, the skeletons appeared to be undisturbed. The adult had been buried in the seated position, while the child was lying on its back with arms crossed on the chest (Figures 12.1, 12.2).

The Adult

According to biological anthropologist Sonia Guillén, the seated man was older than 50 years of age. His body was tightly flexed, with his knees touching his chest. His femur length was 41.5 cm. This man was dressed in a poorly preserved, brown-striped cloth.

No pottery vessels accompanied this burial, but we did find a *mate* or gourd vessel next to the man's feet (Specimen 29) (Figure 12.3a, b, and c) (Smith and Marcus 2016a: Fig. 16.23). Inside this gourd bowl was a complete guinea pig whose coat color varied from 10 YR 7/3 to 10 YR 7/4 to 10 YR 7/6 (different shades of "pale brown") and even 2.5 YR 8/6 ("yellow").

Covering the guinea pig was a mat that served as a lid to protect the food in the bowl. The diameter of the bowl was irregular, ranging from 16.0 to 16.5 cm. Its height was 3.5 to 4.0 cm and its wall thickness was 5 mm. The exterior color of the gourd was 2.5 YR 3/2 ("dusky red").

The Child

According to Dr. Sonia Guillén, the child in Burial 6 was six or seven years of age at the time of its death. The arms had been folded across the chest, where we also found three perforated

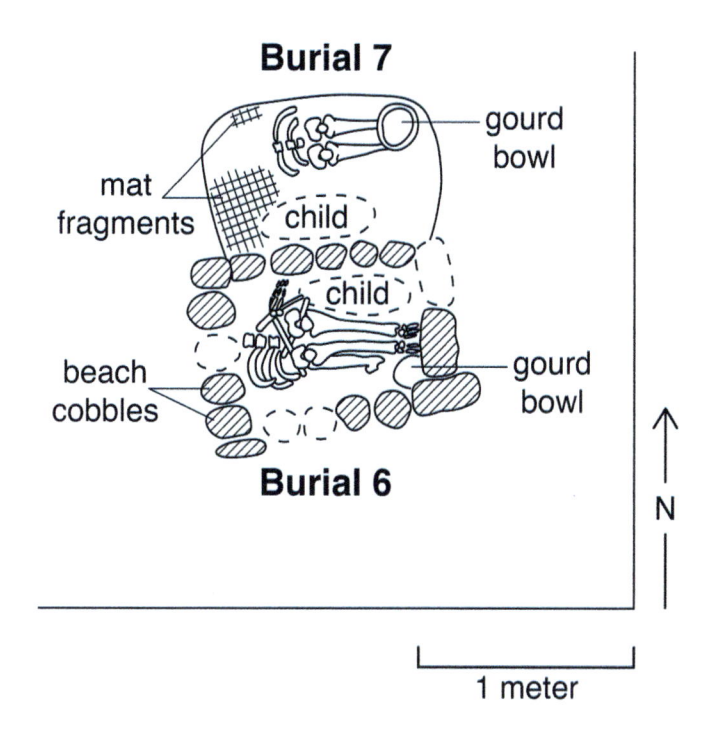

Figure 12.1. Plan view of Burials 6 and 7 at Cerro Azul; each burial included one seated adult male and one child. The skulls of both adults were missing, having been removed by a looters' pit; the rest of the skeleton was undisturbed. Since the children were fully extended, they remained undisturbed just below the looters' pit.

black beans strung on a thin brown thread (Figure 12.4). Botanist C. Earle Smith, Jr. tentatively identified the beans as a species of wild *Canavalia* (Miscellaneous Specimen 34). Given where this string of seeds was found—on the child's chest, but near its wrists—we are not sure whether it was a bracelet or necklace.

Comments on Burial 6

Burial 6 was the first of two burials involving a man, a child, and a gourd containing a guinea pig. The second case was Burial 7 (Chapter 13).

Figure 12.2. Professor Ramiro Matos exposes the remains of the adult in Burial 6.

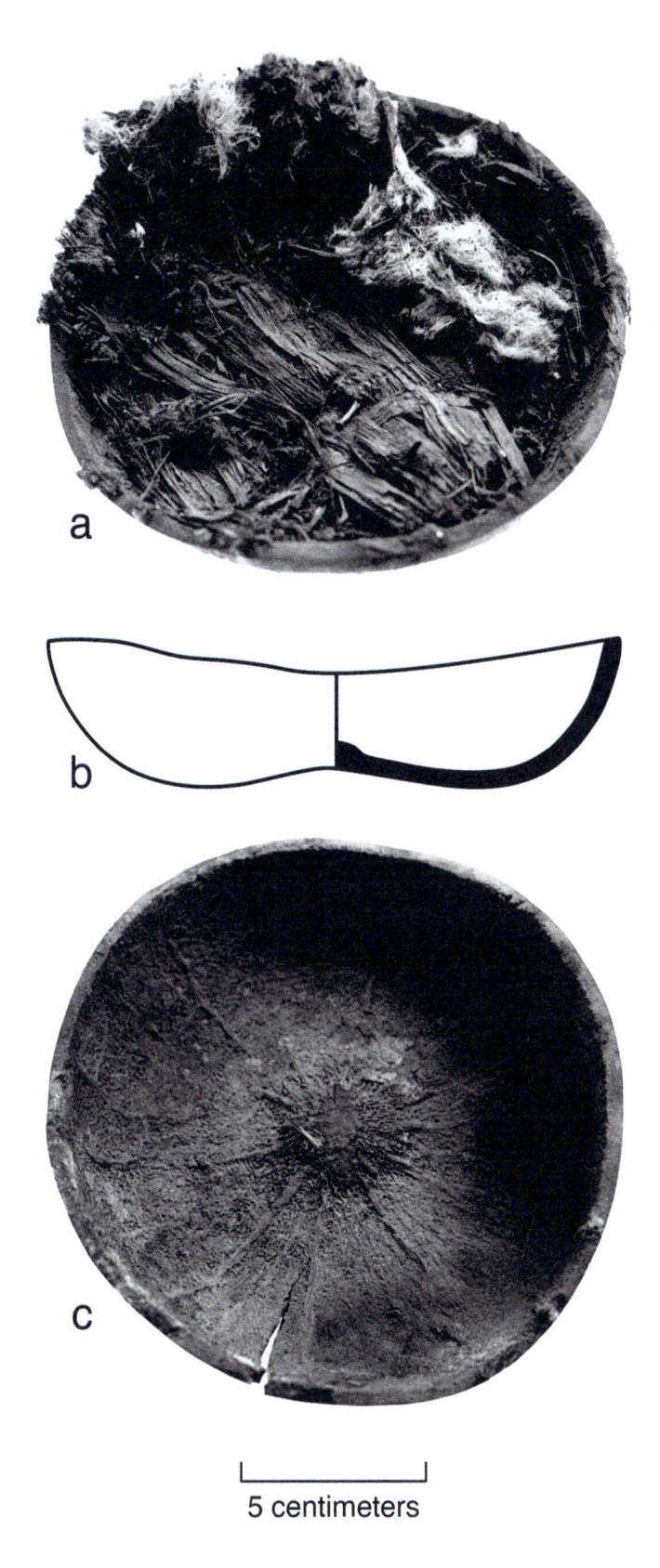

Figure 12.3. Three views of a gourd vessel placed at the feet of the adult in Burial 6; it contained a guinea pig. (a) The bowl, full of food as discovered. (c) The same bowl after its contents had been removed.

266　　　　　　　　　　　　　　　　　　　　　　　　Chapter 12

Figure 12.4. Unidentified beans strung on thread, associated with the child in Burial 6. Based on their placement (near both the child's wrists and neck) this string of beans could have been either a necklace or bracelet.

Chapter 13

Burial 7

Burial 7, which also contained an adult man and a child, was located just north of Burial 6 (see Figure 12.1). As with the man in Burial 6, the adult in Burial 7 had had his skull removed because he was buried in the seated position and a looters' pit was deep enough to reach his head. Like the man in Burial 6, he also had a gourd vessel near his feet, containing a guinea pig covered with a mat.

The Child

We exposed the child's skeleton first. This 14-month-old youngster, buried immediately south of the adult, was accompanied by an unusual ceramic vessel with two appliqué snakes attached to opposite sides of the bowl (Figure 13.1a, b). Part of the child's body had been placed inside the mouth of the vessel. Burials of infants in ceramic vessels is also known from the highlands (e.g., Isbell and Korpisaari 2015:145–146).

The snake's eyes—and the additional eight spots on the snake's body—had been made by pressing the end of a hollow cane tube, 5 mm in diameter, into the moist clay. The vessel is 13 cm high; its rim diameter is 16.8 cm, and its wall is 4–6 mm thick. The clay body of the vessel has a Munsell color of 2.5 YR 5/4 ("reddish brown"); over this reddish-brown clay, the potter applied a cream slip with a Munsell color of 5 Y 8/3 to 5 Y 8/4 ("pale yellow"). After that light-colored slip had been applied, the vessel was double burnished.

This child was also associated with a gourd (Specimen 22), decorated with a delicately incised bird on each side (Figure 13.2a, b, and c). The fact that this gourd was decorated puts it in the minority at Cerro Azul, where most gourds were plain (Marcus 2016f). It has a rim diameter of 17 cm; its maximum height is 5.5 cm, and its wall is 5 mm thick. The Munsell color of the gourd's exterior is 5 YR 3/2 ("dark reddish brown").

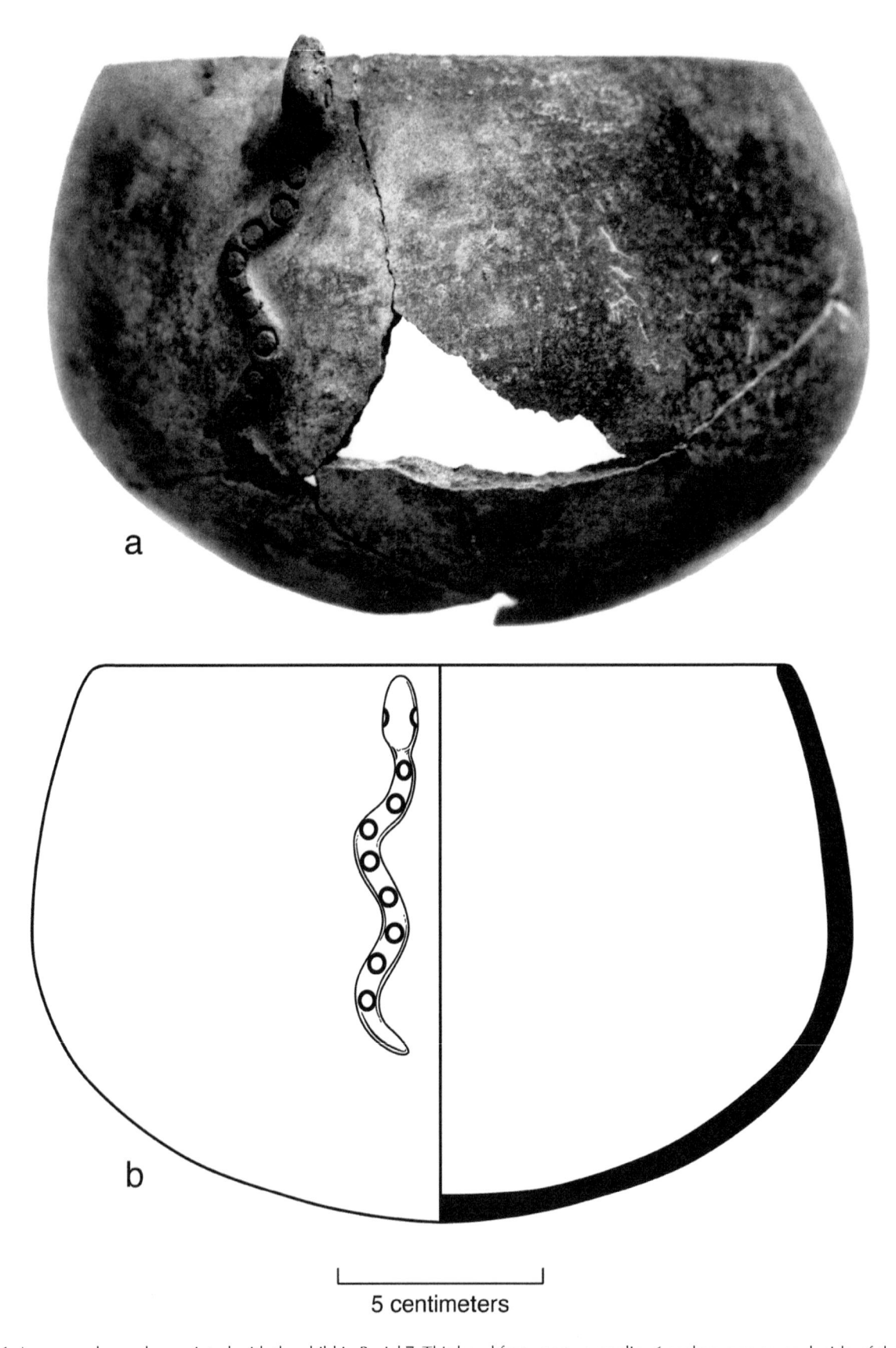

Figure 13.1. An unusual vessel associated with the child in Burial 7. This bowl features two appliqué snakes, one on each side of the vessel. The snake's eyes and its eight spots were made by pressing the end of a cane tube into the moist clay.

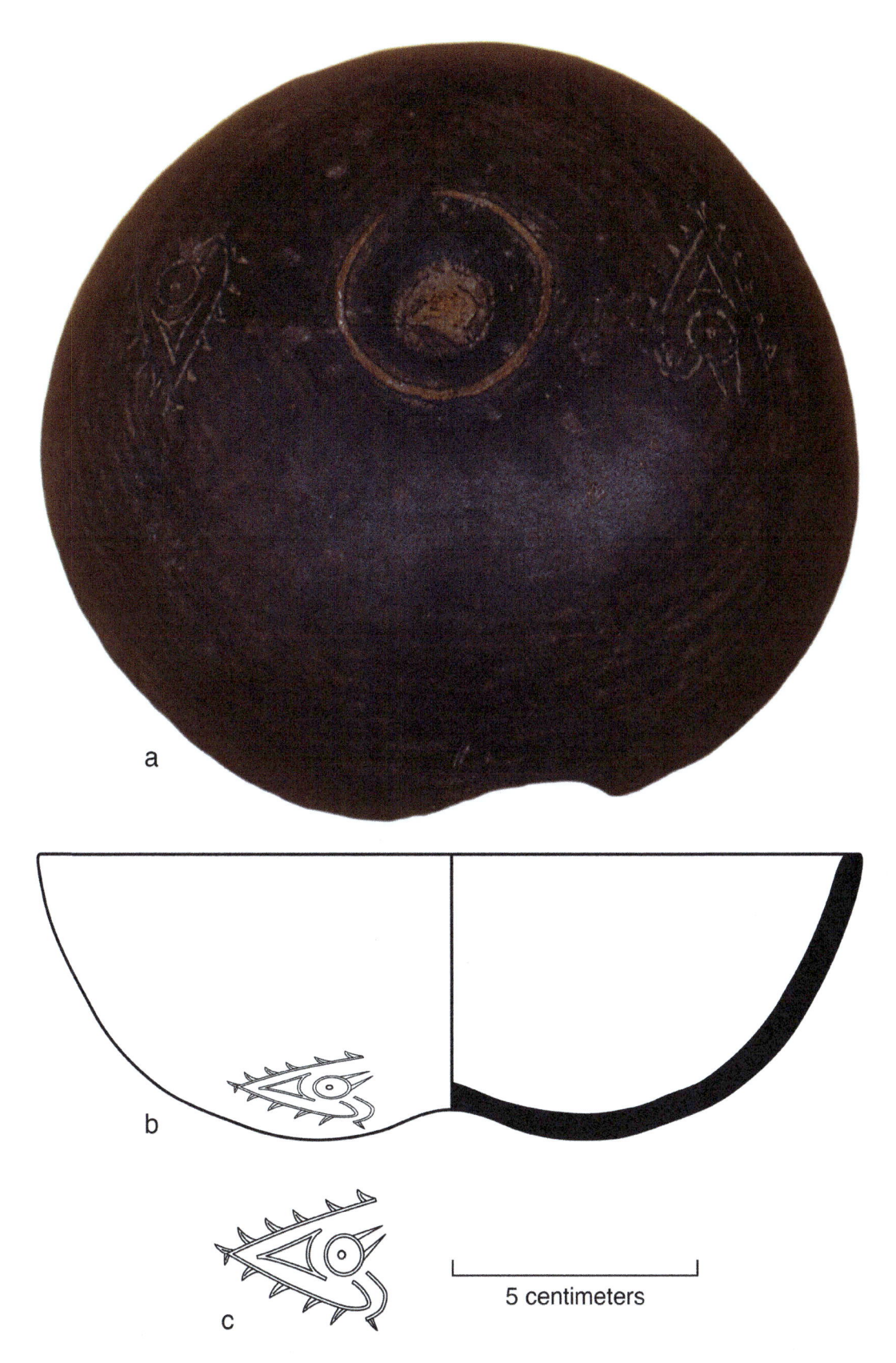

Figure 13.2. Photo and drawing of a decorated gourd vessel associated with the child in Burial 7. This bowl has a bird incised on either side. (a) The gourd turned upside down, showing both incised birds. (b) A drawing of the vessel. (c) A close-up view of one incised bird.

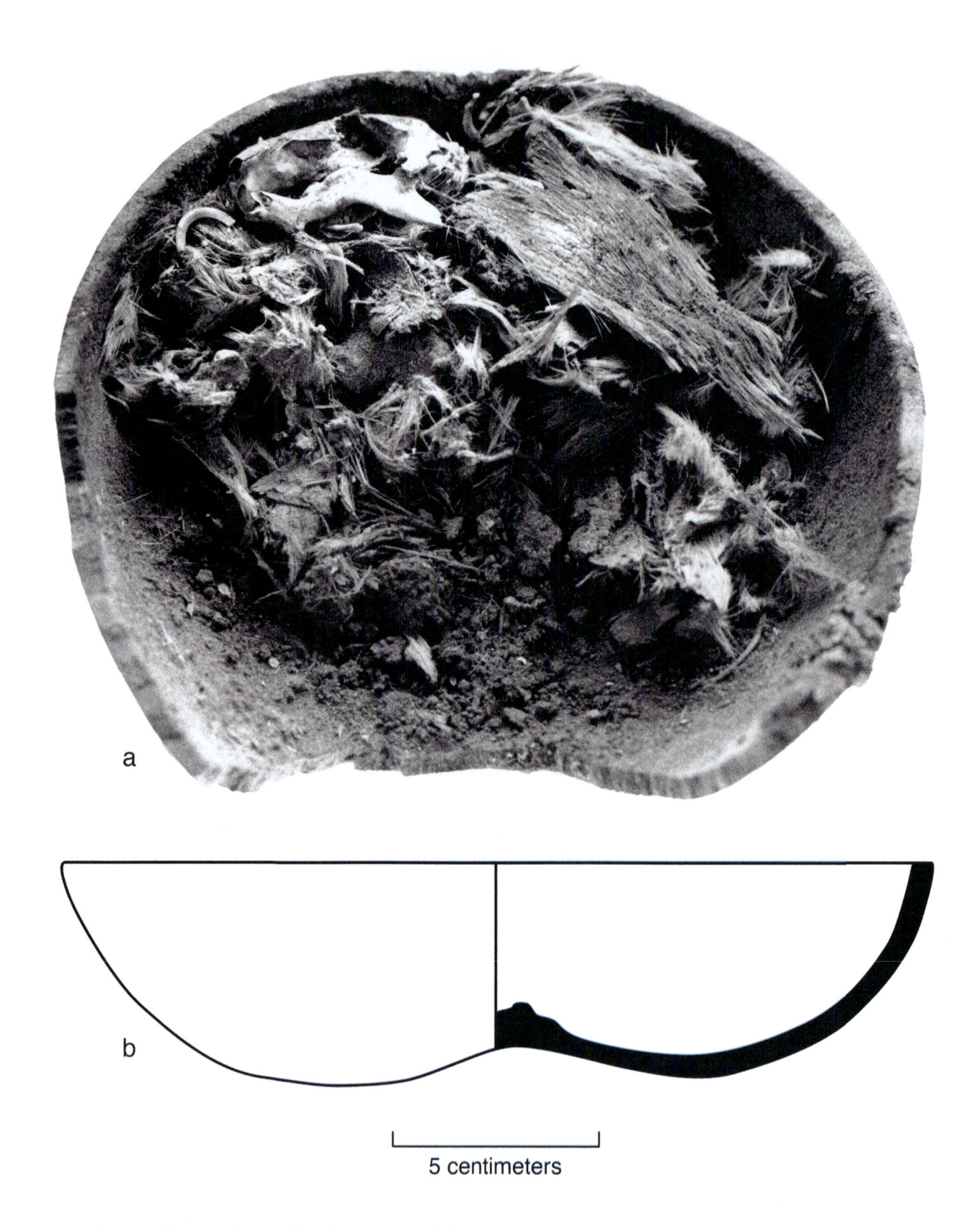

Figure 13.3. Photo and drawing of a gourd bowl associated with the adult man in Burial 7. (a) The bowl as discovered, with the remains of a guinea pig inside. (b) A profile drawing of the empty bowl.

Figure 13.4. Photo and drawing of a Camacho Reddish Brown jar, found with the adult man in Burial 7. The lower half of this vessel was blackened from long-term cooking, making it clear that it was not made from scratch as a burial offering. The jar was damaged by looters.

The Adult

According to biological anthropologist Sonia Guillén, the adult skeleton in Burial 7 was that of a 45-year-old man whose height would have been between 1.66 and 1.68 m. He had been buried in a seated position on a mat; resting on his feet was a gourd bowl containing a guinea pig with a coat color of 7.5 YR 5/6 ("strong brown"). This gourd (Specimen 30, Figure 13.3) was slightly larger than the one placed with the child; it had a diameter of 20.5 to 21.0 cm and its height was 5.0 to 5.5 cm, while its wall thickness was 5 mm. The color of the gourd was 2.5 YR 3/2 ("dusky red"). Like the gourd found with Burial 6, this vessel contained a guinea pig covered by a mat. The guinea pig was so well preserved that we could record the color of its fur as 7.5 YR in the Munsell color system.

This man was also accompanied by a globular jar with flaring neck and a dimple in its base (Figure 13.4). This specimen was one of the common coarseware cooking vessels of the Late Intermediate and belonged to a type called Camacho Reddish Brown. It had a height of 27 cm, a rim diameter of 19.7 cm, and a wall thickness of 6–7 mm. Its clay body was 2.5 YR 6/6 in the Munsell color system and the color of the jar's surface was 2.5 YR 6/6 ("light red"), although it graded into 2.5 YR 4/4 ("reddish brown") and 5 YR 4/2 ("dark reddish gray"). The lower third of the jar was blackened with soot, making it clear that this vessel had seen use and was not made simply as a burial offering (see Marcus 1987a: Fig. 19, Marcus 2008: Fig. 3.6). The base of this jar had been dimpled in such a way that it would have stood upright if it was resting on a ring some 4 cm in diameter.

Overview of Burial 7

Burials 6 and 7 were so similar in layout and content that one suspects these individuals may have been related in some way, or buried close together in time.

Chapter 14

Burial 8

Burial 8 was found between Burials 5 and 4 in the northeast quadrant of our 5 x 5 m excavation (see Figure 7.1). As was the case with Burial 4, the pit containing Burial 8 had once been sealed with a clay cap, but by the time we arrived the seal had been broken by looters. Below that seal was a mummy bundle wrapped in a continuous piece of cloth that had been wound several times around the body.

Accompanying Burial 8 was an amphora, lying on its side; it featured two holes that might have been ritual "kill" holes (Figure 14.1a). As we brushed away the dirt, we also uncovered a cranium with long dark hair and only a few gray hairs. Biological anthropologist Sonia Guillén identified this individual as a woman, and estimated that she was at least 50 years of age at the time of her death.

Burial 8 was found in a seated position, tightly flexed, with her knees against her chest. Found with her were a loom, a workbasket still tied up in a cloth, a gourd bowl containing a guinea pig, two silver *tupus*, silver foil, and two pottery vessels. We also found that she was still holding a small bag in her hand. A marine shell (*Mesodesma* sp.) was found on her left shoulder; this Late Intermediate practice of placing a mollusc on the shoulder of the mummy bundle continued into the Late Horizon, as seen in the cemetery at Puruchuco-Huaquerones and elsewhere (Cock and Goycochea 2004).

Ceramic Vessels

Vessel 1

Vessel 1 was found inside the funerary bundle, just below the first layer of cloth wrapping; it had fallen to a position near the woman's feet (Figure 14.2). This jar had a cotton plug, or stopper, still in place; its three strap handles were spaced equidistantly around the jar's globular body. The vessel's surface color ranged from 5 YR 5/3 ("reddish brown") to 5 YR 4/2 ("dark reddish gray"); however, it had firing clouds as light as 5 YR 7/4 ("pink").

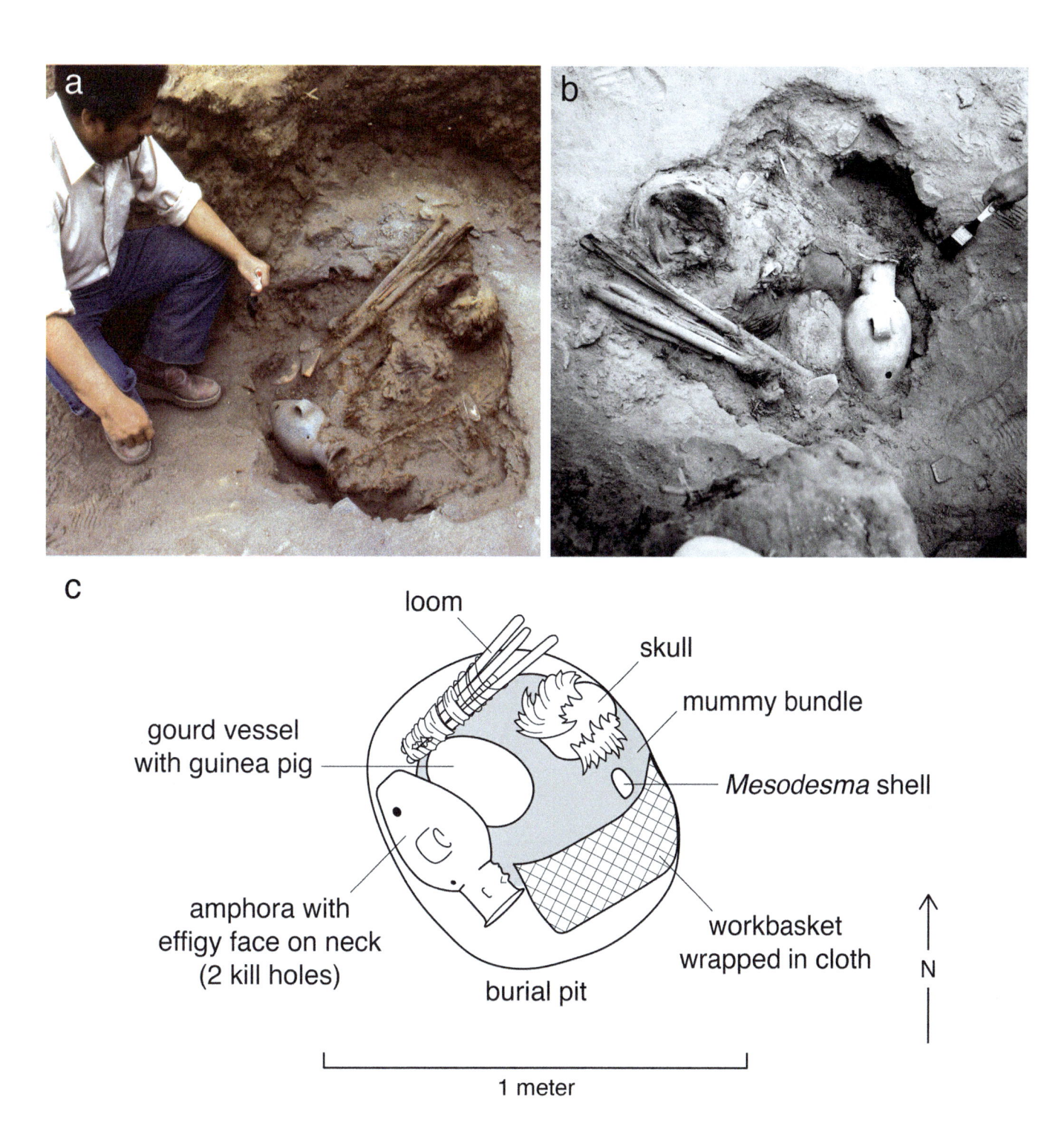

Figure 14.1. Burial 8 from Cerro Azul contained a woman buried with her loom, her workbasket, and a gourd vessel containing a guinea pig. (a) Professor Ramiro Matos has exposed the burial. Two items visible in this photograph are the loom parts and an amphora with its "kill" holes. (b) A view of the burial from a different angle. (c) A drawing by Joyce Marcus of all the items visible after the dirt had been brushed away from the uppermost level of the burial.

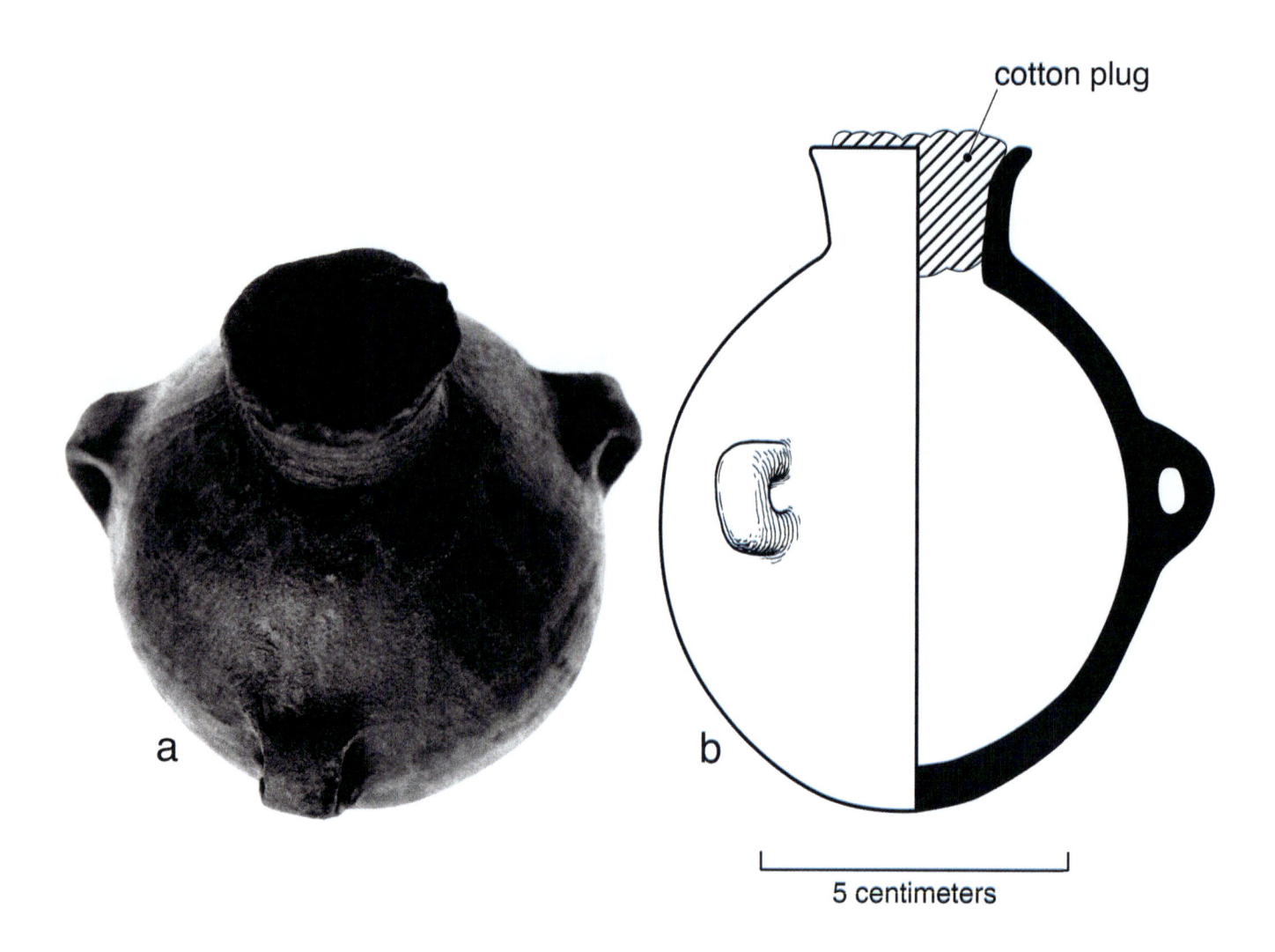

Figure 14.2. Vessel 1 of Burial 8, sealed with a cotton plug and bearing three handles that were spaced equidistantly around the jar. This vessel was found inside the woman's funerary bundle, in the first cloth wrapping and near her feet.

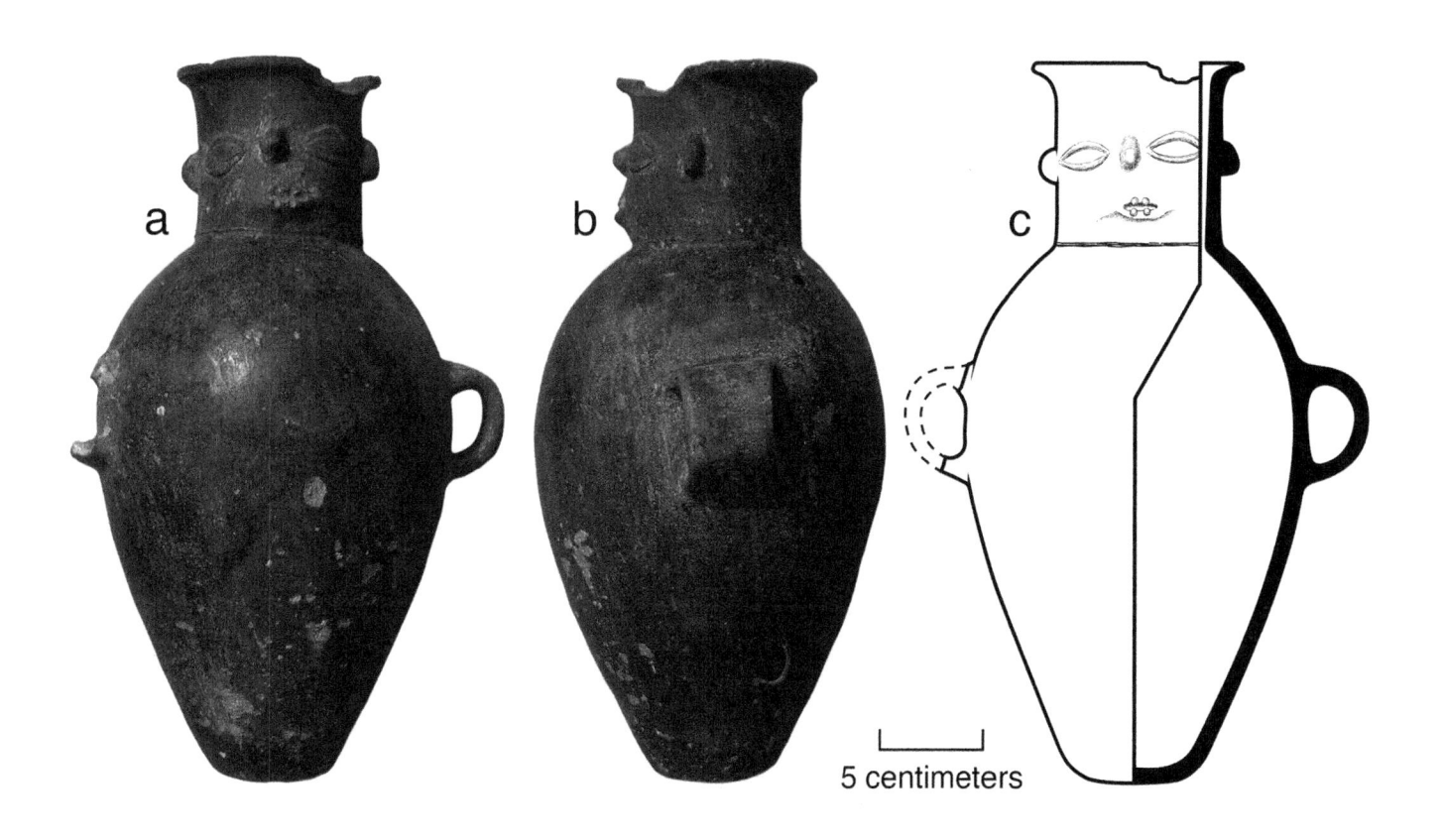

Figure 14.3. Two photos and a drawing of Vessel 2 of Burial 8, a Camacho Black amphora with two possible "kill" holes (see Figure 14.1). The amphora's rim had been chipped in antiquity, and the base was so worn that it clearly was not made as a burial offering.

Vessel 2

Vessel 2 was a Camacho Black amphora with a human face modeled on the neck (Figures 14.1, 14.3a–c). The depiction of the mouth suggests that the lips may have been sewn together, possibly a practice carried out after metal packets had been inserted into a corpse's mouth. Unfortunately, Burial 8's mouth had not been sufficiently preserved to show us whether it had been sewn. Her hand was well preserved, and we could see that her fingers had been tied together; her ankles, too, had been tied with a strip of cloth.

Vessel 2 had two strap handles and two possible "kill" holes. We suspected that this vessel was Burial 8's personal possession, since it had been chipped in antiquity and continued to be used until it was extremely worn on its base. It therefore seems unlikely that it was made especially for inclusion in a burial.

The vessel's height was 32.5 cm, its rim diameter was 9.8 cm, its wall thickness was 6–7 mm, and the width of its strap handles was 3.5–4.0 cm. The Munsell color of the vessel's surface was primarily 10 YR 4/1 ("dark gray"), occasionally grading into 10 YR 5/2 ("grayish brown"). The clay body was 10 YR 7/1 or 7/2 ("light gray"). This vessel was evenly, though moderately, burnished (Marcus 2008: Fig. 3.13).

Gourd Vessel

Vessel 3

Vessel 3 was a poorly preserved gourd bowl (Figure 14.4a, b), which contained a guinea pig with a coat color of 10 YR 6/6 ("brownish yellow"). The bowl was 21 cm in diameter, with a height of 4.5 cm and a wall thickness of 5 mm. The color of the gourd was 7.5 R 2/2 ("very dusky red").

276　　　　　　　　　　　　　　　　　　　　　　　　　　　　Chapter 14

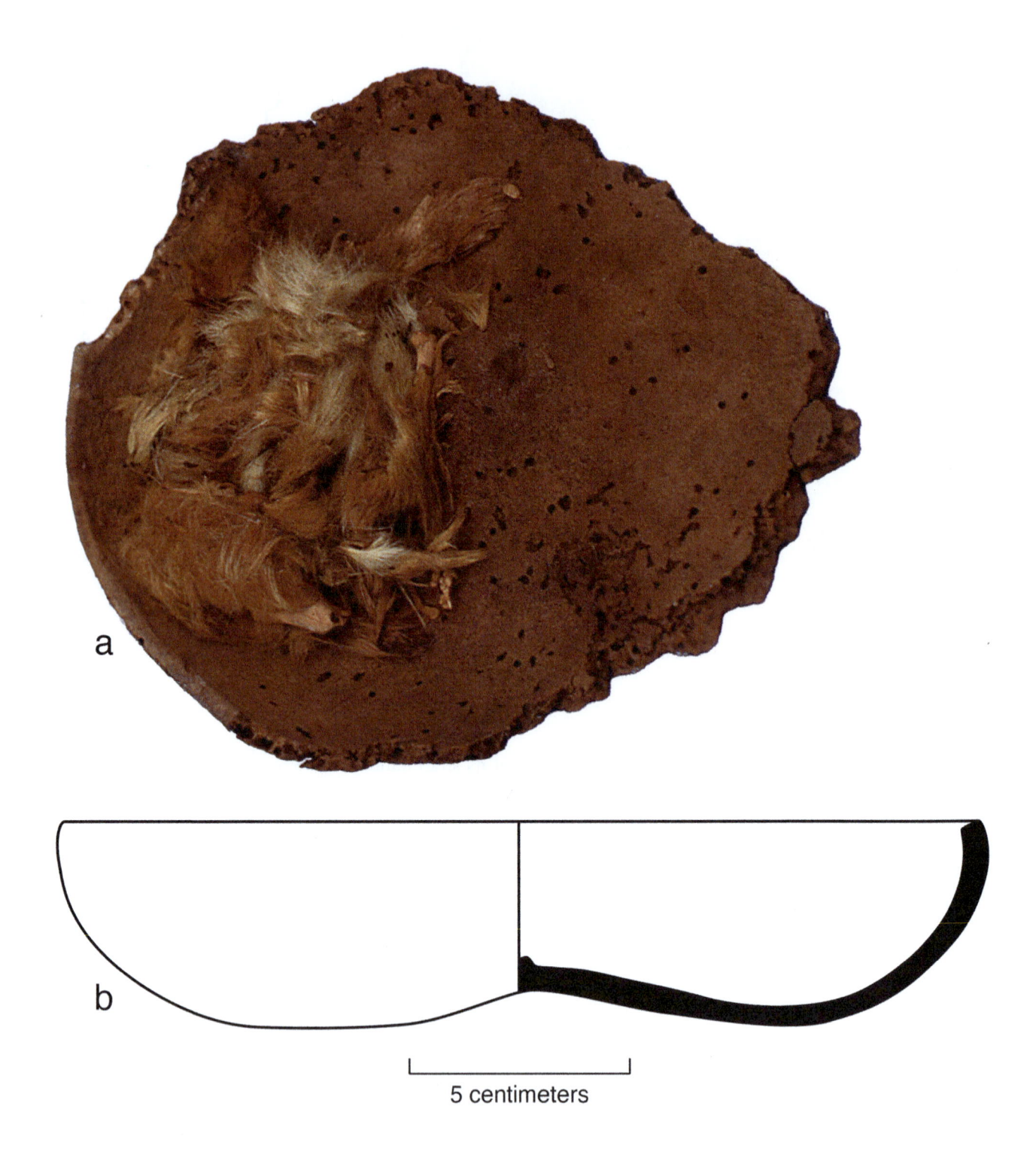

Figure 14.4. Vessel 3 from Burial 8 was a badly broken gourd bowl containing a guinea pig. (b) is an artist´s reconstruction of the bowl.

Artifacts of Metal

As we unwrapped the funerary bundle, the first item we saw was Vessel 1 (Figure 14.2). The next items were two silver *tupus* or cloak pins, one weighing 28 g and the other 24 g. Although these *tupus* were still in use as cloak pins, both were broken (Figure 14.5a, b); one had even been repaired with brown string. These efforts at repair indicate the high regard in which silver *tupus* were held, and perhaps the difficulty of replacing them.

Five fragments of silver foil were found on Burial 8's chest (Figure 14.6). We suspect that these may have fallen out of her mouth, since her mandible had also dropped. The total weight of these five metal fragments was 4 g.

Maize and Cotton

Burial 8 was also accompanied by one sixteen-row maize cob and cotton of two species. Raw padding of both light brown and dark brown cotton was found behind her hips. Two locks of kidney cotton (*Gossypium barbadense* var. *brasiliense*) were also found with her (Figure 14.7; see Smith and Marcus 2016a:280, Fig. 16.31).

Loom

Burial 8 had been buried with a loom (Figure 14.8; Specimen 129) of the type used to weave *mantas*, or larger textiles. The components of this loom were as follows:
—two *qansas* or cane segments with the following dimensions (Figure 14.8, top):
· 81.4 cm long, 3.0 cm in diameter
· 77.8 cm long, 2.5 cm in diameter
—four segments of "estacas" (Figure 14.8, below the two *qansas*) (see also Cobo 1990:223–224)
—four *mini comachas* or narrow sticks (Figure 14.8) with the following dimensions:
· 54.7 cm long, 6.0 mm in diameter
· 60.0 cm long, 8.2 mm in diameter
· 63.0 cm long, 6.4 mm in diameter
· 60.8 cm long, 8.7 mm in diameter
—one segment of *caña brava* (*Gynerium* sp.) (Figure 14.8, bottom)

Textiles

Textile 174 was a dark brown cotton cloth that had been used as the outermost layer of the funerary bundle. It was a plain weave, S-spun.

Also present on her chest were ribbon-like cords of unknown function.

In addition, Burial 8 had multiple fragments of a very badly disintegrated cloth that included two side selvages.

A Woolen Bag in Burial 8's Hand

The contents of this woman's bag (Figure 14.9a) were as follows:
—four yarn balls (Figure 14.9b) with the following dimensions:
· 3.0 cm diameter, weighing 3 g, 5 YR 3/2 ("dark reddish brown")
· 4.0 cm diameter, weighing 9 g, 2.5 YR 2/2 ("very dusky red")
· 4.5 cm diameter, weighing 12 g, 2.5 YR 2/2 ("very dusky red")
· 2.5 cm diameter (wrapped around *algodón pardo*, including cotton seeds), weighing 2 g, 5 YR 3/4 ("dark reddish brown")
—four lumps of white chalk (?), as follows (Figure 14.9b, bottom row):
· 3 x 3.5 x 2 cm, weighing 10 g
· 4 x 3 x 1.5 cm, weighing 9.5 g
· 4.6 x 2.8 x 1.3 cm, weighing 9.5 g
· 4.9 x 2.9 x 2 cm, weighing 12 g
—three pigment pouches. Two of the pigment pouches contain red pigment, 10 R 5/6 ("red"), and one pouch contains blue pigment. The smallest item in Figure 14.9 (row *b*, second from the left) is one of the pigment pouches.

The bag containing all these items (listed above), held in the hand of the deceased, was woven from golden brown and dark brown wool (Figure 14.9a). This plain weave warp-stripe bag had been made from a single textile measuring 25 x 14 cm. By folding that textile in half, they created a bag 12.5 cm wide x 14 cm high.

One of the three selvages was left unmodified, since it was to serve as the open mouth of the bag; the two side selvages were sewn shut with a running stitch using paired yarns. The bag's stripes were achieved by using a four-yarn line, then an eight-yarn line of staggered checkers, and then

278 Chapter 14

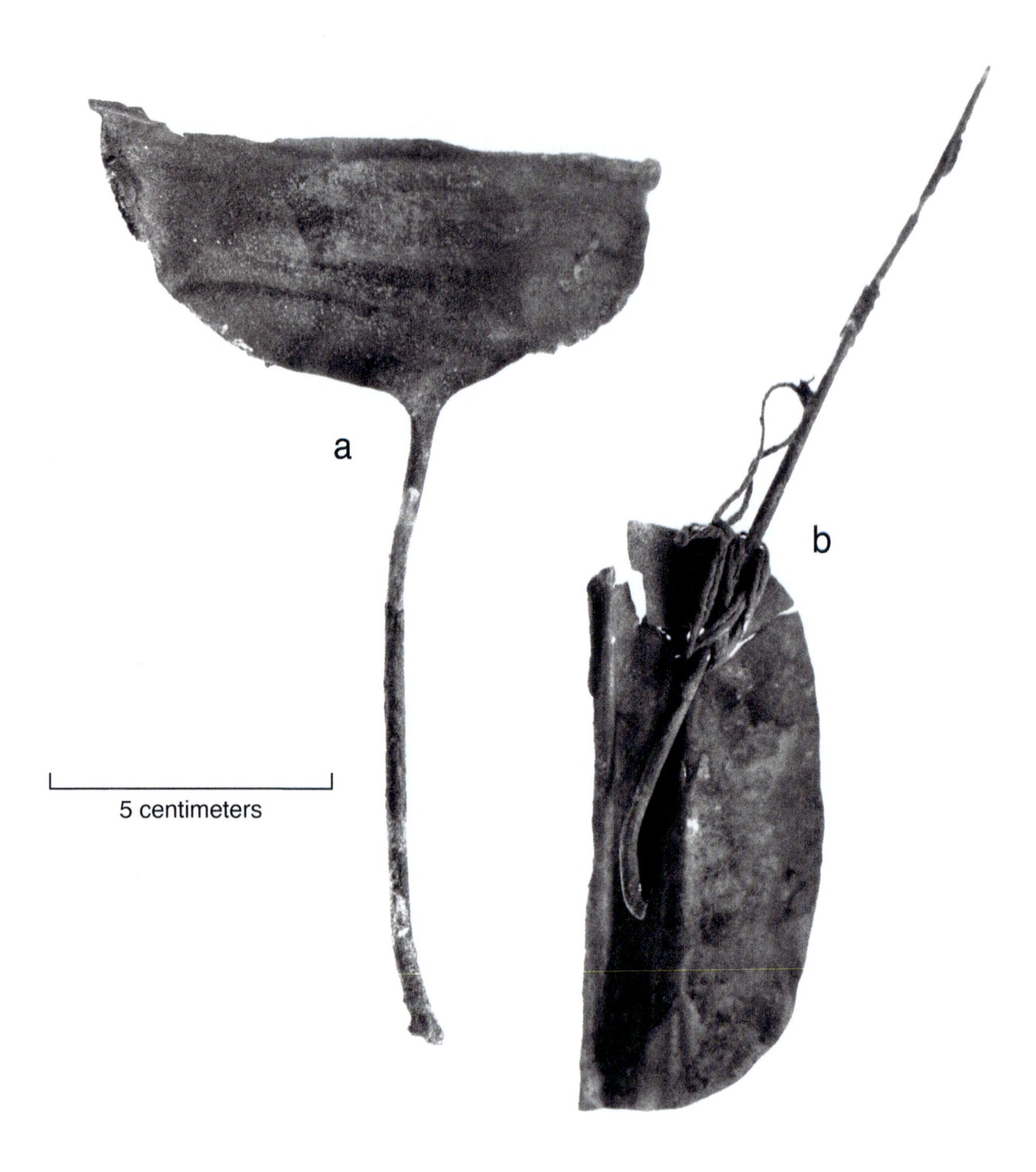

Figure 14.5. Two *tupus* or cloak pins found with the woman from Burial 8. One cloak pin (a) was broken and the other (b) had been repaired with brown string. This woman may therefore have been highly ranked enough for metal *tupus*, but not sufficiently elite to get new ones when the old ones broke.

Figure 14.6. Five pieces of silver foil that had fallen to the chest of the woman buried in Burial 8. We suspect that this silver had been inserted into her mouth, but fell out when her mandible fell to her chest.

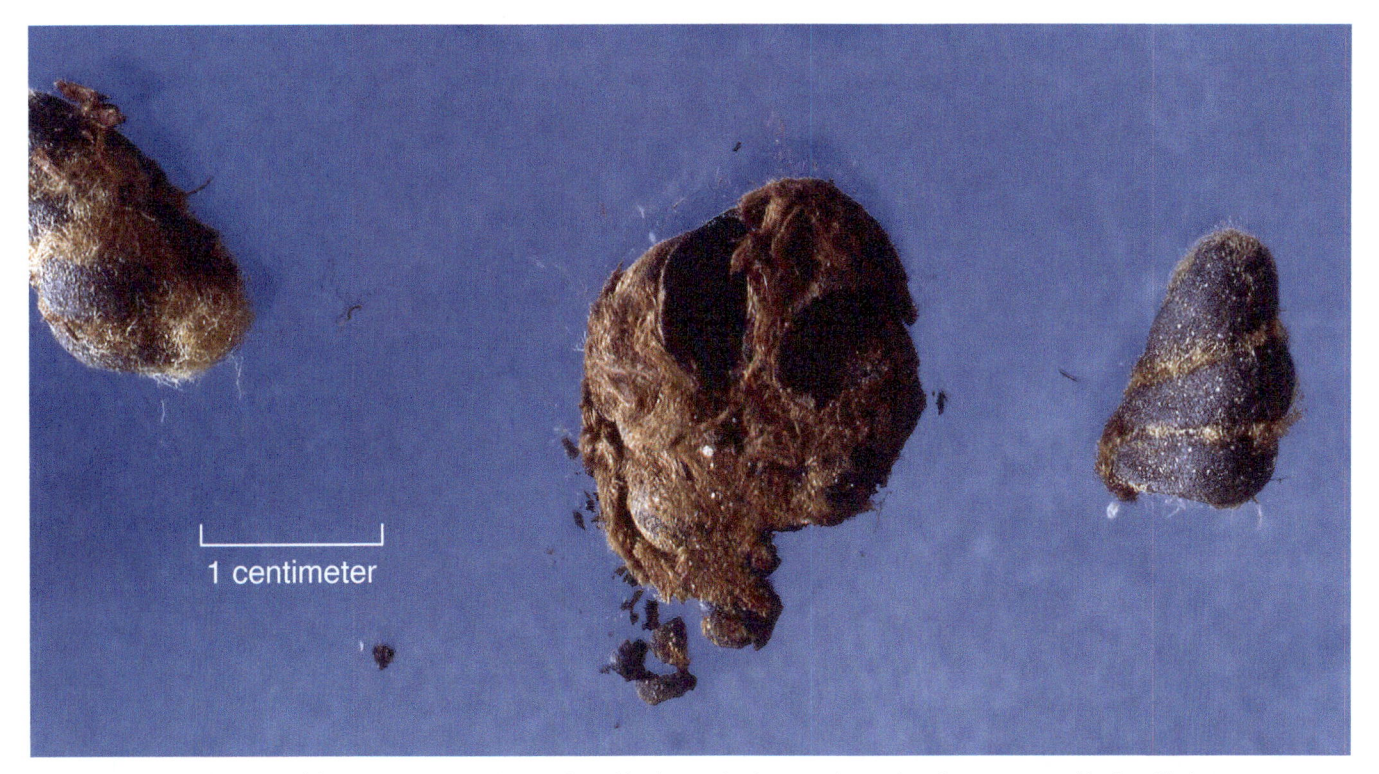

Figure 14.7. Around the hips of the woman in Burial 8 we found both standard cotton (center) and some unusual locks of kidney cotton (*Gossypium barbadense* var. *brasiliense*).

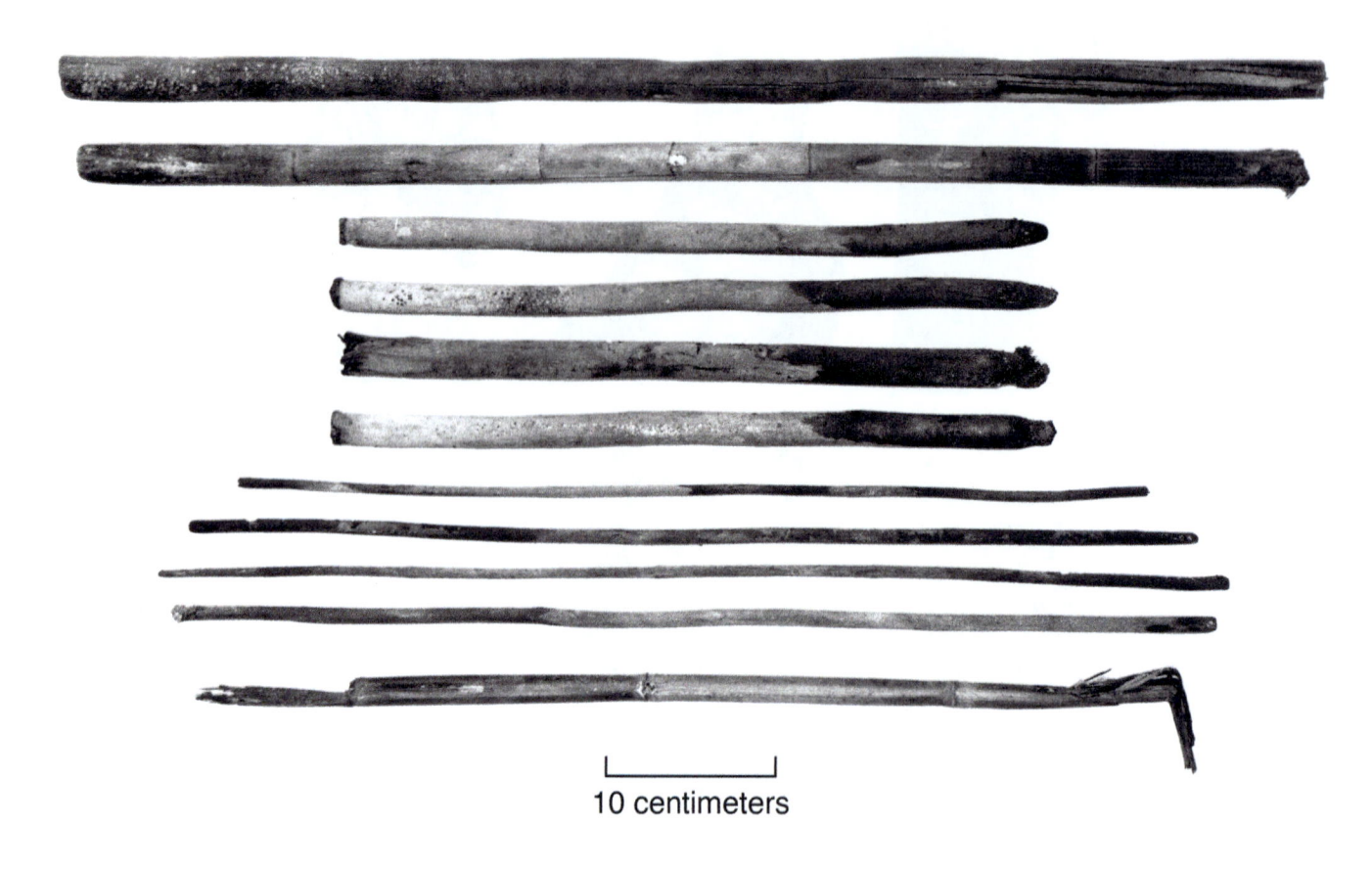

Figure 14.8 (above). Loom parts buried with the woman in Burial 8.
Figure 14.9 (opposite page). The woman in Burial 8 was still holding a bag (a), which contained four yarn balls (b), four pieces of chalk-like material (lower row), and one pigment pouch (the smallest item in b, second from left in the upper row).

twelve-yarn ladder stripes separated by plain gold brown bands. The heading cord was black wool. There were two end selvages and a two-shot heading cord of paired two-ply yarns.

The Workbasket

Like so many other women at Cerro Azul, this woman was buried with her workbasket (Specimen 111). It was wrapped in a cloth, leading us to expect that we would find a workbasket in poor condition and such was the case. Some Cerro Azul women extended the use-life of their workbaskets by wrapping them in an outer cloth. The workbasket with this woman proved to be so fragile that it had virtually disintegrated. Its contents were as follows:

A piece of chalk (6 x 5 x 2.8 cm), weighing 36 g (Figure 14.10a, at right).

Five of the six spindles are shown in Figure 14.10a.

Three of the painted spindles display identical barcoding (Figure 14.10b), the code being eight white stripes between black bands. These three spindles have the same color yarn wound around them, 7.5 YR 5/6 ("strong brown"). In contrast, the thread on one of the unpainted spindles is 2.5 YR 3/2 ("dusky red"). One painted spindle is 24.7 cm long with a maximum diameter of 3.8 to 3.9 mm; a second painted spindle is 20.4 cm long with a maximum diameter of 3.8 to 3.9 mm; the third painted spindle, incomplete, is 17.5 cm long. Only two of the plain spindles are complete. One is 21.5 cm long and 3.8 mm in diameter; the other is 18.1 cm long and 3.7 mm in diameter.

There were three spindle whorls (two complete, one broken). All the whorls are Camacho Black (Figure 14.10). The broken whorl has a squat teardrop shape; its height is 12.7 mm and its diameter is 20.7 mm. The two complete whorls are 16.1 mm in height and 20 mm in diameter.

5 centimeters

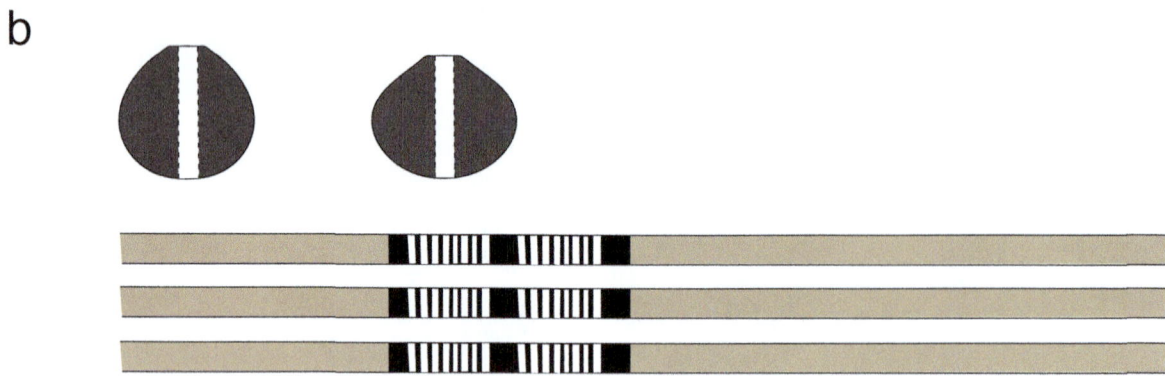

Figure 14.10. Some of the contents of the disintegrated workbasket found with Burial 8. Included are (a) two barcoded spindles with black whorls, three spindles without whorls, and a possible piece of chalk. (b) Artist's rendering of two whorls and the three spindles bearing the identical barcode.

Chapter 15

Burial 9

Burial 9—the last one we salvaged in Quebrada 5a—was found inside the cobblestone construction we called Structure 8 (Figure 15.1). This burial had been inserted into a midden that included abundant mollusc shells. In this part of the terrace, the looters' pits reached a depth of 1.30 m; Burial 9 and Structure 8 were found just below that depth.

Burial 9 consisted of three individuals—a woman, a child, and an infant—and the sequence of interments was clear. First, a woman had been placed at the bottom of the cist; next, a puddled adobe surface was laid down over her. Finally, the bodies of an infant and child were placed on a reed mat above the puddled adobe surface.

The Construction of Structure 8

Structure 8 stood out among all the other burial cists in its resemblance to a keyhole; its entrance was only half a meter wide (Figure 15.2). To construct the cist, the builders had brought *cantos rodados* or smooth cobblestones from the beach nearby (Figure 15.3). To build the walls at the entrance they used four rows of beach cobbles, and along the back wall they used at least six rows of cobbles. From the reed mat on which the infant and child rested, it was 73 cm to the floor of the cist.

The Infant and Child

According to biological anthropologist Sonia Guillén, the bones of the child and infant were too disintegrated to be aged accurately, though she noted that the child had a deciduous cheek tooth that was just erupting.

The infant was not accompanied by any grave goods. The child, however, had been supplied with two ceramic vessels, as follows.

Vessel 1 (Figure 15.4a, b) was a Camacho Black jar with two handles, found next to the child's head. It has two strap handles. A possible "kill" hole was found in the vessel. Its height was 18.1 cm, its rim diameter 5.6 cm, its maximum diameter 15 cm, and its wall thickness 5–6 mm; one strap handle was 2.1 cm wide. The jar's surface color ranged from

Figure 15.1. Structure 8, which housed Burial 9, was the last looted burial cist we salvaged in Quebrada 5a at Cerro Azul. Here we see the cobblestone cist after its contents had been removed.

black to dark gray to very dark gray, and its clay body was gray to light gray.

Vessel 2 (Figure 15.5a, b) was a miniature Camacho Black amphora, found near the child's legs. Although largely disintegrated, a fragment of rope was still detectable in the vessel's strap handles. The amphora's height was 11.3 cm, rim diameter was 3.8 cm, its wall thickness was 4.0–4.5 mm, and its strap handles were 8–9 mm wide. The surface color of the vessel was black wherever it had been burnished, and dark brownish gray where no burnishing occurred.

The Adult Woman

Individual 3 of Burial 9, the adult woman, was an exception to the usual Cerro Azul pattern of women whose loom backstraps had been folded and then placed one above another in their burials, resembling stacks of towels in a laundry basket. She was found still wearing her backstrap, in the perfect position for her to continue weaving in the afterlife. The backstrap—wrapped around her lower back and hips—was padded with unspun cotton, still full of cotton seeds. This thick padding provided a cushioned backstrap that would make weaving on a backstrap loom, with the frequent rocking forward and backward, a more comfortable act.

According to biological anthropologist Sonia Guillén, this woman had died between 35 and 39 years of age. Each of her fingers had been carefully tied to the adjacent finger, and a cord was tied around her wrists and arms. That cord (T243) was a braid of four strands, Z-spun S-twisted, apparently made from a fiber in the bromeliad family.

This practice of tying fingers and limbs together is known from other coastal sites (e.g., Owens and Eeckhout 2015). After Individual 3's wrists and arms had been tied, they were crossed in front of her chest. She was then wrapped in a cloth wound several times around her body.

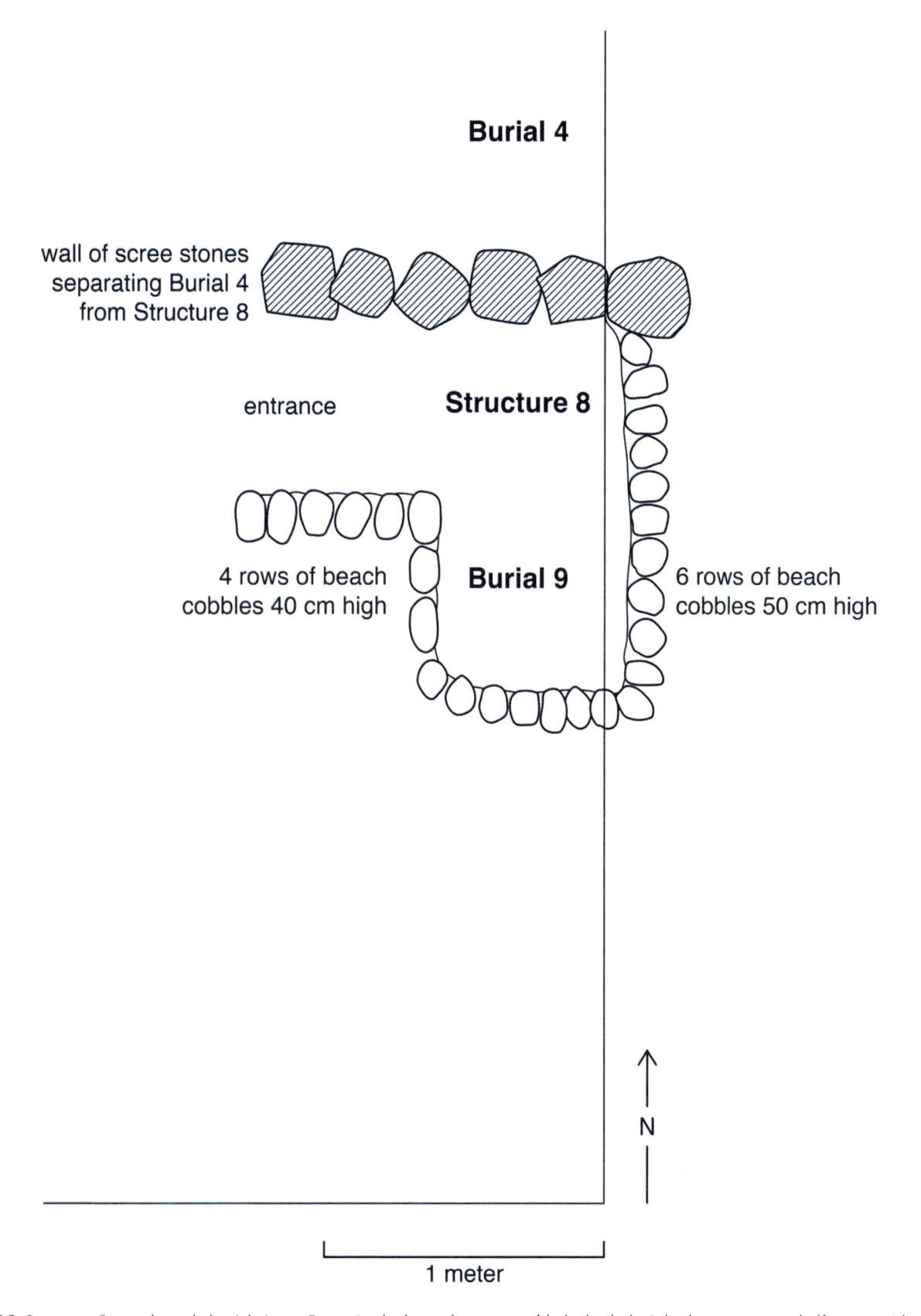

Figure 15.2. Structure 8 was the only burial cist at Cerro Azul whose shape resembled a keyhole. It had an entrance a half meter wide and walls made of *cantos rodados,* or smooth cobblestones, brought from the beach nearby.

286   Chapter 15

Figure 15.3. Burial cists at Cerro Azul were built from *cantos rodados* like these, which are abundant and readily available on the type of beach the local fishermen call *costa*.

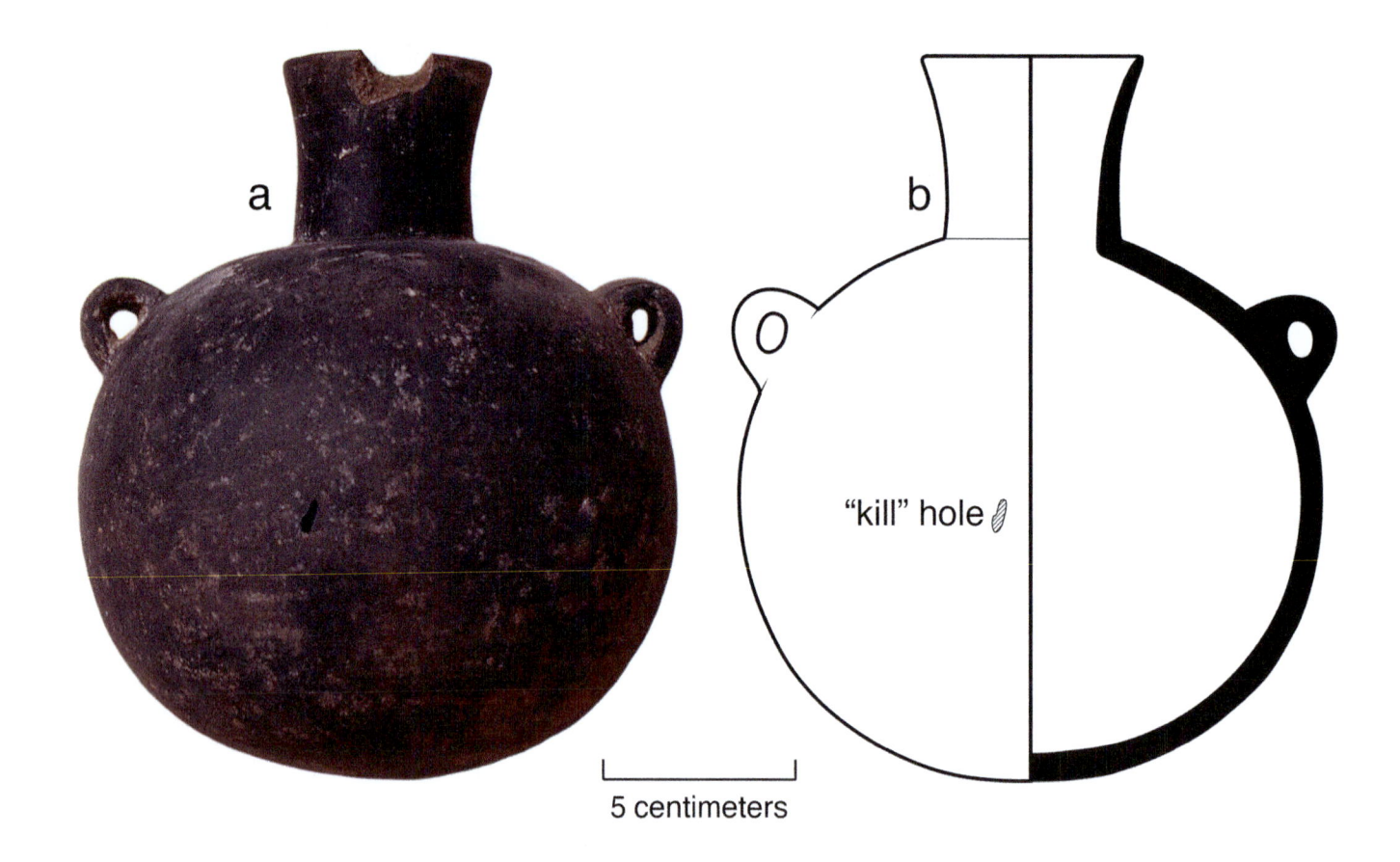

Figure 15.4. Vessel 1 from Burial 9 was a Camacho Black jar with two handles, found next to the child's head. Two possible "kill" holes, one of which is shown here, were found in this vessel.

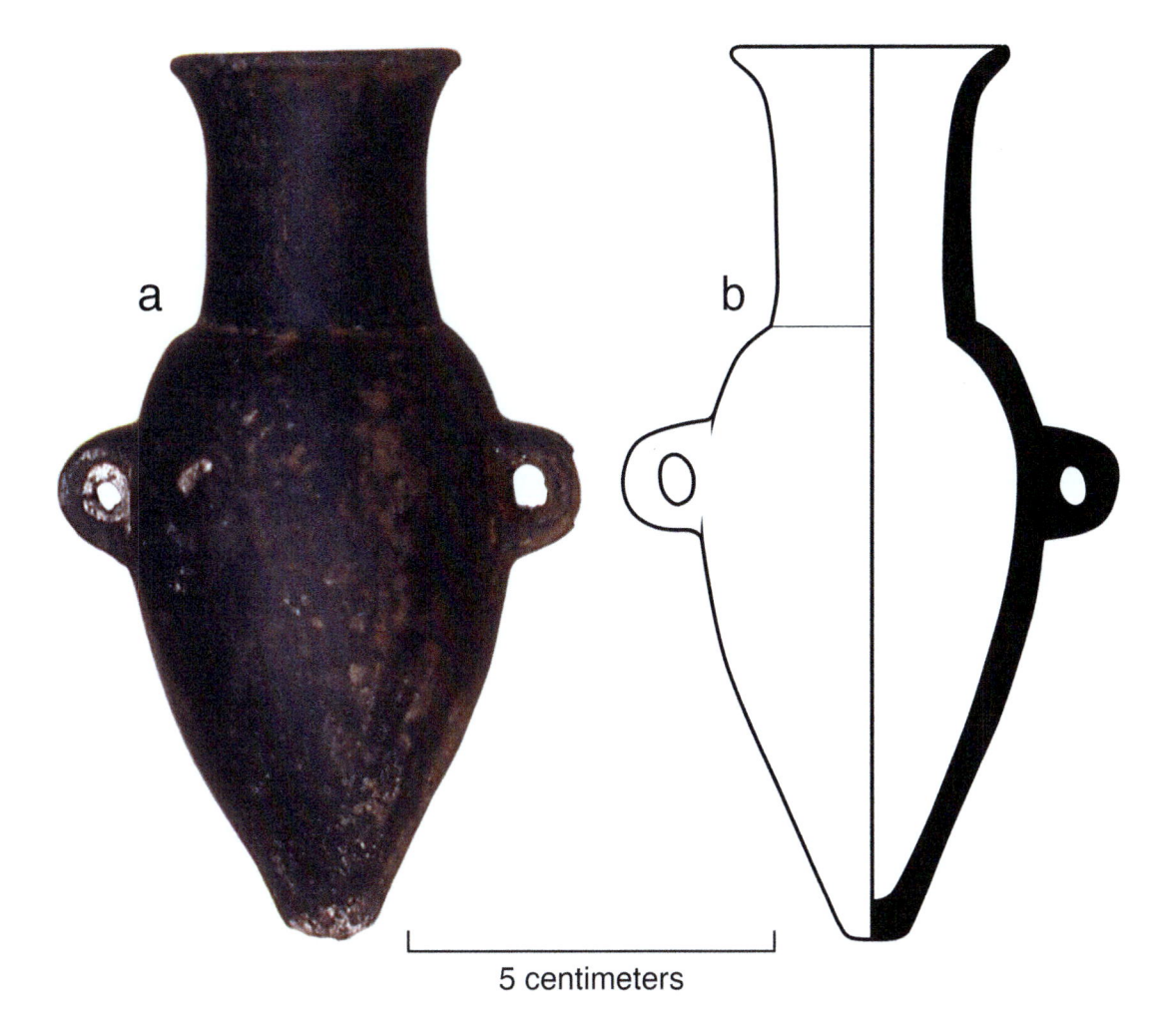

Figure 15.5. Vessel 2 from Burial 9 was a miniature Camacho Black amphora, found near the child's legs. Although considerably disintegrated, fragments of rope could still be detected in the vessel's strap handles.

Figure 15.6. This gourd bowl from Burial 9 (a) contained two guinea pigs, three complete sardines, two razor clams, two mussels, one false abalone, one bean pod, two pod fragments of *pacay*, one *lúcuma* seed, one maize cob, and the maize tassel shown in (b).

Food for the Afterlife

Individual 3's food for the afterlife was found in a shallow gourd bowl (Figure 15.6a; Specimen 20). This bowl had a rim diameter of 21.5 cm, a maximum height of 5.5 cm, and a wall that was 6 mm thick; its Munsell color was 2.5 YR 2/2 ("very dusky red"). Inside the bowl were two guinea pigs. Guinea Pig #1 was represented by its left mandible, left scapula, right humerus, right radius, four cervical vertebrae, and one thoracic vertebra. Guinea Pig #2 had been pregnant and was accompanied by the left mandible of a late-term foetus. It was represented by its cranium, left mandible, right and left innominates, left femur, one lumbar vertebra, and pieces of yellowish-brown fur (Glew and Flannery 2016b:331).

In addition to the guinea pigs, this woman's gourd bowl was packed with other food: three complete sardines, two razor clams, two mussels, one false abalone, one bean pod, two pod fragments of *pacay*, one *lúcuma* seed, and one cob and one tassel of maize (see Figure 15.6b).

In addition to the gourd filled with food, Individual 3 was accompanied by a second gourd bowl containing a neatly prepared bundle of *totora* (*Scirpus* sp.) (Figure 15.7). The diameter of this bowl (Specimen 33) was 24 cm, its height was 4.5 cm, and its wall thickness was 6 mm. The surface color of the gourd was 7.5 R 2/2 ("very dusky red"). The *Scirpus* bundle (18 x 5 cm in length and width, and 2 cm thick) consisted of long strips of *totora*, folded back on themselves and tied together. We suspect that these strips of *totora* might have been saved by Individual 3 to weave a mat or some other item in the future.

Individual 3's Last Meal

Owing to the fact that there was a coprolite still present in her intestines, we can say something about Individual 3's final meal. Coprolite specialist John Jones (2016) reports that this well-preserved specimen included nine small fish bones, crayfish shell fragments, corn kernels, a few seeds

Burial 9

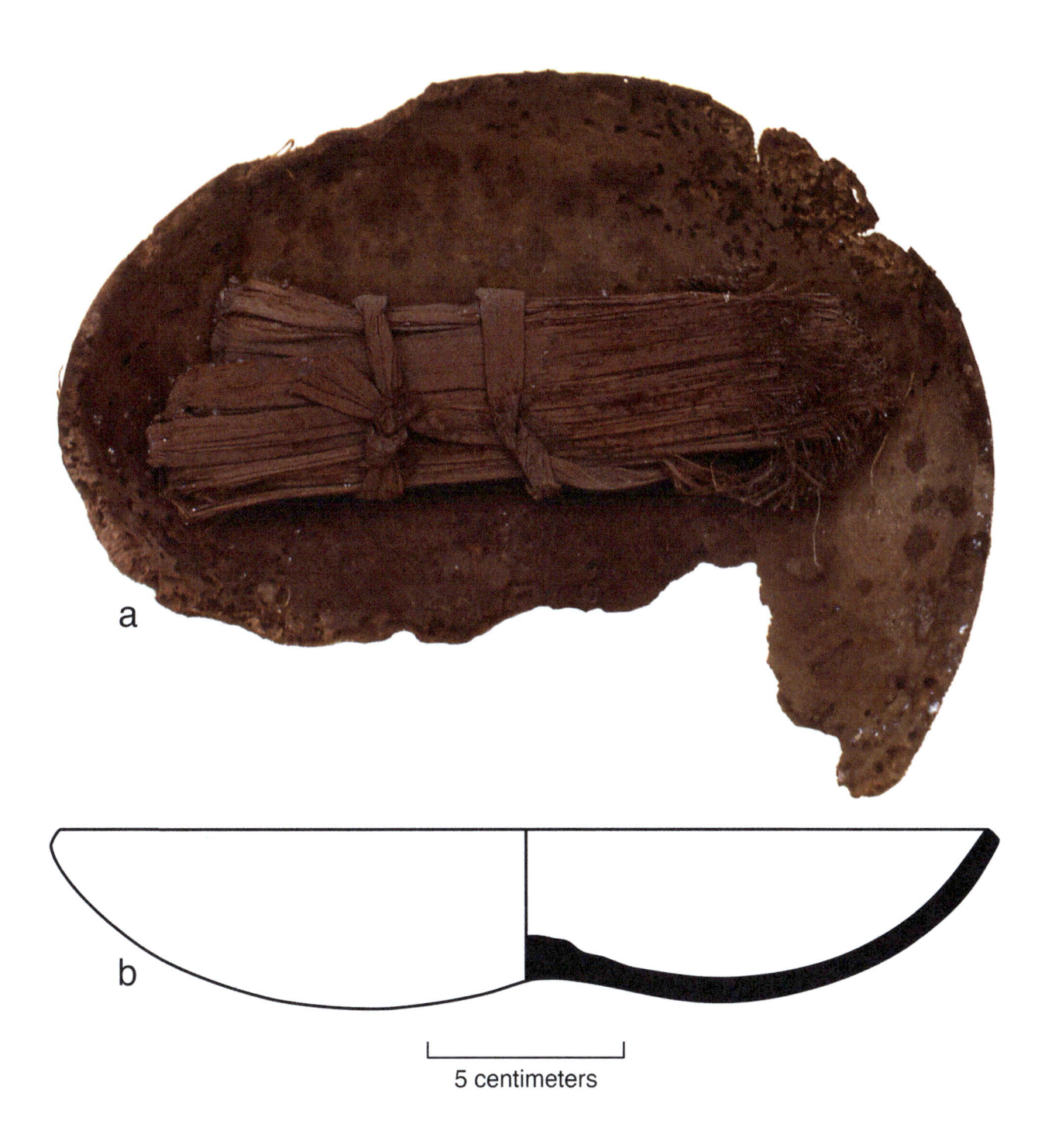

Figure 15.7. Individual 3 of Burial 9 was accompanied by a badly damaged gourd bowl containing a bundle of *totora* (*Scirpus* sp.). At (b) we see an artist's reconstruction of the bowl.

and fibers that could not be identified, and some animal hair. The fact that there were no fish scales in any of the Cerro Azul coprolites he examined suggested to Jones that the scales had been removed from fish more frequently in Late Intermediate times than in the earlier periods he had studied, such as the Preceramic (John Jones, personal communication). In this woman's coprolite, Jones also found pollen of the Solanaceae, Chenopodiaceae, and Amaranthaceae families, as well as several pollen grains of *Tillandsia*, a plant native to the coastal *lomas*.

Dog

Burial 9 also included the left maxilla and premaxilla of a dog, with all its teeth present except for a few incisors (Flannery and Glew 2016:319). In addition to the dog, found at the base of the burial pit, there were masses of *totora* mat fragments, tied bundles of reeds, and loose piles of *pacay* leaves, all perhaps serving as bedding.

Textiles Associated with Individual 3

Individual 3 was accompanied by two backstraps from a belt loom. One, Chumpi 10, was well preserved (Figure 15.8) and still in place around her hips. The other, Chumpi 11, had deteriorated so much that it was impossible to determine its motif.

Chumpi 10 measured 64 x 11 cm and had a warp and weft of camelid wool, 22 warp yarns per centimeter and 6 weft yarns per centimeter. The warp was Z-spun S-twisted, with yarns of several colors—green, red, black, white, and yellow. The weft was also Z-S, but constructed of only brown camelid wool.

Chumpi 10 had two decorated sides, each with different motifs and colors. Side A had narrower than usual warp-faced bands (2.5 cm wide), located to either side of its multicolored central tapestry panel (6 cm wide). These bands were one solid color—reddish brown—with only four black yarns visible at the outer edges.

The weaver used black yarn in the central tapestry panel to outline the multicolored design, which consisted of diagonal rows of geometric fish; each fish motif was within a diamond. In one row we see reddish-brown fish with white eyes against a gold background. The next row has reddish-brown fish with gold eyes against a white background. In other words, two color schemes alternated.

Fish motifs are known from incised needlecases at Cerro Azul (see Burial 4 in Chapter 10), from painted pottery and textiles at Cerro Azul (e.g., Figures 5.28c, 16.24b; see also Marcus 2008: Figs. 3.32, 4.22a, 6.6b, 9.45), and from pottery and textiles from the Chincha Valley (Garaventa 1979; Kroeber and Strong 1924: Fig. 6; Marcus 2008: Fig. 10.2a, b). Farther afield, a similar geometric fish motif is known from a double-cloth textile reported to be "from graves in the neighborhood of Lima" (Bunt 1918: Fig. 4).

Side B, in contrast to Side A, had two dark brown bands flanking its central panel. The motif on Side B was birds, rather than fish. Set within diamond-shaped units are birds with intertwined necks, as well as floating triangles and squares with dots inside them. As was the case with Side A, the color scheme on Side B repeated itself every other diagonal row. One row had orangish-yellow birds with brown eyes on a forest green background; the next row had orangish-yellow birds with dark brown eyes on a light brown background.

Chumpi 10 (Textile 149a), like those found with other Cerro Azul women, was a two-sided complementary warp weave with single-face warp float figures. Except for Individual 3's unique color choices and the narrower bands flanking its central tapestry panels, Chumpi 10 was identical in construction to those made by the women of Burial 4. Such similarities in construction suggest that Cerro Azul women shared information about how to construct backstraps; nevertheless, each woman clearly had the freedom to express herself by selecting her own colors and motifs.

Textiles 114a and 114b

Among Individual 3's other textiles was **Textile 114a**, a warp-stripe plain weave cloth that consisted of two webs sewn together so expertly that the sewing thread was barely visible (Figure 15.9). Each web had a different width—one 74 cm, the other 65 cm. This all-cotton garment was 138 cm long. The sewing thread is S6Z and 1.7 mm thick. A wide variety of colors were used—brown, black, tan, blue, white, dark brown, and purplish brown. The design consists of wide bands and narrow stripes in the following sequence: a brown band, then a black stripe, a tan band, a black stripe, a brown band, followed by a tan band, a black stripe, a brown stripe, a black stripe, and then another tan band, a blue band, a brown stripe, a tan band, a brown stripe, a medium blue band, a black band, a brown stripe, a white stripe, and black band.

Textile 114b (41 x 35 cm) was a warp-stripe plain weave that had been repaired with a light brown thread

Figure 15.8. Chumpi 10, a double-sided loom backstrap, was found in place around the hips of Individual 3, the woman in Burial 9. The tapestry on one side (a) featured fish, while the opposite side (b) depicted birds with their necks intertwined.

Figure 15.9. Textile 114a, associated with Burial 9 of Cerro Azul, was a multicolored warp-stripe plain weave cotton cloth consisting of two webs sewn together. Each web had a different width—one 74 cm, the other 65 cm.

Figure 15.10. Textile 171, associated with Burial 9 of Cerro Azul, appears to be a bag. It was made from dark brown cotton, and on three sides it had been sewn shut with single-strand cotton yarn.

(S4Z and 1.2 mm thick). It seems likely that the same woman made both Textiles 114a and 114b, since the complex stripe sequences were nearly identical. A few details (including the spacing between stripes) were different, and it is clear that Textile 114b was an independent item rather than a fragment of Textile 114a. Textile 114a used a medium blue yarn; in contrast, Textile 114b used dark blue and greenish blue yarns. Textile 114b had a color sequence of bands and stripes as follows: navy blue, dark blue, turquoise, dark brown, medium dark brown, medium brown, and white.

Two Cotton Bags

Textile 171 (Figure 15.10) appears to be a plain weave cotton bag made from dark brown cotton. On three sides it has been sewn shut with single-strand cotton yarn, S-spun.

Textile 173 (Figure 15.11) is a dark brown plain weave bag that contained food.

Cords

T149b consisted of two types of decorative cords, knotted together (Figure 15.12). Type 1 was a 0.95 m long cord with over 2 under 2 plaiting of paired yarns, worked in a spiral on a foundation that appears to have been a dark brown cotton (now disintegrated).

The Type 1 cord is all red in one direction, blue and yellow in the other direction; that pattern creates longitudinal red bands with alternating blue and yellow checks in between. The base of the cord is thicker, approximately 11 cm in diameter.

Figure 15.11. Textile 173, also associated with Burial 9, was a dark brown plain weave bag containing food.

Type 2 consists of four cords resembling hair ribbons. Each cord was approximately 1.2 m long, and all were tied together using an overhand knot. All the cords were spiral cross-knit looping, on a core that had an ovate cross section. Two rows of stitches appear on opposite sides with one in between, giving the cord an asymmetrical cross section. The middle row of stitches is also offset, creating a chevron effect. The design involves sets of four chevrons of alternating colors in the following sequence: red-blue, white-yellow, white-red, and white-yellow. This sequence is then repeated; black lines occur between the areas of color.

T243 was a four-strand braid, found binding this woman's wrists together. This braid was made of four fiber bundles, two of which were 4 mm thick and two of which were 3 mm thick.

Individual 3's Workbasket (Specimen 112)

Individual 3's workbasket included the following items:
- two skeins of yarn (Figure 15.13a, top row), with a total weight of 2 g. The Munsell color of the yarn was 7.5 YR 6/6 ("reddish brown")
- two unpainted spindles (Figure 15.13a). Both spindles had the same type of yarn, which was 5 YR 4/2 ("dark reddish gray")
- six spindle whorls (three whorls are shown in Figure 15.13a, b). One whorl was black, burnished, and globular with a weight of 6 g. Two others were broken, black, and burnished. A fourth whorl—broken and threaded on a broken spindle 16.4 cm long—was black, burnished, and had incised lines that created diamond shapes (shown in both Figure 15.13a [lowest whorl on line 5] and Figure 15.13b [lower left]). The fifth whorl was burnished black and shaped like a gear (Figure 15.13b, lower right); it was painted red and white, weighed 7 g, and was 15 mm in height. The sixth whorl, also black and burnished, is shown in Figure 15.13b in the middle of the row.
- one unpainted spindle, 17 cm long and 3 mm in diameter
- two unpainted spindle fragments, one 4 cm long, and the other 4.5 cm long
- fragment of spindle, 9 cm long, containing yarn that is 5 YR 4/2 ("dark reddish gray")

Figure 15.12. Textile 149b, associated with Burial 9, consisted of two types of decorative cords, knotted together.

Comments on Burial 9

Individual 3, identified by biological anthropologist Sonia Guillén as a woman, was apparently buried with her workbasket and other personal possessions. Her basket was poorly preserved, but its contents were recovered. They included spindles holding yarn, whorls on the spindles, and unused yarns of different colors. Inside her mummy bundle were wads of unspun cotton containing cotton seeds. The backstrap that she used in conjunction with her loom was still in place around her lower back. Thus it appears that Individual 3 had all she needed to continue weaving in the afterlife. She was placed at the bottom of the cist and above her were the bodies of a child and an infant.

Figure 15.13. The contents of a disintegrated workbasket associated with Burial 9 included two skeins of wool (at top of a), six spindles (a), and a number of whorls (a, b).

Part IV

Excavations in Quebrada 5-south at Cerro Azul

Chapter 16

The Structure 12 Burial Cist

As Quebrada 5 nears the end of its descent from the slopes of Cerro Camacho, it widens to the point where a southern extension can be distinguished. We have called this extension Quebrada 5-south and noted that it seems to have been closed off by an ancient tapia wall. As shown in Figure 16.1, there were a series of looters' pits in the Quebrada 5-south area.

Wind erosion in Quebrada 5-south had partially exposed a stone-lined cist that we designated Structure 12 (Figure 16.2). This exposure had evidently attracted looters, who removed items from the cist and left human remains and textiles lying on the surface.

Excavating Structure 12

Structure 12, which measured 2.0 x 1.4 m, had walls 15 cm thick (Figure 16.3). The creators of this cist had excavated down through a midden until they reached uneven bedrock. At an average depth of 1.28 m below the surface, the builders had poured a clay floor to create a level surface over this irregular stone foundation. The walls of the cist utilized unmodified scree stones that were readily available on the slopes nearby. The stones could be stacked to create walls, and once stacked, they were held in place by a layer of clay plaster. The back wall of Structure 12 was the natural bedrock of Cerro Camacho. Structure 12, partially lined with mats, had been supplied with diverse kinds of food. The form of the cist roof, if one existed, is unknown.

Our excavations showed that prior to the construction of Structure 12, this particular terrace had been used for the drying of beans and the storage of fish and crabs. A substantial midden had eventually been created by carrying basketloads of refuse to this location, and at some point in time the occupants of Cerro Azul deemed the terrace sufficiently deep to allow Late Intermediate burials to be inserted into the midden.

Although disturbed by looters, the Structure 12 cist included the partial remains of at least one child and one adult accompanied by two food-filled gourds still lying on the floor. We also found a possible medicine bundle, a *mallero*, a

Figure 16.1. A view of Quebrada 5 and its terraces, descending from the summit of Cerro Camacho. At the center of the photo, our workmen are shown salvaging material discarded by the looters of Structure 12.

balanza, a silver disc, a *quena* or flute, a wooden toy, several ceramic vessels, numerous fragments of textiles, rope, and cords, and two nets, one of which had a sherd weight attached.

Judging by the presence of bones from several individuals, we conclude that Structure 12 once contained multiple persons. Two of the skulls left on the surface near the opening of the cist had green discolorations on the upper palate, suggesting that pieces of metal had been placed in their mouths.

Ceramic Vessels

In the looters' backdirt adjacent to Structure 12 we found a broken and badly eroded amphora (Figure 16.4). Its clay body was uniformly gray, but its surface bore traces of pinkish and reddish burnishing marks.

We also recovered a highly burnished Camacho Black vessel that shows incised human ribs and a modeled vertebral column (see Figure 16.5a, b). We immediately saw a similarity between this "fat skeleton" vessel and one that we found in Structure D (Figure 16.5c, d).

In addition, we found a Pingüino Buff shallow dish (Figure 16.6a, b) that had been given a cream slip, then painted black and white on the exterior; its interior was burnished and left a natural buff color.

Gourd Vessels

Two gourd bowls filled with food, plus a lid made from a gourd, were still resting on the floor of Structure 12.

Gourd #1 had a diameter of 20.5 cm, a height of 4.5 cm, and a wall 0.7 mm thick; its color varied from 2.5 YR 4/6

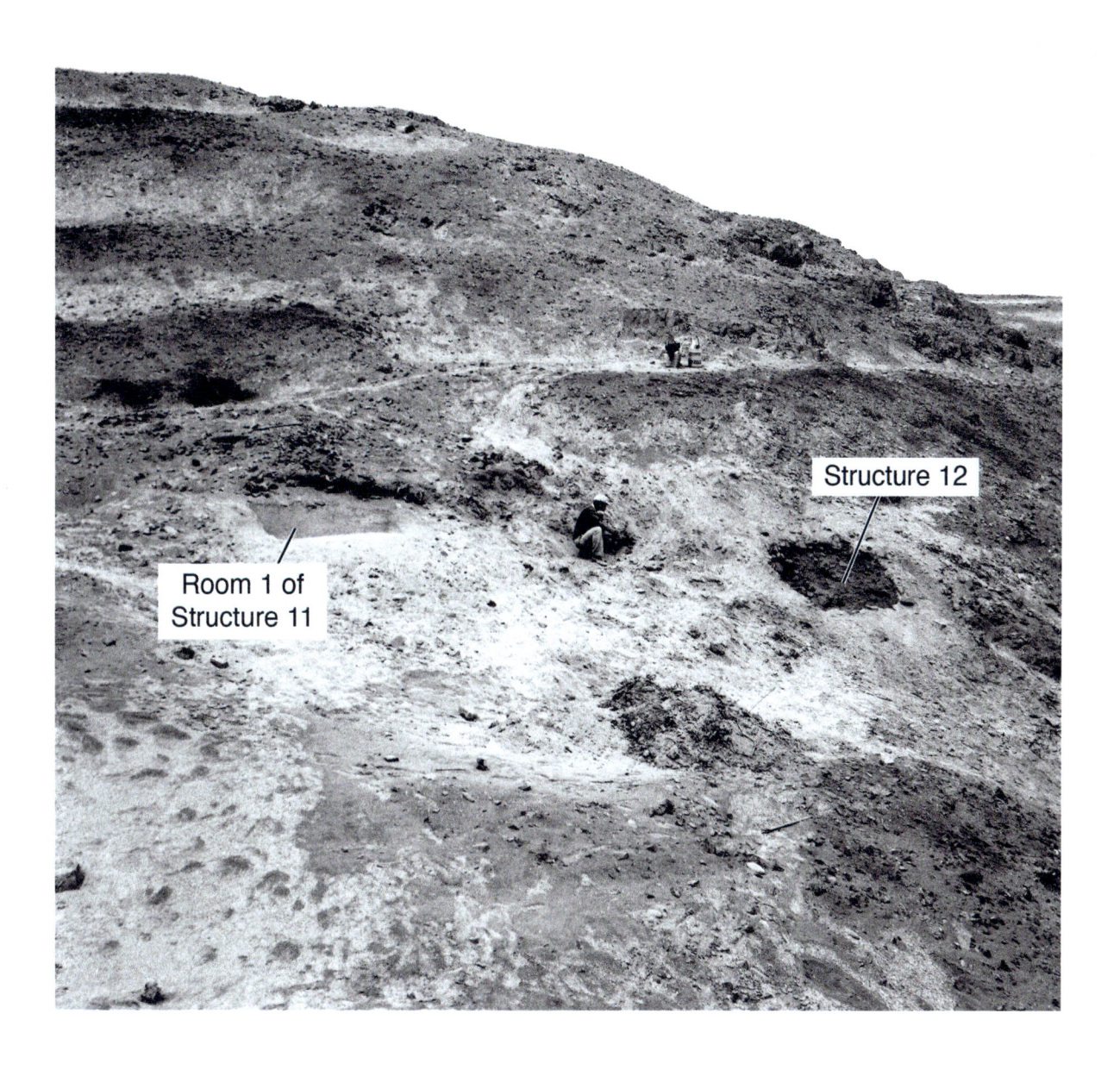

Figure 16.2. Quebrada 5-south, showing the locations of Structure 11 and Structure 12. The latter proved to be a looted burial cist.

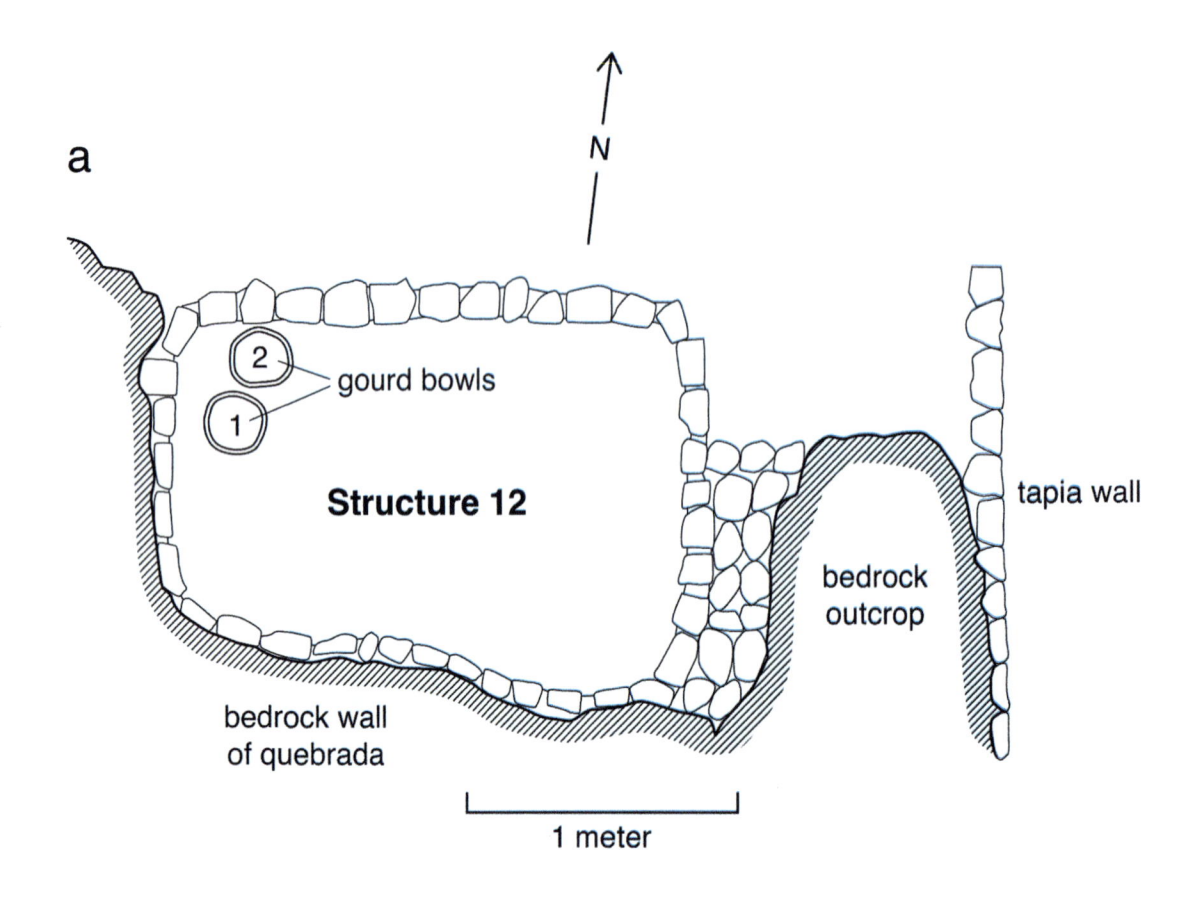

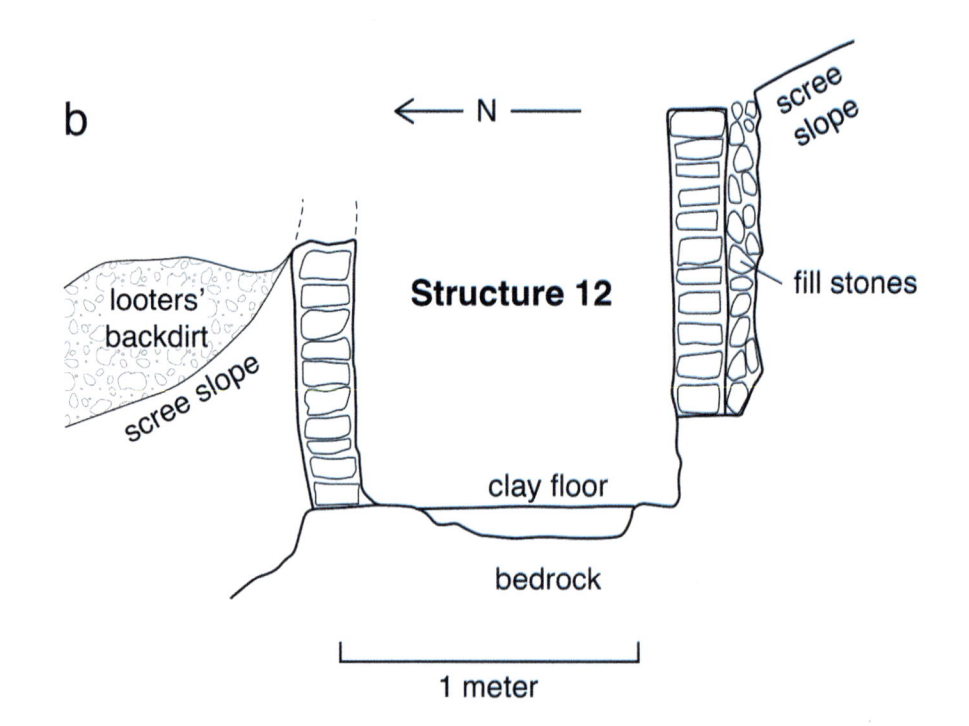

Figure 16.3. Two views of the Structure 12 burial cist. (a) The plan view, showing the gourd bowls left on the floor of the cist. (b) A north-south cross section of Structure 12, the scree slope, and the backdirt pile left by looters. In their haste the looters discarded many items, including a silver disc and several ceramic vessels.

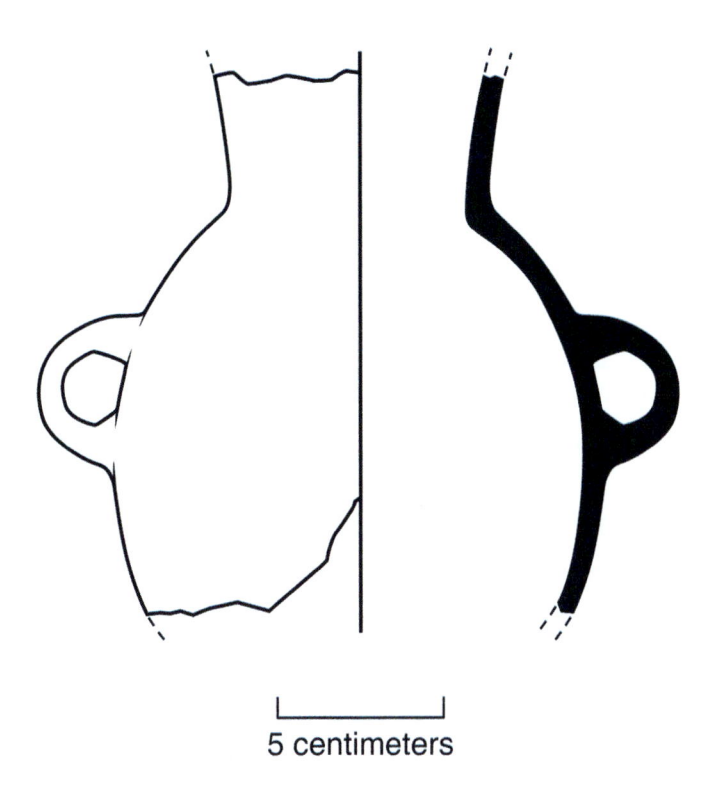

Figure 16.4. A broken amphora, found in the looters' backdirt next to Structure 12.

("red") to 5 YR 4/6 ("yellowish red") (Figure 16.7a, b, c). The food in this gourd had been placed on a thin layer of maize husks. There were three ears of maize, two *lúcuma* seeds, two small mussels (one *Perumytilus*, the other *Semimytilus*), and at least 30 dried anchovetas. Local rice rats (*Oryzomys xanthaeolus*) had made their way into the cist and eaten most of the kernels on the maize cobs; two of the rats had even died in the cist.

A vessel lid carved from a gourd was found near Gourd #1; its diameter was 11 cm and its height 2.5 cm (Figure 16.8a, b). This lid did not fit any of the vessels we found, leading us to suspect that it may once have covered a pot removed by looters.

Gourd #2 measured 23.6 cm in diameter, 6 cm in height, and 0.7 mm in wall thickness (Figure 16.9a, b, c). Its exterior color varied from 2.5 YR 2/2 ("very dusky red") to 5 YR 2/2 ("dark reddish brown").

This gourd contained a guinea pig with a coat color of 10 YR 6/4 ("brownish yellow"), as well as five dried anchovetas and two *Semimytilus* mussels. Hidden below the guinea pig were the remains of 52 beans (*Phaseolus* sp.). Possibly because the cist had initially retained some moisture, many of these beans had sprouted before becoming desiccated.

In addition to the complete guinea pig in this gourd bowl, we recovered a few more *Cavia* specimens from Structure 12. Included were two right mandibles from two different guinea pigs; one left mandible; miscellaneous ribs and vertebrae; and the desiccated skin of a brown and white guinea pig.

Our excavation crew also recovered miscellaneous plants (presumably left in Structure 12 as food for the afterlife) that had fallen from their gourd bowls. Included were:

—1 immature ear of maize, still in its husk, plus 155 loose kernels
—1 pod and 1 loose seed of *Phaseolus vulgaris*
—4 *Canavalia* beans
—1 seed of butternut squash
—12 *lúcuma* seeds

Finally, in Gourd #2 we found a complete cotton bag, fragments of red cloth, and a dirty white cloth (see below).

304   Chapter 16

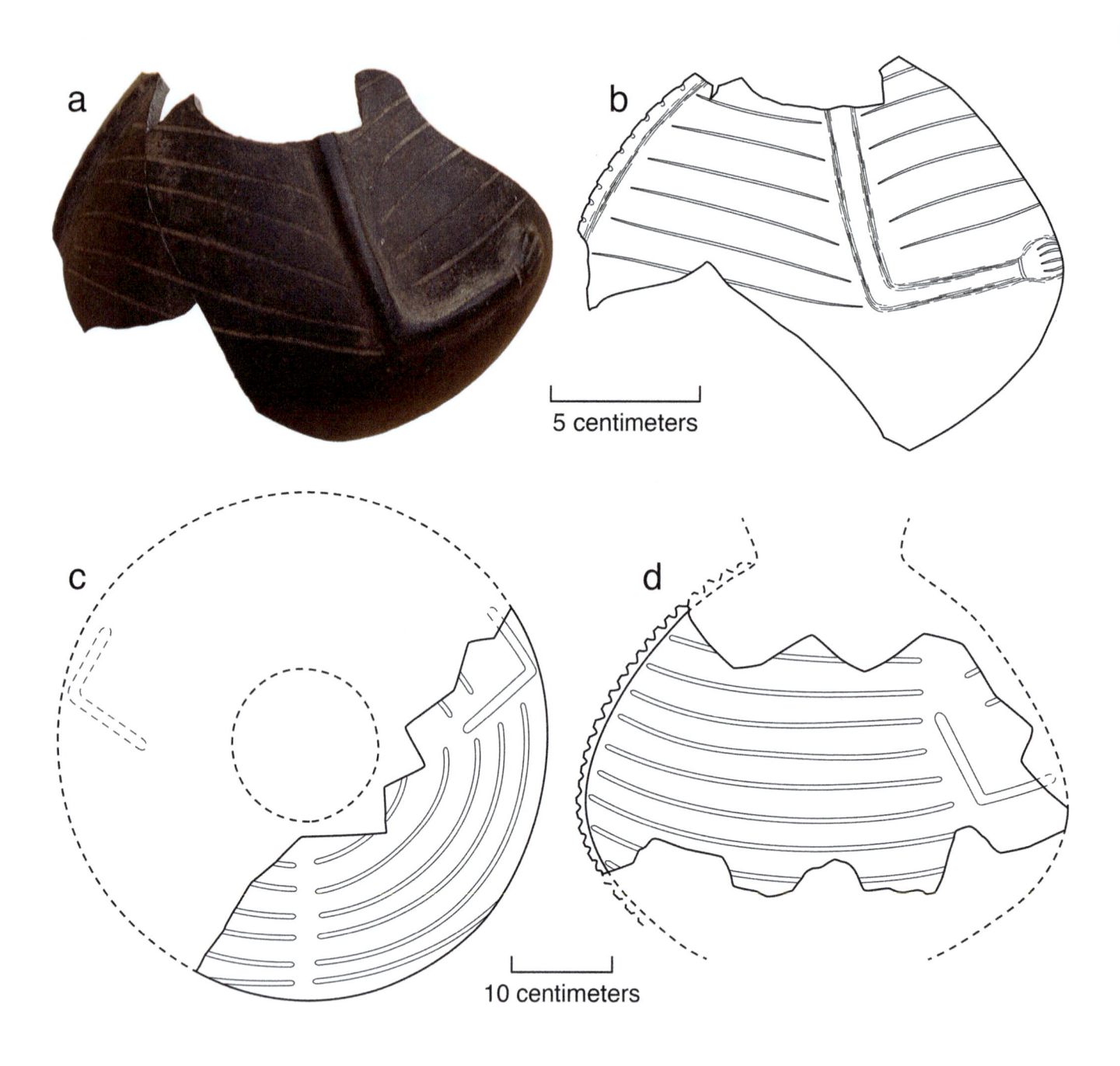

Figure 16.5. Two vessels from Cerro Azul depicting the "fat skeleton," a motif featuring incised ribs, modeled arms, and modeled vertebral columns. (a, b) Two views of a vessel from Structure 12. (c, d) A comparable vessel from Structure D (see Marcus 2008: Fig. 7.13).

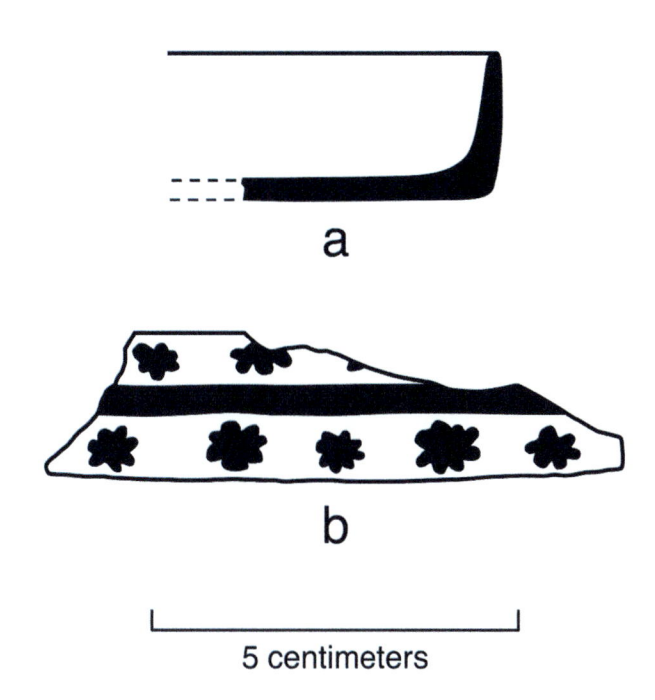

Figure 16.6. A broken Pingüino Buff shallow dish from Structure 12. This vessel was slipped cream white, then painted in black and white on the exterior (b), but left natural buff on the interior (a).

Textiles From Gourd #2

Textile 131a was a plain weave cotton bag with a cord handle (Figure 16.10). This bag (mentioned above) was found in Gourd #2 (see Figure 16.9). The bag measured 11 x 10 cm, while the handle was 37 cm long.

Textile 131b (16 x 18.5 cm) was a fragment of plain weave cloth that was also found in Gourd #2. It was cotton and light red to salmon in color.

Textile 131c was the dirty white cotton cloth found in Gourd #2.

A Possible Medicine Bundle

One of the most remarkable items left behind in Structure 12 was a possible medicine bundle that might have been used by an indigenous *curandero* or curer (Figure 16.11a). The bundle weighed 800 grams and consisted of a series of plants inside a cloth that was tied by bringing together its four corners in a knot (Figure 16.11c).

This unique bundle contained (1) a lock of *algodón pardo* or brown cotton; (2) a lock of *algodón blanco* or white cotton; (3) a twist of human hair; (4) a cluster of *Euphorbia* and other herbs that were identified by botanist C. Earle Smith, Jr. as "hierba Golondrina" (see Figure 13.4 in Smith and Marcus 2016b). Smith said this genus was often used to treat gastrointestinal problems and tissue inflammation; (5) four fragments of achira leaves; (6) one bundle of achira leaves tied up in a twisted maize leaf; (7) two splints of *caña hueca* or *Phragmites australis*; and (8) approximately 53 cloth strips that could be used to tie up small bags or bundles (Figure 16.11b). Of the 53 strips, some 46 had warp and weft yarns that were S-spun; the other seven strips had warp and weft yarns that were Z-spun. Several of these potential ties seem to have been torn from the same piece of cloth.

It is possible that one of the individuals buried in Structure 12 had been treated with these potentially medicinal herbs before his or her death, and that the bundle was simply buried with the corpse. Not many medicine bundles have been reported in the Andean literature, but Wassén (1972) reported on a "medicine man's" implements and plants found in a Tiahuanaco tomb. During Inca times an enormous variety of plants were used as medicines, and many of these are listed by Cobo (1890–1895, Books 4–6). In Quechua, a *hampi camayoq* or "medical specialist" is

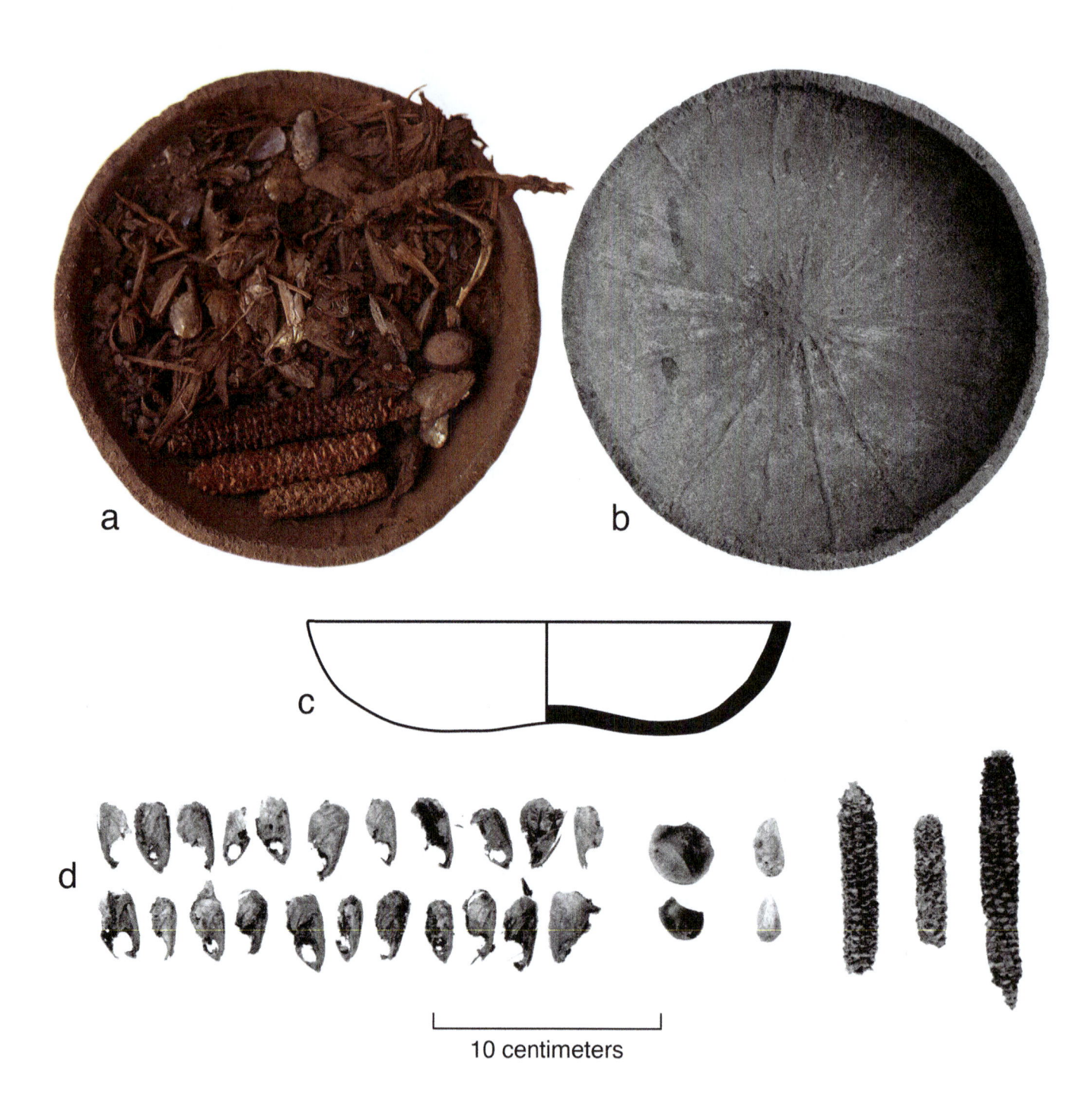

Figure 16.7. Gourd #1, one of two gourd bowls found on the floor of Structure 12. (a) The gourd as found, filled with food. (b) The empty gourd. (c) A cross section of the gourd. (d) The gourd's contents—more than twenty dried anchovetas (whose heads are shown here), two *lúcuma* seeds, two tiny molluscs, and three maize cobs.

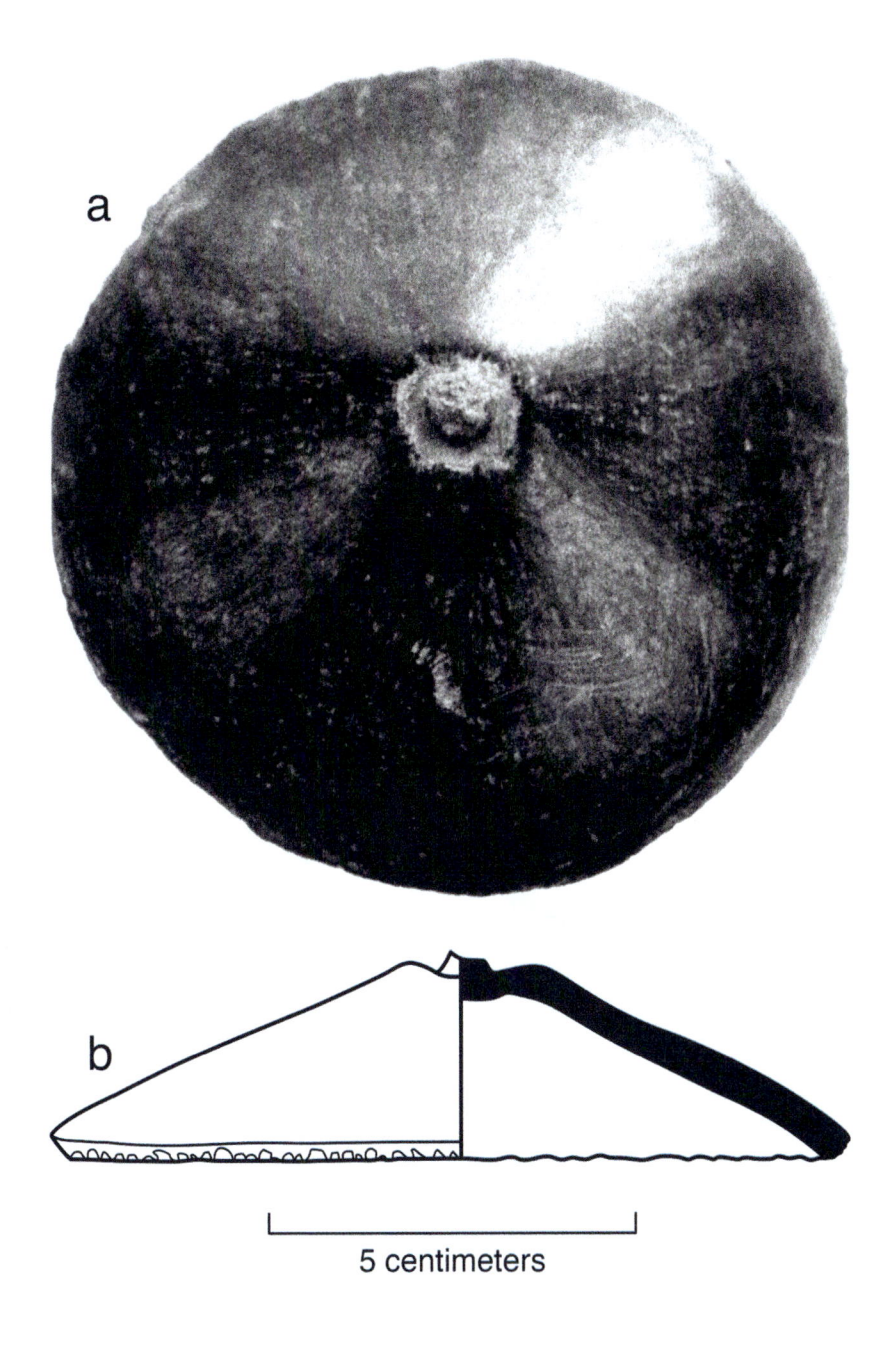

Figure 16.8. A vessel lid made from a gourd, found in Structure 12.

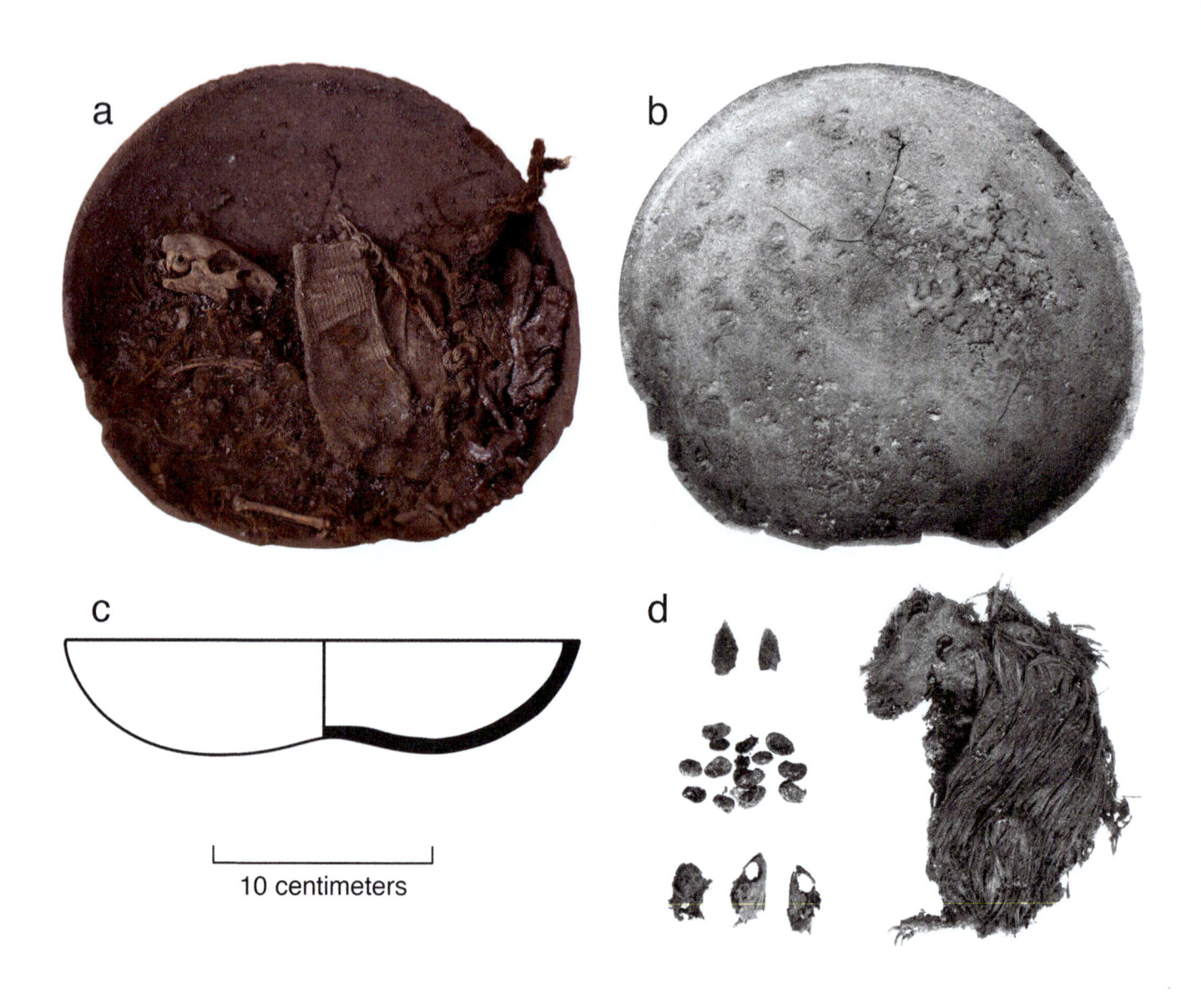

Figure 16.9. Gourd #2, the second of two gourd bowls, found on the floor of Structure 12. (a) The gourd as found, filled with food. (b) The empty gourd. (c) Cross section of the gourd. (d) The gourd's contents included 52 beans, several anchovetas, a guinea pig, and the white cotton bag shown in Figure 16.10.

Figure 16.10. A white cotton bag found in Gourd #2 of Structure 12 (see also Figure 16.9a).

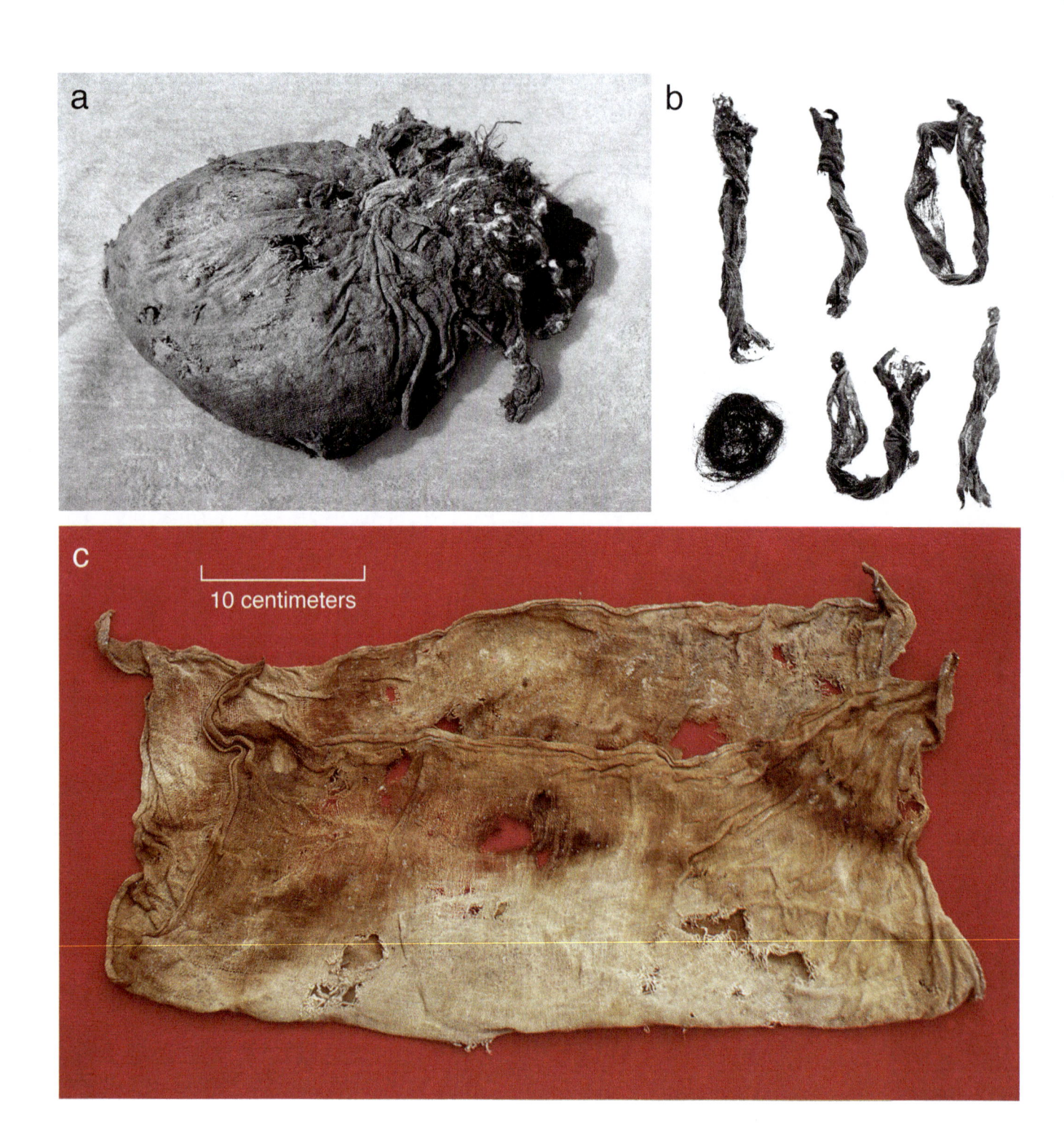

Figure 16.11. A possible "medicine bundle," discovered in Structure 12. (a) The unopened cloth bundle. (b) Five cloth strips and a clump of human hair (lower row, left) found in the bundle. (c) The outer cloth wrapping of the bundle. (The medicinal plants, including *Euphorbia* sp. and achira, found inside the bundle are illustrated in Smith and Marcus [2016b: Figure 13.4].)

described as a diviner who treated and diagnosed illnesses (J. Rowe 1946:312).

Silver Disc

Another remarkable item recovered from the looters' debris in Structure 12 was a large silver disc, wrapped in a dirt-encrusted cloth (Figure 16.12). The dirty cloth, whose unattractive appearance probably kept the disc from being noticed by the looters, was a warp-stripe plain weave cotton textile tied with a square knot. The cloth features a series of wide and narrow brown and tan stripes.

The silver disc itself is 9.5 cm in diameter and 2.1 to 2.4 mm thick; it weighs 68 g. This was by far the heaviest single piece of silver we recovered, but some of the pieces we found in the mouths of the deceased might have been cut from a disc like this.

Balanza

In earlier chapters, we have discussed three of the four *balanzas* found at Cerro Azul (see Figures 3.5 and 10.44). We found this fourth *balanza* in looters' backdirt, next to Structure 12.

We find it noteworthy that all four *balanzas* differ in size; they also differ in raw material (three are of wood, one of bone). We suspect that the size reflects the raw material being weighed, and wonder if the raw material of the *balanza* itself reflects social status. After all, the only person associated with a decorated bone *balanza* was the high-status woman (Individual 3) in Burial 4 (see Chapter 10).

The Structure 12 *balanza* is made of wood and measures 16.8 x 2.4 cm (Figure 16.13). A two-ply Z2S cotton cord is still attached to it; from knot to knot, the cord measures ca. 52 cm. This *balanza* is similar in construction to the one from Room 2 of Structure D (Figure 16.14). The four Cerro Azul *balanzas* (Figures 3.5, 10.44, 16.13, 16.14) are similar to the Late Intermediate *balanzas* from La Centinela in the Chincha Valley. Dalton (2020) reported on several Late Horizon *balanzas* from the Chincha Valley; some were made of bone and decorated with 10 birds, a possible allusion to the Andean decimal system (Kendall 1973; J. Rowe 1946). Donnan (2009), too, calls attention to artifacts that occur in units of 10 or multiples of 10.

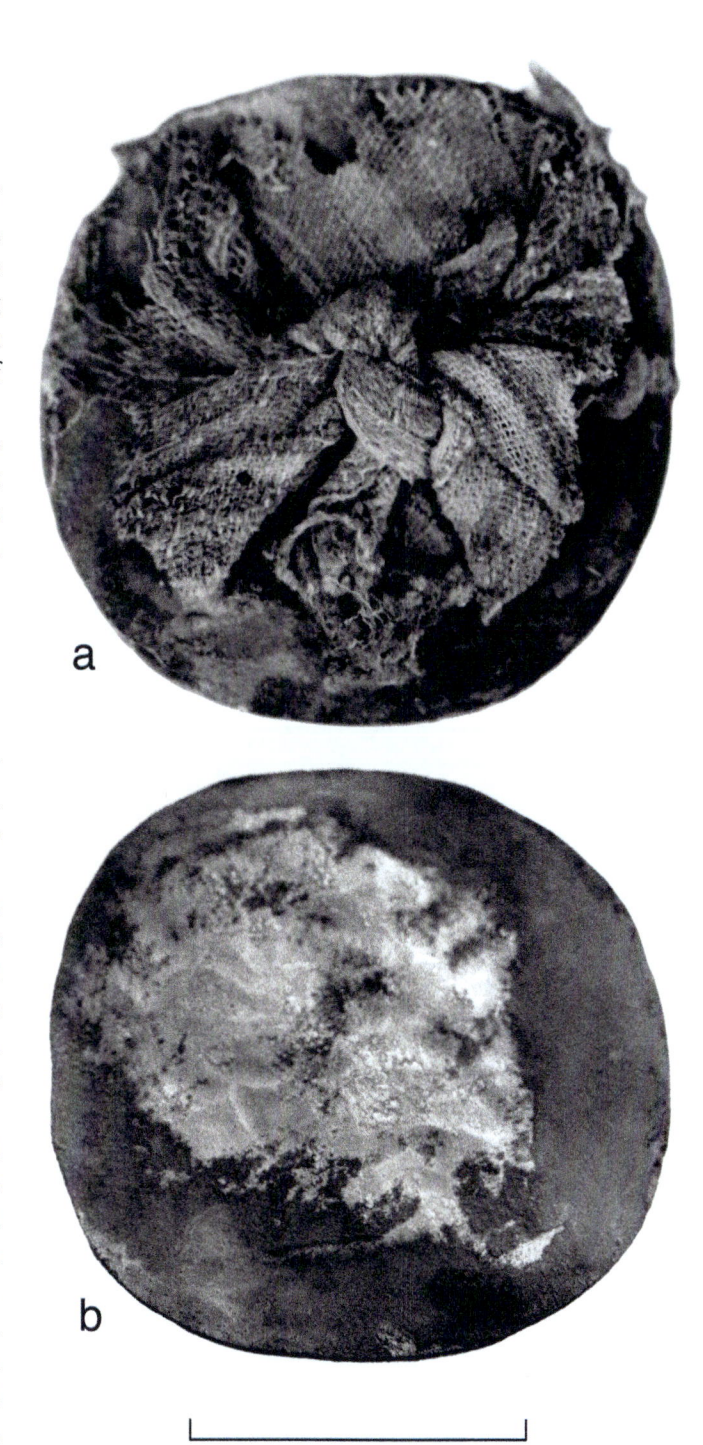

Figure 16.12. Two views of a silver disc, tied up in a striped cloth, found in looters' backdirt adjacent to Structure 12. Apparently, the cloth was so covered with dirt that the looters assumed it contained nothing of value.

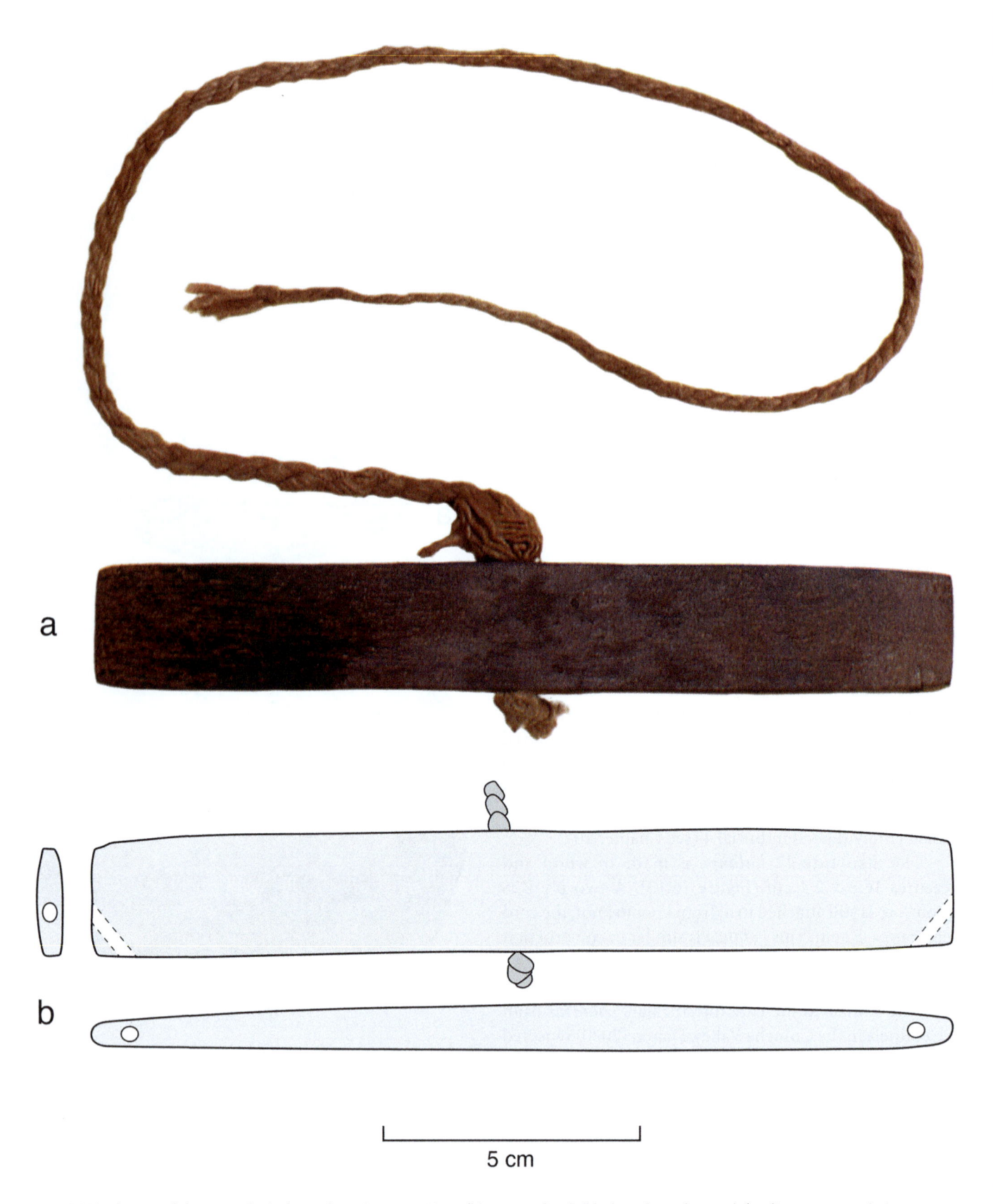

Figure 16.13. Photo and drawing of a *balanza* from Structure 12. At (b) we see the drill holes where the cords leading to suspended nets or pans could be inserted.

The Structure 12 Burial Cist 313

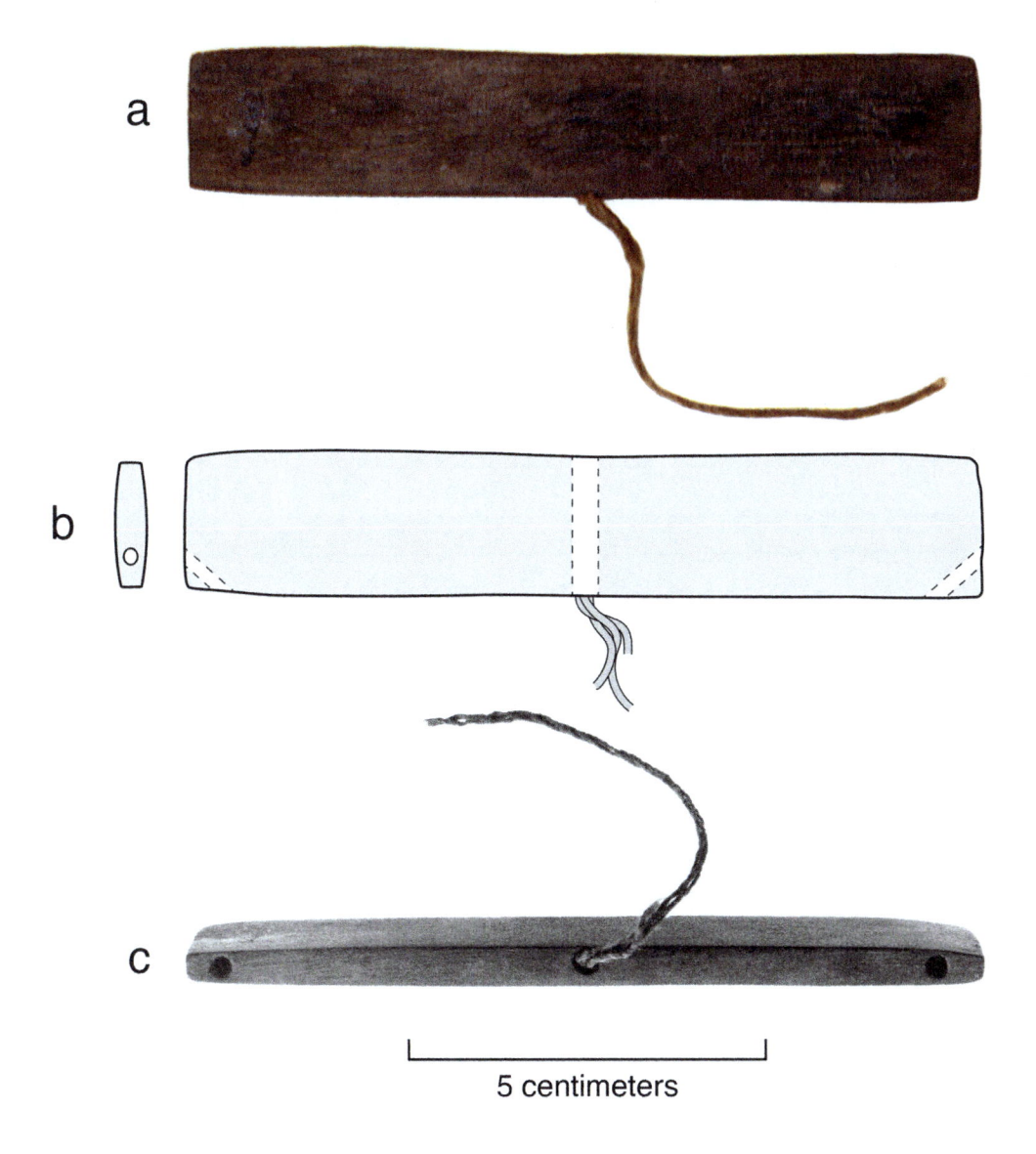

Figure 16.14. Two photos and a drawing of a *balanza* found in Room 2 of Structure D at Cerro Azul (Marcus 2008: Fig. 4.1). (b) shows the drill holes for the central and side cords; the latter were used to suspend nets or pans to weigh items. (c) shows the underside of the *balanza*, with its three drill holes (the cord shown is merely the tail end of the one that originally suspended the wooden beam).

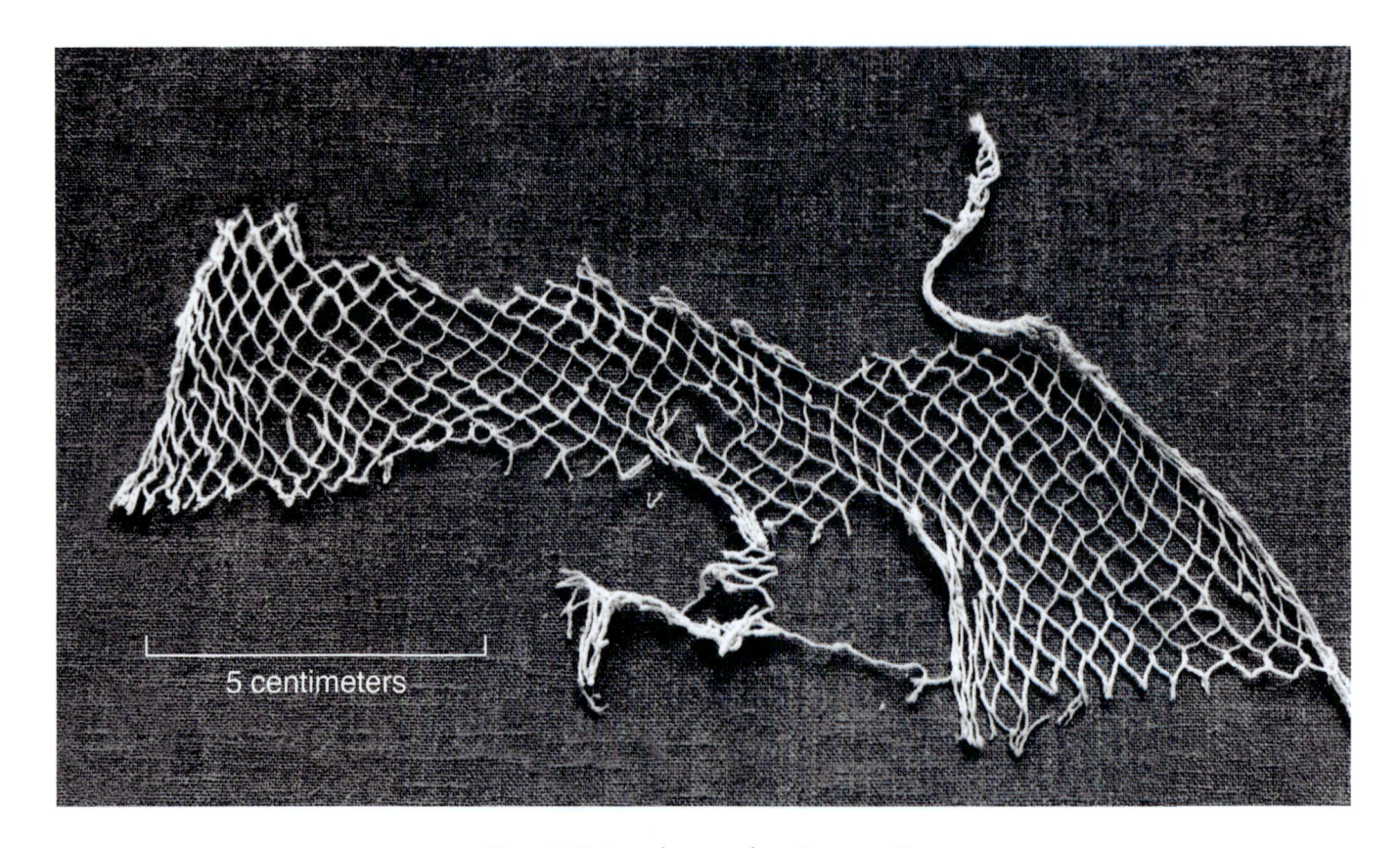

Figure 16.15. A net fragment from Structure 12.

Fishing Nets and Weights

In Structure 12 we found the remains of two nets and two net weights. One net fragment is shown in Figure 16.15. The second net fragment (Figure 16.16a) was particularly interesting, since one of its weights was still attached. This net weight, which measured 3.2 x 3.5 cm, was an 11 g body sherd from a Camacho Reddish Brown jar. The net itself was probably a trammel net.

The second net weight from Structure 12 (Figure 16.16b) was also a body sherd from a coarse jar, probably Camacho Reddish Brown. This second weight measured 3.8 x 3.0 cm and weighed 15 g. Although it was no longer attached to a net, a brown-dyed string was still attached to it.

Malleros

Wooden *malleros,* or mesh-measuring templates, vary in size because the desired mesh size in fishing nets varies. Figure 16.17 shows the one we recovered from Structure 12, which measured 6.8 x 4.6 cm. The other *mallero* found at Cerro Azul measured 8.7 x 2.3 cm.

Malleros have been found at other coastal sites, but their sizes are not always given; Squier, for example, found a *mallero* in a fisherman's mummy bundle at Ancón, but did not provide its dimensions (Squier 1967[1869]). Fortunately, Sandweiss (1992:73–74) gives the dimensions for the *mallero* he found in Late Horizon deposits at Lo Demás in the Chincha Valley; it measured 12.75 x 2.39 cm and was 1.0 cm thick. In speaking of Pacatnamu's *malleros*, Donnan (1995:150) says, they "appear to have been as exclusive to male graves as weaving implements were to women's graves."

A Drilled Astragalus

An unusual artifact found in Structure 12 was an ungulate astragalus, drilled through its condyles (Figure 16.18a, b). Kroeber (1937:252, Plate LXXXVII-1) found 43 similar

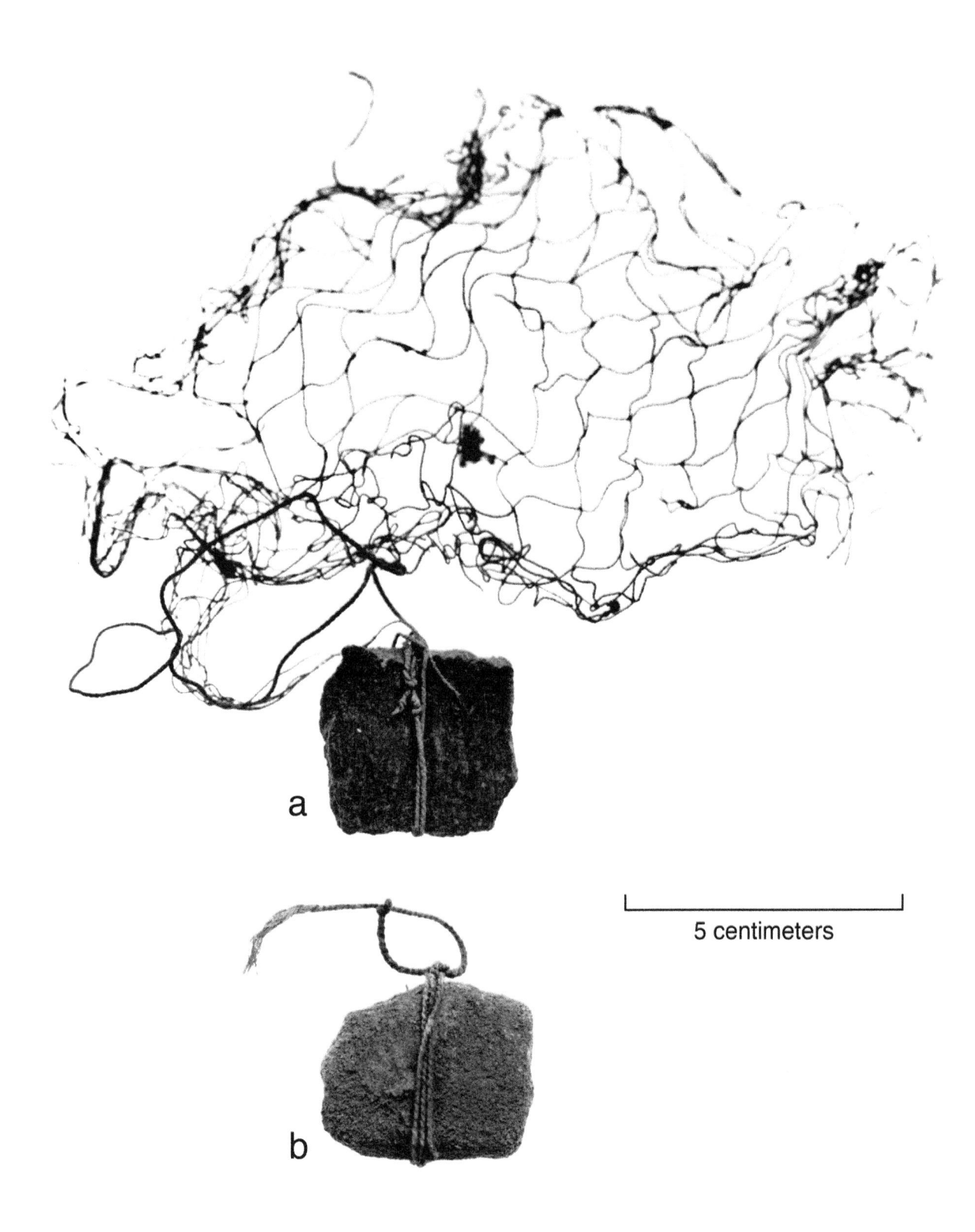

Figure 16.16. Potsherds from Structure 12, used as net weights. (a) A portion of trammel net with potsherd weight. (b) A second potsherd weight, also found in Structure 12.

316 Chapter 16

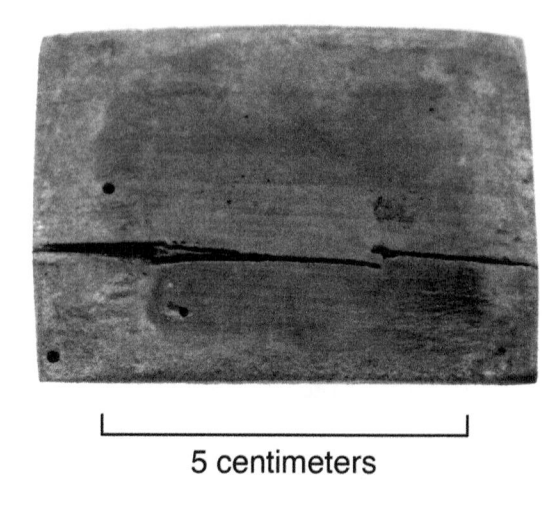

Figure 16.17. A *mallero* (a wooden template used to create uniform mesh in fishing nets) discovered in Structure 12.

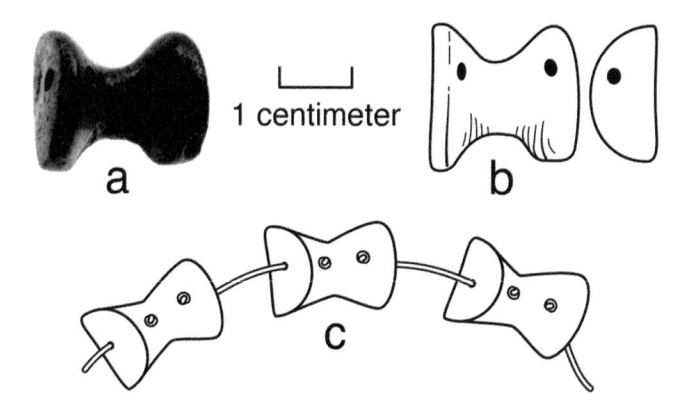

Figure 16.18. Photo (a) and drawing (b) of an ungulate's astragalus, drilled through the condyles; this item was found in Structure 12 of Cerro Azul. (c) Three similar items found by Kroeber (1937:252, Plate LXXXVII-1) in Quebrada 1 of Cerro Azul. Kroeber found 43 of these unusual artifacts, whose function is unknown.

items in a cache in Quebrada 1 at Cerro Azul, calling them "half-spools." These artifacts had been strung on three separate cords which, when combined, had a total length of 1.55 m (Figure 16.18c). Kroeber noted that a knot was used to keep the string from slipping out of its hole. Kroeber suggested that his artifacts were made of *huarango* wood (*Acacia* sp.), rather than bone.

Sandweiss (1992:90) found twenty similar items at Lo Demás, and all but one of his were made of clay. He described them as shaped like a spool of thread standing on one end, and cut in half along a vertical plane. Like those at Cerro Azul, his had holes that allowed them to be strung on a cord. Sandweiss (1992:92) referred to these items as "half-bobbins" and concluded, "if the objects had a single function, it was one that could be equally well fulfilled by ceramic, bone, or wood."

Miscellaneous Textiles from Structure 12

Textile 107 is a cotton cloth that had been tied with a simple overhand knot, resulting in three sections (Figure 16.19): a central pouch that measured 18 cm, one end section that measured 31 cm, and another end section measuring 29 cm. Inside the tied-off pouch were maize fragments that may have been sieved from *chicha* (corn beer) during manufacture. The moderately open weave of this cloth would make it appropriate to catch and remove the floating maize fragments. One possibility, therefore, is that someone buried in Structure 12 was involved in *chicha* making.

Textile 110 (Figure 16.20) was another square cloth (74 x 74 cm); its dimensions are the actual loom dimensions. Like Textile 107, Textile 110 was a tied cloth with a central pouch holding corn, possibly from sieving during *chicha* production. This plain weave cloth would have worked well for that purpose. It was made of cotton with 11 warp yarns per centimeter and 5.5 weft yarns per centimeter. There is a repair yarn S3Z (1.0 mm thick) that contrasts with the warp yarns, weft yarns, and the heading cord.

Textile 158 is a fragment of a multicolored band that now measures 15.8 x 9.0 cm (Figure 16.21). It features a motif with interlocking frets of stepped triangles and dots. This obverse side of the band has extra-weft patterning. The band is one warp by one weft, with 19 warp yarns per centimeter and 12 weft yarns per centimeter. The warp is cotton S-spun, Z-plied, and 0.6 mm thick. The weft is cotton Z-spun and S-plied, with yarns of four colors (red, yellow, black, and brown). The decorative yarn is wool, S-spun, and Z-plied. The heading cord is cotton, S6Z. The red background wefts pass from side to side within a 7-cm-wide float pattern; floats are three over and one under on the front surface.

Textile 222a was a dark brown plain weave, Z-spun S-twisted, with 18 warp yarns per centimeter and 11 weft yarns per centimeter.

Textile 222b was a fragment of a warp-stripe plain weave bag that had wide brown and white stripes. It had a warp of wool yarns and a weft of cotton. On the sides of the bag was *soumak* edging or *cordoncillo* that featured red, black, white, and yellow wool.

Textile 222c was a warp-stripe plain weave, all cotton cloth. It features a series of 10.5-cm-wide stripes in different colors that have now faded to different shades of brown, each separated by a set of blue-white-blue stripes 9 cm wide.

Textile 222e (Figure 16.22) was a round cord using a *soumak* technique; it measured 27 cm long and 14 mm in diameter. Both the warp and weft are wool yarns, Z-spun and S-twisted. The design is a series of rectangular panels that alternate in color, each 5 cm rectangle featuring a bird. One set of birds has triangular bodies with wings up over their heads.

Textile 222f was a 6 cm segment of white bast, Z-S, made of three bundles; it includes two eight-strand square braids made of bundles of apparently untwisted bast. The longest braid is 27 cm.

Textile 222g was a braided cord.

Textile 222h was a four-strand round braid, made of bast fiber. It is 5.6 mm thick and 37 cm long.

Textile 242 was a four-strand circular braid 32 cm long. This may have been part of a sling, since it ends in a tassel like that seen on slings elsewhere.

Wooden Top: A Possible Toy

In the looters' debris next to Structure 12 was a conical wooden artifact that measured 5.2 x 2.9 cm (Figure 16.23, upper right corner). Similar items have been found at several coastal sites, and we found more of them in the residential structures at Cerro Azul, especially in the *canchones* or large open workspaces in Structure D.

Valdez and Bettcher (2020) have made a convincing case that these wooden artifacts were children's tops. To reinforce their interpretation they call attention to an illustration from Guaman Poma de Ayala ([1615]1980: Vol 1, pp. 184–185), showing a five-year-old boy playing with a similar-looking top (Figure 16.23, lower left). That illustration closely resembles the conical wooden artifacts found at Cerro Azul and elsewhere (e.g., Sandweiss 1992; Valdez and Bettcher 2020).

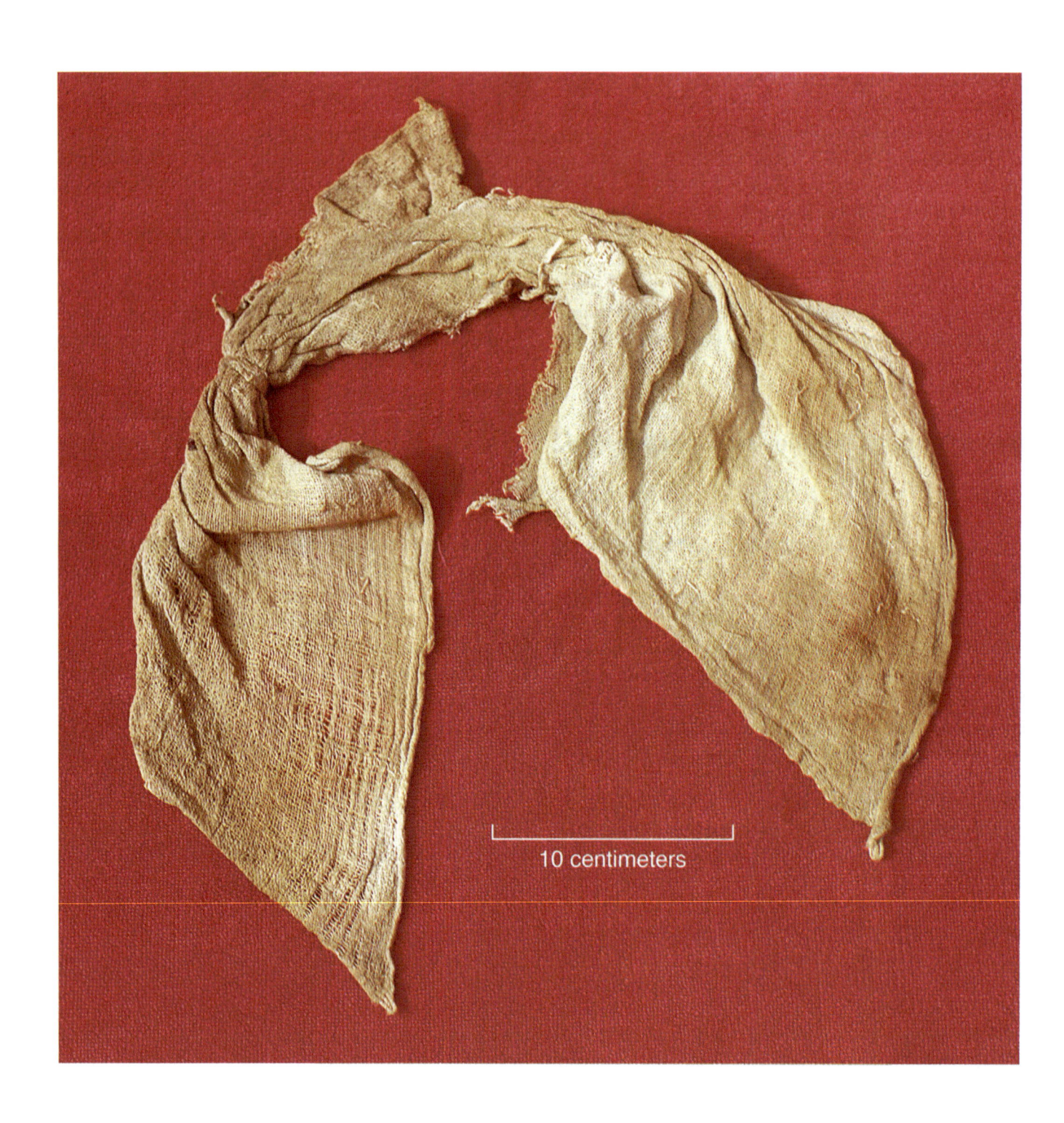

Figure 16.19. A cotton cloth from Structure 12 at Cerro Azul, in whose central tied pouch we found fragments of maize.

Figure 16.20. A second cotton cloth from Structure 12 that contained maize fragments. There is a repair yarn (upper left) that contrasts with the warp yarns, weft yarns, and heading cord.

Figure 16.21. A cotton band with colorful decorative wool yarn, discovered in Structure 12.

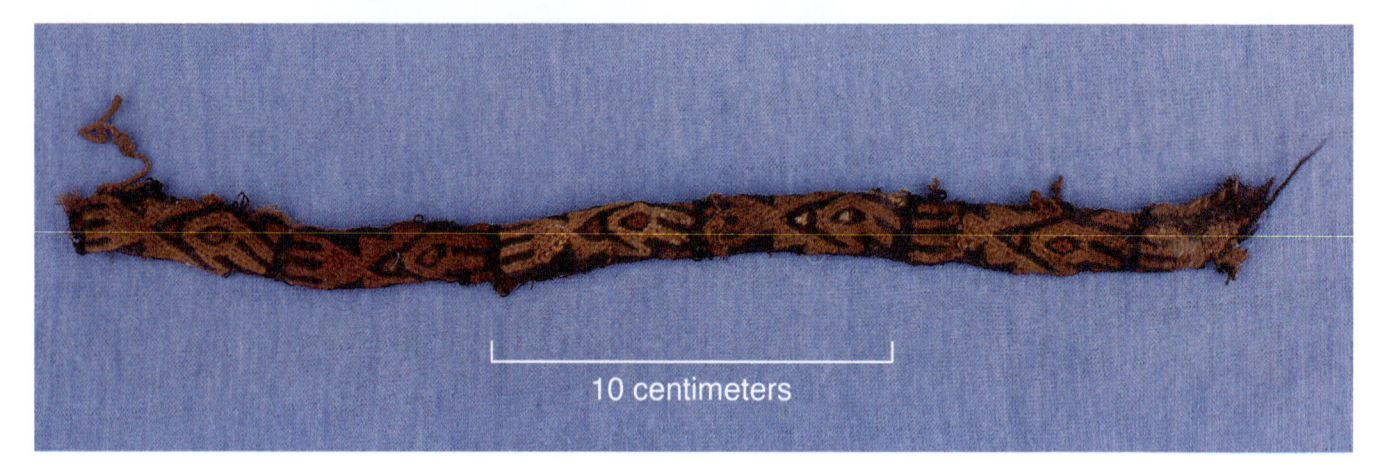

Figure 16.22. A round cord featuring bird motifs, found in Structure 12.

Opposite page: Figure 16.23. These wooden artifacts are possible children's toys from Cerro Azul. The specimen in the upper right corner was found in Structure 12; all others came from the *canchones* of Structure D (Marcus 2008: Fig. 4.1). At lower left we see a drawing from Guaman Poma de Ayala ([1615]1980, Volume I:184), which shows a young boy spinning one of these wooden tops.

The Structure 12 Burial Cist   321

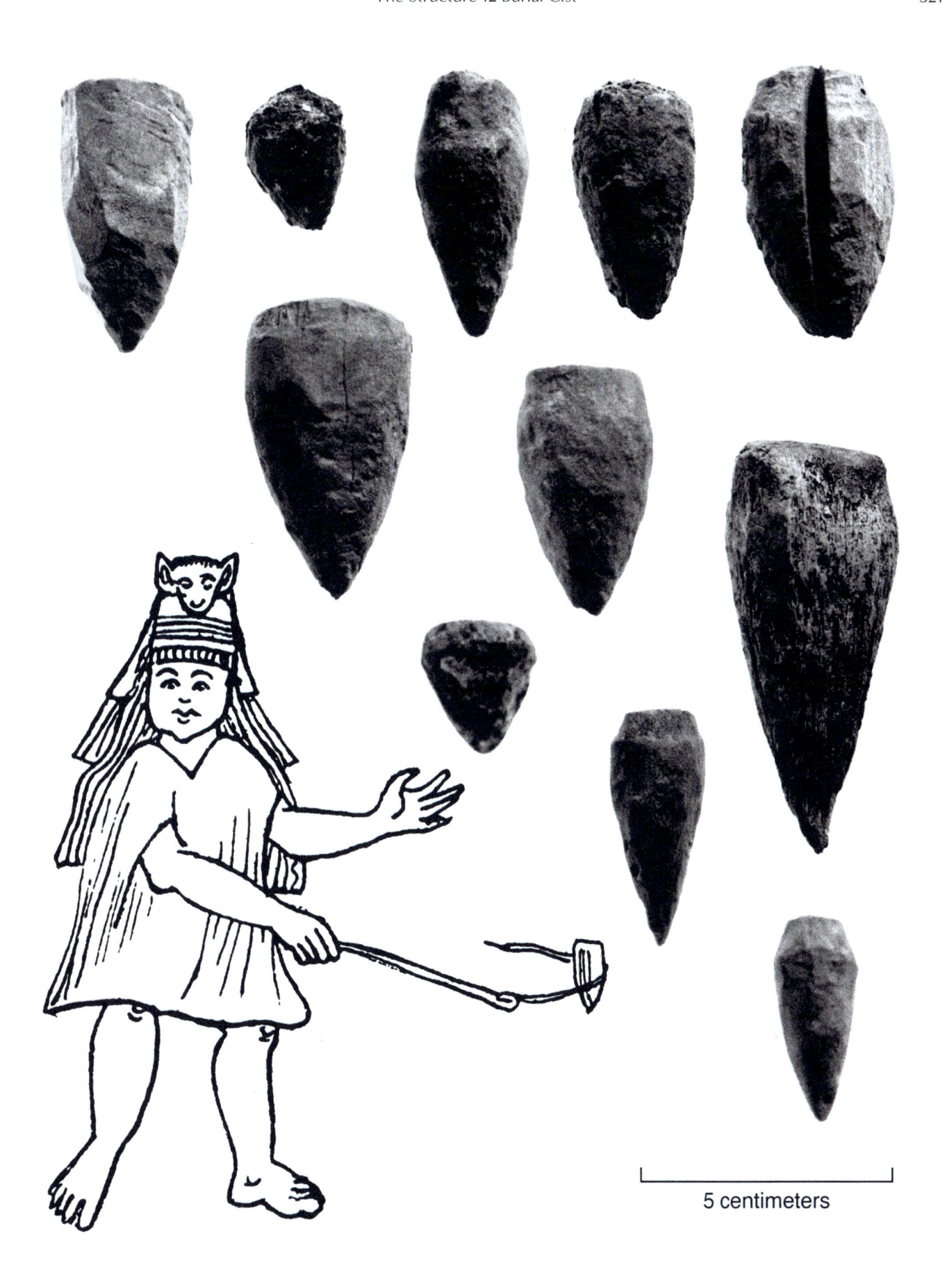

5 centimeters

The Quechua word for "top" has been variously given as *pisqoynyo, piscoynu,* or *pisqoyñu*. In speaking of Andean children, Kendall (1973:53) says that they were supposed to occupy themselves in useful ways, but "There were, however, a few simple toys and games"; as an example, she mentions that "*Pisqoynyo* was a top which was spun by whipping it with a lash." John Rowe (1946:288) also mentions that the Inca "made a top (*pisqoynyo*) which was spun by whipping." Cobo (1990:243) adds that "*piscoynu* was a game that corresponds to whipping and spinning a top."

The flat floors of Cerro Azul's *canchones* would have been appropriate venues for spinning tops. It seems likely to us that this might have been a form of play engaged in by children whose mothers were weaving in the *canchón*.

Two other artifacts found at Cerro Azul may reflect the activities of children in the *canchones*: I am thinking specifically of small, fully dressed figurines and "practice webs." In the Northeast Canchón of Structure D we found several wooden tops, as well as one tiny fully dressed figurine (see Figure 5.12d). In addition to a weaving sword just over a meter in length, yarn balls, backstrap loom stakes, spindles, and a woolen bag (Figure 16.24a), this storage bin in the Northeast Canchón contained multiple "practice webs" that might have been produced by young girls who were learning to embroider (Figures 16.24b and 16.24c).

The all-woolen bag was created from a textile measuring 21 x 14 cm, carefully folded in half. The bag had both a drawstring and decorated edging. The edging or piping around the bag was a 5.5 mm circular *soumak* that featured white, dark brown, and black diamonds.

Inside the storage bin associated with the Northeast Canchón we found some clear practice webs. One, shown in Figure 16.24b, is a piece of cloth 23 x 10.5 cm with two side selvages and two end selvages. Designated Textile 111b, it is an all-cotton cloth, except for the decorative wool embroidery showing colorful triangular fish in red, gold, dark brown, and yellow-brown yarns. When I showed two Quechua-speaking weavers this textile, they both described it as an "embroidery effort," done by "a beginner just practicing"; they based their conclusions on the placement of the embroidered figures and the presence of one very crude fish.

Another of the "practice webs" from the same storage bin can be seen in Figure 16.24c. Designated Textile 148b, it is a plain weave cloth with embroidered designs; the cloth strip has two side selvages and two end selvages. The warp and weft are cotton and show variable thickness, which my informants described as "the result of less-than-skilled spinning." The thread used for embroidery was light brown cotton, S-Z, and 0.5 mm thick; the work shows at least one case of split yarn and one error in stitching. The inexpert motif consists of two small birds with triangular elements.

Given the aforementioned circumstantial evidence from the Northeast Canchón of Structure D and its associated storage bin, I suspect that the women engaged in weaving there were accompanied by their children, some of whom (girls?) practiced embroidery and others of whom (boys?) played with tops.

Musical Instrument

Structure 12 also included a damaged *quena* or flute, made from a hollow cane tube (Figure 16.25). When complete, this flute would have been longer than 16.17 cm. The flute has seven finger holes, each 5 to 6 mm in diameter. A second flute from Cerro Azul, found by Kroeber (1937:250), was 19.5 cm long and had seven stops.

Workbasket Contents

We found the contents of one or two disintegrated workbaskets strewn across the floor of Structure 12 (Figures 16.26–16.30). Included in these remains were the following:
— one complete spindle (Figure 16.26, top). This spindle held 8 g of extremely fine white yarn. The spindle is 27.7 cm long and has a maximum diameter of 4 mm.
— fragment of a weaving sword, 12.4 cm long (Figure 16.26, second from the top).
— one spindle (Figure 16.26), 18.9 cm long and 3.2 mm in diameter. Its faded barcode is white and red.
— one spindle (Figures 16.26, 16.29), 26 cm long and with a diameter of 3.5 mm. Its barcode consists of narrow black stripes and wide yellow and brown bands.
— one spindle (Figure 16.26), 21.5 cm long and with a diameter of 3.6 mm.
— one complete spindle (Figure 16.27), holding at least 13 g of light brown yarn (7.5 YR 6/4).
— one complete spindle (Figure 16.27), holding ca. 10 g of extremely fine yarn, with a Munsell color of 2.5 YR 3/ 4 ("dark reddish brown").
— one complete spindle (Figure 16.27), holding ca. 8 g of very fine yarn, colored 10 YR 8/4 ("very pale brown").
— one painted spindle (Figures 16.27, 16.29) whose barcode features black and white bands.

Figure 16.24. The women of Structure D at Cerro Azul did their weaving in the Northeast Canchón and kept their equipment in Collca 1, a nearby storage bin (Marcus 2008: Figs. 5.1, 6.1, and 6.3). Included were loom parts, a woolen bag with drawstring (a), and "practice webs" showing embroidered fish (b) and birds (c). Many of the toys shown in Figure 16.23 were also found in the Northeast Canchón.

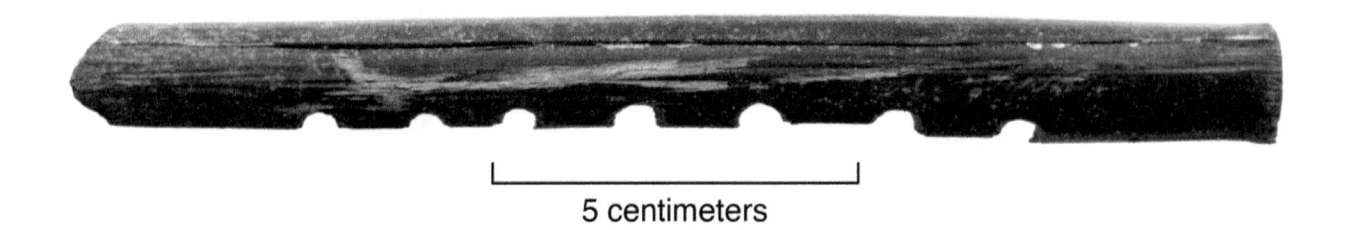

Figure 16.25. A broken *quena* or flute from Structure 12. This was one of two flutes found at Cerro Azul.

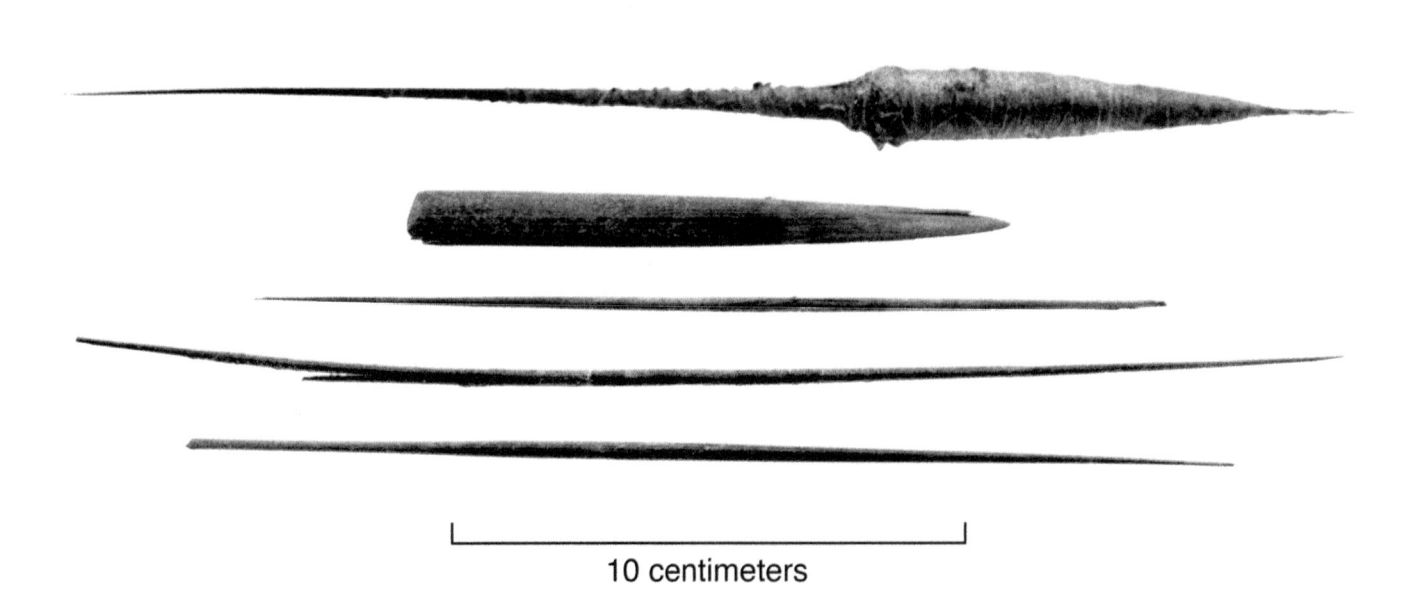

Figure 16.26. Some of the contents of a disintegrated workbasket found in Structure 12. The topmost item is a spindle holding ca. 8 g of yarn; the second is a fragment of broken weaving sword. Below are three spindles, one of which shows traces of a painted barcode.

The Structure 12 Burial Cist 325

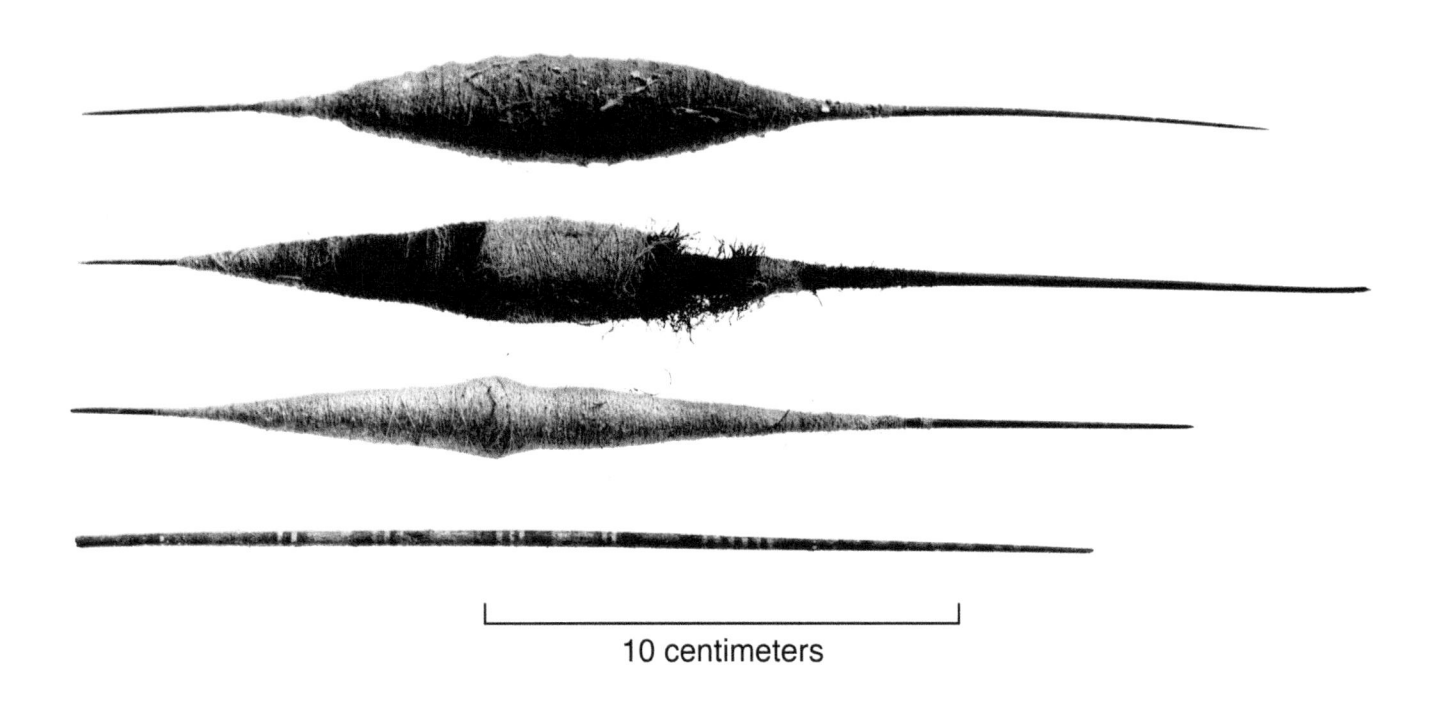

Figure 16.27. Additional contents of a disintegrated workbasket found in Structure 12: three spindles holding yarn, and one spindle painted with a barcode.

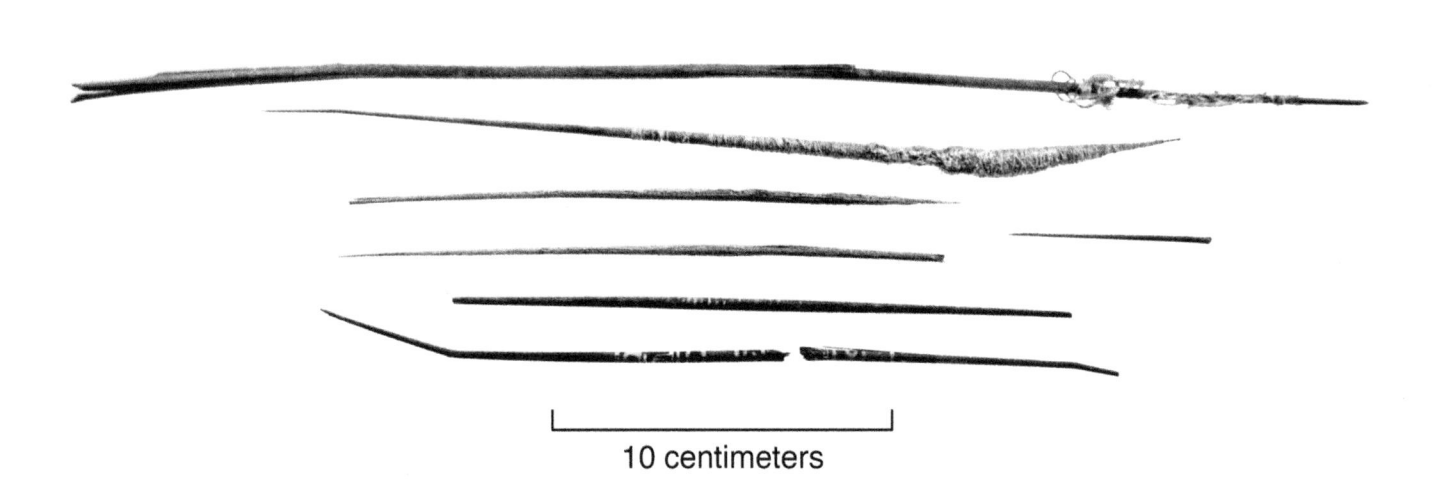

Figure 16.28. More spindles from a disintegrated workbasket found in Structure 12. Note that some spindles were barcoded.

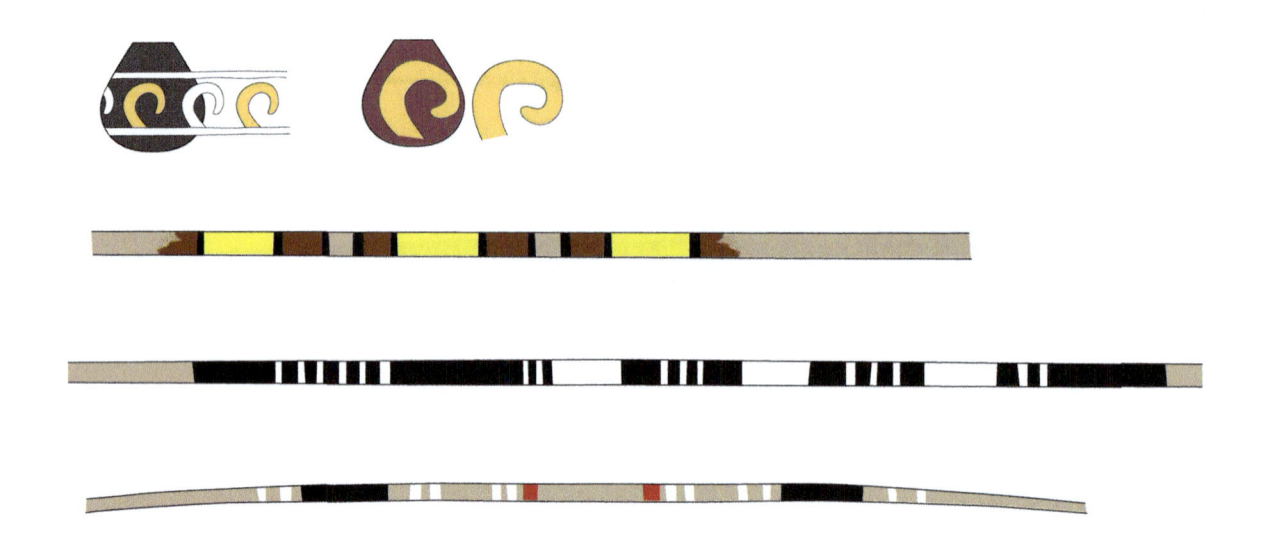

Figure 16.29. Artist's rendering of some of the spindles and whorls from Structure 12. Two whorls were painted with yellow hooks or spirals; all three spindles are painted with different barcodes, suggesting that the owner of the workbasket sometimes exchanged spindles with her co-workers.

Figure 16.30. Three yarn balls from one of the disintegrated workbaskets found in Structure 12. The smallest (at the top) consists of yarn wrapped around a segment of corncob 1.5 cm in diameter. At the lower left is a ball of white yarn; at the lower right is a ball of white yarn dyed blue.

Figure 16.31. Structure 12, as it looked after all salvage operations had been completed.

—large spindle (Figure 16.28), broken; a maximum diameter of 0.5 mm; bearing one gram of very fine yarn, 0.2 mm in diameter.
—painted spindle (Figure 16.28), bearing two grams of fine white thread.
—two plain spindles, and the tip of a third (Figure 16.28).
—one broken, painted spindle (Figure 16.28).
—painted spindle (Figures 16.28), broken but apparently complete; its barcode features both yellow spirals and black and brown bands.

Figure 16.29 shows two painted whorls and three barcoded spindles; the whorls have yellow hooks or spirals, and each painted spindle bears a different barcode.

Three of the well-preserved yarn balls are shown in Figure 16.30. The smallest consists of yarn wrapped around a corncob segment 1.5 cm in diameter; together, the yarn and corncob weigh 1.5 g. At the lower left in Figure 16.30 is a ball of white yarn 4.5 cm in diameter. At the lower right is a ball of white yarn dyed blue, 4 cm in diameter, weighing 21 g.

Figure 16.31 shows Structure 12 empty, after we had salvaged everything we could.

Comments on Structure 12

Structure 12 was a multiperson burial. Bones left inside and scattered nearby include those of men, women, and children. Many of the associated grave goods are similar to those seen in Quebrada 5a. However, Structure 12 included a few items not present in any of the Quebrada 5a burials, such as a possible medicine bundle, a large silver disc, a flute, and a child's wooden top.

Part V

Cerro Azul's Burials in Regional and Historical Perspective

Chapter 17

Mortuary Archaeology and Andean Culture

Having done our best to salvage Cerro Azul's burials, let us now try to place them in the context of mortuary analysis and Andean ethnohistory. These burials should contribute to our understanding of men's and women's identity and division of labor. To be sure, looted burials present more challenges than undisturbed burials, both in documentation and interpretation. Burial offerings may be broken or missing, human remains commingled, and many objects not assignable to a specific individual (e.g., Adams and Byrd 2008; Adams and Konigsberg 2008; Bongers 2019; Bongers et al. 2018, 2022; Boz and Hager 2014; Dalton 2020, Dalton et al. 2022b; Gerdau-Radonic and Herrera 2010; Lozada et al. 2013; Lozada and O'Donnabhain 2013; Parker Pearson 1993, 1999, 2002; Rengifo Chunga and Castillo Butters 2015; Weinberg et al. 2015).

Linking objects to a specific individual is usually crucial if we want to offer convincing interpretations about that individual's identity, and given that many of Cerro Azul's burials had been looted it was often difficult to establish such associations. Fortunately, in spite of all the information that had been lost, the Cerro Azul burials not only reinforce inferences made by investigators working in other coastal cemeteries, but also provide new insights about the society of A.D. 1000 to 1470.

Important Steps in Mortuary Archaeology

Most scholars rightly cite James Brown's 1971 memoir, entitled *Approaches to the Social Dimensions of Mortuary Practices*, as a turning point in the field of mortuary archaeology (e.g., Chapman 2003; O'Shea 1984; O'Shea 1995:125). One reason is that it focused on a social framework, rather than simply using burials to establish a chronological sequence (J. Rowe 1962). In Brown's edited memoir, Binford (1971:14–15) proposed the following: "other things being equal, the heterogeneity in mortuary practice which is characteristic of a single socio-cultural unit would vary directly with the complexity of the status hierarchy, as well as the complexity of the overall organization of the society with regard to membership units and other forms of sodalities."

Binford (1971:17) evaluated this hypothesis in the second part of his chapter. He argued that we have to consider the social persona, "a composite of the social identities maintained in life and recognized as appropriate for consideration at death." The main dimensions of the social persona were age, sex, social position, status, and subgroup affiliation. Binford tested his hypothesis against societies drawn from the Human Relations Area Files. He used ethnographic data to search for cross-cultural generalizations and link mortuary practices to social organization. Notably, however, he did not utilize archaeological data. That task has been undertaken by many others, including Saxe (1970), Brown (1971a, 1971b), and O'Shea (1984, 1995).

Rather than buying into Binford's framework, Parker Pearson (1982) argued that burials do not directly reflect status and wealth, but rather reflect the agenda and budget of the living, who manipulate the dead for their own purposes. Parker Pearson and other postprocessualists often looked at society from the bottom up, viewing descendants and individuals as the active agents. Instead of focusing on the deceased's status, they featured symbolism, economics, beliefs, and meanings. By 1995 Brown accepted that his 1971 position, whereby treatment at death was determined by status in life, might apply in some situations but not all. For example, it might obtain when relatives wanted to retain inherited rights and offices (Brown 1995). Brown also presents examples of societies that used ancestors to validate claims to critical resources. Charles and Buikstra (1983:119–120) add important propositions that (1) corporate groups will be distinguished by inclusion in separate cemeteries or distinct areas within a single cemetery, and (2) inclusion of individuals in the cemetery implies inclusion of those individuals in the corporate group. Brown concludes by calling for analysis of the total set of funerary rites, not just a narrow focus on the contents of a grave. The Andean coast lends itself to this kind of holistic analysis.

To understand both the living and the dead in the Andes, we often turn to ethnographic monographs and ethnohistoric documents to complement what we learn from archaeology. One enlightening ethnohistoric passage about the active role of mourners is revealed in a sixteenth-century work by Bartolomé de Las Casas (2010[1550]). In discussing Andean mummy bundles, he says that a narrator stood next to the bundle to relate the accomplishments and deeds of the deceased; this rite was accompanied by sad melodies played on the flute. Mourners came with objects in their hands, including cloth that they placed on the bundle, all the while crying and singing. The mourners made offerings of food and placed other objects useful in life with the mummy bundle. These offerings were later renewed inside the tomb.

In this example, it is clear that the contents of mummy bundles could be augmented or altered by mourners; thus, we should consider the roles played by the deceased, the mourners, and the community (e.g., Buikstra 1995; Deetz and Dethlefsen 1971). Furthermore, although burials in one society (or one era) may primarily reflect the deceased's status, profession, or gender, in another society there might be less correspondence.

Another key point is that mortuary practices change over time. Those changes often co-occur with other kinds of change, especially economic and sociopolitical. In other words, some mortuary practices may have endured from the Late Intermediate Period to the Inca era, but new rites also emerged in tandem with the Inca conquest and the reorganization of subjects and local societies (e.g., Bongers et al. 2022; Dalton 2020; and Dalton et al. 2022a, b).

Archaeological Examples that Contribute to Gender Studies

Andean archaeology supplies abundant information on mortuary rites and gender identity; it is a region where being buried with certain implements can convey or reinforce identity. Many such associations are described by sixteenth and seventeenth-century sources (e.g., Arriaga 1621; see also Costin 1993, 1998, 2018; Murra 1962, 1975). In speaking of women, Murra (1962:711) says, "she spun the thread and made most of the cloth in which she dressed herself and her family and took the spindle into her grave as a symbol of womanly activity." Writing in 1616 about items placed in Andean burials, Arriaga (1968[1621]:27–28) says: "they leave with them [in the grave] the implements they [the deceased] used during their lifetime. The women have their spindles and skeins of spun cotton, the men their *tacllas* or hoes to work the fields, or the weapons they used in war."

Speaking of coastal Peru in the nineteenth century, Thomas Hutchinson was one of the early archaeologists to note that slings often came from the graves of males; he says "with the men I generally found slings; and with the women almost invariably needles and buttons, frequently some woollen thread and a distaff" [a distaff was used in spinning and often had fibers wound around it] (Hutchinson 1874:312).

Even before Hutchinson and other early excavators found slings with boys and men, and looms, workbaskets, needles, spindles, and whorls with women, archaeologists had been thinking about gender-specific artifacts and the sexual division of labor. When infants and children were found with these items, archaeologists sometimes used the latter to infer the sex of the child (e.g., Dorsey 1894; Hutchinson 1874; Reiss and Stübel 1880–1887; Safford 1917; Squier 1869; and Uhle 1903). That era, to be sure, occurred before biological anthropologists came along to study the skeletons and determine the biological sex of burials.

Murra (1962:711), in speaking of the Inca and early Colonial era, differentiated the "ideal" from the "actual" when he said that:

> in practice, the sexual division of labor was less rigidly defined. Spinning and weaving skills were learned in childhood by both girls and boys. While wives and mothers were expected to tend to their families' clothing needs, all those who were 'exempted' from the *mitta* labor services—old men and cripples and children—helped out by spinning and making rope, weaving sacks and "rough stuff" according to strength and ability. Modern ethnologic research confirms this impression: both sexes weave, but different fabrics. Specialized craftsmen tended to be, and still are men.

Abundant research has demonstrated that although the division of labor along gender lines was often how work was organized in prehistoric societies, such gender-specific idealized roles did not always play out as rigidly as idealized. The Late Intermediate era was probably no different. Thus, objects selected for inclusion in graves can reinforce idealized male and female identities, but do not necessarily do so at every site, every time period, or in every burial.

Nineteenth-century excavations continue to offer insights on gender and the objects buried with each. In 1869, in *Frank Leslie's Illustrated Newspaper*, Ephraim George Squier published an account of his 1864 excavations at Pachacamac. In one grave he found five individuals, which he interpreted as a family consisting of a man, his wife, a daughter about 14, a son some years younger, and an infant. Buried with the father was a fishing net, fishing lines of various sizes, copper hooks, copper sinkers, corn on the cob, and a piece of copper that had been left in his mouth. "This was all discovered belonging exclusively to the fisherman, except that suspended by a thread around his neck was a bronze tweezers, for plucking out the beard…" (Squier 1967[1869]:212).

Squier describes the man's wife as having long hair and holding a comb in one hand and a fan with feathers in the other. Around her neck were triple strands of shells, and resting between her torso and her bent knees was her spinning paraphernalia—a spindle half covered with spun thread, which connected to a mass of raw cotton "as if death had overtaken the matron with her last task of industry in life but half finished." In addition to the evidence for spinning, this woman was buried with a "wallet" containing lima beans, locks of cotton, two discs of silver, and tiny beads of chalcedony.

When Squier found a child with a sling tightly bound around its head, he inferred that this was the body of a boy. When he found an infant with a seashell containing pebbles, he inferred that the infant was a girl with a rattle. When Squier found a child sitting on a workbasket, he assumed that this was the body of a girl. In the workbasket were a fan, a comb, needlecases, needles, strips of cloth, spindles, skeins, threads, bags, the hollow bones of a pelican (or other large bird) with wads of cotton plugging each of them, a pigment palette, and a pestle and mortar to grind pigment. "There were many other curious things in the poor, withered girl's work-box," such as a badly crushed gold ornament, bronze needles, a bronze knife, and a *mallero* which Squier interpreted as "indicating that, like a good daughter, the girl of Pachacamac helped make nets for her father." Finally, there were silver spangles on the headband wrapped around the head and a dried parrot between her feet. Although many of Squier's inferences have been confirmed by more than a century of excavations, today we would want a biological anthropologist to confirm Squier's guesses about the sex of each individual.

Another example of inferring gender from associated objects comes from Dorothy Menzel. Some scholars have cited Menzel (1977:14) as providing evidence that men could be buried with workbaskets, so let us look at the evidence. Menzel was not actually reporting on her own excavations, but rather interpreting Uhle's 1901 excavations in the Ica Valley. She started her interpretation of two sacrificial burials, Td-1 and Td-2, by saying that "neither has been identified by sex." To this day, no biological anthropologist has studied these skeletons to determine their sex. Menzel says that Td-1 had a belt or sash, a twill workbasket, a cloth "two feet square," and two pottery vessels (a jar and a bowl filled with peanuts). The other burial, Td-2, was associated with ear ornaments, a sling, a workbasket, and coca leaves wrapped in a finely woven cotton cloth "two feet square." Menzel says, "at least one of them may have been a woman, as suggested by an item of apparel," allowing for the possibility that both were women; however, she then goes on to say that Td-2 "was almost certainly that of a man." Apparently, she inferred this from an x-ray that seems to show that the individual was wearing ear ornaments and associated with a sling. (As a point of comparison, a prominent woman with elaborate ear ornaments was buried in a tomb at the Castillo de Huarmey in the Huarmey Valley, so the presence of ear ornaments in some periods was more an indicator of status and could be worn by both women and men [Więckowski 2019]).

Because Td-2 had a workbasket with weaving and sewing equipment, Menzel goes on to say, "This probably means that both men and women could engage in weaving and sewing, though such activities may have been done for different purposes or in different contexts." Why not also consider the possibility that Td-2 was a woman with a sling, since women are known to use slings? The bottom line is that we cannot know the sex of Td-1 or Td-2 until biological anthropologists study their skeletons; it is always risky to deduce biological sex from objects in the grave (Marcus 1978:130).

The Ychsma polity, whose capital was Pachacamac, has yielded Late Intermediate mummies that have been studied by biological anthropologists. Men were interred with slings, tweezers, loincloths, and *unkus* or tunics; women were buried with looms, spindles, spindle whorls, workbaskets, *tupus*, and metal strips held in the women's hands (e.g., Díaz Arriola 2015; Eeckhout and Owens 2015).

Changes Over Time: Late Intermediate versus Late Horizon

There are noteworthy differences between Late Intermediate mortuary practices (A.D. 1000–1470) and those of the Inca era (A.D. 1470–1534). One example of Late Horizon practices can be seen at the coastal site of Puruchuco-Huaquerones in the Rímac Valley, a site located on land once controlled by the Late Intermediate *señorío* of Lati. The palace of Puruchuco, built during the Late Intermediate as the residence of the local lord, was remodeled in the Late Horizon. In their analysis of 1,300 Late Horizon mummies, Haun and Cock Carrasco (2010) showed that roughly half were of women from the highlands, while two-thirds of the men were from the coast. This movement of highland women to the coast had been occurring during the Late Intermediate but such movement substantially increased in the Late Horizon, showing that the Inca could expand or amplify an existing practice. The mummy bundles at the site show a great deal of variation, but the vast majority were accompanied by tools relating to textile manufacture.

Absent from the cemetery were potters' tools, farmers' hoes, and metallurgical tools.

Both Late Horizon men and women have been found with weaving tools or with spun fibers of cotton and wool. One possible explanation is that whole families had to get involved in order to meet the high demands for cloth imposed by the Inca. In Late Horizon, as well as in Colonial times, Diez de San Miguel (1964:61) says that old men, children, and others not capable of hard work helped with the plying (final twisting) of yarn.

Other cases of community specialization existed in the Late Horizon. For example, near Puruchuco-Huaquerones is the site of Rinconada Alta, which provides evidence for specialization in metal smelting (Frame et al. 2004). A third Late Horizon site, Cerro Puruchuco, was found nearby; there, Cock's excavations revealed abundant flutes, panpipes, and agricultural implements left with the burials, but only a few weaving implements (Haun and Cock Carrasco 2010:205).

Haun and Cock Carrasco argue that the Inca's increased demands for cloth could have caused *curacas* or local lords to instigate the changes we see, such as aggregating weavers at Puruchuco-Huaquerones and burying both men and women with spinning or weaving implements. By concentrating more highland weavers in his community, the local lord could meet Inca demands and still maintain his status (Haun and Cock Carrasco 2010; Spurling 1992; Urton and Chu 2018).

For the Inca, the production of cloth was intimately tied to notions of control, both of people and resources; this control could be direct (when girls were brought from the provinces to live and work in the *akllawasi* under the watchful eye of Inca administrators) or indirect (when local lords were left in place and authorized to organize labor to produce more cloth for the state) (Murra 1962, 1989; Niles 1992:51).

The Inca created a new institution, the *akllawasi* ("House of the Chosen Women"), so that girls and women would live and work together under state control. Ethnohistoric sources say that the "chosen women" were taught spinning, weaving, cooking, and *chicha* making. Cobo (1990) and Guaman Poma de Ayala (1980[1615]:300) note that after four years of instruction, these girls were ready to serve as *mamakuna* or "consecrated women"; while some continued to reside in the *akllawasi*, others were given as wives to nobles that the Inca emperor wished to befriend (Cobo 1990:172; Morris 1998; Silverblatt 1987). Although these *akllawasi* were more common in the highlands, the Inca seem to have established both a Temple of the Sun and an *akllawasi* at the coastal site of Huacones-Vilcahuasi, a site in the Cañete Valley that is approximately equidistant from Cerro del Oro and Canchari (Areche Espinola 2019; Campos Napán 2007; Larrabure y Unanue 1935[1893], Vol. II:309–321). In other coastal valleys, however, the Inca seem to have delegated the task of overseeing weavers to the *curacas* or local lords (Costin 2016; Haun and Cock Carrasco 2010).

Costin (2016) has discussed in some detail the Inca's increased demand for cloth. She contrasts the Late Intermediate era (when textile production was a household activity, motivated by family needs) to the Late Horizon (when the Inca Empire imposed top-down demands). "Regarding the sex/gender of LIP [Late Intermediate Period] domestic textile producers," Costin says, "we can turn to the burial data." "Of sexed adults from a range of cemeteries throughout the empire, only females had tools related to textile production (loom parts, weaving baskets, and/or spindle whorls), although not all female burials contained these items" (Costin 2016:35–36). Based on this evidence, we see that Late Intermediate women were more likely to be buried with weaving implements; in contrast, Late Horizon burials of both men and women could include artifacts used in cloth manufacture (Haun and Cock Carrasco 2010).

During Late Intermediate times, the women in most communities could probably meet their family's needs for cloth; by Late Horizon times, some communities had added male weavers to meet the increasing demands imposed by the Inca. For example, Costin (1993, 2018) has shown that the number of tools associated with textile production doubled in Wanka elite households during Inca times. As demand increased, women, men, commoners, and elite all contributed in some way to the many stages of cloth production, "yet spinning and weaving were largely women's work, and, indeed, making cloth was the iconic female activity" (Costin 2018:13).

The idealized social identity of women was similar in both Late Intermediate and Late Horizon times; they were regarded as spinners and weavers (Costin 2016; Guaman Poma de Ayala 1980; Murra 1975). This gender association had time depth and symbolic importance. "Whether or not women were the primary—or only—cloth producers in actuality, the fact that the close association between women and weaving was so consistently reinforced in charged settings such as mortuary contexts suggests there was symbolic importance in this connection" (Costin 2016:36–37). Such was the importance of establishing identity in death that some looms—made specifically for inclusion in the graves of women—were not even functional (Skinner 1975:69).

The Impact of the Inca Conquest on Local Ethnic Groups

As is well known, the Inca conquest led to the reorganization of local populations, the relocation of whole communities, the exaction of labor service, and the establishment of new institutions (Covey 2006, 2015; Morris and von Hagen 2011; Murra 1975; J. Rowe 1946). Ethnohistoric documents indicate that the Inca utilized diverse strategies to administer scores of other ethnic groups, each of whom had skills of interest to the Inca (Burger et al. 2007; Malpass and Alconini 2010; Marcus 2017).

The Inca insisted that each ethnic group wear distinctive attire so that they could be identified and confined to their region, unable to flee the demands for their labor service (Alconini 2004; Burger et al. 2007; Covey 2006, 2015; D'Altroy 1992, 2002; Malpass 1993; Malpass and Alconini 2010; Murra 1975, 1980; Shimada 2015).

Niles (1992:53) notes that clothing was an important statement of its wearer's social identity, and that people in different towns were expected to retain their native costumes. Betanzos ([1551], *primera parte*, chapter 40, 1987:179; Betanzos 1996) tells us that when the Inca emperor Huayna Capac assumed office, he sent emissaries to visit the provinces to deliver Inca-style clothes as gifts. The new emperor visited each province shortly thereafter, but before he entered a provincial town he was met by the local lord, who gave him the regional attire; the emperor then dressed himself in the local style, so that he would look as if he were a native when he met its townspeople. John Murra (1989:293) emphasized that such gifts of cloth were initiated by the king and served as "the initial pump-priming step in a dependent relationship."

Changes in the economy imposed by the Inca especially affected the lives of *curacas* (local lords) and their role in arranging marriages. Those marriages often came to be orchestrated by Inca officials, and brideservice became a key component of Inca state policy. As Gose (2000:92–93) notes:

> There was a dramatic asymmetry in how marriage changed the lives of Andean men and women. For women, it meant downward mobility, removing them from the ranks of the aqllas [chosen women] in which they were identified with the state, and returning them to obscurity in the ranks of the tributary populations. For men, however, marriage

was key in the status transformation from marginalized bachelor into recognized adult. … By establishing itself as a force capable not only of bestowing but also withholding women, the Inka state politically actualized the "wife-giver" position. … By conspicuously providing its tributaries with food and drink, the Inka state culturally elaborated its role as provider and partially displaced the household as a unit of consumption. … By making brideservice a vehicle of state policy, the Inkas also prevented households from emerging as an ideologically "private" domain.

In addition to creating a new category of female workers (the "chosen women") who lived in a well-guarded *akllawasi*, the Inca Empire created the *qompicamayoc*. These *qompicamayoc* (or *cumbicamayoc*) were said to be the weavers of the finest cloth. By A.D. 1562 in the Huánuco census, we see that some of the weavers listed were men and some were widows (Levine 1987; Murra 1972). Although John Rowe (1979:239) maintains that only men wove *cumbi*, Murra (1980:73), Niles (1992:52), and Stone-Miller (1992b:172–173) argue that the "chosen women" were the ones who wove *cumbi*. *Cumbi* was a finer cloth restricted to garments worn by "the kings, the great lords, and all the nobility of the kingdom, and the common people could not use it" (Cobo Book II, Chapter 11; Cobo 1990:225).

Of great significance is the fact that *cumbi* cloth was not woven on a backstrap loom, but rather on a vertical frame of four poles built against a wall (Guaman Poma de Ayala 1980, tomo 2:81; Stone-Miller 1992a: Fig. 1.14); *cumbi* weavers worked on large cloths, and did so while standing (Cobo 1890–1895, Book 14, Chapter 11; Garcilaso 1966, part 1, Book 5, Chapter 6; Guaman Poma de Ayala 1980:647). Weaving wide tapestries was a task that could even involve three or four men at the same time; it was thus different from the work of the backstrap weaver, who sat on the ground while creating narrow belts, bands, and tapestry strips. The number of *qompicamayoc*—the specialists weaving fine cloth on vertical looms—seems to have been amplified by the Inca, so that labor would be easier to control and much more cloth could be produced.

All the looms found so far with Cerro Azul women were of the portable backstrap type. As noted by Hernández Escontrías (2016:84), "the condition of being a female weaver for the state or empire did not remain consistent across time." The huge cloth demands of the Inca (and later the Spaniards), as revealed in the ethnohistoric data, thus cannot be uncritically projected back in time to the Late Intermediate Period. It does not appear that the institution of "chosen women" and the exceptional top-down imperial demand for standardized garments existed before the Inca.

At the least, it appears that the Inca greatly amplified extant practices.

Standardization of Inca Garments

For many years, scholars have remarked on the impressive standardization and "austere geometry" of Inca and Late Horizon garments (e.g., Phipps 2015:197 and 2018; A. Rowe 1978, 1992, 1997; A. Rowe and J. Rowe 1996; J. Rowe 1979). For example, the Inca army dressed in standardized tunics, with a red yoke in the upper zone and a black-and-white checkerboard pattern in the lower zone (Morris and von Hagen 2011:99).

Scholars studying Inca clothing have typically relied on two lines of information: (1) the depictions of garments in Felipe Guaman Poma de Ayala's work and (2) the well-preserved *unkus* or men's tunics from Pachacamac or those stored in museums. Until the last two decades few scholars had spent equal time studying the standardization of garments worn by women, simply because fewer had been preserved. That situation changed with the discovery of textiles worn either by female figurines or by young girls found sacrificed at high-altitude ritual sites (Ceruti 2004; Duviols 1976; Eeckhout 2018; Morris and von Hagen 2011; Reinhard 2005; Reinhard and Ceruti 2010; Wilson et al. 2013).

Prior to these more recent discoveries, much of our archaeological information about women's dress was restricted to Max Uhle's 1903 excavations in the Temple of the Sacrificed Women at Pachacamac (Tiballi 2010; Uhle 1903; VanStan 1967; Wardle 1936). Since then, these studies of Late Horizon garments at Pachacamac, as well as fully dressed girls and female figurines on high-altitude mountaintops like Ampato and Llullaillaco, have provided new information on the woolen mantles, feathered headdresses, belts, *tupus*, and multicolored cords that held these female garments together.

The standardization of men's and women's attire was the result of imperial policies that specified the kinds of garments the Inca Empire needed in order to clothe official government personnel. To ensure this production of standardized garments, the Inca plucked girls out of the provinces at ages 10 to 12 (Cobo 1990:172), and then secluded them in well-guarded *akllawasi* where the girls were taught how to spin and weave standardized garments. Guaman Poma de Ayala (1980[1615]) describes the tasks the Inca expected of these females: young girls were to gather flowers for dyeing; adolescents and elderly women were to spin yarn; and adult women were to weave (Zuidema 1990, 1991). Given women's seclusion and supervision by the *mamakuna*, it is not surprising that the clothing manufactured by and worn by Late Horizon females displayed greater uniformity of design and construction than garments worn by Late Intermediate women.

Honoring the Dead during Inca Times

Cobo (1990:42) says, "The dead were worshiped only by those who were descended from them in a direct line. Therefore, they took great care to worship their father, grandfather, and great-grandfather and so on as far back as their information reached." "When an Indian died, his relatives performed great lamentations and ceremonies before the burial, and if it was a lord and *cacique*, all of his vassals participated. These lamentations or funeral rites were longer or shorter according to the social status of the deceased" (Cobo 1990:250).

Ethnohistoric sources such as these provide key information on burials, though we must be cautious about projecting that information onto earlier times. Since mortuary practices do change, the Inca data can only be a starting place for comparison and contrast with the earlier archaeological record. It remains for archaeologists to determine which Late Intermediate burial practices endured, and which new practices emerged during the Late Horizon. One new practice emerging in the Late Horizon was that of threading human vertebrae on a reed or stick, a trait that Bongers et al. (2022) call "vertebrae-on-a-post" (see also Dalton et al. 2022b: Fig. 15). Stringing together vertebrae was a Late Horizon practice known for 192 individuals from coastal and mid-valley sites in the Chincha Valley, and this custom continued into the Colonial period.

The Social Persona of Men, Women, and Children

In state-level societies the roles played by men, women, and children are many. As we have seen, south coast graves were often multiperson—as early as Paracas times, if not earlier. However, even when a burial cist contained several people, each person was likely to be separately wrapped in his or her own mummy bundle (Tello and Mejía Xesspe 1979). If found intact, each bundle has the potential to tell a story about an individual, usually an adult.

Late Intermediate and Late Horizon Children

Although children were a key component of Andean families and communities, they tend to be underrepresented in ethnohistoric documents and in cemeteries. Often treated differently in life as well as in death, children were sometimes buried under a house floor or placed inside a jar; their grave goods were sometimes different from those associated with adults. In some cases, grave goods were entirely absent in the burials of infants and children.

At Pachacamac, for example, "age and status [were] irretrievably linked to one another in that children under the age of about seven do not appear to have been recognized as individuals in their own right; those above this age were buried with considerably more care and in conjunction with artefacts deposited as grave goods (perhaps reflecting their roles in life—such as weaving)" (Owens and Eeckhout 2015:183). Owens and Eeckhout report paleoentomological research indicating that some subadults were exposed in the open air for a time before burial. It is therefore possible that some deceased children may have been kept above ground for a while, eventually having their bodies added to the grave of an adult. It would be valuable in such cases to have DNA evidence regarding the possible relationship of the child and adult.

In the case of Burial K1 at Cerro Azul, 14 children were buried with four adults. Since it is unlikely that all 14 children died at the same time, it is possible that some of these children had been stored for a time. Although adding bodies gradually over time cannot be ruled out (e.g., Middleton et al. 1998; Millaire 2004; Miller 1995), Burial K1 at Cerro Azul does not appear to have been reopened; it would appear that all 18 individuals were buried at the same time.

The Late Intermediate treatment of deceased children at Cerro Azul contrasts with that of the Late Horizon children at Pachacamac. The latter lacked grave goods, while most of the infants and children at Cerro Azul *were* associated with grave goods. Some of the Cerro Azul children had metal packets inserted into their mouths, while others had been given an incised gourd, miniature ceramic vessels, seed bracelets or necklaces, or even a wooden top.

One possibility is that the Inca regarded children under seven as less than full members of society, and thus not in need of grave offerings. A child in Inca society did not receive its name until it reached one or two years of age; and on that occasion, the child's oldest "uncle" cut its hair and nails and carefully preserved them. A boy's "uncle" gave him a shield, a sling, and a mace at about 14 years of age, and at that time the child was also awarded a breechclout (*wara*) and a new name that replaced his former name; that ceremony for boys was called *waracikoy*, a term that included the word for breechclout (J. Rowe 1946:283, 1958).

Whether similar rites were conducted prior to the Late Horizon is not known. Rowe (1946:282) says that Inca children were considered a great economic asset and most "learned only by helping their parents, which they began to do almost as soon as they could walk."

How The Cerro Azul Data Contribute to Documenting Individual Style Preferences

The textiles of Late Intermediate Cerro Azul contrast with the more standardized versions woven in the Late Horizon. Typically, the Late Intermediate has been regarded as a time when women had greater individual freedom to create their own designs. Young-Sánchez (1992:49) says that "the fabrics of the Late Intermediate Period exhibit a liveliness and freedom quite foreign to some of the rigidly formal Wari and Inca styles of the Middle and Late Horizons." She notes that Late Intermediate women had wide scope for individual expression in the choice of color, pattern, and color sequencing; their designs were "adjusted at will" and "small filler motifs were arranged to suit the weaver's fancy." Young-Sánchez emphasizes the impressive variety and exuberance of the diverse and colorful motifs created by Late Intermediate women.

The above characterization is consistent with the Late Intermediate textiles we recovered from Cerro Azul burials. The women at Cerro Azul expressed themselves in their choice of motifs and colors, and even barcoded their spindles to personalize ownership. Individual style was especially evident in the *chumpis* and other fabrics a woman might be creating at the time of her death; often, her half-finished products were buried with her so she could complete them in the afterlife.

To establish a woman's personal style, we can look at the following:

1. her preferences in raw materials (camelid wool, cotton, bast, etc.)
2. her choice of colors
3. her sequencing of colors
4. her choice of designs and motifs
5. the items in her workbasket (dyed yarn balls; yarn still threaded in needles; yarn stored on spindles), especially if they match the yarns in the unfinished textile on her loom and any unfinished cords held in her hand
6. the barcoding that each woman painted on her own spindles
7. the contrast between her choices and those of other women buried nearby

The mummy bundles buried in Quebrada 5a provided us with the ideal opportunity to recognize individual style and personal choices made by each woman (Hill and Gunn 1977a, b). The mourners responsible for creating a woman's burial helped us in our recognition of individual style by including her unfinished weavings in her mummy bundle.

How the Cerro Azul Data Contribute to Gender Studies

Past mortuary studies have been concerned with the intersection of social roles, identity, status, age, and gender. Many ancient societies created idealized categories to reflect their views on the roles of men, women, and children. The ideal, to be sure, did not always match reality.

In some societies, men's identity and women's identity were associated with specific implements needed for the kinds of work they were expected to do. For example, a woman's identity might be exemplified by a potter's wheel, and a man's by a crucible for molten metal. However, both men and women might participate in different aspects of the same production sequence. For instance, although Navajo potters were considered to be women, men often helped with various facets of pottery production (e.g., Tschopik 1941:45). Women, nevertheless, got all the credit for making pottery, since pottery making was considered part of women's identity. Similarly, although Navajo men were traditionally associated with silversmithing, women participated in various stages. After considering the Navajo case, Kelly and Ardren (2016:9) concluded that "women's participation in silversmithing, which is not considered a female task, would not confer advantages to specialized production by women. A woman who invested more time or attention to silversmithing would not receive the same societal recognition or credit as a man who engages in the same tasks because her actions fall outside idealized gendered expectations."

The burials of Cerro Azul add to our understanding of the fishermen, weavers, and others who lived and worked in this community from A.D. 1000 to 1470. From the burials we learn that most fishermen used more than one kind of net, and that women—especially elite women—were associated with implements for spinning, weaving, and sewing. Elite women also had access to dyed camelid wool, which presumably came from farther away and was consequently more highly valued. For example, the women in Burial 4, with their gold foil, camelid wool bags, pigment pouches, and multiple slit tapestry *chumpis*, can be contrasted with women of lower status, buried with less elaborate cotton textiles. Interestingly, ceramics did not reflect social inequality as clearly; both high-status and low-status burials were likely to include the same kinds of jars and receive the same kinds of food in gourd bowls.

In other words, if one were to rely heavily on the number of ceramic vessels in a burial as the primary indicator of status, he or she might be misled; instead, at Cerro Azul, the number of woolen textiles and items of gold and silver were better indicators of status.

The gourd bowls found with the Cerro Azul burials —often filled with food—provide a cautionary tale for those of us who have worked in Mesoamerica. Gourds are not preserved there, and Mesoamericanists often rely heavily on ceramics to infer social identity and status. At Cerro Azul, even elite individuals might have their food for the afterlife left in a humble gourd bowl.

Who was Buried in the Quebradas of Cerro Azul?

Who was buried at Cerro Azul? The seven graves (totaling 37 individuals) that Kroeber excavated provided important background information for the University of Michigan's salvage efforts. For example, Kroeber found that even when grave offerings appeared to be meager, each individual in a multiperson grave might be buried with metal of some type in his or her mouth.

Kroeber had the advantage of finding his burials before the looters did; we did not. Even after looting, however, we were able to see that when a cist contained several people, each person was often wrapped separately in his or her own mummy bundle. We found that a specific mummy bundle could include a man with his breechclout and/or fishing nets, or a woman with her workbasket, loom, unfinished weavings, and a number of bags containing her personal possessions. We would like to have DNA evidence to establish the relationships of the men and women in each cist, but the bones were often so scattered that it is not clear whom we would be sampling.

The women's burials at Cerro Azul show us that (1) there was a regional Late Intermediate style of weaving, but (2) each woman had her own color and motif preferences. Each woman appears to have barcoded her spindles, but since women worked in groups in open patios, there were times when spindles were shared or exchanged. Once again, we wish we had DNA to establish the relationships of all the women in Burial 4.

We deplore the looting at Cerro Azul, but without it we would not have found these burials. We would know less about gender, status, identity, agency, individual color choices, and division of labor (see also Dobres and Robb 2000; Hodder 2000; Knapp and van Dommelen 2008; LeVine 1987; Sewell 1992).

To summarize the data we salvaged:

Some perishable items, such as camelid wool tapestries, may be better indicators of an individual's status than the ceramic vessels buried with that person.

Late Intermediate black amphorae—even the highly burnished variety—do not seem to be good indicators of status; they are simply a widespread diagnostic ware of the era (Figure 17.1).

Typical foods for the afterlife included protein sources (guinea pigs, sardines, and shellfish) and carbohydrate sources (maize and *lúcuma*).

Numerous textile motifs (such as fish and birds) were shared by the women buried at Cerro Azul and other coastal towns, and together they provide the basis for a "regional style."

Documenting the individual style of a woman is possible by studying the barcoded spindles and spindle whorls stored in an individual's workbasket at Cerro Azul.

Individual color choices and color sequencing are also evident when we compare the textiles of one woman to another.

Twill workbaskets, with their sewing and weaving implements, take on greater significance when their contents can be compared to unfinished textiles buried with the same person.

It seems likely that the tattoos on Late Intermediate women in coastal communities were also a component of their identity (see Allison et al. 1981; van Dalen Luna 1981; Vásquez et al. 2013). Although only one of the women at Cerro Azul had such tattoos, the subject is worthy of further study.

Like the mummy bundles at Ancón and elsewhere (see Dorsey 1894; Hutchinson 1874; Reiss and Stübel 1880–1887; Safford 1917; and Squier 1967[1869]), fishermen buried at Cerro Azul were likely to be associated with fishing nets, *malleros*, slings, and bolas.

Figure 17.1. Four miniature Camacho Black vessels, allegedly from the Cañete Valley, as exhibited in the Museo de Arqueología y Antropología, Pueblo Libre, Lima, Peru in 1985. Although no context or site provenience was given, these vessels resemble the black miniatures from Cerro Azul's Late Intermediate burials. All four may have been looted from Cerro Azul or some other site in the valley.

In contrast to women of the Inca era, the Late Intermediate women on Peru's south coast seem to have had significant freedom in selecting motifs, colors, and designs for their textiles. As Young-Sánchez (1992:49) notes, "the fabrics of the Late Intermediate Period exhibit a liveliness and freedom quite foreign to some of the rigidly formal styles" of the Late Horizon.

As Donnan (2022:138) has noted, "The looting of antiquities always results in a tragic loss of information about the past, but turning away when looted material can be recorded only compounds the loss." In fact, salvage excavations are more important than ever today, since cemeteries are being destroyed at an alarming and accelerated pace. By presenting the material we salvaged at Cerro Azul, we hope to inspire others to turn looted cemeteries into sources of useful information.

References

A

Acosta, José de
1954[1590]. Historia natural y moral de las Indias. *Biblioteca de Autores Españoles*, Tomo 73. Ediciones Atlas, Madrid.
2002[1590]. *Natural and Moral History of the Indies*. Edited by Jane E. Mangan, translated by Frances López Morillas. Duke University Press, Durham, North Carolina.

Adams, Bradley J. and John E. Byrd, editors
2008. *Recovery, Analysis, and Identification of Commingled Human Remains*. Humana Press, Totowa, New Jersey.

Adams, Bradley J. and Lyle W. Konigsberg
2008. How many people? Determining the number of individuals represented by commingled human remains. In *Recovery, Analysis, and Identification of Commingled Human Remains*, edited by Bradley J. Adams and John E. Byrd, pp. 241–256. Humana Press, Totowa, New Jersey.

Agai, Jock M.
2015. Resurrection imageries: a study of the motives for extravagant burial rituals in ancient Egypt. *Verbum et Ecclesia* 36(1), Article #1457, pp. 1–7.

Aguirre Morales, Manuel
2008. Arqueología y etnohistoria de los periodos tardíos del valle de Chilca-Cañete-Lima. In *Arqueología de la costa centro sur peruana*, edited by Omar Pinedo and Henry Tantaleán, pp. 147–180. Avqui Ediciones, Lima.

Aland, Amanda
2018. Fishing economies and ethnic specialization under Inca rule. In *The Oxford Handbook of the Incas*, edited by Sonia Alconini and Alan Covey, pp. 247–262. Oxford University Press, New York.

Alconini, Sonia
2004. The southeastern Inka frontier against the Chiriguanos: Structure and dynamics of the Inka imperial borderlands. *Latin American Antiquity* 15:389–418.

Allen, Catherine J.
1982. Body and soul in Quechua thought. *Journal of Latin American Lore* 8(2):179–196.
1988. *The Hold Life Has: Coca and Cultural Identity in an Andean Community*. Smithsonian Institution Press, Washington, D.C.
2015. Worship, ancestors. In *Encyclopedia of the Incas*, edited by Gary Urton and Adriana von Hagen, pp. 304–307. Rowman and Littlefield, Lanham, Maryland.

Allison, Marvin J., Guillermo Focacci, Bernardo Arriaza, Vivien Standen, Mario Rivera, and Jerold M. Lowenstein
1984. Chinchorro, momias de preparación complicada: métodos de momificación. *Chungara, Revista de Antropología Chilena* 13:155–173. Universidad de Tarapacá, Arica, Chile.

Allison, Marvin J., Lawrence Lindberg, Calogero Santoro, and Guillermo Focacci
1981. Tatuajes y pintura corporal de los indígenas precolombinos de Perú y Chile. *Chungara, Revista de Antropología Chilena* 7:218–225. Universidad de Tarapacá, Arica, Chile.

Alva, Walter and Christopher B. Donnan
  1993. *Royal Tombs of Sipán*. Fowler Museum of Cultural History, University of California at Los Angeles.

Aponte Miranda, Delia
  2000. La vestimenta femenina en la costa central del Perú durante el período Intermedio Tardío. *Estudios Atacameños* 20:91–101.
  2006. Presentación de los materiales del fardo funerario 290 de Wari Kayán, Paracas Necrópolis. *Arqueológicas* 27:9–99.

Appadurai, Arjun
  1986. *The Social Life of Things: Commodities in Cultural Perspective*. Cambridge University Press, Cambridge, UK.

Areche Espinola, Rodrigo
  2019. Las primeras evidencias arqueológicas de Huacones-Vilcahuasi, Cañete, Perú. *Actas del V Congreso Nacional de Arqueología*, Volumen I, pp. 187–197. Ministerio de Cultura, Perú.

Arriaga, Pablo Joseph de
  1621. Extirpación de la idolatria del Piru. Geronymo de Contreras, Lima, Peru.
  1968[1621]. *The Extirpation of Idolatry in Peru*. Translated and edited by L. Clark Keating. University of Kentucky Press, Lexington.

Arriaza, Bernardo T.
  1995a. Chinchorro bioarchaeology: chronology and mummy seriation. *Latin American Antiquity* 6(1):35–55.
  1995b. *Beyond Death: The Chinchorro Mummies of Ancient Chile*. Smithsonian Institution Press, Washington, D.C.
  2016. *Cultura Chinchorro: Las momias artificiales más antiguas del mundo*. Editorial Universitaria, Santiago de Chile.

Arriaza, Bernardo T., Matthew Doubrava, Vivien G. Standen, and Herbert Haas
  2005. Differential mortuary treatment among the Andean Chinchorro fishers: social inequalities or in situ regional cultural evolution? *Current Anthropology* 46:662–671.

Ashley, Clifford W.
  1944. *The Ashley Book of Knots*. Doubleday, Doran and Co., Garden City, New York.

Ashmore, Wendy
  2013. Mobile bodies, empty spaces. In *The Dead Tell Tales: Essays in Honor of Jane E. Buikstra*, edited by María Cecilia Lozada and Barra O'Donnabhain, pp. 106–113. Monograph 76. Cotsen Institute of Archaeology Press, University of California at Los Angeles.

Aufderheide, Arthur C.
  2003. *The Scientific Study of Mummies*. Cambridge University Press, Cambridge, UK.

Aufderheide, Arthur C., Iván Muñoz, and Bernardo Arriaza
  1993. Seven Chinchorro mummies and the prehistory of northern Chile. *American Journal of Physical Anthropology* 91(2):189–201.

B

Baessler, Arthur
  1902–1903. *Ancient Peruvian Art: Contributions to the Archaeology of the Empire of the Incas from his Collections*. Translated by Augustus H. Keane. A. Asher, Berlin.

Bailey, Douglass and Steve Mills, editors
  1998. *The Archaeology of Value: Essays on Prestige and the Processes of Valuation*. BAR International Series 730. British Archaeological Reports, Oxford, UK.

Baines, John
  2014. Not only with the dead: banqueting in ancient Egypt. *Studia Universitatis Babes-Bolyai-Historia* 1:1–34.

Barraza Lescano, Sergio, Rodrigo Areche Espinola, and Giancarlo Marcone Flores
  2022. By stones and by knots: the counting and recording of chili pepper stored during the Inca occupation of the Guarco administrative center of Huacones-Vilcahuasi, lower Cañete Valley, Peru. *Andean Past* 13:221–264.

Barrett, John C.
  2001. Agency, the duality of structure, and the problem of the archaeological record. In *Archaeological Theory Today*, edited by Ian Hodder, pp. 141–164. Cambridge University Press, Cambridge, UK.

Bartel, Brad
  1982. A historical review of ethnological and archaeological analyses of mortuary practice. *Journal of Anthropological Archaeology* 1:32–58.

Bastien, Joseph W.
  1978. *Mountain of the Condor: Metaphor and Ritual in an Andean Ayllu*. Waveland Press, Prospect Heights, Illinois.

Bauer, Brian S.
  2004. *Ancient Cuzco: Heartland of the Inca*. University of Texas Press, Austin.

Beck, Lane Anderson, editor
  1995. *Regional Approaches to Mortuary Analysis*. Plenum Press, New York and London.

Becker, Marshall J.
  1992. Burials as caches, caches as burials: a new interpretation of the meaning of ritual deposits among the Classic period lowland Maya. In *New Theories on the Ancient Maya*, edited by Elin C. Danien and Robert J. Sharer, pp. 185–196. University Museum Monograph 77. University of Pennsylvania Museum, Philadelphia.

Bennett, Wendell C. and Junius B. Bird
1949. *Andean Culture History*. Handbook Series, Number 15. American Museum of Natural History, New York.

Bernal, Ignacio
1976. The jaguar façade tomb at Dainzú. In *To Illustrate the Monuments: Essays on Archaeology Presented to Stuart Piggott on the Occasion of his Sixty-Fifth Birthday*, edited by J. V. S. Megaw, pp. 295–300. Thames & Hudson, London.

Betanzos, Juan de
1987[1551]. *Suma y narración de los incas*. Edited by María del Carmen Martín Rubio. Ediciones Atlas, Madrid.
1996[1551–1557]. *Narrative of the Incas*, edited and translated by Roland Hamilton and Dana Buchanan. University of Texas Press, Austin.

Binford, Lewis R.
1971. Mortuary practices: their study and their potential. In *Approaches to the Social Dimensions of Mortuary Practices*, edited by James A. Brown, pp. 6–29. Memoirs of the Society for American Archaeology, Number 25. Washington, D.C.

Bird, Junius B.
1952. Appendix 3. Textile Notes. In *Cultural Stratigraphy in the Virú Valley, northern Peru: The Formative and Florescent Epochs*, edited by William Duncan Strong and Clifford Evans, Jr., pp. 357–364. Columbia University Press, New York.

Bird, Junius and Louisa Bellinger
1954. *Paracas Fabrics and Nazca Needlework 3rd century B.C.–3rd century A.D.* The Textile Museum Catalogue Raisonné. The Textile Museum, Washington, D.C.

Bird, Junius B. and John Hyslop (in collaboration with Milica D. Skinner)
1985. *The Preceramic Excavations at the Huaca Prieta, Chicama Valley, Peru*. Anthropological Papers of the American Museum of Natural History, Volume 62, Part 1. New York.

Bird, Robert McKelvy and Emilio Mendizábal Losack
1986. Textiles, weaving, and ethnic groups of highland Huánuco, Peru. In *The Junius B. Bird Conference on Andean Textiles, April 7th and 8th, 1984,* edited by Ann Pollard Rowe, pp. 339–349. The Textile Museum, Washington, D.C.

Bittmann, Bente and Juan R. Munizaga
1976. The earliest artificial mummification in the world? A study of the Chinchorro complex in northern Chile. *Folk* 18:61–92.
1979. El arco en América, evidencia temprana y directa de la cultura Chinchorro. *Indiana* 5:229–251.

Bloch, Maurice
1971. *Placing the Dead: Tombs, Ancestral Villages, and Kinship Organization in Madagascar*. Seminar Press, London.

Bloch, Maurice and Jonathan Parry
1982. Introduction: death and the regeneration of life. In *Death and the Regeneration of Life*, edited by Maurice Bloch and Jonathan Parry, pp. 1–44. Cambridge University Press, Cambridge, UK.

Bolton, Ralph
1979. On coca chewing and high-altitude stress. *Current Anthropology* 20:418–420.

Bongers, Jacob L.
2019. Mortuary practice, imperial conquest, and sociopolitical change in the middle Chincha Valley, Peru (ca. AD 1200–1650). Unpublished PhD dissertation, Cotsen Institute of Archaeology, University of California at Los Angeles.

Bongers, Jacob L., Colleen O'Shea, and Alan Farahani
2018. Communities of weavers: a methodology for analyzing textile and cloth production. *Journal of Archaeological Science: Reports* 22:223–236.

Bongers, Jacob L., Juliana Gómez Mejía, Thomas K. Harper, and Susanna Seidensticker
2022. Assembling the dead: human vertebrae-on-posts in the Chincha Valley, Peru. *Antiquity* 96:387–405.

Bongers, Jacob L., Vanessa Muros, Colleen O'Shea, Juliana Gómez Mejía, Colin A. Cooke, Michelle Young, and Hans Barnard
2023. Painting personhood: red pigment practices in southern Peru. *Journal of Anthropological Archaeology* 69:1–20.

Booth, Thomas J., Andrew T. Chamberlain, and Mike Parker Pearson
2015. Mummification in Bronze Age Britain. *Antiquity* 89(347):1155–1173.

Boz, Başak and Lori D. Hager
2014. Making sense of social behavior from disturbed and commingled skeletons: a case study from Çatalhöyük, Turkey. In *Commingled and Disarticulated Human Remains: Working Toward Improved Theory, Method, and Data*, edited by Anna J. Osterholtz, Kathryn M. Baustian, and Debra L. Martin, pp. 17–33. Springer, New York.

Braun, David P.
1981. A critique of some recent North American mortuary studies. *American Antiquity* 46:398–416.

Brown, James A., editor
1971a. *Approaches to the Social Dimensions of Mortuary Practices*. Memoirs of the Society for American Archaeology, Number 25. Washington, D.C.

Brown, James A.
1971b. The dimensions of status in the burials at Spiro. In *Approaches to the Social Dimensions of Mortuary Practices*, edited by James A. Brown. Memoirs of the Society for American Archaeology 25:92–112. Washington, D.C.

1995. On mortuary analysis—with special reference to the Saxe-Binford research program. In *Regional Approaches to Mortuary Analysis*, edited by Lane Anderson Beck, pp. 3–26. Plenum Press, New York and London.

Bruce, Susan Lee
1986a. The audiencia room of the Huaca 1 Complex. In *The Pacatnamu Papers 1*, edited by Christopher B. Donnan and Guillermo A. Cock, pp. 95–108. The Museum of Cultural History, UCLA, Los Angeles.
1986b. Textile miniatures from Pacatnamu, Peru. In *The Junius B. Bird Conference on Andean Textiles, April 7th and 8th, 1984*, edited by Ann Pollard Rowe, pp. 183–204. The Textile Museum, Washington, D.C.

Buikstra, Jane E.
1995. Tombs for the living….. or…. for the dead: The Osmore ancestors. In *Tombs for the Living: Andean Mortuary Practices, a symposium at Dumbarton Oaks 12th and 13th October 1991*, edited by Tom D. Dillehay, pp. 229–280. Dumbarton Oaks Research Library and Collection, Washington, D.C.

Bunt, Cyril G. E.
1918. Studies in Peruvian textiles: double-cloth weaves. *The Burlington Magazine for Connoisseurs* 32(180):109–112.

Burger, Richard L., Craig Morris, and Ramiro Matos Mendieta, editors
2007. *Variations in the Expression of Inka Power: A Symposium at Dumbarton Oaks, 18th and 19th October 1997*. Dumbarton Oaks Research Library and Collection, Washington, D.C.

C

Cahlander, Adele (with Elayne Zorn and Ann Pollard Rowe)
1980. *Sling Braiding of the Andes*. Weaver's Journal Monograph IV. Colorado Fiber Center, Boulder, Colorado.

Cahlander, Adele and Suzanne Baizerman
1985. *Double-Woven Treasures from Old Peru*. Dos Tejedoras, St. Paul, Minnesota.

Campos Napán, Carlos
2007. Vilcahuasi o Los Huacones: La otra capital de la sociedad Guarco en peligro de desaparición. *Tukuy Rikuq* 4:60–62.

Carbajal, Pedro de
1965[1586]. Descripción hecha de la Provincia de Vilcas Guaman… año de 1586. In *Relaciones Geográficas de Indias*, edited by Marcos Jiménez de la Espada, pp. 205–219. *Biblioteca de Autores*, volume 183. Ediciones Atlas, Madrid.

Carmichael, Patrick H.
1988. Nasca mortuary customs: death and ancient society on the south coast of Peru. PhD dissertation, University of Calgary.
1995. Nasca burial patterns: social structure and mortuary ideology. In *Tombs for the Living: Andean Mortuary Practices, a symposium at Dumbarton Oaks 12th and 13th October 1991*, edited by Tom D. Dillehay, pp. 161–188. Dumbarton Oaks Research Library and Collection, Washington, D.C.
2019. Stages, periods, epochs, and phases in Paracas and Nasca chronology: Another look at John Rowe's Ica Valley master sequence. *Ñawpa Pacha: Journal of Andean Archaeology* 39(2):145–179.

Caso, Alfonso
1969. *El tesoro de Monte Albán*. Instituto Nacional de Antropología e Historia, México, D.F.

Castro, Cristóbal and Diego Ortega Morejón
1936[1558]. Relación y declaración del modo que este valle de Chincha y sus comarcanos se gobernaron antes que hobiese ingas y despues que los hobo hasta que los cristianos entraron en esta tierra. *Historia y Cultura* 8:91–104. Museo Nacional de Historia, Lima.

Ceruti, María Constanza
2004. Human bodies as objects of dedication at Inca mountain shrines (northwest Argentina). *World Archaeology* 36(1):103–122.

Chan, Keith
2011. Life in the Late Intermediate Period at Armatambo, Perú. PhD dissertation, University of Missouri, Columbia.

Chapdelaine, Claude and Gérard Gagné
2015. A temple for the dead at San Juanito, lower Santa Valley, during the Initial Period. In *Funerary Practices and Models in the Ancient Andes: The Return of the Living Dead*, edited by Peter Eeckhout and Lawrence S. Owens, pp. 34–54. Cambridge University Press, Cambridge, UK.

Chapman, Robert
1987. Mortuary practices: society, theory building, and archaeology. In *Death, Decay and Reconstruction: Approaches to Archaeology and Forensic Science*, edited by A. Boddington, A. N. Garland, and R. C. Janaway, pp. 198–213. Manchester University Press, Manchester.
1995. Ten years after—megaliths, mortuary practices, and the territorial model. In *Regional Approaches to Mortuary Analysis*, edited by Lane Anderson Beck, pp. 29–51. Plenum Press, New York and London.
2003. Death, society and archaeology: the social dimensions of mortuary practices. *Mortality* 8(3):305–312.
2005. Mortuary analysis: a matter of time? In *Interacting with the Dead: Perspectives on Mortuary Archaeology for the New Millennium*, edited by Gordon F. M. Rakita, Jane E. Buikstra, Lane A. Beck, and Sloan R. Williams, pp. 25–40. University Press of Florida, Gainesville.
2013. Death, burial, and social representation. In *The Oxford Handbook of the Archaeology of Death and Burial*, edited by Liv Nilsson Stutz and Sarah Tarlow, pp. 47–57. Oxford University Press, Oxford, England.

Chapman, Robert, Ian Kinnes, and Klavs Randsborg, editors
  1981. *The Archaeology of Death*. Cambridge University Press, Cambridge and New York.

Charles, Douglas K. and Jane Buikstra
  1983. Archaic mortuary sites in the central Mississippi drainage: Distribution, structure, and behavioral implications. In *Archaic Hunters and Gatherers in the American Midwest*, edited by James L. Phillips and James A. Brown, pp. 117–145. Academic Press, New York.

Chase, Diane Z. and Arlen F. Chase
  1996. Maya multiples: individuals, entries, and tombs in Structure A34 of Caracol, Belize. *Latin American Antiquity* 7(1):61–79.
  1998. The architectural context of caches, burials, and other ritual activities for the Classic period Maya (as reflected at Caracol, Belize). In *Function and Meaning in Classic Maya Architecture*, edited by Stephen D. Houston, pp. 299–332. Dumbarton Oaks Research Library and Collection, Washington, D.C.
  2003. Secular, sagrado, y revisitado: La profanación, alteración, y reconsagración de los antiguos entierros mayas. In *Antropología de la eternidad: La muerte en la cultura maya*, edited by Andrés Ciudad Ruiz, Mario Humberto Ruz Sosa, and María Josefa Iglesias Ponce de León, pp. 255–277. Publicación 7. Sociedad de los Estudios Mayas, Madrid, Spain.
  2011. Ghosts amid the ruins: analyzing relationships between the living and the dead among the ancient Maya at Caracol, Belize. In *Living with the Dead: Mortuary Ritual in Mesoamerica*, edited by James L. Fitzsimmons and Izumi Shimada, pp. 78–101. The University of Arizona Press, Tucson.

Chiñas, Beverly
  1973. *The Isthmus Zapotecs: Women's Role in Cultural Context*. Holt, Rinehart, and Winston, New York.

Chu, Alejandro
  2015. La plaza y el *ushnu* mayor de Incahuasi, Cañete. *Cuadernos de Qhapaq Ñan* 3(3):92–110.

Cieza de León, Pedro de
  1932[1553]. *La crónica del Perú*. Espasa-Calpe, S.A., Madrid.
  1959[1553]. *The Incas of Pedro de Cieza de León*. Translated by Harriet de Onis and edited with an introduction by Victor Wolfgang von Hagen. University of Oklahoma Press, Norman.

Cobo, fray Bernabé
  1956[1653]. *Obras del P. Bernabé Cobo. Historia del Nuevo Mundo*. Edited by Francisco Mateos. *Biblioteca de Autores Españoles*, Tomos 91–92. Real Academia Española, Madrid.
  1990[1653]. *Inca Religion and Customs by Father Bernabé Cobo*. Translated and edited by Roland Hamilton. Foreword by John Howland Rowe. University of Texas Press, Austin.

Cock, Guillermo A. and Carmen Elena Goycochea Díaz
  2004. Puruchuco y el cementerio inca de la Quebrada de Huaquerones. In *Puruchuco y la sociedad de Lima: un homenaje a Arturo Jiménez Borja*, edited by Luis Felipe Villacorta Ostolaza et al., pp. 179–197. Concytec, Lima, Peru.

Coe, William R.
  1959. *Excavations in the Great Plaza, North Terrace, and North Acropolis of Tikal*. Tikal Report 14. University Museum Monograph, Number 61, University of Pennsylvania, Philadelphia.

Coker, Roberto E.
  1908. Condición en que se encuentra la pesca marina desde Paita hasta Bahia de la Independencia (conclusión). Chapter 7, La pesca en Chilca, Bujama (Mala), y Cerro Azul. *Boletín del Ministerio de Fomento* 6(5):99–115. Dirección de Fomento, Escuela de Artes y Oficios, Lima.

Conklin, William J.
  1975a. Pampa Gramalote textiles. In *Irene Emery Roundtable on Museum Textiles, 1974 Proceedings: Archaeological Textiles*, edited by Patricia L. Fiske, pp. 77–92. The Textile Museum, Washington, D.C.
  1975b. An introduction to South American textiles with emphasis on materials and techniques of Peruvian tapestry. In *Irene Emery Roundtable on Museum Textiles, 1974 Proceedings: Archaeological Textiles*, edited by Patricia L. Fiske, pp. 17–30. The Textile Museum, Washington, D.C.
  1979. Moche textile structures. In *The Junius B. Bird Pre-Columbian Textile Conference, May 19th and 20th, 1973*, edited by Ann Pollard Rowe, Elizabeth P. Benson, and Anne-Louise Schaffer, pp. 165–184. The Textile Museum and Dumbarton Oaks, Washington, D.C.

Costin, Cathy Lynne
  1993. Textiles, women, and political economy in late prehispanic Peru. *Research in Economic Anthropology* 14:3–28.
  1998. Housewives, chosen women, skilled men: cloth production and social identity in the late prehispanic Andes. In *Craft and Social Identity*, edited by Cathy Lynne Costin and Rita P. Wright, pp. 123–141. Archaeological Papers of the American Anthropological Association, Number 8. Archeology Division of the American Anthropological Association, Washington, D.C.
  2016. Political, social, economic, and ideological dimensions in the late pre-hispanic gendered division of labor on the north coast of Peru. In *Gendered Labor in Specialized Economies: Archaeological Perspectives on Female and Male Work*, edited by Sophia E. Kelly and Traci Ardren, pp. 27–60. University Press of Colorado, Boulder.
  2018. Gender and status in Inca textile and ceramic craft production. In *The Oxford Handbook of the Incas*, edited by Sonia Alconini and Alan Covey, pp. 283–302. Oxford University Press, New York.

Covey, R. Alan
- 2006. *How the Incas Built Their Heartland: State Formation and the Innovation of Imperial Strategies in the Sacred Valley, Peru*. University of Michigan Press, Ann Arbor.
- 2008. Multiregional perspectives on the archaeology of the Andes during the Late Intermediate Period (ca. A.D. 1000–1400). *Journal of Archaeological Research* 16:287–338.
- 2015. Inka imperial intentions and archaeological realities in the Peruvian highlands. In *The Inka Empire: A Multidisciplinary Approach*, edited by Izumi Shimada, pp. 83–95. University of Texas Press, Austin.

D

Daggett, Richard E.
- 1988. The Pachacamac studies: 1938–1941. In *Multidisciplinary Studies in Andean Anthropology*, edited by Virginia J. Vitzthum, pp. 13–21. Michigan Discussions in Anthropology 8. University of Michigan, Ann Arbor.

Dalton, Jordan A.
- 2020. Excavations at Las Huacas (AD 1200–1650): exploring elite strategies and economic exchange during the Inca Empire. Unpublished PhD dissertation, Department of Anthropology, University of Michigan, Ann Arbor.

Dalton, Jordan A., Juliana Gómez Mejía, Noemi Oncebay Pizarro, Iride Tomažič, and Emilie M. Cobb
- 2022a. The dead do not unbury themselves: Understanding posthumous engagement and ancestor veneration in coastal Peru (AD 1450–1650). *Journal of Anthropological Archaeology* 66: article #101410.

Dalton, Jordan A., Colleen O'Shea, Juliana Gómez Mejía, and Noemi Oncebay Pizarro
- 2022b. Mortuary practices amid sociopolitical changes: interpreting a large communal ossuary at Las Huacas, Chincha Valley. *Ñawpa Pacha: Journal of Andean Archaeology* 42(2):235–260.

D'Altroy, Terence N.
- 1992. *Provincial Power in the Inka Empire*. Smithsonian Institution, Washington, D.C.
- 2002. *The Incas*. Blackwell, Malden, Massachusetts and Oxford, England.

Davies, Jon
- 1999. *Death, Burial, and Rebirth in the Religions of Antiquity*. Taylor and Francis, New York.

Dean, Carolyn
- 2010. The after-life of Inka rulers: Andean death before and after Spanish colonization. In *Death and the Afterlife in the Early Modern Hispanic World*, edited by John Beusterien and Constance Cortez. *Hispanic Issues On Line* 7:27–54.

Deetz, James
- 1967. *Invitation to Archaeology*. Natural History Press, Garden City, New York.

Deetz, James and Edwin N. Dethlefsen
- 1971. Some social aspects of New England Colonial mortuary art. In *Approaches to the Social Dimensions of Mortuary Practices*, edited by James A. Brown. Memoirs of the Society for American Archaeology 25:30–38. Washington, D.C.

Degano, Ilaria and María Perla Colombini
- 2009. Multi-analytical techniques for the study of Pre-Columbian mummies and related funerary materials. *Journal of Archaeological Science* 36(8):1783–1790.

DeLeonardis, Lisa
- 2012. Interpreting the Paracas body and its value in ancient Peru. In *The Construction of Value in the Ancient World*, edited by John K. Papadopoulos and Gary Urton, pp. 197–217. Cotsen Institute of Archaeology, University of California at Los Angeles.

DeLeonardis, Lisa and George F. Lau
- 2004. Life, death, and ancestors. In *Andean Archaeology*, edited by Helaine Silverman, pp. 77–115. Blackwell Studies in Global Archaeology. Blackwell Press, Malden, Massachusetts.

Desrosiers, Sophie
- 1986. An interpretation of technical weaving data found in an early 17th-century chronicle. In *The Junius B. Bird Conference on Andean Textiles, April 7th and 8th, 1984*, edited by Ann Pollard Rowe, pp. 219–233. The Textile Museum, Washington, D.C.

D'Harcourt, Raoul
- 1934. *Les Textiles Anciens du Pérou et Leurs Techniques*. Les Éditions d'Art et d'Histoire, Paris.

Díaz Arriola, Luisa
- 2015. The preparation of corpses and mummy bundles in Ychsma funerary practices at Armatambo. In *Funerary Practices and Models in the Ancient Andes: The Return of the Living Dead*, edited by Peter Eeckhout and Lawrence S. Owens, pp. 186–209. Cambridge University Press, Cambridge.

Díaz Carranza, José Luis
- 2015. Hallazgos de coca en colcas del valle medio del río Cañete correspondientes al Horizonte Tardío. *Cuadernos de Qhapaq Ñan* 3:128–147.

Diez de San Miguel, Garci
- 1964[1567]. *Visita hecha a la provincia de Chucuito por Garci Diez de San Miguel en el año 1567*. Edited by Waldemar Espinoza Soriano. Documentos Regionales para la Etnología y Etnohistoria Andinas 1. Casa de la Cultura del Perú, Lima.

Dillehay, Tom D., editor
- 1995. *Tombs for the Living: Andean Mortuary Practices. A symposium at Dumbarton Oaks, 12th and 13th October 1991.* Dumbarton Oaks Research Library and Collection, Washington, D.C.
- 2017. *Where the Land Meets the Sea: Fourteen Millennia of Human History at Huaca Prieta.* University of Texas Press, Austin.

Dobres, Marcia-Anne and John Robb
- 2000. Agency in archaeology: paradigm or platitude. In *Agency in Archaeology*, edited by Marcia-Anne Dobres and John Robb, pp. 3–17. Routledge, London.

Donnan, Christopher B.
- 1995. Moche funerary practice. In *Tombs for the Living: Andean Mortuary Practices, a symposium at Dumbarton Oaks, 12th and 13th, October 1991*, edited by Tom D. Dillehay, pp. 111–159. Center for Pre-Columbian Studies, Dumbarton Oaks Research Library and Collection, Washington, D.C.
- 2009. The Moche use of numbers and number sets. In *Andean Civilization: A Tribute to Michael E. Moseley*, edited by Joyce Marcus and Patrick Ryan Williams, pp. 165–180. Cotsen Institute of Archaeology, University of California at Los Angeles.
- 2012. Dressing the body in splendor: expression of value by the Moche of ancient Peru. In *The Construction of Value in the Ancient World*, edited by John K. Papadopoulos and Gary Urton, pp. 186–196. Cotsen Institute of Archaeology, University of California at Los Angeles.
- 2022. *La Mina: A Royal Moche Tomb.* University of New Mexico Press, Albuquerque.

Donnan, Christopher B. and Guillermo A. Cock, editors
- 1986. *The Pacatnamu Papers, Volume 1.* Museum of Cultural History, University of California at Los Angeles.

Donnan, Christopher B. and Sharon G. Donnan
- 1997. Moche textiles from Pacatnamu. In *The Pacatnamu Papers, Volume 2: The Moche Occupation*, edited by Christopher B. Donnan and Guillermo A. Cock, pp. 215–242. Fowler Museum of Cultural History, University of California at Los Angeles.

Donnan, Christopher B. and Donna McClelland
- 1997. Moche burials at Pacatnamu. In *The Pacatnamu Papers, Volume 2: The Moche Occupation*, edited by Christopher B. Donnan and Guillermo A. Cock, pp. 17–187. Fowler Museum of Cultural History, University of California at Los Angeles.

Donnan, Christopher B. and Carol J. Mackey
- 1978. *Ancient Burial Patterns of the Moche Valley, Peru.* University of Texas Press, Austin.

Dorsey, George A.
- 1894. An Archaeological Study Based on a Personal Exploration of Over One Hundred Graves at the Necropolis of Ancon, Peru. PhD dissertation, Harvard University, Cambridge, Massachusetts.

Doyle, Mary Eileen
- 1988. Ancestor Cult and Burial Ritual in Seventeenth and Eighteenth Century Central Peru. Unpublished PhD dissertation, University of California at Los Angeles.

Dransart, Penelope
- 2020. Basket making in the Americas and the value of work: The arts and industries paradigm as a nineteenth-century legacy. In *Basketry & Beyond: Constructing Cultures*, edited by T. A. Heslop and Helen Anderson, pp. 78–91. Sainsbury Research Unit for the Arts of Africa, Oceania & the Americas, University of East Anglia, Norwich, England.

Duviols, Pierre
- 1976. La capacocha: Mecanismo y función del sacrificio humano, su proyección geométrica, su papel en la política integracionista, y en la economía redistributiva del Tawantinsuyu. *Allpanchis* 9:11–57.

Dwyer, Edward
- 1979. Early Horizon tapestry from south coastal Peru. In *The Junius B. Bird Pre-Columbian Textile Conference, May 19th and 20th, 1973*, edited by Ann Pollard Rowe, Elizabeth P. Benson, and Anne-Louise Schaffer, pp. 61–82. The Textile Museum and Dumbarton Oaks, Washington, D.C.

Dwyer, Edward and Jane P. Dwyer
- 1975. The Paracas cemeteries: mortuary patterns in a Peruvian south coastal tradition. In *Death and the Afterlife in Pre-Columbian America*, edited by Elizabeth P. Benson, pp. 145–161. Dumbarton Oaks Research Library and Collection, Washington, D.C.

E

Eeckhout, Peter
- 2000. The palaces of the lords of Ychsma: An archaeological reappraisal of the function of pyramids with ramps at Pachacamac, central coast of Peru. *Revista de Arqueología Americana* 17–19:217–254.
- 2003. Ancient monuments and patterns of power at Pachacamac, central coast of Peru. *Beiträge zur Allgemeinen und vergleichenden archäologie* 23:139–182.
- 2004a. Reyes del sol y señores de la luna: Incas e Ychsmas en Pachacamac. *Chungara* 36(2):495–503.
- 2004b. La sombra de Ychsma: Ensayo introductorio sobre la arqueología de la costa central del Perú en los períodos tardíos. *Bulletin de Institut Français d'Études Andines* 33:403–423.
- 2010. Nuevas evidencias sobre costumbres funerarias en Pachacamac. In *Max Uhle (1856–1944): evaluaciones de sus investigaciones y obras*, edited by Manuela Fischer, Peter Kaulicke, Peter Masson, and Gregor Wolff, pp. 151–163. Fondo Editorial de la Pontificia Universidad Católica del Perú, Lima.

2012. Inca storage and accounting facilities at Pachacamac. *Andean Past* 10:213–239.

2013. Change and permanency on the coast of ancient Peru, the religious site of Pachacamac. *World Archaeology* 45(1):119–142.

2018. *Inca Textiles and Ornaments of the Andes*. Ludion, New York and Los Angeles.

Eeckhout, Peter and Enrique López Hurtado
2018. Pachacamac and the Incas on the coast of Peru. In *The Oxford Handbook of the Incas*, edited by Sonia Alconini and Alan Covey, pp. 179–196. Oxford University Press, New York.

Eeckhout, Peter and Lawrence S. Owens
2008. Human sacrifice at Pachacamac. *Latin American Antiquity* 19:375–398.

Eeckhout, Peter and Lawrence S. Owens, editors
2015. *Funerary Practices and Models in the Ancient Andes: The Return of the Living Dead*. Cambridge University Press, Cambridge.

El-Shahawy, Abeer
2005. *The Funerary Art of Ancient Egypt: A Bridge to the Realm of the Hereafter*. Farid Atiya Press, Cairo, Egypt.

Emery, Irene
1966. *The Primary Structures of Fabrics: An Illustrated Classification*. The Textile Museum, Washington, D.C.
1980. *The Primary Structures of Fabrics: An Illustrated Classification*. The Textile Museum, Washington, D.C.
1995. *The Primary Structures of Fabrics: An Illustrated Classification*. Watson-Guptill Publications, Incorporated.

Engel, Frédéric
1957. Early sites on the Peruvian coast. *Southwestern Journal of Anthropology* 13:54–68.
1960. Un groupe humain datant de 5000 àns Paracas, Pérou. *Journal de la Société des Américanistes* n.s. 49:7–35.
1963. A preceramic settlement on the central coast of Peru: Asia, Unit 1. *Transactions of the American Philosophical Society* 53(3):3–139.
1970. Exploration of the Chilca Canyon, Peru. *Current Anthropology* 11(1):55–58.
1981. *Prehistoric Andean Ecology: Man, Settlement, and Environment in the Andes: The Deep South*. Humanities Press, New York.

Espinoza Soriano, Waldemar
1987. *Artesanos, transacciones, monedas y formas de pago en el mundo andino. Siglos XV y XVI*. Tomo I. Banco Central de Reserva del Perú, Lima, Perú.

F

Feinman, Gary M., Linda M. Nicholas, and Lindsey C. Baker
2010. The missing femur at the Mitla Fortress and its implications. *Antiquity* 84:1089–1101.

Feldman, Robert A.
1986. Early textiles from the Supe Valley, Peru. In *The Junius B. Bird Conference on Andean Textiles, April 7th and 8th, 1984*, edited by Ann Pollard Rowe, pp. 31–46. The Textile Museum, Washington, D.C.

Fernandini Parodi, Francesca
2018. Peopling the Cañete Valley circa AD 600: A view from Cerro de Oro. *Ñawpa Pacha: Journal of Andean Archaeology* 38(2):135–156.

Fester, Gustavo
1940. Los colorantes del antiguo Perú. *Archeion* 22:229–241.

Fester, Gustavo A. and José Cruellas
1934. Colorantes de Paracas. *Revista del Museo Nacional* 3:154–156.

Fitzsimmons, James L.
1998. Classic Maya mortuary anniversaries at Piedras Negras, Guatemala. *Ancient Mesoamerica* 9:271–278.
2002. Death and the Maya: Language and Archaeology in Classic Maya Ceremonialism. PhD dissertation, Department of Anthropology, Harvard University, Cambridge.
2006. Tomb re-entry among the Classic Maya: Archaeology and epigraphy in mortuary ceremonialism. In *Jaws of the Underworld: Life, Death, and Rebirth among the Ancient Maya*. Proceedings of the 7th European Maya Conference, British Museum, London, edited by Pierre R. Colas, Geneviève LeFort, and Bodil Liljefors Persson, pp. 35–42. Acta Mesoamericana Volume 16. Verlag Anton Saurwein, Möckmühl, Germany.

Flannery, Kent V. and Christopher P. Glew
2016. Domestic dogs. In *Coastal Ecosystems and Economic Strategies at Cerro Azul, Peru: The Study of a Late Intermediate Kingdom*, edited by Joyce Marcus, pp. 318–323. Memoirs of the Museum of Anthropology, University of Michigan, Number 59. Ann Arbor.

Flannery, Kent V. and Joyce Marcus
2005. *Excavations at San José Mogote 1: The Household Archaeology*. Memoirs of the Museum of Anthropology, University of Michigan, Number 40. Ann Arbor.
2016. The fish resources of Cerro Azul in the 1980s. In *Coastal Ecosystems and Economic Strategies at Cerro Azul, Peru: The Study of a Late Intermediate Kingdom*, edited by Joyce Marcus, pp. 72–97. Memoirs of the Museum of Anthropology, University of Michigan, Number 59. Ann Arbor.

Fleming, Stuart
    1986. The mummies of Pachacamac: An exceptional legacy from Uhle's 1896 excavation. *Expedition* 28(3):39–45.

Fortes, Meyer
    1976. An introductory commentary. In *Ancestors*, edited by William H. Newell, pp. 1–16. Mouton Publishers, The Hague and Paris.

Frame, Mary and Rommel Ángeles Falcón
    2014. A female funerary bundle from Huaca Malena. *Ñawpa Pacha: Journal of Andean Archaeology* 34(1):27–59.

Franquemont, Edward and Christine Franquemont
    1988. Learning to weave in Chinchero. *Textile Museum Journal* 26:54–78.

G

Garaventa, Donna Marie
    1977. Ancient Textiles with Grave Association from Chincha, Peru. PhD dissertation, Department of Anthropology, University of California, Berkeley.
    1979. Chincha textiles of the Late Intermediate period, Epoch 8. In *The Junius B. Bird Pre-Columbian Textile Conference, May 19th and 20th, 1973*, edited by Ann Pollard Rowe, Elizabeth P. Benson, and Anne-Louise Schaffer, pp. 219–238. The Textile Museum and Dumbarton Oaks, Washington, D.C.

Garcilaso de la Vega, "El Inca"
    1966[1609]. *Royal Commentaries of the Incas and General History of Peru* (Primera parte de los *Comentarios Reales* [1604]), edited and translated by Harold V. Livermore. University of Texas Press, Austin.

Gasparini, Graziano and Luise Margolies
    1980. *Inca Architecture*. Translated by Patricia J. Lyon. Indiana University, Bloomington and London.

Gayoso-Rullier, Henry and Santiago Uceda-Castillo
    2015. When the dead speak in Moche funerary customs in an architectural complex associated with the Huaca del Sol and the Huaca de la Luna. In *Funerary Practices and Models in the Ancient Andes: The Return of the Living Dead*, edited by Peter Eeckhout and Lawrence S. Owens, pp. 87–116. University of Cambridge Press, Cambridge.

Gayton, Anna H.
    1967. Textiles from Hacha, Peru. *Ñawpa Pacha: Journal of Andean Archaeology* 5:1–14.

Gerdau-Radonic, Karina and Alexander Herrera
    2010. Why dig looted tombs? Two examples and some answers from Keushu (Ancash highlands, Peru). *Bulletins et Mémoires de la Société d'Anthropologie de Paris* 22 (3–4):145–156.

Glew, Christopher P. and Kent V. Flannery
    2016a. Camelids and *ch'arki* at Cerro Azul. In *Coastal Ecosystems and Economic Strategies at Cerro Azul, Peru: The Study of a Late Intermediate Kingdom*, edited by Joyce Marcus, pp. 287–317. Memoirs of the Museum of Anthropology, University of Michigan, Number 59. Ann Arbor.
    2016b. The raising of guinea pigs. In *Coastal Ecosystems and Economic Strategies at Cerro Azul, Peru: The Study of a Late Intermediate Kingdom*, edited by Joyce Marcus, pp. 324–333. Memoirs of the Museum of Anthropology, University of Michigan, Number 59. Ann Arbor.

Goldberg, Phyllis and Constance Orcutt
    1979. Appendix. Technical analysis of the Chucho textiles. In *The Junius B. Bird Pre-Columbian Textile Conference, May 19th and 20th, 1973*, edited by Ann Pollard Rowe, Elizabeth P. Benson, and Anne-Louise Schaffer, pp. 76–81. The Textile Museum and Dumbarton Oaks, Washington, D.C.

Goldstein, Lynne G.
    1976. Spatial Structure and Social Organization: Regional Manifestations of Mississippian Society. Unpublished PhD dissertation, Northwestern University, Evanston, Illinois.
    1980. *Mississippian Mortuary Practices: A Case Study of Two Cemeteries in the Lower Illinois Valley*. Northwestern University Archaeological Program, Scientific Papers, Number 4. Evanston, Illinois.
    1981. One-dimensional archaeology and multi-dimensional people: Spatial organization and mortuary analysis. In *The Archaeology of Death*, edited by Robert W. Chapman, Ian A. Kinnes, and Klavs Randsborg, pp. 53–69. Cambridge University Press, Cambridge.
    1995. Landscapes and mortuary practices: a case for regional perspectives. In *Regional Approaches to Mortuary Analysis*, edited by Lane Anderson Beck, pp. 101–121. Plenum Press, New York and London.
    2006. Mortuary analysis and bioarchaeology. In *Bioarchaeology: The Contextual Analysis of Human Remains*, edited by Jane E. Buikstra and Lane A. Beck, pp. 375–387. Academic Press, New York.

González Holguín, Diego
    1952[1608]. *Vocabulario de la lengua general de todo el Perú llamada lengua Qquichua o del Inca*. Edited by Raúl Porras Barrenechea. Instituto de Historia, Universidad Nacional Mayor de San Marcos, Lima.

Goodenough, Ward H.
    1965. Rethinking "status" and "role": toward a general model of the cultural organization of social relationships. In *The Relevance of Models for Social Anthropology*, edited by Michael Banton, pp. 1–24. ASA Monographs, Number 1. Tavistock Press, London.

Goody, Jack
    1962. *Death, Property and the Ancestors: A Study of the Mortuary Customs of the Lodagaa of West Africa*. Tavistock Press, London.

Gose, Peter
　1996. Oracles, divine kingship, and political representation in the Inka state. *Ethnohistory* 43:1–32.
　2000. The state as a chosen woman: brideservice and the feeding of tributaries in the Inka Empire. *American Anthropologist* 102(1):84–97.

Guaman Poma de Ayala [Waman Puma], Felipe
　1980[1615]. *El primer nueva corónica y buen gobierno*, edited by John V. Murra and Rolena Adorno. Translated by Jorge L. Urioste. Three volumes. Siglo Veintiuno, México, D.F.

Guillén, Sonia E.
　1992. Chinchorro Culture: Mummies and Crania in the Reconstruction of Preceramic Coastal Adaptation in the South Central Andes. PhD dissertation, Department of Anthropology, University of Michigan, Ann Arbor.

H

Harth-Terré, Emilio
　1923. La fortaleza de Chuquimancu. *Revista de Arqueología* I(1):44–49. Órgano del Museo Víctor Larco Herrera, Lima.
　1933. Incahuasi. Ruinas inkaicas del valle de Lunahuaná. *Revista del Museo Nacional* II(2):101–125. Lima, Peru.

Haun, Susan J. and Guillermo A. Cock Carrasco
　2010. A bioarchaeological approach to the search for *mitmaqkuna*. In *Distant Provinces in the Inka Empire: Toward a Deeper Understanding of Inka Imperialism*, edited by Michael A. Malpass and Sonia Alconini, pp. 193–220. University of Iowa Press, Iowa City.

Haviland, William A.
　1969. A new population estimate for Tikal, Guatemala. *American Antiquity* 34:429–433.

Hecker, Gisela and Wolfgang Hecker
　1992. Huesos humanos como ofrendas mortuorias y uso repetido de vasijas. Detalles sobre la tradición funeraria prehispánica de la región norperuana. *Baessler-Archiv* n.s. 40:171–195.

Hernández Escontrías, Pilar Margarita
　2016. Crafting feminine subjects: a diachronic interrogation of gendered production in the Andes. In *Gendered Labor in Specialized Economies: Archaeological Perspectives on Female and Male Work*, edited by Sophia E. Kelly and Traci Ardren, pp. 61–90. University Press of Colorado, Boulder.

Hertz, Robert
　1960[1928]. *Death and the Right Hand: A Contribution to the Study of the Collective Representation of Death*. Translated by Rodney Needham and Claudia Needham. Free Press, Glencoe, Illinois.

Hill, James N. and Joel Gunn, editors
　1977a. *The Individual in Prehistory: Studies of Variability in Style in Prehistoric Technologies*. Academic Press, New York.

Hill, James N. and Joel Gunn
　1977b. Introducing the individual in prehistory. In *The Individual in Prehistory: Studies of Variability in Style in Prehistoric Technologies*, pp. 1–12. Academic Press, New York.

Hodder, Ian
　2000. Agency and individuals in long-term processes. In *Agency in Archaeology*, edited by Marcia-Anne Dobres and John Robb, pp. 21–33. Routledge, London.

Houston, Stephen D., David Stuart, and Karl Taube
　2006. *The Memory of Bones: Body, Being, and Experience Among the Classic Maya*. University of Texas Press, Austin.

Huntington, Richard and Peter Metcalf
　1979. *Celebrations of Death: The Anthropology of Mortuary Ritual*. Cambridge University Press, New York.

Hutchinson, Thomas J.
　1874. Explorations amongst ancient burial grounds (chiefly on the sea-coast valleys) of Peru. Part I. *The Journal of the Anthropological Institute of Great Britain and Ireland* 3:311–326.

Hyslop, John
　1977. Chulpas of the Lupaca zone of the Peruvian high plateau. *Journal of Field Archaeology* 4(2):149–170.
　1984. *The Inka Road System*. Academic Press, New York.
　1985. *Inkawasi, the New Cuzco, Cañete, Lunahuaná, Perú*. British Archaeological Reports, International Series, Volume 234. Oxford, England.

I

Ikram, S. and A. Dodson
　1998. *The Mummy in Ancient Egypt: Equipping the Dead for Eternity*. Thames & Hudson, London.

Isbell, William H.
　1997. *Mummies and Mortuary Monuments: A Postprocessual Prehistory of Central Andean Social Organization*. University of Texas Press, Austin.

Isbell, William H. and Antti Korpisaari
　2015. Bodies of evidence: mortuary archaeology and the Wari-Tiwanaku paradox. In *Funerary Practices and Models in the Ancient Andes: The Return of the Living Dead*, edited by Peter Eeckhout and Lawrence S. Owens, pp. 137–157. Cambridge University Press, Cambridge.

J

James, T. G. H.
1976. *An Introduction to Ancient Egypt.* Harper & Row, New York.

Jiménez de la Espada, Marcos, editor
1965[1881–1897]. *Relaciones Geográficas de Indias: Perú.* Biblioteca de Autores Españoles 183–185. Editorial Atlas, Madrid.

Johnson, George R.
1930. *Peru from the Air.* American Geographical Society, Special Publication Number 12. New York.

Jones, John G.
2016. Macrofossil and palynological analysis of the coprolites from Cerro Azul. In *Coastal Ecosystems and Economic Strategies at Cerro Azul, Peru: The Study of a Late Intermediate Kingdom*, edited by Joyce Marcus, pp. 334–339. Memoirs of the Museum of Anthropology, University of Michigan, Number 59. Ann Arbor.

Joyce, Rosemary A.
1998. Performing the body in prehispanic Central America. *RES* 33:147–165.
2005. Archaeology of the body. *Annual Review of Anthropology* 34:139–158.
2008. *Ancient Bodies, Ancient Lives: Sex, Gender, and Archaeology.* Thames & Hudson, New York.

K

Kaulicke, Peter
1997. *Contextos funerarios de Ancón. Esbozo de una síntesis analítica.* Fondo Editorial Pontificia Universidad Católica del Perú, Lima.
2000. La sombra de Pachacamac: Huari en la costa central. *Boletín de Arqueología PUCP* 4:313–358.
2015. Inka conceptions of life, death, and ancestor worship. In *The Inka Empire: A Multidisciplinary Approach*, edited by Izumi Shimada, pp. 247–261. University of Texas Press, Austin.

Kelly, Sophia E. and Traci Ardren
2016. Craft specialization and the comparative advantages of gender. In *Gendered Labor in Specialized Economies: Archaeological Perspectives on Female and Male Work*, edited by Sophia E. Kelly and Traci Ardren, pp. 3–25. University Press of Colorado, Boulder.

Kendall, Ann
1973. *Everyday Life of the Incas.* B. T. Batsford Ltd., London and G. P. Putnam's Sons, New York.

Kenyon, Kathleen
1960. *Archaeology in the Holy Land.* Frederick A. Praeger, New York.

Knapp, A. Bernard and Peter van Dommelen
2008. Past practices: rethinking individuals and agents in archaeology. *Cambridge Archaeological Journal* 18:15–34.

Kopytoff, Igor
1971. Ancestors as elders in Africa. *Africa* 41:129–141.

Kroeber, Alfred L.
1937. *Archaeological Explorations in Peru. Part IV: Cañete Valley.* Field Museum of Natural History Anthropology Memoirs, Volume II, Number 4, pp. 220–273. First Marshall Field Archaeological Expedition to Peru. Field Museum of Natural History, Chicago.

Kroeber, Alfred L. and William Duncan Strong
1924. The Uhle collections from Chincha. *University of California Publications in American Archaeology and Ethnology*, Volume 21, Number 1, pp. 1–54. University of California Press, Berkeley.

Kroeber, Alfred L. and Dwight Wallace
1954. Proto-Lima: a middle period culture of Peru. *Fieldiana Anthropology* 44, Number 1. Chicago Natural History Museum, Chicago.

Kula, Gulli I.
1988. Chancay textiles in the Young Peruvian Collection. A thesis in anthropology/archaeology for Masters of Liberal Arts in Extension Studies, Harvard University, Cambridge, Massachusetts.

L

Larrabure y Unanue, Eugenio
1935[1893]. *Manuscritos y Publicaciones. Volumen II. Historia y Arqueología—Valle de Cañete.* Imprenta Americana, Lima, Peru.

Las Casas, Bartolomé de
2010[1550]. *De las antiguas gentes del Perú.* Estudio y notas por Marcos Jiménez de la Espada (1982). Editorial Nuevo Mundo, San Juan, Puerto Rico.

Lau, George F.
2021. Animating idolatry: making ancestral kin and personhood in ancient Peru. *Religions* 12(287):1–18.

LeVine, Terry
1987. Inka labor service at the regional level: the functional reality. *Ethnohistory* 34(1):14–46.

Lind, Michael D.
　2003. Lambityeco—Tomb 6. In *Homenaje a John Paddock*, edited by Patricia Plunket, pp. 45–66. Universidad de las Américas, Puebla, Mexico.

Lind, Michael and Javier Urcid
　1983. The lords of Lambityeco and their nearest neighbors. *Notas Mesoamericanas* 9:76–111.

Lothrop, Samuel K. and Joy Mahler
　1957a. Late Nazca burials in Chaviña, Peru. *Papers of the Peabody Museum of Archaeology and Ethnology*, Volume 50, Number 2. Harvard University, Cambridge, Massachusetts.
　1957b. A Chancay-style grave at Zapallan, Peru: an analysis of its textiles, pottery and other furnishings. *Papers of the Peabody Museum of Archaeology and Ethnology*, Volume 50, Number 1. Harvard University, Cambridge, Massachusetts.

Lozada, María Cecilia and Jane E. Buikstra
　2002. *El señorío de Chiribaya en la costa sur del Perú*. Instituto de Estudios Peruanos, Lima.

Lozada, María Cecilia and Barra O'Donnabhain, editors
　2013. *The Dead Tell Tales: Essays in Honor of Jane E. Buikstra*. Monograph 76. Cotsen Institute of Archaeology Press, University of California at Los Angeles.

Lozada, María Cecilia, Augusto Cardona Rosas, and Hans Barnard
　2013. Looting: another phase in the social history of a prehispanic cemetery in southern Peru. *Backdirt* 115–123.

Lozada, María Cecilia and Gordon F. M. Rakita
　2013. Andean life transitions and gender perceptions in the past: a bioarchaeological approach among the pre-Inca Chiribaya of southern Peru. In *The Dead Tell Tales: Essays in Honor of Jane E. Buikstra*, edited by María Cecilia Lozada and Barra O'Donnabhain, pp. 114–122. Monograph 76. Cotsen Institute of Archaeology Press, University of California at Los Angeles.

M

Malpass, Michael A., editor
　1993. *Provincial Inca: Archaeological and Ethnohistorical Assessment of the Impact of the Inca State*. University of Iowa Press, Iowa City.

Malpass, Michael A. and Sonia Alconini, editors
　2010. *Distant Provinces in the Inka Empire: Toward a Deeper Understanding of Inka Imperialism*. University of Iowa Press, Iowa City.

Mantha, Alexis
　2015. Houses, residential burials, and identity in the Rapayán Valley and the Upper Marañon drainage, Peru, during Late Andean prehistory. *Latin American Antiquity* 26(4):433–451.

Marcone, Giancarlo, editor
　2022. *Unveiling Pachacamac: New Hypotheses for an Old Andean Sanctuary*. University Press of Florida, Gainesville.

Marcus, Joyce
　1978. Review of "Kaminaljuyú Project—1969, 1970 Seasons—Part I—Mound Excavations," edited by Joseph W. Michels and William T. Sanders. *Pennsylvania State Occasional Papers in Anthropology, Number 9*. *American Antiquity* 43(1):129–130.
　1983. Monte Albán's Tomb 7. In *The Cloud People: Divergent Evolution of the Zapotec and Mixtec Civilizations*, edited by Kent V. Flannery and Joyce Marcus, pp. 282–285. Academic Press, New York.
　1987a. *Late Intermediate Occupation at Cerro Azul, Perú: A Preliminary Report*. Technical Reports of the Museum of Anthropology, University of Michigan, Number 20. Ann Arbor.
　1987b. Prehistoric fishermen in the kingdom of Huarco. *American Scientist* 75:393–401.
　2004. Maya commoners: The stereotype and the reality. In *Ancient Maya Commoners*, edited by Jon C. Lohse and Fred Valdez, Jr., pp. 255–283. University of Texas Press, Austin.
　2008. *Excavations at Cerro Azul, Peru: The Architecture and Pottery*. Monograph 62, Cotsen Institute of Archaeology, University of California at Los Angeles.
　2009. A world tour of breweries. In *Andean Civilization: A Tribute to Michael E. Moseley*, edited by Joyce Marcus and Patrick Ryan Williams, pp. 303–324. Cotsen Institute of Archaeology, University of California at Los Angeles.
　2015. Studying the individual in prehistory: a tale of three women from Cerro Azul, Peru. *Ñawpa Pacha: Journal of Andean Archaeology* 35(1):1–22.
　2016a. Barcoding spindles and decorating whorls: how weavers marked their property at Cerro Azul, Peru. *Ñawpa Pacha: Journal of Andean Archaeology* 36(1):1–21.
　2016b. The ecosystems of the Kingdom of Huarco. In *Coastal Ecosystems and Economic Strategies at Cerro Azul, Peru: The Study of a Late Intermediate Kingdom*, edited by Joyce Marcus, pp. 3–19. Memoirs of the Museum of Anthropology, University of Michigan, Number 59. Ann Arbor.
　2016c. Provenience and context of the plant and animal remains at Cerro Azul. In *Coastal Ecosystems and Economic Strategies at Cerro Azul, Peru: The Study of a Late Intermediate Kingdom*, edited by Joyce Marcus, pp. 20–32. Memoirs of the Museum of Anthropology, University of Michigan, Number 59. Ann Arbor.
　2016d. The drying of fish for export. In *Coastal Ecosystems and Economic Strategies at Cerro Azul, Peru: The Study of a Late Intermediate Kingdom*, edited by Joyce Marcus, pp. 116–119. Memoirs of the Museum of Anthropology, University of Michigan, Number 59. Ann Arbor.
　2016e. The hunting of birds and mammals. In *Coastal Ecosystems and Economic Strategies at Cerro Azul, Peru: The Study*

of a Late Intermediate Kingdom, edited by Joyce Marcus, pp. 158–171. Memoirs of the Museum of Anthropology, University of Michigan, Number 59. Ann Arbor.
2016f. The economy of the Kingdom of Huarco. In *Coastal Ecosystems and Economic Strategies at Cerro Azul, Peru: The Study of a Late Intermediate Kingdom*, edited by Joyce Marcus, pp. 340–351. Memoirs of the Museum of Anthropology, University of Michigan, Number 59. Ann Arbor.
2017. The Inca conquest of Cerro Azul. *Ñawpa Pacha: Journal of Andean Archaeology* 37(2):175–196.
2019. Competitive versus peaceful interaction. In *Interregional Interaction in Ancient Mesoamerica*, edited by Joshua D. Englehardt and Michael D. Carrasco, pp. 341–364. University Press of Colorado, Boulder.
2020. *Zapotec Monuments and Political History*. Memoirs of the Museum of Anthropology, University of Michigan, Number 61. Ann Arbor.

Marcus, Joyce and Kent V. Flannery
2010. En búsqueda de la mentalidad andina: aventuras en el Perú con Ramiro Matos. *Arqueología y Vida* 3:9–22. Lima, Peru.

Marcus, Joyce, Kent Flannery, Jeffrey Sommer, and Robert G. Reynolds
2020. Maritime Adaptations at Cerro Azul, Peru: A Comparison of Late Intermediate and Twentieth-Century Fishing. In *Maritime Communities of the Ancient Andes: Society and Ecology in Island and Coastal Archaeology*, edited by Gabriel Prieto and Daniel H. Sandweiss, pp. 351–365. University Press of Florida, Gainesville.

Marcus, Joyce, Ramiro Matos Mendieta, and María Rostworowski de Diez Canseco
1985. Arquitectura inca de Cerro Azul, valle de Cañete. *Revista del Museo Nacional* 47:125–138. Lima, Peru.

Marcus, Joyce, Jeffrey Sommer, and Christopher P. Glew
1999. Fish and mammals in the economy of an ancient Peruvian kingdom. *Proceedings of the National Academy of Sciences* 96:6564–6570.

Marquet, Pablo A., Calogero M. Santoro, Claudio Latorre, Vivien G. Standen, Sebastián R. Abades, Marcelo M. Rivadeneira, Bernardo T. Arriaza, and Michael E. Hochberg
2012. Emergence of social complexity among coastal hunter-gatherers in the Atacama Desert of northern Chile. *Proceedings of the National Academy of Sciences USA* 109(37):14754–14760.

Marsteller, Sara J., Kelly J. Knudson, G. Gordon, and A. Anbar
2017a. Biogeochemical reconstructions of life histories as a method to assess regional interactions: stable oxygen and radiogenic strontium isotopes and Late Intermediate Period mobility on the central Peruvian coast. *Journal of Archaeological Science Report* 13:535–546.

Marsteller, Sara J., Natalya Zolotova, and Kelly J. Knudson
2017b. Investigating economic specialization on the central Peruvian coast: A reconstruction of Late Intermediate Period Ychsma diet using stable isotopes. *American Journal of Physical Anthropology* 162:300–317.

Medlin, Mary Ann
1986. Learning to weave in Calcha, Bolivia. In *The Junius B. Bird Conference on Andean Textiles, April 7th and 8th, 1984*, edited by Ann Pollard Rowe, pp. 275–287. The Textile Museum, Washington, D.C.

Menzel, Dorothy
1977. *The Archaeology of Ancient Peru and the Work of Max Uhle*. Robert H. Lowie Museum of Anthropology, University of California, Berkeley.

Menzel, Dorothy and John H. Rowe
1966. The role of Chincha in late pre-Spanish Peru. *Ñawpa Pacha: Journal of Andean Archaeology* 4:63–76.

Meskell, Lynn and Rosemary A. Joyce
2003. *Embodied Lives: Figuring Ancient Maya and Egyptian Experience*. Routledge, London.

Metcalf, Peter and Richard Huntington
1991. *Celebrations of Death: The Anthropology of Mortuary Ritual*. Second edition. Cambridge University Press, Cambridge, UK.

Middleton, William D., Gary M. Feinman, and Guillermo Molina Villegas
1998. Tomb use and reuse in Oaxaca, Mexico. *Ancient Mesoamerica* 9(2):297–307.

Millaire, Jean-François
2002. *Moche Burial Patterns: An Investigation into Prehispanic Social Structure*. BAR International Series 1066. Archaeopress, Oxford, England.
2004. The manipulation of human remains in Moche society: delayed burials, grave reopening, and secondary offerings of human bones on the Peruvian north coast. *Latin American Antiquity* 15:371–388.

Millaire, Jean-François and Flannery Surette
2011. Un fardo funerario procedente de Huaca Santa Clara, valle de Virú (ca. 1150 a.D.). *Bulletin de L'Institut Français d'Études Andines* 40(2):289–305.

Miller, Arthur G.
1991. The carved stela in Tomb 5, Suchilquitongo, Oaxaca, Mexico. *Ancient Mesoamerica* 2:215–224.
1995. *The Painted Tombs of Oaxaca, Mexico: Living with the Dead*. Cambridge University Press, New York.

Millon, René
1992. Teotihuacan studies: From 1950 to 1990 and beyond. In *Art, Ideology, and the City of Teotihuacan*, edited by

Janet C. Berlo, pp. 399–419. Dumbarton Oaks Research Library and Collection, Washington, D.C.

Milner, George R.
    1984. Social and temporal implications of variation among American Bottom Mississippian cemeteries. *American Antiquity* 49:468–488.
    1995. An osteological perspective on prehistoric warfare. In *Regional Approaches to Mortuary Analysis*, edited by Lane Anderson Beck, pp. 221–244. Plenum, New York.

Moore, Jerry D.
    1996. *Architecture and Power in the Ancient Andes: The Archaeology of Public Buildings*. Cambridge University Press, Cambridge.

Morris, Craig
    1988. Más allá de las fronteras de Chincha. In *La Frontera del Estado Inca*, edited by Tom D. Dillehay and Patricia Netherly, pp. 131–140. BAR International Series 442. British Archaeological Reports. Oxford, England.
    1998. Inka strategies of incorporation and governance. In *Archaic States*, edited by Gary Feinman and Joyce Marcus, pp. 293–309. School of American Research Press, Santa Fe, New Mexico.

Morris, Craig and Julián Idilio Santillana
    2007. The Inka transformation of the Chincha capital. In *Variations in the Expression of Inka Power: A Symposium at Dumbarton Oaks, 18 and 19 October, 1997*, edited by Richard L. Burger, Craig Morris, and Ramiro Matos Mendieta, pp. 135–163. Dumbarton Oaks Research Library and Collection, Washington, D.C.

Morris, Craig and Adriana von Hagen
    2011. *The Incas: Lords of the Four Quarters*. Thames & Hudson, London.

Muñoz, Iván, Bernardo T. Arriaza, and Arthur Aufderheide
    1993. El poblamiento Chinchorro: Nuevos indicadores bioantropológicos y discusión en torno a su organización social. En *Acha-2 y los Orígenes del Poblamiento Humano en Arica*, edited by Iván Muñoz, Bernardo Arriaza, and Arthur Aufderheide, pp. 107–132. Universidad de Tarapacá, Arica, Chile.

Munsell Color Company
    1954. *Munsell Soil Color Charts*. Munsell Color Company, Baltimore, Maryland.

Murra, John V.
    1962. Cloth and its functions in the Inca state. *American Anthropologist* 64(4):710–728.
    1972. El 'control vertical' de un máximo de pisos ecológicos en la economía de las sociedades andinas. In *Visita de la Provincia de León de Huánuco en 1562*, edited by John V. Murra, pp. 429–476. Universidad Nacional Hermilio Valdizán, Huánuco, Peru.
    1975. *Formaciones económicas y políticas del mundo andina*. Instituto de Estudios Peruanos, Lima.
    1980. *The Economic Organization of the Inca State*. JAI Press, Greenwich, Connecticut.
    1989. Cloth and its function in the Inka state. In *Cloth and Human Experience*, edited by Annette B. Weiner and Jane Schneider, pp. 275–302. Smithsonian Institution Press, Washington D.C. and London.

N

Nelson, Andrew J.
    1998. Wandering bones: archaeology, forensic science and Moche burial practices. *International Journal of Osteoarchaeology* 8(3):192–212.

Newell, William H.
    1976. Good and bad ancestors. In *Ancestors*, edited by William H. Newell, pp. 17–29. Mouton Publishers, The Hague and Paris.

Nielsen, Axel E.
    2008. The materiality of ancestors: chullpas and social memory in the late prehispanic history of the south Andes. In *Memory Work: Archaeologies of Material Practices*, edited by Barbara Mills and William H. Walker, pp. 207–231. School of American Research Press, Santa Fe, New Mexico.

Nigra, Ben, Terrah Jones, Jacob Bongers, Charles Stanish, Henry Tantaleán, and Kelita Pérez
    2014. The Chincha kingdom: the archaeology and ethnohistory of the Late Intermediate Period south coast, Peru. *Backdirt* 36–47.

Niles, Susan
    1992. Artist and empire in Inca and Colonial textiles. In *To Weave for the Sun: Ancient Andean Textiles in the Museum of Fine Arts, Boston*, edited by Rebecca Stone-Miller, pp. 51–65. Thames & Hudson, New York.

O

O'Neale, Lila M.
    1932. Tejidos del período primitivo de Paracas. *Revista del Museo Nacional* 1(2):60–80.
    1936. Wide-loom fabrics of the Early Nasca period. In *Essays in Anthropology, presented to Alfred L. Kroeber*, pp. 215–228. Berkeley, California.
    1937. Middle Cañete textiles. Appendix 6. In *Archaeological Explorations in Peru. Part IV: Cañete Valley*. Field Museum of Natural History Anthropology Memoirs, Volume II, Number 4, pp. 268–273. Field Museum of Natural History, Chicago.
    1946. Mochica (Early Chimu) and other Peruvian twill fabrics. *Southwestern Journal of Anthropology* 2(3):269–294.
    1949. Weaving. In *Handbook of South American Indians*, edited

by Julian H. Steward. Smithsonian Institution, Bureau of American Ethnology, Bulletin 143, Volume 5: The Comparative Ethnology of South American Indians, pp. 97–138. U.S. Government Printing Office, Washington, D.C.

O'Neale, Lila M. and Bonnie Jean Clark
1948. Textile periods in ancient Peru, III: The gauze weaves. *University of California Publications in American Archaeology and Ethnology* 40(4):143–222, Plates 3–22. University of California, Berkeley.

O'Neale, Lila M. and Alfred L. Kroeber
1930. Textile periods in ancient Peru, I. *University of California Publications in American Archaeology and Ethnology* 28(2):23–56. Berkeley, California.

O'Neale, Lila, E. Baker, C. W. Bacon, R. Gemmer, R. V. Hall, Irmgard W. Johnson, C. M. Osborne, and M. B. Ross
1949. Chincha plain-weave cloths. *University of California Anthropological Records* 9(2):133–156. Berkeley, California.

O'Shea, John M.
1981. Social configurations and the archaeological study of mortuary practices: a case study. In *The Archaeology of Death*, edited by Robert Chapman, Ian Kinnes, and Klavs Randsborg, pp. 39–52. Cambridge University Press, Cambridge and New York.
1984. *Mortuary Variability: An Archaeological Investigation*. Academic Press, Orlando, Florida.
1995. Mortuary custom in the Bronze Age of southeastern Hungary: diachronic and synchronic perspectives. In *Regional Approaches to Mortuary Analysis*, edited by Lane Anderson Beck, pp. 125–145. Plenum Press, New York.
1997. A portrait of ancient society on the South Hungarian Plain. In *Analecta Praehistorica Leidensia*, pp. 111–119. Faculty of Archaeology, Leiden University.

Owens, Lawrence S. and Peter Eeckhout
2015. To the god of death, disease and healing: social bioarchaeology of Cemetery I at Pachacamac. In *Funerary Practices and Models in the Ancient Andes: The Return of the Living Dead*, edited by Peter Eeckhout and Lawrence S. Owens, pp. 158–185. Cambridge University Press, Cambridge.

P

Palma Málaga, Martha R. and Krzysztof Makowski
2019. Bioarchaeological evidence of care provided to a physically disabled individual from Pachacamac, Peru. *International Journal of Paleopathology* 25:139–149.

Papadopoulos, John K. and Gary Urton, editors
2012. *The Construction of Value in the Ancient World*. Cotsen Institute of Archaeology, University of California at Los Angeles.

Parker, Arthur C.
1922. Archaeological history of New York. *New York State Museum Bulletin*, pp. 235–238. Albany, New York.

Parker Pearson, Mike
1982. Mortuary practices, society, and ideology: an ethnoarchaeological study. In *Symbolic and Structural Archaeology*, edited by Ian Hodder, pp. 99–113. Cambridge University Press, Cambridge, UK.
1993. The powerful dead: archaeological relationships between the living and the dead. *Cambridge Archaeological Journal* 3:203–229.
1999. *The Archaeology of Death and Burial*. Sutton Publishing, Stroud.
2002. Placing the physical and the incorporeal dead: Stonehenge and changing concepts of ancestral space in Neolithic Britain. In *The Space and Place of Death*, edited by Helaine Silverman and David B. Small, pp. 145–180. Archaeological Papers, Number 11. American Anthropological Association, Arlington, Virginia.

Parker Pearson, Mike, Andrew T. Chamberlain, Matthew J. Collins, C. Cox, G. Craig, Oliver E. Craig, Jen Hiller, Peter Marshall, Jacqui Mulville, and Helen Smith
2007. Further evidence for mummification in Bronze Age Britain. *Antiquity* http://antiquity.ac.uk/ProjGall/313/html.

Parker Pearson, Mike, Andrew Chamberlain, Oliver Craig, Peter Marshall, Jacqui Mulville, Helen Smith, Carolyn Chenery, Matthew Collins, Gordon Cook, Geoffrey Craig, Jane Evans, Jen Hiller, Janet Montgomery, Jean-Luc Schwenninger, Gillian Taylor, and Timothy Wess
2005. Evidence for mummification in Bronze Age Britain. *Antiquity* 79:529–546.

Parker Pearson, Mike, N. Sharples, and J. Symonds with Jacqui Mulville, J. Raven, Helen Smith, and A. Woolf
2004. *South Uist: Archaeology and History of a Hebridean Island*. Tempus, Stroud.

Patterson, Thomas C.
1985. Pachacamac: An Andean oracle under Inca rule. In *Recent Studies in Andean Prehistory*, edited by Peter Kvietok and Daniel H. Sandweiss, pp. 159–176. Latin American Studies Program, Cornell University, Ithaca, New York.

Paul, Anne
1990. *Paracas Ritual Attire: Symbols of Authority in Ancient Peru*. University of Oklahoma Press, Norman.
1991. Paracas: an ancient cultural tradition on the south coast of Peru. In *Paracas Art and Architecture: Objects and Context in South Coastal Peru*, edited by Anne Paul, pp. 1–34. University of Iowa Press, Iowa City.

Peters, Ann H.
2000. Funerary regalia and institutions of leadership in Paracas and Topará. *Chungara: Revista de Antropología Chilena* 32(2):245–252.

2014. Paracas necropolis: communities of textile production, exchange networks and social boundaries in the central Andes, 150 BC to AD 250. In *Textiles, Technical Practice and Power in the Andes*, edited by Denise Y. Arnold and Penelope Dransart, pp. 109–139. Archetype Publication, London.

Petersen, James B., Nathan D. Hamilton, James M. Adovasio, and Alan L. McPherron
    1984. Netting technology and the antiquity of fish exploitation in eastern North America. *Midcontinental Journal of Archaeology* 9(2):199–225.

Phipps, Elena
    2015. Inka textile traditions and their Colonial counterparts. In *The Inka Empire: A Multidisciplinary Approach*, edited by Izumi Shimada, pp. 197–214. University of Texas Press, Austin.
    2018. Garments, *tocapu*, status, and identity: Inca and Colonial perspectives. In *The Oxford Handbook of the Incas*, edited by Sonia Alconini and Alan Covey, pp. 645–668. Oxford University Press, New York.

Polo de Ondegardo, Juan
    1916–1917. Informaciones acerca de la religión y gobierno de los incas por el licenciado Polo de Ondegardo [1571]. In *Colección de Libros y Documentos Referentes a la Historia del Perú*, Tomos 3–4. Edited by Horacio H. Urteaga. Colección de Libros y Documentos Referentes a la Historia del Perú. Imprenta y Librería Sanmartí. Lima, Perú.

Price, Karen E., Catherine Higgitt, Thibaut Devièse, Colin McEwan, and Bill Sillar
    2015. Tools for eternity: pre-Columbian workbaskets as textile production toolkits and grave offerings. *Technical Research Bulletin, British Museum*, Volume 9, pp. 65–86. London.

Prieto, Gabriel and Daniel H. Sandweiss, editors
    2020. *Maritime Communities of the Ancient Andes: Society and Ecology in Island and Coastal Archaeology*. University Press of Florida, Gainesville.

Q

Quilter, Jeffrey
    1989. *Life and Death at Paloma: Society and Mortuary Practices in a Preceramic Peruvian Village*. University of Iowa Press, Iowa City.

Quinn, Colin P.
    2015. Returning and reuse: diachronic perspectives on multi-component cemeteries and mortuary politics at Middle Neolithic and Early Bronze Age Tara, Ireland. *Journal of Anthropological Archaeology* 37:1–18.

R

Rabin, Emily
    1970. The Lambityeco friezes: notes on their content, with an appendix on C14 dates. *Boletín de Estudios Oaxaqueños*, Number 33. Mitla, Oaxaca, Mexico.

Rabinowitz, Joel Bezalel
    1980. Pescadora, the Argot of Chimu Fishermen. Master's thesis, Department of Anthropology, University of Texas, Austin.
    1983. La lengua pescadora: the lost dialect of Chimu fishermen. In *Investigations of the Andean Past: Papers from the First Annual Northeast Conference on Andean Archaeology and Ethnohistory*, edited by Daniel H. Sandweiss, pp. 243–267. Cornell University, Ithaca, New York.

Rakita, Gordon F. M., Jane E. Buikstra, Lane A. Beck, and Sloan R. Williams
    2005. *Interacting with the Dead: Perspectives on Mortuary Archaeology for the New Millennium*. University Press of Florida, Gainesville.

Reese-Taylor, Kathryn, Marc Zender, and Pamela L. Geller
    2006. Fit to be tied: funerary practices among the prehispanic Maya. In *Sacred Bundles: Ritual Acts of Wrapping and Binding in Mesoamerica*, edited by Julia Guernsey and F. Kent Reilly, pp. 40–58. Boundary End Archaeology Research Center, Barnardsville, North Carolina.

Rehl, Jane W.
    2002. Weaving Metaphors, Weaving Cosmos: Structure, Creativity, and Meaning in Discontinuous Warp and Weft Textiles of Ancient Peru, 300 B.C.E.–1540 C.E. PhD dissertation, Department of Art History, Emory University, Atlanta.

Reinhard, Johan
    2005. *The Ice Maiden: Inca Mummies, Mountain Gods, and Sacred Sites in the Andes*. National Geographic Society, Washington, D.C.

Reinhard, Johan and María Constanza Ceruti
    2010. *Inca Rituals and Sacred Mountains: A Study of the World's Highest Archaeological Sites*. Cotsen Institute of Archaeology Press, University of California at Los Angeles.

Reiss, Johann Wilhelm and Alphons Stübel
    1880–1887. *The Necropolis of Ancón in Peru: A Contribution to Our Knowledge of the Culture and Industries of the Empire of the Incas, Being the Results of Excavations Made on the Spot*. Translated by A. H. Keane. Three volumes. A. Asher and Co., Berlin.

Rengifo Chunga, Carlos and Luis Jaime Castillo Butters
    2015. The construction of social identity: tombs of specialists at San José de Moro, Jequetepeque Valley, Perú. In *Funerary*

Practices and Models in the Ancient Andes: The Return of the Living Dead, edited by Peter Eeckhout and Lawrence S. Owens, pp. 117–136. Cambridge University Press, Cambridge, UK.

Ritchie, William A.
  1932. The Algonkin sequence in New York. *American Anthropologist* 34:406–414.
  1938. A perspective of northeastern archaeology. *American Antiquity* 4(2)94–112.

Rivera, Mario A.
  1995. The Preceramic Chinchorro mummy complex of northern Chile: context, style, and purpose. In *Tombs for the Living: Andean Mortuary Practices, a symposium at Dumbarton Oaks 12th and 13th October 1991,* edited by Tom D. Dillehay, pp. 43–78. Dumbarton Oaks Research Library and Collection, Washington, D.C.

Rodríguez Suy Suy, Víctor Antonio
  1997. *Los pueblos muchik en el mundo andino de ayer y siempre.* PRATEC, Lima, Peru.

Romero Molina, Javier
  1958. *Mutilaciones dentarias prehispánicas de México y América en general.* Instituto Nacional de Antropología e Historia, Mexico.
  1970. Dental mutilation, trephination, and cranial deformation. In *The Handbook of Middle American Indians,* Volume 9: *Physical Anthropology,* edited by T. Dale Stewart, pp. 50–67. University of Texas Press, Austin.

Rostworowski de Diez Canseco, María
  1970. Mercaderes del valle de Chincha en la época prehispánica: un documento y unos comentarios. *Revista Española de Antropología Americana,* tomo v, pp. 135–178. Madrid.
  1973. Urpay Huachac y el símbolo del mar. *Arqueología PUCP,* number 14:13–22. Pontificia Universidad Católica del Perú, Lima.
  1975. Pescadores, artesanos y mercaderes costeños en el Perú prehispánico. *Revista del Museo Nacional* 41:311–349. Lima.
  1977a. *Etnía y sociedad: costa peruana prehispánica.* Instituto de Estudios Peruanos, Lima.
  1977b. Coastal fishermen, merchants and artisans in prehispanic Peru. In *The Sea in the Pre-Columbian World, October 26th and 27th 1974,* edited by Elizabeth P. Benson, pp. 167–186. Dumbarton Oaks, Washington, D.C.
  1978–1980. Huarco y Lunaguaná. Dos señoríos prehispánicos de la costa sur-central del Perú. *Revista del Museo Nacional* 44:153–214. Lima.
  1978. *Señoríos indígenas de Lima y Canta.* Instituto de Estudios Peruanos, Lima.
  1981. *Recursos naturales renovables y pesca, siglos XVI y XVII.* Instituto de Estudios Peruanos, Lima.
  1989. *Costa peruana prehispánica.* Instituto de Estudios Peruanos, Lima.
  1992. *Pachacamac y el Señor de los Milagros: una trayectoria milenaria.* Instituto de Estudios Peruanos, Lima.
  1999. *History of the Inca Realm.* Translated by Harry B. Iceland. Cambridge University Press, Cambridge, UK.

Rowe, Ann Pollard
  1977. *Warp-Patterned Weaves of the Andes.* The Textile Museum, Washington, D.C.
  1978. Technical features of Inca tapestry tunics. *Textile Museum Journal* 17:5–28. Washington, D.C.
  1984. *Costumes and Featherwork of the Lords of Chimor: Textiles from Peru's North Coast.* The Textile Museum, Washington, D.C.
  1986. Textiles from the Nasca Valley at the time of the fall of the Huari Empire. In *The Junius B. Bird Conference on Andean Textiles, April 7th and 8th, 1984,* edited by Ann Pollard Rowe, pp. 151–182. The Textile Museum, Washington, D.C.
  1992. Provincial Inca tunics of the south coast of Peru. *Textile Museum Journal* 31:5–52. Washington, D.C.
  1995–1996. Inca weaving and costume. *Textile Museum Journal* 34–35:5–53. Washington, D.C.
  1996a. The art of Peruvian textiles. In *Andean Art at Dumbarton Oaks, Volume 2,* edited by Elizabeth Hill Boone, pp. 329–345. Dumbarton Oaks Research Library and Collection, Washington, D.C.
  1996b. Central coast textiles. In *Andean Art at Dumbarton Oaks, Volume 2,* edited by Elizabeth Hill Boone, pp. 437–451. Dumbarton Oaks Research Library and Collection, Washington, D.C.
  1997. Inca weaving and costume. *Textile Museum Journal* 34–35:5–54. Washington, D.C.
  2011. Evidence for pre-Inca textiles. In *Costume and History in Highland Ecuador,* edited by Ann Rowe, pp. 49–69. University of Texas Press, Austin.

Rowe, Ann P. and John H. Rowe
  1996. Inca tunics. In *Andean Art at Dumbarton Oaks, Volume 1,* edited by Elizabeth Hill Boone, pp. 453–469. Dumbarton Oaks Research Library and Collection, Washington, D.C.

Rowe, John Howland
  1946. Inca culture at the time of the Spanish Conquest. In *Handbook of South American Indians,* edited by Julian H. Steward, volume 2, pp. 183–330. Smithsonian Institution, Bureau of American Ethnology, Bulletin 143. U.S. Government Printing Office, Washington, D.C.
  1958. The age grades of the Inca census. In *Miscellanea Paul Rivet Octogenario Dicata II. XXXI Congreso Internacional de Americanistas,* pp. 499–522. Universidad Nacional Autónoma de México, Mexico.
  1962. Worsaae's law and the use of grave lots for archaeological dating. *American Antiquity* 28:129–137.
  1979. Standardization in Inca tapestry tunics. In *The Junius B. Bird Pre-Columbian Textile Conference, May 19th and 20th, 1973,* edited by Ann Pollard Rowe, Elizabeth P. Benson, and Anne-Louise Schaffer, pp. 239–264. Textile Museum and Dumbarton Oaks, Washington D.C.
  1995. Behavior and belief in ancient Peruvian mortuary practice. In *Tombs for the Living: Andean Mortuary Practices, a symposium at Dumbarton Oaks, 12th and 13th October*

1991, edited by Tom D. Dillehay, pp. 27–41. Dumbarton Oaks Research Library and Collection, Washington, D.C.

Royce, Anya Peterson
2011. *Becoming an Ancestor: The Isthmus Zapotec Way of Death*. State University of New York Press, Albany.

S

Safford, William Edwin
1917. Food-plants and textiles of ancient America. In *Proceedings of the XIX International Congress of Americanists* (held at Washington, December 27–31 in 1915), pp. 12–30.

Salomon, Frank
1995. "The beautiful grandparents": Andean ancestor shrines and mortuary ritual as seen through Colonial records. In *Tombs for the Living: Andean Mortuary Practices, a symposium at Dumbarton Oaks, 12th and 13th October 1991*, edited by Tom D. Dillehay, pp. 315–353. Dumbarton Oaks Research Library and Collection, Washington, D.C.

Sanders, William T. and Barbara J. Price
1968. *Mesoamerica: The Evolution of a Civilization*. Random House, New York City.

Sandweiss, Daniel H.
1988. The fishermen of Chincha: Occupational specialization on the central coast. In *Economic Prehistory of the Central Andes*, edited by Elizabeth S. Wing and Jane C. Wheeler, pp. 99–118. British Archaeological Reports, Oxford, England.
1992. The Archaeology of Chincha Fishermen: Specialization and Status in Inka Peru. *Bulletin of the Carnegie Museum of Natural History*, Number 29. Pittsburgh, Pennsylvania.

Santos, Mariela and Vivien G. Standen
2022. El temprano arte de la tradición de tejer esteras en fibra vegetal en la sociedad Chinchorro (10.000–3500 aP): Extremo norte de Chile. *Latin American Antiquity* 33(2):355–375.

Saville, Marshall H.
1925. Balance-beam scales in ancient Peru. *Indian Notes* 2:266–283. Museum of the American Indian, Heye Foundation, New York.

Saxe, Arthur Alan
1970. Social Dimensions of Mortuary Practices. Unpublished PhD dissertation, Department of Anthropology, University of Michigan, Ann Arbor.
1971. Social dimensions of mortuary practices in a Mesolithic population from Wadi Halfa, Sudan. In *Approaches to the Social Dimensions of Mortuary Practices*, edited by James A. Brown, pp. 39–57. Memoirs of the Society for American Archaeology, Number 25. Washington, D.C.

Sewell, William, Jr.
1992. A theory of structure: duality, agency and transformation. *American Journal of Sociology* 98:1–29.

Sharer, Robert J. and Loa Traxler
2006. *The Ancient Maya*. Stanford University Press, Stanford, California.

Shimada, Izumi
1982. Horizontal archipelago and coast-highland interaction in north Peru: archaeological models. In *El Hombre y Su Ambiente en los Andes Centrales*, edited by Luis Millones and Hiroyasu Tomoeda, pp. 137–210. Museo Nacional de Etnología, Osaka, Japan.
1991. *Pachacamac Archaeology: Retrospect and Prospect*. The University Museum of Archaeology and Anthropology, University of Pennsylvania, Philadelphia.

Shimada, Izumi, editor
2015. *The Inka Empire: A Multidisciplinary Approach*. University of Texas Press, Austin.

Shimada, Izumi and James L. Fitzsimmons, editors
2015. *Living with the Dead in the Andes*. University of Arizona Press, Tucson.

Shimada, Izumi, Haagen D. Klaus, Rafael A. Segura, and Go Matsumoto
2015. Living with the dead: conception and treatment of the dead on the Peruvian coast. In *Living with the Dead in the Andes*, edited by Izumi Shimada and James L. Fitzsimmons, pp. 101–172. The University of Arizona Press, Tucson.

Shimada, Izumi, Rafael A. Segura, and Barbara Winsborough
2022. Pachacamac and water: An interdisciplinary approach to the origins, significance, and resilience of Pachacamac. In *Unveiling Pachacamac: New Hypotheses for an Old Andean Sanctuary*, edited by Giancarlo Marcone, pp. 40–75. University Press of Florida, Gainesville.

Shimada, Izumi, Ken-ichi Shinoda, Julie Farnum, Robert Corruccini, and Hirokatsu Watanabe
2004. An integrated analysis of prehispanic mortuary practices: a Middle Sicán case study. *Current Anthropology* 45(3):369–402.

Sillar, Bill
1992. The social life of the Andean dead. *Archaeological Review from Cambridge* 11(1):107–123.

Silverblatt, Irene
1987. *Moon, Sun, and Witches: Gender Ideologies and Class in Inca and Colonial Peru*. Princeton University Press, Princeton, New Jersey.

Skinner, Milica D.
1975. The archaeological looms from Peru in the American Museum of Natural History collection. In *Irene Emery*

Roundtable on Museum Textiles: Archaeological Textiles, 1974 Proceedings, edited by Patricia L. Fiske, pp. 67–76. The Textile Museum, Washington, D.C.

1986. Three textiles from Huaca Prieta, Chicama Valley, Peru. In *The Junius B. Bird Conference on Andean Textiles, April 7th and 8th, 1984*, edited by Ann Pollard Rowe, pp. 11–18. The Textile Museum, Washington, D. C.

Slovak, Nicole M. and A. Paytan
2009. Fisherfolk and farmers: carbon and nitrogen isotope evidence from Middle Horizon Ancón, Peru. *International Journal of Osteoarchaeology* 21:253–267.

Smith, C. Earle, Jr. and Joyce Marcus
2016a. Industrial plants. In *Coastal Ecosystems and Economic Strategies at Cerro Azul, Peru: The Study of a Late Intermediate Kingdom*, edited by Joyce Marcus, pp. 262–284. Memoirs of the Museum of Anthropology, University of Michigan, Number 59. Ann Arbor.
2016b. Edible, ritual, and medicinal plants. In *Coastal Ecosystems and Economic Strategies at Cerro Azul, Peru: The Study of a Late Intermediate Kingdom*, edited by Joyce Marcus, pp. 201–231. Memoirs of the Museum of Anthropology, University of Michigan, Number 59. Ann Arbor.

Splitstoser, Jeffrey C.
2012. The parenthetical notation method for recording yarn structure. *Textile Society of America*, pp. 1–16. Washington, D.C.
2017. Twined and woven artifacts. Part 1: Textiles. In *Where the Land Meets the Sea: Fourteen Millennia of Human History at Huaca Prieta*, edited by Tom D. Dillehay, pp. 458–524. University of Texas Press, Austin.

Spurling, Geoffrey E.
1992. The Organization of Craft Production in the Inka State: The Potters and Weavers of Milliraya. PhD dissertation, Cornell University, Ithaca, New York.

Squier, Ephraim George
1967[1869]. A plain man's tomb in Peru. From Frank Leslie's Illustrated Newspaper Vol. 28(704):21–22. Reprinted in *Peruvian Archaeology: Selected Readings*, edited by John H. Rowe and Dorothy Menzel, pp. 210–217. Peek Publications, Palo Alto, California.

Standen, Vivien G.
1997. Temprana complejidad funeraria de la cultura Chinchorro (Norte de Chile). *Latin American Antiquity* 8:134–156.

Standen, Vivien G., Bernardo Arriaza, Calogero M. Santoro, and Mariela Santos
2014. La práctica funeraria en el sitio maestranza Chinchorro y el poblamiento costero durante el arcaico medio en el extremo norte de Chile. *Latin American Antiquity* 25(3):300–321.

Stanish, Charles
2012. Above-ground tombs in the circum-Titicaca Basin. In *Advances in Titicaca Basin Archaeology—III*, edited by Alexei Vranich, Elizabeth A. Klarich, and Charles Stanish, pp. 203–220. Memoirs of the Museum of Anthropology, University of Michigan, Number 51. Ann Arbor.

Stephens, S. G. and M. Edward Moseley
1973. Cotton remains from archeological sites in central coastal Peru. *Science* 180(4082):186–188.

Stone-Miller, Rebecca, editor
1992a. To weave for the sun: an introduction to the fiber arts of the ancient Andes. In *To Weave for the Sun: Ancient Andean Textiles in the Museum of Fine Arts, Boston*, pp. 11–24. Thames & Hudson, New York.
1992b. *To Weave for the Sun: Ancient Andean Textiles in the Museum of Fine Arts, Boston*. Thames & Hudson, New York.

Stothert, Karen E. and Eve Yarberry
1978. Preparing a mummy bundle: notes on a late burial from Ancón, Peru. *Ñawpa Pacha: Journal of Andean Archaeology* 16:13–22.

Strong, William Duncan
1933. The Plains culture area in the light of archaeology. *American Anthropologist* 35(2):271–287.
1935. An introduction to Nebraska archaeology. *Smithsonian Miscellaneous Collections*, Volume 93, Number 10. Smithsonian Institution, Washington, D.C.

Sugiyama, Saburo
2011. Interactions between the living and the dead at major monuments in Teotihuacan. In *Living With the Dead: Mortuary Ritual in Mesoamerica*, edited by James L. Fitzsimmons and Izumi Shimada, pp. 161–202. The University of Arizona Press, Tucson.

T

Tainter, Joseph A.
1978. Mortuary practices and the study of prehistoric social systems. In *Advances in Archaeological Method and Theory* 1:105–141. Academic Press, New York.

Takigami, Mai K., Izumi Shimada, Rafael Segura, Sarah Muno, Hiroyuki Matsuzaki, Fuyuki Tokanai, Kazuhiro Kato, Hitoshi Mukai, Omori Takayuki, and Minoru Yoneda
2014. Assessing the chronology and rewrapping of funerary bundles at the prehispanic religious center of Pachacamac, Peru. *Latin American Antiquity* 25(3):322–343.

Tantaleán, Henry, Juliana Gómez Mejía, and Charles Stanish
2022. Los últimos Paracas: fardos funerarios de la tradición Paracas Cavernas de Cerro del Gentil, valle medio de Chincha, costa sur del Perú. *Boletín de Arqueología PUCP* 31:61–80.

Tello, Julio C.
    1929. *Antiguo Perú: primera época*. Comisión Organizadora del Segundo Congreso Sudamericano de Turismo, Lima.
    1959. *Paracas. Primera parte*. Empresa Gráfica T. Scheuch, Lima.
    2009. *Paracas Wari Kayan*. Cuadernos de Investigación del Archivo Tello 9. Museo de Arqueología y Antropología de la Universidad Nacional Mayor de San Marcos, Lima, Perú.

Tello, Julio C. and Toribio Mejía Xesspe
    1979. *Paracas. Segunda Parte: Cavernas y Necrópolis*. Universidad Nacional Mayor de San Marcos and The Institute of Andean Research of New York. Dirección Universitaria de Biblioteca y Publicaciones. Lima, Peru.

Tiballi, Anne
    2010. *Imperial Subjectivities: The Archaeological Materials from the Cemetery of the Sacrificed Women, Pachacamac, Peru*. PhD dissertation, State University of New York at Binghamton.

Tiesler, Vera
    2012. Studying cranial vault modifications in ancient Mesoamerica. *Journal of Anthropological Sciences* 90:1-26.

Tomasto-Cagigao, Elsa
    2009. Talking bones: bioarchaeological analysis of individuals from Palpa. In *New Technologies for Archaeology: Multidisciplinary Investigations in Palpa and Nasca, Peru*, edited by Markus Reindel and G. A. Wagner, pp. 141-158. Springer-Verlag, Berlin.

Tomasto-Cagigao, Elsa, Markus Reindel, and Johny Isla
    2015. Paracas funerary practices in Palpa, south coast of Perú. In *Funerary Practices and Models in the Ancient Andes: The Return of the Living Dead*, edited by Peter Eeckhout and Lawrence S. Owens, pp. 69-86. Cambridge University Press, Cambridge, UK.

Tomczak, Paula D.
    2003. Prehistoric diet and socioeconomic relationships within the Osmore Valley of southern Peru. *Journal of Anthropological Archaeology* 22(3):262-278.

Topic, John R., Jr.
    1982. Lower-class social and economic organization at Chan Chan. In *Chan Chan: Andean Desert City*, edited by Michael E. Moseley and Kent C. Day, pp. 145-175. School of American Research, University of New Mexico, Albuquerque.

Trik, Aubrey S.
    1963. The splendid tomb of Temple I at Tikal, Guatemala. *Expedition* 6(1):2-18.

Tuan, Yi-Fu
    1977. *Place and Space: The Perspective of Experience*. University of Minnesota Press, Minneapolis.
    1991. Language and the making of place: a narrative-descriptive approach. *Annals of the Association of American Geographers* 81(4):684-696.

Turner, Bethany L., John D. Kingston, and George Armelagos
    2010. Variation in dietary histories among the immigrants of Machu Picchu: carbon and nitrogen isotope evidence. *Chungara: Revista de Antropología Chilena* 42:515-534.

Tyler, John M.
    1921. *The New Stone Age of Northern Europe*. Charles Scribner's Sons, New York.

U

Uhle, Max
    1903. *Pachacamac: Report of the William Pepper, M.D., LL.D., Peruvian Expedition of 1896 by Dr. Max Uhle*. Department of Archaeology of the University of Pennsylvania, Philadelphia.
    1924. Explorations at Chincha. *University of California Publications in American Archaeology and Ethnology* 21(2):55-94. University of California Press, Berkeley.

Urton, Gary and Alejandro Chu
    2018. The invention of taxation in the Inka Empire. *Latin American Antiquity* 29(4):1-16.

V

Valdez, Lidio M.
    2019. Inka sacrificial guinea pigs from Tambo Viejo, Peru. *International Journal of Osteoarchaeology* 29:595-601.

Valdez, Lidio M. and Katrina J. Bettcher
    2020. Pichqa and pisqoyñu: Inca gaming paraphernalia from Tambo Viejo, Peru. *Ñawpa Pacha: Journal of Andean Archaeology* 40(1):119-132.

Valdez, Lidio M., Katrina J. Bettcher, and J. Ernesto Valdez
    2002. New Wari mortuary structures in the Ayacucho Valley, Peru. *Journal of Anthropological Research* 58(3):389-407.

van Dalen Luna, Pieter Dennis, Alfredo Altamirano Enciso, and Łukasz Majchrzak
    2018. Marcas para la vida, señales para la muerte. Los cuerpos tatuados de la cultura Chancay en Cerro Colorado, Huacho, Perú. *Revista M.-Dossie Estudos sobre a morte, os mortos o morrer* 3(6):344-377. Río de Janeiro.

van Dalen Luna, Pieter and Łukasz Majchrzak
    2019. Estratigrafía y componentes de un fardo funerario de la cultura Chancay procedente de Cerro Colorado, Huacho. *Arqueología. Investigaciones Sociales* 22(41):79-91. Lima.

van Dalen Luna, Pieter, Łukasz Majchrzak, and Martín Rodríguez Huaynate

2021. La cronología absoluta de los fardos funerarios de la cultura Chancay del cementerio de Cerro Colorado, Huacho. *Arqueología y Sociedad* 35:239–267. Museo de Arqueología y Antropología de San Marcos, Universidad Nacional Mayor de San Marcos, Lima.

van Gennep, Arnold
1960. *The Rites of Passage*. University of Chicago Press, Chicago.

VanStan, Ina
1967. *Textiles from Beneath the Temple of Pachacamac, Peru*. University Museum, University of Pennsylvania, Philadelphia.

Vásquez Sánchez, Víctor F., Régulo Franco Jordan, Teresa Rosales Tham, Isabel Rey Fraile, Laura Tormo Cifuentes, and Beatriz Álvarez Dorda
2013. Estudio microquímico mediante MEB-EDS (análisis de energía dispersiva por rayos X) del pigmento utilizado en el tatuaje de la Señora de Cao. *Revista Archaeobios* 7(1):5–21.

Velasco, Matthew C.
2023. Burying the dead at Ayawiri: Mortuary diversity and postmortem manipulation at an Andean hillfort (AD 1100–1450). *Latin American Antiquity* 34(3):589–607.

Verano, John W.
2003. Trepanation in prehistoric South America: geographic and temporal trends over 2,000 years. In *Trepanation: History, Discovery, Theory*, edited by Robert Arnott, Stanley Finger, and Christopher Upham Murray Smith, pp. 223–236. Swets & Zeitlinger, Lisse and Exton, Pennsylvania.
2016. *Holes in the Head: The Art and Archaeology of Trepanation in Ancient Peru*. Studies in Pre-Columbian Art and Archaeology Number 38. Dumbarton Oaks Research Library and Collection, Washington, D.C.

Vetter Parodi, Luisa María and Paloma Carcedo de Mufarech
2009. *El tupu: Símbolo ancestral de identidad femenina*. Gráfica Biblos, Lima.

Vreeland, James M.
1976. Second annual report, Proyecto de Investigación Textil "Julio C. Tello." Research report presented to the Secretariat for Technical Cooperation, Organization of American States, Washington, D.C.
1978. Prehistoric Andean mortuary practices: preliminary report from Peru. *Current Anthropology* 19(1):212–214.
1980. Mummies of Peru. In *Mummies, Disease, and Ancient Cultures*, edited by Aidan Cockburn, Eva Cockburn, and Theodore A. Reyman, pp. 154–189. Cambridge University Press, New York.
1986. Cotton spinning and processing on the Peruvian north coast. In *The Junius B. Bird Conference on Andean Textiles, April 7th and 8th, 1984*, edited by Ann Pollard Rowe, pp. 363–383. The Textile Museum, Washington, D.C.

W

Wallace, Dwight T.
1960. Early Paracas textile techniques. *American Antiquity* 26(2):279–281.
1979. The process of weaving development on the Peruvian coast. In *The Junius B. Bird Pre-Columbian Textile Conference, May 19th and 20th, 1973*, edited by Ann Pollard Rowe, Elizabeth P. Benson, and Anne-Louise Schaffer, pp. 27–50. The Textile Museum and Dumbarton Oaks, Washington, D.C.

Wardle, Harriet Newell
1936. Belts and girdles of the Inca's sacrificed women. *Revista del Museo Nacional* 5(1):25–38. Lima.

Wassén, S. Henry
1972. *A medicine man's implements and plants in a Tiahuanacoid tomb in highland Bolivia*. Goteborgs Ethnografiska Museum, Goteborg.

Wedel, Waldo R.
1938. The Direct-Historical Approach in Pawnee archaeology. *Smithsonian Miscellaneous Collections,* Volume 97, Number 7. Smithsonian Institution, Washington, D.C.

Weinberg, Camille, Jo Osborn, and Richard Espino Huaman
2022. Marine shellfish exploitation as a means of reducing vulnerability to resource uncertainty in southern coastal Peru (200 BCE–150 CE). *The Holocene* 32 (issue 12):1503–1517.

Weinberg, Camille, Benjamin T. Nigra, María Cecilia Lozada, Charles Stanish, Henry Tantaleán, Jacob Bongers, and Terrah Jones
2015. Demographic analysis of a looted Late Intermediate period tomb, Chincha Valley, Peru. *Andean Past* 12:133–154.

Weiss, Pedro
1932. Restos humanos de Cerro Colorado: Exploración en Cerro Colorado. *Revista del Museo Nacional* 2:90–102. Lima.

Weiss-Krejci, Estella
2001. Restless corpses: "secondary burial" in the Babenberg and Habsburg dynasties. *Antiquity* 75:769–780.
2003. Victims of human sacrifice in multiple tombs of the ancient Maya: A critical review. In *Antropología de la eternidad: La muerte en la cultura maya*, edited by Andrés Ciudad Ruiz, Mario Humberto Ruz, and María Josefa Iglesias Ponce de León, pp. 355–381. Sociedad Española de Estudios Mayas y Centro de Estudios Mayas, Madrid, Spain.
2004. Mortuary representations of the noble house: a cross-cultural comparison between collective tombs of the ancient Maya and dynastic Europe. *Journal of Social Archaeology* 4(3):368–404.

Whalen, Michael E.
1981. *Excavations at Santo Domingo Tomaltepec: Evolution of*

a Formative Community in the Valley of Oaxaca, Mexico. Memoirs of the Museum of Anthropology, University of Michigan, Number 12. Ann Arbor.

Whitley, James
    2002. Too many ancestors. *Antiquity* 76:119–126.

Więckowski, Wiesław
    2019. *Wari Women from Huarmey. Bioarchaeological interpretation of human remains from the Wari elite mausoleum at Castillo de Huarmey, Peru.* Archaeopress Pre-Columbian Archaeology 11. Summertown, Oxford, England.

Williams, Carlos and Manuel Merino
    1974. Inventario, catastro y delimitación del patrimonio arqueológico del valle de Cañete. Two volumes. Instituto Nacional de Cultura-Centro de Investigación y Restauración de Bienes Monumentales. Lima, Perú.

Wilson, Andrew S., Emma L. Brown, Chiara Villa, Niels Lynnerup, Andrew Healey, María Constanza Ceruti, Johan Reinhard, Carlos H. Previgliano, Facundo Arias Araoz, Josefina González Diez, and Timothy Taylor
    2013. Archaeological, radiological, and biological evidence offer insight into Inca child sacrifice. *Proceedings of the National Academy of Sciences USA* 110(33):13322–13327.

Y

Yacovleff, Eugenio and Jorge C. Muelle
    1932. Una exploración en Cerro Colorado: Informe y observaciones. *Revista del Museo Nacional* 1(2):31–59. Lima.
    1934a. Un fardo funerario de Paracas. *Revista del Museo Nacional* 3:63–153. Lima.
    1934b. Notas al trabajo "colorantes de Paracas." *Revista del Museo Nacional* 3:157–163. Lima.

Yarrow, Harry Crecy
    1880. Introduction to the study of mortuary customs among the North American Indians. *Contributions to North American Indians, Contributions to North American Ethnology* Volume 1. [republished in 2007 by IndyPublisher, Boston, Massachusetts]

Young-Sánchez, Margaret
    1992. Textile traditions of the Late Intermediate Period. In *To Weave for the Sun: Ancient Andean Textiles in the Museum of Fine Arts, Boston,* edited by Rebecca Stone-Miller, pp. 43–49. Thames & Hudson, New York.

Z

Zaro, Gregory
    2007. Diversity specialists: coastal resource management and historical contingency in the Osmore Desert of southern Peru. *Latin American Antiquity* 18(2):161–179.

Zorn, Elayne
    1982. Sling braiding in the Macusani area of Peru. *Textile Museum Journal* 19–20:41–54. Washington, D.C.

Zuidema, R. Tom
    1990. *Inca Civilization in Cuzco.* University of Texas Press, Austin.
    1991. Guaman Poma and the art of empire: towards an iconography of Inca royal dress. In *Transatlantic Encounters: Europeans and Andeans in the Sixteenth Century,* edited by K. Andrien and Rolena Adorno, pp. 151–202. University of California Press, Berkeley.

Index

A

abalone, see chanque, false abalone
Acacia sp., 317
acacia spines, 212. See also *huarango*
acequias (canals), 23. See also canals, irrigation
Acha 2 (a Chinchorro campsite), 14
Acha Man (naturally desiccated Chinchorro mummy), 14
achira leaves, 305, 310
Acosta, José de, 202
Africa, 4, 6
Agave, 35, 159
age grade, 6
agriculture, xvi, 16, 21; implements, 16, 334; lands, 16. See also beans, gourds, hoe, maize
aklla or *aqlla* (Quechua term for Chosen Women), 335
akllawasi (Quechua term for House of the Chosen Women), 334, 335, 336. See also *cumbi*
algodón blanco (*Gossypium*), see cotton
algodón pardo; see cotton
alpaca wool yarn balls, imported, 11. See also bag, camelid wool, yarn balls
Amaranthaceae, 290
Ampato, 336. See also Llullaillaco
ancestor, 3, 4, 5, 6, 10, 16, 20, 332; ancestor veneration, 16
anchovetas (*Engraulis ringens*), 61, 86, 114, 115, 121, 303, 306, 308
anchovies, xv, 61
Ancón, 11, 12, 13, 17, 18, 19, 25, 37, 84, 120, 145, 216, 314, 339
anhydrite, 202, 228, 236. See also pigment, pigment pouch
animal fertility, 6
animal hair or fur, 14, 193, 196, 271, 288, 290, 308. See also dog, guinea pig, leather pouch, llama, pelican

animated, lifelike quality, 7
animating substitutes of the emperor, 16
anniversaries, 4, 6
Antisuyu, 9
aparina (Quechua term for backstrap), 153, 156, 160–161. See also backstrap
appliqué snake, 267–268, see Burial 7
Ardren, Traci, 338
Arica, 14
Armatambo, 196, 216
Arriaga, Pablo Joseph de, 202, 332
ash, hot, applied to bones, 14
Ashley, Clifford W., 84
Asia (coastal Peruvian valley), 81, 84, 216
astragalus, drilled, 314, 316
astragalus, llama, 193
asymmetry in the impact of marriage on men and women, 335
atarraya (cast net), 60, 107, 121, 122, 123. See also cast net
aya (Quechua word for the deceased), 8, 10
ayllu members (Quechua term for a corporate group), 3, 20. See also descendants
azurite, 202, 228. See also pigment, pigment pouch, waterproof pouch

B

Bacall, Lauren, 7
backstrap, xvi, 13, 15, 121, 126, 153, 156, 160–161, 167, 184, 196, 204, 205, 206, 207, 208, 234, 242, 245–250, 284, 290, 291, 295, 322. See also Burial 9 (woman still wearing her backstrap around her hips and lower back, 284), *chumpi*, loom, tapestry, weaving

backstrap loom, xvi, 13, 15, 24, 99, 142, 153, 159, 160–161, 273, 280, 295, 322, 336.   See also loom

bag, cloth, 11, 17, 19, 131, 132, 134, 135, 136, 137, 142, 178, 184, 219, 193, 294; net bag, 14; woolen bag, 162, 164, 202, 203, 216, 224, 228, 233, 234, 235, 236, 237, 238, 239, 240, 241, 249, 251, 254, 277, 280, 281, 317, 322, 323.   See also chalk, coca, coca leaves, William Safford, yarn balls

bag drawstring, 235, 236, 238, 240, 251, 322, 323

bagre, 61

Baines, John, 19

balanza (scale for weighing items), 11, 35, 36, 37, 224, 238, 239, 300, 311, 312, 313; of bone, 311; to weigh gold, 37, 238

barbacoas (cane bed), 7

barcode (painted on spindles), xvi, 11, 137, 140, 208, 251, 254, 282, 322, 324–327, 338, 339.   See also spindle

Bartolomé Ruiz, see Ruiz

basketry, 11, 89, 163, 166, 167, 168, 248; twill plaited basketry band, 137, 163, 166, 167, 168.   See also workbasket

bast, 81, 86, 184, 236, 317, 338

bast fibers, 86, 87, 90, 93.   See also milkweed

batán (metate), 182; *mano de batán*, 182, 185

batten, 156, 160–161.   See also *kallwa* or weaving sword

battle, 14.   See also mace, mace head, trauma

beads, 34, 36, 60, 216, 219, 222, 333; of beans, 262, 263, 266; of chalcedony, 333; of gold, 36; of seeds, 196, 203, 227, 228, 337; of shell, 34, 60; of silver, 36; of stone, 216, 219, 222, 333; of turquoise, 219, 222.   See also bracelet, necklace

beans, 9, 17, 263, 266, 288, 299, 303, 308.   See also *Canavalia*, *Phaseolus*

beard, 333

bedding in burial cists, see mats, *pacay* leaves

beetle, golden spider, 115.   See also coprolite

belt, 99, 121, 126, 184, 333, 336.   See also Burials 4, 9, *chumpi*, loom

belt loom (*chumpi awana*), 15, 107, 108, 153, 242, 243, 244, 256–261, 290

Betanzos, Juan de, 335

Bettcher, Katrina, 317.   See also Lidio Valdez, wooden top

beverage, 8, 10, 19; therapeutic, 19.   See also coca leaves, coca tea, maize beer

Binford, Lewis R., 331, 332.   See also mortuary analysis

binni gula'sa' (Zapotec term for ancestor), 20

bird head, 97, 98, 205, 206, 241

Bird, Junius B., 84.   See also Huaca Prieta

Bird, Robert, 159

bird motif, 35, 92, 98, 126, 127, 205, 206, 232, 256, 267, 269, 290, 291, 320; birds incised on gourd, 266, 269

black seeds, 251, 263.   See also beads, beans, bracelet, necklace

Bloch, Maurice, 4.   See also Madagascar, Merina

blouse, 98, 101, 107, 184, 186.   See also cloth, tunic

blue powder (*binços*), 202.   See also pigment, pigment pouch

blunt force trauma, see battle, trauma

Boas, Franz, 31

bobbin, 156, 160–161, 209, 260.   See also loom, workbasket

body modifications, 13–14.   See also piercing, tattoo, trephination

Bogart, Humphrey, 7

bolas (*liwi*), 93, 107, 143, 152, 154, 155, 156, 157, 173, 339; repaired bolas, 152, 156

Bongers, Jacob, 337.   See also human "vertebrae-on-a-post"

bonito (*Sarda sarda chiliensis*), 61, 219, 225

boobies, Peruvian, 21

bouquets of flowers, 19

bracelet, 196, 202; of black beans, 263, 266; of black seeds, 196, 202, 203, 337.   See also necklace

brandishing femora, 6

breechclout, 99, 105, 107, 338, 339.   See also *wara*

brewed beer, xvi, 24.   See also maize

brewery, xvi.   See also brewed beer, corn, maize, maize beer

brideservice, 335, 336

bridgespout vessel, 216, 219, 221

brocaded design, 99, 131, 202, 204

brocading, 98, 99

bromeliad, 89, 121, 284

Bronze Age societies (Europe), 11.   See also John O'Shea

bronze knife, 333

bronze needle, 333

Brown, James A., 331, 332

Buikstra, Jane, 332

built environment, 3, 4.   See also burial tower, *chullpa*

bulrush, see *Scirpus*, totora

bundle, funerary or mummy bundle, see Burials 1–9, Burials K1–K5, Chinchorro cemeteries, fardo, Inca mummy, mummification, mummy, Structures 4–8, 10, 12.   See also *fardo*

Burial 1, 31, 175–186; amphora with a face modeled on its neck, 179; dog, 182, 184; grinding stones, 175, 177, 178, 182, 185; wad of human hair bound at the bottom of vessel, 178, 179

Burial 2, 31, 176, 187–189; llama bone, 187

Burial 3, 176, 190–193; amphora still wearing its harness of grass rope, 190, 191

Burial 4, 36, 119, 176, 184, 194–255, 272, 290, 311, 339; bone *balanza*, 224, 238, 239; figurine, 115, 118, 119, 196, 202, 224, 225, 227, 228, 231

Burial 5, 31, 176, 256–261, 272; flint flake still attached to unfinished textile on a belt loom, 258–261; ungulate long bone with cut marks, 260, 261

Burial 6, 31, 176, 262–266, 269, 271; beans strung on a thread associated with a child, 262, 263, 266; guinea pig in a gourd bowl, 262, 263, 265

Burial 7, 31, 176, 262, 263, 267–271; bird motif incised on gourd, 267, 269; vessel with appliqué snake, 267, 268

Burial 8, 31, 176, 272–282

Burial 9, 31, 176, 184, 205, 283–296; woman still wearing a backstrap, 284, 290

Burial K1, 31–34, 337

Burial K2, 31, 34

Burial K3, 31, 34–38

Burial K4, 31, 36, 38, 142

Burial K5, 31, 36

Burial K6, 31, 36

Burial K7, 31, 36
burial offerings, see Burials 1–9, Burials K1–K7, Structures 4–8, 10, 12
burial tower (*chullpa*), 3, 4
Burton, James, xvi, 202, 219, 228, 236. See also pigment, pigment pouch
butternut squash, 303
buttons, 16, 332

C

caballa (*Scomber japonicus peruanus*), 61. See also *malla, mallero*, nets
Cabeza Larga (Paracas Peninsula), 11, 13, 84
cabuya, 152, 156, 190; *soga de cabuya*, 190
cache, see Alfred Louis Kroeber, Quebrada 1 cache at Cerro Azul
cacica (female ruler), xv; de Huarco, xv
cacique, 337
cactus spine, 27
Cahlander, Adele, 86, 87, 121
Cajamarquilla, 25
Callao, 238
camelid bladder, 202
camelid bone, 153, 156, 205, 209. See also llama, ungulate long bone with cut marks
camelid fur, 14, 86
camelid ribs, 14
camelid wool, xvi, 13, 17, 93, 140, 162, 225, 240, 290, 338, 339. See also alpaca wool yarn balls, bag, *chumpi*, tapestry, woolen bag, workbasket, yarn balls
caña brava (*Gynerium sagittatum*), 145, 153, 277
caña hueca (*Phragmites australis*), 219, 305. See also cane
canals, irrigation, xv, 21, 22, 23
Canavalia, 263, 303; perforated and strung on a thread, 263, 266. See also beads, beans, bracelet, necklace, seeds
Cancharí (Cañete Valley), xv, 22, 24, 335
canchón (large walled room with a level floor, located in a tapia compound) 320, 322. See also tapia compound, wooden top
canchones, 317, 320, 322. See also Structure D
cane, hollow, 267, 268, 322. See also flute, loom bars, needlecase
Cañete River, 21, 22, 24
Cañete Valley, 335. See also Cancharí, Cerro Azul Bay, Cerro Camacho, Cerro Candela, Cerro Centinela, Cerro del Oro, Huarco, Ungará
canopic jars (Egypt), 19
cantos rodados (beach cobbles), 27, 46, 283, 284, 285. See also *batán*, cobblestones, grinding stones, metate
Capsicum, see chile pepper
Carcedo de Mufarech, Paloma, 219
caretakers, of royal mummy, 16
cast net (*atarraya*), 60, 61, 107, 121, 122, 123
Castillo de Huarmey, 13, 334; elite women, 13, spindles and spindle whorls of gold, 13

cemeteries, xv, 9, 331, 332, 335, 337, 340. See also Burials 1–9, Structures 4–7
Centinela, La (archaeological site in the Chincha Valley), see La Centinela
Cerro Azul Bay, 24, 27
Cerro Camacho (Cerro Azul, Peru), xv, 7, 9, 24, 27, 36, 41, 46, 109, 299, 300
Cerro Candela (Cañete Valley), 22
Cerro Centinela (Cerro Azul, Peru), 21, 24, 27, 34, 44
Cerro Colorado (Paracas Peninsula), 11
Cerro Colorado (Huaura Valley), 13, 216
Cerro de la Campana (Oaxaca, Mexico), 6
Cerro del Fraile (Cerro Azul, Peru), 21, 24, 27
Cerro del Oro (Cañete Valley), 22, 23, 24, 31, 335
Cerro Puruchuco, 334
chacra or *chakra* (Quechua term for cornfield), 23
chalcedony, 333
chalk, 11, 23, 251, 252, 253, 277, 280, 282; powdered chalk, 11. See also bag, Vreeland, spinning raw cotton, workbasket
Chancay culture, 216
chanque, 60, 182. See also false abalone
Chapdelaine, Claude, 234
Chapman, Robert, 4
ch'arki (Quechua word for dried meat), 187
Charles, Douglas K., 332
chaupi yunga (piedmont zone), xv, 24
checkered pattern on textile, 204; on wool bag, 202, 235, 238, 277
Chenopodiaceae, 290
Chicama Valley, 216. See also El Brujo, Huaca Cao Viejo, Huaca Prieta
chicha, 5, 317. See also maize beer
chicha making or *chicha* production, 317, 334
Chilca, 84
children placed above the bodies of adults in coastal graves, 178
children's wooden tops, 317, 320, 321, 322. See also canchón, canchones
Chile (the country), 14
chile pepper (*Capsicum*), 115
Chillón River, 25
Chincha, 7, 16, 21, 25. See also Chincha Valley, La Centinela, Las Huacas
Chincha Valley, 7, 11, 36, 86, 105, 120, 219, 238, 290, 311, 314, 337
Chinchaysuyu, 9, 10. See also Antisuyu, Collasuyu, Cuntisuyu, *suyu*
Chinchorro cemeteries, 14; culture, 14; mummies, 14; type of net, 122; populations, 14
chonta wood, 142, 205. See also *kallwa* or weaving sword
Choromytilus, 219, 228, 231, 234. See also shell
Chorrillos, 216
chosen women, see *aklla, akllawasi*
chullpa (burial tower or funerary structure), 3, 4, 5, 8
chumpi (belt), xvi, 15, 196, 204, 205, 242, 338. See also backstrap, tapestry
Chumpi 1, 243, 245. See also Burial 4, Individual 3
Chumpi 2, 246. See also Burial 4, Individual 3

Chumpi 3, 246, 247. See also Burial 4, Individual 3
Chumpi 4, 247, 248. See also Burial 4, Individual 3
Chumpi 5, 248, 249. See also Burial 4, Individual 3
Chumpi 6, 248, 250. See also Burial 4, Individual 3
Chumpi 7, 204, 205, 206. See also Burial 4, Individual 1a
Chumpi 8, 204, 205, 207. See also Burial 4, Individual 1a
Chumpi 9, 204, 205, 208. See also Burial 4, Individual 1a
Chumpi 10, 290, 291; in place around her hips and lower back, 290, 295. See also Burial 9, Individual 3
Chumpi 11, 290. See also Burial 9, Individual 3
chumpi awana (belt loom), 153
Chumpitaz, don José, 60. See also knots
cinnabar, 202, 228, 236. See also pigment, pigment pouch
claims to land, territory, 3, 19. See also ancestor, descendants
claims to resources, 4, 332
clams, 56, 115; drilled for suspension, 56. See also false abalone, mollusc, mussel, palette, pigment, pigment pouch, waterproof pouch
clay cap, see *torta de barro*
clay with finger impressions, 12
cloak pins, see *tupus*
cloth, see *aklla, akllawai, aparina*, backstrap, backstrap loom, bag, belt, blouse, breechclout, brocaded design, *chumpi, chumpi awana*, cotton, cotton seeds, *cumbi*, gifts of cloth, high demand for cloth, Inca demand for cloth, loom, loom backstrap, loom bars, manta, portable loom, spinning raw cotton, standardization of Inca garments, tapestry, tunic, unfinished textile on loom, weaving
cloth, evidence of patching or repair, 212, 234, 290, 317
club, 14. See also mace, mace head, trauma
coastal ecosystems, xv, xvi
cobblestones, 27, 46, 283, 284, 285, 286
Cobo, Bernabé, xv, 6–7, 202, 219, 305, 322, 334, 336, 337
coca, 3, 53
coca bag, 10, 18. See also bag, William Safford, woolen bag
coca leaves (*Erythroxylum coca*), 3, 17, 18, 19, 53, 238, 240, 333
coca, powdered, 10
coca tea, 11, 19, 53
cochineal, 225, 254
Cock Carrasco, Guillermo, 334
coffin, plank, 13
cognitive map, 3
Collasuyu, 9. See also Antisuyu, Chinchaysuyu, Cuntisuyu, Inca Empire, *suyu*
collca (Quechua term for storage structure), see Collca 1, Structure D
Collca 1, Structure D, 118, 156, 323
color preferences, 338, 339, 340. See also personal style
comb, 46, 87, 91, 333
commoner, 4, 7, 19, 27, 38, 335; commoners buried below their houses, 4, 19–20; commoner burials found by Alfred Louis Kroeber, 27, 31, 34, 36, 38
Concholepas concholepas, 182. See also false abalone
condyles, 314, 316
Confite puntiagudo, 116. See also corn, maize

Congo, 4
copper, xvi, 7, 9, 27, 34, 36, 37, 38, 109, 120, 142, 212; gilded copper, 7, 9; copper arsenate hydrate, 236; copper hooks, 333; copper sinkers, 333. See also gold, metal, silver
coprolite, xvi, 115, 288, 290
coquina clam (*Donax obesulus*), 46, 48, 115, 187
cordage, 13, 81, 84, 89, 92, 163, 216, 217, 218, 227, 229, 230, 242, 284, 287, 293, 295, 305, 317, 320. See also cotton, grass rope harness, rope
cordoncillo, 205, 209, 216, 253, 317
cormorants, 21
corn (*Zea mays*), 3, 9, 16, 24, 116, 288, 317; corncob, 46, 52, 326, 327; corn kernels, 116, 288, 303; corn kernels in coprolite, 115, 288. See also *Confite puntiagudo*, maize, *Zea mays*
corn on the cob, 3, 109, 116, 333
corncob used as plug in jars, 46, 52; cotton used as a plug in a jar neck, 46–47, 196–197, 272, 274; yarn wrapped around corncob segment, 326, 327
corporate groups, 332
corvina (*Cilus gilberti*), 60
corvineras (fishing nets for corvina), 60
cosmetic palette, 56
costa (cobble beach), 42, 46, 286
Costin, Cathy Lynne, 137, 332
cotton bag, see bag
cotton fishing nets, 60–86, 109, 314, 333, 339
cotton pads over eyes or face, 13, 16, 19, 109, 212; unspun cotton containing cotton seeds, 284, 295
cotton, raw, 13, 16, 19, 46–47, 109, 196–197, 212, 284, 295, 333; *algodón blanco* (white cotton), 168, 216, 256, 257, 305; *algodón pardo* (brown cotton), 89, 99, 110, 113, 216, 242, 251, 277, 305. See also bag, cotton fishing nets, cotton pads over eyes or face, cotton seeds
cotton seeds, 9, 127, 130, 137, 159, 295
cotton used as a plug, 46, 47, 110, 113, 196, 197, 256, 257, 272, 274
coya (Quechua term for the empress or wife of the Sapa Inca), xv
crabs, 299; storage of, 299
cradle, slit and webbed; see sling, slingstones
craft activities, 3, 11, 21. See also sewing, weaving
crania, removed from tomb, 6. See also reentry
cranial deformation, xvi, 13. See also Cabeza Larga, Paracas Peninsula, Julio C. Tello, John Verano
cranial surgery, see trephination
crayfish (*Cryphiops*), 115
crayfish shell, 115, 288
crayfish soup, 11
crayfish trap, 93
crops, 6, 21. See also agriculture, beans, butternut squash, canals, maize
crucible, 338
crypts, 3, 4. See also Burials 1–9, *chullpa*; Structures 4, 5, 6, 7, 8, 10, 12
cumbi (Quechua term for fine cloth), 336
cumbicamayoc (Quechua term for weaving specialists), 336

Cuntisuyu, 9. See also Antisuyu, Chinchaysuyu, Collasuyu, Inca Empire, *suyu*
curaca (Quechua term for local lord), 334, 335. See also cacique
curandero (Spanish term for "one who cures" or indigenous healer), 305. See also hierba Golondrina, medicine bundle
curtain net (*red de cortina* or trammel net), 60, 61, 82, 107, 122. See also trammel net
Cusco (Cuzco), 7, 16. See also Inca Empire

D

Dainzú (Valley of Oaxaca, Mexico), 6
Dalton, Jordan A., 35, 36, 311. See also Las Huacas
dance, 8; with corpses, 6, 10
darning, 98. See also patching, repair.
darts, 14
Davies, Jon, 19
deceased Zapotec's spirit, 20
decimal system, 311
decorated needlecases, xvi. See also needlecase
deer, 86; deer bone, 205, 209, 213
defensive walls, see fortifications
defleshed bones, 6, 14
defunto or *difuntos* (Spanish term for the corpse or a deceased person), 4, 5, 8, 10. See also ancestor, *aya*
demand for cloth, see Inca demand for cloth
descent group, 3, 20; descent group membership, 3. See also *ayllu*
descendants, 3, 4, 5, 6, 16, 19, 332, 337. See also ancestor, claims to land rights, claims to resources, genealogical claims, territorial claims
Díaz Arriola, Luisa, 196, 202, 216
Diez de San Miguel, Garci, 334
Dillehay, Tom, 84
direct historical approach, 10–11
distaff, 16
divine beings, 6
diviner, 311
division of labor, 3, 331, 333, 339
dog, 175, 182, 184, 186, 290
Donax obesulus, 46, 48, 115
Donnan, Christopher B., 7, 13, 36, 137, 202, 311, 314, 340
Dorsey, George A., 11–13
Dover (the white cliffs of), 21
dressed figurine, 330. See also figurine
dried fish, xv, xvi, 21, 303, 306; processing of fish, xvi. See also export of dried fish
drum, 60. See also fish bone
duhos (low benches), 7
Dwyer, Edward, 17
Dwyer, Jane 17
dyed fishing net, 61; dyed string, 314; dyed wool, 7, 93, 250, 326, 339; dyed yarn balls, 254, 326, 327, 338; dyed yarns, xvi, 225, 228; girls gathering flowers for dyeing, 336; vegetal dye, 61. See also bag, cochineal, pigment pouch
dynastic continuity, 6. See also ancestor, descendants

E

ear ornaments, 333, 334
earth oven, 9
economic specialization, xv, xvi, 21
Eeckhout, Peter, 337
Egypt, 7, 16, 19
El Brujo, 216
embossed motif, 198, 200, 240, 241. See also *inti* motif, metal
embroidery, 322, 323. See also needle, needlecase, *Opuntia* spine, "practice web," sewing
Emery, Irene, 61, 93, 121, 126
emperor, 7, 10, 16. See also Cuzco, Inca, Inca Empire, Inca mummy
enemy, 14. See also mace, mace head, raiding, war
Engel, Frédéric, 81, 84
Engraulis ringens, 115. See also anchovetas
Erythrina, 19, 115, 116
espinel, 122
ethnic groups, 335; distinctive attire, 335
ethnic identity, see identity
ethnic membership, 3
Europe, 4, 11
exchange, interregional, 3; exchange fish for agricultural products, xv, 21
Estete, Miguel de, 238
Euphorbia, 305, 310
export of dried fish to farming communities, xv, xvi, 21

F

false abalone (*Concholepas concholepas*), 56, 60, 288. See also *Concholepas*
false head of mummy, 17, 19, 46, 194, 195, 196, 212. See also bundle, *fardo*
fan with feathers, 333
fardos, 9, 142, 145, 194–195, 216. See also Burials 1–9; Donnan; Dorsey; Puruchuco-Huaquerones; Structures 4, 5, 6, 8, 10, 12
farmers, 21. See agricultural implements
feathered headdress, 336
feathers, 10, 16
feces, see coprolite
femora, removed from tombs, 6
femur, removed from the tomb, 6
fertility, 6
figurine, 45, 115, 118, 119, 196, 202, 224, 225, 227, 228, 231, 322, 336

finger loop, see sling
fingernail, 56, 120, 198, 201, 216, 218, 228, 231; clippings, 16, 337; filed fingernails, 216; fingernail polish, 56, 111, 120, 198, 201, 216, 224
fish bone, xvi, 288.   See also anchoveta, bonito, caballa, jurel, sardines
fisherfolk, xvi, 21
fishermen, xv, 27, 338; as informants, 60.   See bolas, *mallero*, nets, sling
fishhooks, 14, 122; of cactus, 14, 27; of shell, 14, 27
fishhook weights, 14
fish, drying of, xv, xvi.   See also fish storage
fishing community, see Ancón, Lo Demás
fishing community versus agricultural communities, xv, 21
fish motif, 127, 128, 131, 133, 290, 291, 322, 323, 339
fish scales, 290
fish storage, xv, 24, 184, 299
fishing nets, 16, 60–86, 314, 333, 339
Flannery, Kent V., xvi, 202
flasks, miniature, 216, 219, 220, 228, 231.   See also Burial 4
Fleming, Stuart, 20.   See also Max Uhle
flint flake used to cut yarn, 258, 259, 261
flowers, 336
flute (*quena*), 300, 322, 324, 327, 332, 334
food for the afterlife, 6, 9, 10, 16, 19, 110, 115, 116, 117, 187, 262, 288, 290, 303, 306, 308, 336, 339; scheduling of delivery, 10, 19.   See also corn, gourd bowls, guinea pig, *lúcuma*, maize
fortification walls, xv, 21.   See also mace, mace head, sling
Fortress of Ungará (Cañete Valley), 23
frieze, 6; frieze on tomb exterior, 6
funerary bundle, see bundle, mummy
funerary meal, 153.   See also food for the afterlife, gourd bowls, guinea pig, *lúcuma*, maize, sardines
funerary structure, see *chullpa*

G

Gagné, Gérard, 234
Garcilaso de la Vega, "El Inca", 53
gastrointestinal problems, 305
gender, 3, 332, 333, 338; gender-specific artifacts, 332, 333, 339
gender identity, see identity
gender studies, 332, 338, 339
genealogical claims, 4.   See also ancestor, descendants
generic ancestors, 6.   See also ancestor
gifts of cloth, 335; as initial pump-priming step in a dependent relationship, 335
gold, see metal
gold foil, 198, 200, 216, 219, 240, 241, 254, 339.   See also metal
gold ornament, 333
González Holguín, Diego, 202
Gose, Peter, 333

gourd bowls, 3, 9, 16, 54, 56, 57, 58, 59, 109, 110, 114, 115, 178, 184, 187, 188, 193, 196, 199, 262, 263, 265, 267, 269, 270, 275, 276, 288, 289, 300, 303, 305, 306, 307, 308, 339; gourd lid, 303, 307; gourd vessel perforated for suspension, 196; gourd vessels, repaired, 9.   See also anchovetas, corn on the cob, food for the afterlife, guinea pig, *lúcuma*, maize, sardines
gourds or *mates,* 110, 262; decorated, 267, 269; decorated with incised bird, 267, 269; pyroengraved, 7, 11, 54, 58
grass rope harness, 190, 191
grave, see Burials 1–9, Burials K1–K9, Structures 4, 5, 6, 7, 8, 10, 12
grave marker, 194, 195.   See also Burial 4
grind pigment, 333
grinding stones, 143, 153, 158, 175, 177, 178, 182, 184, 185.   See also *batán*
Guaman Poma de Ayala [Waman Puma], Felipe, 4, 5, 8, 9, 10, 19, 317, 320, 321, 334, 335, 336
guano, 24, 26
Guarco, see Huarco polity
Guillén, Sonia E., xvi, 143, 175, 262, 272, 283, 284, 395
guinea pig (*Cavia porcellus*), xvi, 24, 115, 196, 262, 263, 267, 271, 272, 273, 275, 288, 303, 308, 339; foetus, 288; fur, 115, 263, 265, 270, 271, 275, 276, 288, 303; pregnant, 288; with mat covering the gourd bowl, 262, 265, 267, 271
Gynerium sagittatum, see *caña brava*
gypsum, 236

H

Hair, human, 3, 7, 12, 14, 16, 19, 115, 120, 178, 179, 196, 272, 305, 310, 333, 337; animal hair, 290.   See also animal fur, human fur
hair ribbons, 19, 295
hairstyle, 16
half-bobbin, see drilled astragalus
half-spool, see drilled astragalus, Quebrada 1 cache
hampi camayoq (Quechua term for medicinal specialist), 305
hand processing, see cordage, sandals, slings
harpoon foreshaft, 14, 27.   See also Chinchorro
Hastings, Charles M., xvi
Haun, Susan J., 334.   See also Inca demand for cloth, Puruchuco-Huaquerones
head deformation, see cranial deformation
head trauma, see trauma
hearth, 14
heddle rod, 244.   See also loom
heirloom, 7, 19
Herbay, 23
Herbay Alto, 22
herbs, 305
Hernández Escontrías, Pilar Margarita, 336
hierba Golondrina, 305
hieroglyphic text, 6, 19
high demand for cloth, by the Inca, 334, 335

hoe, see *taclla*
hooks, see fishhooks
House of the Chosen Women (*akllawasi*), 334
household head, 20
huaca (Hispanicized spelling of the Quechua term *wak'a*, a sacred locale, mound, or object), 202
Huaca Cao Viejo, 216
Huaca Prieta, 84, 86
Huacones, Los, 22; Huacones-Vilcahuasi, 335
Huancavelica, 202
Huancayo, 25
Huánuco census, 336
huarango (*Acacia* sp.), 35, 317; post, 48
Huarco, xv, 21; *señorío* of, xv, 21, 22, 23; Huarco's resistance to Inca, xv
Huarco polity, xv, xvi, 21
Huarmey Valley, 13, 334. See also Castillo de Huarmey
Huarmey women, 13; as longtime users of backstrap looms, 13; with gold and silver spindles and whorls, 13
Huaura Valley, see Cerro Colorado
Huayna Capac, 16, 335. See also Inca rulers
human coprolites, see coprolite
human hair, 3, 7, 14, 16, 305, 310
Human Relations Area Files, 332
human "vertebrae on a post" (also called "vertebrae on a stick"), 337. See also Jacob Bongers
Hungary, 11. See also John O'Shea
hunting birds, xvi; mammals, xvi
hunting-gathering band or group, 14. See also Chinchorro
Hutchinson, Thomas J., 332, 333
huts, 14
Hyslop, John, 152, 153

I

Ica Valley, 16, 238, 333
identity, 7, 11, 331, 332, 339; ethnic identity, 3, 11, 335; gender identity, 331, 332, 333, 335, 338, 339; social identity, 332, 335; tribal boundaries, 11
imbricated corn kernels, see *Confite puntiagudo*
Inca administrators, 334; army, xv, 336; buildings, 21, 24; burial customs, 5, 6-7, 8, 16, 337; mummy, 5, 7, 8, 10, 16
Inca children, 337-338
Inca clothing, 336, 340; demand for cloth, 334, 335; standardization of Inca garments, 336, 338
Inca conquest of the coast, xv, xvi, 332, 335; attack on Cerro Azul, xv
Inca Empire, 10, 16, 335
Inca Roca, 16
Inca rulers, xv, 16. See also Huayna Capac, Inca Roca
Inca state policy, 335, 336
Inca strategy for annexing lower Cañete Valley, xv
Inca style, 336, 338; Inca-style clothes, 335. See also Inca clothing

Inca tern (*Larosterna inca*), 21
Inca times, 9, 305, 335, 337
individual style preferences, 338, 339. See also color preferences, personal style, style preferences
informant, fisherman, see José Chumpitaz
informant, weaver, 242
Inga feuillei, 109, 144. See also *pacay*
Inkawasi, xv, xvi, 24, 25, 152, 153. See also John Hyslop
interpersonal violence, 14. See also club, mace heads
intestines, 288; removed, 16. See also Inca emperor, Inca mummy
inti motif, 198, 200, 219, 224, 240; perforated silver foil, 224
irrigation, xv, 21. See also *acequias*, canals
Isthmus Zapotec (Oaxaca, Mexico), 20. See also Valley of Oaxaca sites (Dainzú, Lambityeco, Yagul)

J

jade, 7
jade ornaments, 7
Jauja, 7, 25
Jauja Valley, 7
Jiménez de la Espada, Marcos, 202
Jones, John G., xvi, 115, 288, 290. See also coprolite
jurel (Chilean jack mackerel, *Trachurus symmetricus murphyi*), 61

K

kallwa, or weaving sword, 17, 142, 153, 156, 159, 160-161, 205, 209, 238, 322, 324
Kaplan, Lawrence, xvi
Kelly, Sophia E., 338. See also Traci Ardren
Kendall, Ann, 322
kero (Quechua term for a beaker or drinking vessel), 13
kidney cotton (*Gossypium barbadense* var. *brasiliense*), 277, 279
kincha house (wattle or cane, *Phragmites australis*), 36
Kingdom of Huarco, see Huarco
Kingdom of Lunahuaná, see Lunahuaná
knots, *medio nudo* (half knot), 61; *nudo completo* (full knot), 61. See also *mallero*
Kopytoff, Igor, 4
Kroeber, Alfred Louis, xvi, 11, 21, 24, 27-28, 31-36, 38, 41, 87, 91, 107, 142, 238, 314, 316, 317, 322, 339

L

La Centinela (archaeological site in the Chincha Valley), xvi, 25, 311
La Cumbe (archaeological site in the Chincha Valley), 127
la lengua pescadora (dialect spoken by fishermen on the north coast of Peru), xvi

labor, sexual division of; see division of labor
labor service, 333, 334, 335
Lagenaria siceraria, see gourd bowl
Lambityeco (Oaxaca, Mexico), 6
land, modified endowed with meaning, 9
landmarks, 3. See also burial towers, *chullpa*
landscape, see built environment, cemeteries, *chullpa*, landmarks
lanzadera, 156
Las Casas, Bartolomé de, 332
Las Huacas (archaeological site in the Chincha Valley), 36, 238
Late Intermediate and Late Horizon children, 337, 338
Late Horizon burial practice, see "vertebrae-on-a-post"
Late Intermediate versus Late Horizon mortuary practices, 334
Late Intermediate burial treatment at Cerro Azul versus Late Horizon Pachacamac, 337
Late Intermediate investment in mortuary wrapping cloth, 17
Late Intermediate polity, see Huarco, *señorío* de Huarco
Late Intermediate textiles versus Late Horizon textiles, 338
Lati, *señorío* of, 334
leather pouch, 86
Leguminosae, 225. See also beans
lenguado or left-eye flounder (*Paralichthys adspersus*), 61
Lima, 290, 340
lineage rights, 4. See also descendants
lintel, 6. See also hieroglyphic text
lisa (mullet), 60. See also mullet
lisera, 61
litter, 7, 8, 10, 16, 20, 145, 148
litter-bearers, 7, 8, 16
liwi (Quechua term for bolas), see bolas
llama, 10, 188, 193; llama hide with white hair, 193; llama skin, 7; llama wool, 16. See also camelid wool
llimpi, 202. See also pigment
Llullaillaco, 336. See also Ampato
location of Burials 1–9 at Cerro Azul, 176
locks of cotton, 333
Lo Demás (archaeological site in the Chincha Valley), 86, 314, 317. See also Daniel Sandweiss
loincloth, 13, 334. See also *wara*
lomas, 290
loom (*awana*), 159, 160–161, 242, 243, 244, 256, 258–261, 272–273, 277, 280, 333, 334, 335, 336, 339; loom, portable, 160–161, 242, 243, 244, 256, 258, 259, 261, 336; loom backstrap, 107, 121, 126, 184, 196, 205, 206, 207, 208, 234, 242, 243, 245–250, 254, 284, 290–291. See also belt, *chumpi*, Chumpis 1–11
loom bar, 3, 131, 160–161, 242, 244. See also loom
loom belt, 99. See also belt, belt loom, *chumpi*, Chumpis 1–11, *chumpi awana* (belt loom), tapestry
loom stakes (*estacas*), 156, 277, 322
loom strategies vs. hand strategies, 93
Los Huacones-Vilcahuasi, xv, 22
lúcuma (*Pouteria lucuma*), 56, 115, 131, 339; seed, 288, 303, 306; seeds used as miniature containers, 56, 59, 131
Lunahuaná, xv, 21, 23, 24, 153

Lurín River, 25
Lurín Valley, 25

M

mace, 338; mace head, 143, 151, 152, 153. See also club, interpersonal violence, sling, trauma
macha (*Mesodesma*), 182, 272, 273
Mackey, Carol J., 7
Madagascar, 4, 6
maguey, see *Agave*
maize (*Zea mays*), 115, 116; cob, 288, 303, 306; *Confite puntiagudo*, 116; dark red kernels, 17; fragments, 317, 318, 319; husks, 303; kernels, 115, 116, 288, 303; leaf, 305; purple imbricated maize, 115, 116; sixteen-row maize, 277; tassel, 288; varieties, 115, 116; yellow dent, 115, 116. See also brewed beer, *chicha*, corn, corn on the cob, maize beer
maize beer, xvi, 3, 4, 5, 10, 17, 24, 317
Mala River, 25
malla (mesh), 61. See also *mallero*, nets
malla ciega, 60
malla clara, 60
mallero (net-making template), 60, 61, 107, 300, 314, 316, 333, 339
mamakuna, 334, 337
mano de batán (handstone used with metate), see *batán*, grinding stones, metate
manta (large textile), 159, 277
marine motifs, 219. See also bird motif, boobies, cormorants, fish motif, Inca tern, seabirds
marital pair, 6; marital status, 13
marriage, arranged, 335
mass burial, 7, 20, 337. See also Burials 1–9, Burials K1–K9, Structures 4, 5, 6, 7, 8, 10, 12
mates (gourds), 56, 110, 114. See also gourd bowls, gourds
Matos, Ramiro, xvi, 60, 264, 273
mats, 14, 17, 18, 20, 46, 48, 93, 109, 115, 143, 144, 145, 149, 175, 221, 299; cist lined with mats, 45, 46, 48, 143, 144, 175, 177, 299
Maya, 4
meal, see food for the afterlife
medicinal herbs, 305, 310
medicinal tea, 53. See also coca leaves, coca tea
medicine bundle, 300, 305, 310, 327
medicines, 305
memory, 7. See also heirloom, pilgrimage, reentry
Mendizábal Losack, Emilio, 159
Menzel, Dorothy, 333
mercury, 202; mercury sulfide, 202
Merina, 4, 6
mesh size, 27, 314, 316. See also fishing nets, *malla*, *mallero*
Mesoamerica, 4, 6, 7, 11, 339
Mesodesma, see *macha*
metal, xvi, 7, 9, 16, 19, 27, 34, 35, 36, 56, 60, 119, 120, 198, 200, 202,

219, 223, 240, 241, 275, 277, 278, 279, 300, 334, 338; copper, xvi, 7, 9, 34, 36, 142; fishhook, 27, 333; gold, xvi, 7, 9, 35, 37, 219, 240, 241; gold foil, 198, 200, 216, 219, 240, 241, 254, 339; metal smelting, 334, 338; metallurgical tools, 334; silver, xvi, 7, 9, 34, 56, 119, 120, 142, 151, 219, 223, 240, 241, 277, 278, 279; silver foil, 119, 151, 152, 198, 201, 219, 224, 240, 241, 277, 279; wedges or packets of metal inserted into the mouths of the deceased, 9, 16, 275, 300, 333, 337. See also *tupus*, tweezers

metate, 182, 185. See also *batán*, grinding stones

Mexico, 4, 6, 11, 20. See also Isthmus Zapotec, Mesoamerica, Oaxaca, Zapotec

Middle Kingdom of Egypt, 19

milkweed, 60, 81, 84, 86

mineral pigments, 3, 6, 202, 224. See also pigment, pigment palettes, pigment pouch

mineral powders, 238

mines, see Huancavelica

mismis (*Menticirrhus ophicephalus*), 61

mit'a or *mitta* (Quechua term for mandatory labor services), 333

Moche, 7, 9, 13, 36, 202; gold, 9; graves, 9. See also Huaca Cao Viejo

Moche values, 7. See also Christopher Donnan

mollusc, 114, 283, 306. See also clam, *Donax*, *macha*, *Mesodesma*, *Mulinia edulis*, mussel, *Perumytilus*, *Semimytilus*, shell

Morro 1 (a Chinchorro site), 14

mortar, 46, 48, 333

mortuary analysis, see Lewis Binford, Maurice Bloch, Jacob Bongers, James Brown, Jane Buikstra, Claude Chapdelaine, Robert Chapman, Douglas Charles, Guillermo Cook Carrasco, color preferences, Cathy Costin, division of labor, Christopher Donnan, George Dorsey, Peter Eeckhout, Stuart Fleming, Susan Haun, identity, Alfred Louis Kroeber, Carol Mackey, Dorothy Menzel, John O'Shea, Lawrence Owens, Mike Parker Pearson, personal style preferences, Ann Peters, Jeffrey Quilter, William Safford, Arthur Saxe, Charles Stanish, social status, Julio C. Tello, John Verano, Max Uhle, Pieter van Dalen Luna

mortuary archaeology, see cemeteries, *chullpa*

mortuary practices, 334; changes through time, 334

mortuary towers, 3. See also burial tower, *chullpa*

mourners, 20, 332, 338. See also descendants, pilgrims, reentry

Mulinia edulis, 56. See also clam

mullet (*Mugil cephalus*), 60

mummification, artificial and natural, 14, 16. See also Acha Man, bundle, Chinchorro mummies, Egypt, *fardo*, Morro 1, natron

mummy, brought out for periodic display, 16; cults, 16; royal mummies seated in the order each reigned, 16. See also bundle, cloth, Inca emperor, Inca mummy

Murra, John, 332, 333, 335, 336

music, see flute, panpipes

mussel, 56, 60, 115, 224, 228, 231, 288

N

nail polish, red, 56, 120, 198, 201, 216, 218. See also fingernail, pigment palettes

naming Inca children, 337, 338

natron, 16

Navajo potters, 338

necklace, 118, 119, 219, 222, 225; of seeds, 119, 196, 202, 228, 337; of beans, 263, 266. See also beads, bracelet, figurine, seeds perforated for suspension

needle, 9, 16, 107, 142, 205, 207, 210, 212, 214, 219, 224, 251, 253, 333. See also *Opuntia* spines

needlecase, xvi, 11, 107, 219, 333; decorated, xvi, 219, 224, 225, 226; incised, 11, 224, 225, 226

net floats, 122

net-making template, see *mallero*

net repair, 9, 78, 80, 81, 121

nets, see cast net, curtain net, fishing net, *mallero*

nets, nylon, 60

net weights, 14, 82, 84, 85, 121, 122, 300, 314, 315

Nile River (Egypt), 19

Niles, Susan, 335, 336

nopal, see cactus, cochineal, prickly pear cactus

Norte Chico, Peru, 13

novice, 121. See also "practice web"

Nuevo Imperial, 24

O

Oaxaca, 6, 11. See also Isthmus Zapotec, Mesoamerica, Zapotec

obsidian knives, 14; stone knives, 14

occupational specialization, 21

ochre, red, 16. See also pigment, powders

Odontesthes regia regia, see pejerrey, silversides

Old Kingdom in Egypt, 19

Olivella shell, 56

Omas River, 25

Opuntia spines, used to make sewing needles, 107, 140, 205, 208, 210, 212, 214, 219, 224, 251. See also needle, needlecase, spine

orpiment, 236

Oryzomys xanthaeolus, see rice rats

O'Shea, John M., 11, 332

oven, earth, 9

Owens, Lawrence S., 337

P

Pacatnamu, 9, 10, 13, 314

pacay (*Inga feuillei*), 17, 18, 19, 109, 143; leaves, 109, 143, 144, 175, 290; pods, 17, 288; rachises, 145

Pachacamac, xvi, 11, 25, 37, 145, 196, 333, 334, 336; cemeteries, 11; children under the age of seven lack burial goods, 337. See also Ychsma
Pacific sardine, see sardines
pain and pressure, 14. See also trauma, trephination
palace of Puruchuco, 334
Paloma (Archaic site), 19, 84; subfloor burials, 19–20; wrapped in mats, 20. See also Jeffrey Quilter
Pampa Flores, 196
panpipes, 334. See also flute
pans, weighing, 312, 313. See also *balanza*
pans, of copper to weigh items; see *balanza*
Papadopoulos, John, 7
Paracas, 14, 16, 17, 81, 84, 216
Paracas Bay, 84
Paracas Cavernas, 14, 17. See also Julio C. Tello
Paracas cemetery, 84; culture, 16; mummies, 11, 16, 17; Peninsula, 11, 13, 17, 25; populations, 13
Paracas Necrópolis, 17. See also Julio C. Tello
Paracas skulls, 14
Paracas times, 337
Paralichthys adspersus, see lenguado
Páras, 202
paria, 202. See also pigment, pigment pouch, powders
Parker Pearson, Mike, 332
parrot, 333
patching, 81, 84. See also bolas, darning, gourd bowls, repair yarn
peanuts, 17, 36, 333
peat, 16. See also South Uist, sphagnum
pejerrey (silversides), 60, 61, 86
pejerreyera (net for catching silversides), 60
pelican, 333; pelican skin, 14
pendant, 6. See also bracelet, necklace
Perry, Linda, xvi
personal style, 3, 205, 338, 339. See also individual style preferences, style preferences
personal possessions, 20. See also workbasket
personal property, 9. See also workbasket
Perumytilus shells, 115, 131, 303
Peruvian boobies, see booby
pestle, 333
Peters, Ann, 17
petrographic analysis, xvi
Phaseolus vulgaris, 303. See also beans
piedmont, see *chaupi yunga*
piercing, 13. See also tattoo
pigment, mineral, xvi, 3, 6, 207, 233, 238; black manganese pigment, 14; blue pigment, 207, 233, 283; red pigment, 6, 13, 16, 19, 34, 35, 61, 139, 190, 207, 233, 260, 283; vermilion pigment, 207
pigment palettes, 60, 216, 224, 228, 231, 234, 333
pigment pouch, xvi, 3, 202, 203, 204, 216, 219, 224, 228, 231, 234, 236, 277, 280, 281, 339
pilgrimage, 4

pilgrimage destination, 4
pilgrims, 3, 19
pillow, 13, 46, 50, 145, 150
Pisco, 16, 17, 25
pisqoyñu (Quechua word for wooden top), 322. See also Katrina Bettcher, wooden top, Lidio Valdez
pisqoynyo (wooden top), 322. See also canchón, canchones
plank coffin, 13
points, lanceolate, 14
polisher, stone (or smoother), 170, 172
pollen, 115, 290
Polo de Ondegardo, Juan, 6–7
poncho, 159
porotic hyperostosis, 143
portable loom, 242. See also belt, loom
postprocessualists, 332
potato, 115, 117
pottery production, 338
pouch, leather, 86; tied-off pouch with maize fragments, 317, 318, 319. See also pigment pouch, waterproof pouch
Pouteria, see *lúcuma*
powders, of different colors, to be blown in the direction of the sacred huacas, 202, 236. See also pigment, pigment palettes, pigment pouch
"practice web," 131, 133, 322
Price, Karen, 137. See also workbasket
prickly pear cactus, 228. See also cochineal, *Opuntia*
procession, 6. See also *chullpa*, pilgrimage
prying shellfish from sea cliff, 14
pucullo, 5, 10
purple corn, see maize
Puruchuco-Huaquerones, 13, 272, 334; mollusc placed on the shoulder of the deceased, 272. See also Guillermo Cock Carrasco, Susan Haun
puya, 121. See also bromeliad
Pyramids at Moche, 13. See also Moche
pyroengraved gourd bowl, 7, 11. See also decorated or incised gourd bowls

Q

qompicamayoq, see *cumbi, cumbicamayoc*
Quebrada Acha, 14
quebradas as burial sites, 27, 301. See also Burials 1–9; K1–K9; Structures 4–8, 10, 12
Quebrada 1 at Cerro Azul, 28, 32, 34, 87, 91, 316, 317. See also Burial K2, Burial K3
Quebrada 1 cache at Cerro Azul, 87, 91, 317; comb, 87, 91. See also Alfred Louis Kroeber
Quebrada 2 at Cerro Azul, 31, 32. See also Burial K1
Quebrada 8/8a at Cerro Azul, 32, 36. See also Burials K4–K7
Quebrada de Topará, 16

Quilter, Jeffrey, 19, 20
quena, see flute
quicksilver, 202
Quilmaná, 22, 24
Quito, 16

R

raids, 14. See also mace, mace heads, trauma, warriors
raising guinea pigs, see guinea pig
Ramose (Egyptian pharaoh), 19
rattle, 333
raw cotton, see cotton
rayas (rays), 61
razor clams, 288
realgar (pigment), 228, 231, 236
red de cortina, 122. See also curtain net, trammel net
reentry, 6, 7, 34; reentering tombs, 4, 6. See also descendants, mourners
relatives, 3, 4 6, 19. See also ancestor, descendants
repair, 9, 78, 80, 81, 82. See also bolas, cloth, darning, gourd
repair yarn, 81, 82, 317, 319. See also workbasket, yarn balls
representativeness of the sample of burials, 11, 13
rice rats, 303
Rímac Valley, 25, 216, 334
Rinconada Alta, 334
rite of passage, 13
roads, 23
rock crystal, 35
Romania, 11. See also John O'Shea
roof of cist, 145, 148, 299; tomb roof, 17, 18
rope, 86, 87, 93, 121, 134, 156, 216, 217, 284, 287, 300, 333. See also cordage, grass rope harness
Rostworowski de Diez Canseco, María, xvi
Rowe, Ann P., 121
Rowe, John H., 322, 336
Royce, Anya P., 20
Ruiz, Bartolomé, 238

S

sacrificed captives, 13; sacrifices, 7; sacrificial burials in the Ica Valley, 333
Safford, William E., 17, 18
salt incrustations (*salitre*), 196, 199
Saltzman, Max, xvi, 225
sample size, 11, 13. See also Alfred Louis Kroeber
sandals, 95, 121
Sandweiss, Daniel H., 86, 314, 317. See also Lo Demás
San José de Moro, 13. See also Christopher Donnan
San Juanito (Santa Valley), 234

San Luis, 24
San Vicente, 24
Sarda sarda chiliensis, see bonito
sardines, xv, 60, 288, 339
Sardinops sagax, see sardines
Saxe, Arthur, 332
scale to weigh items, see *balanza*
school of fish, 219, 224, 226
Scirpus (bulrush or *totora*), 45, 46, 50, 143, 196, 251, 288; bundle of, 288, 289. See also mats
scissor, flint flake used as, 258–259, 261
scree stones, 46, 285, 299, 302
seabirds, 21, 26. See also cormorants, Inca terns, Peruvian boobies
sea lion, 21, 46, 86, 87; ribs, 14; skin, 14, 87
seal, 34
seeds, see cotton seeds
seeds perforated for suspension, 228
seeds strung on bracelet, see bracelet
seeds strung on necklace, see necklace
seeds that resemble wrinkled peppercorns, 261
Semimytilus, 303. See also shell
Señora de Cao, 216
señorío (polity), see Huarco, Lati, Lunahuaná, Ychsma
servants, 16, 24
sewing, 137, 143, 202, 205, 246, 334. See also needles, needlecases, *Opuntia* spines, sewing needles
sewing needles, 16, 109. See also needles, workbasket
sewing thread, 234, 290. See also needles
sexual division of labor, see division of labor
shark teeth, 219, 224, 226
shed rod, 156, 160, 161, 244. See also loom
shell, 46, 56, 182, 224, 228, 231, 333. See also *Choromytilus, Concholepas, Donax*, macha, *Mesodesma, Mulinia edulis, Olivella, Perumytilus, Semimytilus, Spondylus*
shell bead, 56, 60
shellfish, 339. See also mollusc, shell
shell ornament, 56
shell palette, 56. See also nail polish
sherd weight, 82; stone net weight, 82
shield, 338
shirt, 98
shrine, family, 4
silver disc, 240, 302, 311, 327, 333
silver foil, 277, 279. See also metal
silver packet, see metal, wedge
silver spangles, 333
silverside, see pejerrey
silversmithing, 338
skeins, see yarn balls, workbasket
skull deformation, see cranial deformation
sling (*warak'a*), 16, 46, 86, 87, 88, 89, 90, 91, 93, 107, 109, 121, 124, 142, 143, 152, 154, 173, 317, 332, 333, 334, 339
slingstones, 152, 154
slit tapestry, xvi, 93, 97, 98, 126, 127, 128, 129, 204, 205, 206, 207,

208, 234, 239, 240, 241, 242, 243, 245, 246, 247, 248, 249, 250, 290, 291

slivers of unidentified fiber, 81. See also bast, milkweed
Smith, C. Earle, Jr., xvi, 61, 81, 86, 145, 163, 225, 263, 305
smoother or polisher, 170
snake, see appliqué snake. See also Burial 7
social construction of value, 7, 9
social identity, see identity
social persona, 332, 337. See also Lewis R. Binford, identity
social position, 332
social status, 7–11, 16, 332, 339. See also gold, metal, silver
sodalities, 332
Solanaceae, 290
Sommer, Jeffrey D., xvi
soumak (weft-wrapping), 93, 121, 126, 136, 137, 162, 317, 322
South Uist (Scottish island), 16. See also ancestor, peat, sphagnum moss
specialization, community, xvi, 334
sphagnum moss, 16
spindle, 13, 46, 105, 106, 137, 175, 184, 207, 209, 210, 211, 251, 252, 253, 254, 295, 296, 322, 324, 325, 326, 327, 334, 335, 339; as symbols of womanly activities, 332–333; spindles with barcoding, xvi, 11, 137, 140, 254, 324, 325, 326, 327, 338; spindles of gold, 13; of silver, 13; spindles with crosshatching, 254
spindle whorl, 13, 46, 105, 106, 137, 140, 175, 184, 207, 209, 211, 251, 252, 253, 254, 295, 296, 322, 326, 334, 335, 339; spindle with fruits or seeds, 208, 213, 251; whorl shapes, 207, 211; whorls with crosshatching, 251, 252, 253, 254
spines, *Opuntia*, 107, 140, 205, 208, 210, 212, 214, 219, 224, 251. See also needle
spinning raw cotton, 17, 24, 137, 159, 168, 171, 322, 332, 333, 334, 335. See also workbasket
splint or stiffener, see workbasket
Splitstoser, Jeffrey C., 61, 84, 86
Spondylus shell bead, 56, 60. See also button
Squier, Ephraim George, 120, 314, 333; grave at Pachacamac, 333; tweezers, 333
standardization of Inca garments, 336. See also Margaret Young-Sánchez
statues, 16, 19
status category, 11, 13. See also copper, gold, metal, silver
status hierarchy, 331
stitching, see sewing. See also repair yarn
Stoltman, James B., xvi
Stone-Miller, Rebecca, 336
stone net weight, 82. See also net weights
stopper (end plug) of needlecases, 219, 224, 225, 226
storage bin, 118, 322, 323; facilities, xv. See also Inkawasi, practice web, Structure D
storage of mineral pigments, 3. See also mineral powders, pigment pouch, waterproof pouch
storage room, for bodies kept above ground, 16, 337
Strong, William Duncan, 238

Structure 4 burial cist, 31, 41–108, 109, 142, 143, 144
Structure 5 burial cist, 31, 41, 45, 109–142, 143, 173; figurines, 115, 118, 119
Structure 6 burial cist, 31, 41, 45, 143–174, 262
Structure 7 burial cist, 31, 41, 45
Structure 8 burial cist, 41, 283, 284, 285
Structure 9, 27, 118, 119, 184
Structure 10 burial cist, 31
Structure 11, 301
Structure 12 burial cist, 31, 170, 299–327; *balanza*, 311, 312, 313; *mallero*, 314, 316; potsherds used as net weights, 314, 315; silver disc, 311; wooden top, 317, 321, 322
Structure D, 35, 36, 46, 56, 59, 118, 156, 184, 300, 311, 313, 317, 322, 323; "practice webs," 322, 323; storage bin, 322, 323; woolen bag, 322
Structure F, 41
Structure G, 41
Structure I, 36
style preferences, 3, 19, 338. See also individual style, personal style
substitutes, 16, substitute head, 19
Suku, 4, 6
suirucu (*Sapindus saponaria*), 251. See also seeds
sulfur, 228, 231, 236
supernatural forces, 6. See also *yllapa*
suyu, one of the four quarters of the Inca Empire, 9, 10. See also Antisuyu, Chinchaysuyu, Collasuyu, Cuntisuyu
sword, weaving; see *kallwa*, weaving sword

T

taclla or hoe, 332, 334. See also agriculture, agricultural implements
talismans, 16. See also amulets, 208
Tambo Colorado, 25
Tambo de Mora, 25
Tank site, 84
taparrabo, see breechclout or *wara*
tapestry, xvi, 93, 97, 98, 99, 126, 127, 216, 242, 243, 336, 339. See also belt, belt loom; Burials 4, 9; *chumpi*, portable loom, slit tapestry, unfinished textile on loom
tapia compound, xvi, 9, 24, 27, 41, 184; wall, 299, 302. See also canchón, canchones
tattoo, 11, 13, 16, 216, 217, 339; on Late Intermediate women in coastal communities, 339. See also textile designs, 216, 217
Tello, Julio C., 11, 13, 14, 17. See also Cabeza Larga, Paracas, Paracas Peninsula, Wari Kayan
temple, 4, 19, 334
Temple of the Sacrificed Women, 336. See also Inca, Pachacamac, Max Uhle, Ychsma polity
Temple of the Sun, 334–335
Teotihuacan, 11

terrace, as midden accumulation, 9, 27, 34, 41, 46, 188, 299
territorial claims, 3, 19. See also ancestors, descendants
textiles, see bags, belt, belt loom, *chumpis*, Irene Emery, loom, slit tapestry, tapestry, unfinished textile on loom
throwing sticks, 14
Tiahuanaco (Bolivia), 305
tied ankles, 13, 14, 16, 145, 146, 275
tied arms, 16, 17, 145, 284
tied fingers, 12, 13, 14, 16, 17, 109, 145, 275, 284
tied hands and wrists, 13, 16, 17, 145, 147, 284
tied toe, 12, 14
Tikal (Guatemala), 11
Tillandsia, 17, 290
Tomaltepec (Valley of Oaxaca), 11
tomb door, 4, 5, 6. See also *chullpa*
tomb reentry, see Maurice Bloch, Dainzú, descendants, lintel, mourners
Topa Inca Yupanqui, xv
Topará, 16. See also Quebrada de Topará
torta de barro (clay surface), 194, 283. See also Burial 4
totora (Scirpus), see bulrush, mats, *Scirpus*
tower, stone burial, see *chullpa*
toy, 317. See also Katrina Bettcher, Lidio Valdez, wooden top
trammel net, 60, 61, 79, 81, 83, 85, 122, 314, 315. See also cast net, *red de cortina*
trapezoidal niches, 24
trauma, blunt force, 14; healed skull fractures, 14. See also mace heads, slingstone, trephination
trepanation, see trephination
trephination, 13, 14, 17, 143
tributary populations, 335, 336
Tuan, Yi-Fu, 9
tumuli, 4
tunic (*unku*), 186, 334, 336
tupus (Quechua term for cloak pins), xvi, 7, 13, 216, 219, 223, 254, 272, 277, 278, 334, 336; silver *tupus*, 277; repaired with brown string, 277, 278
turquoise beads, 219. See also beads
Tutankhamun (Egyptian pharaoh), 7
tweezers, 16, 119, 120, 142, 333, 334; bronze, 333; silver, 120, 142; suspended from a cord, 120. See also Ephraim George Squier
twill workbaskets, xvi, 137, 251, 333, 339. See also workbasket
tying digits, 14, 16, 196, 275; tied ankles, 14, 275; tied wrists, 14, 196

u

Uhle, Max, 11, 20, 31, 238, 333, 336; excavations in the Ica Valley, 333. See also Ica Valley, Dorothy Menzel, Pachacamac, Ychsma polity
unfinished textile on loom, 258, 259, 338, 339
Ungará, Fortress of, xv, 21, 22, 23, 24, 25

ungulate astragalus, 314, 316
ungulate long bone, 205, 208, 242, 244, 260, 261. See camelid bone and deer bone
ungulate long bone with cut marks, 260, 261
Urton, Gary, 7

v

Valdez, Lidio, 317. See also Katrina Bettcher, wooden top
value, concept of, 7, 9; body value, 7, number value, 7; object value, 7; place value, 7; social construction of value, 7, 9. See also Christopher Donnan, John Papadopoulos, Gary Urton
van Dalen Luna, Pieter, see Cerro Colorado (an archaeological site in the Huaura Valley), tattoo
vassals, 337. See also Inca
Verano, John W., 14. See also trephination, trauma
vessel depicting "fat skeleton," 300, 304
Vetter Parodi, Luisa María, 219
Virú Valley, 105
visits to burial towers, 3; visits to tombs, 19. See also *chullpa*, descendants, reentry
Vreeland, James M., 11, 17. See also chalk, cloth, spinning raw cotton

w

Wallace, Dwight, xvi, 61, 78, 86, 89; Wallace's system vs. Splitstoser's parenthetical notation method, 61, 78. See also Jeffrey Splitstoser
walls, defensive, xv, 22, 23; defending communities, 14, 21
Wanka, 335
war, see interpersonal violence, mace head, trauma
wara (Quechua term for breechclout), 99, 106, 338. See also breechclout
waracikoy, 338
Wari Kayan (Paracas Peninsula), 11, 17. See also Paracas, Julio C. Tello
Wari style pottery, 13; textiles, 338
Warku, see Huarco
warrior, 14; painted faces and bodies of, 202. See also bolas, mace, mace heads, sling, trauma
Wassén, S. Henry, 305
watercraft, see waterproof rafts
waterproof pouch, 3, 202, 228. See also pigment pouch
waterproof rafts, xv, 87
weapons, 332. See also bolas, club, mace, mace heads, sling, trauma
weather, affected by the ancestors, 6
weaving, xvi, 3, 13, 15, 16, 17, 87, 137, 142, 143, 153, 156, 163, 184, 205, 208, 209, 213, 238, 242, 244, 256, 258–261, 284, 295, 314, 322, 333, 334, 337, 338, 339; weaving implements, 208, 209, 213,

258, 260, 314, 334, 335, 339; weaving in the afterlife, 242, 256, 284, 295, 338; weaving sword (*kallwa*), 17, 142, 205, 209, 238, 322, 324.   See also batten, *kallwa*, loom, loom bars, sewing, shed rod, stakes, unfinished textile on loom, workbasket

weaving sword, see *kallwa*

weft-wrapping, see *soumak*

whistle, 7

whorls, 105, 106, 137, 140, 170, 171, 172, 205, 207, 208, 209, 211, 251, 252, 253, 254, 295, 296, 326, 327, 333.   See also spindle, spindle whorls

Więckowski, Wieslaw, 13.   See also Castillo de Huarmey

wife-giver, 346

wigs, 14, 16, 196

willow twigs, 145, 150

wooden artifacts, 317, 320, 321

wooden block, carved, 35

wooden handles, see obsidian knives

wooden masks, 196

wooden top, 300, 317, 320, 321, 327, 337.   See also *canchón*, *canchones*

wooden toy, see wooden top

woolen bag, see bag

workbasket, xvi, 9, 11, 17, 18, 19, 93, 109, 137, 139, 140, 141, 168, 169, 170, 171, 172, 173, 194, 195, 205, 207, 209, 210, 211, 212, 251, 252, 253, 254, 280, 282, 295, 296, 322, 324, 325, 326, 327, 333, 334, 335, 339.   See also alpaca wool yarn balls, bag, Burials 4, 5, 8, 9, chalk, cotton, needle, needlecase, *Opuntia* spine, sewing, sewing needles, spindle, spindle whorl, Structures 5, 6, 12, weaving, whorls, yarn balls

writing system, 19

Y

Yagul (archaeological site in the Valley of Oaxaca, Mexico), 6

yarn balls, 9, 11, 105, 107, 109, 140, 142, 162, 170, 172, 173, 195, 202, 203, 204, 211, 212, 215, 225, 229, 230, 236, 237, 238, 249, 251, 252, 253, 254, 255, 277, 280, 281, 322, 338, 339; received in trade, 142.   See also bag, camelid wool, spindle, spindle whorl, spinning raw cotton, workbasket

Ychsma polity, 21, 37, 334.   See also Pachacamac, *señorío*, Max Uhle

yllapa (lightning), 4, 5, 10

Young-Sánchez, Margaret, 338, 340

yquima (widow), 10

yunga (Quechua word for coastal plain), xv.   See also *chaupi yunga*

yuyu (edible seaweed), 9

Z

Zapallán, 216

Zapotec (one of the indigenous groups residing in the state of Oaxaca, Mexico), 4, 6, 20.   See also Anya Royce, Cerro de la Campana, Dainzú, hieroglyphic writing, Lambityeco, lintel, Mesoamerica, tomb door, tomb reentry, Yagul

Zea mays, see brewery, corn, maize

Zorn, Elayne, 121

zorrito (*Menticirrhus rostratus*), 61